THE HISTORY OF KING RICHARD THE THIRD

The realization of Arthur Kincaid's intention to create this new edition owes much to the encouragement and support of the Richard III Society's membership. The decision to underwrite its publication indicates the Society's view of its historical importance, and has been made possible thanks to legacy funds bequeathed by its late member Pauline Stevenson. The generous financial support of both donors is gratefully recognized.

RICHARD III SOCIETY
Researching & Reassessing Richard III

SOCIETY OF ANTIQUARIES OF LONDON

THE HISTORY OF KING RICHARD THE THIRD (1619)

by

SIR GEORGE BUC

Master of the Revels

Edited with an introduction and notes

by

ARTHUR KINCAID

THE SOCIETY OF ANTIQUARIES OF LONDON
New edition, 2023

Research Report of the Society of Antiquaries of London No. 83

First published by Alan Sutton Publishing Ltd, 1979, 1982
This new edition published 2023 by
The Society of Antiquaries of London
Burlington House
Piccadilly
London W1J 0BE
www.sal.org.uk

The Society of Antiquaries gratefully acknowledges the financial support of the Richard III Society in the publication of this book.
www.richardiii.net

ISBN 978-0-85431-304-4
ISSN 0953-7163

British Cataloguing in Publication Data
A CIP catalogue record for this book is available from the British Library.

Project management: Annette Carson and Stuart Brookes, FSA
Copy-editing, proofreading and index: Annette Carson
Cover design: Sue Cawood
Page layout and printing: Barnwell Print Ltd, Aylsham, Norfolk NR11 6SU.
www.barnwellprint.com

WORLD LAND TRUST™
www.carbonbalancedprinter.com
Barnwell Print - Reg. 2102
CBP014469

By using Carbon Balanced Paper through the World Land Trust on this publication we have offset 1231kg of Carbon & preserved 235sqm of critically threatened tropical forests.

Cover illustration: Richard III (arched), workshop of artist unknown, probably English. Oil on oak panel, c 1510–40 © The Society of Antiquaries of London

CONTENTS

This edition is for Phoebe,
who started the whole thing off
when we were in school

If we do meet again, why we shall smile.
If not, why then this parting was well made.

Arthur Kincaid, D.Phil.
1942 – 2022

Arthur Kincaid's death occurred while this book was in preparation. He had intended a revised edition for several decades, an intention that took tangible form in 2015, based on updating his research into Richard III which had been a life-long commitment from childhood. It is a commitment he shared with Annette Carson, who has carried the incomplete files through to final publication and must take responsibility for any errors introduced in the process. Dr Kincaid's insightful work comports with the aims of the Richard III Society, which has enabled this publication in tribute to a much-respected academic, and in furtherance of continued research and reassessment of the historical material relating to this monarch.

FOREWORD & ACKNOWLEDGEMENTS

The passage of time and new interest aroused in Richard III by the recent discovery of his skeleton and his re-interment make this an appropriate time to produce a new edition of Buc's *History of King Richard the Third.* Sir George Buc is the first author to have tried to rescue Richard's reputation through serious scholarship. Unfortunately he has been steadily dismissed because no one reads his original work, which, until my first edition came out in 1979, was known only in a heavily altered, much shortened, plagiarized version by a young relation whose name was essentially the same as his. That edition, apparently against all reason, but probably because it is shorter and cheaper and now much more readily available, continues to prevail.

To distance the original from the rampant edition of 1646, I feel obliged now to change the spelling of the author's name from 'Buck', which I preferred, to 'Buc', which Sir George himself preferred, though he always used the spelling 'Buck' for his family. This change was forced on me by the reissuing in 1973 – just after I had completed work on the text of the original and was known to have done so – of the version of the work published by the author's great-nephew, who spelt his surname 'Buck' and passed it off as his own. My plea to the then Richard III Society not to back this republication met with the rejoinder that I did not hold the copyright of it. How very different from the response of Professor Berners Jackson in Canada who, as I was starting work on my edition of the original, had been considering beginning one himself but graciously withdrew.

This 1973 republication made no sense of any sort. The 1646 edition (which everyone persists in calling a 1647 edition, though such a thing never existed) had for a long time been known to be useless. It was easily dismissed on the grounds of failings which it did not share with the work of its original author, and thus the damage it had caused to Richard III's reputation may be assessed as incalculable. Also, since Buc was mistaken for its author, it had damaged his reputation as well for 330 years and goes on doing so when given a new airing. I shall deal in more detail with the damage caused by this ill-advised republication in Chapter VI of the Introduction. It plagued initial sales of my edition and has plagued second-hand sales, since Amazon led people believe it and my edition were the same work, though I tried in vain for over 10 years to get them to stop doing this. A.R. Myers, chosen as a suitable person to write what proves to be an exceedingly sloppy preface to it (see below, Chapter VI), had previously demonstrated in print his poor opinion of the original author, based entirely on the 'bastard' edition. More recently a facsimile of another copy of it (again dated 1647) has appeared on the web – ascribed to Sir George Buck! I had no idea when I decided on the spelling 'Buck' that all this was going to happen but was assuming that, with the original finally available, consultation of the bastard version would become a thing of the past.

Looking back with more objectivity at the initial job of doing it, it seems an insane thing to have undertaken, since it is basically impossible, fiddly and demanding expertise in a wider range of areas than is possible. Only a young person would have had that sort of nerve. I can only hope that this time through I've managed to correct most of the errors in the first two editions without introducing many more.

There are a lot of people to thank, many no longer alive, but I want to thank them all, regardless. My gratitude remains due to several institutions and individuals for access to manuscripts, old books, and information: in Oxford the Bodleian Library, the English Faculty Library and Christ Church library (notably Alina Nachescu in the last, and in the first, Sally Matthews has been particularly helpful. It was a delight to see Colin Harris still working in rare books and manuscripts in the Bodleian so many years after I first encountered him as a very young man behind the desk in Duke Humfrey). And thanks to Isabel Holowaty of the History Faculty Library for trying trace reasons for the existence there of the printed edition of Buck without my edition of the original. To the British Library on its original site and its present one. To Trinity College, Cambridge, the University of Toronto Library (Thomas Fisher Collection), and the National Archives. To Sidney T. Fisher of Montreal for lending his manuscript copy of the *History* to the Bodleian and for providing information about it, and recently to Pearce J. Carefoote, Interim Head of Department of Rare Books and Special Collections, Thomas Fisher Rare Books Library, University of Toronto. To Major W. Halswell for lending his manuscript of Buc's *Commentary* to the Bodleian and the British Library (it was subsequently purchased by the Bodleian).

Among those no longer with us, my greatest thanks are due to my mother, who assisted me in my very earliest years of research on Richard III, age 13-17, despite the fact that, as a professional historian, as I am not, her views often differed from mine. That was how I learned to do research. History teacher Agnes Finnie was responsible for initiating the interest in my school which ultimately led to this work. Tremendous thanks to my first wife, Meg, who cheerfully supported both my research and me during the years it took to do it. I also owe inexpressible gratitude to my two Oxford thesis supervisors, R.E. Alton and C.A.J. Armstrong. Reggie Alton, who taught me palaeography, took the time and the notebooks containing my transcript of Cotton Tiberius E.X to the British Museum to double-check my accuracy and resolve the points on which I had queries. That he was rarely able to read what I had failed to is a tribute to his excellence as a teacher of palaeography. And to Professor Charles Ross, who pointed me toward recently published material and read and commented on the first edition before it went to press. To Robert Levens, for identifying several of the Greek and Latin tags, and to Jeannine Alton for assisting me in regularizing the French quotations. And finally I cannot possibly omit expressing gratitude to Isolde Wigram for 50 years of friendship, during which she unfailingly encouraged this work while it was in progress and left me first choice of her collection of Ricardian books.

Among the living I want particularly to thank Annette Carson for persuading me to do a new edition of this work and for reading the previous one carefully before I started, meticulously checking for formal consistency, assisting with research, especially in calling my attention to recent publications, proofreading the final version, and enabling it to be published. A lot of this cannot have been much fun. Tremendous thanks also to my friends Dr John Blundell, Editor at the Thesaurus Linguae Latinae, Munich and Professor Maureen Boulton of Notre Dame University, USA for help respectively with the mediaeval Latin and mediaeval French quotations.

I owe gratitude to Professor Alan Nelson for sending me references to Buc manuscripts he discovered in the British Library after my work came out and to Professor Gustav Ungerer for bringing to my attention his article on Buc's participation in the 1605 festivities in Spain celebrating the success of peace negotiations. Also to my former student, Professor Franklin J. Hildy for advice on references to Spanish theatre practices. And finally to the Richard III Society, especially its tremendously helpful librarians Keith Horry and Marie Barnfield, for allowing me to use their library, to Peter and Carolyn Hammond and Dr James Petre for advice and encouragement, and to Peter Hammond especially for a question that led to a correction in the text (I wish there had been more of those!).

Finally, I owe immense gratitude to my wife, Dr Deirdre Kincaid, for proofreading the most difficult segment of this edition and also for saving me from what would have been an egregious error. We have tried to eradicate *all* the errors. This is an impossible task, and in cases of failure responsibility rests entirely with me.

Arthur Kincaid

ABBREVIATIONS

(see Bibliography for full details)

BIHR	Bulletin of the Institute of Historical Research
B.L.	British Library
Bod.	Bodleian Library, Oxford
Camden	William Camden, *Britannia*, 1607
Cam. Soc.	Camden Society
Comm.	Sir George Buc, *Commentary upon the Book of Domus Dei*
CP	*The Complete Peerage*
Crowland	Crowland Chronicle
CSP	Calendar of State Papers
DNB	Dictionary of National Biography (earlier editions)
ODNB	Oxford Dictionary of National Biography (2004)
EETS	Early English Text Society
EHR	*English Historical Review*
Grafton	Richard Grafton, *Chronicle*, Vol. 3, 1807
Pat. Rolls	*Calendar of the Patent Rolls*
Polydore	Polydore Vergil, *Anglica Historia*
PROME	*Parliament Rolls of Mediaeval England*
RES	*Review of English Studies*
R.S.	Rolls Series
STC	Pollard and Redgrave, *Short Title Catalogue*, 1475-1640
TNA	The National Archives (formerly Public Record Office)

REASSURANCE TO READERS

I have emended the text only in the case of (extremely rare) blatant misreadings and conjectural emendations less good than they should be. And of course I have done my best to get rid of all missing brackets and printers' errors. This should not affect the pagination, so that any existing references which cite the text from my previous editions will still be valid.

Explanation of the notations to the text will be found on p. clxx within.

INTRODUCTION

INTRODUCTION

I. THE LIFE OF SIR GEORGE BUC

There is no need to introduce here a long biographical study of Sir George Buc,[1] since that by Mark Eccles in *Thomas Lodge and Other Elizabethans,*[2] though its organization makes it somewhat difficult to follow, is nearly exhaustive. It should be sufficient to sketch the outlines of Buc's life, filling in only details which have particular bearing on *The History of King Richard the Third* and on his place in English literature and historical scholarship.

Buc traces his own descent in his manuscript *Commentary on the Book of Domus Dei*[3] and again in the *History*. Genealogy in an age when its methods were not yet clearly formulated tended to be based to a considerable extent on guesswork from philological evidence and to take colour from the wishes of the tracer. In the *Commentary* Buc lists his own among families such as Percy, Neville and Vere as examples of those springing from foreign nobility. His is almost the only family below baronial rank which he mentions in this work on families that came to England with the Conqueror. In the *History* he introduces his own genealogy as a digression, for which he asks the reader's pardon with a moving appeal to the honour we owe our ancestors, from whom we have derived our claims to nobility and gentility (see below, text, pp. 115-6). Buc was proud of his status as a gentleman and his pride extended to the descent from which he derived that status. 'Noblemen,' as he says in the *Commentary* (f. 58^{v}), are merely lords, whereas 'gentleman' has more honour in it, signifying descent 'from generous parent*es*'. Buc shared the passion for pedigree which flourished under the Tudors among those newly acquiring court promotion. He needed to feel that in his own promotion at court he was carrying on or restoring a family tradition. For, as he

1 In the previous edition of this work I used the spelling 'Buck', as appearing more familiar to modern readers. 'Buc' was an affectation peculiar to Sir George, probably derived from Lisle de Buc in Flanders, to which he traces his family origins. It also has the advantage of seeming more classical, there being no 'k' in Latin. He does not use this spelling to refer to other members of his family or even to himself in the third person, but only as a signature. Bearing in mind the urgent problem of differentiating Sir George Buc's works from his great-nephew's plagiarized and drastically altered version of his work (*History of the Life and Reigne of Richard the Third*), and how widespread is the use of 'Buc' in current scholarship to refer to Sir George, and also that 'Buc' appears more frequently than 'Buck' in extant documents in Buc's hand, I have decided that it makes sense to change my usage. There is no justification at all for A.R. Myers's unsupported assertion in his introduction to Buc's great-nephew's version of the *History*, that Sir George preferred the spelling 'Buck' (George Buck Esq., *History of the Life and Reigne of Richard the Third*, London, 1973, reprint of a 1647 reissued copy of 1646 ed., cited erroneously as 2nd ed., p. 5. See below, pp. lxiv-lxv, cviii-cxi for discussion of this point).

2 Mark Eccles, 'Sir George Buc, Master of the Revels', in *Thomas Lodge and Other Elizabethans*, ed. Charles J. Sisson (Cambridge, Mass., 1933), pp. 411-506.

3 Bod. MS. Eng. Misc. b. 106. Folio references will henceforth be given in my text. See below, pp. xxxvii-xlii for a discussion of this work.

tells us, his family was at one time prominent in the service of the crown, under King Richard III.

On Camden's authority, Buc cites as founder of his family in England Sir Walter Buck of Brabant, a descendant of the earls of Flanders, who was one of the foreign commanders serving under King John. He derives the name from Lisle de Buc, a town in Flanders on the River Isle, near which Ludovick de Buck, a much earlier ancestor, built a castle called Castle de Buck. The name, he conjectures, comes from the German for beech (*Buche* in modern German), a tree very plentiful in this region. Ludovick married a daughter of the king of France who made him governor of Flanders in 621, and his family became earls of Flanders in 880 through a second marriage with the French royal house. After producing the father of Matilda, wife of William the Conqueror, the male line of the earls of Flanders died out in 1119. Sir Walter Buck was one of its younger descendants.

Sir George disagrees with sources who censure the foreign leaders for taking plunder under King John[4] and approves his ancestor's subduing the Isle of Ely for the king and having 'good spoile' there (*Comm.*, f. 451). Lands were given to Walter, now 'Walter Buck' rather than 'de Buck', in Yorkshire and Northamptonshire as a reward for his service. In the north the family intermarried with another of the same surname, the Lords of Bucton in the Wapentake of Buccross – or, as he says in notes for the *Commentary* in B.L. MS. Lansdowne 310, it was then called 'Buck Wapentake'. He says in the same manuscript that this town was conveyed to Ralph Buck in the charter of the foundation for Bridlington Abbey. Buc seems uncertain of this family's English origin. In the *Commentary* he sees it as a branch of the Flemish family which came over with the Conqueror, a theory convenient to the theme of that work. But in the *History* he applies the German derivation of the name to this family rather than to the Flemish branch, and suggests they had been native in England for a very long time.

A John Buck who lived under Richard II and was married to a Howard served the Earl of Arundel, Lord Admiral of England, and was imprisoned for charging the Spanish fleet without leave of his commander (*Comm.* f. 452^{v}; *History*, text, p. 115, and B.L. Cotton Julius I.XI, f. 97).[5] Arundel was also responsible for his release from prison (B.L. Cotton Cleopatra V, f. 182^{v}). This must be the John Buck who, Buc notes in what seems to have been his own copy of *Cronicon Glasterboriensis*[6] was freed from the Tower by the Earl of Arundel, presumably on this occasion.

About his family's tradition of military service Buc says in his *History*:

> And these Bucks were all soldiers, and so were the rest succeeding these, for Robert Buck . . . followed Thomas, Duke of Norfolk, and was with him at the battle of Flodden. And Robert Buck, my father, served King Henry VIII at the siege of Boulogne, and the Duke of Somerset, Lieutenant General of King Edward VI, at the Battle of Musselburgh in Scotland. *Et nos militavimus et bella*

4 See below, p. cxxxv.

5 John Buck's imprisonment and release into Arundel's custody are also documented in Pat. Rolls (5 Nov. 1389), p. 146.

6 This is now MS. Cotton Cleopatra D.IV, 182^{v}. I am grateful to Alan Nelson for calling it to my attention.

vidimus. [I, too, have fought and have seen war.] G. B.
(text, p. 116, marginal note)

The early Bucks followed not only the Howards but also the dukes of York, soon to become the house of York. Laurence Buck served under Edward, Duke of York, at Agincourt, and his son John Buck of Harthill in Yorkshire died in the battle of St Albans fighting for Richard, Duke of York. His son, Sir John Buck, according to his descendant's account, served the Duke of York's sons as a Gentleman of the Privy Chamber under Edward IV and Richard III and was, Sir George first tells us, Controller of the Household under Richard III. Like his father he died fighting for his lord and, taken prisoner at Bosworth, was beheaded two days later. Along with others of Richard's followers, among them the ancestor of Thomas Howard, Earl of Arundel, to whom Buc dedicated the *History*, and the great-grandfather of Sir John Harington, he was attainted. His three destitute children, Robert, Joan and Margaret, were, Buc tells us, taken into the protection of Thomas, Earl of Surrey (later Duke of Norfolk) and brought up 'liberally' (*Comm.*, f. 453) in his house in Suffolk. Robert Buck, who followed Norfolk at Flodden, married a daughter of Sir Clement Higham or Heigham, M.P. and Speaker of the House. Robert's daughter Margaret was given in marriage by the Duchess of Norfolk to her kinsman Sir Frederick Tilney of Lancaster, a cousin of Edmund Tilney.[7] This was the earliest association of the Bucks with the Tilneys, the last being the succession to Edmund Tilney in the post of Master of the Revels by Sir George Buc, who was son of Robert Buck, Margaret's older brother, by his second marriage to Elizabeth Peterill.[8]

Interestingly, another descendant of Sir John Buck, Sir George's cousin Anne Barrow, was second wife to Sir Charles Cornwallis, who was lieger ambassador to Spain when Buc was there in 1605. Sir Charles was, by his first wife, father of the essayist Sir William Cornwallis, who preceded Buc in writing favourably on Richard III. This unfortunately seems to have no significance apart from being a coincidence, since Buc clearly did not know who the author of Cornwallis's *Encomium of Richard the Third* was (see below, p. cxxiii).

Doubt is cast upon Buc's claim regarding his great-grandfather's position in the government of the Yorkist kings by the absence of any mention of him in either the Patent Rolls or B.L. MS. Harleian 433, the compendium of signet documents from Richard III's reign.[9] That he was neither a member of the Council nor a Justice of the Peace makes it unlikely that he could have become Controller of the Household, and indeed Buc himself in a revision of the *History* (see below, p. cxxvi) retracts his earlier assertion to this effect. The only extant record of Sir John Buck is of his attainder after Bosworth in the Parliament of the first year of Henry VII.[10]

7 According to W.R. Streitberger, 'On Edmond Tyllney's Biography', *Review of English Studies*, 29 (1978), 25, Tilney was not 'Sir Edmund', as his name is given in numerous printed sources of the 18th to 21st centuries (including the previous editions of this work). He was rather 'an esquire entitled to be marshalled with knights in virtue of his position as Master of the Revels'. His epitaph does not cite him as 'Sir'. E.K. Chambers in *Notes on the History of the Revels Office, under the Tudors* (London, 1906), p. 68 states that in the order of precedence the Master of the Revels should walk with Knights Bachelor and refers for this to SP Dom, CCLXXIX 86.

8 A detailed family tree will be found in Eccles following p. 505.

9 B.L. MS. Harleian 433. There now exists an edition of this in four volumes, ed. Rosemary Horrox and P.W. Hammond (Gloucester, 1979-83).

10 *Rot. Parl.* VI, 276.

Possibly Buc was accepting family traditions at face value, not wishing to know that his family's origins were humbler than he liked to believe. That he does not qualify his statement of John Buck's position in Richard's household until late in the process of composing the *History* would suggest as much. The fact that no record of a connection with the Bucs appears in the Howard household books during Richard III's reign need not cast similar doubts on this other family tradition, for the association with the Howards originated after Bosworth. It might of course have continued from their association under Richard II.

George Buc was baptized in Holy Trinity Church, Ely, where his father shortly after became a churchwarden,[11] on 1 October 1560.[12] Robert Buck died in Chichester where, in 1577, he had become Steward and Auditor. He had fought in the Battle of Musselburgh and was described as 'vir pius et prudens'. This description, the date of his death, and details of his career and descent appear in the epitaph provided by his son-in-law, Dr Henry Blaxton, to be seen in a copy by his son George.[13] George Buc followed his family's traditions in adherence to and benefit from the Howards, serving under the Lord Admiral Charles Howard, 1st Earl of Nottingham, in 1596 on the Cadiz expedition and being preferred by him to court favour. That he never lost an opportunity of expressing gratitude to the family is apparent in his historical poem *Daphnis Polystephanos*, in the *Commentary,* and in the *History.* The Lord Admiral, says Buc, treated him more like a friend and kinsman than a follower (*Comm.*, f. 453^{v}). Buc was in close contact with another member of the family, Thomas Howard, Earl of Arundel, who was a fellow scholar and collector. He thus was indebted to the Howards not only for their patronage of himself and his ancestors but also for the use of their books and manuscripts and the *viva voce* information he received from them.

Sir George followed another family tradition in adherence to the house of York. A.J. Pollard has noted Buc's loyalty to the north of England, the place of origin for many of his ancestors, and sees this as a major aspect of his attachment to Richard III, who shared this regional affinity.[14] Perhaps Buc also saw the character of the man for whom his great-grandfather died at Bosworth as a reflection on the honour of his own house, just as he seems to find in the glory of the Howards an opportunity not only to show gratitude but also to rehearse and celebrate his own family. He appears to feel the sting of obscurity, mentioning in the *History* 'noble and worthy kindred' who will not acknowledge his family because they 'flourish not nor are rich' (text, p. 116). He attributes this obscurity to the attainder after Bosworth. In his historical poem *Daphnis Polystephanos* he says, "I am poore, and I am as obscure as *M. Scaurus* was . . . and so haue been euer since the fatall iourney at *Bosworth*'.[15]

Although no evidence exists that documents survived in Buc's family to serve as source material for his *History*, traditions did, for his grandfather was throughout

11 W.H. Challen, 'Sir George Buc, Kt., Master of the Revels', *Notes and Queries*, n.s. 3 (1957), 326.
12 *Ibid.*, p. 291.
13 B.L. MS. Cotton Julius F.XI, f. 97.
14 A.J. Pollard, 'North, South and Richard III', from *Richard III, Crown and People*, ed. J. Petre (Gloucester, 1985), pp. 349-355.
15 G[eorge] B[uc], *Δαφνις Πολυστεφανος* (London, 1605), sig A4^{v}. Further references will be given in my text.

his patron's life closely associated with Thomas Howard, Duke of Norfolk, who survived Bosworth. It is on the testimony of his grandfather that Buc gives his account of Thomas Howard's fortunes after Bosworth, a report which conflicts with those accepted at that time and still in force (text, pp. 108f).[16] The Howards, too, had their traditions, and they also had documents.

Buc was educated as a boy at Higham Ferrers in Northamptonshire under his half-brother-in-law, Dr Henry Blaxton. When Buc's family, including the Blaxtons, moved to Chichester he probably continued his studies at the school there of which Blaxton was master. He thanks Blaxton in the Preface to *Daphnis* (sig. B4^v) for showing him charters at Chichester Cathedral. It seems possible that he was himself a schoolmaster in Chichester for a time. We know, in any case, that he held the title of 'Master', which Blaxton acquired and passed to Buc's father Robert, who passed it on to his son.[17]

There is good evidence of his having gone on to Cambridge.[18] He then proceeded to the Inns of Court, first to Thavies Inn as a probationer in or about 1580, and was admitted to the Middle Temple in 1585 'as late of New Inn, gent., son & heir of Robert Buck of Chichester, gent., decd'.[19] He was an envoy to France in 1587, and in the *History* mentions being there when he heard the news of Mary, Queen of Scots' death (text, p. 184). In 1588 he served against the Armada under Charles Howard, the Lord Admiral. It was through his assistance that Buc became M.P. for Gatton, Surrey, in 1593 and 1597. He tells us in the *Commentary* (f. 453^v) that it was the Lord Admiral who preferred him to Queen Elizabeth.

In 1595 the queen suggested him for the post of French Secretary or Clerk of the Signet, and Howard recommended him to Sir William Cecil for one of these posts, but the latter did not fall vacant, and another suitor gained the former. But Buc had at least won the queen's attention. While serving with the Lord Admiral on the Cadiz expedition on Sir Walter Raleigh's ship, he acted as envoy from the commanders to the queen, taking his instructions directly from the Earl of Essex (B.L. Cotton Otho E.IX). As he says in a letter to Sir John Stanhope (f. 107), Raleigh's valour against the Spanish fleet, 'if o*u*r Soveraign M*istres*s had seen it \it/ would I think have been a sufficient expiation of all his faults. whatsoev*er*'.[20] He thought it 'an honour & happiness' to be part of the expedition, despite having to march in full armour 'in an extreme hot day' (f. 107). In this letter he gives details of the expedition and of his colloquy with Essex. He also reports his reply to a Spaniard who asked about the queen's health: 'I told him that hir ma*jes*ty had as strong & as healthfull a body as the youngest mayd in her court' (f. 108). This is in harmony with the expressions of praise in his works, amounting almost to worship of Elizabeth even after her death, which evidently had some basis in his personal impressions. This letter, and his description in B.L. MS. Cotton Otho E.IX, ff. 349-50 of his colloquy with Essex about what to tell the queen, have

16 All accounts of Thomas Howard's life ignore Buc as a source for his adventure at Bosworth.

17 See Eccles, p. 420 and also his article on Buc in 'Brief Lives, Tudor and Stuart Authors', *Studies in Philology*, LXXIX (1982), p. 18.

18 See below, pp. xxxvi, xxxviii .

19 Challen, p. 291.

20 Bod. MS. Eng. lett. B. 27, ff. 106-108, a 19th-century copy of the letter written 9 July 1596. No original survives.

unusual immediacy.

It seems that as early as 1597 there was mention of Buc's candidacy for the reversion of the office of Master of the Revels, then held by his distant relation by marriage, Edmund Tilney.[21] In the case of both Tilney and Buc, the responsibility for their ultimately holding the post was due to the intervention of Charles Howard, now Earl of Nottingham, whose family was entwined with them both. W.R. Streitberger suggests that in 1595 Howard had backed a plan for Tilney to be raised to a higher court position, Master of Ceremonies, and Buc to take over the Revels,[22] but this did not materialize. Streitberger in an earlier article remarks with regard to Tilney that since the Revels had a direct effect on the monarch's comfort and also on court prestige, 'the burden of choosing candidates . . . was great'.[23] Most references to the choice of officer speak of the necessity for the Master of the Revels to be a learned man: 'the connynge of the office resteth in skill of devise, in vndestandnge of histories, in iudgement of comedies tragedyes and showes, in sight of perspective and architecture, some smacke of geometrye and other thynges . . .'[24]

The playwright John Lyly believed that since about 1585 Queen Elizabeth had led him to expect the reversion. Hearing with consternation of her leaning toward Buc, he complained in letters of December 1597 and February 1601 to Robert Cecil, in a letter to the queen herself, probably in 1598, and in other letters and petitions.[25] For the present, though, the queen found more use for Buc as a diplomat.

In 1599 Buc was appointed Esquire of the Body. In 1601 he was chosen by the queen, 'in respect of [his] good discretion' (B.L. MS. Cotton Galba D.XII, f. 330^{v}) to undertake a diplomatic (basically secret service) mission to the besieged Ostend. An English army under Sir Francis Vere, whom Buc had met on the Cadiz expedition, was supporting a Dutch army led by Prince Maurice of Nassau against the Spanish occupying force. The queen was worried by the delay in lifting the siege and particularly about lack of military provisions and food. Buc was to express her majesty's concern for the wounded Vere's recovery and to ask his assessment of the situation. The queen does not want to do anything 'basely or without sound reason', but she wonders if there 'mought not be some meanes to drowne the Towne' (f. 332) or at least destroy the harbour if munitions suffice. If Sir Francis is not able to write, Buc should offer to write for him. He is also to deliver messages to Prince Maurice and was successful in so doing. After a three-year siege the town was lost, though at great cost to the Spaniards.[26]

In 1600-1 the Duke of Bracciano paid a visit to the English court and was entertained with what Leslie Hotson conjectured to be the first performance of *Twelfth Night*. Buc was chosen to escort the duke, along with Baron Darcy, with

21 It was long assumed that Buc was Tilney's nephew, even by me in previous editions of this book. Richard Dutton, *Mastering the Revels: the Regulation and Censorship of English Renaissance Drama* (London, 1991), p. 265, n. 9 gives a useful survey of this 'widely propagated fallacy'.

22 *Masters of the Revels and Elizabeth I's Court Theatre*, p. 215.

23 'On Edmond Tyllney's Biography', p. 20.

24 Chambers, *History of the Revels Office*, p. 37 (see also pp. 42 and 46 for other such descriptions).

25 Chambers, *The Elizabethan Stage*, I (Oxford, 1923), pp. 96-98.

26 B.L. MS. Cotton Galba D. XII, ff. 330^{v}-335.

whom we later find him exchanging scholarly information.[27]

In 1603, on the accession of James I, Buc became a Gentleman of the Privy Chamber and received a knighthood. He also was finally given the reversion of the Mastership of Revels. In 1605 his cousin Philip Tilney, who owned lands in Lincolnshire, died intestate. Buc claimed the lands as common law heir and won them with the support of Sir Edward Coke as his counsel.

In May to June of that year, Buc went to Spain, apparently in a Revels Office capacity as Deputy Master of the Revels,[28] accompanying the Lord Admiral and Robert Treswell, Somerset Herald, on embassy to Valladolid for ceremonies to celebrate the conclusion of peace negotiations between England and Spain. His observations, if only there were more of them, might be extremely interesting in view of the similarities we now know about between Spanish and Elizabethan outdoor theatres.[29] Along with Treswell, Buc was consulted on matters of precedence for the English contingent at a huge procession into Valladolid and at banquets.[30]

Treswell's account, in a short book,[31] is more detailed than Buc's letters and is extremely interesting. He describes one event which seems reminiscent of *The Castle of Perseverance.* In the marketplace were built stands of 20 yards or more equipped with scaffolds for the English audience. Spanish nobles stood to watch in the windows of the king's statehouse, hung with arras. In the centre was a castle with a lady in it, menaced by monsters. Four knights, to accompaniment of drum and fife, rescued the lady and fired the castle, with a show of fireworks. Enter Venus, Pallas, Juno, and Cupid led by savages, then four other knights in blue and white colours with crosses on their breasts like the knights of Malta, bringing the chariots of Peace, Plenty, and others. Four more knights then entered, followed by trumpets, and 'fell to the Barriers' two by two, first with staves, then with swords. Some of these were English lords encouraged by the Spaniards to join in. The judges included the Lord Admiral. Then followed dinner and impressive fireworks (pp. 21-23). On a later occasion there was morris dancing by 'gypsies', eight men, and eight boys attired as satyrs or shepherds who danced and played (p. 27).

They also saw a performance of Lope de Vega's *El Caballero de Illescas* and three interludes, but unfortunately we do not have any account of them from Buc, and Treswell (p. 41) is little more than tantalizing, only describing the performance

27 Leslie Hotson, *The First Night of Twelfth Night* (London, 1954), p. 180.

28 Gustav Ungerer, 'The Spanish and English Chronicles in King James's and Sir George Buc's Dossiers on the Anglo-Spanish Peace Negotiations', *Huntington Library Quarterly,* 61 (1998), 309. He points out on p. 319 that Tilney had written 'a diplomatic manual of encyclopaedic proportions for the sole use of servants of the crown', which must have stood Buc in good stead. I am grateful to Professor Ungerer for calling my attention to this article.

29 See for example Franklin J. Hildy, 'The Corral de Comedias at Almagro and London's Reconstructed Globe', *Shakespeare and the Mediterranean: The Proceedings of the Seventh International Shakespeare Association Valencia 2001 World Congress*, ed. Tom Clayton, Susan Brock and Vicente Forés (Newark, 2004); Hildy, '"Think When We Talk of Horses that You See Them", Comparative Techniques of Production, New Issues in the Reconstruction of Shakespeare's Theatre in the Elizabethan and Spanish Golden Age Playhouses', *Text and Presentation*, XI (1991), 61-8; and John J. Allen, 'The Spanish *Corrales de Comedias* and the London Playhouses and Stages', in *New Issues in the Reconstruction of Shakespeare's Theatre*, ed. Franklin J. Hildy (New York, 1990), pp. 207-35.

30 Ungerer, pp. 322f.

31 Robert Treswell, *A Relation of Such things as were observed to happen in the Journey of the Rt. Honourable CHARLES Earle of NOTTINGHAM L. High Admirall of ENGLAND His Highnesse Ambassadour to the King of SPAINE* (London, 1605).

space which seems to have been used at least for the interludes: the entertainment took place in a court covered with canvas to keep off the heat, with a fountain in the middle. A stage had been erected 'with all things fitting for a play', and the king watched 'the interlude' from a private space. Because clearly the Spaniards did things lavishly we may suspect that the reference to 'the interlude' might have incorporated all three interludes and perhaps the play as well.

Two letters survive from Buc to Viscount Cranborne,[32] as he addresses Robert Cecil by the title he had received the previous year. He ends the first, in May, with a postscript asking his lordship to 'think of some employment for me when I come home, anywhere it please y^{r} Lp.' (f. 85^{v}). In his next surviving letter, of 3 June, he tells Cecil that though he had said earlier that the league would be sworn next Sunday, on Saturday some vital papers seemed to be missing. By the time they were found it was too late to prepare them for the ceremony, which was thus postponed to the following day. We then have a cameo of Buc in action: he announced that since this was a matter of great solemnity, the very cause of the Lord Admiral's being in Spain, it could not be done upon an ordinary day. To the objection that this might delay their departure, he observed that next Thursday was Corpus Christi day, and that was accepted.

Treswell gives more detail than Buc does of the Corpus Christi day parade which preceded the signing of the oath: there were eight giants (three men, three women, and two moors) playing tabor and pipe and dancing, followed by blue-clad pilgrims, 25-26 crosses attended by representatives of their churches, pictures of saints, precious relics, churchmen and ambassadors (French, Venetian, Savoyard, and Moroccan as well as English), the king (and presumably the queen, who was certainly there), and the Cardinal also with tapers. After this the oath was sworn, with the king's hands between those of the Lord Admiral, and then signed (p. 42). This ceremony was attended, Buc tells Robert Cecil (f. 126), not only by the ambassador and lieger ambassador (Sir Charles Cornwallis), but by '& all the grandes, & noblemen (who were all in black)'. In celebration there was a splendid 'Juego de Toro' (bullfight) 'in a fayre place well built well representing the old Roman Theatres' (f. 126^{v}). Next came the Juegos de Cannas, which were 'presented v. magnificently': 40 drums and trumpets with coloured taffeta and 26 horses clothed in crimson velvet. Following them on horseback were the Spanish dukes and knights, who were 'in habit a la moresca' with short pikes in their hands. Then came the king and the Duke of Lerma and 20 other nobles. But, Buc concludes, 'I am ill advised to relate revelling matters at large to y^{r} Lp.' (f. 126 v).

On 1 June the king invited the Lord Admiral to see a muster of armed men. The guests were then invited to a masque in the banquet house, where thirty musicians in long taffeta garments played and six virgins danced. They were eventually joined by the (masked) king and queen and twenty-eight knights and ladies on a stage made to look like a cloud. Others came forward and danced to the upper end of the hall, then turned and joined the other dancers, and they all danced together. After the king and queen had unmasked they took seats, and lords and ladies danced galliards for them (Treswell, pp. 51-3).

32 TNA SP 94/11/f. 126-27.

On 7 June the Lord Admiral took leave of the king, and his party began the journey home. On their return they were celebrated, mention being made of their success not only in the pulpit but 'euen in their open plaies and Interludes' (Treswell, p. [64] labelled erroneously 42). Despite their collaboration and Buc's later friendship with heralds, Treswell seems not to have interacted much with him on this excursion: he refers to him in listing members of the expedition as 'Thomas Buc' (p. 4), with no reference to his knighthood.

Back in England, though earlier authors have seen Buc as exercising the functions of the Revels Office earlier as Tilney's assistant, Richard Dutton and W.R. Streitberger both argue[33] that there is no evidence at all of Buc's acting prior to Tilney's death in 1610. Possibly the confusion arose because Buc appropriated to the Revels Office in May 1606, perhaps as a source of income while he waited to become Master, the task of being sole licenser of plays for publication as distinct from performance. Between 1607 and 1615 all plays licensed for publication bore his signature, apart from *A Yorkshire Tragedy* (1608). He licensed *Timon of Athens* in 1609, *Coriolanus* in 1610, *Othello* in 1614, *The Tempest* in 1612, and *Twelfth Night* in 1614.

The Master of the Revels was responsible for plays performed at court. Buc selected and supervised court performances by the King's Men of *A Winter's Tale*, *The Tempest*, *Much Ado about Nothing*, *Othello*, both parts of *Henry IV*, and *Pericles*. The players were obliged to present a full rehearsal for his approval before he made selection. What he did not approve had to be altered before the play could appear. The Revels accounts in the National Archives give some idea of the time he spent in exercising his office.[34] In 1612-13, the year of the Princess Elizabeth's marriage to the Elector Palatine, he was in attendance 125 days and 24 nights, then for 10 days and 5 nights he attended the Lord Chamberlain (the Earl of Suffolk) to prepare 'for the entertainm*en*t of the said maryed Princes' (2046, no. 18). In addition, he spent 15-20 days airing the wardrobe in the Revels Office. In 1614-15 he was in attendance 115 days and 16 nights between October and 22 February 'as well as for Rehersalls and making choice of plaies and Comedies and reforming them' (2047, no. 20), 20 days in the summer for airing the costumes, and 23 days for triumphs at Easter in celebration of the king's reign. In 1615-16 he claimed expenses for 'wages and Entertaynmentes of Officers Artificers and other ymployed aboute the finishing making and setting forthe of sundry plaies Commodies feates of activity Maskes and Triumphes at Tylte and in airing the stuffe belonging to the said office' (2047, no. 21). In this year between the end of October and the end of February he attended 107 days and 19 nights, and the next year 127 days and 16 nights. In addition he was on hand for triumphs, Easter celebrations, airing of garments, and the marriage at Hampton Court of Sir John Villiers to the daughter of Sir Edward Coke. The visit of the Earl of Oxford 'to my lodging at Hampton Court' which Buc mentions in the *History* (text, p. 170) must have occurred on this occasion.

There is a scrap backing a note inserted in the manuscript of the *History* (f. 43^{v}) that gives an idea of the day to day running of the office. He lists what he needs:

33 Dutton, pp. 146-151; Streitberger, *Masters of the Revels*, p. xiii.
34 TNA MSS. 1, 2046 (16-18) and 2047 (19-21). Specific references will be given in my text.

'Ink paper pen*ns*', a '<ca>ndlestick' (a prop for a play or an office necessity?), and, needing to reach a decision on a play script or a speech he writes a note to himself to 'allow or suppress all'. Having made selection of a play for a particular holiday or event, he and his four assistants had to fit up the hall for it, supplying the huge number of candles required for lighting, as well as decorating it lavishly and having furniture brought in, then taken away afterwards, for which they had to organize the transport. He was also responsible for setting up venues when native or foreign royalty was to be present, for banquets, dancing, and games of various sorts, from tilting to bearbaiting to football. The Revels Office accounts are a tantalizing mixture of branches with wire, pulleys and long ladders for hanging them, roses and tassels, hooks, candlesticks, pans, and chamber pots.

Eccles gives what is probably a just estimate of Buc's censorship practice:

> From what we know of his acts as Master, Buc seems to have been not at all a severe censor, but to have executed conscientiously and moderately . . . the duties of a difficult office. . . . On the whole perhaps it was as well that Elizabeth chose Buc, a gentleman poet and lover of plays, from the point of view of the Court rather than of the professional playwright, and one who had shown the diplomatic qualities necessary to mediate between the players and authority.[35]

In the controversy over the *Biron* performances George Chapman seems to have recognized Buc's gentlemanly qualities even in the heat of his frustration and anger at the censor's hesitation in licensing the play for publication, though there is perhaps a sting in the tail of his letter. Buc, having licensed it for performance, delayed to license it for publication because he had not yet seen the copy intended for print. He had been bitten once, in that the Children of Blackfriars spoke in their performance of it lines that he had ordered deleted, so his hesitation seems understandable. Chapman writes impatiently about the delay of licensing for the press due to the French Ambassador's objection to the performance, protesting that it is not his fault if actors decide to speak lines that have been censored: 'I see not myne owne Plaies; nor carrie the Actors Tongues in my mouthe'. He ends the letter addressing Sir George directly:

> how safely soever Illiterate Aucthoritie setts up his Bristles against Poverty, methinkes yours (being accompanied with learning) should rebate the points of them, and soften the fiercenes of those rude manners; you know S^{r}, They are sparkes of the lowest fier in Nature that fly out uppon weaknes with every puffe of Power. . . .[36]

Buc's censorship can be seen in practice in the manuscript copies of *The Second Maiden's Tragedy* (B.L. MS. Lansdowne 807, ff. 29-56) and *John van Olden Barnevelt* (B.L. MS. Additional 18653). Though the former, Janet Clare notes, is a highly subversive play, dealing with regicide, Buc allowed it with minor cuts,[37] though more than appear in other plays he censored. This argues for his not being

35 Eccles, 'Sir George Buc', p. 504.

36 *Athenaeum*, 6 April 1901, p. 433.

37 Janet Clare, '*Art made tongue-tied by authority*': *Elizabethan and Jacobean Dramatic Censorship* (Manchester, 1990), pp. 165-71.

an unduly strict censor. He begins by correcting a minor grammatical error of 'hath' to 'haue' (f. 29, l. 2). Several very general derogatory remarks about courtiers he has altered or marked for alteration. The phrase 'Frenchmen's tortures' (f. 55), which might have caused national offence, is altered to 'extremest tortures'. Passages on lust, particularly the king's lust, are cut, and strong references to tyranny are marked. A half-line, 'Y*ou*r kinges poisoned' is crossed out, leaving 'I am poisoned' (f. 55^{v}). At the end of the manuscript he writes, 'This second Maydens tragedy (for it hath no name inscribed) may w*i*th the reformations bee acted publikely. 31. Octob*er*. 1611./. G. Buc.' (f. 56). The play, probably by Middleton, which has similarities to the lost partly Shakespearean play *Cardenio*, is still referred to by the title Buc gave it because of similarities he saw between it and Beaumont and Fletcher's *The Maid's Tragedy*. An interesting apparent idiosyncrasy is evident in his marking for deletion references denigrating the general character of women.

Buc usually puts crosses in the margins where revisions are required, and corrections in his own hand appear in passages regarding overthrow of governments: 'tooke that course / that now is practised on you', which would seem to show too specific a precedent for government overthrow, is changed to 'cutt of his opposites', and 'changed to a Monarchie' was made 'changed to another form' (f. 26). Against one passage he remarks: 'I like not this: neither do I think y^{t} the \pr./ was thus disgracefully vsed. besides he is to much presented. [here.] G.B.' (f. 5^{v}). The law restricted representations of royalty onstage, but besides this, Buc appears to be concerned about historical accuracy, unwilling that even popular literature should misrepresent truth. And in this case, he was on hand at the time the play depicts, on his 1601 embassy to the Netherlands, so he responds from personal experience. T.H. Howard-Hill, who has studied his censorship of this play carefully, says, 'His initial objection was to the ignominy of [Count] Maurice's exclusion from the Council by a mere soldier acting for burghers. His second objection was to the unhistoricity of the incident . . .'[38] (something Janet Clare misses). Buc, as we have seen, had met Count Maurice. Some examples of manuscripts he censored can be seen in Dutton's *Mastering the Revels*, Plates 8 and 9.

An undated letter exists from Buc to the Earl of Salisbury, the Lord Treasurer, seeking an allowance for a house for the Revels Office. He has recently had taken from him the house worth £50 annually, granted to him previously by royal patent, since which time the Lord Chamberlain has hired a convenient house for the office, but at a very high price and told him to put there the wardrobe and other items belonging to the Revels Office. Buc points out that the previous Master had £45 per annum allowance and also £100 for recompense, while not required to hire a house. Finally he pleads,

> further I humbly pray y*ou*r L*ordshi*p honorably to consyder *tha*t this office is the onley reward of my long, chargeable & faithfull service [done] in the court & abroad; by land & by sea; in warr & in peace for the space of wellneere 30. yeeres: & is the best meanes of my living, w*hi*ch to take away is a punishment due to no serious,

38 T.H. Howard-Hill, 'Buc and the Censorship of Sir John Van Olden Barnevelt', *Review of English Studies* XXXIX (1988), 57, an excellent, detailed study of Buc's censorship in this play.

& capitall offendors. & not to loyall & serviceable subiects.
(B.L. Harl. 6850, f. 253)

He concludes by pleading for a favourable response, particularly 'for her sacred sake' (Queen Elizabeth's), who would surely have done more for him.

From 1615 he suffered difficulties with the Exchequer over payment of back wages to himself and his men, who seem to have been in a desperate financial state and who, he felt, were blaming him for not being urgent enough in demanding payment. Late in 1621 or in 1622 Buc went mad, a madness Eccles attributes to the struggles over wages,[39] but which Helen Maurer thinks it makes more sense to attribute to Alzheimer's.[40] John Chamberlain wrote to Sir Dudley Carleton on 30 March 1622, 'Poore Sir George Bucke master of the Revells is in his old age faln starke madd, and his place executed by Sir John Ashley [alternatively 'Astley'] that had the reversion'.[41] His death was not long in coming: he died on 31 October 1622[42] and was buried at Broadwater in Sussex.[43]

In 1618 Buc had contemplated marriage with Elizabeth Meutis of West Ham, but his 'humorous and shie proseeding'[44] was said to have stood in his way. Eccles conjectures that his interest was less in the marriage itself than in reforming or discomfiting his prospective heirs. His only brother Robert had become a Jesuit. Buc's will, later declared a forgery, stated that if the law barred his brother from inheritance his heir should be his nephew Stephen Buck, a son of his sister Cecilia, who had married a William Buck of Lincolnshire (no relation to Sir George's family). Stephen Buck took immediate possession of Buc's lands and goods on their owner's death, but a general pardon was then granted Robert Buck, enabling him to possess his inheritance. There followed a protracted legal battle. Stephen Buck tried to prove that Sir George had conveyed his lands and goods to him and his son George by Deed of Gift. There were doubts, however, as to whether the document was genuine or forged, and whether if genuine it had been made before or after the inception of Buc's lunacy. Stephen Buck had at one time been imprisoned for forgery and had since been in collusion with his uncle John Buck, a notorious forger. There was, furthermore, evidence to show Sir George's dislike of his nephew. Consequently, in 1625 Robert Buck was declared his brother's heir. In the meantime, however, Stephen Buck and his son George had made off with numerous of Sir George's possessions and would soon make use of them.

39 Eccles, 'Sir George Buc', p. 481.

40 'Bones in the Tower: a Discussion of Time, Place and Circumstance', Part 1, *The Ricardian*, VIII (1990), n. 44, p. 491.

41 *The Letters of John Chamberlain*, ed. Norman Egbert McClure (Philadelphia, 1939), II, 430.

42 Eccles, 'Sir George Buc', p. 484, derives the date of Buc's death from the inquisition post mortem, C 142/566/17 and on p. 482 attributes the common error of dating it to September 1623 to Malone and Chalmers, followed by Greg. Despite which the Bodleian online catalogue ascribes the 1646 edition by George Buck Esq. and its 1973 reprint to 'Sir [italics mine] George Buck 1622 or 1623' and John Ashdown-Hill queries the date 1622 in *The Last Days of Richard III and the Fate of His DNA* (Stroud, 2013), p. 92 but does not explain his reason for so doing.

43 Challen, p. 291.

44 Letter from Ambrose Randolph to Thomas Wilson, 5 April 1618, quoted in Eccles, 'Sir George Buc', p. 470.

II. BUC'S LITERARY ACTIVITY

Buc has left us several of his minor works, in addition to the three surviving historical treatises and some references to other compositions which have been lost. For two poems in English he is given a place in Joseph Ritson's biographies of poets.[1] As a poet he is technically adequate but far from brilliant or inspired. His first extant verse is a quatorzain which leads the group of complimentary verses introducing Thomas Watson's *Hekatompathia or Passionate Century of Loue*, conjecturally dated 1581. This competent, conventional poem is entitled 'A Quatorzain, in the commendation of Master Thomas Watson, and of His Mistres, for whom he wrote his Booke of Passionat Sonnetes'. In the Huntington Library copy of Buc's *Daphnis*, we have a six-line verse expressing gratitude to Lord Ellesmere, to whom the author presented this copy.[2] These are Buc's only extant original poems in English, apart from his long poem *Daphnis Polystephanos*, published in 1605. One further long poem, 'A Poem of St George the Famous Champion of England', was misattributed to Buc in 1867 by W. Carew Hazlitt in his *Hand-Book to the Popular, Poetical, and Dramatic Literature of Great Britain*, but this was corrected in his *Collections and Notes*, Ser. 1 (1876), with information that the poem was by a certain Gaudy Brampton of Blow-Norton.

Buc produced several short Latin poems:

1) A manuscript poem on the Armada victory, included in Richard Robinson's *Archippus*, 'newly written oute' (f.2) in 1602 (B.L. MS. Royal 18 A.LXVI). 'Vnto whiche ys allso added . . . Collections of English Voyages from 1580 to 1598' (f. 14). Robinson describes the poem as 'Certeyne Verses given me by one Mr Buck a gent of my Lord Admiralles to be annexed vnto the Action praecedent, as I sett yt downe in the Booke w*hi*ch I gave vnto his Honorable good Lordship in the yeare aforesayd. 1589' (f. 21). Buc entitles the poem 'Aquilae Nigrae Austriacae, et Leonis Albi Norfolcici, pugna, sive Illustrissimi Haerois CAROLI HOVARDI, – Anglia Summi Admirallii, &c Victoria, . . . et Numine DIANAE nostrae ELIZABETHAE DEI GRATIA, ANGLIAE, FRANCIAE et HYBERINAE REGINAE, AVGVSTAE, FAELICISSIME TRIVMPHANTIS FIDEI DEFENSATRICIS. &ct.'

2) A complimentary verse, one of a group by several authors, prefaced to the 1607 edition of Camden's *Britannia*. It reappears in the 1610 translation of that work.

3) A eulogy of London at the beginning of Buc's own *Third Universitie of*

1 [Joseph Ritson], *Bibliographia Poetica* (London, 1802), pp. 146f.

2 The authenticity and biographical import of this verse are discussed in Eccles, 'Sir George Buc', pp. 438ff. A copy appears in W.W. Greg, 'Three Manuscript Notes by Sir George Buc', *The Library* XII (1931), 307-21, Plate V.

England,[3] enumerating the physical attributes, the diversity of arts, crafts, branches of learning, artifice, culture, wealth, and populace of the city.
4) A eulogy of Philip Sidney, praising him mainly as a military figure, B.L. MS. Cotton Julius F.XI, ff. 93^{v}-94.

These, like Buc's English poems, are competent and uninspired, rigid in formality and metrical regularity, and conventional in heroic vocabulary.

Buc was also a verse translator from several languages, as numerous examples in his *History* witness.[4] He claims (text, p. 85) the distinction of having preceded Harington as a translator of Ariosto, but he does not say whether he translated the whole of *Orlando Furioso* or merely portions of it. Probably the latter, for in addition to the Ariosto translation in the *History* he presents a short one in *The Third Universitie*, taking this opportunity to express criticism in terms which suggest that in this case Harington's translation preceded his:

> Which verses I haue aduentured thus plainely to turne into English Octaua, and could haue beene well content to haue spared the Laboure had not Sir *John Harrington* discosted from the Author. And yet I must confesse he hath performed an excellent part of a translator in that his English *Orlando*.
>
> (sig. Nnnnv)

The Third Universitie in the section on painting and cosmetology (sig. Oooo 3) includes a verse translation from a Greek epigram by Lucilius about women painting their faces. This particular translation is exceptionally clever and smooth and reproduces some of the original's wordplay. But ordinarily Buc's translations, generally in rhymed iambic epigrammatic couplets, are trite, lame, metrically incompetent and make no attempt to approximate to the tone of the original.

There is a suggestion that Buc wrote a play. J.Q. Adams[5] presents a late seventeenth-century list of early English plays, all probably in manuscript, compiled by Abraham Hill (1635-1721), a book collector. Among those listed is *The Ambitious Brother* by G. Buc. Adams suggests that Hill may have seen Buc's name as licenser and mistaken it for the author's. Also, Buc was an avid book collector,[6] and this might have been a book he owned. Adams warns that we should look to Eccles's biography for mention of other George Buc[k]s. He considers it possible, however, that this is a dramatization by Buc of the subject of his *History of King Richard the Third* – which in view of his revisionist sentiments seems most unlikely – and cites Buc's devising the dumb shows for *Locrine* as evidence of his direct involvement in playmaking. We may note that such facility was an attribute expected of the Master of the Revels: 'The Mayster . . . oughte to be a man . . . of good engine, inventife witte, and experience . . . for varietie of straunge devises delectable . . .'[7]

We have Buc's own hand to witness that he devised these dumb shows. The play *Locrine* was published in 1595. In the copy now in the Bodmer collection in Geneva,

3 In John Stow, *The Annales or Generall Chronicle of England* (London, 1615), sig. LlII 6. Buc's work runs from pp. 958-88 (sigs. Llll 5-Oooo 3v). Since the page numbering is extremely erratic, quotations from this edition will be identified by signatures.
4 See below, text, pp. 34, 69, 85, 116, 167, 193f, and 208.
5 Joseph Quincy Adams, 'Hill's List of Early Plays in Manuscript', *The Library* XX (1939), 71-99.
6 See below, p. lix.
7 Quoted Chambers, *Notes*, p. 42.

he has written on the title page, 'Char. Tilney wrote *a* Tragedy of this matter *which* hee named Estrild. & *which* I think is this. it was l*ost* by his death. & now s*ome* fellow hath published *it*. I made du*m*be shews for it, w*hi*ch I yet haue. G.B.' Although Samuel Tannenbaum attacked the hand as a Collier forgery,[8] his argument was satisfactorily refuted by R.C. Bald.[9] As someone who has read at least a thousand pages in Buc's several hands, I see nothing in the inscription to suggest any possibility of its being anyone's but Buc's and consider it unlikely to the point of impossibility that a forger could have known Buc's hand so well as to have produced so minutely his every idiosyncrasy and to have done so with apparent fluency.

Two works of Buc's on artistic subjects are lost. One is his *Poetica*, mentioned by Camden in his *Remaines* in comments on Sir Philip Sidney's epitaph, which he says is 'most happily imitated out of the French of *Mons. Boniuet*, made by *Joach. du Bellay*, as it was noted by Sir *George Buc* in his *Poetica*'.[10] Eccles remarks that in this observation Buc surpasses Raleigh's latest editor, who knows no source for the corresponding stanza of Raleigh's elegy on Sidney.[11] This work of Buc's on poets is probably the one he mentions in *The Third Universitie* in the section 'Of Poets and of Musitians' (Oooov) as 'a particular Treatise', though it is difficult to tell from the context whether he is speaking here of a treatise on poetry or on drama. Chalmers states that Buc 'wrote a treatise – "of *Poets* and *Musicians*", which recent Inquirers have not been able to find'.[12] Presumably this is the same treatise, and Chalmers has simply adopted the section heading. Eccles notes[13] that the reference to Sidney suggests that the work discussed contemporary poets. This would not be out of keeping with Buc's interests and activities, for although his antiquarian works and classical education tend to overshadow the other aspects of his career, he was deeply involved in one contemporary art form, the dramatic, was a dabbler in verse himself, and wrote a treatise on contemporary London.

It is fitting that a prolific author who held the post of Master of the Revels and possessed a peculiar sense of the dignity of things pertaining to his own origins and activities should have written about the art of the drama. And indeed he did so, but his work is unfortunately not extant. Only this reference to it survives, in his summary of his comments on the craft of dramatic performance:

> I might hereunto adde for a *Corollary* of this discourse, the Art of *Reuels*, which requireth knowledge in Grammar, Rhetorike, Logicke, Philosophie, Historie, Musick, Mathematikes, & in other Arts (& all more then I vnderstand I confesse) & hath a setled place within this Cittie. But because I haue discribed it, and discoursed thereof at large in a particular commentarie, according to my talent, I will surcease to speake any more therof . . .
>
> (*Third Universitie*, sig. Oooo 3^{v})

8 Samuel Tannenbaum, *Shakespearian Scraps and Other Elizabethan Fragments* (New York, 1933), pp. 51-74. He reproduces this inscription on Plate VIII (the transcript is mine).

9 R.C. Bald, 'The *Locrine* and *George-a-Green* Title Page Inscriptions', *The Library*, XV (1934), 295-305.

10 William Camden, *Remaines Concerning Britaine*, rev. ed. (London, 1614), p. 376.

11 Eccles, 'Sir George Buc', p. 413. Agnes M.C. Latham's edition of 1929 is the one alluded to. Her edition of 1951 has not benefited from Eccles's observation. There has been no edition of Raleigh since.

12 [George Chalmers], *An Apology for the Believers in the Shakespeare Papers* (London, 1797), p. 494.

13 Eccles, 'Sir George Buc', pp. 412ff.

Buc's attitudes to poetry and drama were ambivalent.[14] Poetry was evidently for him, as for other gentlemen of his status and educational background, a fashionable pastime. Various comments in the *History* point to a contempt for fictitious works as frivolous in comparison with history. His remarks on literary men are few and little concern their literary pursuits. Sidney is mentioned twice in the *Commentary*, both times as a valiant soldier (*Comm*. ff. 354 and 370). The same concentration on his military at the expense of his literary skill is apparent in Buc's Latin elegy on Sidney mentioned above. Fulke Greville, whom Buc knew best as a fellow antiquary, is called in the *Commentary* 'a very noble & wis & learned gentilm*a*n' (f. 408) and of Thomas Sackville Buc mentions only his honours and offices and an anecdote regarding his death (*Comm*., f. 248). In a remark in the margin of his own copy of Bishop Godwin's *Catalogue of the Bishops of England*, though, Buc says of Thomas Parkhurst, Bishop of Norwich in 1560, 'hee was a meetly good poet. & his poemes are extant',[15] but there are no other entries of this nature. Buc's comments in the *History* regarding Sir Thomas More's poetic ability (text, pp. 121 and 196) are backhanded compliments, designed to discredit More as an historian. In the prose preface to *Daphnis*, he quotes Lydgate and Chaucer to support an argument that the terms 'England' and 'Britain' are used interchangeably, but passes from them very quickly to Higden. Like the modern historian, Buc is wary of citing fictional sources for factual information:

> *Ion Lidgate* disertly asseuereth in King *Arthurs* complaint in these words, *Great Britain now called England*: and so likewise doth *Geffrey Chaucer* in the *Franklins* tale (viz.) *In England, that Clepid was Britain*: And *Ranulfus Cestrensis* a grauer Authour preremptorily affirmeth that King *Egbert* . . . commaunded . . . that *Britain* should bee called *England*.
>
> (sig. B4)

Nearly all Buc's quotations from poets and playwrights are classical, often evidently from memory since he sometimes misattributes them. But occasionally he quotes foreign Renaissance writers such as Ariosto. English translators fare rather better in Buc's esteem. He several times speaks highly of Harington as translator of *Orlando Furioso* (*Third Universitie*, sig. Nnnnv, *Comm*., f. 417; *History*, p. 168). He also makes reference once to North's translation of Plutarch (*Comm*., f. 426^{v}).

We must be wary of assessing Buc's attitude to the stage, since most of the remarks on it which have been habitually attributed to him may be additions to his *History* by his great-nephew, George Buck Esq. (herein designated the 'Editor': see Introduction IV below), and it is impossible to tell in some cases whether they represent the original author's intention or are merely embellishments. In one case, where we have both the autograph version and the editorial ones, it is clear that a reference to the stage is entirely the Editor's (George Buck Esq.'s) addition. When speaking of Richard's calumniators and their attacking him by reference to his bad dreams, Buc himself (text, p. 128) makes no mention of dramatic versions,

14 See below, pp. pp. cxliii-cxliv.

15 Buc's MS. note in the Bodleian copy of F[rancis] G[odwin], *A Catalogue of the Bishops of England* (London, 1601), p. 355.

nor does Buck, Jnr in his handwritten copies. But in the printed version Buc's great-nephew gives us, 'nay, they will dissect his very sleepes, to finde prodigious dreames and bug-beares, . . . which they dresse in all the fright and horrour fiction and the stage can adde'.[16] Consequently, we must not be too hasty in accepting for Buc's own assessment of the stage, as Frank Marcham does,[17] this remark of which there is no trace in the autograph manuscript, but which appears in some form in all the editorial versions. Its style is strongly redolent of Buc's revising great-nephew's style:

> ffor the ignorant, and never-vnderstandeing vulgare; whose faith (in history) is drawne from Pamphlet and Ballad, and their Reverend and learned Autors, the stage, or those that playe the bauds to it, for a living, Let them fly their owne pitch, for they are but kytes, and Crowes, and can digest nought (soe well) as stench and filth, to which I leaue them.
>
> (B.L. MS. Egerton 2216, f. 270)

It is not at all likely that Buc, whose relationship with the actors was, as Trevor Howard-Hill describes it, collegial,[18] would have been so contemptuous of theatre practitioners. Indeed, as we shall see, Buc consulted two professional theatre artists, William Shakespeare and Edward Juby, about authorship of a play script (see below, p. lix).

It is however natural that, despite his office, Buc should show to some extent a gentleman's contempt for drama, because as fiction it distorts the truth of history and panders to the common people's ignorance. Buc in his own writings appeals specifically to the learned reader. His attitude toward poetry is evident in his remarks on More, when he says that poetry assists in writing fables and relating fantasies, giving authors licence to tell falsehoods.

> And that Sir Thomas More was a good poet and much delighted with poetry and with quaint inventions, his many poems and epigrams yet extant testify; besi[des] the many petty comedies and interludes which he made and oftentimes acted in person with the rest of the actors. . . . And to these his practices fantastical and his *Utopia* may be added.
>
> (see below, text, p. 121)

He is moved by the ancient origins of drama and by the honour it bestows on him and on his city to refer to it as 'That first and most auncient kind of Poesy', and to accord the art as practised in his time the highest praise: 'so liuely expressed and represented vpon the publike stages & Theaters of this citty, as *Rome* in the *Auge* of her pompe & glorie, neuer saw it better performed, (I meane in respect of the action, and art, and not of the cost, and sumptuousnesse)' (*Third Universitie*, sig Oooo^{v}).

Because his place in literature is determined not so much by his own compositions as by the fact that those of so many greater authors passed through his hands, and received the imprint of his directions for revision, we should be

16 George Buck Esq., *History of the Life and Reigne*, p. 78.
17 Frank Marcham, *The King's Office of the Revels* (London, 1925), p. 4.
18 Howard-Hill, p. 43. See also below, p. lix for mention of Buc's relationships with specific theatre practitioners.

glad to possess his detailed observations on the arts he supervised. But since these are lost, we can only pursue in as great detail as possible, by picking them here and there from his extant works, the character, opinions, and intellectual bent of a man who touched many of our greatest dramatic works.

Daphnis Polystephanos

'*Δαφνις Πολυστεφανος*, An Eclog treating Of Crownes, and of Garlandes, and to whom of right they appertaine', is an historical-pastoral poem in fifty-eight stanzas in honour of James I's coronation, although Buc says in his dedication to the new king that he began the work 'long since' (sig. A3). It was published in 1605 but seems to have been prepared in 1602, anticipating James's accession. The British Library's Grenville copy (shelfmark G 11553), presented by Buc to Henry Howard, Earl of Northampton, which includes a genealogical tree tracing the Plantagenets back to Egbert in 802, has a printed note 'Ioan. Woutneel excud. 1602' at the lower righthand corner of this tree, crediting the person who composed or at least drew it. Buc has in pen altered the '2' to a '5'.

Daphnis purports to show the glory of King James's ancestors and sets forth his descent from Henry II through the Tudors. James in reconciling the kingdoms of Scotland and England is reconciler of the intestine quarrel between Albanact and Locrine, the sons of Brute, as Henry VII was reconciler of the quarrel between Lancaster and York. Faced with the necessity of praising the Tudors as James's ancestors, it may seem surprising that Buc is able to speak kindly of Richard III:

> Fame hath been sharp to th'other [Richard], yet bicause
> All accusations of him are not proued:
> And hee built Churches, and made good law's,
> And all men held him wise, and valiant,
> Who may deny him then his *Genest* plante?
> (sig. E4v)

Buc's sense of historical honesty and family pride seem to have combined in compelling him to champion this king. He notes in his Epistle Dedicatory that among faults others have found in the poem is 'that I haue concealed, and coloured the faultes of bad Princes' (sig. A4v). He excuses himself on the grounds of Christian charity. That this statement refers specifically to his defence of Richard is strongly suggested by his proceeding immediately to mention on the same page that his own family has been obscure since 'the fatall iourney at *Bosworth*'.

His attitude toward Henry VII is ambivalent. In one stanza Buc praises him in conventional terms – though he clearly regards the house of York as the older:

> This *Richmont* was a very prudent prince
> And therefore was surnamed *Solomon*.
> The world hath seen great works accomplish'd since
> Which were proiected by this *Theodore*.
> This man of GOD did happily atone
> The ciuil feud, whidh [*sic*] long had been before,
> Betwixt the Rose, which first grew in the wood
> And that which Venns [*sic* for 'Venus'] colour'd in hir blood.
> (sig. F2)

Then in a marginal note to this he says, 'hee extinguished the male line of *Yorke*'.

In addition to his defence of Richard, many other themes developed in his later work are struck here. The poem's title and central image are of a garland made from the *planta genista*, whose origins he discusses, citing, as in the *History* (p. 15), Leonhard Fuchs as authority (sig. Dv). Another of his antiquarian interests, the Stone of Scone, to which he returns at the end of the *History* (text, p. 215f), is briefly mentioned in the dedication (sig. A3v). His own family history appears not only in the dedication but also in a marginal note to the verse on King John, where he speaks of Walter Buck's assistance to this king (sig. E3). A very considerable portion of the dedication is taken up with praise of the Howards for fostering his family, and their genealogy is also touched on.

Buc's heroes are the same here as later in the *History*. He shows particular interest in Henry II, spending on him the major part of the Introduction and beginning the poem with him. He is described as 'the greatest King (of whom there is any credible story extant) which hath been in this Isle of *Britain* since the time of the Romaine Emperous [*sic*]' (sig. B3v). So anxious is he to show the magnitude of Henry's empire that he denies James I his claim to be the first ruler of the whole island: 'a late *Anonymous* in a little book dedicated to his Majesty, affirmeth that neuer any Prince was king of this whole Isle vntill now. But he is deceiued . . .' (sig. B3v). Queen Elizabeth as usual merits an effusion:

A Queene, whose state so happily did stand
That men did say (seeing hir greatnesse such)
This Lady leadeth fortnne [*sic*] in hir hand
A virgin which did keep her lamp still light
And eke for tarenes was a *Phaenix* height.
(sig. f. 3v)

Like his loyalties, his prejudices are the same as in the *History*. He refuses to acknowledge Henry IV's title but grants him to have been a 'princely Knight' (sig. F). His anti-Catholic feeling is strong: 'To sweep out of this land the drosse of *Roome*; / A worke of worth . . .' (sig. F2v). He is wary of the 'British History': 'to haue chosen any of the most ancient Kings, I must haue looked so farre backe, as I should not onely haue made this Eclog ouer-long, and tedious, but also haue lost my selfe in the cloudes of obscurity by soring too high amongst them . . .' (sig. B3). He does mention, parenthetically, that the Tudors were descended from Cadwallader, but in general inclines much more toward the sort of genealogy that can be documented by the heralds.

His methods here are similar to those in his antiquarian prose works. He begins with a genealogical dedication and historical introduction and accompanies both prose introduction and poem with marginal notes which include historical and genealogical information, very exact citation of sources, and classical references. Several sources cited in the poem are used again in the *History*: Buchanan, Giraldus Cambrensis, Camden, De la Hay, De Serres, Du Haillan, Fabyan, Froissart, Ingulf [i.e. the Crowland Chronicle], Liber St Stephani (Caen), William of Malmesbury, William of Newburgh, John of Salisbury, Stow, Walsingham. *Daphnis* is interesting as an example of Buc's literary style and interests and as an indication that as early as about 1602 the methods and extent of historical research and the opinions developed in the *History* were already firmly established. It has in addition a sideline interest because it went through the same process of transformation as the *History*, passing through a manuscript revision and a new edition, published in 1635 with the title *The Great Plantagenet* under the name of Buc's great-nephew, George Buck Esq.[19]

The Third Universitie

> THE THIRD VNIVERSITE OF ENGLAND. OR A TREATISE OF THE FOVNDATIONS OF ALL THE COLLEDGES, AVNCIENT SCHOOLES OF PRIVILEDGE, AND OF HOVSES OF LEARNING, AND LIBERALL ARTS WITHIN AND ABOVT THE MOST FAMOUS CITTIE OF LONDON, WITH A BRIEFE REPORT OF THE SCIENCES, ARTS, AND FACVLTIES THEREIN PROFESSED, STVDIED, AND PRACTISED. Together with the Blazon of the Armes, and Ensignes thereunto belonging. Gathered faithfully out of the best Histories, Chronicles, Records, and Archiues, by G. B. Knight. ANNO DOMINI, 1615.

This work forms part of an appendix to Stow's *Annales* as edited by Edmond Howes, who includes and expands Stow's own accounts of the 'other' two universities in England and adds to them Buc's treatise on London. The work is well organized. It discusses under their headings the numerous 'schools' within the 'universitie': divinity, liberal arts, languages, law, medicine, navigational sciences, poetry, music, dance, painting, heraldry, athletics, and drama. For all these Buc gives the origin and history, gathered from various sources, and where possible he has consulted original charters. The description and history of each foundation is accompanied by a description of its arms, collected for Buc by Clarenceux (William Camden) and Lancaster heralds. Probably in Buc's own manuscript of this work the arms were actually drawn and coloured as they are in his manuscript *Commentary*. So creditable is this treatise that it earnt Buc in William Maitland's estimation a place after Stow as an early historian of London.[20]

It is useful to survey Buc's research methods in this one published and well-organized antiquarian work, for the *History* was not published according to his wishes, never reached a final draft under his hand, and as it stands in his rough draft is not well organized. In addition to original annals, charters and records, he relies in *The Third Universitie* both on printed sources, historical and literary, and on *viva voce* information from contemporary antiquarian scholars such as St Low Kniveton, Sir James Ley, Sir Robert Cotton, Dr (Launcelot) Andrewes, and a Dr Palmer who helped with the chapter on medical studies. One of these *viva voce* references is particularly interesting, since it is second hand: Buc cites information from a fellow scholar whom he trusts, though he himself has not been able to see the document in question, when he speaks of Wolsey's building plan for Doctors Commons according to the information of Cotton, who saw it and told Buc about it (sig. Nnnn^5). There is a famous example of similar practice in the *History* (text,

19 See below, p. lxxviii.
20 William Maitland, *The History and Survey of London* (London, 1756), II, 811.

p. 121), where Buc refers to John Morton's original of More's *History of Richard III* on the information of Sir Edward Hoby, who saw it. That this sort of reference exists here in a published work indicates that such a method of documentation was acceptable practice at the time.[21]

For general information Buc uses a treatise describing London written under Henry II, Stow's *Survey*, the Statutes at Large of Henry VIII, and the works of antiquaries and chroniclers. He refers to Du Haillan and Matthew Paris, as he does often in the *History*. On ecclesiastical foundations, he cites ancient church fathers, Francis Dilingham's *De Comparatione Petri cum Paulo*, Godwin's *Catalogue of the Bishops of England*, and 'an old monument'. His discussion of the legal foundations comes largely from his own experience and through *viva voce* information from his friends and acquaintances also trained in the law schools. He refers to a work in private hands, a book of arms 'enlumined in an auncient manuscripte booke of the foundation and Statutes of this [templars'] order belonging to the right honorable, and most learned noble Gentlemanne the Lorde *William Howard* of Naworth' (sigs. Nnnn-Nnnnv).

He quotes Castiglione on arts suitable for a gentleman and cites a series of Italian authors on riding and fencing. He mentions Ludovico Dulce, Georgius Fabritius, and Julius Caesar Scaliger as people who have written on poetry, and on dancing he cites Tomasso Garzoni's *Piazza Universale*, Discorso 45: *De Ballarini*, as well as Plato. Philo and Aristotle are his authorities on painting, and on cosmetology, described as a branch of painting, he quotes from Lucilius.

The work is sprinkled with quotations, mainly in Latin, as is the *History*. Often these are documented, but sometimes Buc evidently expects them to be well known, as when he mentions an author simply as 'the old poet' or 'our rare countreyman'. Of course many of the quotations may be proverbial, the author not known or considered. Buc's treatment of the Lucilius quotation is interesting in illustrating a practice which appears time and again in the *History*: he states that he 'will set [it] downe in Greeke, because I haue not seen it in Latine' and follows it with his own English translation (sig. Oooo3). Evidently it was usual to find in commonplace books Latin translations of Greek quotations. If a Latin translation were available, it seems to have been proper to give it instead of the Greek original. If none was available, the original was presented, with an accompanying English translation written for the occasion.

The Third Universitie is a useful source of information on Buc's personality and certain biographical details, as indeed is every work he writes. Pride of family, profession and social status lead him to a sense of the dignity and worth of these attributes and a profound regard for and study of their origins. To the Inns of Court, he says, come 'young Gentlemen, the sonnes of the best or better sorte of Gentlemenne of all the Shires of England (and which haue beene formerly bred, and brought vppe liberally in good schooles, and other Uniuersitys)' (sig. Nnnn2^{v}). A man cannot be made a gentleman simply by being on the register of the Inns of Court,

> for no man can be made a Gentleman but by his father. And . . . the

21 See pp. xl, cxxii, cxxxiv .

> King (who hath power to make Esquiers, Knightes, Baronets, Barons, Viscounts, Earles, Marquesses, and Dukes) cannot make a Gentleman, for Gentilitie is a matter of race, and of bloud, and of discent, from gentile and noble parents, and auncestors, which no Kings can giue to any, but to such as they beget.
> (sig. Mmmm6)

As for his own education, the implication is that he attended Trinity Hall, Cambridge, for he mentions 'Maister *Henry Haruey*, Doctor of the ciuill and canon Lawes, maister of Trinitie Hall in *Cambridge*, Prebendarie of *Ely*, and Deane of the Arches, a reuerend, learned and good man whom I being a young Scholler knew' (sig. Nnnn 4^v). As we shall see, a remark in the *Commentary* confirms this suggestion of Buc's Cambridge attendance (see below p. xxxviii). At his 'first comming to London', he was admitted to Thavies Inn as a probationer and then proceeded to the Middle Temple, to which he wishes 'all honour, and prosperity (for my particuler obligation, hauing beene sometimes a fellow, and Student (or to confesse a truth) a trewand of that most honourable Colledge' (sig. Nnnn2). He describes the process of legal study as long and painful but seems to have had time to hear Dr William Padey read an anatomy lecture. However, of music he can give only second hand reports.

The modesty which balances his self-esteem is winning, when he speaks of himself as a truant, of his translation from Lucilius as 'mine own homely translation' (sig. Oooo3), and when he confesses that the art of the Revels demands knowledge of more subjects than he understands.

His style of dedication, as can be seen again in the *History* (text, pp. 3-5), is sincere in its professions of friendship and at the same time preserves the author's sense of his own dignity. Very different it is from his great-nephew's weak, subservient, conventional protestations to prospective patrons of his plagiarized work. Buc writes his dedications to people he knows. To his friend Coke, who was responsible for the *The Third Universitie*'s publication, as well as for his success in claiming land inheritance,[22] he writes, 'and albeit I doe not (in complementing manner) make daily profession of this my obligation (as many vse to doe) yet there is no man shall bee more readie to doe to your Lordshippe any honour, or seruice, then my poore selfe . . .' (sig. Mmmm).

Aside from his description of law study, one of the most interesting items in *The Third Universitie* is Buc's list of proposals for urban improvement, which he provides in case, he says, rich citizens are abstaining from useful works from lack of knowledge of what needs to be done:

> to build a Theater, for the more safe and certaine, and wholesome hearing of the sermons in Paules Church-yard, *Item* to repaire and beautifie Paules steeple, and to refurnish the Belfrey thereof. *Item* to make a faire piazza, or Market place within London, such as is and ought to be in euery good Cittie, and to be placed as the manner is, neere to the Towne hall. . . . *Item* to paue Smithfield. *Item* to erect faire arched gates at the bounds of the Liberties,

22 See above, p. xx.

> where now beast fences or wooden barres and rayles stand. *Item* to enlarge the cumbersome and dangerous straits of the royall and more publike wayes of this Cittie . . . that the hallowed ground of S. *Pauls* churchyard may no more bee trampled and prophaned with beasts, and Cartes, and Coaches. . . . *Item* to deliuer the wals of the Cittie and the Towne ditch, from the pester and encumbrances of tenements, and gardens, & other priuate vses, and to open that Ditch, and to bring a Ryuer or fresh currant into it. And lastly . . . to supplie the suburbes with new parrish Churches, wherein by reason of the exceeding encrease of newe houses and tenements, the people and inhabitaunts are so extremely multiplied, as the old churches . . . are not able to conteyne the fourth part of the people. . . . Of these projects and good workes, the richer citizens . . . may make their choise according to their affections, fancies, deuotions, or abilities . . .
>
> (sig. Nnnn 6)

Buc had a gentle sense of humour too.

The only other printed work by Buc on a contemporary subject is a ten-page abstract of his account of the Cadiz expedition printed in Stow's *Annales* (1601) as 'An Abstract of the expedition to Cadiz 1596, drawne out of Commentaries written at large thereof, by a gentleman who was in the voyage'.[23] Nothing of the original treatise survives.

The Commentary, Archigenealogicon, and The Baron

Three antiquarian works preceded the *History* and provided material for it. Two of them, *Archigenealogicon* and *The Baron*, are lost. The third, *A Commentary on the Book of Domus Dei*, is extant in manuscript. Though some notes survive which may have been for *The Baron* (Bod. MS. Arch. Selden B.66), it is not possible to reconstruct either of the two missing treatises or even to guess at the period of their composition. It is clear, however, that they all partake to some extent in each other, reproducing and expanding at many points the same information, relying on the same sources. We know from *Daphnis* that the research which culminates in the *Commentary* and the *History* was well advanced before 1605.

The Commentary

That the *Commentary* was written in 1614 is attested by numerous statements in the body of the work which mention persons 'now living, 1614'. The manuscript, some 800 pages of Buc's neatest hand (see Plate IV turned upside down), appears to be in finished form, not, like the *History,* still in the process of revision. In later additions to it the dates mentioned are 1616, 1617, and 1618, and the information in one of them dates from 1621. Occasionally a name is left out and dots

23 Stow, *The Annales of England* (London, 1601), sigs. Pppp 3-Pppp 8 (the page numbers within which the treatise is included are pp. 1283-93, but extra leaves in this gathering have made for some repetition of pagination). Although Buc's name is not cited in the *Annales*, Eccles, 'Sir George Buc', pp. 430ff has produced decisive evidence that the work was his.

substituted. Sources are given carefully, normally including page numbers, and there is considerable cross-referencing with others of Buc's own works. He supplies an index. The manuscript is illustrated with shields, some coloured, some merely sketched in. The shields are described, and elaborate family trees inserted in another hand, the same hand in which the genealogical manuscript B.L. MS. Cotton Julius B.XII is written, probably that of one of Buc's herald friends. Later owners of the manuscript have added original notes and material, bringing the information up to date in the 1640s and the 1660s, as Buc himself used the margins of his copy of Godwin's *Catalogue of the Bishops of England* to add information and comments and bring ecclesiastical appointments up to date.

> A COMMENTARY Vpon the New Roulle of Winchester, Comonly called Liber Domus DEI. &c. Especially concerning the Baronage, & ancient Nobility of ENGLAND, TOGETHER WITH A SVPPLEMENT of other ancient noble families of this kingdome not mentioned in the sayd Roulle or Book. faithfully gathered out of royall, & publik archives, roulles, & charters: & out of priuate evidences, histories, & other monument*es* authentik. By George Buc Knight one of the gent. of the Kings privy chamber, & Mast*er* of his highnes office of the REVELLS. Wherin the Authours chef scope is not to mak exact graduall genealogies but to shew the originall ancesterr & first founder of those said noble families w*i*th som*e of* their mo*st* segnall posteres & the stat of them & those w*hi*ch yet continew & florish or els *th*e translations & *th*e period*es* of the said families.

The purpose of the work is to list all noble families in England 'whose ancestors haue bene at the least simple barons, & to shew the origine & continuance of them' (f. 3). Buc bypasses all the alliances and family branches, since he considers this to be a tedious task and more suited to the heralds. He attempts to confine himself to family origins, which he feels have been much neglected, and only summarizes their continuance, noting that Glover has traced genealogies in detail. The work is divided into three sections: Saxon families, families which came in with the Conqueror, and families descending from foreign leaders brought in by King John. His own ancestors come under the last heading.

Apart from the long discourse on his own family, and a few comments on the worth of his friends when he cites them as sources for his information, the most important autobiographical notice regards his studying at Cambridge. Mentioning the name Pinqueney, he says, 'I rem*em*ber that ther was a yong gentilma*n* of that surname a [stud] scholler in Ca*m*bridg in my tyme' (f. 179). This confirms the Cambridge recollection already cited (above, p. xxxvi) from *The Third Universitie.*

He mentions his intended successor in the Revels Office: 'S*i*r John Astley now of the Kings pr. chamber & my successor designed by the Ks patent*es* in reversion' (f. 412). Astley (often known alternatively as 'Ashley'), who was granted the reversion in 1612, did succeed Buc as Master of the Revels when the latter became in 1622, by reason of mental illness, incapable of executing the office. One further bit of interesting autobiographical information concerns his service under the Lord Admiral:

> & as I haue shewed *th*at the most noble Howard*es* have ben principall patrons & benefactors to my ancestor*es* so I haue found them my exceding good & favorable lord*es*: & in p*ar*ticular & most especially my L. Charles Howard Erl of Notingha*m* & high Adm of Engl. whom for more then two yeres I followed as a servant, but he of his most noble goodness vsed me rather like a frend & kinsman, then lik a servant, & in that an*no* mirabile viz. 1588 he p*re*fered me to Q. Elizab. my most gracious mistress . . . (f. 453^{v})

Buc's use of sources, which appears far more carefully documented than in the damaged and unfinished *History*, is interesting. Many of the sources cited in the *Commentary* are also used in the *History*. Because the incomplete state, the damage by fire, the editing of the *History*, and recent scholarly incompetence and prejudice have called Buc's use of sources into question, it would be worthwhile to list here those common to the *History* and the carefully documented *Commentary*:[24] [*Axiomata*] *Politica*; Bale; Bracton; Camden; Cicero; Coggeshall; Coke; Du Haillan; Du Tillet; Erasmus; Froissart; Glover; Godwin; Guicciardini; Hall; Heuterus; Holinshed; Hoveden; Huntingdon; Ingulf; Liber Eliensis; Liber St Stephani, Caen; Meyer; Velleius Paterculus; Prateius; El Reusuerq; Rolls; Scaccarii; Stow; Tower Archives; Walsingham; Wendover; Westminster.

In addition, he refers to several original records and to manuscript books in private hands. He points out the difficulty of documenting such material: '. . . I readd it in an old manuscript book, & nameless as many of them bee . . .' (f. 353). He used private libraries for manuscript material: those of Cotton, his cousin Philip Tilney, the heralds Brooke, Charles, and St George, the Lord Admiral, and Lord William Howard of Naworth. At one point he makes a note to himself, probably to express excitement about some information he has found in a private collection: he says a charter for creating the Earl of Surrey Duke of Norfolk under Henry VIII 'was the first record *tha*t I saught in the Roull being sent by the L. Ad. Ch. Howar Er. of Not.' (f. 23^{v}). He crossed this note out when inserting this page as a late addition to the *Commentary*. Nicholas Charles, Lancaster Herald, searched the records (presumably those of the College of Arms) for information on Buc's family. Camden's *Remaines* is cited in manuscript rather than in its published form.

Buc employs considerable *viva voce* information, both from antiquarian scholars and from representatives of the families whose origins he is tracing, since family traditions, documents, and objects are likely to have been passed down through generations. For *viva voce* information he cites Cotton, Camden, Stow, St Low Kniveton, Ralph Brooke (York Herald), Sir Robert Carey, Lord Hunsdon, Sir Henry Wotton, Sir Thomas Vavasour, Lady Mary Vere, Baroness Willoughby, and particularly the Lord Admiral, and Lord William Howard. Some of the *viva voce* information has apparently been stored in his memory for many years:

> Sir Tho. Tindale . . . beng a very old knight told me beng then a very yong man that the states & barons of Boheme sent to N.

24 See below, pp. cxxviii-cxxix for the authors Buc refers to in the *History*.

> Tindale an ancestor of his to requir him to com to Boheme to take vpon him the Kingdome therof as beng the next heyre, & that in token herof they sent a crown & a scepter & a cloth of Estat & other regall ensignes, & the w*hi*ch as he told me then wer all to be seen yet at his house in Norfolk.
> (f. 384)

In view of his later use of *viva voce* evidence in the *History*, especially the instance already mentioned (text, p. 121), this reference is noteworthy, showing that Buc considered as acceptable documentation in a finished work a reference to verbal information received at some previous time concerning items which his informant described but which he himself had not seen.

Buc's approach to his sources is critical: he does not simply accept what he reads but qualifies it in the light of extensive research. He is at pains particularly to correct recent authors when occasion arises. Often he states that he is accepting William Camden's authority on the basis of Camden's worth as a scholar and because conflicting information cannot be found. This suggests he was in the habit of trying to assess conflicting information before accepting a statement as authoritative. At one point he indicates that reference to a primary source – a deed in the hands of Lord Howard – proves a statement of Camden's to be incorrect. At another he states that Stow is mistaken about a pedigree. Buc's sense of justice to historical figures who were maligned by his contemporaries appears when he cites in Matthew Paris a eulogy saying that Walter de Gray, Archbishop of York, was wise, good and continent: 'I would haue Dr Goodwin well to mark this, bycaus, he hath written nothing of him but scandale in his Catalogue of Bishops' (f. 206).

Nor does he accept information merely because it is old, but he subjects the source to scrutiny. He is willing to credit a nameless manuscript book on the origins of the Herberts 'bycaus I have seen therin many thing*es* carefully, iudiciously & faithfully collected & observed' (f. 353). The Roll of Battle Abbey, on the other hand, cannot be taken as authentic because the monks were in the habit of flattering their patrons by adding them to it. In many places Buc shows a wariness of scribal errors. For example, he knows his own copy of Domesday Book occasionally to have been corrupted: 'I am in dout *tha*t my scribe w*hi*ch copied the book of Domus dei w*hi*ch I haue hath corrupted these names, & in sted of Jury hath put Lury, w*hi*ch is an error easily co*m*mitted by reason of the likenes of j and l' (f. 228).

Buc's attitude to the 'British History' is very cautious, for he is speaking here as an historian, not, as in *Daphnis*, as a poet. He declines to present ancient Briton and Saxon genealogies because 'they ar so high and so remote as that they are either vnknown or els corrupted with fables' (f. 3). Yet he does employ the traditional mythic history in connection with the Tudors to some extent: Tudor, he says, is the oldest of all houses, and he presents a pedigree deriving it from King Cole,

> For the hon*ou*r & religious & im*m*ortal loue w*hi*ch I beare to the most renowned & most Glorious princess Q. Elizabeth who was descended & propagated out of this great & ancient & royall hous

> of Britayn, & hir coming was foretold by the tale of the return of
> K. Artur as some & not absurdly interpret it.
> (f. 4^{v})

His worship of Queen Elizabeth, consistent in all his works, reappears in an autobiographical passage where he calls her 'my most gracious mistress, who now is in Glory in heaven & shall for her war vertues aboue her sex be euer honored vpon the erth' (f. 453^{v}). He quotes a eulogy, evidently composed by himself, which is written on her picture in his house (ff. 8^{v}-9). He is not, however, very charitable to Henry VII, of whom he says merely that he was crowned in the right of his wife.

There are mentions of other personages and families which figure in the *History*. Of people connected with Richard III Buc is not always correctly informed in the *Commentary*, but some of the opinions presented later in the *History* seem already well formed. He gives incorrect information about people peripheral to Richard's story, citing Hastings's first name as 'Edward' and saying Rivers became Lord Scales in right of his wife under Richard III. But he has searched carefully the history of Richard's supporter Francis, Viscount Lovell, presenting his titles on the basis of research done for him by Lancaster Herald and noting that 'this Viscount Lovell was attainted by him who hated all them that his praecessor K.R.3 loved to witt K.H.7.' (f. 141^{v}). Already Buc seems convinced that the individual known as Perkin Warbeck was actually Richard, Duke of York, for he notes that Henry VII executed Sir William Stanley for supporting 'Rich duk of York al*ia*s Perkin Warbeck' (f. 254^{v}).

In the Commentary between ff. 354 and 355 appears a group of set-in pages on the descent of the Herberts which were clearly an early draft intended for the History. When Buc was composing the History, about five years after completing the Commentary, he seems to have discarded these few pages as too digressive and inserted them in the Commentary as more suitable to it. He then rewrote the matter on the Herberts which was to appear in the History, paring it down to dimensions suitable to that work.[25] In only one other place does this use of a discarded page from the History form a late addition to the Commentary. F. 3^{v} of the Commentary is written on the back of an upside down and crossed out draft of the History's title page (see Plate IV), a fortunate occurrence, since no title page appears in the autograph manuscript of the History in its present state apart from a scrap, f. 171^{v} of the manuscript itself, which was presumably cut up to make a paste-over. What is left of it shows portions of the same wording as the discarded page in the Commentary.

The accounts of the Howard family are very similar in the *Commentary* and the *History*, and the same sources are used. The wording is closer to the sources in the *Commentary*'s account, whereas the *History* employs freer paraphrase. The same is true of the accounts of Buc's own family, but in the *History* he corrects some details and makes more plausible conjectures.

Buc mentions the *Commentary* only twice in the *History*. He refers to it as a proving ground for his methods of historical research, informing the reader that

25 See below, p. cliii for further discussions of these revisions.

he will attempt to discover the origins of the name 'Plantagenet' 'according to my small talent of knowledge and reading and according to the methods I have held for the searching of the originals of the most ancient noble families of England, of their surnames in my *Commentary on the Book of Domus Dei,* or *The New Roll of Winchester'* (text, p. 11). He apologizes for his long discussion of Howard family origins by saying, 'I shall be . . . pardoned because I have done the like honour and service to many other the most noble families of this country in my *Commentary* . . .' (text, p. 110).

The provenance of the *Commentary* cannot be traced back very far. During the seventeenth century it was owned by persons who continued to make notes in it. Notes tipped in during the eighteenth century show an interest in lawyers and in Berkshire lands, perhaps indicating the profession and residence of the owners. The first owner who can be traced by name is Major G. Halswell of Devonshire, who died in 1935. R.C. Bald 'discovered' the manuscript in Halswell's possession in 1927, mistaking it for Buc's lost book, *The Baron*.[26] He corrected this assumption when he discussed the work more fully in 1935.[27] Until 1969 Major W. Halswell, son of the previous owner, was unable to trace it and assumed his father had sold it, but that year, while moving to a new house, he rediscovered it[28] and authorized the auction house to which he had consigned it to lend it to the Bodleian Library for me to study. It was purchased by the Bodleian on my recommendation in 1972.

Archigenealogicon

Buc refers several times in the *Commentary* to a manuscript work of his own by the name of *Archigenealogicon*. A reference to both it and the *Baron* in the same passage makes us hesitate in identifying them as the same work: Buc tells us that we may see more of the Howard family in 'Baronor*um* Genealogue in s*ecund*u*m* tempora regu*m* in principio. & in Archigenealogico*n*' (f. 20). What the very few references to it lead us to conclude is that it was a genealogical treatise concentrating on the details of descent and on the various branches of families rather than on the origins of families as the *Commentary* does: 'Ther be divers other Blunt*es* in other shires, the w*hi*ch all you may see in my MS. Archigenealogicon wher I haue deduced at large all *th*e pedegree of the Blounts w*i*th their Alliance w*i*th some Spanish noble houses, & the rest vndiquaq*ue*' [wherever] (*Comm*., f. 127^{v}). We are told to look in *Archigenealogicon* under 'Foix' for the family of Geily, evidently a branch of the Foix family. In the *Commentary*, attempting to avoid considering in detail the numerous branches of families, Buc says, 'Vide . . . in Archigenealo. MS.' for Walter Buc's genealogy (f. 389), and later he refers us to it for a warrant of Robert Buck under Edward II, 'as also for the orderly descent*es* for here for brevity \& my methode/ sake I omitt many. but thyre ar sett down in a strict gradual succession' (f. 452^{v}). We are also to see *Archigenealogicon* for all the issue of Philip, Earl of Arundel (f. 21^{v}).

Clearly the two things that Buc attempts to avoid in the *Commentary,* branchings

26 Bald, 'A Revels Office Entry', *Times Literary Supplement*, no. 1,311 (17 Mar. 1927), 193. He printed photocopies of pages from it in 'The *Locrine* . . . Inscriptions', cited above in n. 8.

27 Bald, 'A Manuscript Work by Sir George Buc', *Modern Language Review*, XXX (1935), 1-12.

28 Challen, p. 290 and private letter from Major W. Halswell.

of families through intermarriages and a minute cataloguing of descent, he dealt with in *Archigenealogicon*. Bald conjectures that this work might be identifiable as the *Collections Historical and Genealogical of Sir George Buck, Kt.*, at one time possessed by John Strype, but this description might equally well apply to the *Commentary* or, as Bald suggests, to 'my Antiquary MS.' to which Buc refers in the *Commentary*, f. 59, though this would seem to me to be part of the *Baron*.[29]

The Baron

From the numerous references to *The Baron, or the Magazin of Honour* in the *Commentary* and the *History*, though it is possible to some slight extent to reconstruct its history and contents, it still remains a very great puzzle. We can judge from the references to it in the *Commentary* that it was unfinished in 1614 and was just beginning to take shape then: 'I have written largely thereof in my \Baron/ [advertisement*es* before Glovers Catalogue, & in my Antiquary MS. sic inscripto] (f. 59). This seems to suggest that the work originated as a commentary on Glover's *Catalogue of Honour* (1610)[30] or as material supplementary to it. Again Buc gives a reference 'vt In meis [as in my] Adv*er*tise*me*nts ante [before] Glover' (f. 254^{v}). Glover's *Catalogue* does contain considerable prefatory material written by other well-known antiquaries such as Camden. It is possible that Buc, too, was writing a treatise for inclusion there, as *The Third Universitie* was included as supplementary material to Stow's *Annales*. This work may have captured his interest so that it grew beyond the bounds of a supplementary treatise and became a manuscript work of several books divided into various chapters.

When Buc was completing the *Commentary*, the *Baron* seems still to have been in process of transition from being a supplement to Glover to being a work in its own right, and Buc has not yet completely settled on its title but sometimes describes it instead of giving it a title: 'Baronoru*m* Genealogue s*ecundum* tempora regu*m*' [Genealogy of barons according to time of reign] (f. 20^{v}) or 'book of Barons' (ff. 369 and 383^{v}). The decisive crossing out of the description 'advertisement*es* before Glovers Catalogue, & in my Antiquary MS.' to substitute 'Baron' suggests that a Glover supplement and another antiquarian work were joined together under a single title. That there are in the *Commentary* a few explicit references to the *Baron* citing book numbers suggests that the work had crystallized during the final stages of the *Commentary*'s composition. By 1619 when the *History* was written there is no longer any indecision in references to it by title, and book and chapter numbers are given. Still, Buc calls it a 'rude work' (text, p. 6), though this may merely display his customary modesty, and the various matters mentioned in it to which he makes reference in the *History* give no idea of its structure.

There seem to have been at least sixteen books. Book I was entitled 'Vicomitu*m* et Baron*orum* Catalogus Genealogicis' [Genealogical Catalogues of Viscounts and Barons] (*Comm.*, f. 383^{v}) and contained among other things eulogies of the Howards. A clue to the material in this early section may be gleaned from a table of contents appearing between ff. 349 and 351 of the *Commentary*. The numbers

29 See below, **The Baron**.
30 Buc's own copy of Glover's *Catalogue* was sold not long ago, but my attempts to trace it have failed.

are evidently page numbers and except for 153, which appears twice, they correspond to the page numbers that are missing at the beginning of the *Commentary*, whose numbering starts with p. 31. It appears that Book I of the *Baron* was at one time the opening section of the *Commentary*. These early pages seem, from the headings in the table of contents, extremely close in content to the prefatory material in Glover's *Catalogue*, as does Buc's statement in the *Commentary* that he has written at length in the *Baron* of the distinction between nobility and gentry. Camden speaks similarly of his own work on the subject: in an antiquarian discourse, 'The Etymology and Original of Barons', he says, 'I have elsewhere said somewhat of *Barones* [i.e., in Glover's *Catalogue*], therefore if now I be shorter, it may be more pardonable'.[31] Perhaps Buc's work was prevented for some reason – possibly duplication by other scholars – from becoming part of the prefatory material for Glover. Such a duplication may have forced Buc to attach these early pages to another work of his own, the *Commentary*. They did not really fit the *Commentary* and so broke off to form part of the *Baron*, which was growing as the *Commentary* was being completed and seems to have served as a sort of catchall. The table of contents refers to material entirely concerned with titles, offices, and estates. Headings include:

Adela
Adeling } 4
Βαρεις 7.8
Baronis ecclesiast. 15
Barones iurisp*er*iti 29.31
Barones forain 17
Barones & } defined 12. &c
  Baronie } 22.16.21.153
Baronia diminuta 23
Baronies claymed
Barons by le*tt*ers pat.
barons by sum*m*ons
Baronetts. 5. Baronuli 5
fief noble quid. 22.153
Honor gift of a Sov*er*[a]in Pr. 19
Judges of the Kingd. 29.31
Knights fee 22.16.153
Marchiae barones
Marchisij
Marchiones } 495
Privileges of barons. 25
Principalities inferior to Baronies. 13
Thane 3
Tain 4
Vavasor 5. in m*ar*g.
Vnderthane
Vpthane } 4
  or Abthane
Writt of Sum*m*ons. 18.24

That the material to which Buc alludes was originally part of the *Commentary* is attested by citation of p. 153. On that page in the *Commentary*, now labelled f. 94, Buc crosses out a passage and refers the reader to the *Baron* for information on what a knight's fee was. In the reference to 'Knights fee' in the index, the page numbers 22, 16, and 153 are given. It thus seems that the index was made before the section at the beginning of the *Commentary* was removed to become part of the *Baron*.

Book III – at least in Chapters 11-13 – seems to have been historical in approach. Perhaps it was a history of the house of York or the houses of York and

31 *A Collection of Curious Discourses*, 2 vols. ed. Thomas Hearne (London, 1773), I, 124.

Lancaster. The *Commentary* has called the *Baron* 'Baronoru*m* Genealogue s*ecund*u*m* tempora regu*m*' [genealogy of barons according to reign] (f. 21^{v}), and this description could perhaps fit this section. Chapter 10 speaks of George, Duke of Clarence's treasons and execution (*History*, text p. 135), and Chapter 13 is particularly notable as the origin of the *History*, whose 'Advertisement to the Reader' opens thus (text, p. 6):

> Before I enter into the story of King Richard. I must advertise the noble and intelligent Reader (for unto such only I write) that the argument and subject of this discourse or story was at the first but a chapter, and the thirteenth chapter, of the third book of a rude work of mine entitled THE BARON, or *The Magazin of Honour*. But the argument of that chapter being so strange and very extravagant and extraordinary (as the affairs and fortunes of this prince were), suppeditated strange and extraordinary matters, and in such copy and variety as that it diffused itself into an extraordinary and unusual largeness, and so much as it exceeded very much the laws and the proper limits of a chapter.

Buc's only specific reference to the material contained in this particular chapter is to Clarence and Warwick's confederacy and its success in expelling Edward IV from England in 1469 (see text, p. 137). There is no way of telling whether or not the discussion of the execution of Sir William Stanley and others for aiding Richard, Duke of York (alias Perkin Warbeck), 'Advertisem*en*ts ante Glover' (*Comm*., f. 254^{v}), appeared in this Book as well.

Book IV, at least in part, treated of King Arthur. Buc claims to have 'handled his story' there and to have 'redeemed him & his knights & paladins fro*m* fables & scandales' (*Comm.,* f. 2^{v}). This comment is a late addition, again suggesting concurrent composition of the *Baron* and the *Commentary*. We know nothing of any material in Books V-XII. It is possible that Buc was leading up to the Tudors by a discourse first on their historical ancestors, the Yorkist and Lancastrian families, then on their legendary ancestors, including King Arthur.

Book XIII, Chapter 16 speaks of tortures (see text, p. 152f). The last two books mentioned by number are fifteen and sixteen, which '[treat of] matters of [armory]' (see text, p. 81). Since Buc states that he has written of all armorial signs in the last five books, there could not have been many more than sixteen.

There are other scrappy references to the *Baron* by book and chapter numbers in Bodleian MS. Arch. Selden. B.66, which is a collection of Selden's mainly concerning the officers of the kingdom. The Bodleian catalogue describes it as a draft of 'The baron', but since book and chapter numbers given clearly refer to that work in its organized form, this is not likely. Some of it consists of notes in Buc's hand, jottings about various ranks and offices in England. One note references the office of Chancellor to Book 4, chapter 6 of the *Baron* (f. 61). Later there is a mention of Signet Knights having originated with seal rings under the Normans, with a reference to Book 11, chapter [22] (f. 64). The work's title is not mentioned, but no other book of Buc's was organized in this way. However this conflicts with a later entry about signet rings as an honour among the Romans, where Book 4, chapter 3 is cited (f. 64^{v}). There seems nothing to support Eccles's statement that Buc's lost treatise on the art of the revels sprang from the *Baron*.[32]

There is one minor antiquarian work of Buc's which exists in manuscript (B.L. Cotton Titus C.I, f. 35^{v}) and is printed in Thomas Hearne's *Curious Discourses*.[33] It seems to be Buc's contribution to a topic under discussion at a meeting of the Society of Antiquaries. The group of manuscripts of which it forms a part considers the office of High Constable of England, on which papers were evidently delivered in the autumn of 1602 (one of the discourses bears the date 27 November 1602). The note subtitled 'Justitiarius Angliae [Justiciary of England]' and signed 'G. Buc' comprises a series of factual statements and Latin quotations documented from Camden, Hoveden, Matthew Paris, John of Salisbury, Selden, and others. There are no transitions, and the organization is very loose, but the conclusion to which Buc's observations lead seems to be that at some stage the Chief Justice exercised the duties of Constable, Marshal, Treasurer, and Admiral as well as his nominal functions. The manuscript is a fair copy not in Buc's hand, but the marginal documentation and signature are his. In the discourses which make up the collection, use of an amanuensis for the body of the paper with signature and date or other notation given in the author's own hand is not uncommon.

That Buc habitually cross-references so many of his unpublished but apparently completed works as if they were readily available for consultation makes it necessary to consider whether he had publication in mind at all.[34] It looks as if he may have been writing exclusively for a coterie of antiquarian scholars who regularly lent and borrowed books, both of their own and others' authorship. This practice, apparently quite common for specialist works at the time, would have meant he was able to avoid considering the question of what sort of reception a full-blown defence of Richard III might have met with in his day and whether publication of it would indeed have been possible had he wished it.

The research involved in composing all his antiquarian treatises and his associations with scholars who assisted him in his searches among original documents made it natural that Lord Darcy should, as Buc says in a letter to Cotton, have 'bene ernest with me to deliuer him some matters concerning the great men of the realm in former tymes' (B.L. Cotton Julius C. III, f. 49). In March 1620 Buc describes himself as actively at work on this research, but no trace of it remains, if it ever materialized. His madness came late in 1621 or early in 1622.

32 Eccles, p. 412.
33 Hearne, II, 88f.
34 Michael Hicks, *Anne Neville, Queen to Richard III* (Stroud, 2007), p. 199, states categorically 'Buck wrote for publication', but does not document the source of his certainty.

III. ANTIQUARIES AND THEIR LIBRARIES

The rise of antiquarianism[1] during the sixteenth century cannot be traced to any single cause; as is usual with new 'movements', several factors coincided in its origin. The dissolution of religious houses destroyed libraries, and the dispersal of valuable manuscripts led to efforts by lovers of learning and of their country's past to collect and preserve them. In 1568 Archbishop Parker received a royal licence to collect books and manuscripts from dissolved foundations, and for their own use and interest private men like Cotton, Camden, and Stow made collections of historical material. Cotton offered his large collection as the beginning of a national library, so it is fitting that the remains of it ultimately became part of what is now the British Library.

With the reorganization of libraries, and as the public records gradually became available for consultation and were classified, the old dependence on 'authority' in history was no longer valid. Documentary evidence had to be reckoned with, and scholars had to learn, crudely at first, to deal with it critically. The skills of palaeography, philology, translation and transcription, sense of chronology and suitability to period were in their infancy, but their importance was gradually being recognized. The antiquaries were discovering and applying the rudiments of these skills and also lending to their studies skills peculiar to the law courts, for most of them had legal training: these skills encompassed research into earliest precedents and criticism of information by logic.

Search for precedent gave the movement impetus. A burning sense of patriotism and nationalism, the desire to reflect on the country's present glory by revealing its glorious past, and the immediate need to justify Protestantism as a reformed religion based on early Christianity, combined in a work like Foxe's *Acts and Monuments*, which looked beyond the common chronicles to seek original sources that could speak in matters of controversy. Old texts were edited to make them available for polemical purposes both in theology and in the conflict with Polydore Vergil over the 'British History'. But standards of editorship were lax and groping compared with those we now know. There was a tendency to fill in and embellish texts, and translation and transcription were often careless, grammar and spelling freely modified.

James I hated being reliant on Parliament, called it only when financially desperate, and there were fears for its survival.[2] In defending it, it became vital to show the

1 For thorough studies of Tudor antiquarianism, see F. Smith Fussner, *The Historical Revolution* (London, 1962); F.J. Levy, *Tudor Historical Thought* (San Marino, 1967); May McKisack, *Medieval History in the Tudor Age* (Oxford, 1971); and particularly Linda Van Norden, *The Elizabethan College of Antiquaries* (University of California at Los Angeles, unpublished Ph.D. diss., 1946) and 'Sir Henry Spelman on the Chronology of the Elizabethan Society of Antiquaries', *Huntington Library Quarterly* XII (1950), 131-60.

2 Andrew Thrush, 'The Personal Rule of James I, 1611-1620', in *Politics, Religion, and Popularity in Early Stuart Britain: Essays in Honour of Conrad Russell*, eds Thomas Cogswell, Richard Cust and Peter Lake (Cambridge, 2002), pp. 84-102.

precedence of common law over royal prerogative and its consequent immunity from the latter. To this end Coke's exhaustive study of common law was written. Coke's library was unusually large, but Cotton with his immense collection was in an even better position to advise the Parliamentary opposition on matters of precedent. In this connection he wrote 'A Relation to prove that the kings of England have been pleased to consult with their Peers in the Great Counsell and Commons in Parliament'. Sir George Buc's arguments for the dignity and prime authority of Parliament are a major side issue in his *History of King Richard the Third*.[3] R.B. Wernham notes that

> the constitutional conflicts of the early Stuart period took somewhat the form of a prolonged lawsuit between King and Parliament and, like other lawsuits, it involved much search among the records by both parties. But the issues raised were so much more generalized that they virtually elevated legal searches into historical research.[4]

Scholars challenged a scholarly monarch in demonstrating the age and authority of Parliament. King James remarked in response to their arguments that if they could seek precedents so could he. The pursuit of this debate was beginning to arouse a new interest in the public records simply as materials for argument as well as for history.

Antiquarian scholars worked closely together on some points and clearly influenced each other. An article by David Weil Baker[5] shows how three antiquaries, Camden, Buc, and Speed, pioneered a challenge to the Tudor view of Richard III in conjunction with their support of Parliament, recognizing the significance of Richard's *Titulus Regius* in setting a precedent for Parliamentary ratification of kingship. He states that the relevance of Richard's use of Parliament to ratify his kingship would have gone unnoticed by future writers had these three scholars not dealt with it (p. 341). Camden, who had already given a more lenient than usual view of Richard in his *Remaines*, was responsible for the first appearance of *Titulus Regius* in print, including mention of Edward IV's bigamous marriage, which resulted in Richard's becoming heir to the throne. After first taking careful notes on it (see below, p. liv), he gave an abstracted version of it in the 1607 *Britannia*. This led to his reassessing Richard as one who, by the time Parliament ratified his kingship, had, against expectation, proved worthy to reign, though he won the crown through evil artifices and crimes (though what Camden took these to be with Edward IV's sons shown to be illegitimate and with no mention of his having murdered them is not clear). He goes on to describe Richard as being, by agreement of the wisest, numbered as one of the worst of men but best of kings.[6]

Camden also mentions Henry VII and Henry VIII's responsibility for the death of Clarence's son and daughter, stating that it is not unusual for a prince to provide for his own and his family's security by removing or oppressing those near in blood.[7]

3 See below, p. cxlv for further mention of the issue.

4 R.B. Wernham, 'The Public Records in the Sixteenth and Seventeenth Centuries' in *English Historical Scholarship in the Sixteenth and Seventeenth Centuries*, ed. Levi Fox (London, 1956), p. 25.

5 David Weil Baker, 'Jacobean Historiography and the Election of Richard III', *Huntington Library Quarterly*, LXX (2007), 311.

6 *Britannia* (London, 1607), p. 261.

7 *Ibid.*, p. 182.

This, according to Baker, leads the reader to understand that

> Here, the founder of the Tudor line is reduced to the same moral level as the supposed child-killer whose throne he took. The contrast between Richard and Henry is no longer between extremes of kingship and tyranny but rather between two rulers perhaps equally inclined to temper good and bad qualities with their opposites. Such an admixture in a ruler is, moreover, scarcely 'uncustomary'. Indeed, the awful truth . . . is that the history of monarchy is full of crimes as heinous as the ones supposed to have made Richard villainous.[8]

Speed inserts the whole of the *Titulus Regius* into his *History of Great Britaine*, first published in 1611, though he borrows his history from More, transitioning from that account by the surprise information that Richard 'by profuse liberalitie, by passing great gravitie, by singular affability, by ministering of justice, and by deep and close devises . . . won to himself the hearts of all', and so was petitioned to be king. Then he gives a copy of the petition as included in the Parliament Roll.[9] Later he calls Richard 'a very honourable, wise, just, and necessarie prince after he was somewhat settled'.[10]

It is impossible to tell to what extent and in what manner these three historical writers/apologists for Parliament were influenced by each other in their treatment of Richard. Camden and Speed, perhaps because they were writing earlier, seem to have felt obliged to give a confused picture of him, trying unsuccessfully to meld the king who made good laws and was apparently a good king with the Tudor accounts of his extreme evil. Buc, who unlike the other two derives the *Titulus Regius* not from the Parliament Rolls but from the Crowland Chronicle, does not make such compromises, perhaps because he felt safer writing later, perhaps because he was not writing for publication – we do not know whether he was or not – and perhaps because he had family loyalty to satisfy.

A specific group whose profession led them to antiquarian study were the heralds. Richard III, of course, was responsible for incorporating the College of Arms. The Tudors' need to justify their claim to the throne led to the production of family trees traced back to Cadwallader, to Brute, even to Adam. Families, many of them *novi homines* under Elizabeth, sought out the ancientry of their origins in deeds and records, some inevitably forgeries. These records, because the sciences dealing in the study of documents were still rudimentary, were often believed even by the most astute of heralds.[11] Some of the most notable heralds were also notable scholars and collectors: Camden, Dethick, Glover, St George, and Brooke. Heralds, according to Buc, who was the friend of many, had to be gentlemen. They also needed to be excellent painters so they could record blazons and ensigns, and 'Their study also is or ought to be auncient hystorie, Chronicles, & antiquities: they must search old roles & scrowles, and peruse authentike records, Archiues, olde Charters, & evidences' to find and preserve genealogical

8 Baker, p. 328.
9 Speed. *History of Great Britaine* (London, 1611), pp. 711f.
10 *Ibid.*, p. 728.
11 See below, General Notes, 77/11-15.

matter and testimony to alliances, issue and the honour of ancestors. 'These *Herauldes* bee the ministers of honour, the Antiquaries of the British and English *Heroes*, and the Messengers of Mars' (*Third Universitie*, sig. Oooo 3). The heralds built up libraries to pass on to their successors and ownership of these materials became confused. In 1568 Thomas Howard, Duke of Norfolk and Earl Marshal, established rules, including the foundation of a corporate library which no one could enter unaccompanied by a herald.[12] Further reform and encouragement to scholarship in the College of Arms came in 1597 with the appointment of Camden as Clarenceux. He, with his fellow scholar-heralds, says A.R. Wagner, 'found that a firm foundation for the study of national and local history and genealogy could only be laid by a laborious analysis of the public records in the Tower and elsewhere and of charters and other manuscripts in private hands'.[13]

There is a suggestion in his relationship with heralds of a striking ability in Buc's nature to get along with difficult people constantly at odds with each other. Sir William Dethick, whom he praises in *The History*, seems to have been perhaps unusually quarrelsome, to the extent at times of violence.[14] And although Ralph Brooke, York Herald, was not on friendly terms with William Camden, having criticized him in print for errors in the *Britannia*,[15] Buc was on good terms with both Camden and Brooke. The attack by Brooke may have led to Buc's adopting caution in the *Commentary* when he assesses Camden's accuracy: he changes 'careful' to 'diligent' and 'faithful' to 'judicious' when mentioning Camden's scholarship (*Comm.,* f. 381: see p. liv below).

The varied interests of the new historians can be observed in Leland's never-completed research plans for recording ranks of aristocracy, officers of the kingdom, topography, place names, history and geography of individual countries, chorography, and origins of royal and noble families. These subjects were most competently handled by Stow and Camden. Stow's *Survey of London* is a supreme example of local history. It relies heavily on records and carefully documents statements from manuscript sources. Indeed, Stow's entry into the world of scholarship was impelled by dissatisfaction with Grafton's adopting wholesale, and without documentation or acknowledgement, accounts from his chronicle forebears. Stow took up the challenge to pursue history based on research and documentation, and though his *Annales* still lean toward reliance on the older chronicles, he acknowledges his use of them, which is supplemented and often contradicted by references to public records. Camden in his *Remaines* added genealogy to his interests after his appointment to the College of Arms. His *Britannia* surveys the whole of the kingdom, county by county, its history and geography and the origins of noble families. Brooke's attack on his accuracy led him to search the records more carefully and document more thoroughly. Buc was thus writing at a time when and among a group of scholars to whom documentation was an increasingly important issue.

Thomas Hearne, editing *A Collection of Curious Discourses*, a compendium of

12 Anthony Richard Wagner, *The Records and Collections of the College of Arms* (London, 1952), pp. 9-12.
13 *Ibid.*, p. 31.
14 See Katherine Duncan-Jones, *Shakespeare: an Ungentle Life* (London, 2010), pp. 114-18.
15 *A Discoverie of Certaine Erroures ... in the Much Commended Britannia, 1594* (London, [1596]).

antiquaries' papers, saw the Elizabethan period as especially fruitful for antiquarian studies, since the queen herself, no mean scholar, was a patroness of learning and preferred learned men to high positions in church and state:

> At this auspicious period, a set of gentlemen of great abilities, many of them students in the inns of court, applied themselves to the study of the antiquities and history of this kingdom, a taste at that time very prevalent, wisely foreseeing that without a perfect knowledge of those requisites, a thorough understanding of laws of their native country could not be attained.[16]

The Society of Antiquaries was probably founded in 1586, the same year, F.J. Levy points out,[17] as the first publication of Camden's *Britannia*, with its membership composed largely of people whom Camden had drawn around himself to assist with his research. It included lawyers (John Dodderidge, Sir James Ley), heralds (Glover, Dethick, Camden, St George), collectors (Cotton), historians (Stow) and archivists (Michael Heneage, Keeper of the Tower Records). After a gap between 1594 and 1598 because of the plague,[18] the participants petitioned Queen Elizabeth to constitute the Society as a British Academy, but her death prevented this. They then for a while entertained hopes that King James would do so.

> Topics dealt with included dukes, marquesses, viscounts, barons, knights, the Inns of Court, the Ancientry of the Laws of England, the office of Constable of England, seals, forests, coats of arms. There were also various topographical considerations, and studies of terms denoting measurement and currency. Sir Henry Spelman described the Society thus in retrospect, probably in 1628:
>
> About forty two Years since, divers Gentlemen in London, studious of Antiquities, fram'd themselves into a College or Society of Antiquaries, appointing to meet every Friday weekly in the Term, at a place agreed of, and for Learning sake to confer upon some Questions in that Faculty, and to sup together. The Place after a Meeting or two, became certain at Darby-house, where the Herald's Office is kept: and two Questions were propounded at every Meeting, to be handled at the next that followed; so that every Man had a Sennight's respite to advise upon them, and then to deliver his opinion. That which seem'd most material, was by one of the Company (chosen for the purpose) to be enter'd in a book; that so it might remain unto Posterity. The Society increased daily; many Persons of great Worth, as well noble as other Learned, joining themselves unto it.
>
> Thus it continu'd divers Years; but . . . so many of the chief Supporters hereof either dying or withdrawing themselves from London into the Country; this . . . grew for twenty Years to be

16 Hearne, Introduction, I, iv.

17 'The Making of Camden's *Britannia*', *Bibliothèque de Humanisme et Renaissance*, XXVI (1964), p. 89.

18 Van Norden, 'Sir Henry Spelman on the Chronology of the Elizabethan College of Antiquaries', 149.

> discontinu'd. But it then came again into the mind of divers principal Gentlemen to revive it; and for that purpose upon the [blank] day of [blank] in the year 1614. there met at the same Place Sir James Ley Knight, then Attorney of the Court of Wards, since Earl of Marlborough and Lord Treasurer of England; Sir Robert Cotton Knight and Baronet; Sir John Davies his Majestie's Attorney for Ireland; Sir Richard St. George Knt. then Norrey, Mr. Hackwell the Queen's Solicitor, Mr. Camden, then Clarentieux, myself, and some others. Of these the Lord Treasurer, Sir Robert Cotton, Mr Camden, and my self, had been of the original Foundation; and so to my knowledge were all then living of that sort, saving Sir John Doderidge Knight, Justice of the King's Bench.
>
> We held it sufficient for that time to revive the Meeting, and only conceiv'd some Rules of Government and Limitation to be observ'd amongst us; whereof this was one, That for avoiding Offence, we should neither meddle with Matters of State, nor of Religion. And agreeing of two Questions for the next Meeting . . . and supping together, so departed.
>
> ....
>
> But before our next Meeting, we had notice that his Majesty took a little Mislike of our Society; not being inform'd, that we had resolv'd to decline all Matters of State. Yet hereupon we forebore to meet again, and so all our Labours lost.[19]

Linda Van Norden calculated that the society was disbanded around 1607. Buc may have been a member at that time,[20] since he was working on antiquarian subjects from at least 1602. There is no extant contemporary record of his membership, but no extant list of members is complete. Not only were many of its members his friends and associates, but notes in his hand in Selden's collection (see above, p. xlvi) appear to be for a presentation he intended to give and perhaps did give to the Society on the offices of High Constable and Chief Justice.[21] Since only members could give such presentations, his membership seems almost certain. In 1620 Buckingham presented to the House of Lords a proposal for the foundation of an English Academy: 'The dissolution of this so well an intended exercise [as the Society of Antiquaries], hath neuerthelesse not happened without the iust griefe of all those worthie patriots who know yo*u*r Ma*je*sties realms afford liuing persons of prime worth, fit to keep vp, and celebrate *tha*t round table' (B.L. Harl. 6143, f. 14). Among those listed in illustration were Thomas, Earl of Arundel; Lord William Howard; Greville; Coke; Dodderidge; Ley; Cotton; Spelman; Dr John Hayward; the heralds Segar, St George, and

19 Quoted by Van Norden, *The Elizabethan College of Antiquaries*, pp. 134f, from Edmund Gibson in *Reliquiae Spelmanniae* (Oxford, 1698), which Van Norden states gives an accurate representation of Bodleian MS. eMus.107, apart from some modernized spelling. The version she gives in her thesis is closer to the manuscript, containing more names of members, so I have chosen it over that in her article.

20 A.R. Myers, 'Richard III and Historical Tradition', *History*, LXXX (1968), 186 states categorically that Buc was a member of the Society of Antiquaries but does not document this assertion.

21 For a discussion of this treatise, see above, p. xlvi.

Brooke; Selden; 'Incomparable Camden'; and 'Sir George Buc knight, Mr. of Reuels'.

Some of the subjects considered at meetings of the society were: the Antiquity, Office, and Privilege of Heralds; the Antiquity of Houses of Law; the Antiquity of Arms; the Antiquity of Seals; the Etymology, Dignity, and Antiquity of Duke, or Dux; the Etymology and Original of Barons; the Office of Constable of England; the Office of Earl Marshal. There were also various topographical considerations and studies of terms denoting measurement and currency.

The Society established and enforced methods and standards of research and documentation. It facilitated access to documents: many of its members were keepers of official records, and there was considerable lending within the Society and its members' immediate circle of friends by those who collected privately. Emphasis was on primary sources, yet often without clear critical interpretation: truth was equated with documentation and facts collected without reference to or understanding of the age in which the documented facts occurred. Since dating methods were not well developed, there was a tendency to antedate, and the illogical method was employed of judging the past by what in the present was regarded as 'custom'.[22] On the other hand, says F. Smith Fussner, 'members were anxious to get behind the chroniclers and explore the masses of original records of English history. Instead of making a virtue of conjecture, as Raleigh did in his *Historie of the World*, the antiquaries condemned the use of conjecture as an historical technique'.[23]

Treatises read before the Society of Antiquaries, as well as other treatises by the same authors, can be seen in Hearne's *Collection of Curious Discourses*. The discourses are precedent-orientated and cite as authority biblical, classical, legal and chronicle references, monuments, and inscriptions. Organization is loose and generally in the form of a barely disguised list tracing a history through records as far back as possible. The discourses are studded with Latin quotations. Sometimes long sections of the official documents are copied out. Etymological speculation abounds. Elaborate documentation is pursued at the expense of style and allusions to imaginative literature are very few. Most of the antiquaries display great modesty and respect for their fellows. Sir James Ley appears exceptional in being an excellent stylist, organizing his material systematically under section headings and writing with a fine sense of linguistic balance and concision.

It may be seen that Buc, in all his antiquarian works, applied often for source material to his 'better-booked friends', as he calls them (text, p. 7). He sought information in the College of Arms from his herald friends and borrowed many manuscript works from Cotton and other antiquarian scholars. He also often cites *viva voce* information from them. This was much more highly regarded as source material in the sixteenth and seventeenth centuries than it is now (indeed it is forbidden to that extremely uneven web information compendium, Wikipedia). Elderly people who had experienced events of the past were interviewed for their reminiscences. That they had experienced these events and known prominent people personally gave them authority. Also it was perfectly acceptable to cite a

22 Fussner, p. 99.
23 *Ibid.* p. 97.

source on the authority of someone who had seen it, even if you had not seen it yourself, so long as you could indicate where it was to be found. Recent historians, immensely fond of stating or at least implying that this method covers up intentional scams, seem oblivious of the ethos of late sixteenth- and early seventeenth-century scholarship, which was dedicated to *sharing* information, not concealing it. With documents widespread in private hands, the reason for documenting sources was to help other people find them (as presumably it is today).

Buc derived information from the most noted antiquaries of the time, some listed among the Society of Antiquaries, others not. Sir James Ley, a founder member and active contributor to the Society, Buc cites as a *viva voce* authority in *The Third Universitie*, where he calls him 'an excellent antiquarie' (sig. Nnnn 2). Another early member who contributed *viva voce* information to that work was Dr Launcelot Andrewes. The heralds Brooke, Charles and St George assisted him with the *Commentary* by giving him access to their private libraries, and Camden and Brooke are cited frequently as sources of *viva voce* information. A scholar who does not figure in the incomplete lists of members for the Society of Antiquaries is St Low Kniveton, who wrote a chorography of Derbyshire and assisted Camden in his researches for the *Britannia*. He merits from Buc the appellations 'o*ur* greatest Reader of Record*es*' and 'our best Archivist' (*Comm*., ff. 63^{v} and 452). 'Our best Antiquaries' (*Comm*., f. 51^{v}) are Kniveton and Camden, the latter described by Buc as 'a [carefull] \diligent/ antiquary and a very [faithfull] \iudicious/ Genealogist' (*Comm*., f. 381), and Buc contributes a complimentary verse to the 1607 edition of Camden's *Britannia*. Camden in turn pays tribute to Buc as early as 1600 by including in the *Britannia* a discussion of his ancestry[24] and thanking him for historical information. He describes Buc as 'vir literate doctus & qui . . . multa in historijs obseruauit & candide imperijt' ['a man learned in letters and who . . . has observed much in histories and generously shared it'].[25]

It is tempting to wonder to what extent Buc was responsible for Camden's temperate assessment of Richard III in later editions of the *Britannia*, and which of them directed the other to the *Titulus Regius*. There are in the British Library some very tidy manuscript notes from the Act in Camden's hand relating to the bigamous nature of the marriage of Edward IV and Elizabeth Woodville, thus leaving Richard as 'undoubted heir' (B.L. MS. Cotton Titus F.VII, ff. 154^{v}-155^{v}). With John Stow, a much older man, Buc was well acquainted, referring to him as a *viva voce* source in the *Commentary* and more prominently in the *History*.[26] Stow, for his part, includes Buc's account of the Cadiz expedition in his *Annales*.[27]

Buc obtained *viva voce* information and manuscript source material from several members of the Howard family. The association was of long standing, beginning, according to Buc's account,[28] directly after the battle of Bosworth. Camden, clearly having derived this information from Buc, repeats it in the

24 Camden, *Britannia* (London, 1600), p. 726 and London, 1607 ed., p. 668.
25 *Ibid*. (1600), p. 726. A reference to Buc's knighthood and receipt of the Revels reversion is added in the 1607 ed., p. 668.
26 See below, pp. cxxxvii-cxxxviii for discussion of Stow's influence on Buc.
27 See p. xxxvii.
28 See above, pp. xvii-xviii.

Britannia.[29] The Lord Admiral, Charles Howard, Earl of Nottingham, who was Buc's commander on the Cadiz voyage and preferred him to Queen Elizabeth, was a direct descendant of the Duke of Norfolk who died fighting for Richard III. Buc uses him as a *viva voce* source in the *Commentary*, where he also acknowledges the loan of several books. To Henry Howard, Earl of Northampton, another antiquary, Buck inscribed a copy of *Daphnis*.[30] Lord William Howard of Naworth (1563-1640) was an avid collector of mediaeval historical texts and manuscripts, editor in 1592 of Florence of Worcester, a member of the Society of Antiquaries, and a friend of Camden's, for whom he collected inscriptions.[31] Buc speaks of him as 'an excellent antiquary and Archivist' (*Comm*., f. 210^{v}) and often refers in the *Commentary* to manuscripts in his possession. His nephew Thomas Howard, Earl of Arundel (1585-1646), to whom Buc dedicated his *History*, was another member of the Society of Antiquaries, one whom Buckingham recommended, as he did Buc, for membership in the proposed English Academy. A major collector of books and manuscripts, Arundel formed a collection dealing with history and heraldry which his grandson presented to the College of Arms. The remainder of his library went to the Royal Society, which sold it.[32] He also possessed a collection of family relics which was dispersed shortly after his death as the result of family feuding.[33] Despite these known dispersals and later damage to the Howard papers, Buc has been persistently attacked because one of the Arundel papers to which he refers can no longer be found.[34]

Amongst these numerous collections, Coke's library was outstanding in size, consisting of 1,227 items. It represents the interests of a legal scholar who was also engaged in historical studies. Buc, who dedicated *The Third Universitie* to Coke, calls him 'an excellent Antiquary' (sig. Mmmm). It is interesting to note how many of the sources Buc habitually used were in Coke's collection: Camden (in Latin and English), Commynes, Fabyan, Gainsford, Godwin, Glover, Holinshed, More, Newburgh, Paradin, Paris, *Rerum Angliae Scriptores,* Speed, Stow, Du Tillet, Polydore Vergil, Walsingham, Westminster. Also in Coke's library was a copy of Buc's *Daphnis*.[35] Coke lent freely to other antiquaries.

The most famous private library of the age – perhaps of any age – was that of Sir Robert Cotton. B.L. MS. Harl. 6018 is Cotton's borrowing register. It shows loans to Camden, Coke, Speed, Northampton, Spelman, Arundel, Greville, and, of course, Buc. Loans are cited to him on ff. 161, 173, and 174^{v} of Papal Bulls, Roger of Wendover and Liber Wigorniensis. This is probably the tip of an iceberg: it is clearly this library which Buc used most. He refers to manuscripts in the Cotton collection more frequently than to material in any other. He uses it even for information on his own family (*Comm*., ff. 450 and 451^{v}). That Buc's Cotton grandmother might have been related to Sir Robert's family does not in itself

29 *Britannia* 1607, p. 261.

30 The Grenville copy, B.L. shelfmark B. 11553, mentioned in Eccles, pp. 455f.

31 McKisack, *Medieval History in the Tudor Age*, p. 61.

32 Seymour de Ricci, *English Collectors of Books and Manuscripts* (1550-1930) (Cambridge, 1930), p. 25.

33 Mary F.S. Hervey, *The Life, Correspondence and Collections of Thomas Howard, Earl of Arundel* (Cambridge, 1921), pp. 456-8.

34 See below, pp. c-civ, cvi-cvii, cxiii, cxvi for further discussion.

35 Information on the contents of Coke's library from *A Catalogue of the Library of Sir Edward Coke*, ed. W.O. Hassall, Yale Law Library Publications, no. 12 (New Haven, 1950).

explain Cotton's possessing material on Buc's genealogy. He also possessed Howard papers. In 1610 Sir Thomas Watson was appointed Keeper of State Papers, and his attempts to collect them were, R.B. Wernham remarks, 'not, perhaps, made easier by the private collecting activities of Sir Robert Cotton'.[36]

The lending activities between Buc and Cotton seem to have been amicable and reciprocal in the main. But on 24 March 1605, just before departing for Spain as Deputy Master of the Revels, and with, he says, more to do than he can fit in before leaving, Buc wrote to Cotton to satisfy a request from the younger man. He has searched out two references dealing with Cotton's particular interest and sends him a copy of them, urging him to 'make frendly use of them, for in the one of them there be some thinges w*hi*ch are not fitt to be knowen but to discreet persons'. He hopes on his return to be 'better acquainted w*i*th y*ou*r rich library'. The favour is offered reciprocally: 'if my small Library may stand you, or y*ou*r studies in any stead you shall not fynd the dore shutt against you. for liberall myndes . . . out [*sic*] not to bee excluded' (B.L. MS. Cotton Julius C.III, f. 47).

Relations between them, however, became somewhat strained when on 10 March 1620 Buc wrote to Cotton upset that a manuscript book belonging to the Lord Admiral which Buc had lent to him had not been returned at his request. When Lord Darcy became 'ernest w*i*th me to deliuer him some matters concerning the great men of the realm in former tymes' (B.L. MS. Cotton Julius C.III, f. 49), Buc searched his own collection and came upon references to a manuscript book belonging to the Lord Admiral which he had borrowed and then lent to Cotton. He had not asked for it back earlier because he wanted to wait until he really had use for it. Finding that he required it to supply Lord Darcy's needs, he wrote to Cotton asking him 'to send me & lend me that book for a few dayes'. But instead of returning it, Cotton

> returned answer & such as much troubled me & *tha*t wheras [I] had told you & very truly *tha*t it was my L. Adm*irals* book, & *tha*t I durst not dep*ar*t w*i*th it or lend it for fear of losing & so purchasing his displeasure . . . , & then you gaue me y*ou*r word faithfully to keep it always in y*ou*r owne possession, & wher it should bee redy at all tymes if it wer called for. But when my \man/ told me *tha*t you sayd *tha*t the book was out of y*ou*r hands, & that you could not send it to me, it much distempered me, & I resolued by all meanes to recouer it, not for the worth [of] it . . . but for the preserving of my credit with my L. Adm.

Had it been his own book, he says, he would not have pressed for its return, but he has always taken care 'to hold my credit with good men', especially 'so good & so great men as my*n* auncient & most noble good L*ord* the L*ord* Noting*ham*'. He reminds Cotton that when he had asked for a book back Buc sent it at once.

Loans were made from Cotton's library to Selden and to Arundel (with whom he became closely associated from 1616),[37] Coke, Bacon, Spelman, Greville, Speed, Harington and Hoby among others. In Harleian 6018, which includes

36 Wernham, p. 22.

37 See Kevin Sharpe, 'The Earl of Arundel, His Circle and the Opposition to the Duke of Buckingham, 1618-1628', in Sharpe, *Faction and Parliament: Essays in Early Stuart History* (Oxford, 1975), p. 229.

notes of lending up to 1653, books when returned are shown as crossed off the lending list. Several not crossed off were evidently not returned, and there is a list of missing books on f. 187^{v} of this catalogue. Evidently Cotton often gave away and sometimes traded manuscripts, so that, as C.E. Wright says, 'It is not surprising that many manuscripts known to have belonged to Cotton are no longer in the library'.[38] Losses occurred in the later history of the library as well. B.L. MS. Additional 5161 records loans in 1638, among them a book on Glastonbury which was never returned and is now in the Wood collection in the British Library. There was a tremendous fire in the Cotton library in 1731, and of 958 volumes supposed to have existed before the fire, 114 were totally destroyed and 98 seriously damaged,[39] one of the damaged works being the manuscript of Buc's *History*.

In studying the contents of Cotton's library, past and present, we must take account not only of the various opportunities for loss but also of the numerous errors in cataloguing. There were several manuscript catalogues: Harleian 6018 was compiled between 1621 and 1653. B.L. MS. Additional 5161 is a manuscript catalogue of cartularies in the library. It is of uncertain date, far from complete, and says of itself, 'This booke was made since the book*es* were new plact & therefore imperfect as to find certaine anie booke almost therefore it were very well another Alphabeticall Catalogue in this kind were made' (f. 11). B.L. MS. Harleian 694, a catalogue made in 1674 of several English libraries, lists books under subject headings and gives their numbers in the library. Additional 8926, a parchment roll, is similar, giving the same subject headings but no classification numbers. The first printed catalogue, Thomas Smith's *Catalogus Librorum Manuscriptorum Bibliothecae Cottonianae*, was published in 1696, and David Casley's appeared in 1734 as a supplement to it, to show the damage and destruction of the books in the fire. Hooper's catalogue of 1777, derived from Harleian 694, criticizes the 'injudicious manner' and 'many defects' with which Smith's catalogue was compiled, and considers itself superior in arrangement by subject.

In formulating all these catalogues there always existed the danger of incorrect copying or printing, listing a manuscript under a wrong number, ignoring an alteration in the library's classification system, and failing to list a manuscript which had been bound with several others. For example, Sprott's chronicle, consistently throughout the catalogue cited as Vitellius E.IV, is mentioned as lost after the fire; but in fact it is still in the collection, numbered Vitellius E.XIV. One of Ailred's works, listed in Harleian 694 as 'Julius A 2', appears in the printed catalogue as A.XI, its correct number. Obviously a roman 'II' was at some point mistaken for an arabic 11. Similar confusions resulting from carelessness and misreading of numbers are frequent. Some items listed in Harleian 694 simply do not appear in the printed catalogues, among them several of the manuscript sources Buc specifically documents as coming from Cotton's collection. Because these works are not correctly listed in the printed catalogues it has been persistently assumed that they were lost or often that they never existed.[40] In fact, despite the

38 C.E. Wright, 'The Elizabethan Society of Antiquaries and the Formation of the Cottonian Library', in *The English Library before 1700*, ed. Francis Wormald and C.E. Wright (London, 1958), p. 4.

39 *A Report from the Committee Appointed to View the Cottonian Library* (London, 1777), Preface, p. v.

40 A.R. Myers, perhaps put off by the need to search for them, was particularly fond of this argument, in 'Richard

numerous allegations that Buc's manuscript sources are in the main no longer extant, there are in fact very few not extant or that cannot be proved to have been extant in his time. For many of those which seem genuinely to be lost, either through borrowing or fire, there are records in manuscript catalogues of the Cotton Library to prove that they were there in Buc's time. But the majority of those apparently lost have either been incorrectly classified, not listed, or too scantily described for identification in the most recent printed catalogues. To locate them it has been necessary to use the listings and descriptions in the early manuscript catalogues of the library and a moderate degree of ingenuity and persistence. Bearing in mind that 400 years have elapsed, and with some historical awareness, it should require no very strong feat of imagination to comprehend that some manuscripts referred to in 1619 would have perished between then and now.[41]

Cotton owned copies of Ailred, Bernard André, *Axiomata Politica*, Coggeshall, the Crowland Chronicle, Gildas, Giraldus Cambrensis, Herd, Huntingdon, Malmesbury, Newburgh, Paris, Rous, and Wendover. He had copies of excerpts from the Patent Rolls, the Public Records and the Treasury records, charters and Papal Bulls, assorted manuscript chronicles of various dates, miscellaneous books of rhymes, apothegms, axioms, epigrams, and numerous classical works. Ultimately the manuscript of Buc's *History* found its way into the Cotton Library.

Buc's antiquarian activity is well illustrated by his extant works. He seems in addition to have collected epitaphs for Camden: ff. 91-97 of B.L. MS. Cotton Julius F. XI, a Camden collection, are in Buc's hand, all but the first filled with copies of epitaphs.

Buc's scholarly methods are evident in his private annotations to his own copy of Godwin's *Catalogue of the Bishops of England*. These notes are as carefully documented as anything in his works. He refers to Bede, Camden, Commynes, Daniel's *History of England*, Liber Eliensis, Erasmus, Florence of Worcester, Foxe, Hall, Holinshed, Hoveden, William of Malmesbury, More, Paris, Parker, Stow's *Annales* and *Survey*, and Wendover. Many references are made to *viva voce* information derived from his fellow antiquaries: Dr Andrewes and Robert Cotton are mentioned as *viva voce* sources. References are made to the manuscript collection of the College of Arms in addition to Cotton's. Buc attempts considerable precision in his references, referring to book and page numbers, but he is often careless with the page numbers and writes over them. He supplies cross-references to other sections of the catalogue itself. In the margins he has given regnal years and roughly sketched coats of arms. His notes in margins and on blank pages contain speculation on names, with evidence derived from heraldry and from birthplace, notes of ownership at different times of lands and houses, correction of names and dates given by Godwin, clarification of the text, and additional information on the bishops included. Buc gives anecdotes of recent bishops, and lists names and dates of the incumbents of each see from the date the book was

III and Historical Tradition' and in his Introduction to the reprint of George Buc Esq., *History of the Life and Reigne*, that they never existed. Alison Hanham, however, having worked with early manuscripts, confirms my view that 'The mere fact that perishable manuscripts no longer exist is not surprising in the normal course of things': *Richard III and His Early Historians, 1483-1535* (Oxford, 1975), p. 96.

41 See below, p. cxxxi, for a list of Buc's sources that I could not find.

published to approximately 1611. He seems to have acquired the book in 1606, for he writes, on the title page, 'Quid retribua*m*?' [What shall I give back?], which is evidently his motto, and his signature; then adds to the author's name (given as 'F.G. Subdeane of Exceter') the note 'and prebendary of Wells vt videtur [as seen] fol. 300. 1601. & now Bishop of Landaff. 1606'.

Buc's scholarly bent was also extended to tenaciously seeking out correct ascriptions for pamphlets and play books. He annotated what must have been his own collection of pamphlets in B.L. MS. 600.d.29 with the author's name and professional status where missing. He also took pains to discover names of authors, titles and even plot antecedents of plays and annotated the title page with as much information as he could discover. Professor Alan Nelson has made a list of sixteen play quartos which he certainly inscribed. When Buc finds a title incomplete, he emends it. For example, he finds a title given as 'THE FIRST PART of Ieronimo' and adds, 'or of the Spanish Tragedy'.[42] He inserts a scene designation in *The Tragedie of Tancred and Gismund* (item 5). When he finds an author's name missing, he supplies one, identifying *The Arraignement of Paris* as 'by George Peele, as I remember' (item 4) and 'Sir Clyomon and Clamydes' as also by Peele (item 9). Two such title page notations have been carefully studied as a result of a mistaken claim that they were forgeries, but there is not the slightest doubt that they are in the hand of Sir George Buc. As previously stated, he annotated the title page of *Locrine* saying that Charles Tilney wrote a tragedy on this subject called *Estrild* which was lost at his death. Buc thinks this is it, '& now so*me* fellow hath published *it*'. He also records that he himself 'made the du*m*be shews for it, w*hi*ch I yet haue'. Of at least as much interest is his annotation of the title page of *George a Greene, the Pinner of Wakefield*: 'Written by .... a minister, who ac[ted] the pin*n*ers p*ar*t in it himself. Teste W. Shakespea[re.] Ed. Iuby saith that this play was made by Ro. Gree[ne]'.[43] This is clear proof of his collegial relationship with professional theatre practitioners.

We have very limited information about Buc's own 'small library' which by the standards of the time was not nearly as inconsiderable as he deprecatingly suggests. Those books which could be traced at his death when the question of inheritance was considered amounted to two trunks, one a very large trunk, one chest, and one deep drawer full. This would probably be around 300-500 books, depending on their size. During Buc's insanity his nephew Stephen Buck is alleged to have embezzled books, plate, and jewels in quantity, among them certainly the manuscript of the *History*. Selden acquired a very valuable book of arms from Buc's collection, and Eccles believes he would have taken care to secure as many as possible of Buc's more valuable books.[44] The shelfmark of one of the two in the Bodleian Library indicates that it was from Selden's collection.

42 Item no. 16 in Alan H. Nelson's list of manuscripts containing Buc's hand in https://ahnelson.berkeley.edu/ under 'Shakespeare "authorship" pages'. The item number will hereafter be given in the text.

43 For a thorough discussion of this text, see Alan H. Nelson, 'George Buc, William Shakespeare, and the Folger *George a Greene*', *Shakespeare Quarterly* 49 (1998), 74-83, from which this transcript is taken.

44 This account of Buc's library is from Eccles, 'Sir George Buc', pp. 494f. The estimate of the number of books contained in the trunks and chests comes from my own very considerable experience of packing books in trunks, chests, and deep drawers.

As I discovered accidentally when calling them up, the Bodleian Library possesses his copy of Bishop Godwin's *Catalogue of the Bishops of England* (shelfmark 4° Rawl. 569), and the Bodleian copy of Bouchard's *Grandes Croniques de Bretagne* (shelfmark B.1.17.Art.Seld.) also shows Buc's notations. Although it does not contain his name, as his Godwin does, it seems fairly certain that Bouchard was also his property. I sought for a while his copy of Glover's *Catalogue*, which had belonged to historian J.E. Neale, but the trail went cold, and Alan Nelson had the same experience with his copy of Chaucer.[45] It is unfortunate that from Buc's complete collection only two books can now be traced.

45 Personal email, 2016.

IV. THE TEXTS

There exist several early manuscript versions of Buc's *History*, but discussion and criticism have so far concentrated on the printed edition (see p. xcviif below) published in 1646, with its reissue in 1647 (see below, lxiv-lxv, n. 5) and again in *The Complete History of England* (1706 and 1719). In the nineteenth century Charles Yarnold collected materials for an edition from one of the manuscript copies. I shall supply a brief description of each of these manuscripts and editions before proceeding to discuss their relationship to each other and the relationship of the 1646 printed text to what Buc actually wrote.

British Library MS. Cotton Tiberius E.X (referred to hereafter as 'Tiberius' or 'Tib.)

[no title page]

Large folio, probably originally the same size as Buc's *Commentary* (36.5 x 23 cm), but now badly burnt around all edges, with greater severity toward the end. The largest expanse of remaining leaves is 30 x 20.5 cm. Tops of pages are better preserved than bottoms. A few pages are greyed by burning, some (ff. 23 and 25) to the point of illegibility. Running heads indicating the number of each book occur at regular intervals. The vertical margins are sometimes ruled, leaving 13-14 cm between rulings. Considerable revision makes it extremely unlikely that this was intended as the final copy.

Two people have made revisions in Tiberius: the author Sir George Buc and his great-nephew, George Buck Esq., herein designated as 'the Editor'. Occasionally the author's additions are written on the backs of scrap paper: Revels Office notes, letters, and early drafts of sections of the work. The later binder has sometimes included several versions of the same page or section and has invariably separated portions once pasted over passages the author wished to revise. There is considerable revision between lines and down margins of pages, and considerable crossing out by both author and Editor. Several stages of authorial correction appear in different inks, the darkest normally the latest. The author's usual ink is dull medium brown, with his corrections nearly black. The Editor's ink is generally more watery and somewhat reddish. The author has made some of his corrections first in pencil then written over them in ink, sometimes having marked with a pencilled 'X' in the margin sections he wished to correct. Occasionally sections are bracketed and starred with pencil in the margin, probably indicating the author's intention to revise.

Contents: ff.1-4^{v} dedication; ff. 5-5v Advertisement to the Reader; ff. 6-265 text. Several different hands appear: (1) Buc's normal hand, secretary with some humanist letter forms. Its slope is irregular and it is not particularly current although apparently written rapidly; (2) Buc's 'erasure hand', normally in reddish ink, used after erased portions; (3) a hand, probably Buc's, which attempts to be more formal, ff. 38, 46, and 62^{v}; (4) a hand similar to Buc's normal hand and probably a variant of it, ff. 31^{v}. 45^{v}. 73, and 73^{v}; (5) a humanist hand which is not Buc's for some long Latin quotations, f. 49; (6) the hand of a scribe, secretary: there are a hundred and seven scribal pages, and Buc has frequently made alterations on them and filled in blanks with unusual or foreign words; (7) the Editor's hand, evident in revisions on most pages. Ff. 126, 167, 173, 174, and 263 are entirely in the Editor's hand.

Page numbers from the printed edition of 1646 appear throughout in nineteenth-century hand, indicating collation of the manuscript with the printed edition with reference to which the manuscript's pages seem to have been arranged – sometimes incorrectly – for binding. Each leaf has been mounted in guards and at some point in the nineteenth century the manuscript was bound in calf and buckram.

British Library MS. Egerton 2216 (referred to hereafter as 'Egerton' or 'Eg.')
The history off Richard / the third / Comprised in fiue books / gathered and written by Geo: Buck / Esqr / [Quotation from Plato – 2 lines] / [Quotation from D. Ambros. – 2 lines] / [sign apparently signifying a bee]. Folio regularly gathered in eights. Paper, 29 x 19 cm. Twenty-five lines to a page, area covered by text on each page 24 x 12.3 cm. Ink medium to dark brown, later corrections in light reddish brown. Running heads noting the number of each book appear regularly at the top of each page. Catchwords are regular. Paragraphs are of considerably varying length, some indented, some not.

Contents: [f. 1] title page, ff. 2-3 dedication, ff. 4-309 text. Two different hands are apparent. The title page, dedication, corrections, and a few marginal notes throughout the text are in the hand of George Buck Esq. (the Editor's hand). The body of the text was clearly written by a scribe. Both are individual mid-seventeenth-century hands (about 1640), having mixed secretarial and Roman characteristics. The Editor's hand slants to the right, the scribe's is perpendicular. The manuscript was bound in leather in the nineteenth century. Condition is excellent.

Interesting feature: Charles Yarnold's notes pencilled in margins pointing out handwriting peculiarities, particular information, and collation with Tiberius.

Provenance: (1) title page has the signature 'William Ashton' at the top. (2) Below the title on the title page in Yarnold's hand: 'Bibliothecam Caroli Yarnold Mensis Novem^{bris} 23mo 1810 An^{no} *intravit!*' (3) Yarnold's library was sold at auction by Southgate of Fleet Street in 1825.[1] (4) 'Purchased at Messrs Sotheby's Jan. Feb. 1873' by the British Museum.

Bodleian MS. Malone 1 (referred to hereafter as 'Malone')
The History of King Richard / the Third. / Comprised in fiue bookes. / Written by Geo: Buck Esqr: / [bee sign] / [Quotation from Plato – 3 lines] / [Quotation from D. Ambros. – 3 lines].

Folio, gathered in eights. Paper, size 28 x 19.8 cm. Twenty-five lines to a page,

1 See below, p. lxxii.

area covered by text 24.5 x 11.5 cm. Ink dark brown, later corrections medium brown. Running heads noting the number of each book appear regularly at the top of each page. Catchwords regular. Paragraphs of considerably varying lengths, some indented, some not. Contents: f. 1 title page; ff. 2-3 dedication, f. 4 blank, ff. 5-318 text. Interesting features: wormholes near bottom of leaves in ff. 1-114, most serious in ff. 13-30, but in margins, so not destructive to the text. The hand is that of Egerton, with dedication and corrections in Editor's hand. The binding is calf, probably seventeenth-century.

Fisher Manuscript, Thomas Fisher Rare Book Library, University of Toronto (referred to hereafter as 'Fisher')

The History of King / Richard the 3.^{d} / By Geo: Buck Esqr.

Folio, gathered in eights. Paper, size 28 x 18.8 cm. Pages have been trimmed around the edges after binding, and occasionally parts of the marginal notes have been cut off slightly. Area covered by text is 23.5 x 11.5 cm, with twenty-five lines of text to a page. The hand is that of Egerton and Malone, with corrections in the Editor's hand. Ink is very dark brown.

Contents: ff. 1-4 blank, ff. 5-314 text, ff. 315-322 blank.

Interesting features: the title page is not in the Editor's hand. This copy contains no dedication.

Provenance: the manuscript was owned by W.W. Greg, who allowed Frank Marcham to quote from it in *The King's Office of the Revels*. Marcham does not mention Greg's name, describing it only as a manuscript in private hands (p. 6). It was sold in 1950 or 1951 to Sidney T. Fisher of Montreal by Alan Keen, London, who informed Mr Fisher that the manuscript had been Greg's. Keen's catalogue for 1949 or 1950[2], p. 6, item 13, gives the following description of it:

> THE FIRST BOOK WRITTEN TO REFUTE WILLIAM SHAKESPEARE'S HISTORICAL ACCURACY . . . The much corrected holograph draft of this book is in the British Museum and does not contain nearly so much matter as this MS. . . . From this draft it is just possible that a cipher copy of the complete book was made. There are two existing manuscripts of this work, one, formerly Yarnold's, in the British Museum, and the present. The discrepancies between these two can be accounted for if they were transcribed from cipher, as they are both undoubtedly written by the same person. The matter could not legally or even safely have been printed in 1620, and even in 1646 it was carefully edited, so that it is but a shadow of itself. . . . The above MS. has six blank pages at the beginning. These pages were probably intended for an address to another friend who would receive the gift. The title has been added *c*. 1670.

Keen dates it 1620 (which is certainly incorrect) and prices it at £200. Mr Fisher gave it to the University of Toronto Library, Thomas Fisher Collection, in 1973. Binding is nineteenth-century calf. Condition is excellent.

2 Mr Fisher, an environmental scientist, recalled that he purchased the MS. in 1950 or 1951 and that the catalogue came out a year earlier (personal correspondence, 1973).

British Library Additional MS. 27422 (referred to hereafter as 'Additional')
The history / of / the life and Death / of Richard the third. / in two Bookes / by Geo: Buck Esq.ʳ / [spiral].

Small folio gathered in eights. Paper 11.2 x 7.4 cm. Number of lines to a page between twenty and twenty-three. Area covered by text on each page 9.5 to 8.5 x 4.5 cm. Light brown ink. Running heads giving number of the book appear sporadically in Book I, but regularly at the top of each page in Book II. Catchwords are regular. There are paragraphs, but little punctuation. The manuscript is evenly written with few corrections in mid-seventeenth-century hand. Most of the letters are in secretary forms, with a generally late appearance because of the short 's' humanist form which often occurs initially and medially.

Contents: f. 1 nineteenth-century description of the manuscript, f. 2 title page, ff. 3-135 text. Contemporary vellum binding. Condition is excellent.

Provenance: 'Presented by Sir W.C. Trevelyan, Bart, 20 July 1866' to the British Museum. Trevelyan describes it thus (f. 1):

> This vol: contains Books 1 & 2 of the Life of King Richard 3ᵈ which appears to have been all the Author had at first intended to write – The 3ᵈ. 4ᵗʰ. & 5ᵗʰ. Books which he afterwards added, not being essential to the History, but containing principally a defence of King R. The contents of this vol. with a short addition at the end of the 2ᵈ book, concerning the authors ancestors, is printed with slight alterations, in 'The complete History of England vol. 1. 1706. pp. 514-545. . . . It was previously published in folio in 1646. –

Printed Edition of 1646
[Within a frame of double rules] THE / HISTORY / of the life and Reigne of / RICHARD / The Third. / [rule] / Compoſed in five Bookes / by GEO: BUCK Eſquire. / [rule] / *Honorandus est qui injuriam non fecit, ſ*ed *qui alios eam facere non / patitur, duplici Honore dignus est.* / Plato de legibus. Lib. 5. / *Qui non repellit a proximo injuriam ſ*i *potest tam est in vitio quam / ille qui infert.* / D. Ambros. offic. Lib. 3. / [rule] / [printer's ornament] / [rule] / LONDON, / Printed by *W. Wilſon*, and are to be sold by / *W.L.H.M.* and *D.P.* 1646.

Facing title page, a print of Richard III with motto 'Royaulte [*sic*] me Lie' and superscription, 'The true Portraiture of Richard Plantagenest, of England and of France King Lord of Ireland and third King Richard', and signed 'Cross. Sculp:'. There are commonly considered to be two editions of this, one of 1646 and another of 1647. Comparison of numerous typographical idiosyncrasies which remain constant in all copies examined (around twenty) and notation of the few press corrections, which exist indiscriminately in copies dated 1646 and 1647, proved that there were two issues rather than two editions of this work. Only the date on the title page has been consistently changed in the copies issued later. Both issues were composed of the same sheets. This indicates that the work was not particularly popular and was a way for the publisher to dispose of the spare sheets.

Small folio gathered in fours, pages 27.5 x 18 cm $2^{o}\pi^{2}$, a, B-O^{4} P^{2} Q-T^{4} V^{3} $*^{4}$. Contents: [i] blank, [ii] title, [iii] blank, [iv-v] dedication, 1-150 text [151-157] index, [157-158] glossary, [158] list of authors cited. First two leaves of each $ signed, B-N; first three leaves of O, R, S, and T signed; P unsigned, Q^{2} missigned X^{2} in some copies. P originally contained 4 leaves: page numbers 108-112 are missing. [P-P_{2}], pp. 105-107, [P_{2}^{v}] blank; P_{3} and P_{4}, which are missing, were evidently blanks; Q is p. 113. Pagination is otherwise regular, in upper outside corners, arabic numerals ruled all round. Running titles enclosed in rules: B_{2}^{v}-O '*The History of the Life and Reigne of* King RICHARD the Third', V_{2}^{v} '*The History of* RICHARD *the Third*';* - [*4] 'The Table'. Running heads also include the number of each book. The text is enclosed within rules, text area 23.5 x 14 cm. Margins are ruled. Catchwords regular except: p. 21 troubles (trouble), p. 23 *Imi* (*Immisit*), p. 27 *Solit* (*Solio*); p. 58 But (but); p. 148 Epi- (EPITAPHIVM); [p. 156] War (Warre). All copies, both 1646 and 1647, have on p. 147 between rows of printer's ornaments, '*Octob. 9.* 1646. / Imprimatur, *Na: Brent'*.

This edition was reprinted by E.P. Publishing[3] in 1973 from a copy dated 1647, with 'a new introduction by A.R. Myers'.[4] Myers refers to the reissue as a '2nd edition' (p. vi, n. 1) and the publishers speak of reproducing 'the 1647 edition'. No such thing ever existed. The publishers, clearly wishing to dispose of their spare sheets, simply bound them and printed a title page with a new date. I established this by taking my 1646 copy to many libraries and comparing it with copies dated 1646 and 1647. The same anomalies appeared in copies dated 1646 as in those dated 1647. The British Library catalogue now lists it correctly as a reissue of the 1646 edition. The Wing STC catalogue, which in the 1970s listed it as a second edition, has now corrected its listing.[4] The Bodleian catalogue does not comment. Myers's claim that 'the edition evidently met with success, for it was reprinted in 1647' (p. ix) is nonsensical. A reissue is a means of using up spare sheets of a work that is not selling. This can indicate lack of success, never success.

The 1646 edition has since appeared on the web from another 1647 copy, attributed to Sir George Buck, and is available in two other computerized versions (see p. cxciii).

Strype's Edition

In 1706 and again in 1719 was published *A Complete History of England*, generally associated with the name of Bishop White Kennett, who wrote the third volume of it, though John Hughes, according the British Library catalogue, was editor of the first two volumes. The first volume is a selection of histories from before the conquest to the end of Henry VII's reign. Authors such as Milton, Daniel, Habington, and Bacon are represented. For the reign of Richard III we are given Sir Thomas More, and as a complement to that, George Buck Esq.'s revised, shortened, printed version of his great-uncle's *History*. This was done, according

3 Wakefield, 1973. Calling the introduction 'new' seems curious. I am unaware of an older one.

4 *Short-Title Catalogue of Books Printed in England, Scotland, Wales and British America*, 1641-1700, 2nd ed., compiled by Donald Wing, rev. and ed. by John J. Morrison et al. (New York, 1994). The 1972 edition had cited the 1647 reissue as a 'second edition', but the 1994 has caught up sufficiently to describe it as a reissue.

to the preface, by editor John Hughes because Buck's

> Relation is particular, and very remarkable for the Pains he takes to wipe off the bloody Stains upon King *Richard's* Character, and to vindicate from common Imputation one of the blackest Reigns in all our Story. Whether he has done it with Reason or not, let the Reader judge; for there are various Opinions about it, and 'tis upon this Account that the Booksellers were advis'd to print it. His Book indeed tho' it were all Truth, is much too loosely writ for a History; 'tis pedantick and full of Harangue, and may more properly be call'd *a Defence of King Richard* than any thing else; yet as he is the only Advocate of Note that has appear'd in so odd a Cause, 'tis well worth the while to give him a Place here, tho' among so many of his Betters. In some things 'tis highly probable he has done the King but Justice; yet 'tis strange he'll neither allow him to have had any Deformity in Mind or Body, for he is angry to find him describ'd by others crook-back'd, and of an ill Visage, and seems to be for reversing his Character throughout. 'Twas not fit to let this Work pass without some Animadversions; and, to set all things as much in the Light as possible: Mr *Stripe*, an industrious Antiquary, has added large Notes and Remarks, from an Authentick Manuscript which he had by him, and from other Authors.[5]

The text is printed, without alteration, from the 1646 edition. Obvious printing errors, misspellings of names (e.g. Bevier for Beaujeu), and incorrect grammar and spelling in foreign quotations are left uncorrected. The only intrusion Strype has made into the body of the work is to translate into English occasional foreign passages, including, one would naturally assume, the epitaph at the end of the book, though John Ashdown-Hill has inexplicably been at pains to attribute this to Sir George (not, curiously, to his great-nephew, the alleged author of the work reprinted here), with no justification or explanation for so doing.[6] Except for noting one 'patch'd Quotation' from Commynes (p. 562), Strype never troubles to check any of the references against their originals. Neither has he bothered to correct or expand marginal notes to historical works, which, in the printed edition, are shoddy.

Strype's notes to the text, far from extensive as claimed, are sporadic, unsystematic, and often inaccurate. In a few places he points out more obvious mistakes. He notes, for instance, Buc/k's incorrect references to Charles, Duke of Burgundy, when this duke was in fact dead (pp. 530 and 553). But he himself makes similar mistakes through failing to consult the sources cited. Strype belabours points which have been made perfectly clear, insisting, for example, that Lionel, Duke of Clarence, be called Edward III's third son, though the text has given sound reason for choosing to style him the second. His usual technique is to claim that Buc/k's assertions are impossible because all the traditional

5 Preface to *A Complete History of England* (London, 1706), I, sig. av.

6 'The Epitaph of King Richard III', *The Ricardian*, XVIII (2008), 31-45 and *The Last Days of Richard III and the Fate of His DNA* (Stroud, 2013). See my article 'Researching Richard III's Epitaph', *The Ricardian*, XXVII (2017), pp. 117-29, which refutes this assumption, and also *vide infra*, pp. cxvii, cxxxvi.

historians (those deriving from More) give contradictory 'evidence' (he counters the mention of Eleanor Butler by citing the fact that More mentioned a liaison only with Elizabeth Lucy in this context, p. 565).

Supplementary illustrative material is occasionally introduced from British Library MS. Harleian 433 – the 'Authentick Manuscript which he had by him' – of which at that time he was the owner, but his researches extend no farther into original sources. Aside from those few additions from the 'Journal of Richard III', as he styles Harl. 433, his 'Animadversions' consist mainly of contradictions based on statements from the chronicles, which he regards as canonical and 'proof' of the 'falsehood' he thinks he spots. Strype seems singularly uncritical of the authority of these authors, because he erroneously assumes them to be contemporary with the events they describe. For example, he counters the statement that no contemporary chronicler charges Richard with murdering Henry VI by saying that More, Hall, and Bacon – who not only wrote after Richard's time but also derived information from each other – all make this accusation (p. 549).

Yet even into these sources Strype's search has not gone far, for though he notices the statement that Richard did not reward Banister is incongruous with the land grant recorded in MS. Harleian 433, he neglects to cite Hall as the source of the misinformation. Similarly he attacks the quotation from Camden that Richard was a bad man but a good king by citing uncomplimentary remarks Camden makes about Richard elsewhere and says suspiciously that in any case Buc/k 'does not tell us where *Cambden* speaks so well of him' (p. 525). Obviously Strype has not wished to take the trouble to look this up in Camden, where he need only have consulted the index under 'Richard III'. Two and a half centuries later A.R. Myers, equally unwilling to look this up, simply echoes Strype's assertion without documenting that he has done so, saying Buc/k 'quotes a statement in Camden that no one has seen since'.[7] When attempting to support a case by using material other than the chroniclers, Strype's reasoning is feeble. The identity of the bones found in the Tower as those of Edward IV's sons he considers 'proved' by the fact that Charles II was satisfied that they were.

Strype ends his shoddy piece of gentleman's editing in a state of some perplexity, unable to reconcile the common chroniclers with the one piece of contemporary material which he possesses. In his concluding note he gives documentary evidence of Richard's regard for learning, religion, justice, and public welfare saying, 'Could this King be brought of [*sic*] from the horrid Imputation that lies upon his Memory, of much Bloodshed, Oppression and gross Hypocrisy, to gain and keep the Crown, one might judge him a good King' (p. 576).

Yarnold's Intended Edition

In the first quarter of the nineteenth century, what was thought to be a new edition of Buc's original *History* went a long way toward completion, edited by Charles Yarnold, a surgeon. Work on this intended edition seems to have extended from

7 Myers is fond of saying of things he has not wished to try to find, 'No one else has ever seen it'. See below, Introduction Ch. VI for further discussion of this quirk. The quotation appears below in text, p. 46, ll. 30-1. In Camden's *Britannia*, 1607 ed. it is on p. 269.

1814 to 1821. Yarnold's collections pertaining to this volume are in the British Library, MSS. Egerton 2216-2220. Yarnold's interest in Richard III was evidently of long standing, for he says in his draft for the preface of his intended edition that '. . . at a very early period a strong interest for research into the manners & history of the 15 Century led me to attend to the several historians who wrote of that period. More particularly however the Person & character & [*sic* for 'of'] Richard – was the constant subject of consideration –' (Egerton 2218, f. 46). It is possible that this interest was aroused by Horace Walpole's *Historic Doubts on the Life and Reign of King Richard III*, published in 1768. Yarnold, as he has written on its title page, acquired Egerton 2216 on 23 November 1810. It is not known how it came to him, for he says in his preface only that he acquired it by 'accident' (Egerton 2218, f. 46), or 'a fortunate occurrence' (f. 48).

In 1818 he expressed an intention to dedicate his edition to the Duke of Buccleuch, and up to 1821 was actively involved in research for it. Yarnold's transcript of Books II-V, which takes up the first volume of his collections (Eg. 2217), is undated, but it includes in the margin collational notes from Tiberius and the printed version. In Egerton 2218, f. 37^{v} he gives the date on which he finished collating Tiberius as October 1815. His notes from the Rolls Office are similarly dated (Eg. 2218, f. 243), while his transcripts from the Harleian MSS. are dated exactly a year later (Eg. 2219, f. 88) and miscellaneous collections from other sources he has dated 1818 (Eg. 2218, f. 107). A discourse and notes on More, obviously intended as commentary for the edition, are dated 1817 (Eg. 2218, f. 121), and a similar discussion of Howes's edition of Stow is dated 1818 (Eg. 2218, f. 199). The latest date given in his collections is 1821, when he records completing his transcript of *The Arrivall of Edward IV* (Eg. 2219, f. 1) and in July of that year someone sent him an extract on Richard III in French (Eg. 2220, f. 73).

There exist in the collections several corrected proof sheets for Book I, numbered pp. 1-32 (sigs. B1-E4). The corrections may provide some clue to Yarnold's motive for suspending the printing. The transcripts of Books II-V (Eg. 2217) in Yarnold's hand follow the manuscript's spelling, though not its paragraphing, punctuation, and capitalization. The printed pages have done the same. However, in the printed pages 1-8 and 25-32 Yarnold has systematically altered the spelling to modern, and he includes a fair copy manuscript in modern spelling to supersede printed pp. 17-24, in which he had first made only general editorial corrections without modernizing spelling. He evidently changed his mind or was uncertain about printing the edition 'in the orthography of the writer' as his draft for the preface indicates was his original intention (Eg. 2218, f. 48).

Clearly Yarnold believed at first that Egerton was Sir George Buc's original manuscript, and in his draft for the preface of his edition he does not mention Tiberius, since he regarded this as merely rough papers for his copy text. He was, of course, drawn to support its originality since it belonged to him. But the more work he does comparing the various texts the more he is stretched to the limit in trying to support his own as Sir George's fair copy. He is far less confident about associating with Sir George the printed version, which he appropriately refers to as 'the Castrated Copy', Eg. 2218, f. 10.

> . . . as it [Eg. 2216] explicitely declares itself the only MS – of this

> historian – I tooke the pains to collate this with the printed copy – published in 1646 – the large curtailments & in many places compressions of which were striking – indeed in some instances omissions are to be detected perfectly unaccountable – if We consider Buck himself to have edited the Work
>
> (Eg. 2218, f. 48)

In his list entitled 'Arguments for the originality of the M.S.' (Eg. 2217, f.1), he is clearly pitting it against the printed edition alone. He remarks on the printed edition's references to books (e.g. *Religio Medici*) published after Buc's death and on its blurring of what appear in Egerton clear personal references, e.g. to Buc's own experiences, to *viva voce* evidence, to other works by Buc. He is particularly puzzled about the writing in his own manuscript of 'Segar' over an incomplete erasure, through scraping, of 'Dethick'. The manuscript's title page ascription to 'George Buck, Esq.' obviously conflicts with the assumption that the work is Sir George's, but Yarnold tries to resolve this confusion by citing the marginal note in Eg. 2216, f. 153 which speaks of 'this S*ir* Geo. Buck'.

Though puzzled, his conclusion, evidently influenced by Edmond Malone,[8] is that although Eg. 2216 was the work of Sir George Buc, the printed edition was published by his son. In a note (Eg. 2218, f. 37^{v}), Yarnold conjectures,

> I should think that Buck the Editor [of the printed edition] never saw my M.S. [Eg. 2216] – and from the comparison of the Printed Dedication with Sir Georges I am led to believe that he crossed out the parts which appeared scored – & took out what he chose to insert in his own Edition wishing as it should seem to pass for the author as in the Pub. Copy he no where acknowledges it to be his father's.

Thus Yarnold takes one step toward Eccles's assertion of alterations by a later member of the Buck family,[9] though he is able to see only a single manifestation of it. His eventual discovery of Tiberius leads him no farther down this path, however, for he judges this to be merely 'Rough Papers' for Egerton, Buc's own fair copy. In comparing the hands of the two manuscripts, he notes that the 'correction hand' of Tiberius is the same as that of the preface and several emendations in Egerton (as of course it is: the great-nephew's). Assuming this is Sir George's, however, Yarnold claims: 'the identity of both as Sir G. Bucks is ascertained beyond doubt' (Eg. 2217, f. 1).

By the time the proof sheets were printed, Yarnold had collated Egerton with Tiberius in pencilled notes in Eg. 2216; and in marginal notes in his transcript of Egerton 2216 Books II-V cited certain matters of interest from Tiberius. His notes from Tiberius can be classified as indicating particular interest in autobiographical information: personal, including religious, opinion, strong statements in favour of Richard, and even more frequently and consistently strong statements against Richard's enemies; and expanded information on figures contemporary with Buc or with Richard. These notes appear much more frequently in the earlier stage of the transcript where Yarnold was evidently paying closer attention to Tiberius.

8 See below, pp. lxxiii-lxxiv.
9 Eccles, 'Sir George Buc', pp. 485-503.

His collections include transcripts of only a small portion of Tiberius, the Dedication and Advertisement to the Reader (Eg. 2218, ff. 35-37 and 50-51). Since he considered the Editor's deletions and additions authorial, there was no purpose in transcribing more of what he considered only rough papers. His transcripts seem at first glance potentially useful to the modern reader of Tiberius, since some words no longer present in the manuscript seem to have been extant in Yarnold's time. However, because these at times do not accord with the sense of the passage, one must conclude that they are conjectural emendations by Yarnold. His observations on the form of Tiberius are negligible. He mentions only that Buc has used the back of a letter for one of its pages. No reference is made to the Revels Office scraps.

Yarnold evidently intended to check the foreign quotations carefully before printing them, for he notes that the Ariosto passage (text, p. 85) is probably not in correct Italian (he was wrong) and should be corrected with a good edition (Eg. 2217, f. 23^{v}). As transcription progresses, his copying of foreign quotations becomes increasingly careless and incomplete, as if he intended to go back over them all. It is possible he planned to check and augment the marginal notes throughout the edition, for in the manuscript fair copy for an early portion of Book I he adds a book's title where Tiberius, Egerton, and the printed edition give only the author's name.

In Yarnold's collection appear several lists of research plans carried out. Egerton 2218 and 2219 include biographical material on Buc copied from the *General Biographical Dictionary* and from Cotton manuscripts, several Paston letters, excerpts from Habington, Rastell, Hutton, Walpole, and Drake's *Eboracum*; Strype's notes to his edition of the *History of the Life and Reigne*, and other printed sources; a discussion of More's authority; and transcripts from the Harleian manuscripts, particularly 433. He has made reference to a book by Sir John Jacob, the dedicatee of Eg. 2216, to *The Great Plantagenet* (George Buck Esq.'s pirated version of *Daphnis*) and to Buc's *Third Universitie*. There are also various notes on buildings and persons of Richard III's period.

Drafts of the Appendix to Book I had been composed. These include Paston references to death of the Bastard of Fauconberg; arguments against the existence of a marriage between Anne Neville and the son of Henry VI; Paston evidence of Clarence's aggression; the doubtful death of Edward IV; discussion of Morton's authorship of at least the outlines of More's *Richard III* (Yarnold makes a note to himself to try to locate Morton's original); quotations from More and the Paston letters on the hatred by the Woodvilles of Edward IV's family; and statements on the authenticity of Richard's election, including More's account of the Three Estates' petition to him and the confirmatory evidence of the *Titulus Regius* in full.

Yarnold's assessment of Buc is that he relies for credibility on his own integrity, social position, and acquaintance with contemporary scholars, and thus sometimes seems offhand and unsystematic in citing his authorities. Yarnold imagines that he must have relied heavily on family tradition, both his own and the Howards', for he shows a fondness for 'ancestorial dignity' (Eg. 2218, f. 116^{v}) and 'a quiet, settled sort of contempt' for the common chroniclers, an attitude which 'has much the appearance of being a common one among the better informed or the Noble, whose private family records probably were often in direct confutation of the erroneous histories in common circulation' (Eg. 2218, f. 117v). Nevertheless, Yarnold observes, Buc has taken pains to corroborate these family traditions with evidence, and with the resources of the public records. 'His stile is censured and I think justly . . . that he participates in the pedantic spirit of the age is evident . . . ' (Eg. 2218, f. 47).

Egerton 2220, a collection of letters relating to the potential publication of Yarnold's edition, indicates that part of it was in press late in 1814. A Prospectus for the work, 'Printed for RICHARD REES, No. 62, Pall Mall', states that the edition is 'In the Press, and speedily will be published', prices £1-11-6 for quarto and £2-12-6 for large paper copies (Eg. 2218, f. 2). A delay occurred in 1815 when Rees retired from business and turned the work over to his brother at Longman's. It is certain that in 1816 the edition was going forward, for in that year Yarnold writes a draft of a letter to someone possessing original documents that he is 'at this moment editing a republication of that singular Historian & apologizer for the unfortunate Richard . . .' (Eg. 2218, f. 184). Throughout the years 1816 and 1817 the printer, Arthur Taylor, attempts to urge Yarnold on, in a letter of 2 May 1816 telling him that another bookseller had undertaken to publish Buck's *History of the Life and Reigne* from the 1646 edition '& *has actually begun it*!!!! We have seen a Sheet of this new Edition!! So the world may lose, for Ever, the advantage of a Manuscript which *you*, the *Zealous* defender of Dickon Plantagenest have had sundry years in your possession!' (Eg. 2220, f. 28). Clearly the assumption was (presaging developments in the 1970s) that the republication of the 1646 edition would bury any new edition of what was believed to be the original. However, Yarnold's publisher negotiated with the intended publisher of the reprint, and clearly, having better luck than I did, succeeded in persuading him to relinquish the project.

But in the meantime another Prospectus for Yarnold's edition takes pains to stress the shortcomings of the printed text: it claims Yarnold's new edition will be from the author's original manuscript, in contrast to the 1646 edition by his 'son', which is 'now rarely to be met with and at considerable price'.

> The intended edition, given literally from the ORIGINAL MANUSCRIPT of Sir George Buck will be found to contain considerably more of interesting matter than the former one. Several omissions, which in the prior edition had occasioned some plausible cavils at his integrity as an historian, or obtained for him the character of a 'lover of paradoxes', are now fully rectified and the imperfect marginal Notes of the printed copy, which had given rise to charges of misquotation, will be supplied by the original references to personal and oral testimony.
>
> (Egerton 2220, f. 111)

For whatever reason, Yarnold never finished his edition. On his death in 1825 his complete library amounted to some 573 items, including the Buck manuscript. It included Bacon's *Henry VII*, Camden, Cotton's Tower Records abridgements, Commynes, Drake's *Eboracum*, Gainsford's Perkin Warbeck, Hall, Habington's *Edward IV*, Hardyng, Hutton's *Bosworth Field*, Lingard, Paradin, Paris, Rapin,

Polydore Vergil, Walpole's *Historic Doubts*, Matthew of Westminster, and a manuscript copy of Sir William Cornwallis's *Encomium of Richard III*.[10] The collection was sold at auction by Southgate of Fleet Street.

Collections of Yarnold's were again advertised for sale at £180 by T. Evans in his 1839 catalogue, which states that the materials for his edition of Buck 'would be a valuable acquisition of any Literary Club to print for the use of its Members'. Finally in 1873 the five volumes of Yarnold's collections associated with his intended edition, including Eg. 2216, were sold at Sotheby's to the British Museum, valued collectively at £21. The sale catalogue confusedly identified Egerton 2216's author as 'GEORGE BUC, Esq. *the original MS'*, and Buc is styled Master of the Rolls [*sic*], a gentleman of the Privy Chamber under James I, and 'a distinguished poet as well as historian' (Eg. 2218, f.1). The catalogue repeated the recommendation to a literary club.

10 For discussion of this work's relation to Buc's *History*, see below, pp. cxxii-cxxv. For further details of this particular MS. copy (now B.L. MS. Additional 29307) see J.A. Ramsden and A.N. Kincaid, Introd. to Sir William Cornwallis, *The Encomium of Richard III*, ed. A.N. Kincaid (London, 1977).

V. TRANSMUTATION OF THE TEXT

Sir George Buc's *History of King Richard the Third* had a curious future. Its author never finished his work on it but left it in a rough state, apparently near completion, heavily revised and often with decisions not made among revisions, but almost ready for copying fair. He had clearly attempted to have a fair copy produced at one point, but this stage had ended in further revision. There is no way of knowing whether he intended to publish it, or whether it would have been possible to do so in his time. After his death it found its way eventually into Cotton's library, by what means is not known. It is listed in the 1674 catalogue (B.L. MS. Harl. 694) as existing in this collection, of which it still forms a part within the British Library. But this was not before it had undergone considerable revision by another hand and a revised master copy had been made from it. From this master, no longer extant, were made three scribal presentation copies, described hereinunder. These were all made for the same reviser, and they exhibited in some places different revisions. The revising hand was that of Buc's great-nephew who, except for the suffix 'Gent.' or 'Esq.' instead of 'Knight', and his preference for spelling his name 'Buck', shared his great-uncle's name and managed to steal a share of his fame as well. He seems to have been ambitious for preferment, and his methods of seeking it were far from ethical.

Mark Eccles suggests that young George Buck got possession of the manuscript through his father's embezzlement of money, books, and other valuables during Sir George's insanity.[1] The younger George's great-uncle, John Buck (no relation to Sir George's family) was a notorious forger who lost his ears and was branded in the business. Possibly John Buck's nephew Stephen shared what seems a family talent for forgery: a version of Sir George's will, which left his goods to his nephew Stephen Buck's family, was disputed as a forgery. This proclivity seems to have been inherited, with certain artistic distinctions, by George Buck Esq.

The authorship of the edition published in 1646 remained a matter of confusion for some time. In 1748 Philip Morant in *Biographia Britannica* said it was the work for which Sir George Buc was best known.[2] This error was 'corrected' by Edmund Malone over 50 years later:

> I take this opportunity of correcting an error into which Anthony Wood has fallen, and which has been implicitly adopted in the new edition of the *Biographia Britannica*, and many other books. The error I allude to, is, that this Sir George Buc, who was knighted at White-hall by king James the day before his coronation, July 23, 1603, was the author of the celebrated *History of King*

1 Eccles, 'Sir George Buc', p. 495.
2 [Philip Morant], *Biographia Britannica*, (London, 1748), II, entry for 'Buc, Sir George'.

> *Richard the Third*; which was written above twenty years after his death by George Buck, *Esq*. who was, I suppose, his son.[3]

George Chalmers follows this, stating that 'he did not write, as it seems, the celebrated History of Richard the 3d, which is said to have been written, after his death, by George Bucke, his son'.[4] But before his next edition he has done more research:

> I was induced, chiefly, by the strong assertions of Mr. Malone . . . to doubt, whether *The History of the Reign of Richard III*, were written by Sir George Bucke [*sic*], the Master of the Revels, or by George Buc [*sic*], his relation. Further inquiry has convinced me, however, that there can be no controversy. . . . In the Catalogue of the Cotton Library, which was compiled before the unlucky fire . . . this MS. is called 'The history of King Richard the third comprized in five books, gathered and written by Sir G. Buc, Knight, Master of the King's Office of the Revels, and one of the gentlemen of his Majesty's Privy Chamber; corrected and amended in every page'. The original MS. which still remains, in the British Museum . . . though it be greatly damaged by fire, clearly proves, that the Catalogue is perfectly accurate. This MS. appears to have been the Author's rough draught; as it is corrected, by interlineations, and erasements, in every page. A part of the Dedication to Sir Thomas Howard, the Earl of Arundel . . . still remains, together with 'an advertisement to the Reader', which is dated 'from the King's Office of the Revels, St. Peter's hill, the of the 1619'. This evidence, then, is decisive, in favour of Sir George Buck, as the real Author, against Mr. Malone. This *History* was first published, in 1647 [*sic*], by George Buck, Esquire, who says, indeed, in his Dedication to Philip the Earl of Pembroke and Montgomery, 'that he had *collected these papers out of their dust:*' Yet, was the publisher, whether he were the Son of Sir George, or some other relation, so disingenuous, as to assume the work as his own: . . . as to publish for his own profit, what, certainly, was the property of another.[5]

A bit later Joseph Ritson in his *Bibliographia Poetica* has picked this up and states in a direct reply to Malone that Sir George Buc was the true author of the 1646 *History* which passed under the name of George Buck Esq., since the original manuscript bearing his name was extant in the British Museum.[6] It was clear that this error persisted because, though there was now awareness of Tiberius's existence, it was impossible to read or assess it while it remained in unbound burnt sheets.

W. Carew Hazlitt was the first to note that more than one manuscript copy existed: 'The original MS. of his Life of Richard the Third, varying considerably

3 Edmond Malone, 'An Historical Account . . . of the English Stage', prefaced to William Shakespeare, *The Plays and Poems* (London, 1790), I, pt. ii, 46f.
4 [Chalmers, George], *An Apology for the Believers in the Shakespeare-Papers*, London, 1797, p. 494.
5 [George Chalmers], *A Supplemental Apology for the Believers in the Shakespeare Papers* (London, 1799), pp. 204f.
6 [Ritson], *Biographia Poetica*, p. 147 (London, 1802).

from the printed copy, 1646, is still extant, and one or two copies of it as well. It was probably written at least 50 years, before it saw the light in a printed shape'.[7] As we have seen in the previous chapter, Charles Yarnold owned one of the manuscript copies and was planning to print it as Buc's original, assuming it to have been a fair copy made for the author. Frank Marcham, who in 1925 had access to two manuscript copies (Egerton and Fisher), followed Yarnold's conjecture that these were fair copies made for Buc,[8] though he does not adopt Yarnold's palaeographical error of assuming the hand of the copies is Buc's own. It was left for Mark Eccles to identify George Buck Esq., and discover the relationship of the copies to the original.[9]

Changes in Tiberius

The younger Buck's first step was to make alterations and corrections in the manuscript itself. These are for the most part stylistic improvements. He simplifies the tortuous constructions and dispenses with the innumerable 'ands' both in series and at the beginnings of sentences. By employing subordination, he makes grammatical constructions more vivid. He sometimes creates immediacy by changing a verb from past to present tense. While in the first half of the book the Editor (which is how I refer to George Buck the Younger) sometimes revises sentences and occasionally larger thought units for the sake of compression, he becomes bolder and more ruthless from the middle of Book III onward and is readier to lop away whole pages of digressive, repetitive or verbose material, sometimes replacing them with a few sentences summarizing their content, sometimes dispensing with them altogether. His stylistic revisions seem to have the purpose of diversifying and tightening the structure and reducing the size of the work.

Some examples of his stylistic changes are:

(1) diversifying the beginnings of sentences or clauses:

'and the which' becomes 'which'

'and now to proceed' becomes 'to proceed then'

(2) removal of 'ands' in series:

'& the L*ord* lovell, & the lo*rd* Graystok, & Sir W*illiam* Parr'[10] becomes 'the Lo*rd* Lovell, the Lo*rd* Graystok, Sir W*illiam* Parr'

(3) subordination within sentences:

'& he demandeth the erldom of Heryford' becomes 'demanding the erldom of Heryford'

(4) rewording and abbreviating to express more compactly:

'forejudge & hardly censure' becomes 'preiudicate'

'who was a man bredd in good letter*es*, & well languaged' becomes a 'man well read and languaged'

7 Hazlitt, *Hand-Book to the Popular, Poetical, and Dramatic Literature of Great Britain* (London, 1867).

8 Marcham, p. 3.

9 Eccles, 'Sir George Buc', in *Thomas Lodge and Other Elizabethans*, pp. 485-503.

10 Tiberius, f. 13^{v}. Square brackets in the examples given in this Introduction indicate crossings out by the Editor, George Buck Esq., and pointed brackets my conjectural filling in of gaps. Italics indicate expansion of abbreviations. Folio numbers from Tiberius will hereafter in the Introduction be given in parentheses in the text when the material in these examples is of any magnitude or interest.

(5) making language and construction more diverse and vivid:

'But to proceede with the affaires of these Armies now th<at> thes two armies i.e.
the army of the king & the army of the rebells Lancastrians were nowe come to Redmore heath, and in the viewe the one of the other, & were approachinge and disposed themselues to fight' becomes 'and nowe suppose you see the King*es* Army and the f<ollowers of Lancaster> at Redmore hea<th> and disposing themselues to fight' (f. 99).

The conversation between Edward IV and his mother (ff. 223-4) is given entirely in direct discourse instead of fluctuating between direct and indirect.

(6) prudery:

'lustful' becomes in one instance 'sweetest' and in another 'amorous'
'wench' becomes 'fair one'
'lusts' becomes 'desires'

Circumstantial detail is deleted, such as that surrounding Dethick's showing Buc the book of sobriquets (f. 10). Some philosophical digressions are reduced or discarded, but this is by no means true of all digressive material. Buc's innumerable pointers to what he has said or what he is about to say, and his cross-referencing of his own statements, are deleted.

So far the alterations must in most cases be described as improvements, making the work more vivid, compact, and readable. One can only regret that Buc did not remain in health long enough to have undertaken similar revision himself. It is fortunate that we have a fair copy of the *Commentary* to show his style in a finished work. Some of the revisions in which the younger Buck indulges, however, alter the content materially. These are of three main varieties: toning down political references, particularly with regard to the treason against Richard III of Henry Tudor and his followers; removing religious references; and concealing the personal aspects of the work to facilitate passing it off as his own. In doing all these things the Editor begins a process which he pursues with increasing severity through his future copies. For example, f. 126 is entirely in his hand, probably a rewriting of an authorial page which is now missing. He revises as he goes along. He particularly wants to avoid references to people currently living. Buc has written about the living Earl of Shrewsbury. So the Editor writes 'the Talbots . . . *th*e [that bee the erle of the erle] \and the late erles/ of Shrewsbury . . . '.

In his political revisions he gives special attention to whitewashing Morton:

'all his secret & trayterous practices' becomes 'all his secret practises'

'almost as badd, & fals, & disloyall as himself' becomes 'almost as deadly as himself'

'Thus the oratour of sedition, & he told his tale so cunningly as that the duke was agayn, & anew stirred vp to <be f>alse, & disloyal \& false hearted to his prince/ & hee was w*it*h these divelish seditious arguments much \more/ encouraged & enflamed with the fyre & fury of rebellion' becomes simply 'as that the duke was agayn incendiated' (f. 57^{v}).

The reference to Morton's gaining advancement through treachery and malice is omitted, as are suggestions of his complicity in the deaths of Edward, Earl of Warwick and Perkin Warbeck (ff. 192^{v} and 202). The remarks about Henry failing to punish the alleged murderers of Edward IV's sons because they were favoured in high places (ff. 205-206^{v}) also disappear.

Henry's other followers fare better with the Editor than with the author:

> 'thes noble rebells' becomes 'his partyes' (f. 66)
>
> 'Welshe and false knights and Esquires and manie perfidious and rebellious Englishmenn of all quallities' becomes 'other of all quallities' (f. 96).

Criticism of Henry himself is diluted by the Editor. Instead of being ambitious and egotistical, his temper becomes 'as other men's' (f. 21^{v}). The remark about his risking his reputation and his soul by following Morton's evil counsel rather than the divine spirit is deleted (f. 79 v), as is the wish that Henry, though destined to be king, had awaited the Lord's leisure (f. 263). Instead of disliking combat and being far inferior to Richard in arms, Henry had 'the advantage other wayes' (f. 103). Examples of kings keeping the crown from their true heirs are deleted (f. 192 v), and what was originally a literal translation of the quotation, 'prosperum scelus virtus vocatur' – '<the> wicked act succeeding well is called a vertew' is softened by judicious crossing out to '<the> act is called a vertew' (f. 20).

The extensive paraphrasing of the particularly diffuse section on Perkin Warbeck in the second half of Book III has a serious effect on its content, which seems intentional: it destroys or dilutes most of the statements that the foreign princes who aided Perkin believed in the justice of his title, as did the majority of the populace. Long religious digressions are invariably excised, though brief references are untouched. As in his earlier revision of *Daphnis*, the Editor tends to alter or remove the name of God, which had been placed under censorship. Clearly his intention was to avoid potentially controversial material in politics and religion.

His alterations in Tiberius take the form of crossing out words, lines, or pages and rewriting above the lines or in the margins, or very occasionally on scrap sheets, reworking, primarily for stylistic improvement, the author's original. There is no evidence of his adding any factual material of his own, though there is some stylistic elaboration. The date of this revision must be placed after 1625, since a reference to King James has been altered to read 'our King', and the description of Arundel as young (f. 239) is discarded. The work was probably done considerably later than this. Perhaps after his publication in 1635 of *The Great Plantagenet*, his revision of *Daphnis*, the Editor felt the challenge of a larger work. Dating the revision of the original manuscript after 1635 would place it nearer the manufacture of the copies, around 1638-40. But there is no internal evidence to permit a closer dating.

In this process of revision an attempt has been made to dispose of the original's autobiographical aspects. The reference to the Earl of Oxford's conversation with Buc about the revenue of his land (ff. 209-10) is deleted and the information given with no personal reference. Nearly all the praise of Queen Elizabeth (f. 134^{v}) is removed. We can see in this only a suggestion of the Editor's scheme to pass off the work as his own. He has not dealt systematically with all the personal references and does so gradually over the course of the successive copies. Eccles seems correct in calling his revisions of this type haphazard.[11] These excisions fit his general revision pattern of cutting down passages which are too circumstantial (as in the case of the Earl of Oxford anecdote) or go on too long after making their point (as in the Queen Elizabeth eulogy). All we can say definitely at this stage is that the Editor was attempting to update the work.

The 'Literary Career' of the Editor, George Buck Esq.

Buck the Younger's life of literary deception seems to have been a succession of appeals to potential patrons in hope of obtaining preferment. He seems never to have met with success. He began at some point after 1625 when Charles I came to the throne, and his first traceable attempt was made on 'Sir John Burrough, K*nigh*t principall Kinge at Armes'.[12] The work he dedicated to Burrough was a manuscript revision of his great-uncle's *Daphnis Polystephanos*. Evidently possessing the original manuscript of this work (which unfortunately does not survive), as he did of the *History*, he seems to have been unaware that it had been published in 1605. His manuscript of *Daphnis*, in a state of revision between the two printed versions, Sir George's of 1605 and his own of 1635, is written in the same hand as the three copies of the *History* made for him. The title page and dedication with its signature are in the same hand (his own) as the title pages, dedication and corrections in Egerton, Malone, and Fisher and the alterations he makes in Tiberius. The title of the manuscript version is '*Δαφνις or the Polyanthine Ghirland*, by George Buc. gent.' Interestingly at this point he adopts his great uncle's surname spelling, a practice he does not repeat. He signs the dedication with one of his usual formulae: 'Your unfeigned honorer and humble Servant George Buc:' (f. 3). The dedication is similar to the one in the printed version of the *History*, where he deprecates his own ability and protests his zeal.

He next publishes the work in 1635, still evidently unaware that it had been previously published, and true to his usual practice in his various copies of the *History*, he dedicates the printed copy to someone else, this time to Sir John Finch, Lord Chief Justice of the Court of Common Pleas, a dedication perhaps suggesting that his own training, like his great-uncle's, had been in law (ironic as this may seem). The poem has been revised to focus on Charles I and has been retitled *The Great Plantagenet or a Continued Svccession of that Royall Name*. The dedication includes self-conscious remarks on the author's ability: 'There wants nothing in the *Subiect* to make an *Historian* and a *Poet*. And had these *Intentions* mett an abler *Pen*, they might (with some desert of Pardon, haue beene admitted the intermission of your *Lordships* more serious Houres . . .' (A3^{v}). He remarks rather slyly, 'in these *Papers* I have but practis'd like a young Limbner, wipt away the *dust* from some *Antiquities*, and by them drawne these proportions . . .' (A3) and closes, 'Your most humble and unfeigned honorer, *George Buck'*.

Ritson had observed early in the nineteenth century that the 1635 edition 'appears to be a reprint of the former, with very considerable alterations, by some

11 Eccles, p. 503.
12 *Δαφνις or the Polyanthine Ghirland*, Bod. MS. Rawl. Poet. 105, f. 2.

fellow who assum'd his name'.[13] In fact, the practice the Editor follows 'like a young Limbner' is plagiarism, and his name, except the spelling and that it lacks the prefix 'Sir', is the same. The great-nephew's changes in *Daphnis* are of several types: general reorganization for the sake of clarity; excision of boring and drawn-out passages; removal of the original's references to God; and making the whole refer to King Charles rather than to King James. The younger Buck shows himself here as in the *History* a good reviser and organizer of another's material. But whenever he drastically revises existing verse or substitutes verses of his own, he shows himself a poor poet. He has no sense of metre, his language is trite, inappropriate and insipid. We shall find similar stylistic flaws in his final revision of the *History*.

One would imagine the younger Buck was running some risk in publishing under his own name and with limited revision a work dedicated to the former king which was already published and in the libraries of great men, and which he had presented in a manuscript of his own with a dedication to another prospective patron. And in connection with this or some similar practice with another work, he does – as we shall see – seem to have been censured for reissuing with different dedications works already in circulation.

Whether the translation of Lipsius,[14] dedicated to Sir John Jacob, one of the farmers of the king's customs, was actually the younger Buck's own work or again a copy or version of one of his great-uncle's efforts is not known. That no translation, published or unpublished, is extant under Sir George Buc's name or in his hand does not preclude the possibility of its existence at one time. Lipsius was an antiquary who spoke highly of Camden, and Buc mentions him (but only as an authority on fencing) in *The Third Universitie* (sig. Oooo 2). A translation of Lipsius would have been a natural work for Sir George to have undertaken. However, the fluidity of the language, not laboured as Sir George Buc's can be, suggests that this very literal translation may really be the work of the man who put his name to it. We know he was a competent Latinist from his corrections of errors (though unsystematically made) in his scribal copies of the *History*. Also pointing to the work being his is that the dedication does not involve subterfuges, as do those of the *History* copies, but rather concentrates on the worthiness of the dedicatee, whom young Buck has clearly not approached before:

> S*ir*: if you aske why this to you, I must appeale to the priviledg of you [*sic*] noble and generall fame, w*hi*ch hath improud itself beyond the touch of envy, and plac'd you so eminently in the esteeme of all good men, that (without thought of flattery I may avouch it) I haue been vnfainedly ambitious (in the thronge of those that hono*u*r you) to offer a zealous vote, to yo*u*r enobled Merritt . . .

His self-deprecation is expressed in a much more confident tone than that which he employs later: 'if my zeale hath been too bold and forward, it will not bee much vnworthy, your fauour and pardon, since (in this) I haue onely sought

13 [Ritson] in *Biog. Poetica*, p. 147.

14 Justus Lipsius / his two bookes / de Constantia / englished / by George Bucke Esqr 1638, Trinity College, Cambridge, MS. O.3.17.

to expresse myself your vnfained and humble honoure^r^, George Bucke'. Young Buck seems to have employed for most of this presentation the same scribe who was responsible for *Daphnis* and the three main *History* copies, with the title page and dedication and corrections and a few pages of the text in his own hand.

After Lipsius, young George began his manipulations of the *History*. From the original manuscript, now bearing his own revisions, he seems to have made or had made for him a master copy which he used in having all his subsequent copies prepared. The first of these, Egerton 2216, is addressed to Sir John Jacob in a dedicatory preface which uses some phrases from Sir George Buc's dedication of his original manuscript to the Earl of Arundel. As Eccles notes,[15] the presentation would have had to have occurred between 1638 and 1642, since it refers to the translation of Lipsius, dated 1638, and Jacob was declared delinquent in his office in 1642. The date can be fixed even closer by reference to Jacob's publication in his own defence: 'To be thought rich', he says in 1654, 'was I hope my greatest Crime, and now to be thought poore, is my greatest Labour', and he claims to have been 'in the midst of those waves these thirteen years', i.e., since 1641. 1640 would have been the last year in which Jacob was secure in his position and 'thought rich', for in that year the farmers had entered into contract with the king and advanced or engaged large sums for his wars. But Parliament had cancelled the contract, appropriated these sums to its own uses, then accused the farmers of delinquency and forced them to submit to composition. From then on came a series of petitions and hardships.[16]

It seems that Jacob received the translation favourably but issued a caveat regarding Buck's having put out a duplicate of some work already in circulation. *Daphnis* is likely to have been the work in question, easily detected since already in print. Probably Buck pressed his version of the *History* on Jacob very soon after that detection to show his good intentions, professing that there is no extant copy but his own rough papers: 'I haue nowe aduentured it, to your noble patronage, and giue mee leaue noblest S*ir* to cleere my self thus farr vnto you (in respect of your former doubt) that (as I respect your worth and fauour) but my rough papers there is no Copy saue this, which I present . . .' (ff. 2^v^-3). The words 'rough papers' probably refer to his great-uncle's manuscript, 'his' probably through theft, and to his own master copy from which his subsequent copies seem to have been made. The dedication includes an ambiguous apology similar to those prefacing the younger Buck's versions of *Daphnis*: he deprecates his own ability and leads the reader to believe, while not actually saying so, that he is the author. His words, 'the history laye vnder a rough draught; w*hi*ch I haue hasted to perfect (f. 2^v^) recall the 'young Limbner' remark in *The Great Plantagenet*.

When Jacob's position became insecure, or possibly even before, Buck looked elsewhere for patronage. He next tried Lord Aylesborough, Keeper of the Privy Seal, to whom he dedicated the copy known as Bodleian MS. Malone 1. Since Aylesbourgh died early in 1640, the year Jacob's position became precarious, it is

15 Eccles, 'Sir George Buc', p. 501.

16 John Jacob, *Publicanus Vindicatus* (London, 1654), pp. 1f. There exists also a petition signed by John Jacob and others, 'A Remonstrance of the Case of the late Farmers of the Customes, and Their Humble Petition to the Parliament', ([London,] 1653).

probably very early in this year that the dedication was made. There was yet a third manuscript copy made, the one now in the Fisher Rare Books Room of the University of Toronto. No dedication exists to show for whom it was intended. Perhaps it was a copy Buck kept on hand in case of future need; indeed Keen's catalogue[17] suggests that the six blank pages at the beginning were intended for a dedication. Manuscript peculiarities indicate that Fisher was made almost concurrently with Malone.

Little else is known of the younger Buck apart from his death in 1645, as Mark Eccles discovered[18] long after he wrote his superbly researched biography of Sir George. In 1647 some laudatory verses of the younger Buck's, along with others by Waller, Lovelace, Webster and Habington, were contributed to a volume of Beaumont and Fletcher's works[19] published by the actor John Lowin, Richard Robinson, and others, and dedicated to the Earl of Pembroke, to whom Buck's printed version of the *History* had been dedicated. That Pembroke had become Master of the Revels in 1641 may indicate that Buck the Younger was seeking an office in the Revels. His final poem is in couplets, the lines not adeptly fitted to the metre, and the wording is sometimes awkward and unsuitable. It ends tritely and is signed 'George Buck'.

> Let *Shakesepeare*, *Chapman*, and applauded *Ben*,
> Weare the Eternall merit of their Pen,
> Here I am love-sicke: and were I to chuse,
> A mistress corrivall 'tis *Fletcher*'s Muse.

The place of George the Younger (the Editor) seems to have been that of a very minor literary figure, occasionally admitted to the society of great names, partly on the strength of his great-uncle's work, pursuing similar acquaintances to Sir George's – antiquaries, heralds, authors – aspiring to court or government preferment, but evidently unsuccessful in obtaining it. Before his death in 1645 came to light it could have been assumed that he had taken advantage of the death in 1646 of the original dedicatee, the Earl of Arundel, to publish his final severely butchered version of his great-uncle's work. But clearly this is not possible, and we have no way of knowing how far along in the final revision process he had progressed before his death. Did someone else take advantage of Arundel's death to publish it, and if so, for how much of the final revision was that person responsible? The published version's Latin is generally more accurate than that of the scribal copies, this being the only area in which this version is at all superior to the manuscript copies. Was it the Editor who saw to this or someone else? We shall never know.

Egerton, Malone, and Fisher

The first three and only nearly complete manuscript copies[20] of the *History* so far

17 See above, p. lxiii.
18 Eccles, 'Brief Lives', p. 19.
19 Francis Beaumont and John Fletcher, *Comedies and Tragedies* (London, 1647), sig. C3.
20 Myers, Introduction to Buck, *History of the Life and Reigne*, pp. vii-ix, claims that Malone preceded Egerton, but provides no analysis to back this claim or reason other than that the dedicatee of Malone died in 1640. From the arguments given above, based on close study of all three manuscript copies, it should be clear that this claim cannot be correct.

as is known, Egerton, Malone, and Fisher, are in the same hand, that of a scribe who clearly had no knowledge of foreign languages or of history, for his errors in foreign quotations and names of persons and places of historical import are numerous. He is obviously following the same manuscript for all three copies, since most of the habitual errors in foreign languages and proper names are the same in all, and words and names with variant spellings are usually spelt in the same way at the same point in the text of each copy. For example, the spellings 'Beajer', 'Beaugeu', 'Beauyer', 'Beaujew' for a name consistently spelt 'Beaujeu' in Tiberius appear in their variant forms at the same points in Egerton, Malone, and Fisher.

The Editor has in his own hand gone through the copies rapidly and made a few minor changes in style and matter, sometimes crossing out personal references which might suggest he was not the author, sometimes deleting uncomplimentary references to Morton and other followers of Henry VII. His proofreading seems to have been very cursory, for he corrects only a very few errors in names and foreign words. When making these minor alterations in Egerton, he seems to have made many of them simultaneously in the master copy so that Malone and Fisher appear corrected at these points. He has done the same when revising Malone, since the alterations he makes in Malone often appear in Fisher, Additional, and the printed edition. It is not clear that he did so in the case of Fisher revisions, since Additional and the printed edition seem closer to Malone than to Fisher.

On first glance one would assume that Fisher is a copy of Malone. However, closer examination proves this impossible. The two copies are very close in their use of accidentals. In spelling peculiarities, placement of commas, and tendency to capitalize they are close to each other, much closer than either is to Egerton. This closeness is shown in the striking regularity with which habitual differences from Egerton in the spelling of common words occur in Malone and Fisher identically:

Egerton	*Malone and Fisher*
authority	autority
howse	house
-c*i*on	-t*i*on
desimulac*i*on	dissimulat*i*on
Earle	Erle
accompte	account

However, errors and unintentional omissions occurring in one do not appear in the other. Intentional alterations made in Malone, including those made by the Editor above the line, sometimes appear in Fisher but just as often do not. Evidence indicates that Fisher is the latest copy: Malone is closer to Egerton in accidentals than is Fisher. Whereas Fisher incorporates changes made in Malone, Malone incorporates none of Fisher's deletions or alterations in wording. Fisher proceeds further than Malone in material changes, in deletion of personal references and derogatory remarks about Richmond's party, especially Morton. The explanation of their closeness seems to lie in (1) their being done around the same time, (2) alterations made in Malone often being put into the master copy, (3) simultaneous correction of the two by the Editor.

We may infer something about the nature of the master copy by comparing the corrections in Malone and Fisher. It seems that the crossings out were not always clear, since often in Fisher the copyist does not realize until after he has written in a word or phrase that it was intended to have been deleted or emended, and then he crosses it out or changes it. For example, at one point Egerton says 'Treachery'. In Malone the word is 'practices'. Fisher gives '[treachery] practises'. This change in Fisher is made instantly, appearing on rather than above the line, and is typical of many similar corrections. This suggests that the emendation was made in the master copy with the new word written above the line and the discarded word only lightly crossed out, or perhaps on occasion not crossed out at all. Some of the Editor's crossings out in his three copies are in the form of pale dashes rather than solid lines through the word, and we can see how unclear these might have appeared to the copyist when he encountered them in the master copy. When he made corrections in the copies themselves, the Editor evidently added many but not all of these to the master copy. And in addition he probably made minor emendations in the master copy between the creation of his various copies. This would account for the fact that Malone and Fisher often produce the same wording in places where Egerton's is different, a factor occurring far too frequently always to be the result of errors in Egerton. That all three copies used the same master can be inferred from the fact that although they are not dependent on each other they very often make the same misreadings in the same places. At one point in Tiberius the word 'contudit' appears. This is given by Egerton and Malone as 'conludit', presumably because the 't' is uncrossed or crossed faintly in the master. In several places some error is made at an identical point in the text in all three copies, but not precisely the same error. This probably occurs in places where the master was difficult to read.

Egerton, Malone and Fisher are so close that they can be discussed together. What we have in them is a fairly reasonable representation at some length of the original manuscript. The three copies differ from each other in that they make different errors at certain points, leaving out short sections by accident or misreading. They differ also in intentional alterations made by the Editor in the copies themselves or in the master between copies. Such changes are not numerous or considerable, but they are progressive except where an alteration has not found its way into the master copy. The copies are approximately two-thirds the length of the original (Tiberius) and show progressive stylistic improvement and material alterations along precisely the same lines as those, already described, made by the Editor in the original manuscript. Just as we saw the Editor making changes in the holograph by removing personal references which might identify the original author or period of composition, as well as religious remarks and derogatory refences to Henry Tudor and his followers, so in the copies we see him making further alterations to these points and making more of them as he progresses from copy to copy.

The stylistic revision shows continuing reduction of the innumerable 'and's, both through deletion and substitution of other linking words. Rearranging word order ensures that modifications are clear and points are not lost in verbal meandering. Verbs are often made more vivid by changing from past to present or passive to active. Pronouns are substituted for repetitive noun references, and unnecessary repetitions of words or ideas are revised. Subsidiary or digressive factual information is often relegated to a marginal note. Repetitions and digressions are discarded and diffuse passages more compactly expressed, sometimes in little more than a brief summary. But though much is given in summary, little of significance is entirely left out, and no new material is added, except possibly at the very end, in the two concluding poems, but it seems likely they were already in that part of the original manuscript which was destroyed by fire.

The Editor gradually becomes bolder in the introduction of his own style, which is less pedestrian and more flowery than Sir George's. Thus Egerton's '. . . were become penitents, and made Confession thereof' becomes in Malone and Fisher, '. . . became so sensible thereof that at length, there penitence broke forthe ['brake out' in Fisher] into confession'. This tendency increases as the copies progress. Young Buck occasionally tries his hand in these manuscripts as in *Daphnis* at revising his great-uncle's verses. He makes a minor improvement in the Ariosto translation (see text, p. 85): for the awkward first line, 'No man ever whilst he was happy knew', a more fluent 'No man whilst he was happy ever knew' is substituted. The copies make a few genuine corrections in their reorganization of material, for example deleting the references to *Utopia* and the eulogy of Queen Elizabeth from the list of contents at the beginning of Book IV. In Egerton and Malone these are written but crossed out and they do not appear at all in Fisher. The Editor had noticed that material on these subjects does not in fact appear in Book IV.

Since religion was not a safe subject, religious references, especially those that might be misconstrued as betraying Catholic ideology, are deleted. A mention of the Pope's 'spiritual power' is crossed out in Egerton, but since evidently the Editor forgot to cross this out in the master copy as well, it is retained by all the others, including the printed version (p. 47). The statement that the Plantagenets all passed one purgatory appears in Egerton and Malone but is crossed out in Fisher.

In these manuscripts, as in his revisions of the original, the Editor's most numerous and consistent revisions occur in passages describing Henry Tudor and his followers. These are reworded so as to soften or eliminate suggestions of sedition and treachery. The word 'treasons' becomes 'inconstancy' or 'practices' and 'rebellion' becomes 'action'. Where Sir George had at one point revised to make an accusation stronger, substituting the word 'evil' for 'mighty', the Editor gradually dilutes this, amending it in the original to 'cruell', then in Egerton, Malone, and Fisher to 'very insolent and strong'. Circumlocution is stretched almost to the breaking point when a statement that Richmond's followers were all rebels in Egerton is in Malone and Fisher turned into a vague comment on their loyalty: 'they could not be called soe' [i.e., loyal], beinge worse'. Henry Tudor's practices, 'seditious & Ambitious' in Egerton and Malone, are only 'Ambitious' in Fisher. King James IV's disaffection to him disappears. At the end of Book III, revision of the criticism of the Tudor monarchy for destroying the rightful heirs who stood in their way is extensive in Fisher, and the statement that the Lancastrians were 'soe vehement, that they regarded noe title, how iuster, or better soever' is crossed out.

Morton himself, once 'perfidious and treacherous' to Richard (Egerton) becomes 'extreamely his Enemy in harte' (Fisher); from 'Malitious Morton' he becomes 'B*isho*pp Morton'; from 'this politique prelate' (Egerton and Malone), simply 'hee' (Fisher). Derogatory descriptions of him, such as 'How Covetous hee was, those examples may giue a taste' (Egerton) are deleted (this one disappears in Malone but reappears in Fisher).

Considerably less deletion of personal references is made in Egerton than in the later copies. That Egerton leaves so many of these intact is very useful for filling in gaps burnt out of the original manuscript. As he progresses in his deception, the Editor becomes more careful. For example, he crosses out in Egerton the last item of Book IV's Contents page, 'An elegy' (which in Tiberius reads 'An eulogy') of Elizabeth, the late Queen of England'. It does not appear at all in Malone or Fisher. But one interesting personal reflection, the mention of Mary, Queen of Scots' death, the end of which is burnt away in Tib., f. 227, does not appear even in Egerton.

In Egerton there is a fascinating alteration, made by scraping rather than the usual crossing out. This concerns Buc's consultation with Dethick. All copies omit the personal detail surrounding this consultation. However, in Egerton the Editor has allowed himself to write the name 'William Dethick', only to scrape out 'Dethick' and write 'Segar', the name of Dethick's successor in office. Yarnold's pencilled note opposite this substitution in Egerton (f. 8^{v}) observes the original manuscript's reading of 'Dethick' and says 'Segar is here evidently an erasure and \its Insertion/ apparently some time subsequent. I think that part of the h. and the final letter k is visible'. Part of the intial 'D' is visible as well. In later copies the Editor is more careful and says merely 'in the rich studdy of a noble, and learned freind, I mett with a Catalogue of such Setbriquetts' (Malone and Fisher). In Additional he reduces it further: 'from a Catalogue of many I have translated these . . .'.

Other examples of *viva voce* information have been tampered with. The marginal note on Don Duarte de Lancastro which describes a conference at which Buc was present reads in the ensuing text, 'Don Duarte de Lancastro, a noble gentleman of Portugal, came to my Lord Admiral ambassador to the King of Spain, and to[ld] him that he was descen[ded] from the Duke of La[ncaster in] Valodolid. G.[B. *teste*]' (see text, pp. 75f). Changes have been gradually introduced into this note by the Editor. He has not touched it in the original manuscript and copies it *verbatim* in Egerton. But in Malone he alters 'came . . . and told him' to 'averred', and 'my Lord Admiral' to 'my Lord Howard'. Fisher repeats the change to 'averred' and deletes 'G. B. teste'.

A reference to material Buc has seen in Cotton's collection, shut down in 1629, is revised in Malone and Fisher but not in Egerton, Additional, or the printed version. Malone has 'which Charter [is] \was/ in the hands of S*i*r Robert Cotton, [wherof I have reade it and] \from w*hi*ch I haue/ transcribed, these summarye notes'. Fisher reads 'w*hi*ch Charter [is] \was/ in the hands of S*i*r Robert Cotton, and] \from thence/ transcribed, these summarye notes, fro*m*'. As can easily be seen the revision was made carelessly, and it was obviously not copied carefully into the master script.

Viva voce information from Stow regarding Richard III's personal appearance is deprived of its firsthand nature. Egerton gives as they stand the words 'as he himself told me'. But in Malone the scribe wrote these words then crossed them out, changing them to 'protested averring', and a marginal note was added identifying the recipient of the information as Cotton: 'ad D: Rob: Cotton'. In Fisher again 'tould mee' is written in but crossed out and altered to 'averred', and the marginal attribution to Cotton is retained. Thus where we originally had a personal confrontation between Stow and Buc, we now have a vague report that Stow averred to Cotton that Richard was not deformed, with no indication of how this hearsay might have reached young Buck. Later on the same page another reference to what Stow 'told me' is retained in Egerton, but Malone has corrected this to '[tould mee] \likewise reported/' and Fisher to '[told me] \added/'. A later discussion with Stow, when Buc pressed him to know his opinion of the evidence for the murder of Edward IV's sons, is altered in Egerton to the nonsensical wording, 'Mr Jo*h*n Stowe affirmed confidently vpon occation, pressing to knowe', making it unclear who was pressing to know. Malone and Fisher remedy the structural awkwardness but do not improve credibility by saying Stow 'hath affirmed confidently to some'.

As for his own family, Buck the Younger is content to be thought the grandson of Robert Buck, the orphan of Bosworth. First Egerton presumably copies the original manuscript: 'This Rob*ert* Buck the grandfather of this Sir Geo. Buck'. Then Malone and Fisher give us 'This Rob*ert* Buck the grandfather of this Author'. References to Buc's other works disappear. That no references to *The Baron* of the five which appear in Egerton appears in Malone and Fisher may indicate that this work was widely known, or perhaps that Buck the Younger had initially planned to issue that as his own work too but changed his mind. The excision of all references to it made in the master after Egerton was completed must have been very plain indeed. A single reference to the *Commentary* remains in all three copies, perhaps as an oversight, perhaps indicating that it was not widely known. The translation of Ariosto, its first line improved, appears in Malone and Fisher with the comment, '\I/ haue adventured thus to translate, without any forfeite to S*ir* Jon Harington as I hope', though in Egerton the remark that the author made his translation before Harington's stands. Since Harington's translation of *Orlando Furioso* was published in 1591, this stands out as unlikely.

Mentions of Sir George Buc himself are tampered with. The instance of deleting 'G.B. teste' indicating the author's presence at a conversation, has already been described. Two marginal notes regarding Buc's family at the end of Book II are emended: 'this Sir George Buc' untouched in Egerton but in Malone and Fisher is changed to 'this Author'. The printed version omits the note altogether. In the note which refers to 'Rob*ert* Buck my ffather', 'my father' appears in Malone but is crossed out there and reappears in Fisher. It does not appear in Additional or the printed version.

Contemporary references or remarks bearing on contemporary situations suffer changes, both for political reasons and for purposes of updating. In Malone and Fisher though not in Egerton the Editor is careful to avoid offence by deleting the note that James I was reputedly descended from a bastard son of Fleance. In speaking of Charles Howard of Effingham, who died in 1624, he changes Egerton's unaltered 'there is one liveing' to 'there was one lately liveinge' in Malone and Fisher. The master copy seems before Egerton was made to have altered a reference to Dr Godwin, 'now Bishoppe of Hereford' by removing 'now Bishoppe', so that Egerton and Malone read 'Dr. Goodwin, of Hereford'. Fisher ignores the crossing out in the master copy and replaces the phrase. A marginal note at this point gives the date 1620. This is crossed out in Malone, and it seems simultaneously to have been crossed out in the master as well, since Fisher does not include it. Thomas Gainsford is described in Book V of Egerton as still alive. He had died in 1624 and Malone and Fisher delete 'yet liueing'.

Though James I was king when the original was composed, he died in 1625. Consequently, though Egerton as usual makes few changes, Malone and Fisher in Book V alter the several present tense references to this king to the past. 'But had S*i*r Tho. Moore, liued in these dayes, hee had knowne a kinge, whose sacred temper, would not haue admitted such an Act' becomes '. . . liued in these latter dayes'. And the ensuing 'hee' is clarified in Malone and Fisher to refer to 'our late kinge of euer famous memory'. But these changes do not indicate that King James died between Egerton and Malone's composition, for even in his alterations of the original manuscript the Editor has changed a reference to King James by name to 'our king', indicating that James was no longer king when the editorial alterations were made in the original.

Additional and the Printed Version

When my first two editions of this book were published it was not yet known that George Buck the Younger had died before publication of 'his' book. Hence it was not noted there that we cannot be certain that all the revisions derived from him. The Latin is in general more accurate in the printed version than in Egerton, Malone and Fisher. As a competent Latinist the Editor would have been capable of revising it. The other changes were in the directions he showed that he was taking in the manuscript copies but are carried farther in the printed edition. My guess is that he had the publication well in hand at the time he died.

Additional and the Printed Edition

The alterations made in the master copy between Malone and Fisher's composition and the printed stage were drastic. Additional,[21] a fair copy of Books I and II, represents a state of revision very close to the printed edition but is neither a direct source for it nor derived from it. It is in a different hand from the earlier copies and the Editor's hand appears nowhere. The purpose for which it was made is not known. The revisions which led to Additional and the printed version do not take account of Fisher: many corrections appearing in Fisher but in neither of the

21 Myers on p. ix of his Introduction to the facsimile of the printed *Life and Reigne* gives the information that 'at least three more of his [i.e., Buck the younger's] copies of the history survive'. Clearly these are in addition to Egerton and Malone, which he discusses in his Introduction, though erroneously assessing which came first. One of these three other copies he identifies as Additional, though this is not a complete copy. Another must be Fisher, which was known to be in Greg's hands in 1925. But Myers gives no clue to the third (or others comprised in 'at least'), of which, in all my research, I have never heard a breath apart from this. All I can say, using a favourite phrase of Myers's, is that no one has ever seen it (or them).

previous copies are not taken up by Additional and the printed edition. That in some places the wording of Additional is closer to that of Fisher than to the two earlier manuscript copies may represent minor revision made in the master copy between Malone and Fisher. Of the three early copies, Malone is the one to which Additional and the printed edition are closest. It seems that they were based on a master copy into which some of the changes the Editor made in Malone but in no later manuscript had been incorporated. There is no reason not to assume that this master copy was the same which served as the basis for the three earlier copies. Presumably the changes made in Fisher were not entered in the master copy.

The alterations in Additional and the printed edition consist most obviously in reduction of material and in drastic stylistic revision both for the sake of extreme compression and to give the Editor's own style freer rein. Since Additional is an offshoot with no important connection to the other copies and seems merely to represent a state very close to the printed edition, and also since it includes only the first two books, there is no purpose in discussing it separately in any detail. Differences between Additional and the printed edition are infrequent up to p. 26 of the latter but increase thereafter. They are changes in wording rather than in material. This pattern can be observed in all the copies: the wording in the early pages is very close to the preceding copy, growing more divergent as the copy progresses. Where differences exist, Additional is closer in wording than the printed edition to Egerton, Malone, and Fisher, and the style of the printed edition is much more flamboyant and careless of sense. Both paraphrase the material in the three earlier copies, but more words and phrases of the earlier copies are retained in Additional than in the printed version. The style of the printed edition is smoother at certain points, carrying further the tendency to eliminate conjunctions and to subordinate. And there is further elimination of apparently inessential detail, of introductions to passages and statements of intention. This suggests that the printed version was created after Additional from the same master copy, which had been further emended. Two examples of stylistic divergence appear on p. 28 of the printed edition in the description of Richard's progress, which reads in Egerton, 'All things thus established, in good order' and in Additional, 'All things thus in good order' becomes in the printed edition, 'All things thus in a happy presage and good order'. And Egerton's 'where hee was very honourably, and delightfully entertained of the Muses', is elaborated in the printed edition: 'where the Muses Crown'd their browes with fragrant Wreathes for his entertainment'. If we were to fall into the error of assuming that the printed edition represented the elder Buc's work, we should think that we had here an interestingly specific masque-like reference from the Master of the Revels.

Whereas Egerton, Malone, and Fisher are about two-thirds the length of the original, the printed edition is less than half its length. The outlines of the work remain, and what we have in the printed version is in some sense a summary of the original. Paragraphs and even pages are summed up in sentences or phrases. Elaboration, explanation and digression are eliminated. Strict cutting removes all apparently extraneous phrases and sentences. Sentence structure is tightened: connectives are eliminated, pronouns substituted for repeated nouns, and pairs of adjectives and verbs reduced to single words. Narrative elaborations are omitted.

Whereas Sir George, using More as his source, created visual setting and action for the scene in which Richard is petitioned to be king, Buck the Younger removes the dramatic elements and gives only the speeches, in slightly reduced form, one after the other with no scene visualized. The original's descriptions of emotion, mood, tone, quality, character and situation are rejected, as are statements of opinion. So that where Buc the Elder represents a speech and asks us to understand that the speaker is undergoing emotional or intellectual turmoil or has scruples about what he says, Buck the Younger does nothing more than present the speech. Where the elder Buc in citing his sources states their qualifications and describes their authors as wise, learned, or specially experienced, or where in mentioning an historical personage he describes him, for example, as honourable and courageous, Buck the Younger merely mentions the name and leaves out any description.

The Editor's creative urge was evidently released in the extended revision process, for he shows at this stage a tendency to add his own stylistic elaborations. Sometimes these are of structural value. He writes short transitional and introductory passages when new material is introduced. And he begins and ends books with a much greater flourish than does the original author. He closes Book I, for example, with the words, 'And thus farre King *Richard*, in the Voyage of his Affaires had a promising Gale; wee will therefore here cast Anchor a while, and claspe up this first Booke, with the Relation of his better Fortunes' (p. 37). He opens Book II with a more intrusive metaphor: 'We left King *Richard* the Third in the growth of a flourishing and promising Estate . . . But Fortune that lends her smiles as Exactors do mony, to undoe the Debtor, soone cald for the Principall and Interest from this Prince . . .' (p. 41). He has a tendency to add moralistic comment, remarking, for example, that Fulke of Anjou's courage and strength are 'two of the best Principles when they have good seconds, and make too a glorious man, where they serve his vertues, not affections, as in this Prince they did' (p. 5). Not a word of this comment is in the original or early copies. The Editor's flourishes are usually incongruous and very often incomprehensible. He describes Richard's decision to offer single combat thus: 'this might taste of a desperate will, if he had not afterwards given an apodixis in the battaile, upon what plat-forme he had projected and raised that hope, which as it had much of danger in it, so of an inconcusse and great resolution, and might have brought the odds of that day to an even bet . . .' (p. 60).

But despite tendencies to clog the sense by incongruous and incomprehensible rhetorical flourish, or puzzle the reader by too drastic summarizing, he is sometimes able, when employing his flair for clarifying and organizing in conjunction with his own euphuistic tendencies, to produce a clearer, stronger, and better turned passage than the author has given us. Where we get from Buc a plodding, diffuse and unvaried construction we sometimes get a varied and interesting construction from the Editor's summary.

Not all his additions are purely stylistic. Whereas in the manuscript copies it is striking that the Editor does not make additions, he gives himself more licence in the printed edition. He adds marginal notes, two purely explanatory, another giving illustrative information, and in one Plutarch and one Suetonius reference he specifies the particular Life from which the example is drawn. He adds one classical quotation and makes two additions to the material of the work, one a letter relating to Don

Sebastian's identity (pp. 98-99) and the other a lame discourse, based on uninformed guesswork, on the etymology of the word 'Parliament' (pp. 124f), which he substitutes for the original's discussion of God punishing Edward IV for his sins.

But his excisions are far more numerous than his additions. They exhibit the same intentions as do the revisions in the earlier copies: to reduce length; to remove derogatory comments about the Tudor faction; to avoid religious questions; to eliminate sexual suggestion; and to destroy personal references. In matters of religion the Editor seems to want to stay clear of all controversy, since he cuts out a reference to the massacre of Protestants as well as removing references to the Pope.

Discussions of Morton are very drastically cut, since the original had little good to speak of Morton. The lists of men Richard III ought to have destroyed are removed. Henry VII is treated more tenderly at this stage than at any other. His responsibility for destroying the Yorkist heirs and emphasis on the Yorkists' right are minimized. The discussion of Perkin Warbeck's tortures is reduced. Henry becomes confident, pure and manly and the discomfort Perkin causes him is shortened. His ability in amorous speech disappears. His government is given the Editor's approval in that the discussion of bad Parliaments is deleted, as well as the suggestion that the Parliament in which Henry had Richard attainted was self-abrogating; and then most strikingly in the alteration (p. 149) of Richard's reign from two years, fifty-two days to two years, fifty-one days, and the date of the Tudor reign's inception from 22 August to 21 August, the day before Richard's death – an adherence to Henry VII's device for backdating his reign to make Richard appear to have been the traitor against the true king at Bosworth. What we have in the printed version is a work purporting to defend Richard III which essentially undermines him by his adversary's means. It is no wonder this book has had so poor a reputation.

References leading to awareness of the original author's period, identity, associates and interests are further deleted in this version, though the Editor still misses a few. A mere mention of Queen Elizabeth's name (p. 77) is substituted for Buc's first long eulogy, and another eulogy of this queen is cut entirely. The marginal reference about all the Bucks, including the author, having been soldiers is gone: presumably soldiering was not one of the younger Buck's activities.

Unfortunately for Sir George Buc's reputation, three centuries ensued during which it was always in the form of the printed *Life and Reigne* that the work was known and heavily criticized for its shortcomings. Even the present attempt at establishing an authentic text, first published in 1979, has been widely overlooked in favour of facsimiles of the younger Buck's regrettable mangling of the elder Buc's work, with readers too often oblivious of any distinction. For this reason it is extremely important to take full account of those alterations within the younger Buck's publication which cast a negative light on the original author's research methods, his care and thoroughness in documentation, his accuracy, and his presentation of his subject. As a result, changes introduced by the Editor which make the work exhibit an apparent lack of scholarship have been largely responsible for Buc's failure for hundreds of years to be taken seriously.

The Editor's changes in documentation, both intentional and careless, give an incorrect impression of Buc's research methods, which are made to look extremely shoddy and far less thorough than they actually were. His long description of how he went about his research into the origins of the name 'Plantagenet', perusing many books and monuments, consulting heralds, ultimately receiving from Dethick the information he cites (text, pp. 11f) is reduced to 'In my Inquiry . . . I met with an ancient manuscript' (p. 5). This makes the research look haphazard and deprives it of any sense of method or authority. Another example of Buc's careful method is lost in the mention of Richard III's charter incorporating the College of Arms (see text, p. 204), when the Editor excludes the words 'I have seen it' and also the marginal reference to Ralph Brooke, York Herald, through whose agency Buc saw the original charter. What Buc says is that the charter was once kept in the College of Arms, but its now being elsewhere is of no importance since he has seen the original in its new place – he cites Brooke in corroboration of this – and says there is in any case a duplicate in the College. The printed edition, on the other hand, simply says the lack of it is not important because there is a copy in the College. Buc, aware that seeing a mere copy is of less value than seeing the original, painstakingly demonstrated his care to see the earliest extant version. The Editor seems easily content with a copy (which, presumably, he himself had not seen) and to consider viewing the original as unimportant.

Again, a statement of Buc's that he will transcribe a charter 'as I have seen and read it in the archives and records kept in the Tower of London' (text, p. 79) becomes 'which Charter . . . I shall exhibite, as it is taken out of the Archives and Tower Records' (p. 48). There is no indication here that the author ever saw this document or that it was of any importance to him whether he had seen it or not.

The references to Cotton's library, by then closed for some fifteen years, necessarily suffer. Whereas Buc had said specifically 'this charter *is now* [italics mine] in the hands of Sir Robert Cotton, where I have seen and read it and transcribed these summary notes from thence' (text, p. 81), the printed edition can give us only the impression of a vague situation quite some time in the past (Cotton had died in 1631): 'This Charter I saw in the hands of Sir *Rob. Cotton*, & from it took these Summary notes' (p. 50). Buc knows the material from recent examination and knows its collector well enough to inform the reader of its present whereabouts so anyone else interested can go and check it. The printed edition, on the other hand, does not tell us where we can see the document and makes it appear that the notes were not taken recently but some time long past. This is only one example of what frequently happens in the case of Cotton material and has made it easy for people like Myers to claim that 'No one else has ever seen' this or that document to which Buc refers. Being all but unfamiliar with Tiberius, he blurs the distinctions between the works of the two Buc/ks.

The Editor's errors and omissions in marginal documentation are numerous, and the effect of this compounds the problem that (a) Buc's documentation is in the margins, and (b) it is the margins that suffer most severe damage from burning, sometimes being burnt entirely away. This means that there is essentially no means of restoring the documentation to anything like what it was, for which Buc's scholarly reputation has suffered severely and will permanently suffer. The following are examples of errors in marginal documentation of the printed version:

p. 5 marginal reference to Du Haillan and Paradin documenting a quotation from Fulke of Anjou is left out
marginal documentation of Zosimus for reference to Constantine and Aegyptus is omitted
marginal reference 'Georgics II' is left out, only a general attribution, 'Virgil', remaining in the text
7 the laudatory citation of Glover is replaced by references in the text to 'Master *Brookes* genealogies of England', but the marginal note, 'In his Catalogue of Honour' (which is the title of Glover's book) confusingly remains
17 'Nyerus' is given for 'Meyerus'
24 only 'Camden' appears in the marginal note for 'Camden in Dobuni' (which the copies had corrupted to 'Dolucu'). Strype criticizes Buc here for not stating where in Camden the reference occurs (*Complete History*, I, 525), a criticism Myers simply borrows, without troubling to look it up for himself (see above, p. lxvii)
28 the references to the Cotton MS. and Fabyan are so misplaced as to seem to refer to the appointment of John of Gloucester as Captain of Calais, not, as they actually do, to Richard's pacifying the country
29 only 'Joan Maierus' is given in a marginal note, without the original's specific reference to *Annales Flandr*. Lib 17
43 textual documentation is omitted citing More, Polydore Vergil, the histories of Brittany, the French writers, and the common chroniclers as the sources on which the account of Henry's first invasion is based
45 reference to Salisbury, Epistle 89 is given as '85'
58 citation of Polydore Vergil for information on Henry Tudor's problems about marriage is omitted
80 'Sir *Thomas Moor apud Harlington'* is the reading given for what must originally have been '. . . Hardyng et Grafton'
81 'Majerus' is twice given for 'Meyerus'
a marginal reference to Holinshed documenting the chronicles' account of Edward, Prince of Wales's death is left out
93 the reader is not referred to 'Grafton, Hall, etc.' for information about Perkin Warbeck's confession
94 in a reference to St Augustine's *Civitas Dei,* 'Lib. 19', is omitted
117 the lost work *El Reuseurq* is made to appear part of the Duke of Milan's title: 'Duke *of Millain el Reuseur*.'
121 a marginal reference to Ovid for a quotation from that author is left out
128 '4. Ebr. Harmon. Evang,' is given as '4. *Evang. Harmon. Evang*.'
130 a marginal reference to Prateius is left out
141 a marginal reference to Çurita and Garibay for information regarding Henry VII's 'capture' of Philip of Burgundy is left out
146 'Edwardus Ethelredus' is confusingly given for 'Edmerus Alvredus'

One begins to see why Myers's opinion of the 'author' of the printed *Life and Reigne* was low, but regrets his propensity for applying that opinion to the author of the original *History*.

Buc's *viva voce* references are so tampered with as to be reduced to the level of apparent hearsay. All awareness is lost that he was working closely with the most eminent scholars of his day and personally gleaning information from people whose professional positions or historical connections made them more authoritative than any published matter on certain subjects. In the original, Buc, speaking of bastards, says, 'I have been informed by a very learned and signal judge of the laws of this land'. In the margin he identifies this judge as Coke, whom he knew (text, p. 78). The printed edition retains the attribution to Coke but depersonalizes it: 'as a Learned and eminent Judge reports' (p. 48), so that one assumes the reference is to a printed work. Buc was able to present his story of Surrey's adventures after Bosworth on the testimony of his own grandfather, Robert Buck, who was with the earl from his own childhood until Surrey's old age 'and was well acquainted with all his actions and his fortunes' (text, p. 108). The printed edition says merely that the information comes 'by warrant of one that well knew him' (p. 64). The information on the value of the Earl of Oxford's lands is given (inaccurately, probably through the Editor's or the scribe's misreading of the original) on p. 105, but without any documentation. This information had been conveyed to Buc in personal conversation with the current Earl of Oxford when the earl paid him a visit (text, p. 170).

Instead of the detailed face to face discussion with Stow about Richard's lack of apparent deformity, the printed edition says only that Stow 'acknowledged *viva voce*' that he had spoken to old men who affirmed Richard not to have been deformed (p. 79). This sounds like hearsay. Another conversation between Buc and Stow we can almost visualize as the original gives it: 'when I pressed much to know and understand' Stow's opinion on the death of Edward IV's sons, 'his answer was this, and as peremptory as short . . .' (text, p. 173). The printed edition robs this confrontation of all immediacy: Stow 'being required to deliver his opinion . . . affirmed . . .' (p. 106). Not once in all these statements of personally derived information is there in the printed version the slightest indication of how they reached the author, and we are led to assume they were little more than hearsay and thus not credit them.

The disputed letter from Elizabeth of York to the Duke of Norfolk regarding her wish to be married is in the printed edition made to look both more important and less reliable by rearrangement of material and exclusion of all details regarding the research which uncovered it. First of all, the question of Elizabeth's objecting or not objecting to marriage with Richard is given a prominence it does not possess in the original. The Editor in reorganizing material has begun the discussion of this contemplated marriage with two forcefully stated points (pp. 126f), as if they are the main things he is aiming to disprove:

Item, *That all men, and the Maid herself most of all, detested this unlawful Copulation.*

Item, *That he made away the Queen his wife, to make way for this Marriage, and that he propounded not the Treaty of Marriage, until the Queen his wife was dead.*

This is quite differently stated in the original, where Buc observes that Richard has been accused of wanting to marry Elizabeth 'and they [the accusers] add' that she opposed the match and that he killed his wife (see text, p. 192). The original gives subordinate rather than primary emphasis to the two later points. In the original, the letter appears as a sideline, a matter of interest, not a crucial proof. It is a digression within the argument that Richard, if he had wished, could have procured a divorce; and the information derived from it is primarily that Elizabeth spoke like a young girl in her letter, in ignorance that a man could remarry without his wife's dying. One may easily suspect that Buc's intention in including the letter was as much, if not more, to pay tribute to Arundel by citing material from his splendid collection as to exhibit the young lady's feelings (as he reads the letter), which he seems to view with gentle amusement. Indeed, his concentration on Arundel is evident from the number of times he revises the reference to him and his rich cabinet (see Plates II-III).

In the compressed printed *Life and Reigne* the letter seems to take on greater significance, standing as it does in a different relation to the surrounding material: it has suffered only slight reduction, but the material around it has been very much compressed. From the letter itself are cut important references to Norfolk's loyalty to Richard III and to the sons of Edward IV. These are replaced by a mere '&c' (p. 128). The words 'in body, and in all' are left out, clearly for the sake of compression, not to make a point. Aside from minor changes, this is all. Yet the circumstantial detail surrounding Buc's viewing of the letter is reduced to a mere statement that this is what Elizabeth said, in her own words, and the letter 'remains in the Autograph, or Original Draft, under her own hand, in the magnificent Cabinet of *Thomas* Earl of Arundel and Surrey' (p. 128). There is no indication here that the author had actually *seen* the letter (indeed, the plagiarist had not). And the expressions of gratitude to Arundel for his kindness and favour in allowing Buc to see it are gone, as are the descriptive details of his 'rich cabinet' and collection. The fact that Arundel was a direct descendent of the letter's recipient is not mentioned.

Rewriting and excerpting by George Buck Esq., the Editor, are sometimes careless of the sense, and often the details omitted are important ones. Some of the details of Archibald Quhitlaw's acquaintance with Richard III are left out, so that we are ignorant of the personal knowledge on which his eulogistic address was based. The Editor also omits the perceptive suggestion that Thomas More transfers to Richard his own deformity, the inequality of shoulders mentioned by Erasmus.

Some violence is done to Buc's methods of argumentation. Compression and omission in the printed edition create a very abrupt leap from deploring Hastings's execution to parallel cases in modern times, 'Let us leave it up on that accompt, and to consider how much more wee forgive the fames of *H*.1. *E*.3. *H*.4. *E*.4. *H*.7. because they had their happy Starres and successe . . .' (p. 13). The Editor then goes backward to cite ancient examples which in this position appear mere pedantry, and cites reason of state at the end. The original, on the other hand, presents a carefully constructed discussion leading from Richard's specific action, which it accepts instead of putting it aside, then discusses reason of state at some length, illustrating it by examples proceeding logically from ancient to modern times and thence back to Richard. In Book III the same abruptness is constantly apparent because of the compression and deletion. Pressing together of accusation and defence deprives the reader of Buc's gradual rational argument with its occasionally whimsical character and makes the defences appear much more polemical – like the harangue for which the book has been justly criticized, in the name of the wrong author.

Revision badly distorts a description of the relationship of More's narrative to the chronicles which followed it. The printed edition merely says that the chroniclers trusted what More said and followed him, not, as the original explicitly observes, that they inserted his narrative into their works. Buc's caution to the reader about the unreliability of the common chronicles and critical discussions of their authority are omitted. Since Buc uses these statements about contemporary historiography to introduce his defence and explain its necessity, the omission not only deprives us of all awareness of his critical acumen but is structurally quite crucial. In the original he tells us, in historiographical terms, why a defence of Richard III is needed. The printed version gives no inkling of any such perception. It is no wonder that John Hughes, in introducing the printed edition reprinted in *The Complete History of England*, seemed to wonder why anyone would want to defend Richard III.[22]

Errors in the printed text are numerous. Some of the foreign words and proper names which are incorrect in the earlier copies are corrected in print, but as often as this happens a new glaring error is made in another place. These errors lend the work an appearance of carelessness and ignorance. Some of the most glaring mistakes in factual information and proper names can be listed, but the errors in foreign quotations are far too numerous.

Pr. ed. p. 9 'Exon' for 'Hexham'
20 'Elizabeth Butler' for 'Eleanor Butler' (in Additional also)
25 'Norfolk' for 'Suffolk' (all other copies are correct)
27 'John Hide' for 'John Herd'
30 'Fieries' for 'Fiennes'
52 'Pe.' for 'Pontus' (Heuterus)
61 'Sir Charles Brandon' for 'Sir William Brandon'
63 'Billington' for 'Pilkington'
67 'Gadys' for 'Cadiz'[23] (Additional gives 'Cadish')
79 'Juliola' for 'Tulliosa'
'Totheringham' for 'Fotheringhay' (copies give 'Fotheringham')
83 'Loualto melie' and 'Loyalty bindeth men' for 'Loyaulte me lie' and 'Loyalty bindeth me' (the latter is also in the earlier MS. copies)
91 'Aylau' for 'Ayala'
92 'Beanely' for 'Beaulieu'
93 'Shrene' for 'Sheen' (Egerton gives 'Shrene', Malone 'Shree', Fisher 'Shreeue')
97 'Walter Blunt' for 'Walter Blewyt'

22 Observed by D.R. Woolf, *The Idea of History in Early Stuart England* (Toronto, 1990), p. 132.

23 Marcham inexplicably seems to consider this spelling acceptable: 'Buc tells us that he was at the siege of Gadys', p. 3. Myers quotes this passage without comment on p. vi of his introduction to the modern reprint of the 1646 edition, though he uses the form 'Cadiz' later. Evidently he considers it a valid variant, but apart from these instances I have never met it as such, and Google does not help.

100 'York' for 'Essex'
129 'Don Alde Mendoza' for 'Don Alonzo de Mendoza' (in copies given as 'Don Al: de Mendoza')
141 '1493' for '1485' as Richard's date of death (*sic* in all copies) 'Edward' for 'Edmund', Earl of Kent, uncle to Edward III

The word 'fifth' is misread as 'first' in all copies except Fisher, and so the printed version absurdly states that Edward III was 'the first King in a Lineall descent' from Henry II (p. 4). A careless compression makes the Bastard of Fauconberg Earl of Kent rather than son of the earl, an error for which Strype criticizes Buc, who did not make it (Strype in *Complete History*, I, 517n). All the Editor's copies, including the printed edition, duplicate the designation 'of Ross' and attach it to Sir William Parr as well as to Lord Parr. Instead of stating that Morton 'and a certain countess' were contemplating the death of King Edward's sons by poison, a not unlikely proposition, the printed edition states that they were plotting the death of Edward IV (p. 102), thus depriving Richard's defenders of another rumour which might add grist to their mill.

The structure of the printed edition is neatly finished with the inclusion of 'The Authors Scope, Peroratio & Votum', a heading which had appeared in Buc's original's list of contents for Book V but had puzzled the Editor in his previous copies and been removed from the list of contents for Book V in the manuscripts. He found it now in Buc's diffuse summing up of Richard's case near the end of Book V so has cut, organized and placed it in a prominent position. Someone has provided a not very painstaking index and a list of sources, a practice Buc had considered unnecessary because, as he says, he cites his authors everywhere. Authorship is cited on the title page: 'Composed in five Bookes by George Buck Esquire'.

Sir George Buc's work, though diffuse, well-documented and researched through various original documents with the personal assistance of the most eminent antiquaries of the age, had been reduced by the Editor to a concise summary, haphazard in its documentation and spellings of proper names and foreign words, and giving as hearsay what was firsthand information from reliable sources. All traces of the original author's identity, his period, his associates, his opinions of scholarship, of Lancastrian treachery, of Morton's evil nature, have been erased. The style, which in the original was plodding and repetitious, has become in places clear and varied, but often shows extreme carelessness and incongruity and is sometimes so high-flown as to be completely obscure. It is in the form of this printed edition that the work is still most commonly known, largely due to the misguided reprinting in 1973 just after the text of my first edition was – and was known to have been – completed. In recent years another copy of the reissue of 1647 has been digitized[24] and erroneously attributed, on the website where it appears, to 'Sir George Buck'!

24 https://books.google.co.uk/books /edition/The_history_of_the_life_and_reigne_of_Ri.html.

VI. THE *HISTORY* AND ITS CRITICS

Buc himself expected that his book 'would find many censors and critical essayers, and those of divers kinds: some curious, some jealous, some captious and peremptory, some incredulous, some scrupulous and some haply malevolent and malicious. But the fairest censure would be that all was a paradox or contr'opinion' (text, p. 3). This censure began to be entertained not in reference to the book as he wrote it but to the edition of it concocted by his great-nephew, George Buck Esq. (alternatively George Buck Gent.), shortly after its appearance in 1646 as *The History of the Life and Reigne of Richard the Third*. It has been subject ever since to conflicting evaluations on the grounds of both content and style.

Bishop Fuller in his *Church History* (1655) is very severe about it:

> . . . I confess it is no heresy to maintain a paradox in history; nor am I such an enemy to wit as not to allow it leave harmlessly to disport itself for its own content and the delight of others. . . . But when men shall do it cordially, in sober sadness, to pervert people's judgements, and therein go against all received records, I say singularity is the least fault can be laid to such men's charge.

Fuller expresses moral indignation that whereas Richard was

> low in stature, crook-backed, with one shoulder higher than the other, having a prominent gobber-tooth, a warlike countenance; . . . yet a modern author, in a book by him lately set forth, eveneth his shoulders, smootheth his back, planeth his teeth, maketh him in all points a comely and beautiful person; nor stoppeth he here, but, proceeding from his naturals to his morals, maketh him as virtuous as handsome . . . concealing most, denying some, defending others of his foulest facts, wherewith in all ages since he standeth charged on record.[1]

A note identifies this modern author as 'George Buck, esq.' In so short a time all consideration of the original author, Sir George Buc, and his reputation for scholarship, learning, integrity and dignity have vanished. It is perhaps ironic that most subsequent accounts should assume that 'George Buck, Esquire' is a misprint or alternative for 'Sir George Buc' and that scholars still confuse the two.

On the other hand, an anonymous writer, whose comments George Chalmers saw in the margin of a copy of Ulpian Fulwell's *Flower of Fame*, 1575, in a hand Chalmers claims to be of James I's era – which, if so, means it could only be a response to the original manuscript or a very early copy – speaks highly of the

1 Thomas Fuller, *The Church History of Britain*, ed. J.S. Brewer (Oxford, 1845), II, 490. The 'prominent gobber-tooth' was invented by Richard Baker in *A Chronicle of the Kings of England* (London, 1643), p. 137. Curious that an invention c. 160 years after Richard's death is accepted as 'received record' by Fuller.

author's treatment of his subject: '. . . a just confutation of all their unjust and false imputations are clearly and with truth wiped of [*sic*] from that innocent prince by the thrice noble and famous scoller S.r G. Buc: in v bookes which hee hath (with special knowledge) written in King Richard's defence . . .'[2] Chalmers, as we may recall, had drawn attention to the younger Buck's forgery (see above, p. lxxiv). Certain antiquarian scholars, probably influenced by Buc's defence (though certainly through the medium of his great-nephew) presented favourable accounts of Richard's life and reign, a prominent example being William Winstanley's *England's Worthies* in 1660.

18th-century assessments

The conflict of opinions inspired the republication in 1706 and 1719 of the younger Buck's *History of the Life and Reigne* in *A Complete History of England.*[3] John Hughes, who wrote the preface to it, mentions that on the grounds of content 'there are various Opinions about it, and 'tis upon this Account that the Booksellers were advis'd to print it'.[4] He goes on to criticize it on stylistic grounds: 'much too loosely writ for a History, 'tis pedantic and full of Harangue, and may more properly be call'd a *Defence of King Richard* than any thing else'. The word 'harangue' obviously alludes to the florid style of Buc's great-nephew, for it is something of which Buc certainly cannot be accused. The suggestion that it is more properly described as a defence, too, is more applicable to the printed edition, with its ramming together of accusation and defence, which obliterates Buc's leisurely reasoning methods.

In the 1748 edition of the *Biographia Britannica*, the annotator Philip Morant agrees with these stylistic flaws and adds that the *History* 'abounds with faults, which, in a man of his [i.e., Buc's] learning, is something unaccountable'.[5] It is accountable, of course, by the alterations the Editor and his scribe made both intentionally and accidentally to Buc's original, of which Morant was unaware. Nevertheless, he states that the *History* was the work by which Sir George Buc most distinguished himself!

Andrew Kippis, reviser of *Biographia Britannica*, gives, in 1780, this addition to the stylistic criticism, tempering it with appreciation of Buc's ability:

> . . . though Buc writes very pedantically, which may partly be attributed to the fashion of the times, he displays considerable abilities. His digressions, in particular, though they are introduced in an improper place, manifest a good portion of antiquarian knowledge. In his Vindication of Richard the Third, he hath offered some things worthy of attention; but he writes in so declamatory a manner, and with so much of the air of a professed panegyrist, rather than of a cool enquirer into truth, that he makes, on that account, the less impression upon the minds of his readers.[6]

2 Quoted in [Chalmers], *Supplemental Apology*, pp. 206f.
3 London, 1706 and 1719. It has been customary to ascribe this whole work to Bishop White Kennett, who wrote the final volume, but there is no evidence of his being involved with the first two volumes.
4 [Hughes], Preface to *Complete History*, I, sig. av.
5 [Morant], 'Buc', *Biographia Britannica*, II, 1005n.
6 Andrew Kippis, 'Buc', *Biographia Britannica* II (London, 1780), 677.

Again it appears that this reference to panegyric style describes the great-nephew's in the printed edition, for Buc's own could generally be described as that of 'a cool enquirer into truth'.

During the eighteenth century the *History* in its 1646 version was not without influence. The most important influence on all historians of the period seems to have lain in its calling attention to the Crowland Chronicle, to a lesser degree in its use of other original letters in public repositories, and to its discussion of Perkin Warbeck. Paul de Rapin in his *History of England* (1728), though generally following More, advises caution in accepting reports by Lancastrian historians when they criticize actions by Yorkists and notes that George Buck Esq., as he correctly terms the Editor, has tried to represent Richard better than tradition esteemed him.

Thomas Carte in *A General History of England* (1686-1754) is of all historians the one who follows the printed edition most closely. He uses it as a source for factual material, for the order of events, and for interpretations. He follows its assessment of Richard's character and the judgment that it was obscured by the interest which Tudor historians had in calumniating him. He makes explicit Buc/k's point that it was necessary for the sons of Edward IV to be believed dead if Henry VII's plan to take the crown was to succeed. He points out the inconsistencies in More's account of their death, adducing the same arguments as Buc/k against Richard's being a murderer and concluding, as does Buc/k, that Edward V died naturally and Richard of York escaped to reappear as Perkin Warbeck. Carte cites Buc/k's references to various manuscript documents without quibble.

'Historic Doubts' about Richard III

David Hume in *The History of England* (1763) is severely traditional and disapproving of Richard's apologists, but his friend Horace Walpole wrote the first full-scale defence since Buc's. In his review of Walpole's *Historic Doubts on the Life and Reign of Richard the Third* (1768), Edward Gibbon has this to say of the Editor's style: 'Un seul critique (Buck) s'est élevé contre le sentiment général, mais son ton de panégyriste a révolté tous les esprits'.[7] [One sole critic has risen against the general sentiment, but all minds are revolted by his panegyric tone.] Walpole, like Buc, (text, p. 3), is sensitive to the risk of being considered a paradoxicalist, and he defends the work against this imputation: 'Buck, so long exploded as a lover of paradoxes, and as an advocate for a monster, gains new credit the deeper this dark scene is fathomed' (p. 20). And he ends his defence with an apology similar to Buc's opening one: 'I flatter myself that I shall not be thought either fantastic or paradoxical, for not blindly adopting an improbable tale . . .' (p. 122).

Compared with Buc's, Walpole's is a paltry effort, too flippant in style to be taken seriously, basing its argument less on original records than on Tudor historians, on Buck the Younger's printed version, and on logical assumption. What Walpole considers logic is not critically informed, and his arguments tend

7 Edward Gibbon, 'Doubtes Historiques sur la Vie et la Regne du Roi Richard III. Par M. Horace Walpole', in *Miscellaneous Works* (London, 1814), III, 333. It is claimed here that this review was published originally in 1761 [*sic*] in *Mémoires Britanniques*.

to be flimsy and capricious, based on idiosyncratic personal opinion. He uses the Crowland Chronicle, but he has not Buc's gift for or perhaps interest in assessing his sources. Walpole describes the chronicler (inaccurately) as merely 'a monk who busies himself in recording the insignificant events of his own order or monastery, and who was at most occasionally made use of, was not likely to know the most important and most mysterious secrets of state' (p. 16). He follows Buc/k in pointing out (also inaccurately) that More was a young man in low office when he wrote his *Richard*, but denies that More had most of his material from Morton, because Walpole's social sense does not admit of intimacy between 'so raw a youth' and 'a prelate of that rank and prime minister' (p. 18). He joins Buc/k in pronouncing More's *Richard*, like his *Utopia*, 'invention and romance' (p. 19).

Like Buc, Walpole makes mistakes in the literary quotations he occasionally inserts as illustrations, and his mistakes are so numerous and considerable as to prove his memory far inferior to Buc's. Like Buc, he is careless in attributing to More material which really comes from the post-More sections of Hall and other Tudor chroniclers. He uses Buc/k uncritically, incorporating the errors of the printed edition into his own references. Walpole says that he 'has gone too far; nor are his style or method to be admired. With every intention of vindicating Richard, he does but authenticate his crimes, by searching in other story for other instances of what he calls policy' (p. 20). This method as used by Buc was not as a defence, but rather as evidence that irrationally disproportionate blame is being attached to Richard by his calumniators. Walpole follows his criticism of this method almost immediately by using reason of state as a defence. Like Buc, Walpole cites classical parallels, at one point listing beautiful men who have done atrocious deeds. Walpole follows Buc/k's lead on the question of Perkin Warbeck, which he examines at length.

The 19th century and Elizabeth of York's letter

Throughout the nineteenth century the original author's integrity and careful methods continued to be ignored. The 1646 edition was the only version consulted in the belief that it was the only version there was. Chalmers examined at least the beginning of Tiberius at the end of the eighteenth century (see above, p. lxxiv) and noted that there was a later George Buck who appropriated Sir George's work, but his observation seems to have had no effect. Nor did an 1850 article in *Notes and Queries*[8] which repeated, though without citing it, what Chalmers had said over fifty years earlier. Nor did the entry on Buc by Arthur Henry Bullen in the 1885-1900 edition of the *DNB*: 'whoever this "Geo. Buck, Gent.", may have been, he did not scruple to claim the authorship of the "Eclog" [i.e. *Daphnis*], and afterwards of the "History of the Life and Reign of Richard the Third" written by Sir George Buc. . . . A charred fragment of a manuscript copy of the work, in the handwriting of Sir George Buc, is preserved among the Cottonian manuscripts'.

Also in the nineteenth century began the focus on the letter written by Elizabeth of York to the Duke of Norfolk requesting his intercession with the king in the matter of her marriage (text, p. 191 and Plates II and III), which Buc had seen in the private collection of Norfolk's heir, the Earl of Arundel, to whom he dedicated

8 Edward F. Rimbault, *Notes and Queries*, no. 35 (1850), 73.

his *History*. According to the Crowland Chronicle, rumours existed that Richard wished to marry Elizabeth. Buc interpreted the letter in this light, understanding by Elizabeth's saying she feared that 'the queen would never die' that she was expressing her wish to marry the king. Commentators tending to approach the letter as Buc did with their minds made up do not take seriously enough the likely possibility that he misconstrued it. Richard's twentieth-century biographer Charles Ross failed to consider that it was possible to read the letter otherwise than as Buc does: that perhaps Elizabeth wished to convey to Richard her wish to marry, not to marry him (for detailed discussion of the letter's meaning see General Notes 191/1-25).

Walpole in 1768 had been the first writer to refer to this letter. Since subsequent critical opinion against Buc has focused on it to such a disproportionate extent, it will be instructive to trace responses to it from Walpole to the present day before turning to consider nineteenth-, twentieth-, and twenty-first century assessments of the *History* in more general terms. Walpole cites it incorrectly, stating that Buc/k says the physicians predicted February as the date of the queen's demise and Elizabeth in her letter complained that most of February was passed and she feared the queen would never die. Walpole defends the existence of this letter: 'Buck would not have dared to quote her letter as extant in the earl of Arundel's library, if it had not actually been there: . . . others of Buck's assertions having been corroborated by subsequent discoveries, leave no doubt of his veracity on this' (p. 129). He was far more generous than more recent writers.

Nineteenth-century writers (and their twentieth-century followers) heaped vilification on Buc/k for his audacity in bringing to light a paper which appeared to cast aspersions on the honour of young English womanhood. This seems to have originated the positive fixation with assuming that if the documents Buc cites cannot be found it is obvious that he made them up. 'If this letter really existed', says N. Harris Nicolas, 'and if Buck has cited it fairly, it would be vain to contend against such testimony, and Elizabeth's fame would be irredeemably affected'. Nicolas goes on,

> The character of Buck as a faithless writer is well known; and even if his notorious inaccuracies and prejudices do not justify the suspicion that the letter itself was never written, it is not too much too suggest that the interpretation which he has given it is at variance with truth. As Buck has inserted copies of several documents of much less interest, it may be asked, why did he not give this most important letter at length?[9]

The answer to this of course is that Buc as an antiquary found legal charters of much more interest than domestic gossip and more worthy of preservation in detail. He does state that he is giving Elizabeth's own words, though he gives them in indirect discourse. And why, Nicolas asks, did none of the other famous antiquaries – Dugdale and Wood – copy it? He does not consider whether or not this was a matter of particular interest to them, on what terms of intimacy they might be with the Howards, and what the state was of the Howard papers at the

9 Nicholas Harris Nicolas, 'Memoir' in *Privy Purse Expenses of Elizabeth of York* (London, 1830), p. li.

time when they wrote, later than both Buc and his great-nephew (see pp. lv, ci). Nicolas goes on in his notes to expound, just in case the letter *did* exist, some tortuous theories of how Buc/k might have misinterpreted it, since he regards it as too prejudicial to Elizabeth to be true as reported.

Nicolas's absurdities on this point are adopted by numerous other writers. John Heneage Jesse in his *Memoirs of King Richard the Third* seems to be following Nicolas when he says,

> Buck is acknowledged to have been a highly prejudiced, and not always trustworthy chronicler. . . . On the other hand, admitting Buck to be a faithless chronicler, and the disappearance of the letter to be a very suspicious circumstance, there is still the difficulty of believing that anyone could so grossly and impudently outstep his duty as a writer of history, as to interlard it with positive fiction.[10]

So in defence of Buc/k's honour this time rather than Elizabeth's, Jesse follows Nicolas's arguments of possible misquotation. He has already 'proved' Buc/k to hold an 'unscrupulous partiality'[11] in showing how his quotation of Richard's epitaph (of which no trace exists in the original manuscript) differs in several points from Sandford's. He ignores the fact that Sandford and Buc copied the epitaph from different manuscripts, takes no account of editorial corruption or printer's errors, and is unaware that the 1646 edition does not come from the original author. (That said, Buc does show a tendency to 'improve' sources so they speak less vituperatively of Richard.)

Caroline Halsted, while expressing extreme scepticism, and speaking of the letter and its source with considerable inaccuracy, admits the possibility that Elizabeth could have been referring to some other potential match:

> If Sir George Buck had himself seen the letter, and spoken of its contents from his own knowledge – if either himself or any other writer had inserted a copy of it, or even a transcript from the 'original draft', then, indeed, it would have been difficult to set aside such testimony. But considering that every search has been made for the alleged autograph, – that no trace of such a document has ever been discovered, or even known to have existed, – that no person is named as having seen it, or is instanced in support of its validity, – and moreover, that Sir George Buck, throughout his history of Richard III, inserts at full length copies of almost every other instrument to which he refers, or gives marginal references to the source whence his authority was derived, but, in this instance, contents himself with merely stating the fact, and giving the substance of a letter which he appears to have received from rumour or hearsay information, the conviction cannot but arise that the letter in question was either not the production of Elizabeth of York, or, if so, that the insinuations referred to in it were misconstrued, and that its contents had reference to some other

10 John Heneage Jesse, *Memoirs of King Richard the Third and Some of His Contemporaries* (London, 1862), p. 316.
11 *Ibid.*, p. 226.

individual, and not, as was supposed, to her uncle.[12]

She then goes on in a note to quote Nicolas's conjectures as to possible misinterpretations of the letter. Halsted seems curiously unaware that even the printed edition gives a marginal as well as a textual reference stating that the letter is in Arundel's cabinet. Had she examined Buc's original, available by that time in the British Museum, she would have found that he clearly states that he did see it and was shown it by Arundel, who must, consequently, have seen it as well, indeed have brought it to his attention. Halsted exaggerates Nicolas's statement when she says that Buck gives copies of every other document he uses. This is far from true: he generally paraphrases and sometimes makes minor changes.

With James Gairdner we return to the sense of outrage perpetrated against English womanhood and a consequent ambivalence in his disposition on one hand to respect Buc/k and his unwillingness on the other to accept Elizabeth's humanity. He begins by saying the letter cannot be ignored, 'however revolting and opposed to natural expectation'. But there are, he says with relief, grounds for incredulity. His statement of them, incorporating by paraphrase then seeming to contradict the errors made by Nicolas and Halsted, is too silly to resist quoting in full:

> Buck does not expressly say that he had seen the letter himself; and we might, perhaps, rather infer the contrary, from the fact that he only gives the substance of it in his own words, whereas he has quoted at full length many documents of less importance. On the other hand, if it is not clear that Buck saw it, there is not a tittle of evidence to show that anyone else did. No reference is made to it by any of the great antiquaries and historians of Buck's day – by Stow, or Speed, or Holinshed, or Camden. No person appears to have seen it before, no person appears to have seen it since, and nothing is known of its existence now. Add to this the fact that Buck, even though not altogether dishonest (and I see no reason to think him so), was by no means an impartial historian, but an essayist bent on justifying a paradox, and that such a letter, if it really existed, was of very great service to his argument. Taking all these circumstances into consideration – together with the further possibility that the letter, even if it existed, may have been misconstrued – we ought certainly to be pardoned for indulging a belief, or, at all events, a charitable hope, that Elizabeth was incapable of sentiments so dishonourable and repulsive.
>
> At the same time it must be remarked that Buck's abstract of the letter is very minute, and such as would follow pretty closely the turns of expression in a genuine original; that he expressly declares the MS. to be the autograph or original draft; and that the horrible perversion and degradation of domestic life which it implies is only too characteristic of the age. Still, it would certainly appear from the little we know of her after life that Elizabeth of York was

12 Caroline A. Halsted. *Richard III as Duke of Gloucester and King of England* (London, 1844), II, 388f.

> not destitute of domestic feeling; and that she could have been eager to obtain the hand of her brothers' murderer is really too monstrous to be believed.[13]

In case, however, the letter should not after all be a forgery passed off on Buc/k, 'or by him upon his readers', Gairdner attempts to explain how it *might* have been written (with a few minor 'errors' such as the substitution of the word 'father' for 'husband') by Elizabeth Woodville!

This account reaches almost the limit of absurdity. Gairdner sees no reason to assume Buc(k?) dishonest, yet this may be a forgery palmed off by him on his readers. 'Not a tittle' of evidence exists that anyone saw the letter, but Gairdner has not bothered to look for evidence in the most likely place, Buc's original work, housed in the British Museum. He fails to consider the interests and methods of Stow, Speed, Holinshed, and Camden (whom he arbitrarily substitutes for Nicolas, Dugdale, and Wood): how far in advance of them Buc was in his treatment of this subject, and his association, which they did not all share, with the Howards. The description of Buc as 'an essayist bent on justifying a paradox' can result only from Gairdner's confusing him with Sir William Cornwallis. Buc wrote in diverse forms, but the essay is not one of them. Clearly both Halsted and Gairdner were relying on their memories rather than recent consultation of even the 1646 edition.

Polarized attitudes to Richard III

The nineteenth and early twentieth centuries saw a close battle develop between two extremes, Richard's defenders and Richard's attackers. Attitudes to Buc/k affected as well as reflecting these extremes. Halsted, the nineteenth century's major defender, follows Walpole closely in appraising Buc/k, except that she credits him because he agrees with Commynes and the Parliament Rolls, whereas Walpole credited Commynes because he agreed with Buc/k and the Parliament Rolls. Halsted observes that Buc/k 'appears to have had access to documents no longer extant'[14] but does not appear to have looked for them. She uses Buc/k as a serious source, though she feels she must apologize for doing so by citing Walpole's approval of him. But she, like Walpole, uses him haphazardly and uncritically, incorporating into her own defence errors in the printed edition and paraphrases of other authors which originated with Buc. Her organization is an improvement on Buc/k's, following chronological order, dealing with accusations according to the order of events. This entails digressing to argue cases in defence, but the overall structure is clearer. She follows Buc/k's method and arguments in defending Richard against the numerous accusations against him, particularly in the matter of deformity, adding to his arguments further evidence discovered at a later date. That this is also the method employed by Sir Clements Markham in 1906 and Paul Murray Kendall in 1955 shows how firm is Buc's groundwork in establishing methods and arraying evidence for later defenders to build upon. Halsted follows Buc/k and Walpole in pursuing the question of Perkin Warbeck's identity.

13 James Gairdner, *History of the Life and Reign of Richard the Third* (Cambridge, 1898), p. 203.
14 Halsted, I, 95.

Gairdner's ambivalent attitude has already been amply demonstrated. He uses the same sources as Buc does, with the addition of MS. Harleian 433, but no more critically than does Buc. He does not differentiate between More and Polydore Vergil and their followers and copiers (Hall, Grafton, Holinshed, Stow). He gives whole passages of More's invented speeches and Hall's battle orations as factual quotations. Examples of Gairdner's carelessness in use of both primary and secondary sources are his lack of awareness that Buc derived from the *Titulus Regius* the information that Eleanor (Talbot) Butler rather than 'Elizabeth Lucy' was Edward's contracted spouse; and his wild statement that a further century and a quarter elapsed after Buc before the *Titulus Regius* was discovered.[15] Gairdner was the first to undertake a large-scale discussion of Perkin Warbeck with intent to prove that he was *not* the Duke of York. He is the first writer to set about trying to prove Richard's alleged crimes by use of historical evidence, and he fails because he cannot or will not examine his sources critically. This is a skill in which Buc, nearly three centuries before, surpassed him.

Sir Clements Markham, Gairdner's antagonist, who was not an historian, links Buc with Stow, Grafton, Hall, and Holinshed as authors who copied from earlier writers and therefore cannot be considered authorities except when they introduce documents as evidence. This is just, to a degree, though it ignores Buc's difference from the other four in that he exercises some critical judgment in the use of his secondary sources, deciding which are most authoritative on which subjects, rather than copying them wholesale as do the other writers on the list. And it also ignores Buc's determination to assess his sources and what they say critically according to the bias of the times in which they wrote. Markham is the first to take cognizance of Buc's original manuscript at all, though he utterly misunderstands the relationship between it and the printed edition, concluding that though the work was published in 1646 under the name of George Buck Esq., the existence of the manuscript in the British Museum citing Sir George as author proved the substitution of 'Esq.' for 'Sir' an error. Contradicting the writers who had noticed the original manuscript and deduced from it Buck the Younger's theft, his theory permits the identification of the printed edition with the original manuscript to persist, both being accepted as the work of Sir George Buc. Markham is at least able somewhat to see Sir George in his own right, as a man Camden praised for his distinction in learning.

Markham follows Buc's structure in dividing his own book: half is a chronological biography, half a discussion of the 'authorities' and a defence of Richard from the accusations against him one by one. Like Buc, he discusses Tudor sources and 'proves' that Morton wrote More's *Richard III*. Thereafter he gives all references to More's work as 'Morton' (as Buc gives many of his as 'Morton and More'). Just as Buc vilifies More to call attention to his unreliability, so Markham vilifies Morton. He agrees with Buc in making Morton the author of all slanders against Richard and even enlarges on this, showing how the slanders travelled with Morton wherever he went, both in England and abroad. Like Buc, he dislikes Henry VII and praises Queen Elizabeth. His general assessment of

15 Gairdner, p. 92.

Richard is the same as Buc's: he attributes to him the same virtues on similar evidence. Buc occasionally sentimentalizes his portrait of Richard; Markham sentimentalizes it even further. He deviates from Buc, however, regarding Perkin Warbeck, for his theory that Henry VII murdered the sons of Edward IV after Richard's death invalidates Warbeck's claim. This theory of murder is certainly as speculative a case as the most speculative Buc propounded. As for the Elizabeth of York letter, 'Buck no doubt was prejudiced, but not more so than the Tudor chroniclers. He blunders and is uncritical, yet there is no reason to impugn his good faith'.[16]

Shakespeare scholarship has, understandably, not been kind to Richard III, Shakespeare devotees often feeling it is necessary to take every word of this writer of dramatic fiction as historical truth. Horace Howard Furness in the first Variorum edition says dogmatically, 'the character drawn by that mighty hand is the one which all of us remember and accept as true, in spite of all apologists'.[17] And he quotes Bishop Fuller's abusive remarks (see above, p. xcvii) to apply to all defenders of Richard, among whom he lists Buc, Walpole, Halsted and Markham. As an assessment of Buc's style, Furness quotes R.G. White:

> As history, it is neither more nor less interesting than the older chronicles. At times the excess of quotations from Latin authors is not only bewildering but exasperating. Sir George apparently belongs to that class of writers to whom the effort of recording their thick-coming fancies presents but slight difficulty . . .[18]

Clearly Shakespeare scholars of the previous century were not concerned with literary styles favoured by writers of their hero's period.

20th-century traditionalists and revisionists

Challenges to Elizabeth of York's letter resumed in the twentieth century, apparently having acquired such great authority through repetition and accretion that in order to attack it seems to have become quite unnecessary to read Buc/k at all by the time David MacGibbon wrote in 1938:

> There does not seem to be an atom of truth in the letter printed by Buck in Kennet's [*sic*] *History of England* . . . in which he quotes a so-called 'authentic' letter written by the Princess Elizabeth to Richard III stating that she was willing to become his wife. It seems rather peculiar that Buck is the only person to mention this letter, and that its contents were invaluable to him in his attempt at defending Richard III's character.[19]

Because of his stylistic carelessness, it is necessary in part to guess at what MacGibbon means. We are expected, it seems, to imagine Buc (or Buck) alive in 1706 and 1719, printing his letter in *A Complete History of England*. Even the text printed there, the most distant version from Buc's original, states quite plainly

16 Clements R. Markham, *Richard III: His Life and Character* (London, 1906), p. 229n.

17 Horace Howard Furness, Jr., in William Shakespeare, *The Tragedy of Richard the Third*, Variorum, 3rd ed. (Philadelphia, 1908), p. x.

18 R.G. White, quoted in Furness, p, 548f.

19 David MacGibbon, *Elizabeth Woodville* (London, 1938), p. 183n.

that the letter was from Elizabeth to Norfolk, not to Richard, and makes no overt statement 'that she was willing to become his wife' (this is, if anything, an understatement of what she is deemed by most commentators to have been communicating by innuendo in the letter as Buc and even Buck cited it). And in fact it has been toned down from what (I am sure incorrectly) may have been Buc's own understanding of it, since the Editor has deleted her commitment to Richard 'in body, and in all'. The contents have assumed such importance only because so many people a) have prurient taste and imagination, b) have used them as a vehicle for attacking Buc/k. They were far from 'invaluable to him in his attempt at defending Richard III's character' but were little more than a sideline in his arguments relating to one of the more minor accusations against Richard. These attitudes resolved themselves, stripped of their grossest absurdities, into A.R. Myers's statement in 1968 that 'it is hard to accept Buc's testimony on this, for no one else has ever seen this document'.[20] Not a single one of these 'experts' takes into account the tremendous difficulties of keeping a manuscript from destruction or loss over centuries and the survival of such a very small proportion of manuscripts known to have existed in that time.

Paul Murray Kendall produced a revisionist biography of Richard III in 1955, He criticized Buc/k in both, basing his remarks entirely on the 1646 edition (*History of the Life and Reigne of Richard the Third*): there is no evidence of his seeking out the original. He considers Buck's work 'so desultory in organization as to make for grim reading'.[21] And again we hear the complaint that Buck is 'blundering and uncritical',[22] echoing Markham's 'He blunders and is uncritical' quoted above. Nevertheless it was Buck who also first pointed out '*some* of the inaccuracies of Vergil and More, . . . sought sources more nearly contemporary with Richard than the Tudor writers, and . . . thus was the first to reveal that the Tudor tradition was not inviolable'.[23]

Kendall followed this with an edition of More and Walpole under the composite title *Richard III: The Great Debate*, in which he includes criticisms of the *Life and Reigne*: its style is 'tiresome', 'cumbersome' and 'capricious'.[24] Some of these criticisms are just: it is, as he says, capricious, though Buc's original cannot be so described – but of course Kendall is not describing the original. Despite Walpole's scholarly inferiority and stylistic inanity, Kendall claims to consider More and Walpole 'the original antagonists of the Great Debate',[25] bypassing Cornwallis and Buc. Naturally he is constrained by More and Walpole being the two authors whose works have been chosen to appear in *The Great Debate* which Kendall is editing here. Yet a few pages later he repeats his observations from the biography, that Buck was the first to undermine Tudor orthodoxy (confusingly, he is actually speaking of Buck the Younger while misleadingly naming him 'Sir George Buc'); this author, he says,

> composed the first full-scale attack on the Tudor tradition . . . For

20 Myers, 'Richard III and Historical Tradition', p. 186.
21 Paul Murray Kendall, *Richard III* (New York, 1955), p. 506.
22 *Richard III*, p. 506.
23 *Ibid.*
24 *Richard III: the Great Debate*, ed. Paul Kendall (London, 1965), pp. 8-9.
25 *Great Debate*, p. 5.

> all his Yorkist partisanship . . . Buc was a friend of the best antiquaries of the day, John Stow, William Camden, and Sir Robert Cotton; he conscientiously searched old records, and was the first to make use of the late fifteenth-century 'Second Continuation' of the *Croyland Chronicle*, a source of great importance, in attempting to discredit More's *History*.[26]

Kendall claims that he 'is driven, like Cornwallis, to dispose of the Tudor tradition by dismissing its charges as improbabilities or justifying them on the basis of *raison d'État'*.[27] This is exactly what Kendall himself does in his biography on occasions when he is unable to prove a point conclusively yet wishes to promote a more balanced judgment of Richard III. Kendall solves the problem of organization by using chronological order and relegating the defences and debates to end notes and appendices. This means one must read with one finger in the corresponding page of notes, which is awkward but allows for an uninterrupted narrative if one does not consult them. He manages at last to achieve near perfection in standards of quotation and documentation. Yet he is not unlike Buc (or indeed More) in inventing, to fill out his picture, speeches, scenes and conjectured emotions and thoughts for which his sources give no actual basis but which are not incongruous with them.

A.R. Myers and the 1973 reprint of Buck '1647' [*sic*]

The historian A.R. Myers wrote about Buc in articles in *History Today* (1954) and *History* (1968). In the second article Myers indicates awareness that the composition of Buc's *History* significantly predated the publication by his great-nephew. And he is aware to some extent of the work's nature, though he has clearly not consulted it except, perhaps, very cursorily.

> Buc clears the king of every charge made against him; he denies that Richard was a villain and asserts that on the contrary he was a good king whose memory had been blackened by Tudor historians. Buc was an antiquary of some note, a member of the first Society of Antiquaries; and it may be through the contacts of this society, especially Sir Robert Cotton, that he was able to consult many of the Cotton MSS. and the public records.[28]

Yet while professing to assess Buc's *History*, Myers has not read even the first pages of the original carefully enough to *know* that it was through Cotton, Camden and Brooke, not to mention Arundel, that Buc gained access to certain of the records mentioned. Myers's tendency is to quote from the printed edition and ignore not only the original author's work, but also the early copies (which preserve much more of his work than does the printed edition), while saying that 'no one has ever seen' manuscripts which Buc carefully documents, such documentation often being available in the manuscript copies. At one point Myers attributes to him a bizarre etymological discourse which is actually an editorial

26 *Ibid.*, p. 8.
27 *Ibid.*, p. 9.
28 Myers, 'Richard III and Historical Tradition', 185f.

insertion in the printed edition, appearing in no other version.[29] His conclusion is that Buc's use of documents is careless, if not downright dishonest, and hence likely to be unreliable where it cannot be checked. Thus 'except for his criticism of More, Buc's defence of Richard III does not amount to much'.[30] It is, he feels, most interesting as an example of contemporary scholarship, which showed 'great erudition, but little critical method'.[31] But Myers fails in arguing this case – in fact has no case – because to illustrate the point he then presents a jumble of examples from both Buc and his great-nephew, without distinguishing between them.

In 1925 Frank Marcham, writing of Sir George Buc's *History of King Richard III*, had said that because 'the edition of 1646 is nearly worthless . . . the *History* should be carefully edited'.[32] Despite this, and although my edition of the original had been in progress for some years and was known to be almost finished, with the text completed, it was decided in 1972 to reprint the 1646 edition. It came out in 1973, the year I completed my edition with introduction and notes. A.R. Myers was chosen to write an introduction to the reprint, which he insisted on describing as the '2nd edition' (to repeat, the reissue of 1647 was simply a means of disposing of leftover sheets of the *sole* edition of 1646, there was thus no second edition).[33] Myers's introduction is extraordinarily careless. Inevitably he relies heavily on Eccles for factual details, sometimes (though less inevitably) very heavily indeed for wording and structure. But by only glancing at the author's original and depending on the printed edition for all illustrations, while presumably trusting no one will consult Tiberius, Myers again makes out a case for the elder Buc's irresponsibility entirely on the basis of his great-nephew's shoddy revision of his work. Ideas referred to as Buc's own are invariably illustrated by a quotation from his great-nephew's version, with all its alterations and misprints. He clearly *wants* to make Buc look irresponsible, and by this method succeeds.

In 'Richard III and Historical Tradition', p. 187, he had attacked Buc for an etymological derivation which exists *only* in the printed version. In his introduction to the printed edition when again he mentions 'Buc's' 'far-fetched etymologies' (p. vii) he is wise enough not to support the statement by quoting from the printed edition: he gives it no support but simply refers the reader to the 'pertinent criticism' of *Biographia Britannica* (see above, p. xcviii), which attacks Buc's style on the basis of his great-nephew's publication. Buc does in fact give 'far-fetched etymologies' at times (different from the ones Myers cites), but Myers makes no allowance for the fact that the science of etymology was only in its infancy in his time. Indeed most historians of the fifteenth century seem ignorant of and uninterested in the ethos and the facts of late sixteenth- and early seventeenth-century scholarship, though not hesitant to make pronouncements on it). Most also seem curiously unaware of the perishable nature of old manuscripts, not grasping what a small fraction survive and why this should be so.

29 *Ibid.*, p. 187.
30 *Ibid.*, p 186.
31 *Ibid.*
32 Marcham, p. 3.
33 Myers, Introduction to Buck, p. vi, n. 1. See above, pp. lxiv-lxv for my proof that the 1647 was a reissue.

Three examples are given to illustrate Buc's unreliability, the first two being quotations from the printed edition, one of them cited with an incorrect page number. One is the omission from a quotation from the Crowland Chronicle of the word 'violenti', which Myers calls the 'crucial word'.[34] In citing this he does not choose the example for himself but follows John Strype,[35] though not acknowledging him. Setting aside the fact that the word 'violenti' is not necessarily crucial in the context, and that Buc was using a manuscript no longer available to us, Myers has neglected to note that there is no way we can determine positively whether or not Buc *did* omit the word, since the section of the passage in which it would have occurred (or not) is burnt away in the original manuscript: the deletion may have resulted from an error on the part of the Editor or his scribe. It may of course have been an example of a tendency Buc demonstrates elsewhere to soften references to Richard. But no firm decision can be made on this quotation, since evidence of the omission is lost.

Again Myers fails to adjust his frame of reference to the period in which Buc was writing and the conventions of that period. Buc tells us when he is quoting exactly, but his usual tendency is to paraphrase, a practice for which he feels no need for apology because he does not claim to do otherwise. Since he tells us what his source is, we can check the original if we so desire.

Myers attacks Buc's use of sources by devious means. Referring to Richard's participation or lack thereof in the slaying of Henry VI's son, he quotes Buc as saying, 'I have seen a faithful Manuscript Chronicle of those times, that the Duke of Gloucester only of all the great Persons stood still and drew not his Sword' and says 'No one else has ever seen this document'. Buc documents it (at least the manuscript copies do, the margin being burnt away in the original) as 'Chronicis in quarto MS. apud Dom. Rob. Cotton' (see text, p. 134, 5th marginal note). Buc mentions this document several times (I am assuming it is the only unnamed chronicle on the relevant period in the collection), and it is the sole document he cites from Cotton's library that cannot now be found, which, in view of the losses by borrowing, vermin, flood, and fire is a quite extraordinary record. Since his purpose in documenting was to lead others to his sources, why should anyone think Buc would not have given them as accurately as possible? Again, Myers shows no historical imagination, judging practices of the early seventeenth century by modern standards.

The next illustration is so blatant an example of either extreme carelessness or extreme perversity that it vitiates everything Myers may have to say in commenting on Buc. Again, he borrows this criticism from Strype (I, 525), again without acknowledgement. It is a claim that Buc 'quotes a statement in Camden which no one has seen since'.[36] Setting aside the impossibility of proving that no one has ever seen any document, the *Britannia* is still Camden's most widely read work. The citation to which Myers refers – one for which Buc even gives the particular

34 Myers, Introduction to Buck, p. vii. See p. 139 in the present text and note thereto. Myers cites it as being on p. 46 of the printed edition. It is in fact on p. 84.

35 *Complete History*, I, 525.

36 Myers, Introduction to Buck, p. vii, n. 4.

section of the *Britannia* where it occurs[37] – can most easily be located in that work by looking up 'Richard III' in the index and turning to the page number there listed: in the 1607 edition it is on p. 261. A not dissimilar remark (that Richard, though living an evil life, made good laws) appears earlier in his *Remaines* (1605, p. 217). It seems that again, wishing to save the trouble of looking it up, Myers has done no more than copy Strype, an editor he himself has criticized, who was equally disinclined to look up the citation in Camden. He concludes his discussion satisfied, despite having given an account of George Buck Esq.'s plagiarism, that the printed edition somehow (he does not say how) represents the original author's intention.

No page number is given for the next example, so it is impossible to trace its source. It is a statement that 'Buc says that Bishop was condemned in Richard's parliament of 1484 of necromancy along with Thomas Nandik and William Knyvet',[38] an assertion that misrepresents information given in the Parliament Roll. No one by the name of 'Bishop' is mentioned anywhere in Buc's *History* or in any of its later versions. It may have been Myers's intention to refer to Bishop Morton. But we can only conjecture, since Buc, like the Act of Attainder he cites, describes only Nandick as a necromancer (see below, text pp. 54, 121, 163, and 188).

Some of Myers's points on texts are extremely confusing or confused. His perverseness in referring to the great-nephew's work as if it were the original author's carries over even to comments on *Daphnis*, and here no lack of accessibility can support him in choosing the version he does: he chooses the least accessible, referring to the work not in Buc's own printed edition or even in his great-nephew's printed version, but inexplicably (and he does not try to explain it) in the great-nephew's *manuscript* reworking. Myers claims that the younger Buck dropped the lines on Richard III from *Daphnis*, though he himself had just quoted them from his manuscript two pages earlier.[39] As for the *History*, the manuscript's being 'heavily . . . erased by the great-nephew' (p. viii) is mentioned, but since no folio references are given, this statement cannot be checked. I am aware of only one erasure (see above, p. lxxxv). Oddly, he speaks of Tiberius as if there were not very much left of the original.

Myers states that Malone preceded Egerton, which my comparative study of the manuscripts shows to be impossible. Not troubling to analyse the manuscripts comparatively, he bases his assertion on Malone's dedicatee dying in 1640 (see above, pp. lxxxii-lxxxiii for consideration of these points).

Further, on the basis of the existence of what he calls a 1647 '2nd edition', he judges that the work must have been popular. But this is only a reissue (see above, pp. lxiv-lxv), not a second edition. A reissue, as opposed to an edition, may indicate the *un*popularity of a work, certainly never the opposite. Myers refers to the printed edition as 'scarce'. It was in 1973 reasonably easy to find in major libraries and also from antiquarian booksellers. Demand certainly did not outstrip

37 Dobuni. This appears in the copies as 'Dolucu'. The printed edition (p. 24) just gives 'Cambden' as a marginal note.
38 Myers, Introduction to Buck, p. vii, n. 3.
39 *Ibid.*, pp. viii and vi. And see above p. xxxii.

supply. He also refers to its 'usefulness', but never explains in what this consists, why anyone would want to read it, what it might be useful *for*. 'No doubt it would be desirable to have a proper edition of the original; but this will be a long and difficult task, in view of the state of B.M. Cottonian MS. Tiberius E.X'.[40] Since Myers was aware that I was at the time engaged in creating such an edition, this is patronizing in the extreme. Long and difficult it was, but by the time this reprint of the *Life and Reigne* appeared it was finished. (It did take six years to be published after that, not an inordinate length of time for finding a publisher for a large work and for the mechanics of publishing it.)

From 1646 to the late twentieth century, criticisms of Buc were muddled not only by worship of More, of the Tudors, of Elizabeth of York, of Shakespeare, of tradition in general. They came also through the misidentification of the 1646 edition as Buc's original work, or the indiscriminate citing of original or printed edition under the assumption that they were similar enough for it not to matter. Yarnold in the nineteenth century never published his intended edition of Egerton 2216. But he was aware that some clarification of inaccuracies would result from the substitution even of this, the earliest extant copy, for the garbled and truncated version of 1646:

> An imperfect edition of this important work . . . which, defective and incorrect as it is, is now rarely to be met with, and at considerable price. The intended edition, given literally from the ORIGINAL MANUSCRIPT of Sir George Buck [*sic*], will be found to contain considerably more of interesting matter than the former one. Several omissions, which in the prior edition had occasioned some plausible cavils at his integrity as an historian, or obtained for him the character of a 'lover of paradoxes', are now fully rectified; and the imperfect marginal Notes of the printed copy, which had given rise to charges of misquotation, will be supplied by the original references to personal and oral testimony.[41]

1973 to the present

When I had completed my edition in 1973 I assumed that the 1646 version would never be used again, existing only in expensive antiquarian copies and rare book rooms of libraries. Even after its ill-advised reprinting (also in 1973), I naively thought the problems of misjudging Sir George Buc's work which it had caused for so long would be at an end. I felt I had shown clearly that the 1646 edition had so little to do with the original author's work as to be not just 'nearly worthless', as Marcham had said in 1925, but now completely so, since someone wishing to consult it no longer had to choose between trying to read the original manuscript with the difficulties it presented, being both in draft and in a damaged state, and settling for a badly edited, extremely sloppy and severely shortened late version.

I reckoned, though, without two factors: that the reprint, particularly one fronted with the name of an historian of repute, no matter how careless,

40 *Ibid.*, p. ix.
41 MS. Egerton 2218, f. 2.

perfunctory, and sometimes downright inaccurate his introduction, remained desirable because, worthless or not, it had the 'advantages' of being half as long, therefore much quicker to read, and was also noticeably cheaper. And finally my edition went out of print, though not before being lodged in university and research libraries worldwide. I next assumed that once the reprint sold out the ground would become more even, but then Amazon came into being. Though I tried for ten years to persuade them to make a clear distinction between my edition and the reprint of the 1646 *Life and Reigne*, they chose not to; and so, not unnaturally assuming them to be the same work, people chose to buy the cheaper version rather than my edition whose price went up absurdly the longer it was out of print. The result has been a great deal of confusion, even people who describe themselves as historians preferring to use the 1646 edition (or rather what they persist in calling the '1647 edition' – something that never existed – though there had at least been a correction in the Wing STC's 2nd edition of 1994).[42] Latterly people have the ease of being able to consult the worthless 1646 edition free on the web as well.

Charles Ross, in his *Richard III*, published in 1981, was the first major historian to use the original in my edition. He points out that

> Until recently, historians have had to rely upon a much truncated and spoilt version of his work published by his nephew [*sic*] . . . in 1646. Now . . . the elder Buck emerges as a more serious defender of Richard's reputation than had hitherto been thought, more careful in his use of sources and less haphazard in his method. . . . Although he remains an irritating author in some ways, crabbed in style, diffuse and prolix . . . his defence of Richard is not without its merits.[43]

He then goes on to mention the Elizabeth of York letter: 'Given the greater conscientiousness of documentation we now know to have been shown by the elder Buck in contrast with his nephew, it is hard to brush aside this circumstantial statement. Yet, since the letter has not been seen since, it is difficult to accept it'.[44]

Jeremy Potter, in 1983, discussing the Elizabeth of York letter, mentions that 'most historians have roundly denounced it as an invention of the deranged Sir George'[45] – an opinion which in fact I have not encountered. Potter is willing to state of Sir George 'it is apparent from Kincaid's edition of his History that he was a genuine scholar'.[46] He goes on to point out that traditionalists might assume the letter to be dictated by Elizabeth Woodville in hope of restoring her status, noting that 'the language of love is formal only'[47] (the first time this had been recognized in print, historical perspective at last being allowed to enter the picture). This, he goes on, makes sense of the resistance to the idea by Richard's

42 *A Short Title Catalogue of Books Printed in England, Scotland, Ireland, Wales and British America, 1614-1700*, compiled by Donald Wing, rev. and ed. by W.A. Jackson, et al., 2nd ed. (New York, 1994). Number 5306 under '[Buck, Sir George]' cites the 1646 edition of *The History of the Life and Reigne of Richard the Third* and number 5307 is given as '[Anr. Issue.] 1647'. This had previously appeared in the 1972 ed. by Wing as 'Second edition'.

43 Charles Ross, *Richard III* (London, 1981), pp. xlviiif.

44 *Ibid.*, p. lxix.

45 Jeremy Potter, *Good King Richard?* (London, 1983), p. 170.

46 *Ibid.*

47 *Ibid.*

northern supporters, who, because they enjoyed profits taken from the Woodvilles, resisted the possibility of their returning to power.

Nicholas Pronay and John Cox in the introduction to their edition of *The Crowland Chronicle* cite Buc as the first person to use the Chronicle, 'a product of that underworld which had grown up by the close of the Tudor period in reaction to the insistent and all-embracing propaganda . . . with which the Tudors sought to establish and legitimate their regime'. While finding the work tendentious, they recognize the author as 'a well-informed and researching historian by habit and a member of the circle of Elizabethan and Jacobean antiquarians and collectors of medieval manuscripts.'[48] They are critical of the 1646 edition, and appear to feel the edition of the original vindicates Sir George: 'As we now know, Buck was a much more serious student of records than he emerged from the pages of the edition which his much less able nephew [*sic*] had published from his . . . draft some twenty years later' (p. 4).

Among historians, D.R. Woolf has clearly read the whole work and the introduction carefully. When he comes to speak of the rehabilitation of Richard III in *The Idea of History in Early Stuart England* he finds Buc's achievement impressive, while feeling that he overstated his case. He calls his book

> one of the most original pieces of historical writing in the early seventeenth century. Through careful research, faultless documentation, and a skilful, lawyer-like erosion of the credibility of the architects of the Ricardian myth (especially Thomas More), Buck single-handedly carried out the first full-scale reappraisal of the king's reign in the history of English historiography.
>
> ....
>
> Unknown except in the pirated version, which makes a much weaker case, the *History* had little influence on later historians, but it is something of a milestone in seventeenth-century historiography nonetheless. Buck had assumed a radically innovative perspective on an important episode in English history, and from that position reordered and reshaped the evidence until it revealed an entirely different picture, while unravelling the arguments of his predecessors; furthermore, he searched beyond the official narrative sources to examine all the evidence related to his case.[49]

David Weil Baker, too, clearly read both the introduction and the text for his excellent article on the contribution made by the defence of Richard III to Jacobean support of Parliamentary authority (see above, p. xlviii for discussion of this).

On the other hand, Anthony Pollard, who attempts in *Richard III and the Princes in the Tower*[50] to achieve a balance between attack and defence of Richard, treats Buc slightingly, attributing to him a desire to portray, because his family

48 *The Crowland Chronicle Continuations*, 1459-1486, ed. Nicholas Pronay and John Cox ([Gloucester], 1986), Introduction, pp. 3-4.

49 *The Idea of History* (Toronto, 1990), pp. 128 and 132.

50 Stroud, 1991.

came from Yorkshire, a northern view of Richard III.[51] Just after mentioning Sir William Cornwallis by full name and title, he refers to Buc as simply 'George'. His one quotation from Buc is not quite accurate and in his two citations the page numbers are both incorrect. He fails to recognize Buc as significant for the sources he introduced to scholarship and basically dismisses him on the grounds that he 'does little more than deny allegations and assert that certain actions were justified by circumstances', an accusation that does not fairly represent Buc and could be much more accurately applied to Cornwallis. Keith Dockray, by contrast, describes Buc thus: 'a conscientious antiquarian-cum-historian who consulted a range of manuscripts including the Crowland Chronicle, produced the first comprehensive assault on Tudor tradition and concluded that the king's "good name and noble memory" had, indeed, been foully maligned'.[52]

In 2005 George M. Logan, a More scholar, recognized that Buc's work, the first serious defence of Richard III, 'was published (in debased form)' in 1646.[53] Annette Carson uses Buc's original extensively in *Richard III: The Maligned King* (editions 2008-2017), and fully discusses the Elizabeth of York letter.[54] She notes that earlier historians discounted *The History* 'as an unreliable source due to the interferences, errors and excisions of his great-nephew, which removed references to the original author's careful personal research'.[55] It is to be expected that defenders should find more use for it than historians who are not defenders, since Buc, not a primary source, is in the main superfluous to the latter.

Some years later, David Baldwin in his *Richard III* revisited the Elizabeth of York letter. He refrains from the accusatory tone which had become customary when considering its disappearance and refers to it matter-of-factly; he is clearly used to old documents: 'the letter has disappeared and Buck', whose work in my edition he curiously references as '*The History of the Reign of Richard the Third*' (a strange combination of the titles of the original and the 1646 edition) 'did not provide us with a full transcript'.[56] Baldwin accepts my suggestion (see below, note to p. 191/1-25) that if Buc's reading is accurately interpreted, Elizabeth Woodville may have seen this as a useful way of gaining back her family's lost power. However he rejects my alternative suggestion (below, note to p. 189/3-4) that it refers to Portuguese marriages contemplated for both Richard and Elizabeth, pointing out that Anne did not die until nearly a month later.[57] This neglects the blatant fact that Richard's first responsibility was to his kingdom, and with his wife apparently dying and without a son, he had no option but to consider an alternative consort. He made official overtures for the Portuguese marriages as early as 22 March,[58] nine days after Anne's death. For his embassy to be that quick it had to have been planned in advance, as the letter, if so interpreted, would suggest.

51 See below, General Notes, p. 240 for further mention of this observation.
52 *William Shakespeare, the Wars of the Roses and the Historians* (Stroud, 2002), p. 146.
53 George M. Logan, introduction to Thomas More, *The History of King Richard the Third* (Bloomington, 2005), p. xlix.
54 Annette Carson, *Richard III: The Maligned King* (Stroud, 2013), pp. 297-303.
55 *Ibid*, p. 347.
56 David Baldwin, *Richard III* (Stroud, 2012), p. 189.
57 Baldwin, p, 193. See above, pp. c-civ, cvi-cvii for discussion of this letter.
58 Barrie Williams, 'The Portuguese Connection and the Significance of 'the Holy Princess', *The Ricardian*, VI (1983), 141.

Michael Hicks used Buc as a sensible source in his article on the Second Crowland Chronicle continuation in 2007,[59] less sensibly in supporting his belief that Richard was a 'serial incestor', a belief which he keeps pounding heavily even in the face of all scholarly evidence to the contrary (see below, n. 18/19-24, and Appendix p. 360 for discussion of this). Anxious to show Richard had designs on his niece, he calls on Buc for support. He starts out with the usual attack on Buc's use of sources: 'Perhaps [the letter] never existed and was forged by . . . the pro-Ricardian Jacobean historian George Buck'.[60] It is unclear why he initially makes this suggestion, since he goes on to contradict it: 'Buck wrote for publication; surely he expected his reference to be pursued'. I never discovered any evidence of Buc's intention to publish (or not to publish) in many years of research, and maddeningly Hicks does not document his assertion. He goes on, 'Moreover it seems to have been overlooked that Buck not only acknowledged the earl's permission to consult the letter, but also dedicated his book to him', proceeding to state that Arundel should have been expected to know what was in his cabinet. He reads Elizabeth's words according to his own theory of Richard as a 'serial incestor', a term he invented and of which he is clearly fond: 'She fancied her uncle as well as wanting the crown', he insists (p. 200). Though Buc's version of the letter was an unclear paraphrase, this does not deter Hicks from making this reading, representing it as a statement of fact rather than an interpretation.

Very recently a book by Chris Skidmore has again considered the letter from Elizabeth of York, sensibly concluding that it sounds more as if she is speaking not of a marriage with Richard but of a marriage he was planning to arrange for her with someone else. But, having taken a step forward he then takes one back by ending the discussion with the comment, 'if the original did indeed exist', not giving his reason for apparently doubting that it did.[61]

It appeared for a while that scholars were tending to consult the original author's work as a matter of course in preference to his great-nephew's, a sensible thing to do, one would have thought, since the latter, completely discredited so long ago, is worthless. This was fortunate for Buc's reputation, as well as for Richard III and his defenders.

But then there is the strange case of John Ashdown-Hill, a professional historian with a clear preference for the 1646 edition, on which he persistently relies, always mis-citing it as published in 1647 – an error Ross, 30 years before, had avoided. In 'The Epitaph of King Richard III' Ashdown-Hill seems almost unaware of my edition and of anything involving the original author, clearly unconcerned about the massive difference between Sir George and his great-nephew and their respective books, often confusing the two. In *The Mythology of Richard III* (Stroud 2015) he is content to call the author of the 1646 edition 'Sir George Buck' and the reprint of this travesty appears in his bibliography under 'Myers, ed.', as if writing an extremely sloppy introduction qualifies one as an editor. What is mystifying is that earlier, in 2009, in *Eleanor, the Secret Queen* he

59 'The Second Anonymous Continuation of the Crowland Abbey Chronicle, 1455-86 Revisited', *EHR*, CXXII (2007), 349-70.

60 *Anne Neville* (Stroud, 2007), p. 199.

61 Chris Skidmore, *Richard III* (London, 2017), p. 322.

used Buc's work sensibly – but then very strangely claimed that his *History of King Richard the Third* was 'published in 1619'.[62] Wishful thinking, perhaps!

In his article mentioned above and his book *The Last Days of King Richard III and the Fate of His DNA* he discusses versions of Henry VII's epitaph for Richard (which are to be found in all four later versions of the *History* but entirely burnt away in the original), though he chooses completely to ignore the three manuscript copies, giving no reason. Also Emily Kearns, in a later article on the epitaph pursuant to Ashdown-Hill's,[63] chooses to use exclusively the 1646 edition (like him invariably referring to it as a '1647' edition) in preference to the earlier and more complete manuscript copies, one of which is conveniently situated in Oxford, where she works. Kearns even goes so far as to describe Sir George's original text as a 'version' of the '1647' edition![64] Ashdown-Hill insists that Sir George Buc (he is quite specific that he means Sir George)[65] was the author of a translation of this epitaph appearing in *The Complete History of England*, which I had assumed – see above, p. lxvi – was by its annotator, John Strype. He asserts it is attributed to Buc by John Nichols in the second edition of William Hutton's *Battle of Bosworth Field*.[66] Nichols in a footnote there cites it as coming from 'Buck's Richard III in *The Complete History of England*, vol. 1, p. 577'[67] – which clearly identifies this work as by *Mr* George Buck. Nowhere, not here or in his mention of it in *Antiquities of the County of Leicester*, does Nichols attribute this translation to anyone. Ashdown-Hill is the sole person ever to have made this – indeed any – attribution, but he never gives his reason for being so anxious to make it.[68]

Even in theatre history, where one would have thought accurate information regarding King James's Master of the Revels might have been *de rigueur*, interest in the 1646 edition rather than the work of the Master of the Revels in question holds sway. Though my edition of *The History of King Richard III* had come out over ten years before, Janet Clare refers to Buck's *History of the Life and Reigne of Richard III* as if it were Sir George's, saying it was 'significantly only published in 1646',[69] though she does not explain what she sees as significant about this. She claims he also wrote something called *The Ancientry of Buck,* of which I have never heard, but does not document her source for it. Richard Dutton's *Mastering the Revels* appeared the next year, a much better book. Dutton also ignores my edition entirely and refers to 'Buc's' *History of the Life and Reign* [sic] *of Richard III*, which he calls 'surprisingly sympathetic', giving no reason for the surprise, even though he, like Clare, has mentioned the (also sympathetic to Richard) *Daphnis Polystephanos* (this time Buc's version rather than his great-nephew's). A very recent book by W.R. Streitberger is alarming in its claim that *The History of the Life and Reigne of Richard the Third* is by 'Sir George Bucke'.[70] The

62 Ashdown-Hill, *Eleanor, the Secret Queen* (Stroud, 2009), p. 165.
63 'Richard III's Epitaph Revisited', *The Ricardian*, XXIV (2014), pp. 75-86.
64 *Ibid.*, p. 75.
65 See my article, 'Researching Richard III's Epitaph', *The Ricardian*, XXVII (2017), pp. 117-29.
66 P. 131. Ashdown-Hill states this on p. 45 of 'The Epitaph' and p. 165 in *The Last Days*.
67 John Nichols in William Hutton, *The Battle of Bosworth Field* (London 1813), p. 222.
68 I have dealt more thoroughly with this invention in my article cited in note 65 above.
69 Clare, p. 14.
70 *Masters of the Revels*, p. 214, n. 143. He cites only the 1973 reprint for the *History*.

spelling of the name is nearly as curious as the attribution of Buc's great-nephew's 'work' to him. It is a spelling Buc never uses, but Streitberger for some reason favours it, applying it in his index also to John and Robert, though not elsewhere to Sir George. Perhaps the reason for his nonchalance is that Sir George's book is irrelevant to his status as Master of the Revels (except, of course, in that its manuscript pages contain several Revels Office scraps). But it still seems surprising that a specialist on the Revels Office of the period, even though his primary interest in Edmund Tilney relegates Buc to a position of less interest, should not be more meticulous.

There is one example from abroad, Andreas Kalckhoff's *Richard III. Sein Leben und Seine Zeit* (Bergisch-Gladbach, 1980). As one of his sources he cites Sir George Buck, diplomat, soldier and 'Sunday poet' (erroneously claiming that he was Master of the Revels from 1603), who, he says, aware that the Tudor chronicles were unreliable, wrote *The History of the Life and Reigne of Richard III*, first published in 1646. He cites it in the 1973 reprint of the 1647 reissue. Thus in mentioning the Elizabeth of York letter he quotes it without 'body', which the 1646 edition omits. Since I know that several university libraries in the general vicinity of Bergisch Gladbach have a copy of my edition, this is a surprising choice. But Kalckoff does make one useful observation (p. 10): that Buc was the 'ancestor' of a considerable number of revisionists to come, including the Richard III Society.

The Oxford History Faculty Library purchased a copy of the 1973 reprint in 2002, presumably at the request of a tutor. Records are too scanty to trace the reason for the purchase. It has not been borrowed since 2010 so will be relegated to the stacks as soon as staff reach the section where it resides.[71]

Attempting to find out what guides the apparently overwhelming current preference for the 1646 version, I asked a student in a British university who had written an undergraduate research essay on Richard III and has since become a Ph.D. candidate. She said her choice came from lack of time and the fact that so many other people used it. It begins to be clear why, because it is now readily available on the web, where there has appeared (if one googles 'George Buck, History' and after calling it up clicks 'other versions') a proliferation of the 1646 edition in various formats, some reproduced by a cheap method that distorts and makes unreadable nearly every word. There are as well two new versions, for one of which (appearing in 2015) we are told that it is essentially the equivalent of a World Heritage Site: 'This work has been selected by scholars as being culturally important and is part of the knowledge base of civilization as we know it'. (One inevitably wonders about the 'scholars' who chose it.) There are six alternative versions of Buc/k listed by the Google site. Half of them, excluding mine, are cited as written by 'Sir George Buck'. The other half, *including mine*, are cited as written by 'George Buck'! Someone has commented as a 'review' of my edition, on the assumption that it is the 1646 version: 'Read the story of Richard III from the point of view of an author who wasn't speaking for the side that overthrew him. Shakespeare was impossibly biased; there is another side to the tale. The

71 My gratitude is due to Isabel Holowaty, Bodleian History Librarian for this information.

book is physically difficult to read due to the style of printing used in the 16th century, but it is worth the effort. This book is referenced in Josephine Tey's book, "The Daughter of Time".' There is not a vestige of awareness that my edition has *no* sixteenth-century printing in it but very clear modern print and that (unfortunately) Tey cannot have seen it, since she wrote years before it came out. This review is clearly intended to refer to Buck the Younger's *History of the Life and Reigne*.

To some extent this favouring of the 1646 edition is perhaps due to a reverence for old books. The blog of Chetham's Library in Manchester (http://chethamslibraryblogspot.co.uk)[72] for 13 February 2013 responds to the discovery of Richard's remains by citing what they call the two earliest defences of him, which are in their collection. These they cite as 'Sir George Buck's' *History of the Life and Reigne of Richard the Third* and Walpole's *Historic Doubts*, neglecting Cornwallis, of which presumably they have no copy. The Edward Worth Library in Dublin featured the *Life and Reigne* not long ago as their 'book of the month' because they had a copy of it.

The preference for the 1646 edition is something I cannot account for. I had naively assumed that scholars were trained, as I was, to seek the oldest, most reliable source. The 1646 edition has absolutely nothing to commend it. I grew up regarding literary theft as one of the greatest crimes. But whereas I run from anything that has a hint of plagiarism about it, other people choose this plagiarized 'work' with their eyes open, and the moral issue (especially, perhaps, with a pirated edition nearly four hundred years old) does not signify.

Possibly the preference for this book and its proliferation are part and parcel of the general attitude toward Richard III.[73] D.R. Woolf mentioned in 1990 that 'the editor of the nephew's diluted version could not fathom why anyone would *want* to defend Richard'.[74] Because nothing can be allowed to stand in the way of Richard's remaining a figure of evil, anyone attempting to defend him *must* be made to seem incompetent. The younger Buck's edition has so completely obscured the longer, more competent original – even now that it is available without the difficulties of trying to sort out the damaged manuscript – that the reputation of Sir George Buc is an easy sacrifice to make in supporting a general attitude to Richard as an archetypal villain: the 1646 edition is easy to dismiss, Sir George not so easy. So the outcome is that Sir George in trying to defend Richard's reputation essentially sacrificed his own, and there seems no interest in defending him – unless truth and accuracy matter. And it appears that fewer and fewer people now feel that they do.

72 Accessed 2017.
73 See below, Appendix, pp. 353-61.
74 *Idea of History*, p. 132. This reference is to John Hughes, who introduces George Buck the Younger's version of Buc's *History*. (There is no evidence of his editing it.)

VII. BUC'S METHODS, ATTITUDES, AND USE OF SOURCES IN THE *HISTORY*

Origin and Genre

Generically, Buc's *History of King Richard the Third* is related both to biography and to the paradoxical encomium, and it is divided into two halves of equal length along these lines of influence. Based on classical and contemporary Continental models, the biographical form in England took its impulse from national consciousness, which inspired antiquaries to search records for the sake of exalting the glories of England's past and England's great men, as the Protestant reformation led to the study of ecclesiastical figures. Donald A. Stauffer cites Buc's *History* as an example of 'biographies of historical figures in the past publishes [*sic* for '-ed'] as parallels and precedents for present political action'.[1] Whatever motives led to his writing the work,[2] this can be seen as in some measure influencing its composition. Buc's *History* enhances the purity and sanctity of kingship by attempting to clear the reputation of a defamed king. As a sideline Buc was making a statement for the authority of Parliament – another institution adding to England's greatness – by defending a king who received confirmation of his title from it. The defence of a maligned monarch would have engaged Buc's strong sense of justice and historical accuracy, and it would also have appealed to his philosophical awareness, for, as M.M. Reese says, 'in theory the Elizabethans believed that no one could be a good ruler who was not also a good man'.[3] Buc's activity as censor was at one with his life as historian: 'The manuscripts he has censored,' says Eccles, 'show curiously mingled his reverence for truth and for princes.'[4] This description could apply equally well to the *History*. And his incidental interest in play scripts, as Alan Nelson has shown more recently, parallels this quest for accuracy in doggedly searching out and recording factual details,[5] something which is also clear in his annotations to his copy of Godwin.

At least one other matter engaged Buc's interest in Richard III: his sense of his own personal worth and his 'interest in the quality gentle or noble' (text, pp. 116f). His ancestors, from whom he derived his status as a gentleman, were partisans of Richard III. Also, as A.J. Pollard points out,[6] many of Buc's ancestors were based, as was Richard III, in the north. The current passion for genealogy led the antiquary Buc to search his own family's past as well as his country's to prove

1 Donald A, Stauffer, *English Biography before 1700* (Cambridge, Mass., 1930), p. 229.
2 Discussed below and see above, pp. xlvii-xlix.
3 M.M. Reese, *The Cease of Majesty* (London, 1961), p. 101.
4 Eccles, 'Sir George Buc', p. 505.
5 See above, p. lix.
6 'North, South and Richard III', 352f.

it glorious and honourable. To do this he needed to exculpate the monarch in whose service his great-grandfather had lost his life.

The subject seems to have been in the air, ready for Buc to take hold of. Interest in the house of York as an extant entity had been aroused in Elizabeth's time, though it is uncertain how strongly or openly. *Leicester's Commonwealth,* a subversive tract widely circulated in manuscript in Queen Elizabeth's reign, makes clear that the Earl of Huntingdon, a friend of the Earl of Leicester and open competitor for the sceptre, based his claim on descent from the house of York, specifically from Clarence, and that Leicester was performing for Huntingdon the role of Warwick the Kingmaker. Comparisons were made with events of Richard's reign: the possibility of Leicester's marrying Queen Elizabeth when he was already married, and the myth of Richard's giving out that his wife was dead, after which she really did die, are mentioned in this connection. The current Hastings is considered likely to suffer his ancestor's fate. Huntingdon's supporters follow Richard III in debasing Edward IV's line as illegitimate to give his own derivation from Clarence precedence. Since this faction reopens the whole question of Lancaster and York, their history, including Richard's reign, is rehearsed in full.

Further interest in Richard III existed among a group of scholars also dedicated to supporting Parliament, with whom Buc shared both interests. These were the antiquary-historians Stow and Camden, whose works began, though very conservatively, to liberalize the view of Richard. Stow was, as we can see from Buc's *viva voce* references to him, making investigations which included interviews with people who had known Richard, and finding many of the charges against the former king unjustified. In his *Survey* he describes Richard's accession as an election, not a usurpation, and in his *Annales* he lists Richard's good works. Buc gives further information favourable to Richard which he acquired from Stow, who was clearly finding out more than he published.

Buc's friend Camden, beginning with his *Remaines* (1605) and more firmly in his *Britannia* from 1607 on, has to concede Richard's potential position among the best of kings, although he still claims he is among the worst of men. He describes the liberality, affability, wisdom, and justice he displayed as Protector, which persuaded everyone, especially lawyers, to petition him to be king. Camden, who took very tidy notes on the *Titulus Regius*, which are in B.L. MS. Titus F.VII, ff. 154^{v}-155^{v}, ultimately judges the marriage of Edward IV to Elizabeth Woodville invalid not because of the precontract but because it occurred without asking of the banns and without the nobility's consent. Thus, with Clarence's children debarred by attainder, Richard was legally heir to the crown. Camden still does not exonerate him of the various murder charges, but only of the great political charge of usurpation. There is no way of knowing how much of this enlightenment concerning Richard, whom Camden had in 1600 described as seizing the realm, is due to Buc's influence and how much Buc owes to Camden in this respect. We can perhaps guess that the influence was Buc's on Camden. The heralds, of whom Camden was one, and many of whom were Buc's friends, had a natural interest in Richard because he had incorporated their foundation, the College of Arms. They gave Buc considerable assistance in his antiquarian works.

Another focus of interest in Richard III found its first outlet in Sir William

Cornwallis's *Encomium of Richard III*, later versions of which tend to be entitled *A Brief Discourse in Praise of Richard III* or variants of this.[7] This interest seems to have existed among a group of literary men all of whom were aware of the existence of a pamphlet by Bishop Morton on which More's history was claimed to be based. This tract is mentioned by Sir John Harington in *The Metamorphosis of Ajax* (1596)[8] as well as by Buc, though there is no evidence that either actually read it. It is quite likely that Harington, like Buc, received his information from Sir Edward Hoby, his closest friend.[9] Hoby died in 1617, and Buc's *History* is dated 1619, but Buc had this information considerably earlier and gives documentary evidence in a statement – clearer than the one in the *History* – which he wrote in the margin of his copy of Godwin's *Catalogue*: 'This Morton wrote \in Latin/ the life of K.R.3, w*hi*ch goeth in S*ir* Th. Mores name – as S. Ed. Hoby saith & *tha*t S*ir* W. Rop*er* hath the originall'.[10] Buc's entries in his copy of Godwin were made between 1604 and 1611, most of them around 1607-9. Buc and Hoby were acquainted at least from 1596, when they were on the Cadiz expedition together.[11] A reference to a non-extant work of Hoby's, *Anatomia de Espagna* (text, p. 160), suggests that Buc remained close enough to Hoby to be among the readers of a work he must have circulated privately in manuscript.

Hoby was evidently so much impressed by the similarities between Morton's tract and More's *History* that he told both Harington and Buc that the two works were all but identical. The Ropers, heirs to both Morton and More, were certainly the likeliest possessors of such a tract. But their status as recusants may have made consultation of the work difficult. Although around 1609 Buc knew that Roper had the manuscript, in 1619 he can say only that he knows Roper had it 'lately', and since, as Myers would say, 'No one else has ever seen this document', it seems laudable that Buc has been so meticulous about it. He documents its existence and nature by citing someone who had seen it. He trusts Hoby's description so completely that he frequently documents something he has derived from More as emanating from 'Morton and More'. These references unfortunately have no significance in tracing the similarity of the Morton tract to More, since Buc is relying on someone else's word rather than on his own observation when he assumes their identity.

Cornwallis knew Harington and probably Hoby, and he could hardly have avoided knowing the Ropers, since the Cornwallises and Ropers, two of the most prominent recusant families, were neighbours and relations by marriage. Cornwallis therefore would probably have had an opportunity to know about and read the Morton pamphlet, assuming its existence. W. Gordon Zeeveld makes a

7 Cornwallis, *The Encomium of Richard the Third*, ed. A.N. Kincaid (London 1977).

8 Sir John Harington, *A New Discourse on a Stale Subject, Called The Metamorphosis of Ajax*, ed. Elizabeth Story Donno (London, 1962), p. 107f: 'the best, and best written part of all our Chronicles, in all mens opinions; is that of Richard the third, written as I have heard by Moorton, but as most suppose by that worthy, and uncorrupt Magistrate, Sir Thomas More'.

9 The associations among the persons involved with this tract are studied by Kincaid and Ramsden, Introduction to Cornwallis *Encomium*, pp. ii-iv. See also Kincaid, 'Sir Edward Hoby and "K. Richard": Shakespeare Play or Morton Tract?', *Notes and Queries*, XXVIII (1981), 124-6.

10 Buc's handwritten note in Bodleian copy of Godwin, p. 115.

11 In his account of the expedition Buc describes Hoby as carrying the Lord Admiral's ensign: Stow, *Annales*, 1601, sig. Pppp5^{v}.

case for Cornwallis's *Encomium* being a direct reply to the Morton tract, and believes the origin of the *Encomium* to be much earlier and Cornwallis only the reviser rather than the author, a theory against which I have argued elsewhere.[12]

But Cornwallis's authorship of the *Encomium* was not known to Buc, who did not use it in connection with the Morton tract. He was not even aware that it had been published, and invariably speaks of it as an anonymous manuscript in defence of Richard III. He refers to it several times, and the structure and argument of his last three books, particularly the beginning of Book III, depend heavily on it. Zeeveld suggests that the *Encomium* was written by a member of the Buc family.[13] He cannot have known how nearly accurate this suggestion was, for, though clearly they did not know each other, Buc and Cornwallis were in some sense related. Sir William Cornwallis was the son by his first wife of Sir Charles Cornwallis, whose second wife was descended from Buc's great-grandfather, Sir John Buck, who was executed and attainted for supporting Richard III at Bosworth. Buc, representing the Revels Office, and Cornwallis's father, Sir Charles, as lieger ambassador, were both on the expedition to Spain for ratifying the peace treaty in 1605 (see above, pp. xvii, xxii). There is an exchange of letters between them in which Sir Charles acknowledges their relationship, thanking Sir George for 'kinde Care of my poore wife yor kinswoman'.[14] The family relationship, though, did not extend to Sir William Cornwallis or to Buc's knowing that he had written the *Encomium*. Had he known, he could not have referred to the work as anonymous or to its author as a lawyer, for he calls him 'Anonymus juris peritus' [Anonymous expert in law]. Cornwallis was not a lawyer and Buc does not give his reason for assuming the author was one. Had he received the document from family sources, family pride as well as care in documentation would have led him to say so. He would also, if he had known the author, probably have known of the essay's publication in 1616. And if he had had private access to an earlier version, as Zeeveld argues, he would not have used – as he consistently does – one of the later versions which incorporates additions both by Cornwallis himself and by those who evidently took over the essay for their own political purposes.[15]

Cornwallis was, unlike Buc, a writer of paradoxes. His book of them was published in 1616, two years after his death.[16] He seems to have written this essay on Richard III as a serious refutation of the accusations against him and tried, with limited success, to fit it into paradoxical form. The concluding remark of the *Encomium*, which appears only in later versions of the work, 'yet for all this knowe I hold this but as a Paradoxe',[17] must be the basis of Buc's fear, expressed in his dedication, that his work might be taken for a paradox (text, p. 3). A paradox was a rhetorical device of classical origin whose purpose was to show off the orator's skill in choosing an absurd topic to defend and his expertise in defending

12 See W. Gordon Zeeveld, 'A Tudor Defense of Richard III', *PMLA*, LV (1940), 946-57; and Kincaid and Ramsden, Cornwallis *Encomium*.
13 Zeeveld, p. 957.
14 Quoted in Eccles, 'Sir George Buc', p. 453 from Harl. MS. 1875, f. 115f.
15 Kincaid and Ramsden, Cornwallis *Encomium*, pp. v-vii.
16 Sir William Cornwallis, *Essayes of Certaine Paradoxes*, London, 1616.
17 Cornwallis *Encomium*, p. 32.

it. Roger Bennett in his doctoral thesis on Cornwallis[18] cites praises of historical or mythological figures not generally considered praiseworthy as being among the oldest types of paradoxical encomium. Rosalie L. Colie in her study of paradoxes gives Cornwallis's *Encomium* as an example that fails because it does not 'surprise or dazzle by its incongruities',[19] for it strikes the reader as an all but serious defence. Instead of appearing skilful, many of its arguments give the impression of being sincere but lame efforts at exonerating Richard.

Buc in his last three books follows methods of Cornwallis's *Encomium*. After the first two books – a biography of Richard which, though digressive, is chronological – he spends three books taking up and replying one by one to accusations levelled by the chroniclers. In his second section of the *History* too he is extremely digressive, but in general outline he uses as his basic structure Cornwallis's technique of posing accusations and following them with refutations and/or comments. In Book III between pp. 127 and 137 we find Buc taking up in order similar to Cornwallis's the accusations regarding Richard's birth with teeth, his deformity, his mother's pangs, then the murders of Henry VI, Edward, Prince of Wales and Clarence. These accusations form groups in Cornwallis; they form groups also in Buc, who, however, arranges them within the groups in more strictly chronological order. Both Cornwallis and Buc pass on to Dr Shaw's sermon and Richard's charging his mother with adultery, and again Buc retains Cornwallis's grouping but reverses the order. Shortly thereafter, both take up the death of Edward IV's sons. As Buc follows the first half of Cornwallis's essay in Book III, he follows the second in Books IV and V. In Book IV he deals with the death of Queen Anne and Richard's reported intention to marry his niece. Both authors use the argument that he could have divorced his wife had he wished to be rid of her. The accusation of unjustly killing Colingbourne follows soon after. Book V deals with Richard's good qualities: his mercy and justice, his care for religion and for his people's safety, his eschewing of taxation, luxury, epicurism, and riot. Again Buc follows Cornwallis in general groupings but not in the precise order in which he takes up particular virtues.

In certain ideas Buc seems to have been influenced by Cornwallis: that Richard should have been less merciful and dealt more harshly with his enemies (Cornwallis mentions only Stanley and the Countess of Richmond; Buc expands the list considerably). That if Richard had won the battle his lasting fame would have been good. That Richard has been made infamous in pamphlets and plays. And that even if he did commit the crimes with which he is charged he is excused by reasons of state.

The debt is primarily structural. Buc expands and improves on Cornwallis in use of argument. He seems to have assimilated Cornwallis's technique of posing and answering accusations, and at times he uses in a very general way a similar argument as defence (as in the case of the divorce suggestion, cited above). But where both authors give examples to support their argument, Buc's are far more numerous and invariably different. And whereas Cornwallis's tendency is to accept the accusations against Richard as true and then argue that they are

18 R.E. Bennett, *The Life and Works of Sir William Cornwallis*, unpublished Ph.D. diss., Harvard, 1931, p. 342.
19 Rosalie L. Colie, *Paradoxia Epidemica* (Princeton, 1966), p. 8.

tolerable, Buc's in most cases is to try to prove the accusations untrue. By so doing he is not, as is Cornwallis, forced to produce ridiculous arguments proving crimes laudable. As a paradoxical essayist Cornwallis attempts to prove praiseworthy something that remains not praiseworthy, not to prove that unpraiseworthy facts are not facts at all, although he shows considerable ambivalence. Buc, though he adopts the accusation-followed-by-defence technique, does so with the purpose of proving the accusations false. Thus he avoids the danger he fears of his *History* being dismissed as a mere paradox. Whereas Cornwallis's arguments are intellectually ingenious, Buc's are carefully researched accumulations of evidence from a wide range of primary and secondary sources. This basis of scholarly research rather than intellectual dexterity makes his structure much looser; as of course do his tendency to digress and the scope which the length of his work allows for digression. Cornwallis, writing a short, tightly argued essay, could not afford this luxury.

Organization

Buc's organization is far from haphazard, and is not purposely rambling, as it may seem at first glance. The author sets out in the Advertisement to the Reader his plan of organization and the scope of his work. First he describes Richard's lineage, birth, youth, training, and private life; then he proceeds to his public life, his coronation and reign; and lastly he tries to redeem him from the slanders with which he has been taxed. He is conscious of a certain decorum or prescription in this organization, for he describes his following of Richard's early and private life with the story of his later public life as being 'as it ought according to method and due order'. His scope is 'to write this unhappy king's story faithfully and at large, and to plead his cause, and to answer and refell the many accusations and calumniations brought against him' (text, p. 8).

In the first two books he feels so dependent on chronology as to see a chronological interim between Richmond's first and second invasions which he must fill up. He interposes mention of certain events of Richard's reign and a discussion of Henry VII's claim, in case 'for lack of them there would be a silence here until we come to the second invasion of the Earl of Richmond' (text, p. 73). He feels the conflicting need to give background material on Henry VII so that his invasions may make sense in the context of Richard's story, while at the same time keeping this material in check, since it is not of central importance to him.

Book I ends with Richard at the height of his prosperity; Book II starts with the beginning of his downfall and the shift in Fortune's favour toward him. Buc makes this structure, influenced by the *de casibus* tradition, stronger as he revises it. The second book proceeds to Richard's death, and with the treatment of his body after death introduces the theme of calumny which will dominate the next three books. Although in the first book chronology now and again compels him to mention Richard's supposed crimes, he touches on these only briefly and says that he will reserve full discussion of them until he comes to the 'fit place' where he intends to clear Richard fully. When he begins his refutations, he prepares the way for them by discussing the unreliability of the sources which have so far dealt with Richard.

Buc's style differs considerably from what Camden propounds as his own ideal: 'Short Sentences I have seldom interlaced, nor adorn'd my Discourse with those nice Observations which the *Greeks* aptly term ΕΠΙΣΤΆΣΕΙΣ [resting places]. . . . Digressions I have avoided'.[20] Buc does use 'short sentences' (i.e., sententious remarks) to support his statements and ornament his work and is extremely digressive and repetitious. He follows the style of 'copia' or 'copy' (copiousness) of which many authors of his period were particularly fond.[21] He is aware of this tendency and defends it in his Advertisement to the Reader as 'a tacit persuasion to the reader or author to remember better, and better to mark the thing so repeated and its causes' (text, p. 7). He is aware also of his tendency to multiply evidence. In the section on Perkin Warbeck he allows that he has already given enough evidence to prove Perkin was the Duke of York, but though more is not needed, more is available, and 'according to the *ancient* principle, *abundans cautela non nocet*' [abundant caution doesn't hurt] (text, p. 160), he adds it. He sometimes allows his enthusiasms to get out of hand. His long genealogical digression on Hamelin Plantagenet has at best a tenuous connection with the subject under discussion, but his digression on Hamelin's false shield has not the slightest relevance in context, although it might be interesting testimony from one acquainted with heraldic practices and malpractices of the period. His long discourse in Book II on Hereward is relevant in his gratitude to his patron's family.

Buc contrasts himself with an author he criticizes by saying 'I am here rather prolix than brief' (text, p. 7). He is objecting, no doubt, to the annalistic style which gives information without explanation and thus considers it better in an historical work to say too much rather than too little. This does frequently prove a virtue, for Buc tends to heap up evidence rather than citing only one authority in support of his assertions, and by so doing he not only arrives at a clearer awareness of the relative reliability of his sources but often in his research uncovers new information which is an original contribution to his study. His digressiveness is annoying in itself, but interesting when he gives information, often firsthand, on sidelines of the story about which no other contemporary information is extant. His sentence structure, strung along with unvaried series after series, 'and' following 'and' with little subordination, is irritating.

Family Tradition

In the case of an author like Buc who has family associations to connect him with the cause of Richard III, we might wonder first of all whether he had access to any private family data which were not available to others. The answer is unquestionably that he did not. He did possess a few family traditions. One was that his great-grandfather was Controller of the House under Richard. In his manuscript he gives this as John Buck's office in a late addition in his own hand to a scribal page, qualifying it by the remark, 'as the tradition of \t/his family is' (Tiberius, f. 52). He must have begun to wonder at once about the accuracy of this tradition, for he crossed the reference out. His doubts probably arose from his research, when he found Sir Robert (whose name he gives erroneously as Thomas) Percy listed as

20 Camden, *The History . . . of England during the Whole Life and Reign of Elizabeth*, in *Complete History of England*, II, 362.
21 See Ross McDonald, *Shakespeare and the Arts of Language* (Oxford, 2001), pp. 27f.

Controller under Richard. But by the time he came to rewrite the page he had resolved the question, perhaps by guesswork, stating that Buck had succeeded Percy in the office. He cites family tradition in the testimony of his grandfather, who was brought up by the Earl of Surrey, about Surrey's adventures after Bosworth. Aside from this there is nothing.

The Howards, it seems, managed to preserve little more. A letter from Elizabeth of York to the Duke of Norfolk (though his interpretation of it is doubtful) is one of Buc's unique contributions to the study of Richard III. This is the single document Buc derived from the Howards. The extent to which family tradition later failed among the Howards to preserve Richard's memory is indicated by the following quotation, expressing gratitude for Richard's generosity but with a report of his actions which relies entirely upon the popular chronicles:

> Rycharde duke of Glocester, finding that so longe as his brother George of Clarence, stoode betweene him & the gole, he coulde not gette the prise . . . caused a certaine prophecie to be suggested to the kyng his elder brother, that G. shoulde one day were the crowne, not doubtinge but the king would rather look to Glocester, then George, aswell in respect of the sayd Dukes former trespasse, and alliance, with the house of Warwicke . . . as because the manner of these prophecies, hath beene rather to regarde the proper name then the dignity. I speake not this to quicken or reuiue the memory of king Rychards heinous fault, which in respecte of all the bountifull and princlye benefites bestowed vppon the family from whence I come, I could rather wish to be drowned in the blacke deepes, and folded vppe in the darke clowdes of obliuion for euer.[22]

This is by Henry Howard, Earl of Northampton (son of the poet Surrey) in 1583. Here family tradition has preserved only a strong sympathy and sense of gratitude, baffled by what had been written about Richard by the 'authorities'. Buc speaks of the Howards' gratitude to Richard in the dedication of his *History* to Thomas Howard, Earl of Arundel (text, p. 3). He possessed a similar sympathy, and it remained for him to approach the authorities critically and combat them with what evidence was available.

Sources

Buc's use of classical and religious works is both decorative and illustrative. His style seems to be very little influenced by classical examples, though of course in following the genre of biographical writing he is influenced by classical historians, as his numerous references show. Apart from this we see some specific influence in his rarely indulged tendency to invent speeches, a classical technique adopted by many other English historical writers who preceded him and were his contemporaries. Examples of Buc's enlarging on a small hint to create brief scenes and speeches can be seen in the conversation of Henry Tudor and Pierre Landois (text, p. 35) and in that of Alexander and Medius in one of the illustrative passages

22 Henry Howard, *A Defensatiue against the Poyson of Supposed Prophesies* (London, 1583), sigs. Hhiiiv – Hhiv.

(text, pp. 166f). He adds visual details to the scene in which Richard is petitioned to accept the crown and constructs speeches using More's phraseology where More's account is in indirect discourse. He adds to this scene a second attempt on Richard by Buckingham and a speech by the Lord Mayor. We may imagine from this tendency that he may have done something similar with the encounter between the Earl of Surrey and Henry VII: relying on his grandfather's report of the general facts and perhaps a few of Surrey's heroic utterances, he imagined the setting and the conversations as a rounded whole. At no point does he distort sense by taking creative liberties. What he does is essentially to convey factual information through direct discourse, rather as Paul Murray Kendall has done more recently and more regularly to create vividness and immediacy. Because Buc's work is so rambling these short scenes or speeches have effect only where they occur and not for the work as a whole.

Buc uses the Alexander and Medius scene, mentioned above, as a parallel to illustrate the case of Richard III, showing how persons in power make innocent men culpable by fastening on them false accusations. Similar anecdotes are drawn from Roman historians, Greek and Roman tragedians, and the Bible. Sententious comments, proverbs, apt quotations are taken from a number of classical, mediaeval and biblical authors. This sort of decorative and illustrative quotation is typical of prose writing in Buc's time. At school, pupils learnt texts from which they were supposed to 'gather the flowers', quotations useful in rhetoric. There existed numerous commonplace books, collections of useful quotations to assist authors and speakers. Erasmus, whose *Chiliades* is probably the most famous of these, gives reasons for their use: they strengthen and clarify the argument and they add ornament and elegance.[23] Buc seems to rely entirely on his memory for many of his rhetorical 'flowers', for he sometimes ascribes them to the wrong authors and changes words to synonyms, usually of the same quantities. He probably used a commonplace book when arraying a long series of quotations on a single subject as, for example, on tyranny at the beginning of Book V. I have not been able to locate a precise book from which he drew his casual quotations. Three collections he mentions seem no longer extant: *Anthologia Sacra*, *Sententiae Arabicae*, and *Axiomata Politica*. He does use and document Erasmus's *Chiliades*. Sometimes he gives, translated into Latin, a quotation that was originally in Greek, a habitual practice of the commonplace book. He drew on his legal background for legal maxims and had some knowledge of commentaries on the scriptures.

By far the greatest number of Buc's illustrative references and quotations comes from the Bible. Seneca is next, with half the references to tragedies, half to prose works. Then Vergil and Cicero, the former used largely for ornament, like Ovid, another author Buc quotes frequently, the latter often for political sentences. Plutarch, both *Lives* and *Moralia*, is used for long illustrative anecdotes, as is Suetonius, whose lives of the Roman emperors provide Buc with political parallels. Terence merits three citations, Plautus none at all. Euripides is the Greek dramatist Buc knows best, though he quotes once from Sophocles and once from

23 Desiderius Erasmus, *Proverbs or Adages*, trans. Richard Taverner, facsimile of 1569 edition, ed. De Witt T. Starnes (Gainesville, 1956), introd., p. viii.

Menander. Aristotle and Homer are the Greek non-dramatic authors with whom he seems most familiar, and he also draws a few references from Plato.

Among the authors he uses less often the largest number are historians: Ammianus, Quintus Curtius, Diodorus, Dion Cassius, Herodotus, Julius Capitolinus, Aelius Lampridius, Livy, Trebellius Pollio, Trogus Pompeius, Valerius Maximus, Velleius Paterculus and Flavius Vopiscus. Next come religious commentators: St Thomas Aquinas, St Augustine, John Chrysostom, Andreas Osiander, Philo, Strigelius and Zosimus. And finally legal authors: first Ulpian, then Vulteius and Prateius, all the legal references almost certainly from memory. Other classical authors who supplied Buc with one or more 'flowers' or anecdotes are Ausonius, Claudian, Demosthenes, Horace, Juvenal, Lucan, Lucretius (not documented), Lycurgus, Philostratus, Pliny, Polybius, pseudo-Quintilian (incorrectly documented as Seneca), Strabo, Suidas, and Publilius Syrus (referred to as 'the old Mimographus').

He uses more recent sources, Hector Boethius and George Buchanan, for early Scottish history. Continental references, Claude Paradin, Jean de la Haye and Gerard du Haillan, trace the genealogy of the Plantagenets abroad. Another small group of sources which Buc uses only once appear in his discussion of More: John Bale, John Foxe, Germain Brie, George Courinus, and Erasmus's letters.

His references to modern legal works are to Henry Bracton and William Staundford. Aside from these he relies on *viva voce* information from famous contemporary lawyers such as Coke. He uses Bishop Godwin's *Catalogue*, a relatively recent work of which he owned a copy, for ecclesiastical biography.

The continental side of the Yorkist and Tudor story he supplements by using continental sources, relying most heavily on Philippe de Commynes' *Memoirs*, Alain Bouchard's *Grandes Cronicques de Bretaigne* (his own copy), Johann Meyer's *Annales Flandriae*, Jean du Tillet's *Recueil des Roys*, and Monstrelet's *Chroniques*. For Spain he refers once each to Çurita, Garibay, Sir Edward Hoby's unpublished and non-extant *Anatomia de Espagna,* and a no longer extant work called *El Reusuerq*, to which he had also referred once in the *Commentary*. He occasionally glances at Froissart, demonstrating an easy familiarity with that author, and refers once to Guicciardini (for his own family history) and once to Jean de Serres (for Edward IV's death).

British topographical references are primarily to Camden, aside from the histories of mediaeval Britain already noted, and a few historical comments are drawn from Camden as well. For English genealogy he uses Glover. The sources on which Buc relies most heavily throughout, however, are the Tudor histories. One of his greatest contributions to the history of the period is his use of the Crowland Chronicle as a source. He would have been able to find the whole of this work, including all continuations, only in manuscript form. It is a valuable discovery in that it does not depend, as do all other available sources, on More or on Henry VII's official sources. Perhaps written by a member of Edward IV's Council,[24] it expresses the attitude of a southerner with a very strong anti-northern bias, politically opposed to Richard's accession, and becomes increasingly less

24 It was at one time thought that the author was Dr John Russell, Richard III's Chancellor, but this attribution is now discounted. See below General Notes for 24 /37 for more recent suggestions.

informative and reliable after his coronation, perhaps because its author or source was no longer constantly at court. Still, it represented more authoritatively than any other work then available the events preceding and to a great extent following Richard's accession. Buc may be said to have discovered this most valuable source for Ricardian history which he uses though it is unfavourable to Richard and biased against the north. He employs it frequently to add to the information of the Tudor chronicles, to substantiate them or to correct their bias. There are more references to it than to any other source except More.

More and Polydore Vergil are the Tudor writers on whom Buc most relies for the general story of Richard III and Henry VII. He often couples these with reference to other accounts derived from them: Grafton, Hall, Holinshed, and Stow, and he links Morton's name with More's assuming Morton to be More's source. Ivo Kamps in *Historiography and Ideology in Stuart Drama*, pp. 177f, points out that 'if these are what Buc had in mind when he mentions "the ancient and large histories" – and there is every indication that he does – then he, like his colleagues, is still with those whose "greatest authorities are built upon the notable foundation of hearsay"'.[25] This strikes me as a not particularly valid argument, since Buc is using them mainly for the general historical outline and in part to poke holes in their arguments on the basis of other sources he has discovered, as he does, for instance, in the case of 'Elizabeth Lucy' being cited by More rather than the historical figure Eleanor (Talbot) Butler as the woman to whom Edward IV was supposed to have been previously contracted. Otherwise he seems to use them mainly for the general historical outline, sometimes using other sources to contradict them.

How he kept up with contemporary material is shown in his use of Thomas Gainsford's *True and Wonderfull History of Perkin Warbeck*, published in 1618 (and also dedicated to Arundel). Other Tudor historians he uses are Fabyan (one reference), Rous (one reference through Stow's *viva voce* information), and André. The reference to André does not appear in the present edition because it occurs in a passage Buc deleted for fuller development later on, and in his later version he does not repeat the reference.

He received *viva voce* information from various antiquarian scholars. He cites Coke on a legal point. John, Baron Lumley, is cited for the description of the Countess of Salisbury's execution under Henry VIII. Arundel is witness that James I had been heard to deplore the execution of Edward, Earl of Warwick and is cited also for the amount of the fine imposed on the Earl of Oxford. The present Earl of Oxford told Buc how much he had been offered annually for use of a part of his lands. Baron Darcy is the *viva voce* source of information regarding Don Sebastian of Portugal. Sir Edward Hoby told Buc about the existence and nature of the Morton tract which was reputedly the basis of More's *Richard III*. Stow on several occasions is cited as imparting information existing in none of his published works from his independent enquiries about Richard III. Buc's grandfather has given him the story of Surrey's escape and pardon, and Buc himself was witness to the conversation between Don Duarte de Lancastro and

25 Cambridge, 1996, p. 177.

Charles Howard, Lord Admiral.

Considering the length of his work and that it exists in a rough state, Buc's accuracy is generally good, so long as we bear in mind that he felt free, in a way that we do not today, to paraphrase rather than to quote precisely. Despite the serious damage by fire to the margins of the manuscript, it is rare that his references cannot be located. I have failed to find the sources of some of the occasional Latin quotations which he uses for ornament and illustration, but I have found so many that any failure is as likely to be my fault as Buc's. Many, of course, are proverbial and their authors unknown. It is worth noting that the ones I have failed to trace are concentrated mostly toward the end of the book, where Buc's marginal documentation is completely destroyed and where the copies of Buc's work are most divergent from the original. Judging from the copies' habit of progressively omitting marginal documentation we may assume, from Buc's standard elsewhere, that most of the references which now appear undocumented were originally documented in the margins.

I have already discussed the use of antiquaries' collections and the general hazards to manuscripts residing in them (see above, pp. lvi-lviii), citing C.E. Wright's remark that it is not surprising so many manuscripts once known to have been in Cotton's collection are there no more. It is a constant surprise that twentieth- and twenty-first century historians are oblivious of what seems so obvious. Loss, borrowing, exchange, sale, division of property, re-cataloguing, fire, water, or activities of rodents and insects could cause a document to disappear. Many Cotton manuscripts which seem at first glance to be lost are actually still in the collection under a different number or bound in with another work. Under these circumstances it should not be a matter of amazement to the reader or of discredit to Buc that, of the huge number of sources he mentions, only nine – not counting commonplace books and collections of proverbs – cannot now be found. Of these fewer than half can be considered of material importance. It should of course be kept in mind that my failure to locate these sources does not prove that they do not exist or never did. Those I have been unable to locate are:

- a copy of a commission for truce and peace with Scotland, giving certain of Lord Howard's titles
- letters about truce and peace between Richard III and Charles VIII
- *El Reusuerq*, from which Buc derives a brief reference to Bona of Savoy's eventual marriage (he cited this work also in the *Commentary*)
- Sir Edward Hoby's manuscript history *La Anatomia de Espagna*, to which Buc makes one passing reference in a generalization about Spanish kings
- a list of sobriquets shown to Buc by Sir William Dethick, mentioned in a digression on the name 'Plantagenet'
- the letter from Elizabeth of York to the Duke of Norfolk seeking support for her marriage, which was during Buc's time in Arundel's collection
- the tract by Morton which is reputedly a source of More's history, not seen by Buc but by Sir Edward Hoby, who reported its whereabouts
- 'an old manuscript book' from which Buc derives a reference to a plot by Morton and 'a certain countess' to poison the sons of Edward IV

– a 'chronicle manuscript in quarto' in Cotton's collection, to which Buc makes six brief references, usually to material that can easily be found elsewhere (possibly this is the same work as the 'old manuscript book' just mentioned)

That so few of his sources have been lost through fire, lending, and the destruction of his own marginal references cannot be considered evidence that Buc is a slipshod or irresponsible author, especially bearing in mind the work's unfinished state. It is not sufficient warrant for A.R. Myers's implication[26] that, since Buc is occasionally careless, his testimony in the very few instances where the source cannot be traced nearly 400 years later is automatically unreliable. Nor does it justify Myers's curious and repeated assertions that 'no one else has ever seen' some of Buc's sources, a statement subject to disproof, never to proof. I have managed to disprove it in most instances by finding these sources, for some (or perhaps all) of which – observing his clanger about the reference to Camden – it appears Myers did not take the trouble to look.[27] Of those few of Buc's sources that I have not seen, we may assume that Cotton himself and others of his readers certainly saw the manuscript chronicle in quarto in his collection to which Buc refers six times, about which Myers specifically says, 'No one else has ever seen this document',[28] prejudicing his statement by failing to cite Buc's marginal note which gives the work's location.

All other items to which Buc refers as being in Cotton's library can still be found there, with the exception of *Axiomata Politica*, whose existence is plainly recorded in the Cotton borrowing list, which designates it as a quarto. It was lent to Mr (Auditor) Povey (Harl. 6018, f. 156^{v}), who passed it on to a Dr Hickman. The record of borrowing is not crossed out, suggesting that it was not returned, and this may well account for its not being able to be found today. The Editor found in one of Buc's citations of it a specific reference, 'cap. 129', which, though now lost from Tiberius E.X, appears in all the copies. To assume that the manuscript history, the only one of the many works Buc cites from the Cotton collection which has been lost without sufficient identifying trace to prove its existence at one time was an invention of Buc's is simply perverse, particularly when information derived from this document is rarely of great importance. On one occasion Fabyan is cited in conjunction with it as supplying the same information. Fabyan, an extant work, can be checked, and this particular reference (text, p. 52) proves to be correct. Several manuscript chronicles covering this period were lost in the 1731 fire in the Cotton library in which Tiberius E.X was damaged (see pp. lvii, cliv). Catalogue descriptions are insufficient to identify the one (or ones) Buc used.

The commission for Scotland still exists in several copies, but none gives as many of Howard's titles as Buc's sources did. The precise copy to which Buc refers was at the time, he says, extant in the Rolls and the letters about the French peace were extant in the Exchequer. He states that he has seen them, and his citing their whereabouts indicates that he is attempting to aid others in seeing them (see text, pp. 46f and 58), in view of which an assumption that he invented them is

26 Myers, 'Richard III and Historical Tradition', p. 186.
27 See above, pp. cx-cxi.
28 Myers, *ibid.*, p. 187.

even more perverse. Bearing in mind our use of footnotes today for precisely the same purpose, it should not take a great stretch of imagination to grasp that internal references and marginal notes (equivalent to our footnotes) served this same purpose in an earlier age.

Dethick saw the list of sobriquets (text, pp. 11-12), for he owned them and showed them to Buc. The Morton tract Buc never claims to have seen, but he refers to a reliable person who has seen it and who told other people he had seen it (see above p. cxxii), and if this reference appears for some reason questionable in the *History*, we should note that Buc has recorded it elsewhere with greater detail and clarity when it was obviously fresher in his mind about ten years earlier, in the margin of a book in his private library (see above, p. cxxii). By the time he mentions it again in the *History*, the exchange is far enough in the past for him to qualify its location with 'lately', since he does not know that its whereabouts are still the same. Buc refers to *La Anatomia de Espagna* on the assumption that some of his readers have seen it: '*he who hath read* [italics mine] the book of Sir Edward Hoby entitled *La Anatomia de* [*Espagna*] . . .' (text, p. 160). Sir Edward had died in 1617.

Arundel, the dedicatee of the *History*, showed Buc the letter from Elizabeth of York, so obviously, despite Myers's claim that 'no one else has ever seen this document',[29] Arundel saw it himself and must have called it to Buc's attention. There is no reason to doubt the existence at one time of this letter. If it were not available at the time in the place where Buc said it was to be found, he would not have documented it as being there, for cooperation in sharing information was one of the hallmarks of antiquarianism, and there is no reason for Buc, contrary to his usual practice of giving very explicit documentation according to the standards which the Society of Antiquaries attempted to foster, to have falsified it, misleading his readers rather than trying as was his custom and, indeed, purpose, to lead them (he was, after all, trying to convince them of something). The whole point of documentation is to make it possible for readers to find a document should they wish, to check the information given by the author. Such a fabrication would have been pointless here, since the letter is of no great importance to Buc's case in this section: his main subject at this point is Richard's disposition to the marriage, not Elizabeth's. And his main interest in using it, as is clear from his multitude of revisions of this specific subject (see Plates II-III), was to compliment his patron. He was bound to be particularly careful in this citation, since the owner of the document was the dedicatee of the work in which he cites it.

That the letter cannot be traced is not extraordinary, for much of Arundel's collection, which had been split up on his death in 1646 because of family feuding, was given away or sold by Henry Howard, sixth Duke of Norfolk. Naworth Castle, where certain of the Howard treasures were preserved, was burnt in 1844, along with many of the treasures it contained. Numerous of these are, however, still in the possession of the various branches of the Howard family. It may still have been available in 1750 when Carte speaks of it as 'preserved in the Arundel collection'[30] without citing Buc/k as his source, as he normally does in the case of

29 *ibid.*, p. 186.
30 Carte, II, 815.

information found in no other place. Henry Howard of Corby, 'who had access to many secret sources of information respecting his house',[31] says: 'there is no reason to doubt his [Buc's] veracity in what must then have been so easily contradicted. I think it very possible that this letter, if sought among the mass of papers at Norfolk House, may still cast up'.[32] The archivist of Arundel Castle gave me a similar response in the early 1970s. Scholars studying the family have expressed frustration at not being allowed to explore the Howard papers.[33] Buc's dedicatee, himself a scholar, collector, and descendant of the recipient, must have been convinced of the letter's authenticity. He would not otherwise have shown it to Buc as historical evidence.

Still unaccounted for are *El Reusuerq*, to which Buc also made reference in the *Commentary*, a completed work in fair copy, and 'an old manuscript book' which said that 'Morton and a certain countess, [conspirin]g the deaths of the sons of King Edward and some other, resolved that <these treach>eries should be executed by poison and by sorcery' (text, p. 163). For this last no documentation remains, which is not to say none existed in Buc's manuscript before it was damaged.

That Buc is consistently concerned that others should be able to locate his sources has already been seen (above, p. xci) in his reassurance concerning the charter of the College of Arms which was no longer to be found in the College itself, where a reader might naturally look for it. In other cases he refers as specifically as possible to the present whereabouts of a document: he states that a particular manuscript is *now* in the hands of Cotton, or in the case of the Morton tract *was lately* in the hands of Mr Roper. When he has been unable to view a primary source, he makes this clear and gives the word of a reliable colleague as the best alternative documentation. This form of second-hand reference by report, to document a work the author has not himself seen, was usual and acceptable in his scholarly milieu. Buc also used it in a published work, *The Third Universitie* (see above, pp. xxxiv, liv). Description of the circumstances in which information was obtained figures as an important part of documentation. It may be partly pride of his acquaintance that has led Buc to describe the Earl of Oxford's visiting him at his Hampton Court lodgings and there telling him about the value of his lands. But the circumstantial detail also serves to support the veracity of his information.

Buc's documentation is copious and painstaking for a period when documentation was still in its early stages, and again we must note that this work remains in an unfinished state. At the beginning, in the Dedication and Advertisement to the Reader, he comments on his method, saying that he has followed other authors, 'And because I follow other men, I cite their names and their authorities either in the text or in the margent, and it maketh more for the credit of the story' (text, p. 4). Later he attacks a particular author for 'neglect of citation of authors and quotations, thus concealing their names and vainly taking all upon himself'. He himself, on the other hand, claims, 'I cite mine authors everywhere' (text, p. 7). That his margins were burnt after his death, thus losing a

31 Gerald Brenan and Edward Phillips Stratham, *The House of Howard* (London, 1907), I, 50n.

32 Howard, *Indications of Memorials ... of the Howard Family* (Corby Castle, 1854), 'Memorials', p. 20n.

33 Melvin J. Tucker, *The Life of Thomas Howard, Earl of Surrey and Second Duke of Norfolk, 1444-1524*, (London, 1964), p. 42.

great deal of his documentation (permanently when the Editor or his scribe failed or decided not to reproduce it) is not his fault.

One of the reviews of my earlier edition of Buc criticized my favourable assessment of his documentation on the basis of its not coming up to the standard of Wood or Dugdale. There are, however, things this reviewer apparently did not consider which need always to be kept in mind: (1) Cotton Tiberius E.X is not a finished work but was still in process of revision when Buc left it; (2) standards changed over time. Wood and Dugdale were later scholars, Dugdale born around 45 years after Buc, Wood around 75 years. It would also be a mistake to impugn Buc's accuracy on the basis of failure to quote his authors word for word according to our standard practice of four centuries later. As E.E. Reynolds says, 'Our strict rules of transcription were unknown in the sixteenth century and for long afterwards'.[34]

Buc's references are generally accurate in terms of sense, but he takes the liberty of introducing synonyms, of paraphrasing, of omitting words and passages, of making corrections, of changing from direct to indirect discourse or *vice versa*, and of adapting the style or grammatical construction to fit his context. He admits to making corrections where his sources 'write false and incongruous English' (text, p. 179). Quhitlaw's speech (text, pp. 205f) is improved by omission of digressive material, some transposition, and grammatical corrections, but there is no change in basic content. On the other hand, the commission to Ralph Ashton as High Constable (text, pp. 55f) differs almost not at all from the version that appears in Rymer's *Foedera*. Herd's poem (text, pp. 50f, 84, and 105) is followed extremely closely, and the longest quotation from it is on a separate sheet pasted in, suggesting that Buc either had it copied or copied it carefully himself from the manuscript. But he has made improvements, filling in an incomplete first line and introducing an emendation for an illegible section.

It must be noted that when Buc feels strongly about a subject he sometimes makes omissions or interpretations which distort sense. An example of his actually slanting an argument occurs when he cites Coggeshall, Westminster, Wendover, Walsingham and Paris as witnesses of his ancestor Walter Buck's worthiness (text, p. 115). In fact, all these references are unfavourable and use Walter Buck's activities to illustrate the destructiveness and violence of King John's foreign mercenaries. This happens too when he makes alterations in passages concerning Richard III. When Camden says that Richard would have been worthy to reign had he not obtained the throne by criminal means and to have been numbered among bad men but good princes, Buc alters the verb to say that Richard *was* worthy to reign and omits mention of devious means and of his being among the worst of men (text, p. 46). In a reference to Johann Meyer, he neglects to mention Meyer's statement that Gloucester was the owner of the sword that killed Henry VI (text, p. 134). It is possible to comment on these distortions because they refer to works Buc used in print. But in the case of the Crowland Chronicle we cannot so securely make such judgements, for Buc used a manuscript no longer extant. So when he uses the verb 'immisit' where Fulman's printed text says 'intrusit', to

34 Reynolds, Trial of St Thomas More, p. 1.

refer to Richard's taking the seat in Westminster Hall (p. 46), where he omits 'violenti' in the passage noted by Strype and adopted from him without acknowledgement by Myers (see above, p. cx), we do not know what the manuscript he consulted said. (In the latter case this section of the passage is burnt away in Buc's original, so we have no proof of what it said, and so, properly, it should not be cited as an illustration.) In other cases too there are examples apparently of his attempting to soften the attitude to Richard, where these might equally reflect a difference between manuscripts. Richard's epitaph, found in a manuscript book in the Guildhall, is quoted 'the faults and corruptions being amended' (text, p. 217). Comparing it to Sandford's version of this epitaph, one finds changes of some words uncomplimentary to Richard (see General Notes 217/33-218/7). Particular caution must be observed with regard to this epitaph, not only because of the difference in sources but because, since Buc's original manuscript is entirely burnt away at the end, the only representations we have of it are in the manuscript copies made for his great-nephew and in George Buck Esq.'s printed edition. There is consequently no proof that these pages were in Buc's original work, though we may surmise they were.

Considering the size and unfinished state of his work, Buc's inaccuracies are not numerous and rarely serious when considered separately, though taken together they clearly improve the view of Richard which some of his sources provide. This he would probably have regarded as justifiable, since the view of Richard as handed down by historians had clearly been warped in the other direction, which means that he is uncovering the truth by removing the effects of hostile propaganda. Small errors are clearly careless. Concerning the house of Burgundy Buc tends toward error because he is working from memory. He once calls Margaret of Burgundy Richard's aunt rather than his sister, and on two occasions he refers to Charles of Burgundy as active in situations which occurred after his death.[35] Like Shakespeare he erroneously makes Peter and Edward Courtenay brothers (p. 100). The errors about Richard's early military career, giving him an active part in battles that occurred in his infancy (another error Shakespeare shares), probably have their basis partly in mistaken recollection, partly in the miscalculation of Richard's birth date. Buc cannot be blamed for this latter error because there was no objective evidence available at the time, so he was forced to conjecture. His methods of conjecture, though producing an incorrect result, are judicious and intelligent. When Buc is in doubt he checks and makes corrections, and when in the process of revision he discovers a mistake, he changes it. For example, on f. 38 in the original manuscript he attributes to the Crowland Chronicle information on Sir Thomas Stanley's part in Richard's Scottish campaign. But on more careful consideration of the source, he discovers that although it does mention the recovery of Berwick, the Chronicle does not mention Stanley's part in it, so he crosses out the attribution.

He sometimes falls into a trap by taking one source as authority and searching no farther. One such occasion is his reference to Banister, who betrayed the traitor Buckingham to Richard (text, p. 65). Buc relies on Hall for his information about

35 See Strype in *Complete History of England*, I, 553.

Banister, but Hall's account is inaccurate. The greatest danger occurs when Buc assumes the accuracy of a document because it is old and in manuscript. In these cases he has not, as with printed sources, much basis for critical appraisal. He often has no way of telling how much of the information he takes from old manuscript chronicles is hearsay. But though his practice with original documents is imperfect, his using them at all is an advance in historical writing of this period. He uses *Titulus Regius* to support the justice of Richard's title, to set forth the circumstances leading to his assumption of the throne, and to correct the chroniclers' references to 'Elizabeth Lucy'. He uses it also, however, in an attempt to prove Richard's nephews were still alive early in 1484, neglecting to observe that what he is reading is a petition of the previous summer which has been bodily incorporated in the business of Richard's first Parliament. And he takes the *Titulus Regius* at face value because, passed by Parliament, it has the status of a legal document, not pausing to consider that political machinations might have affected it. Buc's palaeography is good, though sometimes in manuscripts he misreads names which are not very legible.

Buc is seldom guilty of wildly absurd reasoning, and never in connection with his main theme. The wildest is his derivation of the Howards. He is anxious to prove them descendants of Hereward – a notion with which for some generations they flattered themselves. He is so eager to share in the flattery to his patrons that he must postulate Hereward's having had illegitimate male descendants, since he can find recorded only the existence of a daughter. He says that Hereward's having had illegitimate children is probable because he was noted for physical strength and hardihood and then goes on to give examples of great men descended from bastards (including Jesus Christ) to prove to the Howards that this conjectural descent is no shame to them. He finishes by saying he is sure that if Hereward's arms could be found they would be seen to be the same as the Howards'.

Buc's documentation from memory is sometimes faulty. In his discussion of the name Plantagenet he cites several sources to indicate that it was used prior to the time of the Yorkists. He thinks he has documented this assumption adequately, but only one of his sources – Glover – contains the frequent mention of the name which he claims for four other sources as well. His memory sometimes fails him in the use of More and his followers, because he knows that Hall, Grafton, Holinshed, and Stow have copied More into their works but does not keep careful track of where the portions derived from More begin and end, so that sometimes we find him ascribing to More, along with Hall, Grafton, Holinshed, and Stow, information which is invention by Hall or matter translated by the later chronicles from Polydore Vergil.

Antiquarian Methods

In methods of research, Buc seems most influenced by 'honest John Stow, who could not flatter and speak dishonestly'. In his own tireless researches, Stow, 'a man very diligent and much inquisitive to uncover all things concerning the affairs or works or persons of princes' (text, p. 129) had been finding out things about Richard III. And Buc, whose *Daphnis* was published in 1605, the year Stow died (and which took a charitable view of Richard), had questioned Stow about what he had discovered. Buc knew him as a 'good antiquary and diligent searcher [of] knowledge of the obscure and <hi>dden things appertaining to our story' (text, p. 173), and Stow's collections, now in the British Library, contain a number of tracts and histories of Richard's time. So it was from him that Buc sought the most authoritative opinion about Richard's alleged deformity and about the reputed murder of his nephews (see text, pp. 129 and 173). It is fortunate for our knowledge of Stow that we have Buc's report of his opinions on these matters, for Stow does not make use of them himself. In his *Annales* he describes Richard's accession as an election rather than a usurpation, yet he refers the reader to More's account of his reign, which he prints in his own history. Still he was, at the time Buc began considering Richard, the authority who had gone farthest in original research on him. Stow was 'apparently the first to recover from the fascination' of More, said A.F. Pollard,[36] who attributes this to the form of the *Annales*, which relied on research into documents as well as on accepted authorities.

Buc seems to follow Stow's methods, in which – though F. Smith Fussner points out that they were not original but those required by the Society of Antiquaries[37] – there was not a more exemplary practitioner to serve as a model. Edmond Howes, Stow's literary executor, describes him thus:

> his sight and memory, very good, very sober, mild, and courteous to any that required his instructions and retained the true vse of all his sences, vnto the day of his death, being of an excelent memory, he alwaies protested neuer to haue writt*en* any thing, either for malice, feare, or favour, nor to seeke his owne particular gaine, or vaine glory, and that his only paines and care was to write truth . . .[38]

The feud with Grafton into which Stow was pressed was founded on and brought into prominence the importance of documentation and critical examination of sources. His collecting from various sources unprinted as well as printed material proves his awareness of the necessity for acquiring evidence and judging its accuracy by comparison. His careful observation and collection must be attributed to his own zeal and acuity, not solely to externally imposed standards. He helped to form these standards, and it was in them that Buc grew.

By his tendency to discuss matters about which there was current disagreement among antiquaries, Buc gives us a view of the sorts of subjects they were considering and how they went about attempting to resolve them. An example of this is his discussion of the origin of the surname Plantagenet, about which there were conflicting opinions. After having 'read and searched many books and perused many written monuments', he went to his friends 'learned in heraldry and in history'. Sir William Dethick showed him an old manuscript book on sobriquets, tracing in them the practice of penance. One penitent, an earl of Anjou, took the name Plantagenet. Buc seems to assume this is true not only because the book told him so, but also because there existed an oral tradition to that effect.

36 A.F. Pollard, 'The Making of Sir Thomas More's *Richard III*', in *Historical Essays in Honour of James Tait* (Manchester, 1933), p. 228.
37 Fussner, p. 223.
38 Edmond Howes, in his continuation of Stow (1615), sig. Yyyv.

However, English and French antiquaries had been unable to identify the particular earl. Buc disagrees with those who identify him with Geoffrey of Anjou and gives brief details of Geoffrey's career to prove him unsuitable. He fastens on Fulke, whose history he sets down, using French antiquarian sources. Having proved this earl a penitent, he discusses the nature of the plants and soil around Jerusalem, according to Fuchs, Pliny, and Strabo, to establish the likelihood of the use of a broom plant as an instrument of penance. Buc's conclusions may be incorrect, and the length of this disquisition tedious, but his methods are at least thorough.

Legal argumentation is brought to bear on the question of Henry VII's right to the throne. Again Buc starts from a controversy: whether the Somersets or Beauforts were of the house of Lancaster. He first discusses the families' history, then their legitimation, of which he exhibits the charters of Richard II and Pope Urban. He then considers whether or not legitimation granted the use of royal names and right to the throne. He presents evidence to contradict the genealogists' citation of Hamelin Plantagenet for use of the royal surname by illegitimate children. He discusses the opinions of legal scholars on the Pope's ability to make bastards capable of inheritance, citing *viva voce* evidence from Coke. He counters the argument that the term 'principatus' cannot be taken as an equivalent of 'regnum'. In support of the arguments that the charter was meaningless because Richard II was a reckless king, he refers to the charter of entail which he has seen in the Cotton collection and from which he has 'transcribed these summary notes' (text, p. 81). Buc evidently had not seen Henry IV's interlineation in the patent rolls of the Beauforts' legitimation document, saying they could be admitted to dignities 'excepta dignitate regalis' [except the crown], yet his conclusion is that the Beauforts had no right to the crown before Henry VII became king, and by his sovereign power took all royal titles to himself.

Critical Approach to Sources

Buc has a clear idea of historiographical principles and practice and seems generally to echo the standards Howe attributes to Stow above. His intent in attempting to clear Richard's name is, he says, to make truth emerge:

> . . . the historiographer must be ve[ritable and free from all pro]sopolepsies and partial respects. He <must not a>dd nor omit anything, either of partiality or of hatred. [All which I have endeavoured to observe in] the writing of this story, so that [if my authors be sincere and faithful, my Muse is pure and innocent. For I have imitated the sceptic philosophers,] who of themselves affirmed nothing, but liked the doctrine of the other more renowned and more learned philosophers. <For that> which is said and related in this history is the <true testimony of> honest and faithful writers of former times.
>
> (text, p. 4)

His tendency is to rely for the general thread of his argument on specific main sources, well known histories, using them according to the extent of their completeness and authority for the period or circumstances he is discussing. This involves the exercise of critical acuity, which allows him to follow the common histories 'so long as they err not in the ma<tt>er . . .' (text, p. 179). In details of Henry VII's early years and invasions of England, Polydore Vergil is Buc's basic source. Polydore was Henry's official historian and must have had this particular information from Henry himself. Historians have continued to use him as the basis for discussions of this part of Henry's life.[39] As his main source for events (though not for interpretation of them) from Edward IV's death to Richard's accession, Buc uses More, who he assumed had his information from Morton, a participant in these events.

Buc supports, adds, and fills in with other sources which have a prime claim to authority. He fills in the sections which use Polydore as main source by referring to Commynes, useful because he was in France, moved in high circles, and knew Henry VII. The English sections are backed up and filled in by references to the Crowland Chronicle, also apparently derived from a person in high office during the events the *History* covers. His bolstering More or Polydore by citing the numerous chroniclers who include these authors' narratives in their own is generally meaningless, except insofar as it may be said that the chroniclers who copy others add authority to the original accounts by copying them.

Aside from his main references and supporting references, he uses subsidiary ones to add and confirm details. For matters concerning France he uses Tillet, Meyer, and particularly Bouchard, in addition to the sources already cited. He occasionally brings in Stow and other English chroniclers for dates, and Glover for genealogical excursions. For matters concerning England, he derives considerable support from legal, ecclesiastical, and heraldic manuscript sources. He has done research in the Tower Records, the College of Arms, and the Rolls, and from the last he gives details of various Parliaments, particularly that of Richard III and the first Parliament of Henry VII. He had access to material in the College of Arms through the help of his herald friends, whom he thanks at the beginning of the work. Someone, probably one of the heralds, has copied out for him the commission for the Vice Constableship. He uses a few memorials: the inscription on Surrey's tomb at Thetford and the inscription on the Stone of Scone.

Most of Buc's manuscript sources for the *History* are in Cotton's collection, though he once cites Lord William Howard, of whose private collection he had made use in the *Commentary*, and he once cites a document owned by the Earl of Arundel. The Herd poem, the anonymous manuscript chronicle mentioned six times, the Benedictine history he cites in error as Ailred, the book of St Stephen's, Caen, the list of Richard's officers, many of Richard's foreign treaties, the Bull of Pope Urban for the legitimation of the Beauforts, the charter for entailing the crown on Henry IV's sons, the Bull of Pope Innocent consolidating Henry VII's titles, the charter showing the Buck family's participation in founding Bridlington Abbey, Quhitlaw's speech, and the Crowland Chronicle all come from Cotton's library. Harl. 6018, Cotton's borrowing register, records loans to Buc of a Calendar of Papal Bulls in the Treasury, a Collection of the Cinq Ports, Liber Wigornensis, Radulphus de Coggeshall, and Roger Wendover (ff. 160, 173, and 174^{v}).

His treatment of More is most complex. Buc has perceived about More

39 See S.B. Chrimes, *Henry VII* (London, 1972), p. 19.

something no one had noted before: More writes ironically, and if the irony is ignored and his statements taken seriously, we have a picture of Richard as a good man and a good king which accords with more objective records of his life and reign. Although well aware of More's irony (More 'useth so much to speak ironically and in jest', text, p. 132), Buc generally ignores it in his use of More's statements and habitually quotes him as if he wrote in all seriousness. For example, when More says that the Protector was so much moved with the words of Buckingham persuading him to the crown that 'else as euery man may witte, would neuer of likelyhood haue inclyned to the suit',[40] he means the opposite: he speaks with a knowing sneer. Buc ignores the sneer. In discarding More's stylistic overlay of irony, Buc attempts to uncover the basis of information on which More's *Richard* is founded. Buc quotes More to give favourable evidence when More in context meant to indicate by his quotation of a good sentiment in Richard's mouth the extent of Richard's dissimulation. The facts remain stable; only the interpretation varies, as Buc demonstrates. More chooses to attribute to these facts vicious motives, Buc to apply charity. Any good deed, he says, may be depraved by a foul interpretation (text, p. 127).

Introducing a passage in which More is to be his main source, Buc recommends Morton and More as 'men of near<est> [authority and] b[y all ou]r chroniclers and historians held to be veritable. And it may be thought [they would] <not> [w]rite anything favourably or partially of the Lord Protector nor of [his cause, being the chiefest of those who loved him not]' (text, p. 400). This assessment shows (1) that Buc has a good grasp of the subjects about which Morton and consequently More are likely to be most authoritative; (2) he assumes that what 'they' say in Richard's favour must be true because they hated him. When More praises Richard he is 'loath to speak much in his favour, yet occasion forced him to speak his knowledge, though coldly and sparingly' (text, p. 202). In the last three books Buc deals minutely with unfavourable things More says about Richard, showing them to be absurd or self-contradictory.

He attributes the origin of More's *Richard* to time-serving in a period when it was meritorious to publish slanders of Richard and an offence to write well of him. Buc refers to a book in Latin reporting Richard's actions, accusing him of numerous crimes and suppressing his virtues, believed by fellow antiquaries on good grounds to have been written by Morton in revenge for his political grievances. This book, he says, came into the hands of More, who, desiring preferment, 'translated and interpreted and glosed and altered' it (text, p. 121). He left his book incomplete because he grew tired of practising the detracting style, but he was favoured by fame, which reputed his learning and holiness higher than they deserved (a reputation which Buc misguidedly proceeds to try to shatter), and the book was accepted while it was safer to criticize than to praise Richard. Buc thus implies that this time is past. Yet even now, he cautions, More has so many friends in England and abroad that they will excuse him anything.

The English chroniclers followed More 'step by step and word by word, not having the judgement nor discret[ion to] consider his affections, nor his drifts, nor

40 *The Complete Works of St Thomas More, II. The History of King Richard III*, ed. Richard S. Sylvester (New Haven, 1963), p. 79.

his arts, nor his placentine manners, nor his ends, nor to examine [the truth of] <the> relations which he maketh, nor to search out the truth of his writings' (text, p. 124). Because of their credulity, they 'could swallow any gudgeon and never examine the [style or faith] of those aforesaid authors nor bring th[em to the touchstone of verity]' (text, p. 125). Although Holinshed, Hall, Grafton, and Stow were honest men, he says, they were at fault in importing More's story into their works. Yet they have some excuse in that Morton and More were so highly reputed.

Buc is the first to have perceived a common source for More and Polydore Vergil,[41] claiming that Polydore is at fault in the extent to which he follows Morton's pamphlet. Today it is thought that More read and absorbed the work of Polydore, whom he knew. In general, Buc's opinion of Polydore is favourable: he was 'neither of the House [of York] nor of Lancaster, but only an honest man' (text, p. 204). 'Ma[ny are jealous of him]', says Buc, 'and yet in my opinion not for any <or many> just causes' (text, p. 179). He uses André, in the crossed out reference mentioned above (p. cxxx), to bolster the credibility of Polydore, 'whoe was an honest, and \a/ Learned <man> and liued in the tyme of King Henry:7: . . . (as Bernardus Andreas Tolosanus the Annalist of this King Henry 7 writeth)' (Tiberius, f. 58^{v}).

He has made observations on the authors he uses:

> by way of caution, because they which read their books should be wel <advised to consider> and examine what they read, and make trial of such doubtful things as are written before they give credit unto them. . . . <For it> is a hard thing to find that prince's story truly and faithfully written, who was so hateful to the writers the<n; for when they w>rote they might write no better. And therefore, <th>ese reasons being considered, their writings must be <re>garded and the authors censured accordingly.
>
> (text, pp. 125f)

Buc is ready to correct his sources where they are wrong. By using the *Titulus Regius* he points out the chroniclers' error in citing 'Elizabeth Lucy' rather than Eleanor (Talbot) Butler as Edward IV's first wife. He uses his own knowledge of royal ceremony to correct Polydore's notion of why Richard wore the crown at Bosworth. Using his grandfather's testimony, he disputes the chroniclers' statement that Surrey submitted directly after the battle. Commynes is a 'noble and veritable historian' (text, p. 82), praised several times by Buc, who however wonders at one point if he is not mistaken in saying Stanley's force numbered 26,000 men, since the English historians mention only 5,000.

It is interesting to see how Buc deals with a contemporary historian in his response to 'a new writer', Gainsford, who affirms Perkin Warbeck and Don Sebastian to be counterfeits but 'would have it thought he knew much, and especially matters of [histories] as of other nations and countries. . . . And yet he shows himself pl<ainly ignorant in> stories . . .' Gainsford 'would have us think he took much pains in perusing and sifting [of authors; and indeed I think he did sift them]' (text, p. 156). There is some excuse, Buc says, for his not knowing

41 This is discussed by Sylvester, Introduction to *The History of King Richard III*, *passim*, especially pp. lxxv-lxxvii and by Alison Hanham in *Richard III and His Early Historians*, pp. 164ff.

about Don Sebastian: when he was in Spain the Spaniards concealed the truth ('for they will give many gudgeons to tramontane travellers', text, p. 156). Buc's criticism is in part an expression of contempt for an author writing at the same time as himself whose conclusions differ from his own. But it is also a fact that Buc's research methods are generally far superior to Gainsford's.

Attitudes to Imaginative Literature

'Since the censor constituted one influence on the formation of a play's printed text, the question of Buc's attitude and practices touches upon the history of most of the Jacobean plays before 1622', says Mark Eccles.[42] This statement applies not only specifically to Buc's expressed attitude toward dramatic literature but also more generally to the details of his life and to his attitudes and interests.

It may seem amazing that a Master of the Revels should give so little heed to a major play of his time. We should like him – especially since he knew the author – to refer to Shakespeare's *Richard III*, but he does not. Yet this apparent failure is not remarkable. Buc was writing an historical work based on serious research into historical texts and original documents. Popular literature, which included the drama, could contribute nothing to his research. He did not share the habit of today's readers of deriving their history from the theatre, screen and novel. He uses theatre imagery in the course of his work, viewing to some extent, as his contemporaries tended to do, the events of history as acts played out on a stage, in this case scenes of a tragedy. But his position as censor does not make him more liable to this practice than his contemporaries. He is, if anything, less liable to it, being extremely literal-minded and not often given to flights of fancy.

His references to imaginative literature are either damning or supercilious. He speaks of irresponsible historians as delivering all matter

> upon their own bare and worthless word, and after the manner of fab<u>lous and trivial romancers. And who for <the> most part being idle and sensual persons, will no<t> take the pains to read the ancient and la<rge> histories, but epito<mes> of them, and vulgar pamphlets only. And therefore their stories or ta<les or> romances are accounted as things ambiguous and fabulous.
> (text, pp. 4f)

Because he had a talent for fiction (*Utopia*), More is dismissed as a serious historian: 'many of these accusa<tions> are but fables and fictions and poetical in<ventions. B>esides, he had much intelligence with the <kingdom> of Utopia, and perhaps many of those imaginary <accusations were> advertisements from that strange and uncouth land . . .' (text, p. 196). Stow has told Buc that it was never proved by any evidence 'nor yet by any fine fiction or argument or poetry' that Richard killed his nephews. Buc might have taken this to refer to dramatic representations, but he does not: 'And whereas Mr Stow added fiction and poetry to the proofs, he alluded (as I conceived) to the poetical disposition of Sir Thomas More, because he was a poet and wrot<e a poetical boo>k, to wit, *Utopia* is a

42 Eccles, p. 413.

fable (text, p. 173). Yet *The True Tragedy of Richard III,* Thomas Legge's Richardus Tertius, and Shakespeare's *Richard III* were all well known at the time.[43]

The only mention of plays – and it is not at all certain whether he actually made it, since it does not appear in Tiberius and is in a segment of the text which the Editor has taken some pains to reorganize structurally – is the one quoted previously from Egerton 2216 (pp. xxx-xxxi) about 'the ignorant, and never-vnderstandeinge vulgare' who take their history from the pamphlets, ballads, and the stage. Its style accords much more with the great-nephew than with Sir George. This sort of attitude is not unusual for those of Buc's class and educational status. Cornwallis's was similar: Roger Bennett points out that although he spent time in the playhouse, in his essays he refers to the stage only through metaphorical figures, often contemptuous. And as for vulgar literature, Cornwallis remarks that it is his custom to read it in the privy and then use it as toilet paper.[44] The pamphlets which are linked with plays as vulgar literature are thus described by Stauffer: the 'popular interest in sensational and strange lives . . . produced broadsides and short pamphlets on the disagreeable deaths of every murderer and Newgate criminal, and turned over the pages of old chronicles and foreign histories for lives incredibly criminal or heroic'.[45]

Autobiography and Personal Opinions

Of all Buc's works the *History* contains most biographical information. Yet this is not considerable. Buc speaks of his presence with the Lord Admiral at Cadiz and of taking part in events there. He notes that he was in France when Mary, Queen of Scots died and heard general remarks there on the cause of her death, which seem to have been (this section is burnt away) that she died of a catarrh, the polite way of saying she had been put to death. He speaks of his ancestors, of his great-grandfather, who may or may not have been Richard's Controller of the House and was executed and attainted after Bosworth for siding with Richard; of his grandfather, orphaned by the battle and taken into the care of the Howards, by whom the Bucks had ever since been favoured, who told him the story of Surrey's fortunes after Bosworth; of his father that he, like all his forebears and like his son, had been a soldier.

His acquaintances are revealed in the sources of his *viva voce* information, and we have first-hand descriptions of a number of important personages of the day who were his personal acquaintances: Sir Charles Howard, the Earl of Arundel, the Earl of Oxford, and Queen Elizabeth herself. He is flattered that the Earl of Oxford 'vouchsafed me his personal acquaintance' and came to visit him. He saw the private collections of Lord William Howard of Naworth and his nephew the Earl of Arundel, to whom he dedicates his book, and Arundel relayed to him information by word of mouth, as did Baron Lumley and Baron Darcy. He was assisted by his fellow antiquaries and friends, Cotton, Camden, and Brooke, and

43 On Legge's moral effect, see John Harington, 'A Brief Apologie of Poesie', *Elizabethan Critical Essays*, ed. Gregory Smith (London, 1904), II, 210: 'to omit other famous Tragedies, that that was played at S. *Iohns* in Cambridge, of *Richard the* 3, would moue . . . *Phalaris* the tyraunt, and terrifie all tyrannous minded men from following their foolish ambitious humors . . .'

44 Bennett, pp. 207f.

45 Stauffer, pp. 224f.

also by the herald Dethick, and he records regard and respect for all these men, some of whom were each other's enemies. He is generous in praise of them and also of recently dead scholars such as Stow and Glover. His respect for their learning and wisdom is profound, and his own attitude is humble rather than competitive.

But more than in mere biographical details, Buc is characterized by his attitudes and scholarly methods. His stated intention is generous: to allow truth to come to light. And he proceeds not in an opinionated and emotional manner but in a rational and charitable one, tempered by the lawyer's objective sense of justice. His plea is that a well-balanced, just and charitable assessment be accorded to Richard, and this is the treatment he himself gives his subject. Occasionally he is carried away by hatred of Morton, and he dislikes Henry VII (a dislike which, ironically, he shared with More). He is unfair to More, but he had his sources to blame for this, just as he allows that the historians whose faults he is attempting to unravel have their sources to blame for their view of Richard. He has no sympathy with sloppy, careless, incomplete and inaccurate research in others, and displays contempt for authors of whose methods he disapproves. He himself follows methods he upholds as more responsible. He is proud of this, at the same time humble, deprecating his own 'mean reading'. He has the highest regard for 'chivalry and honour', the lowest for 'policy', 'cunning', and 'treachery'. Upholding the sanctity of kingship, he must condemn rebellion against it.

Buc clearly considers the greatest risk to lie in rehearsing Richard's title according to the rediscovered *Titulus Regius*, which Henry VII had ordered suppressed and destroyed. Twice in speaking of the illegitimacy of Edward IV's children, James's ancestors, he adds a disclaimer protesting that these opinions are not his but those of the times of which he is writing. He also takes pains to show that the various defects in Henry VII's royal claim were 'cured'.

Buc flatters James by rehearsing his titles to the throne, and under this cover he does two things: first he observes how the breach caused by Edward IV's marriage was repaired by Richard's accession, thus placing Richard in the scheme of history, not in his traditional role as interrupter of succession but as the restorer of it, and making James dependent on Richard for his unbroken title. Second he defends the power and authority of Parliament, saying the title to the throne was reinforced by many Parliaments, so that Henry VII (from whom it descended to James) was able to bear it as if it had never been broken. And James has another important claim in his descent from the ancient British kings through Henry VII who 'would have all the titles of this kingdom confirmed to him by the strongest and greatest authority' – and so had them settled in himself and his heirs by Parliament (see text, pp. 214f). This is the culmination of a thread which runs through the entire work. Buc is using the *History* in part as a tract on the authority of Parliament. To suggest that Richard's accession was unlawful was to cast aspersions on Parliament, which 'is or should be a general assembly of all the most [noble] *and m*ost honourable and most just, the most godly and the *most* [rel]igious persons of the kingdom' (text, p. 186). This attitude is useful equally to Buc's defence of Richard and his defence of Parliament.[46]

Buc's judgement of Henry VII and his followers is harsh, but he tries to assume an ambivalent attitude toward Henry himself, partly by using qualifying statements, partly by pushing as much blame as possible onto Morton. About one thing he is clear: those who bear arms against their sovereign in the field are traitors, and their wars are sedition and rebellion, crimes against God as well as against man and against their king. He states this very emphatically in general terms and reinforces it by frequent remarks on the treachery of Henry VII's accomplices, though he tries to avoid applying it directly to Henry mainly by blaming Morton for many of his actions.

At the beginning of the work he claims that one of his intentions is to distinguish between true and false barons and show Morton and More and their followers in their true colours. He uses Morton as a general scapegoat: he is the instigator of rebellion against Richard (this exonerates Henry), and he is the ringleader of Richard's detractors in writing (this clears the writers on whom Buc must rely for general outlines). He sees Morton as an avatar of evil, 'that evil spirit transformed into an angel of light and wearing the habit of religion and sanctity' (text, p. 83). It is he who turns Buckingham against Richard (More gives evidence of this), who stirs up Pembroke, Oxford, and Devon, who poisons Henry's heart with ambition. That Morton, as Buc says, devised the death of Perkin Warbeck and Edward, Earl of Warwick there is no evidence, but the suggestion does remove the blame from Henry. Although Buc admits that the Lancastrians would have been forced to kill the sons of Edward IV in order to clear the way for a king of their faction, he points the accusing finger away from Henry himself by giving evidence from an old manuscript book that Morton and 'a certain countess' (obviously meaning Margaret Beaufort, Countess of Richmond) were plotting the death of these princes and others of the house of York. It may not be carelessness or lack of critical facility which keeps Buc from saying more about this particular document (if indeed he did not – there may have been marginal documentation now lost), but rather wisdom and circumspection.

On the other hand, Henry VII's fault – 'and almost [his] only fault' – was that of hearing and following evil counsel, and for his credulity 'he beareth the blames of other men'. What Buc is really doing is making other men bear the blame for Henry's actions. The account of Henry's early life is straightforwardly factual, though Buc's compliments almost invariably have a reverse side: he was 'a very wary and a very circumspect man, and also somewhat timorous' (text, p. 70). He was obviously good and wise because many people reputed him so and because Queen Elizabeth was said to resemble him. 'Although a very good king' he was guilty of *crimen regale* in disposing of young Warwick, Perkin Warbeck, and other claimants. Buc does not at all mislike his having the crown, but only his not awaiting the Lord's leisure to gain possession of it. His title was made strong by Parliament, so he bore it as if it had never been 'broken by mischance and cunning' (text, p. 214). Henry had faults, but he was nevertheless wise, provident and religious, the restorer of the (legendary) British kings, the nephew of Henry VI

46 See Baker's interesting article, which analyses Buc's use of Richard's story to set forth his praise of Parliament, discussed above, p. xlviii.

– though Buc takes pains to note that this is a tenuous connection through the female – and an offspring of the house of Lancaster. Buc notes that confirmation of the Lancaster title by the Pope was obtained after Henry had taken the crown (text, pp. 88f).

Subtler than these backhanded compliments is another method Buc uses to cast aspersions on Henry and exalt Richard by comparison: that of analogy. He will sometimes adduce a fable or an anecdote from ancient history as an illustrative instance, heap abuse on the character who tacitly parallels Henry in the illustration, and leave the reader to make the comparison. An example of this is the fable of the Eagle and the Scarab (text, pp. 101f). The ostensible motive for including this story is to show the danger of underrating one's enemy. But in addition to this it draws a judgemental parallel between Richard as the royal Eagle ('the king of birds and the chief esquire of the God Jupiter') and Henry as the vile Scarab ('a base and contemptible insect and of no power nor credit') who scores by treachery. Buc disclaims all harm, saying, 'This *is only* a fable, and the moral is easy to be conceived by the *Rea*der' (text, pp. 101-2). The perceptive reader will have gleaned from it, in addition to the moral, his attitude to Richard's antagonists at Bosworth.

Buc does not mince words about what he sees as Henry's serious faults. He was cowardly and unchivalrous in battle and inferior to Richard in skill of arms. His Parliament, in that it attainted of treason the rightful king and his followers, was evil and self-abrogating. He probably would not have resigned the crown to Perkin Warbeck had he known him to be Richard of York, for he (tyrannously, Buc implies) destroyed other royal claimants. On the other hand, Buc's remarks about Henry's grand-daughter Elizabeth, whom he knew, are, as usual in his works, couched in terms almost of worship. He presents in the middle of the *History* (p. 124) a long eulogy of this queen, in which her heroic qualities are exalted, and a shorter one at the end (p. 213).

Buc's general picture of Richard is a temperately favourable one, slightly sentimentalized at times. He sees him as a good and loving brother, husband, and father, deducing the gentleness and faithfulness of his nature partly from his service to his brother as compared with Clarence's treachery. He loved his 'childhood home' (as he accounted the north to be) and had no ambition other than to remain in the north as King Edward's servant, a life in which he was well-reputed by all as generous and hospitable, wise, courageous, and loyal. This attitude Buc sees confirmed by his initial refusal to take the crown, which was, of course, an aspect of tradition. Buc considers him sincere in this, in that feeling for the father dictated loyalty to the son, and putting thoughts in Richard's mind for which there is no evidence regarding reasons for his dislike of sovereignty. But Buc feels that he was forced, by the risk that the Queen Mother's relations would seize power, and also by the threat of foreign invasion, reluctantly to accept it. Buc presents evidence of Richard's moderation and continence in private life, and in public life his wisdom, justice, fortitude, bounty, magnificence, temperance, and piety – which are, he considers, the ideal attributes of kingliness – listing his good works and documenting his exemplary legislation in support of these virtues. By discussing the *Titulus Regius* he justifies Richard's title to the throne, indisputable because it was passed by Parliament.

His arguments against some of the attacks on Richard are based on common sense tempered by a certain degree of ridicule: idiosyncrasies of gesture do not constitute a crime. Nor does being born with teeth, being deformed of body, or for one's mother to have suffered pain in childbirth. And he gives examples of noble and famous men born with teeth, others who were deformed, others whose mothers actually died in childbed. By using ridicule he points up the absurdity of one accusation in particular, the one about the teeth, saying he does not think Morton or More ever spoke with the midwife. The deformity he disproves by Stow's evidence, the failure of all authors who actually knew Richard to mention it, and personal observation of portraits.

Buc's historiography is as morally orientated as was that of his predecessors, but in a different way. He is original in introducing into history the concept of charity. He seems to be one of the first English historical writers to take into account the differences (even if only apparent) between his own and earlier ages, and to see consistently and clearly the distinctions between his own highly chivalric code of honour, which he attributes to his times, and what he interprets as the more opportunistic morality of the fifteenth century.

Buc cannot exonerate Richard of Hastings's death and deplores the '*Artes Imperii*' which justified it. But he mislikes the tendency to blame Richard disproportionately for employing these tactics when other famous and well-reputed men, of whom he gives many examples, are not so harshly censured for doing similar things. He uses the same argument in regard to the general attitude toward Richard. Although he has to his satisfaction cleared Richard of most crimes of which he is accused, he gives examples of several other kings, including Henry VII and VIII, whose disposing of rival claimants is not a matter of mere suspicion but firmly proved. Buc's method is that of a lawyer: he exonerates where possible on the basis of available evidence and where not possible he pleads for mercy on the basis of precedent. 'All King Richard's guilt', Buc pleads, '[is but suspicion. And suspicion is] in la[w no more guilt or culpableness than imagination]' (text, p. 193). The accusations against Richard are not to be credited because they cannot be proved.

Richard is poorly reputed, Buc reminds us, because he lost the battle: 'ill fortune is accounted a vice in military adventures' (text, p. 100), and when fortune is adverse in battle the loser is considered reprobate, whereas the winners are renowned as brave and valiant. Buc voices rational objection to the argument of Richard's enemies that his death in battle betokened divine wrath. His view of history is in a sense providential. Earlier writers had explained Richard's downfall as punishment for his misdeeds. Buc from his Protestant standpoint sees God's determination to destroy the house of Plantagenet and transfer the crown as the basis of Richard's downfall. Richard's actions, good or bad, would have had no effect in altering God's plan and could only serve to help bring it about. It is presumptuous to assume that man's choices and actions can have weight enough to sway God's intent.

Buc sees Richard occasionally as a parallel to Christ, but only in that both, having sacred status, were betrayed and vilified. He is far from setting up Richard as a Christlike figure, and in all cases he deals with Richard's reputation by shrewd analysis rather than emotional harangue. Upon dispassionate examination, one finds less a heated, emotional defence of a hero than a surprisingly cool examination. Buc's passion appears to be rather for accuracy than for Richard III. He shows the same passion for minor historical inaccuracies as for Richard's bad reputation. His final assessment of Richard is judicious:

> [although this prince was not so superlative as to assume the name of holy or best, you see him a wise, magnificent,] and a valiant man, *and a* [just,] bountiful, [and temperate,] *and* an eloquent *and magnanimous and* pious prince; and *a benefactor to the holy* church and to this *realm*. [Yet] for all this it ha[th] been his [fortun]e to be aspersed and fouled *and* to fall into this *malice of those who have* been ill-affected *towards him* . . .
>
> (text, p. 208)

We have no way of knowing whether Buc intended publication. This was a period when long historical tracts circulated in manuscript rather than in print. He sometimes speaks about the reader as if he expected a readership rather than a single reader, the most obvious example being 'An Advertisement to the Reader', text, pp. 6-8, closing with address to 'the just and intelligent and generous and judicious Reader'. Would it have been possible to publish this early the opinions expressed seriously in the *History*? There is no way of telling: we only know that no one did – Stow and Camden, who had revisionist information about Richard, said less in print than they knew. It was an age when completed manuscripts circulated among one's peers, and scholars did not all seek publication as they do now.

Caveat

In surveying Buc's scholarship it has not been my intention to suggest that more complete, better organized, more dispassionate work was not done by later scholars writing on other subjects, or indeed by authors who completed their work and left it in fair copy state, as Buc did his *Commentary*. We must remember that Buc wrote in 1619, not 1646, and his original manuscript – in which, alone, his *History* exists as he wrote it – was still in process of revision when he left it and is very badly damaged. His documentation has been attacked by generations of scholars who either had no recourse to the original or did not wish to attempt either it or the early manuscript copies. They relied instead on the printed edition, in which the Editor and especially his scribe were sloppiest with marginal notes (which was where Buc recorded his documentation), deleting many altogether and copying more of them erroneously. It is difficult to restore them, since it is the margins that suffer most severe burning in the original manuscript. So Buc has been attacked not for his own work but for another person's sloppy rendering of pieces of his work and the impossibility of recovering burnt away text. There is absolutely no sense in considering in the same breath the original – by a competent scholar, but unfinished and damaged – and a truncated work published under false pretences and someone else's name twenty-seven years later.

VIII. METHOD OF COMPOSITION AND THE PRESENT TEXT

Buc completed the dedication of his *History* in fair copy and dated it 1619. Nearly all internal evidence supports this date of composition, but there is some suggestion that he continued to revise and make additions to the work in 1620. This is indicated by the date '1620' in the margin (text, p. 184), elucidating a remark that Francis Godwin is now (i.e. at the time of writing) Bishop of Hereford. There seems to be a vestige of another such dating on p. 98 of the printed edition of the *Life and Reigne* above the marginal note which attributes to Baron Darcy *viva voce* information about Don Sebastian of Portugal. This note reads '162' and has no meaning if it is not assumed to be the remains of a marginal dating '1620', the year in which Buc was doing research for Darcy (see above, p. xlvi).

One may for assistance in dating examine the various scraps Buc has used for late insertions. These are printed in Frank Marcham's *The King's Office of the Revels* and were discussed by E.K. Chambers in his review of that book.[1] Many of them are Revels Office scraps which Buc has crossed out in order to use their blank versos for late additions to his *History*, following his practice in the *Commentary*, where most of the scraps can be proved to be slightly later than the main composition of the work (see above, pp. xxxvii-xxxviii). Chambers in examining the names of the plays on these scraps points out that they cannot be notations of licensing for performance or publication, since some were performed and published before Buc became Master of the Revels. He believes that they were probably being considered by the Revels Office as revivals for court performance and presents evidence pointing to the likelihood of 1619-20 as the period of revival.

The *Commentary* seems to have been composed within a limited time span. Probably the same is true of the *History*. Most of it is in rough draft but at a fairly advanced stage, probably near completion. No gaps are left to be filled in, and the author has gone through the text revising it more than once. In 1619 he seems to have begun making a fair copy. He has written the dedication in a large, neat, rounded hand. Corrections in it are few and are written very clearly. He begins a fair copy of the Advertisement to the Reader as well, but starts to correct it at the end of its first page (f. 5). The next page (f. 5^{v}) is more heavily corrected and ultimately crossed out, probably because the author intended to rewrite it. Book I too begins as a fair copy. Ff. 7 and 7^{v}are written with few corrections in a small, neat hand until the end of f. 7^{v}, where some rewriting first took place over an erasure and the last few lines so rewritten have been crossed out. From then on corrections are numerous, and very few pages in fair copy appear among the

1 E.K. Chambers, review of *The King's Office of the Revels*, *Review of English Studies*, I (1925), 479-84.

others, which are in various states of revision.

What probably happened is that Buc, having completed to his satisfaction a rough draft of the *History* and having made many revisions in it, began to write a fair copy for presentation to his dedicatee, dating the dedication 1619 but leaving blanks for day and month. That these were never filled in proves that he never finished it. He found when he began the fair copy that he needed to revise even further and make further additions. This he continued to do into 1620, probably not long after the beginning of that year, and work gradually ceased altogether because of his encroaching illness.

Buc's methods of composition and revision are difficult to trace, more difficult to generalize about. In his Advertisement to the Reader he states that the 'argument and subject' formed the thirteenth chapter of *The Baron*, a work of Buc's now lost (see above, pp. xliii-xlvi). He mentions *The Baron* frequently in the *History*, but we have not nearly enough evidence about it to reconstruct what he might have included in this chapter and how much he added later. He expanded the material from a chapter to a complete book because, as he says, it existed 'in such copy [copiousness] and variety as that it diffused itself into an extraordinary and unusual largeness, and so much as it exceeded very much the laws and proper limits of a chapter'. Hence he has 'much enlarged' and transferred it to the *History* (text, p. 6). Now, he says, the chapter can serve as argument for the *History* and the *History* as gloss on the chapter. Evidence of this enlarging and transferring process is lacking. Buc does say specifically that he intends to 'transcribe hither from the said thirteenth chapter some particular *matters*, and especially the beginnings and first times of this Prince Richard, comprehending *the prince*ly lineage of the king and his parentage, his birth, his education, his [tirocin]y, and all the conditions of these acts, and of his youth, and of his [private] life' (text, p. 6). But apart from this, and even within this section, we have no way of knowing which is newly written material and which is old.

Buc has left a small page of notes (Tib., f. 145^{v}) including page numbers referring to material in Gainsford's *History of Perkin Warbeck*. It is impossible to surmise from this one page much about Buc's note-taking practice, particularly since Gainsford had been published very recently (1618). One may observe only that on this page he organizes his notes according to source rather than subject and the ordering of it in various parts of the *History* occurs at a later stage. Aside from this, we can observe the markings in his own books, his notes in his copy of Godwin, underlinings in his copy of Bouchard, and in some of the Cotton manuscripts his underlinings and pencilled 'X's in the margins opposite material he intends to use. Once he inserts a whole page which he has apparently had someone copy for him: f. 19, the charter for creating Vice Constable, is in another hand. But occasionally he pastes in a quotation he has copied out separately in his own hand.

What we lack is anything to represent the intermediate organizing state. Probably the lists of contents were written before the books to which they refer were completed, as an attempted outline, from which the material in the book itself sometimes deviates. At one stage in composition Buc employed a scribe to make fair copies of some pages from f. 55 to the end, perhaps intending that the scribal pages should form part of the presentation copy. One hundred and seven scribal pages remain, all but one scribal on front and back. Buc has gone over them and filled in or corrected foreign or difficult words for which the scribe has left blanks or in which he has made mistakes. His proofreading, though far more painstaking than the Editor's in his own scribally composed manuscripts, is not perfect, and many more errors have occurred on the scribal pages than on those in Buc's own hand. Hence I have in the ensuing text marked the scribal page numbers with an asterisk, so that errors which might otherwise be attributed to Buc may be seen as copying errors by the scribe. Frequently he was not satisfied with the scribal pages and began to cross out and revise them. Often his revision was so heavy that he was forced for the sake of legibility to copy the whole page again, incorporating his revisions. Thus at times we have at least three representations of a passage or page: (a) Buc's first draft, revised by him in the process of and after composition, discarded by him but retained in the manuscript because he had later used its back for rewriting something else; (b) a more legible and coherent rewriting, often scribal, in which Buc makes heavy revisions between lines; and (c) a further copy in his own hand, incorporating further revisions made by him either during or after writing it.

Thus the manuscript is a collection of pages in various states:

1) Buc's own early drafts;
2) discarded pages whose material has been rewritten but which have been preserved because Buc wrote on their blank backs and pasted them over other material he wished to revise (these have been taken apart in the binding process and bound as separate pages);
3) scribal pages, which make up one fifth of the collection;
4) Buc's own revised versions of these pages, themselves bearing revisions between the lines and in the margins;
5) at the beginning and infrequently thereafter, fair copy pages in Buc's hand;
6) very few pages in other hands: material copied for him;
7) reworkings in the hand of the Editor, George Buck, Junior.

Buc rewrites to reorganize material, to put ideas in better chronological order, or to bring together separate discussions of related topics. He rewrites to make expression smoother and more vivid, or to make a cleaner, expanded copy of a page in which a series of small and not always complete revisions above the lines and in the margins have destroyed coherence and left him no further room for expansion. His revising of large sections is effected by crossing out, by rewriting whole pages, or by rewriting portions of a page on separate sheets or fragments of paper and pasting them over the portion he wishes to replace.

When transferring material which fits better elsewhere, he sometimes writes new transitional passages on separate sheets and pastes them in, but sometimes he fails to create new transitions. An example of such failure occurs in Book III, the book in which, because of the extreme difficulty in organization, most rewriting occurs. Originally the anecdote about the Earl of Oxford immediately followed the story of Perkin Warbeck, but Buc has revised to insert more material before it and has failed to write a new transitional passage when he introduces it later, so it appears stuck on. On the other hand, he improves the transition from Book I to

Book II, making the opening of the second book an induction, in place of the abrupt plunge into the continuation of Book I's events which he had originally given.

Buc rewrites the story of Hereward on ff. 115-16 to give it much greater detail. But in other cases he feels he has given too much detail for the context and rewrites to reduce it. An example of this is the discussion of the Herberts, which deals with the family history from the fifteenth century to the present. He crosses this out and reduces the material to a short paragraph employing considerable subordination (f. 25). There was originally in the *History* an even more expanded discussion of the Herberts, but he discarded this and inserted it instead into the *Commentary* (see above, p. xli), where he considered it more appropriate to deal with the origins of families at length.

Buc also rewrites the Morton-Buckingham intrigue. He had first given only pure facts and had not organized them well. The rewriting on ff. 56f is expanded to make the scene clearer and more immediate, giving details of the story, some in direct discourse. Psychological and conversational steps are followed in a clear and logical order, so that the stages in the process of Morton's convincing Buckingham become clear.

Buc's smaller revisions are stylistic, tending toward expansion. He seems obsessively concerned with stating everything as completely and explicitly as possible. Toward this end he substitutes one word for another or adds one or two words above the line as possible alternatives for one he found not perfectly satisfactory, and in doing so he often neglects to cross out any of the alternatives. Perhaps he was never able to decide. He does the same with phrases. He adds explanatory clauses above the line in an attempt to eliminate vagueness and duplicates nouns, verbs, and adjectives to reinforce his meanings. He designates, explains, specifies, often more than once. Frequently he makes these revisions and expansions in the process of what started as a simple attempt to make a clearer copy of a page. On f. 69^{v} he has the words, 'But if it be here obiected that albeit <tha>t this be the law of france yet it is not obserued in England'; which in revision on f. 20 becomes, 'But if it be here obiected that albeit <tha>t this be the law & custome of france, yet it is not in vse nor \hath it bene/ observed in England'. F. 95^{v}, rewriting part of the scribal f. 96, gives in place of 'Countryman' the words 'frend, & countryman, & kinsman'.

Revisions occur for the sake of accuracy. Buc had, in discussing Surrey's fortunes on f. 111^{v}, originally stated that he received his promotions in the time of Henry VII. These promotions were in fact rewards for his Flodden victory. When Buc realized that they were events of Henry VIII's reign, he tried to rectify the error by making above-line additions, which produce a very confused and awkward effect. Had he rewritten the page, he would certainly have made this section smoother and integrated the revisions. On f. 8 he corrects an error in the text but apparently forgets to correct the same error in the marginal note. He alters '<this> was foulk the first erl of Anjow' to '<this m>an was the first foulk w<hi>*i*ch was erl of Anjow'. The marginal note (which survives only in the copies) is left to say 'Foulke first Ear. of Anjow' (Egerton, f. 10^{v}).

Buc very occasionally revised his own material to remove indecorous references, on f. 224, for example, changing 'prostitute' to 'yield'. This seems in keeping with his practice as censor (see above, pp. xxiv-xxv). It is a tendency the Editor carried much farther.

When the manuscript was damaged in the Cotton fire of 1731, the report on the library after the fire described Tiberius E.X thus: 'A few Leaves of this Book are left, burnt round'.[2] This pessimistic view is echoed in Casley's 1734 catalogue – 'Bundles of Leaves so burnt as to be of little use'[3] and Hooper's of 1777.[4] It was inset and bound in the mid-nineteenth century. 265 leaves survive, and only a very few (indicated in the Textual Notes) can be shown to be entirely missing – whether always because of fire it is not known. Only two surviving pages have been almost obliterated by fire, f. 23 and f. 25; they are intact, but the pages are so greyed with smoke that the writing has faded away.

The editing process

My intention in the present text has been to produce something as close as possible to what Buc himself would have written had he made a fair copy of the work. The manuscript as it stands presents a number of problems to an editor: it has been severely damaged by fire; the author has made portions of the text illegible by striking out and revising; the author's revisions are often incomplete and produce duplications and syntactical breakdown; the author has frequently failed to make a final decision – normally stylistic – among alternative wordings; finally, George Buck Esq. has made his own alterations in the manuscript, thus providing two sets of crossing out, and it is often difficult or impossible to ascertain whether his or the author's hand was responsible for a particular deletion. In addition, the manuscript has been rebound in modern times. The binder has guarded each leaf and has removed revised sections (there are ninety-eight of these) from the place where Buc had pasted them down. They have been bound in as separate leaves, sometimes divided from their proper place in the text by several intervening leaves. I have dealt with these problems in the following ways:

A) Damage by fire

All leaves of the manuscript are burnt around the edges, increasingly as the text progresses from beginning to end, so that a large proportion of the marginal notes and the beginnings and ends of pages are lost. I have restored these lost portions whenever possible by reference to the other versions of the same material which Buc sometimes gives in his numerous rewritings. Where there is in the original manuscript no representation of the missing material, as is more often the case, I have supplied the gap from the early manuscript copies in order of their composition. Hence Egerton has supplied nearly all the additions which derive from the copies. When I have used Malone and/or Fisher because of obvious errors and omissions in Egerton, this has been indicated in the Textual Notes. Additional MS. 27422 has made no contribution to the filling in of gaps, but sometimes the printed edition of 1646 makes a felicitous correction in the reading

2 *Report from the Committee Appointed to View the Cottonian Library*, p. 35.
3 David Casley, et al., *A Catalogue of the Manuscripts in the King's Library: an Appendix to the Catalogue of the Cottonian Library, Together with an Account of the Books Burnt or Damaged by a Late Fire* (London, 1734), p. 314.
4 Samuel Hooper, *A Catalogue of the Manuscripts in the Cottonian Library* (London, 1777), sig. Rv.

of an obscure word or the grammar or spelling of a word in a foreign language, particularly Latin, and in such cases I have adopted its reading.

In Egerton, George Buck Esq. has a habit of tightening the author's constructions. This means that sometimes a short emendation from Egerton will not fit the structure of the sentence into which I have inserted it without omission of a word or two, generally a relative pronoun. In such cases I have considered that nothing could be gained from placing dots in the emendation from Egerton to show the excision, since it is the syntax of Tiberius, not Egerton, which I am attempting to reconstruct. An indication of how Egerton has changed the author's style in minor points is of no interest in the creation of a text as close as possible to the author's intention, and such indication could only break continuity to no advantage. Aside from these occasional small omissions, I have cited in the Textual Notes any changes I have made in sections taken from Egerton.

The copies, as previously indicated, are roughly three-fifths the length of the original. This means that there are portions of the original which they do not include. In such cases, where no other source represents the destroyed material, I have supplied very short passages by conjecture – based on the sense of the surviving portions of the passage and on knowledge of Buc's ideas and style. Some marginal notes have vanished irrecoverably. There are a few short passages without other representation, either in the original or copies, which are so badly damaged that only a word or two survives here and there, so that conjecture regarding their meaning, purpose or author's intention to retain or reject them is impossible. These I have omitted from the text and given in the Textual Notes.

B) Incomplete revision

Buc often leaves sections in a state of partial revision, with portions partly crossed out, additions above the line, and several alternatives given. Revision in these cases is invariably stylistic and not material to the sense of the passage. Buc's style is his weakest point, and to have noted all these partial revisions would have produced more notes than text.

Where Buc gives several alternatives of the same page, word, or phrase, I have had to decide which to accept. Whenever possible I have used the latest version given. Where Buc has several nearly synonymous words, probably as alternatives, intending to make a choice eventually, I have usually not felt able to make the choice and have tended to include them all. This repetition of meaning by use of several synonyms is consistent with period style: 'copy' was geared to showing off one's leisure, a sort of verbal conspicuous consumption.

I have not invariably followed the order in which the folios are bound in Tiberius because:

- where several alternatives exist, one or more has been crossed out or pasted over by the author
- the clearer and later alternative has sometimes been bound in the manuscript before the less clear and earlier-composed alternative
- the pasted-on fragments have not been bound in logical order, since they have been separated from the pages to which they were attached, and their backs and fronts come from different parts of the work
- whole folios are occasionally misbound.

I have decided among alternative pages by comparing the various drafts to see which seems most complete and finished and includes the revisions made in other drafts. On the rare occasions where two drafts for a page are so close as to necessitate considering them as alternatives rather than revisions one of the other, I have chosen the one containing the fuller information more fluently expressed. Drafts which formed the backs of pasted-on-sections I have excluded, since Buc, by using them as scrap paper and pasting them down, has rejected them.[5] I have matched the pasted-on revisions with the pages to which they were originally pasted by observing subject matter, position of paste marks, size, and shape. In arranging the text I have considered the early manuscript copies, since George Buck Esq., who was responsible for them, saw the original intact, as I have not been able to do. I have sometimes been guided by and often received corroboration from them and have thus been able to achieve a continuity of material not always evident in the order in which the Tiberius folios are bound.

A few pages have been bound in the wrong order and make more sense if their order is shifted. F. 4 is clearly the conclusion of the Advertisement to the Reader rather than of the Dedication. F. 10-10^{v} was almost certainly intended to precede f. 8 in the author's original, and all manuscript copies arrange them thus. The binding, however, follows the printed edition's reversal which destroys clarity by placing the more specific adoption of Fulke of Anjou as founder of the name 'Plantagenet' before Buc's description of the research that led him to adopt it, i.e. the process of positing the qualities requisite to the possessor of a sobriquet and the rejection of Geoffrey of Anjou, the usual candidate, for not possessing these qualities, thus making necessary a search for someone more likely.

In Buc's incomplete revisions his intentions are usually obvious from the partial revisions he has made. Incomplete revisions occur in the following ways:

(1) He has made his revisions so hastily that they are syntactically incongruous with the unrevised portions.

(2) He has begun revisions but failed to complete them: dissatisfied with his original wording, he has given several alternatives of a word or phrase, probably intending at some later point to make a final decision among them.

(3) In the process of revising all or part of a page he has crossed out most of it, having cluttered it too much to complete his revisions where he began them, or having decided to move the material to another place. His intention was certainly to rewrite the whole passage later, but since he never does so, I have had to depend on incomplete extant versions and select the clearest and most coherent, with the most informative wording. I have also attempted to create coherent grammatical constructions in passages Buc left partially revised by restoring words he has crossed out, deleting words he has failed to cross out, and occasionally reversing the order of phrases. In doing so I have not altered the sense but made its expression coherent by continuing a revision along

5 In the case of the title page, which comes from another manuscript work of Buc's (see Plate IV), I have deviated from the practice of ignoring pages used as scrap paper, since this is the sole complete representation in his own hand of what Buc intended for his title page. It is the only authorial source which tells us that the title of his work was *The History of King Richard the Third* (fragmental f. 171^{v} seems to have been a version of the title page but is not complete). Malone confirms the book's title and Egerton nearly does, only omitting 'King'.

lines suggested by the author.

In the present text I have modernized spelling and regularized punctuation. This has been unavoidable because of the number of hands, all with different spelling and punctuation conventions, which have contributed to the present text:

(1) the author in various moods in which he is more or less careful and in which his spelling is more or less formal
(2) the author's scribe
(3) another hand in which a document has been copied for the author
(4) George Buck Esq. in his revisions in the original manuscript
(5) George Buck Esq.'s scribe in the copies Egerton, Malone and Fisher
(6) his (the Editor's) own corrections in these copies
(7) the compositor of the 1646 edition
(8) the present editor

There are in the original manuscript numerous gaps which have had to be filled in with non-authorial material, either from copies or by conjecture. It would have been foolish either to present a conglomeration of spelling styles or to arrange all insertions so that their spelling approximated Buc's own. Modernization of spelling and punctuation eliminates yet another confusion and difficulty from a text already complicated with emendations.

I have followed the same procedure with foreign languages. I have modernized French and normalized Latin spelling. The scribal pages in Tiberius and the emendations derived from manuscript copies show a very large number of errors, whereas those in the author's hand show almost none. Buc himself makes two minor grammatical errors in Latin, the language from which he quotes most frequently, none in French, from which he quotes often, three minor ones in Greek, from which he quotes a few times, and none in Spanish and Italian which he quotes rarely. He made attempts to correct his scribe's numerous errors in foreign passages but missed many of them. The Editor's scribe in the copies distorts most of the foreign passages. When grammatical errors occur in foreign passages I have corrected them in the text and given the erroneous version in the Textual Notes. However, these alterations apply to grammar only; when Buc documents a passage as 'Cicero', what he gives is, more often than not, a paraphrase of Cicero adapted grammatically to suit his context. In such cases I have not substituted in the present text a correct quotation for Buc's paraphrase but have given in the General Notes a reference to the correct quotation. Equally I have left as they stand lines from Latin whose lineation is not as in the original. To aid readers in weaning themselves from looking at Buc's references as *quotations* (as in a modern historical work), the present edition does not use quotation marks except for direct discourse: it does not turn Buc's references into quotations.

I have corrected Buc's few accidental misspellings without citing them in the Textual Notes. Proper names used by Buc which vary in spelling throughout the manuscript I have regularized and given as they are spelt today, as well as names such as 'Richmont' and 'Plantagenest' whose habitual spelling by Buc differs from that to which we are now accustomed. I have invariably given 'Joab' as 'Joas'. But if Buc has mistakenly given 'Thomas' as the name of a man who is in fact Robert, I have let the error stand in the text and given the name correctly in the General Notes.

In keeping with the modernized spelling, I have regularized the punctuation and other accidentals. Buc's punctuation is irregular, sometimes non-existent. I have, consequently, tried to punctuate the work so that thought units stand out as clearly and distinctly as possible and so that sense is as clear as possible in so diffuse a work.

I have provided as samples in this edition (Plates I-III) pages from Cotton Tiberius E.X which I feel would be of most interest to readers, rather than, as I did last time, giving examples of pages which illustrated Buc's revision techniques. These are (Plate I) the passage about the ape dying in the Tower and his bones being mistaken for those of the missing sons of Edward IV (this may serve as a typical page as well), and (Plates II-III) the Elizabeth of York letter, most of which appears on a scribal page. As the reader can see from these examples, the manuscript is not immensely legible. Fire, constant and often incomplete revision, and sloppy handwriting make reading difficult. It is not entirely outside the realm of belief that despite much checking of my transcripts against the original I have made some errors. I cannot claim that my conjectures filling in areas of text damaged beyond recovery always represent Buc's exact wording. These are inevitable hazards in dealing with a badly damaged manuscript in draft state. All one can do is exercise the greatest care and attention in the hope of recovering something as close to the author's intention as possible. I have also provided in Plate IV the (upside-down) page of the *Commentary* which shows the title page of this book, mainly because I'm rather proud of having discovered it. This page turned right side up also provides, from a finished work, an example Buc's most legible hand.

The Third Edition

Revisiting the text more than forty years after having established it, and fearing greatly for errors, I have had to make very few corrections, much to my relief. The pagination of the text is exactly as in the earlier two editions. However, on one or two occasions (almost literally) I have had to change the configuration of a very few lines up to the end of a paragraph to accommodate a correction, and on one occasion (I think) this has resulted in adding an extra line to the page. The most frequent corrections have been to supply dropped brackets. Two revisions (only) are of serious import:

– 40, ll. 40f now read: 'made Richard of Gloucester, his base son, [knight, after Captain of] Calais'
– p. 191, ll. 10f now read: 'she prayed him as before to be a mediator for her to the k*ing* in the cause of [the marria]ge'. (See Plates II & III and, for discussion, General Notes, 191/1-25.)

In this edition I have provided, within square brackets, translations of passages in languages other than English.

In the transcripts which follow:

Square brackets indicate deletion. (Note: it sometimes seems almost certain that specific deletions are the work of the Editor rather than of the author. But it is also possible that such conjectures might be wrong. I have decided to make no distinction in case of being wrong on some occasions.) Underline = expansion of abbreviation.

LIST OF PLATES

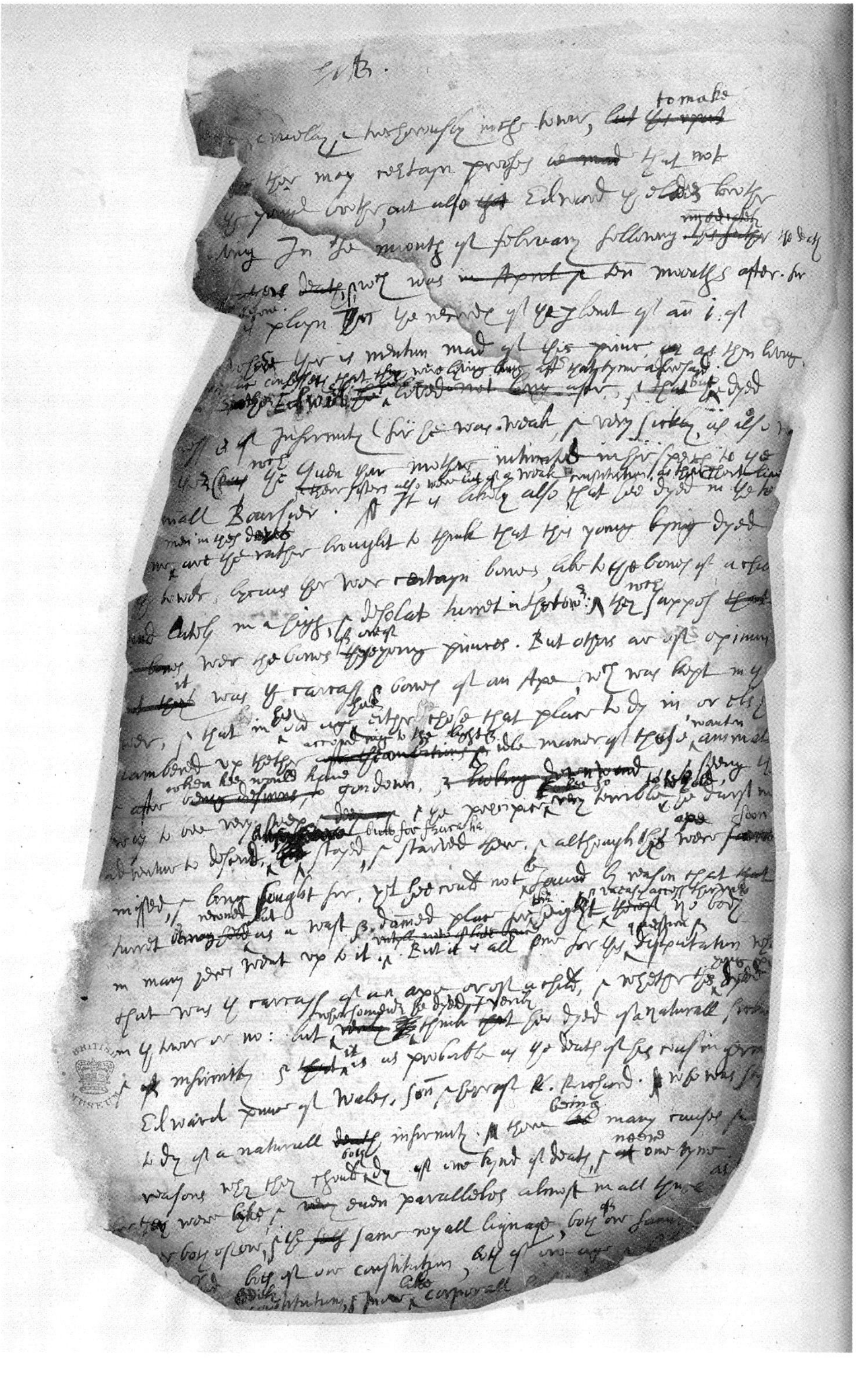

PLATE I: (Cotton Tiberius E.X, f. 153v) – discovery of the ape

\to make/
dered &, cruelly & treacherously in the tower, [but this report]
for ther may certain proofes [be mad] that not
the younger brother, but also [that] Edward the elder brother
\[immediately]/
living In the month of February following [his father] the deth
r fatheres [death], &, which was [in April &] ten mooneths after for
\before/
is playn In the recordes of the parlement of anno i. of
that ther is mention mad of this this princ, [and] as then living,
\place confesseth that they were lyving long after that tyme aforesayd./
brother Edward [he ^ lived not long after, & that] \but/ he dyed
ness & [of] Infirmit (for he was weak, & very sickly, as also w
\which/
other ([and as] the Quen ther mother intimated in hir speech to the
\& their fathers also were but of a weak constitution, as their short liue/
inall Boursier. [&] It is likely also that he dyed in the to
\men in thes dayes/
me ^ are the rather brought to think that the young kyng dyed
the tower, bycaus ther were certayn bones, like to the bones of a chi
\which/
ound lately in a high, & desolat turret in the tower: & they ^ suppose [that]
\of one of/
[bones] wer the bones these young princes. But others ar of opinion,
\it/ \of one of/
at [they] those yong princes. But others ar of opinion,
\it/
[t thes] was the carcass & bones of an Ape, which was kept in th
\his/ \hee/
wer, & that in ^ old age ^ either chose that place to dy in or els h
according to the light & \wanton/
lambered vp thether [after the ambitious &] idle maner of those ^ animals
\when he would haue/
& after [being desirous, to] gon down, [& looking downward,] & seeng th
\[to bee] so/ \to behold,/
way to bee very steep [& deep, &] & the precipice ^ very terrible ^ he durst n
\[but for feare] butt for feare he/ \ape/ \soon/
adventur to descend, [but] stayed, & starved there, & although this were [soone]
\be/
missed, & beng sought for, yet hee could not found by reason that [that]
renowned but \the/ \& uneasy access thervnto/
turret beeng [held] as a wast & damned place for ^ height [therof], no body
\[vntyll now of late &cc.]/ \question &/
in many yeres went up to it. But it is all one for this ^ disputation wh
\yong pr/
that was the carcass of an ape or of a child, & whether this ^ dyed
\whersomever he dyed and verily/
in the tower or no: but ^ [verily][I] think [that] hee dyed of a naturall sickn
\it/
& [of] infirmity & [that] is probable as the death of his cousin germ
Edward prince of Wales, sonn of K. Richard. [&] who was say
\being/
to dy of a natural [death] infirmity. [&] there [be] many causes &
\both/ \neere/
reasons why they should ^ dy of one kynd of death, & [at] one tyme
\as/
for they were lyke & [very] even paralleles almost in all thinges
\of/
er both of one, & the [self] same royall lignage, both one family
d both of one constitution, both of one age & b
\bodily/ \like/
constitution, & In [one] ^ corporall h

PLATE II: (Cotton Tiberius E.X, f. 238v scribal page) – 1st page ref. Elizabeth of York letter

e et in aeternum. Et
ibi a me datus libellus
umentum libertatis, iuxta
wering & to relate/
ere [which] the answere which was
concerning. or death
[witt] the life ^ of the Queen Ane & the
& which was very neare at an end.
es life would be noe ympediment of any
woman [and] in a consumption and
\according to the opinion of hir physitianes/
hat ^ she could not lyve [mus] muche
\in which/
y next following [and] they guessed
\month/
Queene dyed in the next ^ viz: M
\dayes/
st and more of ffebruarie wer [gone]
zabeth beinge verie desirous to be marie
\not onely/ \but also [haply] suspicious of the/
e impatient of delayes ^ wrote a Letter to the [Duke]
\Intimating first therein that/
Howard. Duke of Norfolk, [one] in whome she most
[e], because she knewe the Kinge her Ffather much lov
\had been/ \him & to/
[and] that he [was] a very faithfull servant vnto [him before]
[ing] \most loving &/ \K. Edwards/
[inge, and [verie] serviceable to ^ [his princely] Childrenn)
\congratulates/
[st] she [thancked] him ^ for his many Curtesies and friendly
\desires/ \as before/ to be a in the cause of
nd then she [prayed] him ^ to bee a mediator for her to the K
ge
whoe (as she wrote) was her onely ioye and her maker in
worlde, and that she was [in] his, in harte, in thoughts in
in
and ^ all, and then she intimated that the better halfe of Ffe
was paste, and that she feared the Queene would neu
all written with her own hand
[and] ^ these bee her owne wordes, ^ and this is the summe of
originall d
Letter, whereof I haue seene the autograph ^ vnder hir
and
hande, [and] by the special ^ honorable fauour of the mo
\and cheef of his family]/
[and the first counte of the Realme] ^: Sir Thomas Howarde
\&cc) & as it is [aboue in my dedication] /
[and Baron Howarde, Mowbray and Segraue, Fitzallen and
\[& of Surrey]/
[travers] Erle of Arundel ^ and the immediate and lyneall
of this [foresayd] John Lord Howard &c and Duke of Nor
\[??????]/ of this Lady inexperience] albeeit she be but yong ??????/
age & for his cau= [and my singular good lorde and the which letter \t/h[e]is bee
\capable of any honorable employment, & redy to vndertake [most rare] & to embrace an/
tion but also [amongst other pretious Jewells in his rych rare Cabinet
[??? but also he keepeth that letter aforesaid [& noted] in his rich Cabinet].
[ary of this story] letter [?????] in his rich and rare Cabinet amo
this letter it may bee observed, that she was ignorannt how
\wife lyving mought mary another./
[to be made for such marriadges], as if there were
former
waie but the death of the [Kinges] Wife. But there
and spake like to her selfe (that is to saye) like to
simple Ladie, ??? experienced in the affaires
\es & repudiations [& hath bene before declared]/
Insomuch as shee seemed

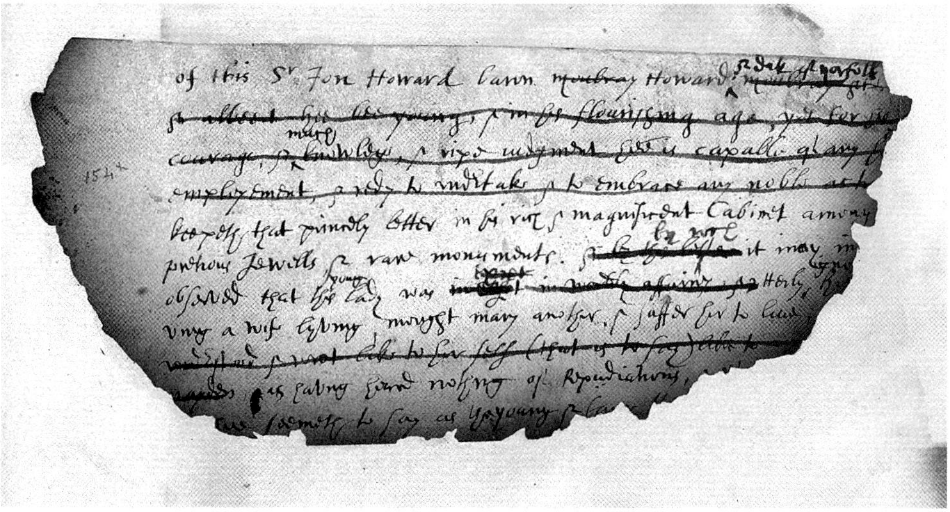

PLATE III: (Cotton Tiberius E.X, f. 239) – 2nd page ref. Elizabeth of York letter

& duk of norfolk
of this Sr John Howard baron [moubray] Howard ^ Mowbray &cc,
[albeit hee bee young, & in his flourishing age, yet for his]
Much
[courage, &^ knowledge, & ripe iudgment hee is capable of any h]
[employment, & redy to vndertake & to embrace an noble acti]
keepeth that princely letter in his rich & magnificent Cabinet among
\by which/
pretious Jewells & rare monuments. [& by this letter] it may in
young [expert] igno
observed that this lady was [in expert in worldly affaires, & I] tterly ^ ha
ving a wife lyving mought mary another, & suffer hir to liue,
[understood & wrot like to hir self (that is to say) like to]
[mayden] [&] as having heard nothing of Repudiations, & of
hee seemeth to say as the young & fayer

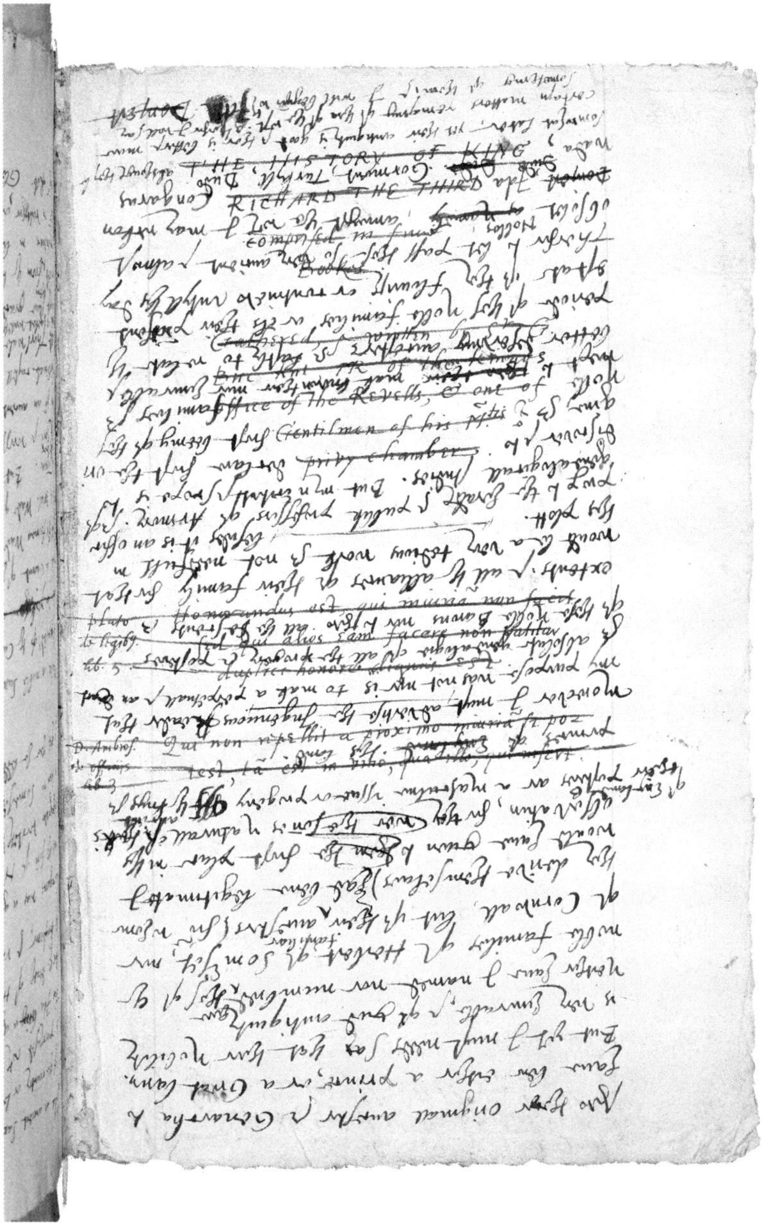
THE HISTORY OF KING
RICHARD THE THIRD
compiled in fower
Bookes
Gathered & written by
the Office of the Revells, & one of
Gentilmen of his Mties
privy chamber
plato
de legibus
lib. 5
Honorandus est qui iniuria non facit,
sed qui alios eam facere non patitur
duplici honore dignus est
D. Ambros.
de officiis
lib. 3
Qui non repellit a proximo iniuriam si potest, tam est in vitio, quam ille, qui infert.

PLATE IV: (Bodleian MS Eng. Misc. B. 106, f. 3^{v}) –
Buc's title page

Buc has written a draft of the title page of the *History* then reused it,
turning it upside-down
to write a page of the *Commentary* over it.
The original draft title page reads:

[THE HISTORY OF KING]
[RICHARD THE THIRD]
[comprised in fiue]
[Bookes]
[Gathered and written by Sr G.]
[Buc Knt, MR of the Kinges]
[office of The Revells, & one of]
[Gentilmen of his M*aje*^{tis}]
[privy chamber.]

[Honarandus est qui iniuria non facit]
[sed qui alios eam facere non patitur]
[duplici honore dignis est.]

[Qui non repellit a proximo iniuria*m* si po-]
[test, ta*m* est in vitio Qua ille, qui infert.]

[FLOURISH]

PLATE V: Houses of Clarence, York and Lancaster (simplified)

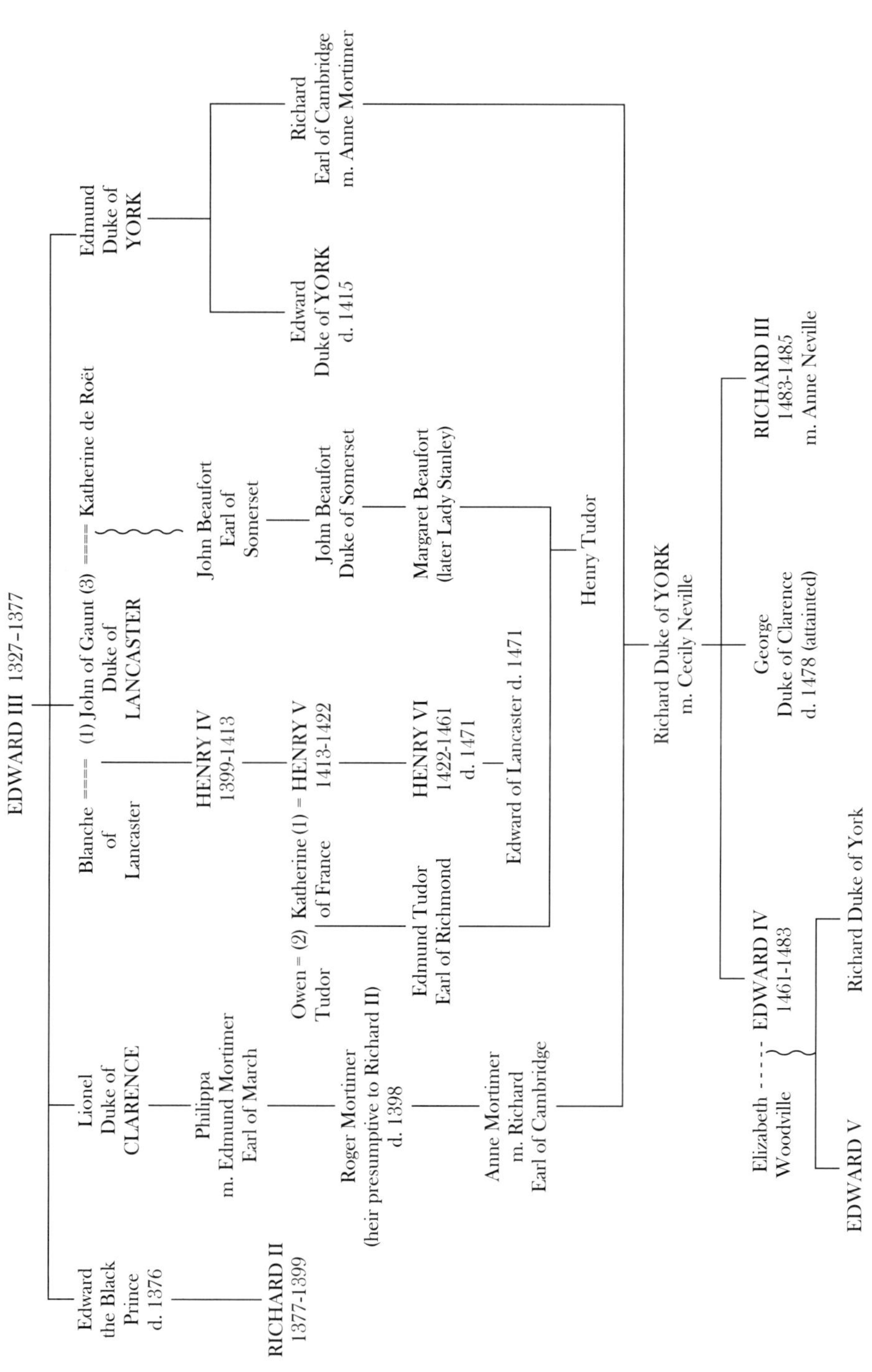

TEXT

The following notations have been used in the present text:

Italics:	conjectural emendations
Bold face:	'quotations' (which may be paraphrases), foreign words, and book titles.
[ ]	surrounds an emendation made from another copy of the work. These are from Egerton unless designated in the Textual Notes as being from Malone and/or Fisher.
[ ]	surrounds a portion bracketed in the original manuscript.
/	when used mid-line, indicates the end of a folio in the original manuscript.
*	following a folio number in the margin indicates a page in the hand of Buc's scribe.
**	follows the folio number of a page entirely in the Editor's hand.
*****	a series of asterisks in the text indicates a lacuna for which no satisfactory conjectural emendation can be made.

The numbers of folios in Tiberius from which material is taken are given in the margins throughout. When a long section such as a whole page or a leaf has been lost, the text has been given from Egerton and the folio numbers from Egerton given in the margin.

THE HISTORY OF KING RICHARD THE THIRD

Comprised in five books.

Gathered and written by

Sir G. Buc, Knight,
Master of the King's Office of the Revels
And one of the Gentlemen of His Majesty's Privy Chamber

****

Honorandus est qui inuriam non facit, sed qui alios eam facere non patitur duplici honore dignius est. — Plato, **De Legibus,** Lib. 5

****

Qui non repellit a proximo iniuriam si potest, tam est in vitio quam ille qui infert. — D. Ambrosius, **De Officiis,** Lib. 3

To the Most Illustrious Lord, Sir Thomas Howard, Premier Count of this Realm, Earl of Arundel and of Surrey, Baron Howard, Mowbray, Segrave, Breus, Fitzalan, Maltravers, etc., Knight of the Garter, etc., a Marshal and Counsellor of the King and of the Kingdom of England.

*Mos*t illustrious count, and my most honourable *good* lord: when I had finished this strange and uncouth [story] of King Richard III (and the which had been *form*erly, and often, written by sundry men, and [in a s]tyle and character very different and *very* contrary to this, and yet received for the *story* of this king), I began to suspect *that this* my book would find many censors *and cr*itical essayers, and those of diverse *kinds: some* curious, some jealous, some haply malevolent and malicious. *But* the fairest censure would be that all was [a pa]radox, or countr'opinion. It *seemed* very necessary and behoveful for *me* to seek the protection of *a patron who is noble not only* / in blood but also in mind *and in* vir*tue*: that is, wise, learned, judicious, and magnanimous*; and who* must be potent: that is, great in authority, in grace, and *in honour*. And all these, in mine opinion, and without flattery, concur copious*ly and* completely in your lordship, and as I could demonstrate if this place *and* your modest ears would admit.

1v

Con*struere est mani-*fes*tis et irrefragibili-*bus* argumentis et testi*moniis* solidis rei cognit*ae* * veritate*m* indic*are*. Johannes Veteranus talis **** hui*us* verbi ubique.**

And this is one cause, and a chief cause, why I should appeal to your lordship, and why your lordship should with a good will and with all noble alacrity entertain this charge and undertake this honourable office. And one is in regard that the prince whose story is here related and whose cause is here pleaded was a most magnificent and a most gracious patron of your most nob*le* and illustrious ancestors. For he (besides many other prince*ly* bounties and benefits bestowed upon them) advanced th*em to* the estates and titles of earls and of dukes, and to the quality of *princes*. And for these causes, he may by good right and by due *merit have* all the honour and right and good offices which your lordship may *afford* him.

Another cause why I dedicate and give this boo*k to your* lordship is because I hold it to be proper and due unto you, *for that* you are more interested than any other noble person *of this* kingdom. For herein be many honourable menti*ons and* fair eulogies of your heroical progenitors and of your *ancestors*, and to whose honours, dignities, titles, fortunes *you* most worthily succeed and rightly inherit. And *you are not only the* lineal and immediate heir and successor, but a*lso the* lively image, so that whatsoever is said *to be* theirs is also yours.

And the fourth and last cause *of this my* dedication hereof to your lordship groweth from the ancient and *noble* custom of offering and dedicating the spiritual *fruits and* the offspring of the best and divine part of men, and *the rewards of* their long and painful studies to honourable person*s to be* esteemed a token and testimony of the reverent
2 *care and* affection which they bear to *them. And this represents / the esteem* and love which I bear, and am bound to bear, to the *noble* house of the Howards, and chiefly to you, as the *pr*ince or head thereof, for the many great favours and good benefits which mine ancestors and myself have received of your most illustrious and magnificent ancestors, and whereof (as I might conveniently) I have made honourable and thankful mentions in some places of this book.

And now that I have declared the many good causes which I had to pray your protection and to grave your most noble name upon the frontispiece of this historical fabric, I doubt not of your most noble and favourable propensiveness to the patrociny and *p*rotection hereof, against the sharp and sinister censures and against the *jea*lous and calumnious spirits of such men as I suspected and *form*ulated in the beginning. For I fear not the generous, *nor th*e learned, nor the candid, nor the judicious readers, *for* they out of the goodness and justice of their dispositions are *res*pectively and modestly careful not to mistake nor *mis*construe anything, and much less to forejudge and hardly *censu*re the honest endeavours of studious persons. But, *being* wise, they will rather find means not only to resolve and to *satisfy the*mselves, but also any other curious, scrupulous, *malicious* and ill-affected men.

I know not what he is who can justly take *any of*fence at this work, if he know what a story is [and ought to be,] for, as your lordship well knoweth, a story must be true [and faithful], must be a plain and perspicuous narration of [things memora]ble and remarkable which have been done or [execute]d before. And the historiographer must be ve[ritable and free from all pro]sopolepsies and partial respects. *He must not a*dd nor omit anything, *either of partiality* or of hatred. [All which I have endeavoured to observe in] the writing of this story, so that [if my authors be sincere and faithful, my Muse is pure and innocent. For I have imitated the sceptic philosophers]
3v who of themselves affirmed nothing but [liked the doctrine of the] other more renowned and more learned philosophers. Fo*r that* which is said and related in this history is the *true test*imony *of* honest and faithful writers of former times.

B*ut* I use (and that seld*om, and only* upon necessity) to make some illustrations, and not *inter*pretations, and some *appa*rent and probable conjectures, and to no other end but for the better un*der*standing of some obscure passages and of some ambiguous words. And that is common and commendable licence and of very ancient use. And because I follo*w* other men, I cite their names and their authorities either in the text or in the margent, and it maketh more for the credit of the story.

Whereas on the other side the relations of stories of some other writers are of little cred*it* because they deliver all their matters of what time and antiquity soever upon their own bare and worthless word, and after the manner of fab*u*lous and trivial romancers. And who for *the* most part being idle and sensual persons, will no*t* take the pains to read the ancient and la*rge* histories, but epito*me*s of them and vulgar pamphlets only. And therefore their stories or ta*les or* romances are accounted as things ambiguous and fabulous. Where*fore I* like very well the counsel of the wise Cicero and follow it as [occasion] requireth. And that is this: **Testimonia et exempla ex veteri memori[a et mo]numentis antiquis deprompta plurimum solent** auctoritatis [habere].

Cicero ***In Verrinum***

And thus much for the account which I held myself bound to r*ender of* my style in this work. And here I purposed to end this dedica*tion*. But in the passage to the close thereof, I was admonished by my Genius *firmly* to answer (and by way of the orator's preoccupation) an objection *and ex*ception which may be made to me for a general word which I *said* but now and too peremptorily, as I confess, and I recant it. And that was *where I said* that I know not any man who might justly take excep*tion to this* history. And wherein it might be said that this my case was like to *that* famous Mantuan shepherd who was reprehended by Apollo for dealing too high for him:

Cum canerem reges et proelia, Cynthius aurem
Vellit et admonuit: 'Pastorem, Tityre, pingues', etc.

Vergil in ***Eclogues***

And I confess that my *sty*le reached too high and was too general *to* have excepted ONE, and that *is* a rare and a peerless One, and [of a singular] and sacred quality, for he hath no peers nor paragons eith*er* in *nature or in* condition. Neither hath he any peers or equals *in judgemen*t, in justice, and in clemency. And *this* one may take exceptions at me as at one who *without a great share* or portion in fortunes and in fame and as small in lear*ning* and but slightly initiated in the mysteries of poli*cy should presume* to write of his royal ancestors and to examine their actions, to rip up their vices, and to treat and to d*iscourse of* crowns, of majesty, of *kingdoms*, of royal rights and tit*les*, and of those *who a*re supposed to be nob*le*.

***Id* est unicus**
*******pri-**
**********pro*prius**
**********De*us**

4v

AN ADVERTISEMENT TO THE READER

5 Before I enter into this story of King Richard, I must advertise the noble, courteous, and intelligent Reader (for unto such only I write) that the argument and subject of this discourse or story was at the first but a chapter, and the thirteenth chapter, of the third book of a rude work of mine entitled THE BARON, or **The Magazin of Honour**. But the argument of that chapter being strange and very extravagant and extraordinary (as the affairs and fortunes of this prince were), suppeditated strange and extraordinary matters, and in such copy and variety as that it diffused itself into an extraordinary and unusual largeness, and so much as it exceeded very much the laws and the proper limits of a chapter. *Wherefore* being also much enlarged and transferred hither, it may pass here *under* the title of a discourse or historiola, and it may serve *as a* gloss and a paraphrase of the foresaid chapter, and that chapter for an *argum*ent of this story of King Richard III; and not of Perkin Warbeck, *as mine* host of *Westminster* (and now a worshipful shallow magistrate) hath idly and add*ledly alleged.*

But to let these sycophantisms pass, and to proceed, I must now draw out *and* transcribe hither from the said thirteenth chapter some particular *matters*, and especially the beginnings and first times of this Prince Richard, comprehending *the prince*ly lineage of the king and his parentage, his birth, his education, his [tirocin]y, and all the conditions of these acts, and of his youth, and of his [private] life. And this being done, and as it ought according to [meth]od and due order, I will next address my style and my *labour*s to the story of his public person and of his regal state, *and to* relate his election and coronation and affairs and actions and the more signal acci[dents of hi]s reign and time until his death.

Publica [persona est] prince[ps, vel magistratus,] qui Re[ipublicae vel parti eius] praeest. [Heironymus Vulteius

And lastly, and because he hath been accu[sed of] great crimes, and slanderously (as I verily believe), and even at such times as envy is accustomed [to cease barking] and malevolence *to leave men* at rest in their graves, *I shall make* [endeavo]ur to answer for him, and to clear and [redeem] *him from those improbab*le imputations and strange and spiteful [scandals] *and rescue* him *entirely* from th*ose* wrongs, and *to make truth*
5v (*hereby* / concealed and oppressed and almost utterly suppressed) present herself to the light, according to her desire, and by the opportune taking of the fair advantage of these happy and just times of a king by whose favour and furtherance Truth hath here safe conduit and free passage and prevaileth and flourishes. And these shall also see the calumniators and false accusers of this prince detected and convinced of slanders and of lies. And the good and loyal barons shall be distinguished from the bad and false barons. And Morton and More and their apes shall be delineated and painted in their own colours, every *one* of them, and shall receive here and

Beatum Sancti Regis Jacobi regnum.

hereafter **propriam mercedem** and **referet unusquisque propria corporis prout gessit sive bonum, sive malum**, if I might so say.

And as truth and justice shall direct and help to answer by way of *refuta*tion an objection against some repetitions which shall occur in this story by the curious carpers, battologies and tautologi*es*, I answer and I say confidently that such repetitions as are here are not *only proper* and allowable, but also needful. And they be such as the ancient *and* grave jurisconsults defended thus in their axiom: **Verba gemina repetita enixam et constantem voluntatem indicant**. And su*ch* that other repetitions are a tacit persuasion to the reader or *author to* remember better, and better to mark the thing so repeated*, and its* causes. The divine Plato was of opinion that *Plato* **Quod bene dicitur, *repetere* non nocet**: and it is much used by him. And in brief, repeti*tion was* allowed in the Holy Scripture and authorized by good reasons. And thus for my repetiti*ons*.

I must not for*get* gratefully to commemorate the courtesies and ingenious prompt*ings of* some of my learned friends to help and to further my studies and *labours* on this enterprise and by whom *I have* profited, besides the nomenclation and quotation of the names of mine *authors* and records which I have followed, and for my better warrant. For I like not that t*he right* and privilege of **ipse dixit** should be allowed to any *but* Pythagoras, or to such another whose words were as orac*les*.

****

[*There follows here a criticism of an individual historian, the beginning of which is missing. Buc has evidently made two points already: that the unnamed author reports events too briefly and that he neglects to cite the dates of the occurrences which he relates*.]

****

******** year and of the years of the reigns of kings. The third wa*s* his **4**
neglect of citation of authors and quotations, thus concealing of their names and vainly taking all upon himself.

Therefore I have avoided their faults. For as concerning brevi*ty*, I am here rather prolix than brief, and I observe times and years, and I cite mine authors everywhere. And therefore I shall not need to make here a catalogue of them as many do vainly also and to no purpose. But as I in*tend* to make a thankful remembrance of the more signal courtesies and of the better help which I have had of some of my more learned and better-booked friends, as namely Mr Camden, Clarensius; and the good herald Mr Brooke, York; and chiefly the noble and learned knight and baronet, Sir Robert Cotton, whose rich and plentiful library hath still been open to me, and very freely and friendly, and as *in* like manner it is to all his honest and studious friends and lovers of good monuments and of rare antiquities. And therefore his cabinet *and* library may worthily have the same inscription and title which *was* set upon the gate of the School of the Sacred Muses, and *to th*eir immortal honour and glory: **Apertae semper Musarum ianuae**.

And if it be objected that I have omitted anything of *the* story of King Richard, I answer that I have omitted nothing of *great* matter or moment, nor anything else but some slight *matte*rs, and such as are to be seen in the common and vulgar chronic*les* and stories, and which are in the hands of every idiot or mere *fool*ish reader, *and to no pur*pose, and for the most part not worth the reading. And my scope was to write this unhappy *king's* story faithfully and at large, and to plead his cause, and to answer and refell the *many* accusations and calumniations brought against him. And if I have performe*d this as* I hope and I *believe* I have, then I have done a work of charity and won the goal and prize *which I sought.*

The just and intelligent and generous and judicious Reader must be there*with satisfied*, and so wishing him all right, and that with favour, I bid him farewell.

From the King's Office of the Revels, Peter's Hill,
the .... of .... 1619.

The Argument and Contents of the First Book 6

The lineage, family, birth, education, and tirociny of King Richard III.

The royal house of Plantagenet and the beginning of that surname.

What sobriquets were.

The antiquity of surnames.

Richard is created Duke of Gloucester; his marriage and his issue.

His martial employments; his prowess and skill in military affairs.

His journey into Scotland and his recovery of Berwick.

The death of King Edward IV.

The Duke of Gloucester is made Lord Protector, and soon after King of England by the earnest and importunate suits of the barons and of the people, and as the right true and lawful heir.

Henry Tudor, Earl of Richmond, is suspected of practice against the king and the state, and not only by King Richard, but also [long] before by the king his brother.

He is conveyed into France.

The noble lineage and [wor]thiness of Sir William Herbert; his employment; he is made Earl of Pembroke.

King Edward IV first, and after King Richard, solicits the Duke of Brittany and [treats] with him for the delivery of the young Earl of Richmond, his prisoner.

T[he success] of that business.

The quality and title of the Beauforts and Somersets.

[The] lineage and family of the Earl of Richmond.

The solemn coronations of King R[ichard] and of the queen his wife, his first at Westminster and his second at York; the no[bles], knights and officers made by him.

The Prince Edward his son is [invested] in the principality of Wales, and the oath of allegiance is made to him.

King R[ichard] demandeth a tribute of France.

His progress to York.

His careful and godly [charge] given to the judges and magistrates for the administration of justice.

He hold[eth a] Parliament, wherein the marriage of the king his brother with the Lady Gray is decla[red and] adjudged to be unlawful, and their children to be illegitimate and not capa[ble of] the crown.

Morton, Bishop of Ely, and Dr Nandick, a conjurer, and the Earl of R[ichmond] and divers others are attainted of treason, and many good laws are m[ade,] and the king is declared and approved by the Parliament to be the only true and lawful [heir] of the crown.

The king h[ath secret] advertisement of seditions and of treasons.

He createth a Vice-Constable of E[ngland.]

His sundry treaties with foreign princes.

Dr Morton an excellent politician [and a] chief sower of sedition.

The Duke of Buckingham is corrupted by Morton and en*vious and* malcontent, and he entereth into disloyal practices, and he demandeth the earldom of Hereford, [with the] Great Constableship of England.

He taketh arms; he is taken and put [to death] by martial law.

7

THE FIRST BOOK OF THE HISTORY OF RICHARD THE THIRD, OF ENGLAND AND OF FRANCE KING, AND LORD OF IRELAND

The [house and] tit[le of York]

Richard Plantagenet, Duke of Gloucester and King of England and of France and Lord of Ireland, the third King Richard, was the younger son of Sir Richard Plantagenet, the fourth Duke of York of that royal family, and King of England designate by [King] Henry the Sixth and by the High Court of Parliament: that is by the most noble senate and by the universal [syn]od of this kingdom.

The mother of this Richard, Duke of Gloucester [was] the Lady Cecily, daughter of Sir Ralph de Neville, Earl of Westmorl[and] by his wife Joan de Beaufort, the natural daughter of [John] Plantagenet (alias de Gand), Duke of Guienne and of Lancaster, [King] of Castile and of Lyons, and the third son of King Edward the Third [(for in t]hat order this duke is best accounted, because William of Hatfield, [the seco]nd son of King Edward III, died in his infancy). And this Duke of York [and King] Designate was propagated from two younger sons of the same King Edward III. And whereby he had both paternal and maternal title to [the crow]ns of England and of France. But his better and nearer title was the [materna]l title, or that which came to him by his mother the Lady Anne de [Mortim]er, the daughter and heir of the Lady Philippa Plantagenet, who was the sole daughter and heir of Lionel Plantagenet, Duke of Clarence, [secon]d son to King Edward III, according to the account and order aforesaid. And this Lady [Philipp]a was the wife of Sir Edmund Mortimer, the great and famous Earl [of Marc]h. And that Duke Richard, King Designate, by his father Richard Plantagenet, Duke [of York] (surnamed also de Conisbrough), issued directly and in a masculine line [from Edm]und Plantagenet (alias de Langley), [the] first Duke of York, and the [fourth son] of King Edward III. And thus much briefly for the princely house [and title of] York.

[Plantagenet]

[And here it] may [se]em fit and convenient to make a report of the stem and lineage [of that most r]enowned and glorious progenitor of these princes of York and [Lancaster,] namely the often before mentioned King Edward III, [which is thus: this king] was the fifth king in a lineal and masculine descent [from the great Henry surnamed] Plantagenet, famous for his great [prowess and many victories. He was the second Henry, King of England, in the right of his mother the Empress Matilda, or Maud, daughter and heir of King Henry I, and styled **Anglorum Domina,** and
7v sometime wife of the Emperor Henry V, whereupon he was] / also
surnamed **Filius Imperatricis**. And the Frenchmen called him Henry **du Court Manteau**, or Curtmantle, because he wore a cloak shorter than the fashion was in his times. And by his father Galfrede, or Geoffrey,

Plantagenet he was Earl or Duke of Anjou (for then **Dux** and **Comes,** and **Ducatus** and [**Comitatus**] were synonyms and promiscuous words). And he was also Earl of Maine and of Touraine and hereditary Seneschal or High Steward of France. And by his marriage of Eleanor, Queen of France repudiate, and the daughter and heir of William, Duke of Gascoigne and of Guienne and Earl of Poitou, he was duke and earl of those principalities and signories, and he was also by the empress his mother Duke of Normandy. He was Lord of Ireland by conquest, and confirmed by [Pope Adrian.]

[The empire of King Henry II]

But these were not all his signories and dominions. For after that he was King of England he extended the limits of his empire and principate so far as they were bounded in the south by the Pyrenean Mountains (the confines of Spain and France), and in the north with the Isles of Orkney, and in the east and west with the oceans. And for his greatness he was styled **Regum Britanniae Maximus** (as Giraldus Cambrensis, Gulielmus Novobrigensis, and Johanne[s] Sarisberiensis, grave and creditable authors, affirm). And doubtless he w[as] the greatest king of Britain since King Arthur reigned.

[Giraldus in **Topographica Hiberniae**; Sarisberiensis in **Polycratico**; Neubrigensis, **Liber** 2.]

But whereas some say that the foresaid Geoffrey Plantagenet, [Earl of] Anjou, father of this Henry, was the first Earl of Anjou which bore the sur[name] of Plantagenest (or Plantagenet after the common and vulgar [orthography)], that must not be allowed. For certainly that surname ha[d the] beginning from a much more ancient Earl of Anjou, and [for other reasons and better causes] than can be found in the foresaid Geoffrey, as it shall be made apparent.

It is controverted amongst the antiquaries and the heralds which Ear[l of Anjou] first bore the name and sobriquet of Plantagenet. And upo[n what] occasion and for what cause it was so taken and borne, and also [in what] time or age it had beginning, I think I shall be able to determine according to my small talent of knowledge and reading and ac*cording* to the methods I have held for the searching of the originals *of the* most ancient noble families of England, of their surnames, in my ***Commentary* upon the Book of Domus Dei, or The New Roll of Winche*ster***. And for the accomplishment hereof I must not only use the he*lp of* good historians and learned antiquaries but also of traditions and of pro*ced*ures, and those fortified with reasons and with arguments of force and credit sufficie*nt* for the beginning of this surname of Plantagenet.

For after I had read and searched many books and perused many written **10**
monuments for the knowledge of this matter, I went to some of my friends learned in heraldry and in history, and I conferred with them and desired to be better informed by them. And amongst these, I addressed myself to Sir William Dethick, Prncipal King at Arms, who was a man bred in good letters, and well languaged, and a generous person, and one of the best heralds of his time. And he had good means to be a good antiquary and a good herald, for he had a library very well furnished with rolls and good books, manuscripts and other and diverse monuments and stories, and such as were fit and proper to a man of his profession.

And I desired this honest officer of arms to declare to me the first beginning and first bearing of the name of Plantagenet. And he answered very courteously that he both could and would show *me* much good matter for that purpose. And he took me with *him* into his library, and he took down a fair old book written o*n p*archment, wherein he said there was some matter concerning *the be*ginning of the name of Plantagenet. And he turned to a brief *glo*ss or paragraph which was written of those strange and fantasti*cal n*ames or words which the Frenchmen call sobriquets, which, according to the learned Nicot and other French writers, *were use*d sometimes seriously and in good part, and sometimes as *nick*names and names of scorn. And there was a jolly catalogue *of* sobriquets in that book. And I made choice of some of *them*, and I transcribed them into a piece of paper and from thence hither, and these they are.

[Sobriquets]

[Berge]r: shepherd
[Grise]gonelle: grey coat
[Teste d']Estouppe: head of tow
[Arbuscu]la: shrub
[Martell]: hammer
[Grundebo]euf: oxface
[La Zouch]: a branch upon a stem
Houlette: sheephook
Hapken: hatchet
Capelle: hood
Sansterre: lackland
Geffard: **iuvencus**, or heifer
Malduit: ill taught
Filz de Fleau: the son of a flail

and many othe*rs*. [And amongst them] was Plantagenet: that is, the plant or stalk [of a broom.

[And the g]loss upon the text was that anciently these so[briquets and the like base and ridiculous] names were taken by great persons [and by other noble and signal persons who had been great and heinous sinners, and had committed murder, blasphemy, treason, sacrilege, incest, perjury, rapes,]
10v and all kind of sins and abominations; and now at the last, by the merciful goodness of God, were become penitent for them, and in all humility and hearty sorrow confessed them to God and to the holy priest, their confessor or ghostly father; and whose manner was to enjoin them some penance for the better appeasing of the divine wrath, and for some amends and satisfaction for their so great and enormous offences, as they supposed.

[After this manner, and long after, King Henry II, the heir and successor of this Earl Fulco, was enjoined by the Pope to go to the Holy Land and to fight against the infidels. Hoveden, Rievall, etc.]

And the priests also enjoined them to punish their bodies with fasting and with sackcloth and with whipping and with other kind of rigours and austerities, and also to undertake some hard and painful labour; or to go a long and dangerous journey upon their bare feet; or to take the cross and to bear arms against the Saracens, Turks, and other infidels; or to go in pilgrimage to som*e* far remote saint's temple or shrine of some special saint, as to St Iago of Compostella, to our Lady of Gua*da*lupe or of Loretta, etc.; but chiefly to the Holy Sep[ulchre] of our Lord and Saviour in Jerusalem.

And furthermore, these lords which [undertook] these penances, to the end to show by this ou[t]ward sign their great hu[miliation] and inward direction wrought by their contrition and hearty peniten*ce* did not only abstain from all matters of pleasure and of po[mp,] of delicacy and of bravery, but also took upon them the c[onditions] and qualities and habits of mean and base and ignoble pers[ons.] One of them would be apparelled and disguised like to a carpen[ter], and another like to a smith, and another like to a fisherman, *or* like to a mariner, and another like to a shepherd, another like to [a mourner,] and another like to a woodman, and another took the title and habit and the ensign [of] a broom man. And he was the ancient Earl of Anjou befo[re intimated.]

And this opinion is general. But none of the heralds nor antiquaries, French or English, [tell how that earl] was called, nor when he lived, nor whose son he was. These be the doubts which remain, *and* I shall be able to unfold and resolve them. And, as I intim*ated*, I m[ust dissent] from them who make Geoffrey Plantagenet, who was the f[ather of King Henry II, to be the first which bore the broom stalk or took the device thereof, for it will be found, I doubt not, that he which first took it was a much more ancient Earl of Anjou, and a man more religious, one that had been in pilgrimage at Jerusalem.]

But Geoffrey Plantagenet was never so pious nor so religious, nor had **8** never so much remorse of his sins, for he was an amorous knight and a jovial, and a gallant courtier, and spent his time in the courts of princes, and in feasting and in tournaments and in courting of fair ladies, and those of the highest quality, for Lewis le Gros, King of France, suspected him with the queen his wife, and not without cause. And he did not only make love to the Empress Matilda, but also won her favour and love with his amorous devices and married her. And doubtless he neither had nor would have any leisure [for] such humble and penitent and mortified thoughts, nor had he any so goodly disposition as to resolve to go in a poor and perilous pilgrimage to Jerusalem.

Therefore I will let him pass and find another and more ancient Earl of Anjou, who was doubtless the man we seek, and his ancestor. And he was a great sinner, and in the [end] repented himself of his sins and vowed to do bitter and austere penance. And for his penance he undertook *a* poor and vile and obscure and hard pilgrimage to the Holy Sepulchre. *This m*an was the first Fulke which was Earl of Anjou, and who lived above a hundred years before the Norman Conquest of England. And I will [set] down his story briefly, as I find it in the chronicles of [Anjou.]

[Fulke, first Earl of Anjou

This Fulke was the son of Godfrey, or Geoffrey, Grise[gonelle,] the first Earl of Anjou, according to du Haillan. [And] *he* was an ancestor and progenitor to the foresaid Geoffrey Plan[tagenet,] and some seven or eight degrees in the ascending line (as Para[din] accounteth). And he was a man of great courage and of much strength, *and* [of] a warlike disposition. And he was also very ambitious [and] covetous, and would do anything to fulfil and to satisfy his [desires.] And, amongst other crimes, he committed two more heinous than the rest, and the [one was a wilful]l perjury, and the other a treacherous murder of his young [kinsm]an Drogo, Earl of Brittany. His perjury was for the defrauding and spoiling of a [church of certain] rights. [And he caused his nephew Dr]ogo to be murdered to the end that he might have and possess his lands and [his co]unty and principality.

And he, being grown old and having much solitary time [and man]y heavy and sad thoughts, which naturally accompany old age and suggest better considerations of a [man's] former life and of his sins committed in his y[outh], *he be*came much grieved and troubled in mind, and he was tormented [with the s]ecret scourges and stings of these his great and heinous [crimes.] And at shrift, or confession, he discovered his grief to his confessor and made his *obeissance*, and desired him (as great Constantine [Zosimus] did Aegyptus) to devise some means to help him [in his trou]bled and afflicted mind.

And this good priest, perceiving [his remorse] (*which* is a token of God's grace), bade him be of good comfort. And he t*old him that to cure him* of 8v his soul's diseases was not hard, if he *would undergo a penance*. / And forthwith this earl in all humility and sorrow confessed his sins and professed to be most heartily sorry for them, and that in taking his true penitence he would endure any pain or penance to have pardon for his sins and to be absolved of their great guilt. Then this priest told him that he should be pardoned and absolved, but with the condition that for the making of some amends for [satisfaction] of Almighty God, he should go in humble and hard pilgrimage to the Holy Sepulc*hre* of our Lord and Saviour at Jerusalem, and there most humbly and penitent*ly* to make his confession of his sins and to crave pardon for them.

And the earl gladly and willingly accepted this penance and resolved to perform that pilgrimage, and in all lowly and contemptible manner. And the better to express his humbled and dejected spirit, he clad himself in the habit of a peasant and base fellow. And he left and dismisse*d* all his gallant followers and courtly train, and went his jour[ney as a private m]an, and took with him only two of his meanest but honest servants. And not to th*e* end to be holpen or eased anything by their services in his poor *pilgri*mage, but rather that they might be witnesses of his true *and* faithful performance of the penance enjoined on him and of s*ervice to* be done by them to him when he was come to Jerusalem.

And he was come to Jerusalem, and then he made the first use of those two f*ellows*, and that was a very strange use. For he employed the one of them [to get] a strong cord, such as is used for the strangling and hanging o[f] *traitors* and criminals. And he commanded the other to provide a bun*dle* of such twigs as wherewith there might rods be mad*e*; and they fulfilled his will and commandment. And then he caused [them] to strip him and to accouter him as a condemned person. And then *he* willed the one to put the halter about his neck and to draw *and* lead him to the Holy Sepulchre. And he commanded his other serv*ant* to follow him close with his rods and to scourge him most sha*mefully*, and without any favour, until he came to kneel before the [Holy] Sepulchre.

[Accoutré en] criminel [et condamné.] Paradin

[The second] Henry King of England *from these s*courges of his [ancestor] took example to [submit] his body to be scourged [by the] monks of Canterbury [for the death] of Thomas Becket. [Du Haillan; Paradin]

And when he came thither he bowed himself and [prostrated] himself before that sacred monument of Jesus Christ. And he said to the Lord in this manner: '*I have been wa*ndering from thy holy ways, and I am here as an assassin or traitor to be hanged for my spiritual treasons commit*ted*'. *And* anon, and after much sorrow and many tears, he raised himself upon his knees and confessed all his sins; and chiefly and with most remorse these his two great [sins] of per[jury and] of murder, and in all sincere and hearty repentance, he p*rayed for mercy* and pardon for his sins. Amongst other his zealou[s and devout words, he u]ttered these: **Mon die[u et seigneur reçois** 9 **à pardon le parjure et homicide et misérable Foulques.]** / And he returned home w[ith a sa]tisfied [conscience,] *and lived* [many] years in his country in all [prosperity and honour of all men.]

And there be many more exa[mple]s, and they *be* of many princes [and noble persons who] lived about the year of our Lord 1000, and somewha*t* in some three or four ages after; who, having been great and famous [offenders, and after,] feeling by the divine mercy a remorse of their gr*eat sins in t*heir consciences, ha[ve under]taken long and painful pilgrimages to sundry holy places, to *Canterbury and* to Jerusalem, the holy city, where the shrine or glorious sepul*chre* of our Lord and Redeemer Jesus Christ was and is. And amongst thes*e* sinful and penitent princes, this first Fulco (or Fulke), Earl of Anjou, and the son of Godfrey Grisegonelle, earl of that country, w[as] one of these noble sinful and penitent persons [who went this pil]grimage to Jerusalem, and expressly to visit *the Holy Sepulchre*, about the year of our Lord 1000.

And in consideration *th*irdly, we may observe here that as they did wear an outward habit of *humility, they wrought and* laboured to have the true and perfect humility in their hearts and souls. But *the signs of* their inward humility and of their *outward submission* were in their plain and coarse and p*oor attire, and* in their base disguises of shephe*rds, peasants* and the like And we find also that according to this dis*guise they took* igno*ble* and contemptible names or nicknames and c*alled themselves by sobriquets. And i*t hath also been made apparent that this old Earl of A*njou* then *took* the sobriquet of Plantagenest, **ut supra.**

And to conclude, by all these particulars being *com*pared and considered, it is apparent and mani*fest* that the foresaid Fulke, the first Earl of Anjou, and the son of *Geoffrey* Grisegonelle, was that noble *pers*on which first took that sobriquet of Plantagenest, or *Broomstalk*. And that now it remaineth that we seek *the* reason why the Count Fulke chose the genet [plant or broomstalk] before any other vegetable or other thing; *and this may* also be resolved. And the reasons of *it* [which I conceive] may be [first in respect the] / broom, [in the hieroglyphical learning, is the] symbol **9v** of hu[mility,] *because it grow*eth not in high, but in low places. [And therefore the] poets, and parti[cularly] Vergil, the best poet, [giveth it] the epithet of **humilis: humilisque genista.** **Geo[rgica,] Lib. [II].**

[And the etymolo]gists say that it is derived from the word **genu**, [the] knee, [which of] all the parts or members of man is most applied, and (as [it were]) dedicated unto lowliness and to humble offices, and to the chief act [of rev]erence: that is, kneeling (as all men know). And the natural Leo[nard] Fuch-[sius.] philosophers affirm [there] is so mutual a correspondency and so natural a sympathy [bewt]een **genu** and **genista**, as that the broom is of all other plants [or] vegetals the most comfortable and the most medicinable thing [to] the pains and diseases of the knees. And Pliny, a great master amongst Pli[ny,] **Lib**. 2[4] [them sai]th, **Genista tusa cum**, etc. **genua dolentia sanat**. **cap**. [9]

*More*over, broom is a natural and actual instrument of pur*ifying and c*leansing places which are foul, and therefore it may serve well for a type of the *instrumen*ts which are proper to purge and to cleanse the soul, *which corr*ections and chastisements be distasteful and b*ring forth evidence of cleansing in the* flowers of the genet. Or in consi[deration] *the stalk*s or branches of the broom m[ay be made a fit instrum]ent of correction (such as the rod [is), it may be defined and conclu]ded [that the] rods or scourges wherewith the n*ewly* [penitent earl was chastis]ed were made of broom tw[igs, and not for that cause only,] but for the necessity the which the[re was to make rods of broom.] For in regard that the earl was *a penitent, there were* rods necessarily to be provided, and t*here* could *good quantity* of rods be made at or near to Jeru[salem.] And those trees which are the most proper to such uses (as namely [the] birch and the willow and the withy) because they covet to be in *rich* and watery and moist soils, or else they will not grow, and the so[il] o[f] Jerusalem was contrary to their [Strabo, **Lib.** 16] nature, for (as Strabo, [a fa]mous geographer, writeth) the soil about Jer[usalem] is stony and sandy and dry and barren; and that kind of soil is [grate]ful and very pleasing to the genet; and therefore, as it is most like, the earl's m*en who* provided and prepared the rods made them of the stalk *or the* twigs of broom about Jerusalem, as the virtues and s*trengths of that plant* were well known to the Earl Fulke.

[And from hence it must take the beginning of that honour which afterward his noble and princely posters continued in making it their chief surname of all other. Nor had they reason only to honour, but also to maintain and continue the fame and honour of the demise of that good earl, [Du Haillan] because they prospered and lived in greater felicity for his sake, as the pious people of that age, and long after, said and verily believed and observed, that God so blessed him and his progeny that they became afterwards dukes and princes in sundry other places. And some of them were kings, namely of Jerusalem, of England, France, Ireland and Scotland, etc.

[And now give me leave to say with Mr Camden, for the continuance of this device, that the father of Henry Plantagenet, King of England, would wear a broomstalk in his bonnet, as also many other nobles of the House of Anjou did, and used it for their surname. But because some men make a doubt and question of the continuance thereof, I will say something which shall be of sufficient importance to determine the question.]

11 Some men (who pretend to see furt[her and better in the dark than] / other men as clearsighted as they) [affirm that the name or surname of] [The surname of Plantagenet very ancient and continuate.] Plantagenet was not used by the kings and [princes of] the Angevin race in the ancient times, but [to be taken of late time.] But *that* [is] a false opinion, [and the] contrary is so tr[ue and manifest, and the testimonies] so many [that it were tedious] to cite and to adduce them. And whosoever shall be [pleased but to] fo*ll*ow and pursue the excellent collection of a[ll the princely and] royal genealogies of England in the **Catalogue of Honour** made by that learne[d and diligent] antiquary, and one of the best and most skilful heralds which [have been] from the first foundation and institution of the College of Heralds and of the officers at arms, and namely Robert Glover, Somerset Duke at Arms, he shall see nothing more obvious nor more frequent in the deductions of the princes of the House of Anjou than the [a]ddition of the surname of Plantagenet to their forename, or Christian name. As for example there you have Thomas Plantagenet, Edmund [Plan]tagenet, George Plantagenet, John Plantagenet, Edward Plantagenet, [Lion]el Plantagenet, Humphrey Plantagenet, and a great many more such. And in the French [histori]ans and antiquaries, and namely in John du Tillet and Gerard du [Haill]an and Claude Paradin and Jean, Baron de la Hay, and in others, you [shall] very often meet with Geoffrey Plantagenet, Arthur Plantagenet, [Rich]ard Plantagenet, and divers the like, all of the first age, and when the [Angev]in princes first became English, and some before.

And Mr [Cam]den, a very learned and judicious writer, maketh mention of some [ancient Plantagenets, as of Rich]ard Plantagenet and of John

Plantagenet, and of others more, in his [immor]tal **Britannia**. And many more such authorities and such [exam]ples might be brought for the ancient use of the surname [P]lantagenet, but it were in vain and needless *to do this, for* the case is so clear and not called in question by any. *So much for the* bearing and use of the surname Plantagenet. And *nevertheless we* may not leave the name of Plantagenet, *and of which I sha*ll have other occasions to speak in the [next book, where] also I will by the way show, and by good authority, [that the surname] of Plantagenet was continually borne by all the [lawful sons, nephews, and] legitimate posters and progeny of the foresaid [king, and the second Henry,] surnamed Plantagenet and FitzEmpre[ss, and that none else] might bear that surname.

11v

Enough has been said for the genealogy and *lineage* of *Plantagenet*. And whereunto might be added that [those earls of Anjou were] descended out of the great house of Saxon [in Germany, which h]ath brought forth many kings and emperors [and dukes, and that they] were of kindred and alliance to the ancient [kings of France] and to sundry other princes. [There nee]d no more to be said here therein, but to conclude for the great and high no[bilit]y of King Richard, as the good old poet did for another noble and heroical person, **viz**:

[Ovid]

***Deus est in utroque parente.**

[*Deus, id est Rex.]

And now to proceed with other matters of the king's private story, and the first as concerning his birth and native place. He was born in the Castle of Fotheringhay, or, as some write, in the Castle of Berkhamsted, both castles and honours of the duke his father, *and* about the year of our Lord 1450. And the which I discover by the cal[culation] of the birth and reign and death of the King Edward, his brother. For Edward was born about the year of our Lord 1441 or 1442, [and he] reigned twenty-two years, and he died at the age of forty-one years, **[Anno] Domini** 1483. And the Duchess of York, his mother, had five [children] betwixt King Edward and King Richard his brother, so that R[ichard] could not be less than seven or eight years younger than King Edw[ard]. And he survived him not fully three years.

[The place and time of the birth of King Richard.]

And this Richard Plantagenet and the other children of Richa[rd, Duke] of York were brought up for the most part in the Castle of Middleham in Yorkshire, until [the duke their fathe]r, together with his son Edmund Plantagenet, E[arl of Rutland,] were slain in the battle of Wakefield, **Anno D[omini** 1461. And then th]e Duchess of York, their mother, much fearing that [her two] sons could not be safe in any part of England, [by reason th]e faction of Lancaster, after the slau[ghter]r of the Duk[e of York, was gr]own very insolent and also very strong and evil, and di[d] bear [a mortal hatred t]o the house of York, she secretly and sudden[ly conveyed her two son]s, the Lord George Plantagenet and [the Lord Richard Plantagenet, out o]f this land, and sent them / [by shipping into the Low Countries, to their aunt, the Lady Margaret, Duchess of Burgundy, wife of Charles, Duke of Burgundy and Brabant, and Earl of Flanders etc., where they were very kindly and honourably received and were brought to Utrecht, the chief city then in Holland, where they had liberal and princely education, the young Lord Richard being about the age of ten years at his going into Holland. And there they continued until Edward, Earl of March, their eldest brother, had revenged the death and slaughter of his father and had put down King

Egerton 16v -18v

Henry VI and got possession of his kingdom and crown, as it was his right.

[Then he recalls his two brothers, and being desirous to make them soldiers, caused them to be entered into the practice of arms, and was not long ere he made them knights, of which honour their towardliness and aptness to military affairs made them worthy, time making them very valiant and expert captains, especially the Lord Richard, who in his riper years was reputed one of the best captains and greatest soldiers of his time. Soon after the king had made these two young princes knights, being desirous still to demonstrate his affection towards them, he gave to them the most honourable titles and estates of dukes and earls, investing the Lord George into the duchy of Clarence and the earldom of Richmond, and the rather conferred that title and earldom of Richmond upon him because he was in great mislike of the young Earl of Richmond, Henry Tudor. The Lord Richard, his brother, had the dukedom of Gloucester and earldom of Carlisle, as I have read in an old manuscript story, but the heralds do not acknowledge this creation.

[The king was also very careful in their advancement other ways, as well as giving lands and signories unto them, as in procuring most noble and rich marriages for them. For after the great Earl of Warwick and Salisbury, Richard de Neville, was reconciled to the king's favour, these two brothers obtained, by the king's means, to marry the two daughters and heirs of this Earl of Warwick, George, Duke of Clarence, married the Lady Isabel (or Elizabeth), the elder daughter, and Richard, Duke of Gloucester, married the Lady Anne; which ladies, by their most noble mother the Lady Anne de Beauchamp, daughter and heir of Sir Richard de Beauchamp, Earl of Warwick, were also heirs of that earldom.

[But Anne, the wife of Richard, although she were the younger sister, was the better woman, having been a little before married to Edward Plantagenet, Prince of Wales and Duke of Cornwall, only son to King Henry VI, and was now his princess and dowager. The Duke Richard loved her dearly and had by her a son called Edward, who after, when his father was king, was created Prince of Wales, as it shall appear in another place.

[The crimes of the Duke of Clarence]

[And here I may insert the great difference between the disposition of these two dukes, George and Richard, the Duke of Clarence being of a sullen and mutinous disposition, very apt to quarrels, nor would forbear to offend the king his brother, raising slanders of him and of the good duchess
12 his mother, becoming an utter foe and professed enemy to the king,] / and confederated and joined with the disloyal and rebellious adversaries of the king. And he took arms against the king and fought a battle against him, and he practised with the French king to break league with the king his brother and to send forces against [England,] and he obtained his *effect* with these French forces and with those of other rebels. He assaulted the king and fought a battle with him and overthrew him, and made him fly into Flanders, *and of which I* shall say hereafter and in a more convenient place.

Richard, Duke of [Gloucester,] his [love and constancy to his brother.]

But the Duke of Gloucester was of a more kind and gentle nature, and very loving and obsequious to the king his brother, ever conformable in all *humble* and dutiful manner to the will and pleasure of the king. And he ever followed him with all fidelity and love in all his fortunes, adverse and prosperous, and never departed from him but when the king employed him

[in] some honourable and weighty affairs, civil or military, *so* much as that when all the king's friends forsook him, the duke was still as [his] most faithful and perpetual Achates, and willingly partaked [of a]ll the calamities and troubles of the king his brother, so [truly] and so equally and so nobly his love and his fidelity and his [cour]age and magnanimity were tempered together.

And as he accompanied the king in all his troubles, quarrels, conflicts and *batt*les, so he was most forward and most adventurous *in the* bloody and perilous congresses and encounters *of war*. And witness hereof are the many battles wherein he fought with and for h[is brother:] in that battle and victory *which the* king had at Barnet, where the duke entered so far and so boldly into the enemy's army that two of his esquires, [Tho]mas Parr and John Millwater, being nearest unto this *duke*, were slain instantly; but the duke by his great courage [and val]our and skill not only saved himself, but also put the most part of the enemies to flight and the [rest to the sword.] And so likewise he behaved himself at [the bat]tles of Hexham and of Doncaster and at St Albans and at Blore Heath and at Mortimer's Cross [and at Te]wkesbury, and still thought that he could never essay or attempt to *encounter* perils enough to succour and defend his brother and to advance his cause and his fortunes. [And when he] was employed in any expedition sent forth by [the king,] *who commanded* above in chief, he so behaved himself and showed his [skill and courage that he still returned with good success] and with honour and with victory.

12v

The Bastard of Fauconberg.

And in this manner and in this kind, this duke did many good services to the king and to the commonwealth, and especially in the expedition into Scotland, whereof I will write more particularly by and by. And he also in this did very good service, taking of the seditious rebel, the famous and mischievous pirate Thomas Neville, alias Fauconberg, the base son of Sir William de Neville, Lord Fauconberg and Earl of Kent. And who, being well entertained and much caressed by Sir Richard de Neville, Earl of Warwick, and the near kinsman of the Earl of Kent, his natural father, he wo*uld undertake* any adventure, how difficult soever, for that proud earl and for his friends. And Warwick esteemed him the *more* because he was a skilful and valiant soldier either by land or sea, and where*of King Edward* had had good trial. For he had by his prowess and valour done good service not long before to King Edward and the House of York, and from where he was nor basely nor *dishonourably descended*.

But being become a Lancastrian, he followed the part of King Henry VI and rebelled against King Edward and bore arms against him. And King Henry VI, by the counsel of Warwick, who feared much the forces and help which King Edward might have from his friends beyond the seas, and also being desirous to rob and to spoil the subjects and [parties] of the king passing along or through the narrow seas, and to take or to destroy their ships, made th[is Fauconberg] admiral, or chief captain, of a warlike fleet. And *this* Admiral Fauconberg did not fail the hopes of the k*ing* and his new friends in this service, in this employment, but robbed and spoiled and took and sunk as well the ships of the king as of his [friends and subjects,] and put very many of the men to the sword.

Edw[ard] had no means then to subdue or to suppress him at [sea,] whereupon the Duke of Gloucester found out another way to meet with him and [to prevent] his mischiefs, rapines and slaughters. And that was by the means of *an a*dvice and stratagem which he had to catch Fauconberg suddenly and unawares. And he had advertisement that the Captain Fauconberg came sometimes ashore and lurked in some of the ports of the *south, and where* he had good friends. And the king, understanding hereof, committed *the taking* him to his brother Gloucester. The duke went *in*[to Ha]mpshire, and there he understood that Fauconberg would ere long [privily visit;] and he lay in wait for his landing. And ere long he came ashore to Southampto[n,] and there Gloucester suddenly surprised and apprehended *him* and brought him to London, and from there he was c[onveyed to] Middleham Castle. And after that he had told some ta[les, and being] well sifted and sounded, he was put to death and *executed*.

[But for the most part the employment] of th[is Duke of Gloucester was
13 in the north parts, where] / he much lived and did good service according to his charge and duty. For he was Lord Warden of all the marches, eastern, middle and western, and earl and governor, or captain (as they then said) of Carlisle. And he liked well to live in those parts of the north for sundry good causes. For besides that Yorkshire was his native country; and that is clear to every man, and most esteemed, for the birth in any place breedeth especial love and affection to the place, and that by a natural instinct, as the poet said well:

[Ovid] **Natale solum dulcedine cunctos mulcet.**

And for that they were the native country both of the duke his father and of the duchess his mother, and by whom he had most noble alliance and very many great friends and mu*ch* love in those parts. And certainly he was generally well beloved and honoured of all the northern people, his countrymen, not [o]nly for his greatness and alliance, but also (and chiefly) because he was [a] valiant, a wise, and a bountiful and liberal prince, and a good and a magni[fic]ent housekeeper, and the which bringeth not the least love of the people, but rather the most and greatest good will, for they and all men love and admire liberality and good [hosp]itality. And thirdly, he liked best to live in these parts *because* his appanage and patrimony was there chiefly, and he had [besid]es goodly possessions and lordships by the hereditary right of [the du]chess his wife in the north parts.

[G. Camden in **Cumberland]** [D. William H*o*ward] **Co**[**mes: id est**] **Praes**[**es.**]

And amongst them he had the signory of [Penri]th (**vulgo** 'Perith'), a chief port in Cumberland, and where he either built or very much [repa]ired the castle, and there he much resided; and much also at the city [of C]arlisle, and where he was made **Comes** by his brother, as [I sa]id before. But whether he were **Comes** after the [anc]ient Roman understanding – that is, the governor – or **Comes** [or c]ount after the common taking it by us Englishmen and other nations now – and that is for [a special titular lord – I] will not take upon me to determine. But I boldly affirm *that* I have

[**Liber MS. in quarto apud D**. Rob. Cotton]

read he was **Comes Carliolensis**. And lastly, he had the *love of* these countries because the noblemen, and of the greatest, much honoured and loved him. And especially the Earl of Northumberland professed much love [unto him.]

And for these many good causes he was so much in *the* good liking of the north countries as that he desired *only* to finish his days there and in the condition of a subject and of a servant to the king. And his ambition and other worldly *aims extended* no further. And he governed those countries very [wisely and justly, both] in time of peace and of war, and preserved [concord and amity between the] Scots and English so much as he could. [But the breaches between them could not so strongly be made up to continue long.] / And especially the borderers, whose best means of living **13v** grew out of mutual spoils and common rapines, and for the which cause they were ever very apt to enter into brawls and feuds. And whilst the Duke of Gloucester lay in these northern parts, and in the last year of the reign of the king his brother, the quarr[els] and the feuds and despoils were much more outrageous and more extreme than before. And thereby there grew so great unkindness and so great enmity, and such hostile hatred between the kings of England and of Scotland, and so irreconcilably as that nothing but the sword and open war could compose or determine and extinguish them. And the cause hereof [was] the unjust detaining of the tribute which King James was bound yearly to pay, as Polydore [thus writeth.]

And [King Edward] IV took it very ill at the hands of James IV, King of **14** Scotland, that he [refuse]d to pay the tribute whereunto he was bound by covenants. And therefore he resolved by arms to [com]pel him to perform and pay it yearly. But King Edward being di[strac]ted with the care of his watching of the practices of France, neglect[ed that] business of Scotland. And in the meantime, Alexander, Duke of Albany [and brother] to King James, pretending to go upon some earnest business into Franc[e, passi]ng through England as his nearest way, he came to King Edward and s[olicited him] to take arms for the wrong which the king his b[rother] *did* him. And he promised to return soon out of France and to raise a pow[er in Sco]tland for his aid.

[An army sent into Scotland under the Duke of Gloucester.]

And hereupon King Edward sent his best brother, the Duk[e of Gloucester, with] a good army into Scotland. And he marched master of the [field, even near to] Berwick, having a little before sent thither Sir Thomas Stanley to besiege it. And the duke came and soon took [it.] But the Duke of Albany fail[ed him,] for he secretly made a peace with the king his brother. But yet Richar[d of Gloucester] accomplished the business of the Scottish expedition very honourably and happily. Thus [Polydore.] [**Anno** 24 Edward IV]

But to proceed in the narration of that story which I instituted, to enlarge **14v** that which Polydore abridgeth and reporteth defective[ly:] King Edward, notwithstanding his negligence, noted before by Polydore, *caused* good and great forces to be levied. And the King of Scotland was as diligent there in that business. And King Edward, as was said before, made his brother Richard Captain General of all the English forces. And under him the chief commanders were sundry noble persons, as namely S[ir Henry] / Percy, Earl **13v** of Northumberland, and the Lord Stanley (after [Earl] of Derby), and the Lord Lovell, and the Lord of Graystock, and [the Lord] Scroop of Bolton, and the Lord Fitzhugh, and Sir W[illiam] Parr, a [noble] and a valiant knight, and father of [the] Lord Parr of Ross, Kendal and Fitzhugh, and grandfather to Sir William Parr, Earl of Essex and Marquis of No[rthampton.] There was also in the army Sir Edward Wood[ville,] Lord Rivers and brother to Queen Elizabeth, with many other signal and noble and worthy men, and too long to rec[ord.]

And the duke marched with this army to the borders and to the frontier, *and met* with those which encountered or resisted, overthrew them, and then

he went [to the] strong town of Berwick, which was then possesse[d] by the King of Scotland, and by the folly and base surrend[er of] King Henry VI. And he, having beaten and slew or else chased those tr[oops of the] enemies which he met and found about the town, he *came to* Berwick and battered it, and he summoned the tow*n and* the defenders thereof to yield. And [after a short siege, the besieged, upon summons and parley, finding
15 themselves not able to resist so strong a power,] / were easily persuaded to be at quiet and in safety upon very ordinary poor conditions, to render the town and the castle of Berwick and themselves into the duke's hands.

Chronicon Croyland And thus he got and recovered Berwick, as it is recorded in the Chronicle of Croyland. And this was held a very honourable and very acceptable achievement by the king and by all the English nation. And after the duke had placed a captain and officers and soldiers in that town, forthwith he marched towards Edinburgh, the chief city of Scotland, and with a purpose to besiege and to take, and also to sack it. But before he was past the half way toward that city, there were certain signal persons sent as ambassadors to the duke and they craved and they obtain*ed* audience, and it was [granted] them. And they told him that the city *of* Edinburgh, and that furthermore the king and the whole nation of Scotland, desired the love and friendship of the duke and of the [King] of England, and to have league and peace made, or at the [least a tru]ce made [bet]wixt both the kingdoms. And they offered so fair conditions for [it] that the general favourably hearkened unto them, and after [some] ripe deliberation and consultation he granted [to] suspend or to cease or intermit his hostile proceeding. And he [gave] good and courteous entertainment and audience to these ambassadors, and then instantly he commanded and gave order [by] public edict proclaimed throughout all the army that no [Eng]lishman should offer any violence to any Scot, *nor* to make any spoil of them nor of their goods, *nor* to do the least offence or hurt unto them. And thus the great [mischief]s of war and bloodshed (which then seemed terribly and heavily [to impend)] were stayed and prevented, and there was a truce taken, [which truce] was the preface of that famous league [after]ward made and concluded by this duke (and that was after [he was king) and James IV,] King of Scotland.

15v There were other martial accidents and exploits and military actions which were put in practice and acted in this expedition made by the Duke of Gloucester into Scotland. But I will willingly omit them, as well because they were not needful in this work, as also because they are written copiously and largely by Polydore Vergil, Ralph Holinshed, Edward Hall, John Stow, Richard Grafton, and other public and vulgar historians and chroniclers, and all that which I desire therein (and *be*cause it maketh best for my purpose) is that *the* indifferent and judicious Reader will take knowledge
16 of those said writers of the affairs and actions of this duke in the north parts ten*ding* to his praise and honour wholly and entirely. And it is so certain as that it may not be denied that this wise and valorous prince had
15v still good success and good fortune in the execution of his designs / and services of the king his brother, and with love and true affection undertook such designs, and *to* perform and act such deeds. And undoubtedly the love and faith of this duke to the king his brother was most inviolable. Wherefore he was very careful and *diligent* for the safety and honour of the

king and for his welfare and prosperity. Therefore it was an unhappy thing for the king that the duke was absent so long, and especially when he fell sick. For he would have pried so narrowly and cunningly into all the practices and treacher*ous* machinations against the king as that he might have discovered and prevented the practices thereof and so have saved the king's life, the which (as som*e* authors write) was shortened by violent treachery, which shall be discuss*ed* more at large in another place.

[The doubtful death of King Edward IV: **vide Lib.** 4]

But so unhappily it fell out that when the king died, the Duke of Gloucester was in [Scotland,] and the news thereof came very speedi[ly unto] him (for, as the proverb is, ill news flyeth apace upon the wings of fame). The barons and [nobles] who were at London and in the south parts seconded that fame, and they sent secret letters in [post] unto him, wherein they advertised him that the king his brother [had] committed the guard and tuition of his sons, Prince Edward and his brother Richard, Duke of York, to him and had ordained him to be the Lord [Protector] of them and of the kingdom**: Rex Edwardus IV filios suos Ricardo duci Gloucestriae [in tutelam] moriens tradidit**, as Polydore testifieth, and those lords also that they approved the [king's election].

[Polydore **Lib.** 23]

[The Duke of Gloucester made Lord Protector]

Hereupon the d[uke] *became* the more careful of the good and safe estate of the young prince and of the kingdom, and made the more hasty return to London. For he stayed no*t, but* [dispo]sed of the army and set in good order the affairs [of these parts, and came to York, where, for some good respects of honour] / and of piety, he made a stay for some few days. And in that time he performed certain charitable and religious offices to [his] brother deceased, and with such honourable and sacred ceremonies proper to princes as the place and the shortness of time would afford. And this being done, he hastened to London, and he was very nobly attended. For besides his own and ordinary train and followers, he was guarded or accompanied all the way to *London* with six hundred voluntary gentlemen of the north parts, and who were brave horsemen of Yorkshire, and of *good appare*l and gallantly mounted, as he passed in his train. So great their love and devotion were unto this duke.

17

And upon the way he dispatched *cer*tain signal and trusty gentlemen toward the prince *or* young king, who was then at Ludlow Castle in Wales. [And the] duke very carefully provided for his more safe conveyance and for his more honourable *re*pute *on coming* into London. And the Lord Protector was not long there arrived *when* also the prince came thither. And he was with all honour and state [receiv]ed at London and conducted to the Bishop's Palace, *where* he was lodged and entertained some days very magnificently *in a* manner as *was* fit and due to such a prince.

[Prince Edward cometh to London]

And being there, he desired to see [his br]other, the young Duke of York, and to have his company, *and he* sent for him. But the queen his mother, being then in the [Palac]e of Westminster, kept him with her, and would not [let hi]m depart from her. And because she would be the more [assure]d of him, she took sanctuary in the Abbey and carried [the y]oung duke her son with her. And then the Protector sent to her to pray and to require her to send or bring the young duke to the [king] his brother. But they could not prevail. And then the Lord [Protec]tor, by the advice of the Duke of Buckingham and of the [other gr]eat lords, made choice of Cardinal Bourchier, [Archbishop] of Canterbury, for their messenger, as a man of more authority by reason of his call[ing.] And they sent him to the queen and willed *him to entre*at and to persuade her by all means to send the Duke of York to the *king at Lon*don. And with much mediation and very earnest persuasions, at length *he made her* consent to deliver her son to him, and he [brought him to the king] his brother in London.

[But the king could not make any longer] abode in the Bishop's House, **17v** [and ancient manner and custom being that the prince] / who was next to succeed the deceased king and to possess and to enjoy *the* crown should go to the Tower of London, being n*ot only* the chief house of the king, but also the castle of the greatest strength and of the most safety i[n this] kingdom. And he was to keep his court there until such time as the more weighty affairs of the kingdom were well ordered and settled and the troubles and seditions, if any happened (and the which often happen at the alteration of reigns and at the death of princes) were composed and appeased. And of which kind of evils some were discovered and reformed before the Protector came to London, and as you shall understand more particularly anon. And moreover, this new king was also to stay in the Tower until all things of royal ap[parel] and of pomp, and necessary and proper to his consecration and co[ro]nation, were duly prepared.

[The observance] of the Lord Protec]tor *for* [the king his neph]ew

And here the Protector attended the king his nephew very dutifully and carefully and very reverently, and he was *not* only very kind and loving unto him, but also most obseq*uious* and serviceable, as to his master and to his liege lord and sovereign. And he mo*st humbly* did homage unto him. And this is testified by the good and honoura[ble] Philip de Commynes, and in these words: **Le duc de Gloucestre avait fait hommage à son neveu comme** à **son roi et souverain seigneur**. But the testimony of that and other obsequious duties will be of mor[e credit] being made by one who loved not the Protector, but much hated him.

[Philip de Commynes in **Lodovicus** xi]

[Sir Thomas More]

When the young king approached near to London, the Lord [Protector] his uncle rode barehead, and in passing before the king said [in a] loud voice to all the people which stood to see and to [welcome] their new king, 'Behold your prince and sovereign lord'. [And] in brief, there was no humble nor dutiful office, w*hether* of the lowest and meanest kind, and due from any se[rvant] or vassal, which he did not readily yield and perform to this [young king. And] all is affirmed and confirmed by a man of good cr[edit, and] a religious man, and one who lived in those times, and n[amely] the Prior of the Abbey of Croyland. And thus he write[th]: **Ricardus Protector nihil reverentiae quod capitis n[udato, genu] flexio, aliusve quilibet corporis habitus in subdito [exigit regi] nepoti suo facere distulit aut recusavit.**

[Chronicl. Abbatiae Croyland]

[And as I believe these relations so I also believe the duke performed those humble officious services faithfully and sincerely. Whereof he **18** gave good] / testimony hereof soon afterward, and that was when he was very earnestly and importunately solicited and prayed to take the crown upon him: whereunto his answer was (and with solemn protestation) that he much rather desired to serve his nephew as his humble vassal, holding it to be much more safe and more happy to be a subject and in good favour with the king than to be a king. So true and clear he was from aspiring to sovereignty and from ambitious thoughts.

The Lord Protect[or] prayed to be [king]

And it is also manifest that the duke was drawn by earnest persuasions and, as it were, enfor[ced] by continual importunities to hearken to their motion [and] to raise his thoughts so high as to a crown. And when the barons saw that their requests would not serve, they used threats [and] menaces of imminent evils, and which should soon fall upon him. And the reasons for these their importunate persuasions to have him to be king were these, as they intimated. And first in respect that they utterly misliked that the son of King Edward should reign [o]ver them, and not only because he was too young to govern his kingdom, but also, and chiefly, because they held him and the rest of [t]he children of King Edward to be illegitimate, and not born [i]n lawful matrimony, and therefore not capable of the crown.

[But] on the contrary side they esteemed the duke to be not [o]nly the true and next heir of the crown, and his title to be pure [and] right and without crack or flaw; but also they knew hi[m] by long and tried experience to be a wise, a just, a bountiful, a valorous and a religious prince, and in regard there[fore, they held him] to be the most worthy to wear the crown. [And they did not only] desire him most earnestly and required importunately that he would be their king, [but they] seem[ed in an imperious manner to call] him to the crown. But still the Protector withstood and refused their election of him to be king. And he stood a long time upon those wilful and ingrate and distasteful terms, but yet then he rendered many good reasons in excuse of his refusal – of his obstinacy, as the barons censured it. And here I give but a taste of these aff*airs*; *and pa*ssages of them shall be related and discoursed at large anon.

And in the mea[ntime i]t must be understood that the Protector during these his *continual* refusals of the crown, and, as it were, in the interreign, *omitted not* any business of the state nor any service to the [young king] *to* be done, and he was very careful, and doubtless, / as I said before, he was **18v**
very dutiful and obsequious to the young prince, and very careful and studious of his safety and welfare. And I think verily that he was so far from seeking to hurt him as no man could justly and directly charge him that he gave any offence to the pr*ince* or practised or attempted any ill against him. And the reason thereof was because his love was so kind and constant to the king their father as that he could not nor would *not* entertain or nourish any evil and treacherous thought against this prince his son. But contrariwise, he was an utter enemy to all practices and to all such men as were suspected to be guilty of them or were apt to sedition and tumults, or might be dangerous members of the commonwealth and pernicious or mischievous to him or to his estate.

And in due consideration of the premises, he began betimes to remove some dangerous stumbling-blocks out of the prince's way. And he dispatched and made short work with these men whom he vehemently suspected to be over-ambitious, and m[en] insolent, and who arrogated and usurped such high authority and great power as was not proper unto them. And therefore he made clean riddance of such persons as were not *only* ill-affected to the prince or to the government, but also to the governors, and of whom he was the chief. And therefore he had the more reason to fe*ar* *those that h*ated him and were turbulent and seditious persons, and who extremely ther*efore* envied and maligned and hated him for his very high authority and greatness, but also, and most *of* all, for his justice.

And long before, in the time of King Edward, th[ere was] great mislike

and enmity between those of the Duke of Gloucester's blood, [whose party] the most ancient and most noble barons of the kingdom favoured and defended, and between those of the queen's kindred for the many wrongs and outrages done to the nobles and gentlemen of England. And this was so notorious as that all the people murmured and mut[inied] against them. For besides the pride and insolency of these Reginists, they were so malicious and so evilly affected to the princes of the blood and to the great and chief noblemen as th*at* they, by false tales and slanders, many times incensed the king against them and alienated his love and favour from them and provoked his displeasure and wr*ath*. And these were chief[ly] the Grays and the Woodvilles and their kinsmen and partisans, and they made full accompt to have greater power and greater au*thority* with the young king their kins[man than] they had before. And then there was no doubt but that [they would have acted more and higher rhodomontados and injuries] than before, and they would *have* [removed the princes of the blood and at their pleasures swayed and ruled all things during the minority of the king; after,
19 too, so long as the Queen Mother could usurp the sovereignty.] / Wherefore the Duke Protector and the Duke of Buckingham and some other of the more ancient nobility, consulting of these dangers and mischiefs hanging over their heads and threatening dangers and evils to the state, resolved to give timely remedy unto them.

[The insolency of the queen's kindred]

Sir Thomas More in **[Edwa]rd V [et] Richard III.**

And Sir Thomas More acknowledgeth all this to be true, and he confesseth that the nobles of the kingdom had reason to suspect, and also to fear, that the kinsfolks of the queen would bear more sway and do more mischief when their young kinsman was king than before, in the king his father's time, although their insolencies and outrages were then intolerable. And further, the author acknowledgeth that there had been a long time a grudge and an heartburning between the queen's kindred and the king's blood in the time of King Edward, and the which the king, although he were partial of the queen's side, yet he endeavoured to compose that hatred which was between them, and yet he did what he could by all means to reconcile *them, but he* could not effect it.

And Master More further telleth that after that king was dead, the Lord Gray, Marquess of Dorset, and the Lord Richard Gray, and the Lord Rivers made a full accompt to rule the young king and to usurp the government of the kingdom. They had learned that it was best fishing [i]n a troubled sea. They therefore, the better to accomplish their plots and designs, practised to set variance and debate amongst the great men of the kingdom, and that then whilst th*at* they were occupied in their own quarrels and particular revenges, these cunning and ambi[tious] politicians *by the* [opportun]ity thereof might assault the noble barons, whom they hated, and supplant and destroy the ancient noble blood of the realm.

Moreover, Sir Thomas More intimateth that those proud and *haughty kindred of the* queen, for the better effecting their designs, had made warlike preparations and were purposed to use means of for[ce] to bring the plot to effect and to maintain it by force and by arms and bloodshed; and for the better provision of such warlike instruments, the marquess had secretly taken great quantity of the king's treasure [o]ut of the Tower; and also that the Woodvilles had provided [goo]d store of armour, and whereof some part was soon after [ta]ken upon the way, as it was carried close packed [up] in carts.

It was therefore high time for the Protector [and] the ancient nobility to look well to themselves, and to neglect *no* [o]ccasions to prevent the mischief of these treacheries. And in their consultation they found that there w*as no way* to prevent and avoid these evils but by taking away the lives of those *noblemen. It was* therefore resolved that the Marquess Dorset and the Lord Richard [Gray, and their uncle] Sir Anthony Woodville, Lord Rivers, and some [other of the queen's kindred and faction] should be suddenly a[pprehended and safely guarded until their heads paid the forfeit of their seditions.] *And justice* / was executed upon them all except the **19v** Marquess Dorset, who, as it w*as thought*, was by a friend of his *who was* present at the Council secretly advertised of their plot. And hereupon he presently fled to sanctuary and so was saved. But the rest were taken and sent to Pomfret and there put to death.

And at the same time the Lord Hastings, one who much honoured and [Lord Hastings] favoured and loved the queen and her kinsfolks, and especially the marquess, and he was therefore the more suspected to be dangerous, and for that cause he was arrested of High Treason in the Tower, and instantly his head was chopped off upon a block in the Green yard. And this may seem a more strange and a barbarous and a tyrannous act than the other, he being supposed to be a good subject, and also generally thought to love and to honour the Protector and the Duke of Buckingham. And Sir Thomas Sir Thomas More More affirmeth also that the Protector undoubtedly loved the Lord Hastings very well and was loath to have lost him, had it not been that they feared that he might take part with [their] enemie[s and so] his life might dash and quench their purpose. Thus Sir Thomas More. And this was a dilemma. But he telleth n[ot] disertly what that particular purpose was, and what they had in hand at that instant again[st the Protec]tor and against his friends. But by other places of his story and of his followers' it may be they well understo*od* [that they suspected ve]hemently the Protector's affection of the sovereignty and the practice of th*e* making away of the young prince and of his brother. For these be the crimes which Sir Thomas More and the rest of the calumniators continually objected against the Prote[ctor.]

But let us admit it to be so, and we will also acknowledge that the Protector [was] now grown very suspicious and jealous of the Lord Hastings. And it is true that for tha[t cause] he sent Sir William Catesby, [a man] in gre[at] favour and credit with Hastings, to sound him and to learn what conceit or opinio[n he held] of the title and claim which the Protector might have to the crown and to b*e king. And he perfor*med this task. And the Lord Hastings, presuming of Catesby's secrecy and aff*y*ing in his love and in his fidel[ity] (*for* Catesby had been advanced by him), told Catesby without any colours or circumstances, and also plainly, and eve[n with some] indignation, that he utterly misliked the plot and the title, and that he would resist it and withstand it by all the means and power which he had. And he [added peremp]torily that he had rather see the death and destructions both of the [Protector] and of Buckingham than to see or to suffer the young king *to be* deprived of the crown and of the sovereignty of the kingdom by *them*.

[Now] Catesby, forgetting the dutiful respects which he owed to the Lord Hastings, and the [regard of his safety,] made report of this answer to the

Protector, who was much troubled and perplexed therewith, as well bec*au*se he loved the Lord Hastings, and for good *reason that he* [knew no man could stand him in more stead than he, could his faith and love be assured.
20 But being his adversary, and opposing] / his power and his authority and his council and his friends and his forces, he knew or vehemently suspected
The Lord Hasting[s] his power
that Hastings was able not only to resist him, but also to oppress and to suppress him and Buckingham and all their confederates. And hereupon these two dukes resolved to dispatch Hastings out of the way, and he was presently arrested and beheaded, as is aforesaid. And this is the greatest bloody crime of King Richard and whereof there may weak proof be made. And yet proofs be not so clear but that there may be packing and juggling and frauds in them.

But admit that this bloody deed was the practice and plot of the Protector, yet in reason of state and of policy, and by the rules of those arts which are called **Artes Imperii**, this also may be excused, and it may also *be* authorized or countenanced by many great examples. For it hath been usual for many ages, and even since the Ogygian times, for these men
[**Artes Imperii**]
which affect and seek reign and sovereignty never to strain courtesy at the doing of a*nything, or to* forbear to take the life of any man who standeth in their way or is against them and their attempts, insomuch as the father cannot be a servant of his son, nor one brother of another, and whereof there be too many examples, and even in our own stories. And this is an old observation, and general in all foreign countries:

[Seneca, in tragedies]

Regnum furto
Et fraude adeptum antiquum est specimen imperii.

And as King Atreus said by his own experience,

[**Idem** Seneca]

Ut nemo doceat fraudis et
Sceleris vias, regnum docebit.

This is the censure of a king. [But] when these fraudulent and bloody practices succeed well, *and* when the actors prevail, then **prosperum scelus virtus vocatur**: the wicked act, succeeding well, is called a virtue; and the actors are held to be wise, valorous, and most renowned and happy men.

I would have the virtuous and discreet Reader to think that I write not this as approving and allowing such cruel and perfidious practices *as per*tain to sovereignties and principalities; but I abhor them. So on the other side, *I dislike that* the prince King Richard should of all men *besides be* condemned in such *manner* for the exercising and practice of [these Imperial Arts, and even above all other, considering others have used them with credit.

20v [And it is a very ancient axiom in politic philosophy that] / **Via ad**
[**Axiomata Politica**]
potentiam est tolere aemulos et premere adversarios. And the great master of policy disalloweth not this manner of proceeding, as he intimateth, and
Aristotle, **Politics**
not obscurely, in a similitude taken from a painter and a prince or an ambitious man. For he saith that a painter, when he maketh a horse, must take heed that he make not one leg longer than another, nor one buttock higher than another, and that if he happen to commit such a fault, that he must make these members shorter and take them down. And that so likewise a prince must not suffer any man who approacheth near to him in authority or in titles, or rivalleth him in his ambition, to overtop him, nor to outgrow him, nor in any wise to suffer him to be higher nor greater than himself, but straight to lop him.

And this reason made Julius Caesar to take arms against the great Pompeius, and wherein he prevailed and was and ever shall be reputed a wise captain and a great conqueror, although his emulation cost an infinite quantity of excellent human blood. And in like manner his nephew Octavius Augustus never ceased proscribing and banishing and massacring until he had dispatched all his proud emules, rivals of sovereignty, and all his danger*ous* adversaries out of the w*ay*.

And our King Henry I and Edward III and Henry IV and Edward IV and Henry VII took the like courses and used the same arts of empire, as all the world knoweth. And yet these fa[ults] ar[e forgiven them, and they are] reputed and renowned for good and wise and virtuous princes. And only Richard, who is an innocent in comparison of some of them, is cried down and utterly condemned for cruel practices of taking away his rivals in authority and in empire, and such as *threatened him*, and al*though* there were never yet any lawful proofs made that he c*ommitted thos*e crimes whereof he is accused. Yet he of all men hath been in those matters so injuriously and so slanderously dealt with, and that in so grossly false a manner as that he *hath not only* been suspected, but also charged and directly accused of the slaughter of his two nephews and of *others*, albeit some of them *were* living many years after that King Richard was dead and buried, which will be hereafter, and in the third book and elsewhere, declared.

But suppose that he took away some of his most da*ngerous* adversaries, and such of the nobles as are before named. *Notwith*/standing, he may be **21** taxed of gross error and also condemned as a man guilty of his own blood and ruin and much more reproved and blamed for not taking away the other his impediments and his other emules and adversaries than for his cutting off these lords and nobles aforesaid. For if he had dealt with Dr Morton, Bishop of Ely, and with Peter Courtenay, Bishop of Exeter, and with the Marquess of Dorset, and with the earls of Richmond, of Pembroke, of Oxford, and of Northumberland. And likewise with some principal gentlemen, as namely Hungerford, Bourchier, Digby, Savage and Talbot, Mortimer and Rice, and [Blount, wh]o, although they were no lords, yet were lords in their lordlike possessions and in their noble alliances. To these may be added Bray, Poins, Sanford, the young Stanley, Fortescue, and the crafty doctors Morgan, Lewis, and Urswick. And if King Richard, I say, had dealt with his enemies and foes entered into conspiracies against him as he did with the Grays, Woodvilles, Hastings, and Buckingham, he had been out of danger and had preserved in safety his life and his fortunes and his crown; and of all the which they afterwards deprived and utterly bereaved him.

Therefore it is plain that his error in sparing them was in politic consideration and in human providence a much greater crime than the killing of the other. But I confess that he spared some of them because he suspected them not, nor did he fear them, for he had no cause to suspect Northumberland, by reason of the old acquaintance and amity and good [Northumberland] correspondence which was between and had long been between King Richard and him. And albeit he knew that Oxford hated him in his heart [Oxford] and was a nobleman of such power and riches and greatness as that he was to be feared, yet because he was a prisoner in the strong Castle of Hammes,

and very safely and strongly guarded, he was secure of that earl and did not fear him nor his forces. But he feared and suspected Jasper, Earl of
[Pembroke] Pembroke, and his nephew Richmond, and not without good cause, and as was apparent to all the world afterward. But they were out of King Richard's reach and were safely in France.

And the king feared Morton, and he had greater cause and reason to fear him than any other man, for he was not only treacherous and perfi[d]ious, and one who much hated the king, but he was a subtle and a chief persua[d]er of others to be seditious and treacherous; and in a word he was of all [the m]ost practick and politic **boutefeu** in those affairs of treachery and of sedition and *re*bellion. And although the king had no certain intelligence of all his secret [workings] *and* traitorous practices, yet he knew enough to hold him [suspected and also] to remove him from the council table [and restrain his liberty,] and to commit him to prison. And all this the king did, [committing him to the custody] of one whom he suspected to be *his close* and inward friend, the Duke [of Buckingham; though he was deceived and betrayed in trust by the duke, who was then secretly
21v malcontent and alienated in his heart.] / And he did continually plot treasons against the king, and as you shall see and know at large anon and in the next book, when I come to speak of the rebellion of that duke.

And when Morton had made the duke almost as bad and as false and disloyal as himself, he stole away from Brecknock Castle and went to Ely, and there he found good means for good store of coin and safe means for his passage into France. And whither he had a great desire and vehement longing to go, and to the end that he might fashion and confirm an ambitious and seditious wind in the Earl of Richmond, and under the pretence and colour of a Lancastrian title in him to the crown. And for the achieving and acquiring whereof he persuaded and counselled and vehemently animated him to take arms and to invade England. And for his better encouragement, he assured the earl that he had so many and so mighty friends in England as that the enterprise would be facile and of very little danger or difficulty, and this politic prelate did with so many artificial
22 and eloquent words recommend this design and attempt to *persuade* / the earl.

And he that being, as other ambitious men, apt to be persuaded of his own virtues and powers and titles, and to hope well of his own fortune, as that he did not only hearken unto him and accept well his persuasions and counsels, but also he soon put on a resolution to take arms and to invade this kingdom and to put down King Richard. And this purpose was not held in any great secrecy, but it was well known to very many as well in France as in England. And the King Richard himself had certain intelligence thereof, and also of some particular practices and plots which we[re] kept more close. And he came to understand what friends and confederates he had, and amongst them he found some who professed great love and fidelity to him, as namely the Duke of Buckingham, the Countess of Richmond and others whose names shall be seen afterward.

And now, therefore, the king had good cause to have a watchful eye upon the Earl of Richmond and upon his confederates and the conspirators against him and his estate, and he now well considered that albeit the king his brother su[spected] and feared the Earl of Richmond, and had sought by

su[ndry means to get him into his hands,] / yet that king had not so great **24**
cause to observe and to watch the earl and to provide defences against his designs as Richard had, because now the practice of the earl had taken deep root and was spread very far; and by this time the earl had drawn many noblemen and gentlemen of England into his conspiracy, but also he had so cunningly in[sinu]ated himself into the good favour of some foreign princes as that he obtained their promise and their me*ans* to aid and to assist him in his enterprise of the conquest of England.

But during all the time of King Edward this conspiracy and practice was not of any strength nor of any danger, as well because he was very strong and rich as also be*cause* [the earl's title] of no man w[as preferred.] But yet King Edward without that had cause enough to use means to take and to seize upon Richmond, in respect that he and his friends had adventured to report and give out that he was an heir of the House of Lancaster, and the nearest kinsman to King Henry VI. And thereupon King Edward, and as John Hardyng hath well observed, was in fear that the young Earl of Richmond would claim the crown as the nephew and next heir of the blood of King Henry VI. And the king in regard of these *v*aunts, albeit he knew well that the barons and the gentlemen and the wiser sort of Englishman, and also the French king Lewis XI, and Francis II, Duke of Brittany, and the other foreign princes knew and understood of how little worth the title of Richmond was, and he could in right claim little in the crown by his blood of Lancaster, and that on the other side they also knew that the title of York, whereof King Edward was the head and the most true and certain heir, was a title sound and fair and just and without all default or exception.

But yet this prince, being very wise and provident, conceived well that some foreign princes ill-affected to him, and some of his own falsehearted and seditious subjects, bearing envy or malice or both to his house and to his blood and to his prosperous estate, would make use of any pretended or defective title to trouble his [pe]ace, and to raise seditions and rebellions in his kingdom. Wherefore, this king was desirous to have the Earl of Richmond *safe* and to hold him fast in his own custody. And he put this his
plan in practice very early, for / when the earl was very young, [the king **23v**
committed him to safe custody. And Philippe de] Commynes saith that [when he] came first [acquainted with this earl, being then a prisoner in] Brittany, [he] told him he had been either in a prison [or under strait guard ever since he was] five [years old. And I believe it. For I find he was] but yo[ung] when he [was committed to the custody of Sir] William Herbert, [Lord of Raglan Castle in Monmouthshire, where he was] not long.

For [Jasper, Earl of Pembroke, uncle to Henry Richmond, being then in France, whither he fled after the overthrow of the Lancastrians at Tewkesbury (as John Stow), having advertisement that his nephew was a prisoner with] Sir William Herbert, [with whom he had alliance and friendship, came secretly out of France into Wales,] to Raglan Castle, [where he found] the Lady Herbert, [her husband being with the king.] But in the meantime, [the earl] had so cunningly practised with the lady of the castle as that he got his nephew out of that castle [and conveyed] him to his own castle of Pembroke, the young earl's native place, presuming that he should be a*ble* to keep him safe there, *because it was* a strong castle, and also

[The flight of Richmond with his uncle Pembroke]

[The Earl of Rich-]mond [born in Pem-broke] Castle

becau*se* the people [of] that country [were much affected to] him and his [nephew.] But he overweened in this opinion and hope. For as soon as [the king was adver]tised of the escape of this Richmond, [he commanded Sir William Herbert to levy forces and take both the earls.]

25 This Sir William Herbert was a wise and valiant knight [of] rich and of fair and large possessions, much beloved in those parts because he was of a very noble and ancient family and descended from Herbertus, who was Chamberlain and Treasurer to the kings William Rufus and Henry Beauclerk. And this Sir William was created Earl of Pembroke afterward. And from this noble Herbertus are also descended the noble Herberts, earls of Pembroke and of Montgomery, and many other worthy Welsh gentlemen of that surname and family.

But to proceeed with the employments of this noble knight Sir William Herbert for the surprising and apprehending of two *a*foresaid earls of Pembroke and Richmond, and who then held the Castle of Pembroke for their better safety and more security. As soon *as* those two earls had advertisement *th*at Sir William Herbert was coming, and with a good and strong *pow*er of soldiers, and was near at hand, they, distrusting their own strength and forces, fled *secre*tly in the night out of the castle and rode in great *pos*t to the port of Tenby, and there lurked and kept *the*mselves close and unknown until they had gotten [fit] opportunity for their transportation and escape of this kingdom.

Th[is flight of theirs was in **anno** xi] Edward IV. [John Stow.]

And they soon [got] a ship and [pu]rposed to go into France and to land at [Diep]pe, and from thence to go to the French court, [wher]e the Earl of Pembroke had been not long before, and very [well] entertained. But they failed of this purpose by rea[son of a v]iolent and unhappy storm which arose in the night whilst they [were at] sea [and forced upon them] to run [another course upon the coasts of Little Britain, which fell out as a sad disaster and cross to them and their fortunes for a long time after, the Duke
26v of Brittany being not their friend.] / And how they sped, you shall hear more hereafter. And of this their flight and of many other noble Englishmen which followed the unlucky and unju[st] party of King Henry VI and were fain to fly when he was overthrown by King Edward IV, there is this memorial in the histories of Brittany: **Plusieurs des seigneurs d'Angleterre qui tenaient le parti du roi Henry VI s'en fuyant par mer hors du royaume et entre autres le comte de Penbroke fuyant sauva un jeune prince d'Angleterre nomme Henri comte de Richmont**.

And whilst these earls made some stay in St Malo to refresh themselves after their tempestuous and dangerous passage, Francis II, Duke of Brittany, was advertised in post of their landing and arrival. And he sent in as great post and haste a commandment to the governor of that port to arrest those earls and to keep them so surely as that they might not escape nor depart. And this commandment was duly executed accordingly. And because it seemed strange and also an injurious act of the duke thus to make prisoners those noblemen, being the subjects of a prince with whom the duke was in league and good amity, therefore to give some colour to the arrest, the duke pretended that he had good cause to detain the Earl of Richmond until he had received satisfaction of him for the wrong which he did [to] him in the usurping the title and state of Earl of Richmond and in detaining that earldom from him, which was belonging to the ancien[t] earls

[Earl of Richmond prisoner in Brittany]

[The last duke of Bri]ttany [who was Earl of Ric]hmond and [possessed the earldo]m was [John de Montfort, who]

and dukes of Brittany, his progenitors (and whereof they had been disseized by the spac[e of thirty years),] whose heir and successor he was. And for this cause he resolved there to detain them both as his prison*ers* until that he had restitution of his earldom of Richmond, or composition and satisfaction for it.

flourished [**Anno Domini** 1340] and had sons, [but no Earl] of Richmond, [as Robert Glov]er writeth.

And for their more safe custody, he took order for conducting of these earls to his city of Vannes, where he often resided, and he caus*ed* them to be put into the castle and to be kept as prisoners w[ith] a good guard, and the rather and in truth because the duke h[ad] advertisement that the young Earl of Richmond was a *prince* of England, and nephew to King Henry VI, and that he [laid claim] and title to the crown and kingdom of England [by the blood of Lancaster, for which he, notwithstanding, made their imprisonment more honourable, as is testified by Philip Commynes: **Le duc**, saith he, **les traita doucement pour prisonniers.** And this their imprisonment was such] / an one as Jean Froissart calleth, and fitly, **Prison Curtois.**

[And now this] Francis II [renewed the] claim to the *earldom of* Richmond, and [a]bout thirty [years after] John de Mont-[fort, Duke of] Brittany.

27

And now when the duke considered and deliberated what good use he might make of these his noble prisoners, and what benefit and profit might arise to him by them, he conceived that this their captivity would be very acceptable to the King of England, especially the holding and safe-guarding of the younger, to wit, the Earl of Richmond, because his liberty might turn the thing to great trouble and prove very perilous and pernicious unto him and to his estate. And he hoped not only to have great rewards and great sums of money of the King of England for keeping of the Earl of Richmond, but also that he should be assured of his love and amity. And which is [more,] if you will believe Jacobus Meyerus, that King Edward should stand so much in awe of him by this means as that he would not dare to displease nor to offend the duke: **Propter Henricum Richmontiae comitem non audebat Anglus ab amicitia Britanni discedere.**

[Jacob Meyerus in **Annales Flandriae, Lib.** 17]

And that author was not much mistaken. For it is true that the king would have done anything to have had Richmond delivered unto him. And he was much troubled when he heard that these earls were fled, for he suspected that they would go to some of his enemies, who would make such use of the young earl as *might br*ing *t*o him danger and damage. For from hence might spring an invasion, and whereby all should be in tumults and in combustions. But when the king heard that they were in Brittany, his mind was not only well quieted and his cares well eased, but also he was glad that they were in the hands of his friend and ally, the Duke of Brittany, and detained by him as prisoners. And the king had so good affiance *in* the duke's love and friendship as that he presumed that he would, especially [upo]n some good and golden conditions to boot, send them home to him *to* England.

King [Edward treateth] for [the delivery of the Earl of Richmond]

But if the earls had gone to any of the king's enemies, *and* especially to the French king Lewis XI, the king must [have expe]cted any evil which the French king could contrive for and in the behalf of the young earl, who pretended title to the crown of *England, as has* been before declared. For King Lewis, although he [were then in truce and league] with King Edward, yet he was but in hollow ho*pe. For* he was a mere politician, and studying only to his own ends, yet fearing King Edward, *who was very valiant* / and very famous for his prowess and for his victories, and also for that withal he

27v

The eulogy of King *E*dward IV.

was very rich and very well stored with treasure, as also because he had threatened to enter France with fire and sword for the recovery and reconquest of his ancient hereditary principalities and signories: namely, the duchies of Normandy and of Aquitaine, and counties of Poitou and of Touraine, and other lands. And for these causes King Lewis did not only fear but also hate King Edward in his heart, and so consequently wished and desired his ruin and destruction. For as the good old Ennius said, and it is of the credit of an oracle,

Ennius **ap[ud] Ciceronem in Officii[s]**

Quem metuunt oderunt;
Quem oderunt perisse expetunt.
Whom men do fear and dread, they hate likewise,
And wish them to fall, and never to rise.

Wherefore doubtless the French king would gladly have taken the protection of the Earl of Richmond and his title and cause into his hands, and he would have furnished him with money and arms to attempt the conquest of England, or at the least to have so occupied the king with so many and so dangerous seditions and rebellions as that he should not have had leisure nor been able to invade France, nor to enterprise anything against King Lewis or his kingdom.

[King Edward sendeth for Richmond]

And therefore the king, to prevent and to avoid the said dangers and mischiefs which might happen by the practices of the French king or any other his enemies with the Duke of Brittany for the de*livering of* the Earl of Richmond to them, or for making him an instrument of any troubles, dispatched with all speed a wise and discreet gentleman to the Duke of Brittany, and sent by h*im* a rich present to the said duke. And partly by his kind letters and partly *by the* speeches of his messengers, he earnestly entreated and solicited the duke to send the two earls, of Pembroke and of Richmond, into Engl*and* and to him. And for the which favour he made offers of furth[er] *and* better gratifications, together with his love and the best offices of friend[ship] that he could do to the duke.

28

The duke received [the commendation of these] letters to him, and his present, and the recommendation of the king's love and *friendship in* honourable thankfulness, and entert*ained* [the messenger, assuring him that he was as ready to do the King of England any pleasure as any other whatsoever.] / But he prayed the king to excuse him that he granted not his request nor fulfilled his desire for the delivery of the earls and for the sending them to England to his highness. Because it was a thing which he might not do with his credit and honour saved, in regard that it was against the law of nations and scandal to princely hospitality and to the privileges of sovereignty. Besides that, it were a kind of discharity and impiety for him or for any other prince to deliver to any man, and much less to their enemies and persecutors, such d*istressed* persons as fled to him for succour and craved his safeguard and protection. He was of opinion that if any wrong or violence were offered unto them, that he should be guilty of their afflictions and pains, and also of their blood if it were shed or if they were put to death. But therefore excepting and setting aside this sending of them home, the duke promised faithfully that he would do anything that might be most advantageable and most agreeable and most safe to the king, and that he would keep them so safe as that they should have no more power to hurt or offend the king than if they were his close prisoners in the Tower of

London.

When this answer of the duke was returned to the king, albeit [i]t was not according to his desire nor to his expectation, yet because *he* perceived and considered in his wisdom that the answer was not *un*reasonable, but agreeable with honour and with reason, he well accepted it. [And] thus this cause rested by the space of eight years, as I calculate. [F]or the king made this request and propounded this suit to the duke in the twelfth year of his reign, and **Anno Domini** 1472. And the king was careful all this while to preserve mutual love and his league with the duke, and he entertained the duke's promise bountifully and *to* his great cost, for he sent to him into Brittany every year [g]ood sums of money and fair presents. And all the time the king was *o*ut of any fear of danger or hurt that might come to him by the earl.

[After,] in the twentieth year of his reign, and **Anno Domini** 1480, the king having [inte]lligence of certain new and secret practices and conspiracies, the which the Earl of Richmond and [some of his frie]nds had in the French court and in England, and that he was grown [every day] more and more ambitious, and much aspiring to the crown of England, [the] French king by the solicitations and mediations of the Earl of [Pembroke] and of his other noble friends practised to get [the Earl of Richmon]d into his hands, and had already offered great sums of money for him to the Duke of Brittany, and had promised to aid and assist the [earl in his enterprises] of England. The king then was afresh [trouble]*d* with [this news,] and he presently resolved to [renew his old suit to the duke by the best means that he could.]

[**Histoire de Bretagne**]

28v

Dr Stillington sent for Richmond

The king made choice of Dr Stillington, Bishop of Bath, a very wise and learned and eloquent man, and the king's secretary, and one who had ancient acquaintance and good credit with the Duke of Brittany, whither he was sent with convenient speed. And he came to the duke, who entertained him very honourably and with all courtesy. And the bishop forthwith declared the cause of his employment by the king unto him, and that was, in brief, earnestly to pray the duke to send the Earl of Richmond into England. And the bishop did not only persuade and press this suit with good and artificial words, but also with precious presents and with golden rewards, and at that instant presented the duke with a very rich and sumptuous gift from the king. And the duke liked well the present and also the promise made of more and better gifts. But he liked not the suit, but contrariwise he distasted it much, as before, and was very averse unto it. But the bishop would not leave him so, but with more eloquence and with more import*unate* persuasions and mediations he pressed the duke.

And to make yet hi*s* suit more acceptable and plausible, he told the duke that the king his sovereign gave him in charge to tell him that in token of his *go*od will toward him, and to make their mutual love and amity perpetual and durable, he had chosen him *into* the noble society of the Order of the Garter. Moreover, and to captate the duke's good will, and also the earl's, he told the duke that the king was des*irous* to have the Earl of Richmond with him for the love which he ba*re* unto him, as well because he was his kinsman, also for the desire which he had to advance him and to bestow one of his daughters upon the earl in marriage.

And to be brief of the eloquence and rhetorical flowers and the fair presents, of the charm of gold and jewels which this orator offered and gave to the duke, so farfort*h* and at the length *he* prevailed with the duke as that he faithf[ully] promised and also firmly covenanted that he would deli[ver] the Earl of Richmond to him, and that he would see him sa[fely] conveyed to the port of St Malo, and where four good sh[ips] *of* the king waited and attended upon the bishop's embassag*e a*bout these affairs. And the bishop with his letters [sen]*t* [the king this word, which came not without exceeding welcome to the king.

[And the duke forthwith cause]*d* [the earl to be strongly guarded from
29 The heaviness of the Earl of Richmond
the castle of] / St Malo's. And all the way as the earl passed he was very heavy and sad. And that was well observed by some of the convoys, and especially by Pierre de Landois, a noble gentleman of Brittany, and treasurer to the duke, who had the chief charge of bringing the earl to St Malo's and to deliver him to the English deputies and captains who were to receive him there. And this Monsieur de Landois, being a kind and a courteous and honourable gent*le*man, had compassion of the sorrow of the earl. He would needs know the cause thereof, and promised to give remedy unto it if it lay in his power. And the earl, being thus happily and fairly provoked by M. Landois to discover the cause of his grief and sadness unto him, willingly exposed and imparted it unto him, and in this manner:

'Sir, it is true, and as you have observed, that I am very sad and sorrowful, and I have great cause to be so, for I am now enforced to return into England, where I shall find and feel nothing but prisons and bonds and captivity, or else the lesser and the last evil, that is, death. For although the King of England, knowing well how to dissemble, pretendeth to love me and to have a purpose to do me good and to advance me (as he hath insinua*ted* to the duke your master by his ambassador), [y]et I know most assuredly that he hateth me, and so mortally and irreconcileably as that he will never receive me to favour *o*r ever be satisfied with anything but with my blood and death'.

[And] thus this sorrowful earl, with many tears and deep sighs, disco*v*ered and reported the cause of his heaviness and pensiveness to the treasurer Landois. And he at the hearing thereof was much moved and greatly [piti]ed him. And he exhorted the earl to *put aside* his [fears] and *doubts* and to be of good comfort, and he assured him that [he woul]d find means to free and deliver him from these evils and calamities which he *feared*. *Wi*th which Monsieur de Landois made relation by writing to the duke of this [lam]entable and miserable estate of the earl, and being pressed *for time*, and because he knew that the Baron of Chandait [stood well affected to the
29v
earl, and that there had been a long and reciprocal love betwixt them,] / and also that this baron was a man in great favour and credit with the duke, he went to him (having a house near to St Malo) and acquainted him with the fears of the earl, and he desired him earnestly to go to the duke and to persuade him to have compassion of the earl and to stay him, or else he was utterly lost and cast away.

And this noble and friendly Baron Chandait rode in post to the duke's court at Vannes and recounted to the duke the lamentable tale, and with such passion and vehemence as that he moved much the duke, and brought him to have commiseration of the miserable state of the earl. And then the duke had remorse of [his contrac]t made with the king, was very sorry that be granted to the king's request, and he was much offended at the king for having so cunningly drawn him into these false trains and so much abused and wronged his credulity and his good affection to the king. And the duke sent a messenger in post to stay the earl and not to suffer him to be shipped for England.

And in the meantime, Peter Landois, studying how he might help the earl, devised that the earl should make an escape from his keepers, whom he would corrupt[t,] and that he should fly to the Abbey Church in St Malo's and there to claim and crave the benefit and privilege of the Holy Asyle *of that* place, and the which he obtained easily. And the duke also, bec*ause* he would not be suspected for some packing and impostures used in this business by him, and be*cause* he would not have the king preoccupied nor possess*ed by any mes*senger before with any distasteful or reproachful news of this business and of prejudice of himself, he presently sent [Maurice] Brumel, one of his most discreet and *honest* servants, to the king to a*dvise* him that according to his promise and covenant he had sent th[e] Earl of Richmond to St Malo's and that he was there delivered to the serv[ants] of the king, and that they had negligently let him to escape, and that he had taken sanctuary. Then the duke further intimated to the king that he had sent to the [abbot] and to the king to require or pray them to deliver the earl ag[ain] unto his officers in St Malo. And that the abbot's answer w[as] that he neither might nor would deliver the earl to them nor to the king of England, nor to any man unless he have sufficient caution and security that the earl should [not be ill entreated or delive]red nor put into the hands of his enemies, but at the w[orst, to be sent back] to Va[nn]es and to be kept [a prisoner, but with as much courtesy as formerly.

Egerton 46-50

[And being the case was fallen into such strict and peremptory terms, and within the contumacy of such lawless persons, he prayed the king to rest contented. And although he could not send the earl into England, he faithfully protested there should be so watchful a guard placed upon him as should prevent all means of escape or ability to offend and hurt him, and that no suit from the French king nor any other should move him to the contrary. The king was content perforce to take this answer in good part, and the duke kept his word religiously, still holding the earl as a prisoner whilst King Edward lived, his imprisonment being, as Philip de Commynes writeth, for the space of twelve years. In which vicissitude of time, as you may observe, how strangely the earl was preserved, and doubtless **Providentia Dei**, though some thought according to Lucanus,

multos servat fortuna nocentes. [Lucan]

and made it Fortune's fantastickness.

[King Richard reneweth the suit to the Duke of Brittany for Richmond]

[Soon after King Edward died, the Duke of Gloucester, being crowned, renewed and continued the suit and treaty with the said Duke of Brittany. And in this negotiation the king employed Sir Thomas Hutton of Yorkshire, a wise and worthy gentleman, giving him all fit instructions for his embassy, with such sums of money and with presents as he thought might engage the continuance of his former promise. But nothing could overcome him to deliver the earl. But perceiving the king's fear of his claim, and the importance of such trouble as might arise that way, he again solemnly promised and assured him there should be no liberty given to the earl which might in any way give him advantage to disturb his peace.

[Yet not long after, the duke broke his promise, and so dishonourably that it then appeared he had kept it with Edward more from fear than love or honour. And indeed the name of Edward and of the Earl of March was counted terrible, and he esteemed the thunder and lightning of arms where his keen and victorious sword was drawn. Nor was this perfidious dealing of the Duke of Brittany left unpunished by a divine revenge. For he having married Margaret, daughter and coheir of Francis de Montford, Duke of Brittany, she dying without issue, he married another Margaret, the daughter of Gaston de Foix, King of Navarre, by whom he had one only daughter, Anne, who was married to the French king Charles VIII. And the Duke Francis died thus without issue male, the duchy being swallowed up and drowned in the lilies or **crapauds** of France irrecoverably. And so his family ended, and the duchy of Brittany was lost and absorbed eternally.

[Edward IV **fulmen belli, ut Seleucus, Rex inde ceraunus: fulmen dictus.**]

[Claude Paradin]

[And thus much for the fears and jealousies of those two kings and their endeavours to get the earl in their custody. But all their counsels and practices were vain and against the ordinances of heaven. For as Henry the Saint foretold, the Earl of Richmond must be King of England, to which it pleaseth God to bring him safe through all those hazards, dangers and difficulties. And no doubt he was animated and prompted by his better genius.

[The Earl of Richmond ordained to be king]

[But it must be supposed here that the House of York flourished and reigned, and that, King Edward being dead, his brother, the Duke of Gloucester, constituted by his brother Lord Protector, was soon after made King of England. Now because his adversaries have censured him very harshly and bitterly for his wearing the crown and for the sinister means by which, as they pretend, he obtained it (in which opinions I verily think they have cast much wrong and slander upon him), to clear the truth whereof I will make a plain and faithful declaration of the manner and means of his getting and coming to the crown, that by a direct and lawful way, not by such frauds and practices as is charged upon him by his enemies. For it is most manifest that he was freely chosen to be king by the estates of the kingdom and was also very earnestly solicited to take the crown – nay, in a manner constrained, as shall be proved by irrefragable testimonies.

[That the Duke of Gloucester came lawfully to the crown]

[And the better to prepare the way, first it must be understood that the barons and commons, with one common an general dislike and with an universal negative voice, had utterly refused to have the sons of King Edward to be their king, for diverse reasons, as shall be produced; the sum of which was that neither the barons nor commons held those children to be legitimate, nor the Queen Elizabeth Gray (or Woodville) to be the lawful wife, nor yet a woman worthy to be the wife of a king, in regard of her so extreme unequal quality. And therefore they would in disdain say, as Sarah did, **Eiice ancillam hanc et fili]*u*[m eius**. And it is most certain the nobles and people were so resolute in this opinion that no arguments could persuade them to the contrary.

[Know, Reader, those assertions be not mine, but of those times.]

[And the Protector was as difficultly persuaded on the other side to take the crown, though some have made it his only aim and practice, which objections are without sense and against reason. For it was not possible, and therefore not credible, the Lord Protector could by any practices attain so suddenly to so great power and credit that he should be able to procure and persuade all the barons spiritual and temporal and all the commons and clergy, as it were in a moment, to renounce and abandon the sons of King Edward and become vassals and liege people to him, and make an only and unanimous choice of him for their king with such continual and instant suit to him to take the crown, and then to put it on his head with all due solemnity and authentical public ceremonies proper and due unto a legitimate and true inauguration. But this will not seem strange if their reasons both for the one resolution and the other be well considered, which will appear to be very important and just. For they rejected those children not for any ill will or malice, but for their disabilities and incapacities of the crown, as also because they had known his wisdom and valour and that he was a magnificent and worthy prince, able to rule and govern the kingdom, which opinion was afterward allowed and confirmed by the high and whole court of Parliament, which I shall come to by degrees.

[But first you must know how the noble barons, the prelates and the rest came to the Duke of Buckingham, who was a very wise, honourable and well-spoken man, with one voice and general consent, and solicited him to go to Baynard's Castle (then York House) to the Lord Protector, who was newly removed from Crosby Place, where he lay before, to the Tower, where the prince was. According to the request of those prelates, the duke, accompanied with many of the chief barons and other grave and learned men, went to the Protector, humbly desiring access unto him, who came into the Great Chamber, and saluting the duke and the rest, sat down, giving respective audience to the duke, their orator.]

30

The Duke of Buc[k-ingham] orator to the [Lord Protector in behalf of the three] estates

And first of all, the duke in all humble manner prayed the Lord Protector to give him leave to propose to his Grace the intent and cause of their coming, of himself and of the rest, and withal insinuating that without his Grace's licence and pardon they durst not to offer nor to report that matter to his Grace's ears. Because albeit they meant as well all good and honour to his Grace, as also welfare and wealth to the realm, yet because they would prevent his displeasure, they most humbly required that his and their pardon might be before granted by his Grace. The Lord Protector then in answer hereof, and briefly, told them that he well loved them, and that he knew that they well loved him also, *and* that he was content that they should declare their business free and securely. And then the duke, this leave and pardon being obtained, and most reverently, and first making humble obeisance to the Protector, spake it in manner as followeth:

Sir Thomas More

[Bishop Morton, Sir Thomas More, Holinshed, Grafton, Stow, Hall]

'Sire, may it please your Grace to be informed that after much and grave consultation and long and well-advised deliberation being had amongst the noble barons and other wise and worthy persons of the realm, it was concluded and resolved that the sons of King Edward should not reign, as well because it was a miserable fortune and a most dangerous state for the kingdom where a child was king, and the which was by a wise and holy man observed and testified: **Vae tibi terra cuius rex est puer**. And as also and chiefly, because they were not born in lawful marriage, the king their father having then another wife alive, namely Dame Eleanor Butler, besides the great dishonour and reproach which he incurred by dispa[ra]ging his royal blood with a woman so full unmeet to match *with* him. And for these and other causes they have refused and utterly renounce to have the children to reign over them and to be king of the realm. [And] because they would not have the realm unprovided and destitute *of* a king,

[The common pub-lished] st[ories have Elizabeth Lucy] but [that is false.]

and that of a good king, these nobles and knights *and* worthy and grave persons have made choice of your Grace to be king, and with [whom no subjects more w]illingly nor with more alacrity concur than the lords and people of the northern [parts. And in like manner] the Lord Mayor and the aldermen and commons of the City of London [have a]ll [a]llowed and gladly embraced this general choice of your Grace. And in testimony thereof they [are come h]ither and are desirous to join with us in the said humble [suit, well un]derstanding that now the crowns of England and of [France, with the] *just course* of inheritance, the right and title of the same, and the [which were by the high authority of Parliament entailed] to the [royal blood and issue of Richard, Duke of York, father unto your Grace,
30v are by just course of inheritance,] / and according to the common laws of the land, devolved and come unto your Grace, as to the very lawfully begotten son and heir of the fore-remembered most noble Duke of York.

'And the thing being well considered and pondered, together with the great kingly and knightly virtues which in your Grace singularly abound, the nobles and also the commons of the realm, being not willing (as hath been afore showed) that any bastard blood should have the rule of the land, have agreed and resolved and fully determined to make your Grace King of England. And they pray your Grace most earnestly to accept their choice, and for that they have made me their advocate and solicitor of this their weighty and great suit to your Grace, deputed me *the*reunto with one voice and common consent and general suffrage of them all. Wherefore I must *beg* humbly before your Grace, in the behalves of all, that you will be pleased of your accustomed goodness and of your wonted zeal unto the good of the realm, now with your eyes of pity and compassion to behold the long and continual distress and decay of the same estate, and set your happy hands to redress and amendment thereo[f.] And the which work is only to be done and to be effected by your takin[g] the crown and by taking upon you the governance of the realm, acco*rding* to your right and title lawfully descended unto your Grace. And this shall be to the l[aws] of God, and to the profit of the land, and to your Grace's so much the more honour, and so much the less pain by how much that never any prince reigned upon any people which was so gla[d] to live under his obeisance and in his allegiance as the people of this land are and will be glad to live under your rule and governance.

'And again and lastly I am bold in their n[ames] most humbly to pray and beseech your Grace to take the crown and government of this kingdom upon you. And we hope and desi*re* and humbly, most earnestly, to have your gracious and favourable answer'.

This speech was made thus by the Duke of Buckingham, and sincerely and truly, as we oug[ht to think.] And it is recorded by Bishop Morton and by Sir Thomas More, men of nea*rest* [authority, and] b[y all ou]r chroniclers and historians held to be veritable. And it may be thought [they would] *not* [w]rite anything favourably or partially of the Lord Protector nor of [his cause, being the chiefest of those who loved him not. And therefore,] whosoever shall detract from [the sincerity and ingenuity of this oration, it may justly be conceived and censured to proceed from envy and malice.

31 [And it is] *not only* [most uncharitable,] / but also very injurious to judge

so hardly of any man not detected of falsehood and forgery, and much more of this noble duke, who was a man which much respected his honour and his word and the credit thereof, and for many years might not speak anything but as he thought it just, according to the truth. And it is to *be credited*. And certainly (as we must believe that he did) in his secret thoughts *he* held and accounted the Lord Protector to be a wise and a just and good man, and never said other[wise] until he himself became false and a malicious and a perfidious man.

But to let these censures and observations to pass, we will now make report of the answer of the Lord Protector to this speech of the Duke of Buckingham, and the which answer was very distasteful and unpleasing to the duke and to all the nobles and commons, because that the Protector accepted not their election of him to be king, but refused it and profess*ed* much mislike thereof. And he stood up, and with a sad and discontented countenance spake these words, and as they are set down by the credible, gracious and much appli*ed* authors aforesaid:

[The answer of the Lord Protector] to [the Three Estates]

'My most noble lords and my most loving friends and dear countrymen. Albeit I know and I must confess that I hold your request and suit made now to me is both reasonable and favourable, and that the things therein and the necessities alleged and urged are true and certain, yet because I bear such entire and faithful love and tender respect unto my most noble and most dear brother, the king deceased lately, and to his children, my sweet and princely nephews, for his sake I cannot find in my heart to yield to your favourable motion nor to condescend to take the crown and the kingdom unto myself. [And] because also I much more regard mine honour [an]d good fame in other realms and foreign countries *which* are round about this land than I do a crown, *or to* take the kingdom or any sceptre.

'For if I should [accept] the crown and take the kingdom into *my possession* and into my own hands, it would *distaste and disg*ust those foreign nations [where the truth and certain proceedings herein are not known, that it may be] / my plot and politic device to procure the rejecting and deposing of the young prince, King Edward, and to the end to take the crown unto myself. But these be such matters of infamy and of reproach as that I would not have mine honour and good name stained therewith for all the crowns in the world. Besides that (I have long perceived and well observed it) there is more labour and more pains in the government of a kingdom than pleasure or delight, especially to the prince who would use the kingly authority and royal office as it ought to be used. And therefore, and for these and the like causes, I protest I never desired the crown; neither can I now find in mine heart to take it, nor to incline to your desires.

31v

'But yet I think myself much beholding to you all for your favourable election of me, and I give you all the most hearty thanks for your great good will and true hearty love, which I find hereby you bear to me. And I promise here that for your sakes, it shall be all one whether I be your king or no, for I will serve the young king my nephew faithfully and diligently and carefully and will live under him his subject and vassal; and I will endeavour with my best counsels and with my sw[ord] to defend him and to preserve him and this kin[g]dom in peace and prosperity. And furthermo[re,] I will be willing and ready to attempt the recov[ery] of the hereditary signories and provinces in France which belong to the King of England, and lately and negligently unhappily lost'.

And here the Prot[ector] became silent and sat down again in his chair, and thought [not] safe nor a politic course to tell them all the distastes and dislikes which [he] had of the condition of sovereignty and of reigning and *especially* in England, because that would have been a matter of exprobation of [the barons] and would have much offended them. And
32 therefore, he c*oncealed his* dislike. / *And* they many times much afflicted and vexed the kings, and brought them into great distress and fear of their lives. And further yet, all their raging fury was sometimes so outrageous and excessive as that they ceased not until they had either deposed or killed and utterly destroyed their sovereign lord. And he knew well, and there were fresh examples hereof in the reigns of his brother King Edward and of King Henry VI, and not long before in the time of King Richard II and of his grandfather, King Edward II. He knew that more anciently the troubles and desperate distresses and calamities of the kings John and Henry III, caused by their barons, were dreadful warnings and [monu]ments of the insolencies and of the rhodomontados and of the disloyal levity of those seditious Bashaes. This was **alta mente repositum** with this wise prince. And he was desirous to avoid and to prevent the dangers and miserable mischiefs following it. But for the causes here showed, he concealed his objection and supposed that he had said enough in his foresaid speech and should not need other arguments.

[The barons, etc., press the Lord Protector to take the crown]

But the barons and the other grave and worthy persons would not admit any answers or excuses of the Lord Protector, nor rest satisfied therewith, but they continued resolute in their purpose, in their choice of him to be king, and then instantly they conferred with the duke their orator, and they gave him instructions and directions sufficient to answer and to refute all the objections. And the duke prayed audience again, and did very fully and eloquently answer and confute the Protector's objections and avoided all his tergiversations and refelled all his arguments and exceptions, as it may be seen in our stories, and in effect as tedious and super*fluous to re*peat. And then in silence the duke attended the answer of the Protector.

But he was also silent and mute, and he *neither* [repli]ed nor said anything to him (as at the least in public), but he [turned to] the Lord Mayor of London and to the Recorder, being [near unto] him, and that which he said, and in a low voice, [tended to] *th*e dislike and disgust which he had of their *entreaty con*cerning his taking of the crown and had *delivered already.*
And [the Lord Mayor, with reverence and discreetly, repre]hended the *which*, [intimating how much the change of his opinion would give requital
32v and satisfaction to the] / barons and to the commons and to the City of London, who all had so earnestly and so importunately besought his Grace to take the kingdom and to be their king and only sovereign lord.

And when the Lord Mayor had ended his short speech, and which the Duke of Buckingham had overheard with close and diligent listening, and thereby had observed and perceived how slightly the Protector entertained the Mayor's advice, and how lightly he regarded his good and grave speeches and his profitable persuasions of the Mayor, and also with the like careless manner he heard those speeches which more at large and more effectually had been uttered by himself, he seemed to have much mislike and indignation thereof, and, as it were, in indignation and in a kind of scorn of the Protector's neglect and of the many repulses and many obstinate refusals of their love and of the election of the *barons and commons of* him to be their king. And being also wearied, and even tired with the perverse and cross proceedings herein, stood forth and craved leave of the Protector to spe*ak* but two or three words more. And he said that he would from thenceforth cease from troubling of his Grace any more in that *vein*. And the duke being licensed to speak what he would for his epilogue and his **ultimum vale** to this motion and suit, spake in this manner:

[The bold and round conclusion of the Duke of Buckingham]

'Sire, since it hath pleased your Grace to give me leave to speak again, the which leave I have ta*ken*, it must also be allowed to me in a bolder and rounder style, because I am bound by this mine employment and by my duty to my cou[ntrymen] to declare plainly in this cause, and to the end to rid the noble barons and the commons out of suspense and out of doubt, **quia dubia plus torquent mala** (i.e., doubtful things more torment the mind), and I must therefore finally and peremptori*ly* advertise your Grace that the most constant and final determination and last and irrevocable *resolution* of the barons and of the people are that the line of King Ed[ward] shall not reign over them, and for the reasons before *stated*, and also because these estates have entered so far and [proceeded so off]ensively to other men and so dangerously to t[hemselves as is now too late to recant or retire. And therefore they have fixed their election upon you, as on the man whom they think most able and careful for their safety.]

'But if there be no end of these your repulses and denials and of your 33
contempt or light regard of our suit, and you be so obstinate and so inexporable and inflexible as that you will never be persuaded nor by any petitions or by any reasons or arguments inanswerable, or by any request or solicitation, nor by prayers and humble petitions be brought to like and embrace and to put on the condition of a king, then we hope and we desire that you will be pleased to declare once more your mind plainly and sincerely and definitively therein, and to give unto us your peremptory and final answer. And if there be no remedy but that it shall and must be as it hath hitherto been – that is, very distasteful and discomfortable and very bitter and grievous unto us – then we humbly pray your Grace that you will be content and give your consent that we seek out some other most noble and princely person who shall be fit and worthy to undertake the great and stately and imperial charge and will gladly and willingly accept our offer and our election of him to be king. And this request we trust that your Grace will grant, considering our great necessity and desperate case. And we hope yet that by these means and by God's good favour to find out one, and such an one, and so well affected unto us, and so princely qualified as aforesaid. And this is all, and the last that we have to say or will say in this matter. And all that we crave and desire now is that you will be pleased once again and finally to give us your perem*p*tory and definite answer, and instantly and without delays'.

The Protecto[r] *considered the* matters of this speech, and he was much troubled also, and almost distracted with this plain and round and braving conclusion *and as it were from* a castle of defiance. And he seemed as one that had been roused out of a drowsy slumber or awaked out of a frightful dream. [For] certain it is that the Protector was much altered with the bold speech of the Duke of Buckingham. As Sir Thomas More disertly confesseth tha*t* the Protector was so much moved with those words as that otherwise and of likelihood he would never have inclined to the suit of the barons and of the commons. This Mr More, and the same author proceeding herein, saith that the Lord Protector saw that there was no other remedy but that he must [e]ither take the crown now and at this instant, or else that both he and [his] heirs forever forgo it and lack and lose it irrecuperably, *and th*at it also should pass to another, who might be his enemy and a scourge and ***mal*us genius** to him and to his. And especially (and so it is to be understood) if the crown went to the *Earl of* Richmond, between whom and this prince Richard the hatred and the malice was equally extreme *an*d irreconcilable, he might be assured that he should *have care*s and evils and mischiefs greater and more than he could conceive. And *when he had his* desire now therefore at last considered and forecast and forefeared, then almost too late for the *safety of sovereign*ty and of empire, now, therefore, *with* better and more advised judgement he / signified unto them in these words:

33v

The Lord Protector yieldeth to the barons

'My most noble good lords and my most loving and faithful friends, I must confess that upon better considerations of your *offer* and of the dangers and evils which were insinu[ated] now at the l*ast* to me by your noble speaker, and also upon the plain and wise words which he last spake, I better apprehend the benefit of your offer and election and [proffer,] *and* I find some alteration in my mind, as well for the causes aforesaid, and also because I perceive and consider that all the realm is set against the sons of King Edward, and which much grieveth us, and will not suffer in any wise King Edward's line to govern them; and that I likewise know that the nation is a people of that stout stomach and courage as that no earthly man can govern them against their wills; and also forasmuch as that we certainly understand there is no man to whom the crown can by just title be so due as to ourself, being the very rightful and lawful gotten son and heir of our most dear and princely father, Richard, Duke of York, and unto which true titles of blood and of nature now by your favour is joined another title, and that is the election of me, made by you, and the which title we take and hold to be the most safe and the most strong and the most effectual title of all other titles. And because also I cannot *nor* ever will endure that that one at whom you glanced, mentioned and without a name in your last speech, being mine utter enemy, should sit in the throne of my kingdom and usurp my royal heritage; and that so I should become a vassal to mine unworthy and hateful subject.

'And therefore, according to the necessities of those causes, there is no remedy but that w*e* must needs consent and agree, and to take your favourable offer of the cro[wn,] and to incline to your petition, and to accept your election of us, and to yield to your earnest and importunate requests to have me to be your king. We therefore, according to the same requests and suits and to our right, do now in the place and at the instant accept your choice and take upon us the royal state and the regal pre-eminence and the r*ule* of these two noble kingdoms of England and of France from this day forward, and by us and by our heirs to rule and to govern and to defend the one (that is, England), and by God's grace and by your good aid to redeem and recover the other (that is, France) and to resubdue it to the rea[lm,] and to restore it to the ancient allegiance of the kings of England, and to es[tablish] it in due obeisance of this kingdom forever. And we ask not of any longer to live than so long as we intend and endeavour to [procure] and labour the advancement and flourishing estate of this [kingdom’. At which they all cried, ‘Go]d save King Richard’, [and thus he] became king, and so all *the people departed*.

And here the ingenious and judicious Reader may see how much the detractors and cavillers wrong and slander the noble prince Richard, and also all the proceedings in the business before related, and who are not ashamed to say that all that hath been said and done, and all the proceedings of state in these affairs of the election and making of him king were but dissimulations and tricks and arts of impostures. And if that be true, then they may as well say (**adsit reverentia dicto**) that all the barons and all the worthy and grave gentlemen and all the better commons, who were the only actors herein, were fools and knaves, **aut utrumque**. And that were a most impudent and an intolerable scandal, and the which also would light upon all the high and most grave and wise and religious court of Parliament, for it was not long after ere all that which was handled and alleged and persuaded and acted and concluded in the same treaties and colloquies and suits aforesaid was allowed and approved and ratified and confirmed by the court of Parliament. But these be so gross cavils as that they serve for nothing but to discover the extreme envy and malice of the contrivers and patrons of them. And therefore they need no answer nor refutation. Then to let them pass with this passport, and to proceed with the story. **34**

And for it is not to be omit[ted] that whilst these matters of the election of King Richard were handled (as is aforesaid) that the northern gentlemen who had joined with these southern friends of the Protector’s had an advertisement that there were some difficulties and some obstacles and crosses in the effecting and accomplishment thereof, and those proceeding out of the will and w[ilfulness of the Protector.] Whereupon they caused a bill supplicatory to be made and to be directed and addressed to the barons spiritual and temporal which were at London or near abouts and were occupied in the foresaid business of the election. And in this bill they signified to them their great desire to have the Protector to be their king, as well for his good title and for his virtues and princely worthiness as also because the children of King Edward and his marriage were unlawful, and also that the blood of the young Earl of Warwick was attainted and his title confiscated by Parliament. And they intimated that for these causes they had chosen the Duke of Gloucester to be their king.

T[he general caution of] th[e author.] **E[t vide in Lib.** 2.]

[He]re, and once for all, because I shall have occasion to speak often of this [mar]riage of King Edward and of these children’s birth, and how that they were reputed *unlaw*ful and illegitimate, I pray the noble and discreet Reader to conceive that [I em]brace not those hard opinions, but I only relate that such opinions and such *beliefs* [were the censures of those times generally believed, and they were of good use for the better effecting of that great business in hand. For to the world it is all one to seem and to be.]

This bill was delivered to th[e] lords being assembled in the Great Hall at Westminster, and the Lord Protector sitting in the chair [of] marble amongst them, upon the 26th day of Jun[e,] and which was some six or seven days after the Protector had accepted the cr[own and was] proclaimed **36v** king. And this is the tenor of this bill, as I *have seen it* written in the Chronicle of the Abbey of [Croyland]:

[**Lib.** Abb. Croyland] **Ricardus Protector eodem die, quo re[gim]*ine* [sub] titulo regii nominis sibi vendicav[it, viz., 26] die Junii, anno Domini [1483, se apud magnam Aulam** 37 **Westmonasterii, in Cathedram Marmoream] / immisit, et tum mox omnibus proceribus tam laicis quam ecclesiasticis et ceteris assidentibus et astantibus, etc., ostendebatur rotulus, quidam in quo per modum supplicationis in nomine procerum et populi Borealis exhibitae, primum quod filii regis Edwardi erant bastardi, supponendo illum praecontraxisse matrimonium cum quadam domina Alienora Boteler antequam reginam Elizabetham duxisset in uxorem. Deinde quod sanguis alterius fratris Georgii (scilicet) Clarentiae ducis, fuisset attinctus, ita quod nullus certus et [i]ncorruptus sanguis linealis ex parte Ri[ca]rdi ducis Eboraci poterat invenire, [n]isi in persona Ricardi protectoris, ducis [G]locestriae, et tum eidem duci supplicabant, [ut] ius suum in regno Angliae sibi assumeret, [et c]oronam acciperet, etc.** Thus that C*h*ronicle of Croyland.

[Bu]t this suit of the northern men was not then very n[eedful, for the barons] were all accorded before the bill came and was presented, all went [well,] and all men were [contentedly] and cheerfully disposed. And now there were preparations of festival [solemn]ity and pomp *ma*de for the coronation. And in the month [of Ju]ly next following, and in the year 1483, all things being r*eady,* [with all st]ate and magnificence, the Protector was very solemnly and most [lawfully] crowned and consecrated, with all the *ancie*nt and pompous rites and royal and sacred [ceremonies apper]taining to the crowning, [anointing, and inaugur]ation of a sovereign 37v king, [and received] / for king with so joyful and general applause, in such favourable acclamations, as any other king was or had been in England for many years before. And that doubtless was done and yielded heart*ily*, without dissimulation, by good right and reason. For as a grave man writeth Cam[den] in **Do*buni*** of this king, **Fui[t dign]issimus regno, et [non in]ter malos, sed inter bonos principes prudentum consensu connum[erandus]**: He was most worthy to be numbered a[mongst the g]ood and not [bad pri]nces.

The Queen Anne also, his wife, was there crowned with him. And she accompanied him with pompous proceeding all the way from the Tower to Westminster. And besides the nobility, greater and lesser, of the south parts which attended at this solemn inauguration feast, there were fou[r] thousand gallant gentlemen of Yorkshire [and of] the north parts in the train. And for the more magnificent and more honourable celebration of this great feast, there were creations and investitures of noble perso[ns] and of knights.

And first the king, some days befo[re] the coronation (viz., 28th day of June) invest[ed] Sir John Howard, who was made Lord Howard and a Knight of the Garter by K[ing Edward IV], in the duk[e]dom of Norfolk, in a favourable ad[mi]ssion of the right of the Lady Marg[aret] his mother, and daughter of Sir Thomas [Mowbray,] Duke of Norfolk and heir gen[eral] of the most noble Mowbrays, [dukes] of Norfolk and earls of 38 [Surrey,] and descended from the Lord Th[omas Plantagenet,] / the first Earl of Norfolk and Marshal of England. And he was also as well and as Style of the Duke of Norfolk rightly Lord Mowbray and Lord Segrave and Lord Breus as Lord Howard, and so I have seen him styled, and by good and royal warrant, namely in a commission in a treatise of truce and peace with Scotland, in the Rolls kept in [t]he Chapel of the Convertites.

[In Rot]ulis [in] domo [conver]sorum

And then also the king created Sir [Th]omas Howard, eldest son of the [sa]id duke, Earl of Surrey, and he made him a Knight of the [Garter.] And this king [ma]de William, Lord Berkeley, Earl [of] Nottingham; and the Baron [Lo]vell was made Viscount Lovell and [Lo]rd Chamberlain; and he took the [Lo]rd Stanley out of prison and made [him] Steward of his house. And Sir Henry Stafford, Duke of [Buc]kingham, was made Constable of [En]gland for term of life, albeit [he] claimed that office as belonging [to hi]m by inheritance. But Sir Thomas More writeth that the Lord Thomas Howard, Earl of [Surrey,] executed the office, and after the Duke of [Buckingham was] dead the king gave that office [of cons]tableship to the Lord Stanley, [with an] annual fee of £100, and *who* [became a most] ingrate, and fatally *served* [the king, his good master.]

[Rotuli in capella conversorum]

And Dr Thomas Rotherham, Lord Chancellor of England and Arch- **38v**
bishop of Canterbury, having been committed to prison for delivering the Great Seal to the Queen Widow, was now pardoned and set at liberty and restored to grace and to his place. And in brief, many knights were created and adubbed of the old Order, and seventeen knights of the new Order or
habit of the Bath, whose names I have here set down, / to show what regard **39**
was had of the choice of those kind of knights in those times which are accounted to be so evil and disorderly and tyrannous:

[Knights of the Bath made by King Richard III]

Sir Edmund de la Pole, son of the Duke of Suffolk
George Gray, son of the Earl of Kent
William Souch, son of the Lord Souch
Henry Neville, son of the Lord Abergavenny

Christopher Willoughby	William Berkeley
Henry Baynton	Thomas Arundel
Thomas Boleyn	Breus of Clifton
William Say	Edmund Bedingfield
William Enderby	Thomas Lewkenor
Thomas of Vernon	John Brown

William Berkeley i.e. another Berkeley

And now I think it very necessary to make a ful[l and] true relation of all **40**
the solemn ceremonies and regal pom[p] which were used and exhibited at the consecration and corona[tion] of this King Richard III. And for two causes, the one for th[e credit] of my word, because I have in some places here before [affir]med the coronation of this king was [most] lawfully and authentically and solemnly and publicly and regularly, and accor[ding] to the ancient custom used therein, celebrated and performed. And the other ca*use*, that they may see their error and the wrong which they ha[ve done] to the king and to all the barons and nobles and people o[f this kingdom] who say that this king came indirectly and irregularly to the cr[own and like a thief] he crept in at the window secretl*y*, [climbing to the throne by] treacher[y and evil acts. The authors which I will follow herein be all the best chroniclers and writers of our stories, all public and well allowed.]

Richard, the third of that name, took upon him to be King of England the **41**
19th day of June, **Anno Domini** 1483, and in the twenty-fifth year of the reign of the French king Lewis XI. And the morrow after, viz., 20 June, he was proclaimed king, and he then made for London to Westminster, with

More, Grafton, Hall, Polydore, **Croylandensis**, Holinshed, Stow, etc.

great solemnity, and there sat in the seat royal and called before him the judges of the realm, straightly commanding them to execute the law, without favour or evil will or delay, and with many other good exhortations. And then he departed toward the Abbey, and at the church door he was met with the procession, and the sceptre of St Edward was delivered to him by the abbot. And then he went to St Edward's shrine and offered there, the monks in the meantime singing **Te Deum**. From the church he returned to the palace, where he lodged until his coronation.

[Monstrelet, Commynes, **Anglicos Scriptores**]

Upon the 4th day of July, he went to the Tower by water with the queen his wife, and being there upon the next day, he created Edward, his only son, being ten years old, Prince of Wales. And then Sir John, Lord Howard, a man very loyal and of great knowledge and experience, and as well in council as in bat[tle, and deservedly therefore in gr]eat favour with King Edward IV, and by him made Lord Howard, was created Duke of Norfolk. And Sir Thomas Howard, his eldest son, was created Earl of Surrey. And William, Lord Berkeley, was then created Earl of Nottingham. And Francis, Lord Lovell, was then made Viscount Lovell and Chamberlain to the king. And the Lord Stanley was delivered out of durance and made Steward of the King's [House]hold. And Thomas Rotherham, Archbishop of York, [was pardone]d and set at liberty. But Bishop Morton was sent for [his treachery to Brecknock C]astle, and to be kept safe [by the Duke of Buckingham. And that same day the king made these seventeen knights of the Bath before named.

[The next day he rode from the Tower through London in great state and pomp, most gallantly attended. The Duke of Buckingham was of most **41v** eminent note and most extraordinarily rich and gallant,] / his habit and caparison of blue velvet embroidered with golden naves of carts burning, and trappings, were supported by footmen in brave and costly garments suitable to the rest.

And on the morrow, being the 6th day of July, the king proceeded in state toward his coronation, and he came into Westminster Hall, where all the prelates, mitred and in their **pontificalibus**, to his chapel received him. And there attended upon the king in this proceeding three dukes, nine earls and twenty-two viscounts and simple barons, and about eighty knights, and esquires and gentlemen without number.

And the great officers of the crown and of the king which had special services to do upon that Great Day went in their order and manner, viz.: next after the procession followed the Earl of Northumberland with a pointless sword naked. The Lord Stanley bare the mace of the Constableship, but he waited not for Constable there, as you shall see by and by. The Earl of Kent bare the second sword naked upon the right hand of the king. The Lord Viscount Lovell bare another sword on the king's left hand. Next came the Duke of Suffolk with the sceptre, and the Earl of Lincoln bare the ball and cross. Then the Earl of Surrey with the sword of estate in a rich scabbard, and in the place of the Constable of England. His father the Duke of Norfolk went upon his right, bearing the crown. And now next came the king himself, clad in a surcoat and a robe of purple velvet, and over his head there was a canopy borne by the barons of the five ports. The king was between the bishops of Bath and of Durham. Next the king came the Duke of Buckingham, bearing up the king's train, and he served with a rod and staff for a Seneschal or High Steward of England.

And now the queen came in her estate, *and* in the forefront of her attendants cam[e the Earl of Huntington, bearing the queen's sceptre, and the Viscount Lisle the rod with the dove. The Earl of Wiltshire] / bare the 42
queen's crown. Then followed Queen Anne in robes like to those of the king, between two bishops likewise, and also with a canopy borne over her head by the barons of the ports. And upon her head she wore a rich coronet set with precious stones and pearls, and the Lady Margaret Somerset, Countess of Richmond, bare her train. And then followed the Duchesses of Suffolk and Norfolk and many countesses and baronesses and other ladies, etc. And in this order this whole procession passed through the palace to the Abbey and entered at the west door.

And then the king and queen took their seats of state, and they stayed there until divers holy hymns were solemnly sung. And then they both descended and went to the high altar, and they shifted their robes and put on others, which were voided and open in sundry places for their anointment. And they, being anointed, put on other robes of cloth of gold and returned to their seats, and where the Cardinal of Canterbury and other bishops crowned them, according to the ancient and solemn customs of the realm. And these prelates put the sceptre in the left hand of the king, and the ball and cross in his right hand. And they put the queen's sceptre in her right hand, and the rod with the dove in her left hand. And on each hand of the king there stood a duke, and before him stood the Earl of Surrey, bearing the foresaid sword in his hands. And upon each hand of the queen stood a bishop and a lady kneeling.

The cardinal said mass and gave the **pax**, and then the king and queen descended, and they were both houseled, with one host parted between them, at the high altar. And this being done, they [bot]h offered at St Edward's shrine, and there the king laid down [St] Edward's crown and put on another crown. And these [cere]monies of inauguration and royal consecration being thus *performed*, [t]he king and queen and the noble*s* and all the train returned to Westminster Hall in the same [order as they we]nt forth, and then they dispersed themselves [and retired for a little season to] their chambers. And in [the meantime, the Duke of Norfolk, Marshal of England, came mounted upon a brave horse richly trapped with cloth] / of 42v
gold down to the ground, and he submoved the press of the people and voided the hall.

And by this time it was near four of the clock, and then the king and queen came into the hall and sat down at the royal table to dinner. And the king sat in the middle of the table, and the queen sat upon the king's left hand, and she had two countesses attending upon each side of her, holding a cloth of pleasance (or rat[her] of essuyance) for her cup. And upon the king's right hand sat the Archbishop of Canterbury. And all the ladies sat on one side of a long table placed in the middle of the hall. And over against them at another table sat the Lord Chancellor and all the nobles and barons. And at the table next to the cupboard sat the Lord Mayor of London and the aldermen. And at another table behind the barons of the kingdom sat the barons of the ports. And there were divers other tables, whereat also many noble and worshipful persons sat and dined.

And after that all were set, then again came in the Duke of N[orfolk,]

Marshal of England, and the Earl of Surrey, his son, Constab[le **pro ille vice tantum**,] and next came the Lord Stanley, Lord Steward, and Sir William Hopton, Treasurer of the Household, and Sir Thomas Percy, Controller. And they served the king's board with one dish of go[ld] and another of silver. And the queen was served all in gilt vessel*s*, and the Archbishop Cardinal had all his diet in silver dish[es.] And as soon as the second course was served into the hall, there came Sir Robert Dymock, the King's Champion, making proclamation that whosoever would say that King Richard III was not lawfully king, he would fight with him at all outerance. And for the gage hereof, he threw down his gauntle[t.] But then all the hall cried, 'King Richard, God save King Ri[chard.]' And in this manner the Champion acted the part in three several parts of the hall. And then an officer of the ki[ng's] cellar brought to him a gilded bowl, covered and full of wine. And the Champion drank some of the wine and ca[st] out the rest, and carried the cup away with him as his a[ncient fee.] And after this, the heralds cried 'largess' thrice and retu[rned to] their scaffold. And lastly came the Mayor of L[ondon and the sheriffs with a voider,] and served the king and queen, [and with sweet wine, or hippocras. By this time the day was spent and it grew somewhat dark, when the king and queen rose from the table and went into their lodgings.

[And this is a brief and true relation of this solemn coronation, which I have the rather reported because (as I intimated before) the malicious adversaries of the king have not shamed to say he was not lawfully and rightfully crowned and anointed king.]

44 And the king gave strait charge to the justices, magistrates and officers of the courts and jurisdictions that they would deal so uprightly as that there might be no corrupting nor frauds nor injustices nor abuses found or used in them. Moreover, and as he had done before, and as it hath been
[Sir] Thomas M[ore] remembered before, he gave strict commandment to the lords spiritual and temporal who were then to take their leaves of the king and to return to their countries, and had charge of justice and jurisdiction in the countries, and all other magist[rates] which had like charge of justice, to be careful to distribute justice and right to every man, as well to the poor as to the rich and great, and equally and indifferently. And also that they would have great and chief regard that God might be duly and rightly served and worshipped in all places.

When the judges of oyer and terminer were [to] depart from Westminster and to ride their summer [circu]its, the king sent for them and gave them *direction, and* required and charged them to administer indiffe[rently] justice to all his subjects and liege people. *And of* all these good and godly exhortations and *instruc*tions given by this king to the honourable *cou*rtly magistrates and to the judges and justi*ces*, this testimony was made by Mr John Herd, a learned m[an and Docto]r of Physic, and a good poet, in a manuscript poesy of his which I have seen:

43 **Solio Juris [rectique minist]ra**
Ille sedens alte, tali sermone profatur:
Moses consilio soceri persuasus Ietro,
[So]lus quod populi nequit componere lites,
Constituit populi praefectos atque tribunos.
[Sic] cum me praecelsa premant fastigia regni

[Ardu]a magnarum teneatis munera rerum.
[Et] primum a vobis p[ra]vos secludite motus,
[Aequis Just]itiae trutinis appendite causas.
[Ob paupertatem,] miserum ne spernite civem;
[Nec vota in cassum fundat pu]pillus in auras.
[Denique largitio ne vos corrumpat iniqua, etc.]

All things being set in good order, the king departed from London, being 44v accompanied with the queen his wife and Edward, Duke of Cornwall, his son, and attended upon with many lords and ladies and other worthy servito[rs,] and amongst other, and chiefly, with the Duke of Buckingham. And the king made the castle of Windsor the first gifts of his progress, where he for some few days took the pleasure of the fresh air and the green woods and of the red and fallow deer of that forest, as he did also at his manor and park of Woodstock, which was his next place of lodging. And from thence he went to the University of Oxenford, where he was very honourably and delightfully entertained of the noble and courteous Muses. And he visited soon after his titular city of Gloucester and thanked the citizens for the love and loyalty which they showed in defending and holding the castle and town, and so constantly [and] stoutly, against the Queen Margaret and the forces of King Henry VI for him and for the king his brother. And he bestowed large privileges and immunities upon that city. And here the Duke of Bu[ckingham took his leave of the kin]g and went a[way to Brecknock, very] well content, [as it seemed.]

The king made small stay anywhere, saving only [at] Coventry, until he came to the goodly and ancient [city] of York, a place much esteemed and beloved *of* [him.] And whilst he was in York, he was crowned the [second] time by Dr Rotherham, Archbishop of York, with gre[at solem]nity and all festivity in the cathedral, where also his son Edward was invested in the principali[ties of] Wales, and with all due pomp and ceremonies, and as it [is] reported by the Prior of Croyland, and thus:

Eodem die [quo] Ricardus coronatus est rex in ecclesia metr[opoli]tana Eboracensi, mox filium Edwardum in [princi]patum Walliae cum insigniis virgae aureae, et se[rti in] capite erexit, et pomposa et sumptuosa festa [et] convivia ibi fecit.

And indeed, this was a day [of great] state and of great pomp, and very glorious. For u[pon this] day (as saith Polydore) there were three princes adorned with crowns, namely, the king, the q[ueen and prince. In acclamation whereof,] there were stage plays and tournaments and other triumphal sports, as Sir Thomas More writeth. And at this city also, as some say, [the king] made Richard of Gloucester, his base son, [knight, after Captain of] Calais, who was a valiant young gentleman, of whom I shall [have occasion to speak more anon.]

[Richard the bastard of] Gloucester [Captain of Calais]

In this progress the king graced many worthy gentlemen of the north 45 parts with the title and order of knighthood. And albeit this was a time of great feasting and of revelling and of pleasure, yet the king neglected not the duty and charge of his royal office, but still as he travelled he had a care that justice should be duly done, and in sundry places, and gave commandment that the more facinorous malefactors should be executed. And after some convenient time bestowed in this progress to York, he bade farewell, and as it unhappily happened, **longum aeternumque vale**, as the poet said of

[Chronicle MS. **in quarto apud** Robert Cotton, **et** Robert Fabyan]

[Vergil, **Aeneid**]

Aeneas, to that good city of York so much beloved of him, and to all those northern countries and people. And he came to Nottingham Castle, and from there to London.

And being returned, and whereas he had admonished and friendly warned the [Fre]nch King Lewis XI to continue the payment of the tribute [and] pension which he was bound to pay the king and some noble [and] worthy persons of England, now he went more roundly [to] work and required that payment with threat and stout menaces, the which tribute 45v was raised by King Edward IV. But / the Frenchmen would not have it called a tribute but a pension, as Philip Commynes insinuateth. And the tribute and pension was paid in lieu of the profits and revenues of the duchies and counties of Aquitaine and of Normandy and of Maine and of Poitou and of other signories in France, ancient heritages of the kings of England, and whereof the French had disseised the kings of England and usurped the title and right and possession of those said lands and signories.

And King Richard vowed that he would either have the said tribute paid or else he would adventure to recover those lands with his sword, and by such means as his brother the king had before obtained and gained that tribute. For he enforced King Lewis XI to acknowledge his right unto those lands and provinces and to pay a tribute to him for his occupation [of] them. And he made him to give good caution and security [for] the payment 46 thereof in the city of London, and it was covenanted and agreed that / the King of France and his heirs and successors should yearly pay to the King of England and to his heirs and successors the sum of fifty thousand crowns (or after John Tillet and John Meyerus, seventy-five thousand crowns), and that to be brought in the Tower.

Du Tillet saith that this French tribute or pension was three score and fifteen escus or crowns, and **chaque écu valant trente-trois sols.**

And the French king granted to give or to pay certain chief noblemen and other men of special credit and favour with the king the sum of sixteen thousand crowns, and that in the name of annual pension, and to these noble persons by name, viz.: to Sir Thomas Gray, Marquess of Dorset, [t]o William, Lord Hastings, Chamberlain to the king, [to D]r Thomas Rotherham, Bishop of Lincoln [and] Lord Chancellor of England, [an]d to John, Lord Howard, and to Sir [Jo]hn Cheyney, Master of the Horse, and to Sir [T]homas Montgomery, and to the Master [of] the Rolls, and to Mr Challoner and others. And the chiefest of these had [two] thousand crowns apiece per annum, And [bes]ides these pensions King Lewis gave [gr]eat rewards and rich presents to [ce]rtain of those lords to whom he was most beholding for their good affection to him [and] their advancing of this accord and agreement.

Joannes Meyer, **Annal. Fland. Lib**. 17, *p*. 469

The Lord [Howard] favoured h[ighly of King] Edward IV

[Du Tillet]

And Enguerrant [de] Monstrelet writeth that the Lord Howard and the Master [of the] Horse were the chiefest of the English medi[ators] of this accord and peace. And his reason is because, [as he sai]th, they were the most in favour with [King E]dward. And this is also another great reason that the Lord Howard might be one of them. [And King Edward IV made this Sir John Howard a baron and a Knight of the Bath: he was installed in **anno** 17, Edward IV. Philip de Commyn]es writeth that King Lewis gave to the [Lord Howard in less than two] years the value of [2400 crowns in plate and coin and jewels, over and above his annual pension, and that this] 46v king gave to the Lord Hastings at one time to the value of 2000 marks in plate, besides also his pension. And to these may be added Sir Richard de

Neville, the great Earl of Warwick. For if it be true which I have read in the French stories, the King of France gave much greater rewards to him than to any other English nobleman. And the author of the Chronicle of Brittany saith that the Earl of Warwick cost King Lewis very great sums of money.

King Richard, according to his promise and protestation in this behalf to the Lords and Commons (and before remembered), demanded this French trib[ute] *of King Lewis* and his son, King Charles VIII, if my memory fail me not. And if he had not been by horrible sed[ition] and most unnatural treason prevented, he would have compell[ed] the kings of France to have performed and continued the due paym[ent] thereof, and of the pensions besides, or else he would have transported and led a ne*w expedition* into France for the recovery of those duchies and sig[nories,] the ancient heritage of the kings of *England*, as is aforesaid. But yet as cross and as thwart as fortune was to this king, he brought King Lewis to give him good words, and seemed but to [crave respite] and longer time for the payment hereof, as Commynes not obscurel[y intimates.]

47

The Queen [Mother and] King Richard [made friends]

[Not long after] that, by the good, honest and charitable mediation of [som]e honourable and good persons, the king and the Lady [Eliz]abeth, Queen Dowager, were reconciled, and a friendly accord and mutual amity was made between them. And then she, being out of fear and in secu*rity, left* the sanctuary. And in token of his good affection she sent her five daughters soon afterward to the court, where they were very [honou]rably entertained, and with all princely [kind]ness, as you shall understand in a *more* fit place hereafter.

The Parl[iament] of King Ric[hard III]

[The] king kept a very great and magnificent Christmas feast this [year] at Westminster, and as soon as that was ended [he s]ummoned a Parliament, viz., 23rd day of January, [in] the first year of his reign, to be holden at Westminster. [In] that Parliament, many great and grave and honourable matters [were] handled, and many very good laws were made, and *of which I shall give* instances hereafter. [And in this Par]liament the marriages of King Edward were de[ba]ted and tried, *and* his marriage with the Lady Gray was declared [and] adjudged to be unlawful, and his children [begotten upon her] to be illegitimate and bastards be[cause he was formerly contr]acted and also married to the Lady [Eleanor Talbot, daughter of the old Earl of Shrewsbury, and relict to the Lord Butler of Sudeley, then living and long after.]

47v

And all the foresaid matters objected and pleaded by the Duke of Buckingham in his speeches and orations made in the name of the nobles and commons against this marriage of the Lady Elizabeth Gray, and against the unlawfulness and bastardy of the children of King Edward, and against the attainder and incapacity of reign of the children of the Duke of Clarence; also the matters contained in the bill supplicatory of the deputies of the northern people were rehearsed, and those, and all the foresaid objections and accusations, were approved and allowed, and judgement was given and pronounced against that unlawful second marriage of King Edward and against the illegitimacy and bastardy of his children and against their incapacity of reigning, as also of the Earl of Warwick and his sister, the Lady Margaret Plantage[net.] And this judgement and sentence was decreed, ratified and confirmed b[y] Act of Parliament. And therefore it must be thought that this court o[f Parliament] dealt justly and rightly, or else the detractor may say (and which were an extremely foul sca[ndal) t]hat there was [neither one hone]st or [just nor godly man in that] Parliament, but *all were corrupt*ed.

Moreover, in this Parliament public knowledge was taken of the [seditious] and highly ambitious practices of Henry, Earl of Richmond and [of his] treasons, and of his false claim made to the crown and kingd*om* by a title derived from his kindred to the House of Lancas[ter,] and how that this earl was at that time in France, practi[sing] and labouring by all means to persuade and to draw [the] French king and the Duke of Brittany to enter into his quarrel and to aid him to inva*de* this land, and to put down and to destroy the lawful and rightful king.

[It was fur]ther declared in the court of Parliament that he to the effecting hereof, and for the better colour and pretext [to] bring his disloyal purpose to pass, practised, and by all me[ans] sought and promised to marry the eldest da[ughter] of King Edward, supposing thereby to join the titles [of] York and Lancaster together, and pretending by *means* of this marriage to compose and atone *and bring* to an end all the quarrels and questions which had been between those two [princely] Houses. But it rather proved to be the end of the line of th[e House] of York. And yet the true and rightful Lancaster had no fi[nger in it. For it] was not then granted this earl was of the House of Lancaster until the Pope by hi[s Bull had given him the style of Lancaste]r, and that he himself, after he was king, had by his prerogative royal made himself [of that house, which I will *turn* to in the next book, when I come to report all the titles of this Earl of *Richmond*.

[But] in the meantime, whilst this earl was most busily occupied in his seditious practices and treasons [again]st the king and his estate, he was attainted in this Parliament [of High Treason, as also many of those English
48 noblemen and gentlemen who were] / his confederates and had entered falsely into the conspiracies and treacherous practices with him and for him, and namely John, Earl of Oxford, Thomas, Marquess of Dorset, Jasper, Earl of Pembroke, Lionel, Bishop of Salisbury, Piers, Bishop of Exeter, the Lady Margaret, Countess of Richmond, mother to the earl, Thomas Morton, Bishop of Ely, and jointly with him one Thomas Nandick (by the style of Thomas Nandick of Cambridge, conjurer), and William Knevet of Buckingham, smeared with the like pitch. Then George Brown of Beckworth, Thomas Lewkenor of Tratton, John Guildford, John Fogg, Edward Poynings, Thomas Fiennes of Hurstmonceaux, Nicholas Gainsford, William Clifford, [J]ohn Darrell, and many other gentlemen and knights of Kent and of the West Country and of other parts. All these were attainted of treason with the Earl of Richmond in the Parliament. Then also for the approbation and confirmation of the true [and law]ful title of King Richard to the crown of England, there [is thi]s clause or sentence enacted by the whole court of [Parli]ament, viz.,

The friends and confederates of the Earl of Richmond

[It] is declared, pronounced, decreed, confirmed, and esta[blish]ed by the authority of the present Parliament that King [Richa]rd III is the very true and undoubted king of [this r]ealm, as well by right of consanguinity and of heritage, [as by] lawful election, consecration and coronation.

[T]hus much briefly of the Parliament of King Richard. And whereunto [I will] add that I observe in a place of the Roll of [Par]liament that there is

The sons [of King Edward] living [in January and February following the death of King Edward IV]

argument to be gathered from thence [that the] two sons of King Edward IV were living in [the time] of that Parliament, and that was (at the least) nine [months after the] death of King Edward and six months after Richard was crowned king. And hereof we [may make also this] observation that if King Richard, being [then lawfully and quietly possessed of] the crown, had suffered them [to live so long after his coronation, there is no reason why he should after make them away; for their lives could not rectify their bloods nor their titles, so that their lives could not hurt him nor their deaths advantage him. Neither are the lives of bastards dangerous or prejudicial to the just and true titular lords, nor to the lawful and rightful proprietary,] be he prince or subject. Witness France and other countries and even 48v England itself, as I could demonstrate by many examples. For bastards a[re] not capable of heritage nor of honour nor offices. But I will say no more of this matter, because it is handled, and more properly, in another place of this story hereafter.

To proceed then in those causes. In the month of February and toward the end of that Parliament aforesaid, the king, out of a tender fatherly love of the prince his son, and in a provident care of his future royal fortune and sta[te], and to establish the succession of the kingdom in him, and to draw and to build the affection and love of the barons and of his liege people unto him, thought it very important and needful in this case to require the prelates and the noblemen and many knights and gentlemen of quality to come to the Palace of Westminster and there in **interiori caenaculo** (as mine author saith) to offer unto them an oath of fealty and of allegiance in writing, and ten*dered unto t*hem by the Duke of Norfolk; and they took and swore the oath willingly and readily. And then the Duke of Norfolk prayed and required them to put their hands and subscribe their names unto this writing, and the which also they will[ingly] accomplished.

The special occasion and cause of the tenderi[ng] and of the requiring this oath proceeded and grew from the jealous[y] and fear which the king had of the secret and seditious practices *of* the Earl of Richmond and of the Duke of Buckingham, and whose con[sorting] and conspiring with the Earl of Richmond was now discovered, and more plainly and certain[ly] known, as also their confederates. And because these conspirators and their confederates were many, and fit to be *sought out*, and in that it was time that they were apprehended and suppressed, therefore the king *had* erected a new and a great officer some months befor*e* [in] the name of Vice Constable of England, to whom he [gave] ample power and authority to search and to seek and also *to* chastise and to suppress all such persons as were known [or] vehemently suspected to be of the said traitorous conspira[cy.] And this office was committed to the wise and stout and vali*ant* knight Sir Ralph Ashton by the king's letters pa[tents] and made by the king himself **ore tenus.** And because [the] precedent is rare, and the office very great, I think fit [to let] the reader see a true copy of the said commission o[r letters] patents, and taken verbatim as they stand recorded [in the] Chapel of the Convertites, or Rolls:

[Vice Constable of Eng]land

Rex dilecto et fideli suo Radulpho Asheton militi, salutem. Sciatis quod 49 **nos de fidelitate, circumspectione, et probitate vestris plenius confidentes, assignavimus, deputavimus, et ordinavimus vos hac viceconstabularium nostrum Angliae ac Commissarium nostrum, dantes et concedentes vobis**

[Vi]ce Constabulario [Ang]liae constituto. Patentes de anno 1, Richard III, **parte** 1, **mem.** 2

tenore praesentium potestatem et auctoritatem generalem et mandatum speciale ad audiendum et examinandum ac procedendum contra quascumque personas de crimine laesae nostrae regiae Maiestatis suspectas et culpabiles, tam per viam examinationis testium quam aliter prout vobis melius visum fuerit ex officio mero seu promoto, necnon in causis illis iudicialiter et sententialiter, iuxta casus exigentiam et delinquentium demerita, sine strepitu et figura iudicii appellatione quacumque remota*m* quandocumque vobis videbitur procedendum iudicandum, et finali executioni demandandum cum omnibus etiam clausulis, verbis et terminis specialibus ad executionem istius mandati et auctoritatis nostrorum de iure vel consuetudine requisitis, quae etiam omnia hic expressa habemus, assumpto vobiscum aliquo tabellione fide digno, qui singula conscribat una cum aliis quae in praemissis vel circa ea necessaria videbuntur, seu qualitercumque requisita mandantes et firmiter vobis iniungentes quod aliis quibuscumque praetermissis circa praedicta quotiens et quando opus fuerit intendatis, causasque antedictas audiatis examinetis, et in eisdem procedatis ac eas iudicetis et finali executioni ut praefertur demandetis. Damus etiam omnibus et signulis quorum interest in hac parte, tenore praesentium firmiter in mandatis quod vobis in praemissis faciendis pareant assistant et auxilientur in omnibus diligenter. In cuius, &c., teste Rege apud Coventr., 24 die Octobris, anno regni primo. Per ipsum Regem ore tenus.

50 [What] / success this commission and new office of Vice Constable of England [had I] have not found reported. But I doubt it came too late, or that the new officer was *negligent*. For the [faction]s and conspiracies of the king's enemies, or rather traitors against King *Richard*, [sough]t to corrupt and to win all men to them, and [were] secretly and suddenly grown to such a strength and such [height tha]t nothing then but more mighty forces and greater armies and a sharper sword *could have the pow*er to oppress and to extinguish them, *and to which I shall give further considera*tion in the next boo*k*.

50v [Yet surely, in my opinion, the institution of this new office] / was very politic and of great importance, howsoever it succeeded. And it is a pl[ain] *portrait* and ritrat or image, and hereafter, of the office and authority of the Great or High Constable of England, and the which office being in the hands of a valorous, wise and faithful baron and exercised in fit and due time is of great good use and of the highest importance. And sithence that I have made mentions of these offices and of the officers exercising and enjoying them, and also of some other officers of this King Richard, it shall not be a parergon in this void place, but rather a just and necessary work to add and supply the rest of the king's officers, and not only the chief but also the rest, at the least if their offices were places and charges of honour or of dignity, or the administrators thereof were men of some special *quality*. And I have already told who was the High Constable, the Great Marshal, the High Admiral, the Lord Chancellor and the Lord Chamberlain of this king, and therefore I shall not need to ma*ke* repetition of them. But the rest (not mentioned before) are th[ose] which follow, namely, Sir John Wood, knight, the eld[er,] was Lord Treasurer, J[ohn] Tuchet, Lord Audley, was Lord Treasurer during the rest [of] the reign of the king. The Great Seal was committed to Dr Russell, [Bishop of Lincoln.] Thomas Barowe was Master of the Rolls. And because he was a very

Other officers of Richard III

*suffici*ent and serviceable minister, and a wise man, King Henry VII, *successor* to King Richard, retained and continued him in his office and place, [and made] him one of his Privy Council. Mr John Kendall was principal Secre[tary, Sir] William Hopton was Treasurer of the Household, and Sir Thomas Percy was Controller to King Richard, and after [him] John [Buck] *was that* officer. And John Gunthorp was Keeper of the Privy Seal. Sir William Hussey was Chief [Justice,] Thomas Tremain and Roger Townsend were the King's Serge[ants,] and Morgan Kidwelly was his Attorney, and N. Fitzwilliam [Recorder of London.] And I have already remembered that his base son was Captain of Calais.

And now I will treat of the rest of the treaties which were *en*tertained betwixt this king and some foreign princes concer[ning] matters of state and of honour and also of profit. I have found a memorial of a treatise for intercourse [and] commerce between King Richard and Philip, Duke of B[urgundy] and the estates of Flanders, and who in the record are called **[mem]bra Flandriae**. And these princes and states had each [of them] three commissioners to confer and to treat and to deter[mine the] affairs. And I find also that they came to good [agreement] and dispatched and concluded those affairs [with approbation of the princes, their masters. And there] was about that time also a commission directed to certain grave and learned men to hear and redress the complaints made to the king by the subjects of the kings of France and Denmark, and they were well expedied.

[**Thesau. Scaccar**. 1 Richard III]

*Artic*les for league [and comm]erce with [Flanders,] etc.

52*

[In] Roll [**anno**] 1 Richard III

In the next year of this king, viz., **anno regni** 2, that treaty of peace and league with Scotland, and begun before (as I have intimated), was continued and finished by [ce]rtain ambassadors and commissioners sent from James IV, King of Scotland, and by other commissioners [d]elegate for the King of England. The ambassadors *and* commissioners for Scotland were these: Coli, [Ear]l of Argyle,* Chancellor of Scotland, N., Bishop [of] Aberdeen, the Lord Lisle, the Lord Drummond [of] Stobhall, Mr Archibald Quhitlaw, Archdeacon [of] Lodon and Secretary to the king, *item*, Lion [K]ing at Arms, and Duncan of Dundas. And *the*y were honourably received by the king in the [Gr]eat Chamber in the said castle, where the said [M]r Archibald Quhitlaw, stepping before the rest, and somewhat [ne]arer to the king, who then sat under his Royal [Cl]oth of Estate and attended by many noble barons, knights and other worthy persons, made a very [elo]quent oration in Latin, and for the most part [in] the praise of martial men and of the Art Military. [And bec]ause there is also much in it tending to honour and praise [of] King Richard, I have chosen and selected some of *the choic*er flowers thereof. And I will reserve them *until I dec*lare of the other his particular honours, and that toward the end, *and where I wi*ll make it the corollary of them.

A[nno Domini 1484, a treaty with the] King [of Scotland]

*Erg[ile in record]

And here I will proceed with the occasion of *the visit* of these ambassadors, and the which was to treat [partly about m]atters of truce and of peace, and partly [about a marriage of James,] the prince of Scotland, [with the Lady Anne, daughter of John de la Pole, Duke of Suffolk, and niece to King Richard. The] / commissioners of the King of England who treated with these Scottish ambassadors for this truce and peace were John, Bishop of Lincoln, Richard, Bishop of St Asaph, John, Duke of Norfolk, Henry, Earl of Northumberland, Mr John Gunthorp, **Custos Privati Sigilli** (i.e., Keeper of the Privy Seal), Sir Thomas Stanley, Lord Stanley, Sir N.,

52v*

Lord Strange, Sir N., Lord Powys, Sir Henry, Lord Fitzhugh, Sir Humphrey, Lord Dacres, Mr Thomas Barowe, Master of the Rolls, Sir Richard Ratcliff, William Catesby and Richard Salkeld. And the other English ambassadors for the other treaty (and concerning the matter of alliance and of marriage) were Thomas, Archbishop of York, John, Bishop of Lincoln, John, Bishop of Worcester, John, Duke of Norfolk, John, Earl of Nottingham, John Sutton, Lord Dudley, N., Lord Scroop of Upsall, Sir William Hussey, Chief Justicer of the King's Bench, Sir Richard Ratcliff and William Catesby.

[The Lady Anne de la Pole a nun]

An*d* this treaty had had good success if the manifold troubles, tumults and seditions [of the] fickle barons had not come on so fast as that they interrupted the treaty of the marriage and man[y] other good works. And the Lady Anne de la Pole, being discouraged with the ill success here[of,] resolved to hearken to no more motions nor [trea]ties, but forthwith took a religiou[s] habit and became a nun in the monastery [of] Sion.

[Treaty] with the [Duke of] Brittany

53*

[Ibi]dem in [Sc]accario

There was also a treaty of truce and pea[ce] in this second year of King Richard between him [and] Francis, Duke of Brittany, or at least gi[ven out to] be held for a peace; but that was but a part, and ra[ther] a pretext and colour of the treaty, for the ma[in] negotiations of the king's part was about the means to get the E[arl] of Richmond out of his hands and to have h[im de]livered to him, or else kept a[s he] was in the time of the king his brother. The chief [negotiators] and mediators in this t[reaty were the Bishop of Lincoln and Sir Thomas Hutton for the king, and the Bishop of Lyons and others for the duke.] / This treaty for the truce and peace was begun **Anno Domini** 1484 and finished and ratified in the year following. But yet the duke broke and violated it immediately. For he gave aid to the king's enemies and rebels, **ut supra**.

Treaty with the King of Fr[ance]

And in the same year there were letters made (and are yet extant in the Treasury of the Exchequer) about matters of truce and peace moved between King Richard and Charles VIII, King of France, and wherein [it] must be understood that the matter of the tribute aforesaid was one article.

Trea[ty of marriage of] King [Richard] with [the Lady] Eliz[abeth]

There was also in the year before passed another treaty, and the which I may not omit, and that also was a treaty for the marriage, and that a close and secret treaty, and it was for marriage of the Lady Elizabeth, eldest daughter to King Edward IV, and even with King Richard himself. And what the success of this treaty was, and how far it proceeded, I will defer to declare until I come to the scandals and crimes objected against King Richard, because *th*is treaty is accounted and reputed amongst *th*em, though very unjustly.

[Th]is place and time also require that I should here make commemoration of the charitable and good works of [this] king, and of his founding of churches and colleges, *an*d of the erecting of other good and beneficial monu[men]ts, but I have determined to reserve them for the [end,] and to the end they may accompany his other [pio]us, honourable and magnificent and profitable *wo*rks, and other matters of his praise and honour. And the chief or special cause w*hy I have* thus deferred the report of those *his* good deeds and virtues is because they will have *smal*l credit and small grace to be reported and to be remembered in such honourab*le wise* until the many slanders and false crimina*tion*s brought against this king be answered and confuted.

This is a fit time and place to relate the conspiracy and treason *and* rebellion of Henry, Duke of Buckingham and *th*e other inconstant and seditious barons and *those* who joined with him. For this was the **preparatif** [and] **fourrier** of the rest. This [duke, togeth]er with his complices, pretended the [cause of their] discontentment and mutiny [to be for the reformation of the ill government and tyranny of the king, and under this colour (for treason is ever] / fairly palliated) they resolved to take arms against the king and to bereave him both of crown and life. And here they discovered their ancient and native vice and fault and taint, to wit, their inconstancy and disloyalty and variableness and also perfidiousness, and the which the prince supposed in the beginning, as I intimated *before*. And herein those false barons imitated the ingrateful and perverse Jews, who one while cried very kindly **Osanna**, and **Osanna in altissimis** and **Benedictus qui venit in nomine Domini**, and anon they cried **Crucifige, crucifige. Tolle, tolle, crucifige eum**. Thus inconstant are men, and even to the best of men and most deserving love and loyalty.

The treas[on of the] Duke of Buc[king-ham]

53v*

Mat. 21. John. 19.

And this duke, who made the first overture and demonstrations of the false heart of a seditious baron, departed malcontent from the court and retired himself to his strong castle of Brecknock in Wales. But he made not that general and publicly pretended cause of sedition, to wit, the king's great crimes and tyranny, to be all his quarrel, but he also challenged the king for some private wrongs, as namely for the king's denying to give o[r] to restore (as he would have it) to him the earldom of Hereford and the Constableship of England (for they went together a long time), and the which he said belonged to the partage which fell to his grandmother, the Lady Anne, daugh[ter] and heir of Thomas de Woodstock Plantagenet, alias Duke of Gloucester and Earl of Buckingham, and of his w[ife] Eleanor, daughter and coheir of Humphrey de Bohu[n,] Earl [of] Hereford and Constable of England.

[The Duke of] Buck-ingham [first riseth in] rebellion

[The quarrel of] the [Duke of Bucking]-ham [against King] Richard

But this claim of the duke was not unjust. And because that clai[m and] this [con]troversy may the better be understood, I wi[ll] set down the cause and case according to the truth t[hereof,] and the rather for the king's justification. An*d of this* kind of good offices this story hath most need. This is the case: Humphrey de Bohun, Earl [of] Hereford, of Essex, and of Northampton, and Lord of Brecknock, and Constable of Englan[d] in the time of Edward III, and the [last] earl of the family of the Bohuns, had by th[e] Lady Joan his wife, daughter of Rich[ard] Fitzalan, Earl of Arundel, two daughters and heirs, Eleanor and Mary. E[leanor was] married to the same Thomas P[lantagenet, **alias** de Woodstock, youngest son of King Edward III, and Duke of Gloucester and Earl of Buckingham.]

[The titl]e of the [earldom] of Here-ford [and of t]he Constable[ship o]f England

Mary, the second daughter, was married to Henry Plantagenet, Duke of Lancaster, and after King of England by the name of Henry IV, and the earldom of Hereford fell to his wife. And in regard and favour thereof, he was created Duke of Hereford by King Richard II. And this earldom (now a duchy) and the rights thereof remained in the king and in the king's heirs and successors until the death of King Henry VI, who died without issue. And then all the estate of Lancaster escheated to King Edward IV, and from him it came to King Richard, as heir to his brother the king, and to all the kings his ancestors.

54*

And this Duke of Buckingham craved and required that earldom of King

Richard, pretending a title to it by his said grandmother Anne, who was one of the daughters and heirs of the foresaid Lady Mary, wife of Thomas de Woodstock, Duke of Glou[c]ester and Earl of Buckingham. And she was the wife of Edward Stafford, Ear[l of Stafford, and grandfather] to this duke. The [d]uke the rather presumed to make the claim because [th]e issue of the other sister, Eleanor, being extinct, he took hi[mself to be] her heir. But King Richard, not liking this suit because it savoured of the like secret ambition and [aff]ectation of royalty and sovereignty as was in Henry of B[olingbroke, ans]wered the Duke of Buckingham and told him that [th]e earldom of Hereford was the inheritance of *Ki*ng Henry IV, and which was also King of England *and France*, but by tort and by usurpation. 'And will you, my [Lo]rd of Buckingham', quoth the king, 'claim to be heir to [King Henry IV? Then you w]ill also haply assume his spirits, and then you will also [cla]im the crown, and by the same titles'.

The answer was very displeasing and bitter to the duke, and it was doubly [ill] taken of him, first because it came with a repulse of his suit, *and* then next because it seemed to proceed from a [sus]picion which the king had of his high ambition and *affec*tation of the crown, and as a tax also of his disloyal mind. [With this, the] duke pretended another cause of grievance *and of* injury, and that was the breach of the king's promise and *declaration* whereby he bound himself to join the prince [his son] *in* marriage to the Lady Anne Stafford, daughter [of the Duke of] Buckingham. But these exceptions and challenges [were but pretences] of his revolt, and [the true cause was well divined and found out by the king, which was his ambition and aim to be sovereign, springing from that] / overweening which the duke had of the royal blood which he supposed to [be] in himself and in his descent from the said Thomas of Woodstock, Duke of Gloucester, and son of a king.

54v*

The ambition of the Duke of Buckingham

But he was not resolutely determined to make his claim to the crown, nor to attempt the kingdom by rebellion and seditious arms until he was earnestly incited and animated and persuaded thereunto by the factious and seditious clerk, Dr Morton, Bishop of Ely, and the[n] also a Privy Counsellor, but in disgrace, and committed to the custody of the duke as a prisoner (as hath been said), and for his treachery and seditious practices against the king. And at this time, and particularly, amongst other offences of the prelate, one offence of his was greater, for because that he, being a Privy Counsellor, gave secret advertisement to the Earl of Richmond of all that passed in the secret council of the king; and that is double treason.

[Dr Morton per]suadeth [the Duke of Buck]ing[ham to rebel]

[And] thus he, being ill affected to the king and perceiving the duke's discontentment and his ill affection also to the king by sundry of his speeches which passed in the often conferences betwixt them, as also finding his aspiring mind and ambition and his great good opinion of his royal bl[ood] *and* stem, took the advantage thereof, and finely fed his vain and proud humour, and wrought diligently upon th[ose tickling] grounds. For the drift and chief desire of Mor[ton] was to prepare the duke to rebellion at any ha[nd,] but not that he should seek to get the kingdom and comp*ass* the crown thereby for himself. For Morton had [destined that to another, whom he] loved much better, and as you have heard and shall hear better. But this prelate, to draw the duke on the faster into his net and to m*ake him* apt to rebel, first he persuaded earnestly the duke to claim his title to the crown and to take the advantage of the presen[t] times, in respect that now he which reigned was [an] usurper and a murderer and a tyrant, and hated of all men, and that he would ere long be pulled fro[m] the royal throne by a most noble and worthy person.

The ambitious and silly duke bit at this cunning, deceitful bait and swallowed it. And in a word, he was much encouraged and incensed [by] these mutinous motions and treacherous exhortations of the bishop. And after he had a while ruminated or meditated of the b*ishop's* speech, he desired to know of him who [that] brave and noble and worthy person was who would pull the ty*rant* King Richard out of his royal throne. [The bishop] answered that it was the noble Earl [of Richmond,] and who, upon his certain k[nowledge, was resolved to invade this land. And] *to help him to* / accomplish this his enterprise, it was resolved by the Queen Widow of King Edward IV to give her eldest daughter Elizabeth to him in marriage and therewithal to bring all the friends and lovers of the House of York who were at her service and devotion into this action, and that by the means also of this marriage, the titles of York and Lancaster should be united, and so all claims should cease and vanish away. And further, this prelate added that many great and potent lords and many worthy and valiant knights and resolute and adventurous gentlemen were entered into this confederacy (or rather conspir*acy*) and faction, and had faithfully promised to the Earl of Richmond and to his mother and to the queen and to his other chief friends that they would join their forces to his forces and assist him to their uttermost and at all hazards in this attempt for the crown of England, and that also some foreign princes ha[d promised to assist him.]

***of the Earl *of Rich*mond

55*

[Sir] Thomas More

And as it hath been intimate*d*, when the bishop had spoken these words and thus [wi]th much art and treacherous and crafty rhetoric set forth, declared and advanced the cause and the forces and *promis*ed and accomplished power *and the* greatness of the titles of the Earl of Richmond, York and Lancaster being so *conjoined, and* then had *urged an*d insinuated the great hope and fair possibility of the good success of this earl in *his en*terprise of England.

The duke withdrew a little *and* was much troubled and perplexed with this *ad*vertisement, and he then, being [entered into] a wrong way, *be*gan to consider, and more advisedly, and that his titles and claim would be nothing. [If] the titles of York and Lancaster were united and joined together, *they* would be so mighty *and* be so strong – because then they would draw all the *factions together* – as that neither he nor any much more mighty m*an* should by no means be able to resist and *to* encounter with them, and much less to prevail against them. And he *had wandered into a fool*'s paradise, and he apprehended that the grass was [cu]t under his feet, and in a word, he doubted that he was abused. And thereupon he grew out of liking with his [ow]n cause and of his title, and into utter despair of the *goo*d success thereof, as well because the Earl of Rich[mon]d was not only so resolute to attempt the gaining of the *roya*l goal, and at all perils, but also, and chiefly, because he was so strong and *was we*ll furnished with arms and with forces and guarded *and* aided with such multitudes of great and puissant friends as well foreign as *native*. And when this duke had weighed well the state of these affairs and well considered, he found plain*ly and conc*eived that to contend with the Earl of Richmond and *be his* rival for the crown were but to seek his *own* ruin and destruction, and nothing else to be hoped or expected.

56v And now it may be conceived that the duke, after due consideration and meditation upon these plots and evil counsels, could have been content to have been silent, and doubtless that he wished to have been reconciled to the king and to have his love again and to enjoy his favour as he had in former times, and his *trust*. The duke in his reply to Morton somewhat discovered all this in effect, for therein he bewrayed his disgust and distaste of the prelate's counsel and perilous *arguments* and persuasions, and that he suspected that they were not only cunning and ambiguous, but also very dangerous. And he smelled some spice of fraudulent practice, in that the prelate first persuaded and advised him to take arms against the king and to make his title to the crown to be the pretence and colour thereof; and after that he had brought him to resolve to undertake that great business, the duke thought it strange that Morton should anon use such arguments to divert him [and] *terri*fy him with the amplification of the greatness of the great aspirer and with the impossibility [to resist him]; *and* [so] from thence to come by degrees to persuade the duke to be the earl's follower and his fellow conspirer: he would have the duke to love and to join with him in his rebellion and perfidious enterprise. And in brief, the duke thought (as he had *reason to think*) that these things did not well hang together. And the duke acknowledged that he should not be ab*le to* over*come these doubts*, for*********** he*********** and***********.

And therefore, as soon as the subtle prelate perceived the dislike and the alteration of the duke, and having a ready and a nimble wit and an eloquent tongue, he found instantly a device to salve the disgust of the duke and to correct and *over*come that his alteration, and then to retain still the duke in his former false purpose and inclination to rebellion. Wherefore he insinuated *to this* duke that albeit [he knew his title] to the crown was very good, and that he wished with all his heart that he might possess it, but yet h[e would] not conceal the plot and the power of the Earl of Richmond from him, because as he said there was no reason to suppose that so great strength and forces which that no*ble earl possessed*, and so *many* great and powerful friends as he had abroad and at home, should fail or not happily and absolutely prevail in that his enterprise of England and of his getting of the crown. And that therefore on the other side it was not to be hoped that the duke should be able to make forces sufficien[t to encounter] with him and to resist, and much less to suppress him and thereby to catch or snatch the gar*land* or crown from the earl's head, there being no hope or possibility thereof. Yet he would not have the duke to change his mind and to forbear to take arms for any such doubts of *ha*zards or losses and so high and great fortunes as seemed to trouble and to alter him.

Because (he tol*d* the duke) that albeit he forbore his claim, yet there were other reasons, and very important, although he had no cause or [claim to the crown,] why he sh[ould] be resolute in his taking of arms against the king and to join [with] the earl, and to assist him in his attempt and royal ambite. 'For', quoth he, 'by [this] enterprise, and by the most certain victory which will ensue, you [shall be] revenged of Richard, and you shall have full satisfaction of all *the* wrongs done to you by him. And besides, I dare assure [you] that the earl, as soon as he is king, shall in all kinds of h[onourable] and princely gratitude acknowledge his great obligation, [and] shall not only restore all the honours and titles, [office and signories to you which you] claim, which Ri[chard hath unjustly detained, but shall advance you above any other nobleman'.

[Further, he engages the duke] / that as he was a great man and a chief peer of the realm, so in regard thereof, his principal and most honourable obligation was to help and to relieve the oppressed subjects, and to reform abuses, and to purge the land of impiety and of tyranny, and to provide carefully for the good and prosperous estate of the kingdom. And he then inculcated that by how much a man is greater, that by so much the greater is his obligation and bond to do good to his country and to redress wrongs and oppressions, at any hazard of his person and f[ortune. And he, being the] grea[test and most eminent person in the kingdom, was therefore] bound in honour to be the most forward in this work, and that for what difficulty or danger somever, he ought to exp*ect* to use his power and his forces for the defence or preservation of the people and of the commonwealth.

57

Nobiles sunt spes miserorum. Seneca **Declam**. 12

And then again and afresh this prelate urged and, [as it were refr]icated [t]he sundry and particular wrongs done to him by King Richard. For [h]e finely found that argument to be the most vigorous and forcible, and the sharpest *s*ting to incense and stir up the duke to rebellion; and the which wrongs he un*d*erstood partly by his often conferences with the duke and by the duke's many and bitt*er c*omplaints of the injuries done to him by the king, and partly by his own observations thereof, and by other means. And he intimated *and* aggravated the greatness and the extremeness thereof, and that [t]hey were so intolerable as that they were cause enough alone *fo*r him to endeavour and to seek by all means the overthrow *and* ruin of the king. And that therefore, although neither he (nor y*et any other st*raight and clear eyes) could see that by his taking of arms in the cause of [his] title and for the advancement of his claim to the kingdom *th*at he might prevail in his hope and attempt thereof, *for* the reason of the ever strong and mighty opposition and vehement and violent ambite of the Earl of Richmond (which would be *irresisti*ble and insuperable, and as was before intimated more than once). Yet he would in no cause have [the duke] be an idle spectator in so great and so *noble and* so meritorious an action, especially considering disturbing the king from the throne and his overthrow, and *that* it *promised* a good amending and fair satisfaction [for his wrongs, and his more assured and greater honours.]

Thus the orator; I will not say the **primus motor**, for that were to profane a hol[y word, but he may be sa]id to be **primus molitor**, and in French, **le premier mutin**, and chief mover of sed[ition]. And he told his tale so cunningly as that the duke was again and anew stirred up t*o be* false and disloyal, and he was with these argument*s* much more encouraged and inflamed with the fire and fury of rebellion. And now therefore he entered into the conspiracy and plots and practices of treasons, and he became a chief actor in them, al*lowing* both the reasons of his **malus genius**, as well for the taking of his own revenge, as also fo*r* the assisting and advancing of the Earl of Richmond.

57v

And it was not long ere the duke made a journey to visit the C[oun]tess of Richmond, and to confer with her about these treacher*ous* matters. For she was entered far into them, and none better plunged in them and deeply

[This Margaret,] Countess [of Richmond, was d]aughter [and heir to John

Beauf]ort, first Duke [of Somerset, and] Margaret [Beaufort,] mother of [the Duke of] Buckingham, was [daughter of] Edmund, Duke [of Somerset.] And thus were [the Earl of Richmond] and the Duke [of Buckingham ak]in. Robert [Glover, in **Ca]talogue**.

58*

acquainted with th*em*. And she was a politic and subtle lady. And he made open to her of the propositions and motions Dr Morton had made to him concerning the royal design of the earl her son for England, and of the great and mighty means which he had to accomplish and effect it. And he told h[er] also how earnestly the bishop had dealt with him, and how the bishop had persuaded him to ass*ist the* earl in his said enterprise for England. And then the duke *told the* countess of the intelligence of the prelate in these [design]s, *to know if they* might be credited.

She answered and pr[otest]*ed* [it was really true, yet short of the full, which she then report]*ed*, [and fell into a cunning captation of the affection and endearment of her son ever towards him, closing her argument upon the nearness of blood and kindred betwixt, affirming the duke's mother was a Somerset, concluding that consanguinity, a great and just bond of mutual love and friendship – for that cause and the ancient and constant affinity and respects] / which was between the Duke of Somerset, her father, and the Duke of Buckingham, his father – that he would be kind and loving to her son and join his love and his forces with those of her son and of his most noble friends, and who were very many and very great and mighty, etc., and who had determined and vowed to put down King Richard, the tyrant and usurper, and to put her son up in his place and to make him king, but provided and upon condition that he would marry the Lady Elizabeth, and the which to perform he had taken solemn oath. For it must be understood that this cunning countess had, by the mediations and the ministry of Dr Lewis, conciliated the love and friendship of the Queen Mother and persuaded her t[o acc]ept that alliance by marriage, and also drawn her into this conspiracy. And yet in that time the countess, knowing well to dissemble great love to the king, to desire and to effect the love of King Richard, came in all h[umility] *and* besought him to call home her son and to be gracious to him and to vouchsa[fe him the honou]r as to marry him to any of King Edward's daughters.

But to pr*oceed* with this conference of the duke and of the Countess of Richmond and ret[urn. She,] having prevailed with him (he being apt to rebel against King Richard) as that he promised her faithfully that *he* would join with her son and give him all the *hel*p and succours that he could. And then he took his leave of the countess *and entered* forthwith *into* consultation and conjuration with the chief friends of *the* Earl of Richmond: namely the Lord Stanley, [the] Marquess of Dorset, Edward Courtenay, Earl of Devon[shi]re, and his brother, the Bishop of Exeter, Sir John Bourchier, [Sir J]ohn Wells, Robert Willoughby, Edward Woodville, Thomas [Aru]ndel and others, and they resolved the rebellion, and they made ready their [force]s in all haste, and they appointed their rendezvous [nea]r to Gloucester. And the duke with his Welshmen and *othe*rs, and the marquess with his northern men, and [the] Courtenays with their western men, and Sir Richard [Gui]ldford and Sir John Cheyney and other knights of Kent [and] of the south parts, marched towards Gloucester. And if [thei]r power had been joined, it was so very great as that it had been very dang[erous.] And they made full and sure account to have given [King] Richard a terrible and fatal blow.

The con[spirators with the] Duke of [Buckingham] for the [Earl of Rich]mond

But the king, having good intellige[nce of all the plots and] counsels of this rebellion, and he having a good army, made as much haste to meet them, and before all their forces were united, and a*lso before* the Earl of Richmond should c[ome to the coast of D]orsetshire, where [he was to fight] with them. But the armies never met, for by strange accidents, and both by the element of water, their designs and attempts thereby [were] checked and made frustrate. For the English forces were kept asunder by [a su]dden and very huge inundation, which not only [overflowed] the ways and passages so deeply and so dangerously as the forces *of Buckingham* [c]ould not come together nor pass the River [Severn; but] besides which the suddenness and strangeness and fright thereof [struck such a terror into] the soldiers that [the most part of them forsook the duke and ran away, leaving him so weak and slenderly guarded that himself was glad to fly too and provide for] / his safety with the swiftness of his heels.

[The overthrow of the Duke of Buckingham]

58v*

And the accident which overthrew the earl's *attempt* by sea was a great storm and tempest which took him upon the coasts of England, as you shall hear an*on* and at large. But the king, who was an excellent captain, took the advantage instantly which was offered him, and he pursued the disarmed duke, and not only with posting and galloping armies but also with edicts and proscriptions, offering thereby to give a thousand pounds in money (and whereunto some writers add so much land as was worth £100 by the year) to any man who would bring in the duke.

Polydore, **Lib**. 25

And thus first by that disastrous inundation, and next by the diligent chase of the pursuit and thirdly by the golden charm of reward, this rebellious army and enterprise was defeated there. And the duke was taken and brought to the king (being then at Salisbury) by Humphrey Banister, the duke's false servant. And there the duke being examined, he freely and foolishly confessed all the treason and he discovered all the conspirators, as well the Earl of Richmond as the rest. And this being done, his head was struck off, [according to] martial law used in armies and in the field in November, **Anno Domini** 1484 and **anno** 2 of King Richard III.

[King Richard shar]ply rebuked *and* [re]prehended [Banister for] apprehending [his master] which argued [a noble min]d.

And this unhappy end had that seditious and incons*tant baron*, and by the means of Bishop Morton, who, as Sir Thomas More confesseth and affirmeth, [by his politic drifts and] pride [advanced himself and brought the duke] to destructi[on.] And the rest of his fellow conspira[tors] fled, some into sanctuaries, and some into Brittany to the Earl of Richmond and some into Flanders. And all were glad to hide thems*elves*.

And because that hitherto all things have gone well [with] King Richard, and that his affairs have well prospe*red*, we will close here these his good fortunes and this fir[st] book together.

Explicit Liber I

60

THE SECOND BOOK OF THE HISTORY OF KING RICHARD THE THIRD

The Contents of this Second Book

The Earl of Richmond, vehemently affecting the crown, practiseth with foreign princes and with the English nobles for assistance and for forces to make his first and second invasions of England. He came first to Poole, and with all success, and secondly to Milford, **bonis avibus**.

What bastards are and whereof they are capable.

Who be of the House of Lancaster; how Lancaster and Beaufort and Somerset differ.

Bastards of kings must not take the surname of the king nor the kingdom.

The honourable privileges of the name of Plantagenet.

The Prince E[dward and Queen Anne die.] John de la P[ole proclaimed heir] of the kingdom [by King Richard III.]

Bastards of John, Duke of Lancaster, made legitimate and capable of offices, of honours and of heritage [by] King Richard II and by the Parliament.

What legitimation of the Pope is.

Arms [and names of princes' bastard]s.

[The] nobility of King Henry VII; he affied not much in the titles of York and [of L]ancaster.

The Pope giveth to him the title **de jure belli [et] de domo Lancastriae**.

The greatness of the title of York.

Of counsel and counsellors.

The conspirators joining with the Earl of Richmond.

Dr Morton's character.

[Th]e prerogative of the king in judgements and controversies.

[The E]arl of Richmond landeth at Milford Haven; his good enter[tai]nment there and in Wales.

His aptness for diverse wives.

[H]e marcheth to Bosworth.

The King Richard and he fight.

[Ri]chard overcome and slain, and also the Duke of Norfolk, and [by] the Earl of Oxford (**ut creditur**).

The Earl of Richmond is straight [crow]ned king in the field (**θεοῦ δῶρον**).

The fatal errors of King Richard.

[King]s loved combats.

The titles of King Henry VII.

[King]s go not now to the wars.

Cruelties executed [upon] the corpse of King Richard.

He was attainted of treason (though against the laws of [nature and of royal] majesty, and hereof see more **Lib.** 4), with many noble and faithful and valiant gentlemen. [His fol]lowers and servants and subjects also attainted.

The Earl of Surrey, how released [out of pris]on.

[Hi]s genealogy from Hewardus.

His goodness to the children orphans [of Sir John Buck.]

The description of Hewardus.

[The nobility and grea]tness of the House of Howard.

[Walter de Buck and his progeny.]

60v

THE HISTORY OF KING RICHARD III
THE SECOND BOOK

61v We left King Richard III in a flourishing and glorious estate, and reigning in peace (*a* never enough desired and blessed state), and he enjoyed all worldly prosperity for a time. But Fortune, that inconstant and variable and unfaithful dame, will suffer no joys nor honours nor pleasures, no prosperity nor any worldly good thing to last long, and much less to be permanent and perpetual in this world. And therefore this was well called by the expert **Heros** in Euripides, **Fortuna diurna**: fortune of a day's life;
[Euripides in **Heraclides**] and especially if she be extraordinarily gracious and favourable, for then she is most wavering and inconstant. And when she is in her best mood, she is brief in her favours and tedious in her mischiefs, as it was well observed by a grave man: **fortuna adversas res cupido animo inducit secundas parco**.
[Valerius Maximus, Lib. VII] And she is a mother but a little while, but a stepdame a long time, and ever to s[ome.]

And indeed she was very sparing and very brief in her favours towards this King Richard, and merely nov[ercal to him.] For he enjoyed them but a little while, and then she changed her countenance, and she frowned upon him, and she much and grievously afflicted him. And times of calamity and adverse chances came galloping and posting upon him. And in this *way* they oppressed and accabled him – but not forever. For Fortune hath no interest no*r* estate in perpetuity: neither can she give permanence or any hig*h* time to anything in this world. But that is only proper to Virtue; for she, like to a go*ddess*, maketh the men which serve and honour her to live long and to flourish still and to leave a true fame and name of their virtues behind them, according to that wise sent*ence*, **Efficacior est ad b*reve* tempus Fortuna, ad longum Virtus.**

But it may haply be thou*ght that I neglect the will of God* in ascribing so much to Fortune. But yet I pray you to think that I know *not that puni*shment which is not the will of God and by his divine privilege.

Bu[t] now we are ent*ering* [into] *the story o*f the troubles and tumults which angry Fortune hath raised, [which were the end and period] to the
62 story of the unhappy times [of this king and of his reign.] / The invasions of this land of England attempted and made by the Earl of Richmond were the formal and efficient and final cause of all the mischiefs and calamity. I will begin this second book with his invasions, and I say invasions plurally because he twice invaded this kingdom, but through error and ignorance or negligence of our common chroniclers and vulgar historians they are confounded and made one journey or one invasion. And these have thereby corrupted and maimed the story and concealed or omitted some things well

worth the knowing and very remarkable. And particularly by error and by this negligence, the true and certain cause of the ill success of the enterprise of Buckingham and his defeat is misunderstood or not at [all] known. Wherefore I think it necessary to make a brief relation of those first preparations and of the first attempt of invasion made by the said Earl of Richmond.

First then it must be understood that after it was resolved by him and by the Duke of Buckingham and by the Lord Stanley and other that he should come to make his claim of the crown, and that they assured him by Bishop Morton and other their secret treacherous instruments that he should lack no means nor friends for the accomplishment of his design and for the attaining to the crown, and he were able to bring but so much power and force with him as thereby the*y* might land safely and to defend himself in any sort until his friends of England came to him, and who would be with him with all speed possible.

Hereupon he propounded this his cause and enterprise to the Duke of Brittany, and told him what good friends he had in England and how great possibilities he had to win the crown and the kingdom. The duke gave him favourable hearing and wished good success unto him and to his designs, but he pleaded first h[is amity and leag]ue with the King of England, which in honour and justice he might not violate; and then *he* alleged his poverty and want of growing, by the long and cruel wars which he had with his barons of Brittany; and he *to*ld the earl that therefore he was not able to furnish him as (at the least) [in] any short time, and as his cause required.

But the earl, having a great affiance in h[is] own [good] fortune, would not leave the motion and suit thus. But he resolved to rene*w* it to the duke by some of his most honourable and most gracious and po[werful friends.] The truth is that the earl had many and great friends. / But yet I must **62v** confess for that the ingenious behaviour, and with sharp and pleasant wit, and the fine, insinuating, also courtly arts of the Earl of Richmond were such, and so agreeable and so plausible to all these noble persons with whom he conversed and to whom he had favourable access, as that he won the favour and the good will and well wishing of them and of many private persons of the best estimation and of the greatest authority; and in brief, of all men and of women likewise.

And he was so good and so cunning an Amoret as that when he came amongst ladies, [he ob]tained and (as I note) he stole their affections and favours from them, so that he was with them very gracious. And he could not only speak French well but also excellently and best in the amorous and courtly and insinuating style. And to grace that the better, he was, as Philip Commynes, who knew him, testifieth, a very complete and well-featured gentleman. And then the rule is certain and well-ominating: **Gratior est** Vergil **pulchro veniens e corpora virt[us]:**

The beauties of the mind more gracious are,
Whereas the body's features are more fair.

And amongst the many ladies with whom he became acquainted during his fair and courteous imprisonment, he obtained the favour of tw[o] ladies, and these great ladies, and in great *esteem*. And the one, and the first of them, was the Lady Margaret, Duchess of Brittany, and the daughter of Gaston de Foix, a great man in those western parts of France, and whose

ancestors were very well affect[ed] to the English nation, as John Froissart
63 and Pa[radin] / and sundry French historians report. And the other lady
Histoires de Bretagne (and his most gracious lady) was Madame de Beaujeu, and of whom I will speak in the second invasion.

This duke had by this lady his daughter Anne, who brought the duchy of Brittany into France.

And it pleased this Lady of Foix, the Duchess of Brittany, to be so favourable to him and to his cause as to afford and to yield [him] help and succour of men and of money and of ships and of arms and of other necessary provisions for his enterprise of England. And the duke consented and granted to furnish the earl with all these things, and in such quantity as his store and ability would afford, and all the bonds and cautions and pledges which the earl gave and put in for these aids and succours were only that the earl was to go to the cathedral and chief church of Vannes, and there, kneeling at the high altar and before the Lord's sacrament, should faithfully and religiously promise and vow that he would justly and truly observe such covenants and promises for restitution or satisfaction as he had made to the duke and to the duchess. And the protestation was accordingly made by the earl.

And then, and immediately thereupon, these warlike implements and instruments were delivered unto him: to wit, three great ships, well-equipped and ready rigged and copiously furnished with arms, men and victuals, and as in these few words of my British author it may be seen: **Au**
[**History de Brittany**] **comte de Richemont furent aux dépens du duc trois gros navires de Bretagne chargés de gens, d'armes,** etc., **et qui se mirent en mer.**

64 [But] by the favour and leave of this British writer, I must tell you that the earl stayed many days at the seaside and at St Malo. And the cause of his stay was that [in the meantime he might] give advertisement and warning to the Duke of Buckingham and the rest of *his* loyal barons and other his consorts in this conspiracy that he was *furnis*hed with soldiers and with a convenient fleet for his invading this land and for landing *in Englan*d, and that his best and most experienced friends had advertised him to land in [Hampshire] or in Dorset, because he might descend so near to London and [in] such plac[e] *of safe*ty and convenience. And he also advertised them that he would [loose from St Malo's in] the beginning of October, and prayed them [to have the forces ready at his landing,] and without fail. And thus h*e advised them*, [and had answer from them that they were ready and would not miss nor fail] to receive him [with good power in those western]
65v parts, according to his direction and desire.

The earl being thus satisfied in all things, to wit of the English sides there for the observing of their time and of the place, he weighed anchor and departed from the port of St Malo in the beginning of October, **Anno Domini** 1484, and accor*ding* to his promise. And he sailed toward England, and he came before the port of Poole in Dorset, and he cast anchor in the road or harbour and prepared to land there with all convenient speed, but yet with safety, or else not. For he was a very wary and a very circumspect man, and also somewhat timorous.

And therefore, and to prevent and to avoid all dangers and damages, he made choice [of] some stout and well-experienced soldiers to go ashore in their [skiff]s or cockboats, and in the manner of explorers or spies to go spy into the *situation* on land and to survey the coasts, and to learn what news there was ashore, [and get some intelligence] where [the] armies of his friends were, how near they were, and what *King Richard did*, and where he was and how armed; and other such instructions he gave to them. In the meantime the earl stayed aboard.

But these messengers could [l]earn no certainty, especially of those matters whereof the [e]arl desired chiefly to hear. But they understood that there were many armed men in [the] country and thereabouts – no news of the Duk[e of] Buckingham nor of his forces in those parts. Hereupon the earl grew susp[icious] *and un*happy, and was [weary of] staying in that harbour, and resolved to go to some other port.

And it happ[ened] *suddenly* [the] night following an unhappy and adverse accident, but it was very, very happy to him and to his fleet. For there arose so wh*irling and so* terrible a tempest of winds and of foul weather as that he was driven for the safety of his fleet and for the safety of himself and of the life of all his companies to weigh anchor and to go into the wind and main. And with this storm the ships in the darkness of [the ni]ght were severed and dispersed in the sea, and some were driven upon the coasts of Brittany. And the earl's ship fell upon the coasts of Normandy, and the first invasion failed and quailed.

But this storm (as I noted even now) was a happy disaster for the earl, for if he had gone on land at Poole or thereabouts, or if he had stayed but till the king's ships came, and which were not far of[f,] he had been a lost man every way, and he had been brought to the king, and then all his high and ambitious hopes had been cut off, and his head also, without all doubt. For *the* king hated him exceedingly, and was well provided to be revenged of him, and that was *by* the good intelligence which the king *had* of the *p*lots and counsels of the earl and of his consorts at that time from a faithful and secret friend. And thereby the king so well ploughed with their hay for as that he knew all that they either debated or deliberated and resolved. And by this means and at this time he was too hard for the earl and [the Duk]e of Buckingham and for the Earl of Devon and for the other conspirators. And *thus he over*reached them and overshot them in their plots and practices.

For after that he understood what their counsel was, and where their **66**
rendezvous should be, and where they were appointed to meet and when, the king by his great wit and industry and skill in martial affairs found good and certain means to prevent all their plots. For whereas it was resolved by these noble rebels that first the forces of the Duke of Buckingham and of the Earl of Devon and others should meet in Gloucestershire and near Gloucester, and that as soon as they were joined they should march in their full and united strength toward the seacoasts of Dorset, there to receive and to entertain the earl with all their forces – him whom they had chosen and ordained to be their chief captain and also their king, to wit, the Earl of Richmond – the king finely, and like to a skilful captain prevented and crushed all these purposes and designs. For first, and as soon as he heard that the Duke of Buckingham was armed and that his army was afoot, the king made all haste to meet and encounter him before his forces of his friends and fellow rebels were joined. He perfor[med] *all this* according to his project and desire: for he made such haste to meet with the Duke of Buckingham and to fight with him, and [he encountered him] and beat him and cut off his head before his friends could come to him.

And the king also, to prevent that the Earl of Richmond should not do any harm at his landing, nor join with the said duke and with the rest of the rebels, he took order that the ordinary bands of the West Countries should be appointed to guard the coasts. And he gave directions to the [sold]iers and guards of the coasts that if [the] Earl of Richmond or any of his French forces came ashore that they should entertain them courteously, and to say that they were soldiers and bands of the army of the Duke of Buckingham, and how that he (having overthrown the king and chased him away) had sent them thither to receive the earl and his companies and to conduct them to London. And then the earl had been caught and [ensnared] if the sudden *a*ccident of the great storm aforesaid, together with the good fortune of the Earl *of* Richmond, *had* not preserved and saved him from that trap which the king had set for him so subtly.

But yet [this] first expedition and first invasion by sea miscarried and all was lost, as also the Duke of Buckingham. *But the* earl and the rebels and the conspirators mended all these faults and errors of th*is first invasion by the* other *and* second invasion. And for the better accomplishing thereof then, they kept their counsel and purpose so *secret that neither the* king nor any of his true friends could come to any matter of moment of their designs, *and as you sha*ll better know when I come to the relation thereof.

[And for my warrant of this] *which I have* here written, I have followed [Sir Thomas More, Polydore Vergil, and the authors of the story of Little Britain,] and some other [French writers, and our common chroniclers.]

66v And now here very fitly the strange fortune of the Earl of Richmond may be considered and observed. And it is very remarkable, for he did not only thrive by the good success and by the prosperous events of his practices and enterprises, but also by the adverse accidents and by the evil and cross fortunes thereof. For it was good and happy for him that the storm arose at Poole, and that it scared and chased him from the coasts of England.

It was also good for him that the Duke of Buckingham was overthrown and defeated in his absence, and utterly. For if the duke had then prevailed in his rebellious attempt and had overcome the king in the battle and utterly vanquished and suppressed him, and in the absence of the Earl of Richmond (for here he was to be not only present in person, but also chief commander and Captain General of all the fo*rces which we*re levied and assembled for him and in his behalf). But he being absent, then the Duke of Buckingham (who pretended title to the crown and claimed the kingdom as due to him by right of blood and by lawful inheritance) without doubt would not have reserved the honours and the fortunes and the glorious and rich prize of the victory and of such a conq[uest] to the earl, but he would have kept all and seized all to his own use and for himself, and put the crown upon his own head and made himself king.

And the reason hereof is ready, and not to be contradicted: and that is that great men have not been accustomed to part with such stately purchases nor to surrender any such princely requisitions nor any sovereign possessions to any man during their lives – and n*ot* to any man but then to their own sons and to their next heirs. And not to go far for any examples, we have a very famous example thereof: this very Earl of Richmond, who, when he had gotten the kingdom and, albeit he knew that the children of the Duke of Clarence and others h[ad] better right to the crown than he, yet he would not resign it to any of them; no, not yet his own son so long as [he] could hold it. He had many precedents for his warrant and authority, as a[ll men know who know anything.]

And now I will proceed with the other matters of *the* story which happened in the times following these acc*idents* and occurrents herebefore related. And if for lack of them there *should be* silence here until we come to the second invasion of the Earl *of Richmond* (and which is the main matter of all), we will discourse *at this* time of other things, and which shall not be impertinent to this [story] *and* [may well supply the interim and the Reader's observation.]

And first I must declare and relate that in the interim, amongst many **67** other accidents, there happened unhappily the untimely death of the most towardly young prince, and the king's most dear and only son (at the least legitimate), viz., in the month of April, **Anno Domini** 1484. And he died in the Castle of Middleham in Yorkshire. And when [the] heavy news was brought to the king and to the [qu]een, they were then in the Castle of Nottingham, and they took the death of this their only son so grievously *and so* impatiently that (as mine [auth]or saith) **subitis doloribus insanire videbantur:** that they were ready to run out of their wits [and] be mad for grief.

The [death of Edward,] Prin[ce of Wales, son of] King R[ichard III]

[Croyland Ch]roni[cle]

[**Ibidem**]

But yet the king, being [a] man of much moderation and temperance, and abounding with great courage and true magnanimity, did as easily and in as short time *ov*ercome the grief and the care as he had done many adverse *acc*idents and worldly calamities before: [and a]s it was said of Julius Caesar when the evil and *heavy* news of the death of the dear and only daughter [Ju]lia was advertised to him, he soon passed it over. **Et tam facile dolorem [hun]c, quam omnia vicit.** And the King Richard, [as t]he Prior of Croyland [tell]eth, neglected not his business. Notwithstanding this cause *he* [did] all things as gravely and as orderly as before. **Rex Ricardus [nihilo]minus tamen suarum partium defensioni vacaverit**.

[Seneca]

But the queen, being [more passionate, according to the] tender sex, took the death of her son so grievously and so passionately, *and it* pierced her so far and afflicted her *so deeply that there*withal she grew very sick and very weak and in such extremity *as that she nev*er recovered her health, but she *languished until she* died, and that was not long after this [prince's] *death*, [and added not a little to the king's sufferings and sorrows, though his adversaries belied him in that, as in the rest.] *And* [I will not only prove against them this] / assertion anon when I come to the fit place for it, but **67v** also I will show how much they slandered him who reported that he poisoned or otherwise treacherously made away the queen his wife. And because this is a great crime, I will also reserve the answering thereof to that place where I am purposed to do my best to clear him of the false accusations and unjust criminations and slanders which are brought and laid against him.

But now we will return to this government of the state. And there we shall find that *notwithstanding* h*is grief* and great sorrow, yet his care for matters of importance, and even then (and as I noted before) was well discovered, and that he was a man not only endowed with true fortitude and void of passion, and a wise man, but also that he was a true lover and father of his country. For as soon as his son was dead and he issueless, he delibe[rated] of his successor in the kingdom to himself, and his care was to nominate such an on[e that was] not only next heir of the crown, but also a man worthy for his [virtues.] And thereupon without delays he nominated and chose, with the cons[ent] of the barons, Sir John de la Pole, Earl of Lincoln, son and heir of John de la [Pole,] Duke of Suffolk, and of the Lady Elizabeth Plantagenet, Duch[ess] of Suffolk, the sister and heir of this King Richard. And he was forthwith [de]clared and proclaimed heir apparent of the kingdo[m.]

[John, Earl of Lincoln, and] after [Duke of Suffolk pr]oclaimed [heir apparent]

But this was a **countrecoeur** to the faction of Ric[hmond,] and it much troubled and offended them, and it was as a t*horn* or pin in the eye of Buckingham, of Pembroke, of Morton and of the Countess of Richmond, and *as a* crown of thorns set upon his head who affected *the party* of the golden Richmond, *who lan*guished after the golden and precious crown and imperial diadem of this kingdom. And what mor*e* extreme and intolerable injury might b[e] offered to the Earl of Richmond if these gentlemen of the House of Lancaster or of [Beaufort] w[ere] the next heirs to the crown (as the friends of the Earl of Ri[chmond] a[ffirmed]), and that he was **caput et princeps familiae gentis Lancastriae**. But [they could not prove] that, nor hardly that he was **membrum illius familiae**, until he was [king.]

And this is a question heretofore much arg[ued] and disputed, to wit, whether the Beauforts or Somersets were of the House of [Lancaster or no, and never determi]ned so long as the House of York flourished. But how it was decided and determ[ined afterward I could say something,] but I will not pre[sume to speak indifferently] of this controversy, but I will deliver the argu[ments which] have been brought about it, and about the claim [which those of Somerset or Beaufort] made [to the crown by the title of Lancaster.]

68

The differences between the houses of Lancaster and of Somerset

And first, and if I may be bold to tell mine opinion, I will first say that there was much difference held to be between Lancaster and Beaufort, alias Somerset, and that so long held to be such until pride and usurpation on the one side, and parasitism and gross error on the other side confounded them and made them one and the same. For there is no doubt but that the houses of Lancaster and of Beaufort differed as much as royal and feudal, as much as legitimate and illegitimate, and as sovereignty and suzerainety.

For the children of the House of Lancaster, being lawfully born, and after Henry Plantagenet, Duke of L[ancaster, had conque]red and also [deposed Richard II,] were held to be princes of the blood royal and capable of the crown in their natural and due order. But those of Beaufort (or Somerset) were as people say, **filii populi**, or as the imperial jurisconsults say, **liberi vulgo quaesiti**; and who by the old Greeks were termed **ἀπατορες: sine patre**; and as the doctors of the spiritual law say, these kind of children had their **originem ab illicito et damnato coitu**, and of the polluted and adulterous bed.

[John Sarisberiensis, **Epistula** 89]

And those Beauforts, begotten by John of Gaunt, as he believed and said, were according to the laws to be reputed the children of Otho Swinford, for Catharine, the mother of these children, was the wife of Sir Otho Swinford, and the daughter of Sir Payen Rouet, a Frenchman dwelling in Beaufort, a town in Anjou, and he was Guienne Herald to the Duke of Lancaster. And albeit this duke was straitly bound by the sacred bands and duties of holy and honourable matrimony to his most noble and virtuous wife, Dona

Constantia, daughter of Don Pedro, King [of] Castile, yet nothingstanding that zealous religious bond and that solemn vow of conjuga*l faith* at his marriage, this duke kept as his **pellex**, or leman, or concubine *the* said Catharine a long time in the life of the noble and virtuous lady his co*nsort*, in which time he begat his four Beauforts, three males [and one fe]male, upon the said Catherina, and whose husband also, [Sir Otho Swinford,] was then also living.

And because the Duke of [Lancaster might not] give to these children the princely [name of Plantagenet nor of Lancaster, he surnamed them from the town of Beaufort, a town of his own where they were born. And they bore that name of Beaufort,] / and with good liking and contentment, until **68v** that the children of that John de Beaufort, the eldest brother of those base children of John of Gaunt being made Earl of Somerset, assumed the name of their father's greatest honour and earldom for their surname, viz., Somerset. And the rest afterward, following their example, left the name of Beaufort and took that of Somerset.

And to speak a word more of the frailties of their father, he added error to error and crime to crime (as the poet saith), for he, after his wife the duchess and after Sir Otho Swinford were dead, and when he was old and had lived out all the time of his life within one year, he would needs marry Catharina Swinford and make her a duchess, and against the liking of the king and of all his noble friends. Besides that, such a marriage as this, and between such men and women as have lived in adultery, is forbidden by the common law. And there was much wondering and scoffing at it in the court, as Thomas Walsingha[m writeth.]

Thomas Walsingham in R[ichard II]

And albeit that these base children of John de Gaunt were made legitimate first by Pope Urbanus VI, and next by the charter of King Richard II, and both of these indulgences and graces afterward allowed and confirmed and enlarged by Parliament, yet neither of these four legitimated children of the Duke of Lancaster, **Nec qui nascebantur ab illis**, were allowed and permitted to take the princely familiar title and the gentilitious surname of Plantagenet, for that was the p[eculiar or] capital surname or surname in chief of the kings of Engla[nd and of their] lawful children, since the time of the second King Henry, son of the Empre[ss Matilda,] and surnamed Plantagenet, and the founder and author of that sur[name] in the royal family of England, **ut in Libro Pr*imo***. And [none] but the princes and princesses of the blood royal and of le[gitimate] birth might take the surname of Plantagene*t*, [(as all our] *goo*d heralds and antiquaries) [of which honours were partakers the princely families of Wales, of Brotherton, of York, of Lancaster, of Clarence, of Woodstock, of Gloucester and others.

[Parliament **anno** 20 Richard II]

[Plan]tagenet

And there be yet some noble gentlemen in Portugal who, being descended **69** from John, Duke of Lancaster, bear that surname and are called and written de Lancastro. And other having the like origin and title may do the like, and not else. And therof this is a good argument and testimony: to wit, that neither King Henry IV, nor King Henry V, nor King Henry VI, all being kings of the line and race of Lancaster, and albeit they much respected and favoured these their kinsmen of the house and lineage of Beaufort or Somerset, and advanced them to many honours and called them cousins, yet these kings would not endure that those base children nor

Don Duarte de Lancastro, a noble gentleman of Portugal, came to my Lord Admiral ambassador to the King of Spain and to[ld] him that he was descen[ded]

from the Duke of La[ncaster in] Valodolid G.[B. **teste**]

their posters should bear the name or surname of Lancaster, for they held that to be an arrogation and usurpation of royalty and of royal right and title, and not due to them.

Th[e particular sur]na[mes of the] b[astards of the] an[cient kings of England]

And herein these kings followed the example of their royal ancestors, who would not suffer their base children to bear the royal name of Plantagenet, but other surnames were devised and appointed to them. And as, for example, the divers bastards of sundry kings were called Fitzroy Oxenford, Fitzherbert Clarendon, Fitzhenry Longuespee Cornwall, as after the same manner the base children of the foresaid Duke of Lancaster were called Beaufort and Somerset, **ut supra**, and not Plantagenet nor Lancaster, and for the reasons before showed.

And this ancient manner and laudable law of [giv]ing meaner names to the bastards of kings was an imitation of the kings [o]f France, as I conceive. For I have observed that the kings of France since the time of Hugh Capet never permitted nor vouchsafed any of their base [so]ns either to be capable of the crown of France or to have the [**ad**]**veu**, as they call it, or approbation of lawful children, nor the surname of France. [B]ut the female bastards or illegitimate daughters of these [kin]gs may take and bear the surname of France, or 'de France'. This is thus witnessed by Mr Jean [de Tillet, a] learned man and one of the best antiquaries of France: **[La troisième lig]née a du tout rejeté les bâtardes non seulement [de la couronne, mais aussi] de l'aveu et surnom de France, [quelle concession est permis aux bâtardes des rois,]** etc.

70 But if it be objected that albeit this be the law and custom of France, yet it is not in use nor hath it been observed in England. And for the better maintenance and authority of this their objection, they bring the example of Hamelin, whom some silly and negligent heralds who have forged his arms call Hamelin Plantagenet. This therefore importeth nothing nor may have any more credit than an error or a fiction. For the truth is that the said Hamelin (who was the base son of Geoffrey Plantagenet, Earl of Anjou) was simply called Hamelin, and bastard of Geoffrey Plantagenet. And his son William took the surname of his mother, Dame Isabel de Warren, daughter and heir of William de Warren, Earl of Surrey. And their posters were also called Warrens, as Johannes de Warrena the first and Johannes de Warrena the [second, both earls of Surrey,] and Isabella de Warren, and Eleanor de Warren, etc., as I have seen in charters and good records – and never Pl[antagenet.

[Camden in **Surrey**]

[This is confirmed] plainly by our best herald and our most learned antiquary, Mr William Camden, whose words be these: **/Isabella/ [fi]lia sola Gulielmi de Warrena comitis Surreiae, Hamelinum nothum Galfredi Plantageneti, etc. titulo comitis Surriae maritum adornavit: Hamelinus Gulielmum Surriae comitem genuit, cuius posteri ascit[o] Warrenorum nomine eundem titulum gesserunt.** And I make no doubt but tha*t* they took the name of Warren because they might not be suffered to b[ear] the royal surname of Plantagenet, it seems.

71v But if it be further objected / the base son of Edward IV was commonly call[ed] Arthur Plantagenet, this example, if it be well and duly considered, can give no authority nor credit to their assertions. And the reason is because that in the time wherein this Arthur lived, the name of Plantagenet, being only left in the House of York (for the Lan[castrian Plantagenets] were extinguished), was of little or no reputation nor of any honour, but rather held in contempt, and they which bore [it] were despised and hated, and the White Rose daily faded and withered and *perished*. So that the case stood then with the Plantagenets as it stood with the unhappy children of Baby[lon] when the prophet said, **Beatus qui tenebit et allidet [parvulos] suos ad petram**. And as a learned gentleman hath well [ob]served, it was not safe in that time to be a Plantagene[t.] He was held in disgrace and scorned and oppressed with wrongs, and *others* were imprisoned, and anon they were made away by one mischief or a*nother*, and as it shall be better demonstrated in th*e next book*.

Ψalm. 1. 36

[Thomas Gainsford]

And it also shall be fit to note and to advertise that [our poetical heralds have forged and given a false surname to Hamelin and to his posters. So they have also assigned to him by the like fabulous] / **73** art a shield of familiar ensigns, which he never bore, nor yet any of the ancient earls of Anjou nor any of their progeny. And that is the arms of France, bordered with an orle of Normandy or of Guienne, albeit that not any earl of Anjou of the antique lineage, nor any of the progenitors of our kings of England ever bore the arms of France – that is, the l[ilies of gold] in the azure field – until King Edward claimed the crown of France and assumed the arms of France in the right of the queen Isabella de Valois, his [m]other. And he first of all bore them, and quarterly with [his] arms of England.

But the arms of the [ancie]nt earls of Anjou were a scarboucle: that is, a golden [buc]kle of a military scarf or belt, set with precious stones, and not a car[bunc]le, or more precious ruby, for that is erroneous, and also [absu]rd if the form be considered, as I have demon[stra]ted in the fifteenth book of my **Baron**. And the princes of Anjou bore this [sc]arboucle in a shield, **parti per chief**, argent and [g]ules. This will not be denied by any good an[ti]quaries and learned heralds, either English or French.

[15] B[ook of] **Ba[ron**, etc.]

And the heir[s of this Hameli]n, and who took the surname of Warren (**ut supra**) bore also the arms of the house of Warren in the[ir shields and capar]isons. But in token that they were descended out of the house of Anjou they bore the **epipo[ma] scarboucle** upon their [helmets for] their crests: and [this I have] seen upon a [seal of John] de Warrena, Earl [of Surrey,] at a charter dat[ed 20] Edward III, **Anno Domini** 13[46] **apud Dominum** Robert [Cotton.] And you shall see at large in the 16th [Book of my] **Baron**, where I [treat of] matters of [armoury].

[16th Book **Baron**]

[Bu]t the herald or painter which forged that coat of flower **de [lis** and] lions for [Hame]lin was but a silly and ignorant animal. For [the fo]rgery is so gross as it may easily be detected by [any] mean armorist, and who was, or would be able to say that [neither] Hamelin nor Geoffrey Plantagenet his father could by right [and jus]t title bear the arms of France or Normandy, or of [Guienne,] either simply or compounded. And thus much for this error [and fiction.]

And now I will return to the Beauforts or Somersets, [and in comm]endation of their modesty and discretion I must [needs acknowledge] that they have not to my knowledge and in my [mean reading anywhere adv]entured / **73v** or presumed to take the surname and title of Lancaster until Henry Tudor, descended from the Somersets, and Earl of Richmond, came. And what would not he presume to do, being a man of so high ambition? And in the end, what might he not do, or what and how great and royal titles might he not take upon him when he had won the crown and when he was King of England and lord of all the regal titles and rights thereof? And whereof more anon.

The first Beauforts which were legitimated by the Pope and by King Richard II have no other surnames but Beaufort in either of the instruments apostolical or royal for their legitimation, nor any words to give or to ensure to them any capacity of royal title or state of sovereignty in the crown. As for that Bull of Pope Urbanus which he made for the legitimation of these Beaufort[s,] the which I have seen, it conferreth no honours nor titles up[on them] but only purged and cleansed them by his spiritual pow[er from] the foulness and infamous note of bastardy. And he a[llowed] them to be held and reputed as children legitimate [and] lawfully born. And in that Bull they have no other sty[les] but these: Joannus de Beaufort, **Miles**; Henricus de Beauf[ort,] **Clericus**, Thomas de Beaufort, **Domicellus**, Joanna de [Beaufort,] **Domicella**, and in brief only dispensed with thei[r bas]tardy.

And more the Pope cannot do, as the doctor[s] of [Sorbonne] and some other of the best canonists hold and affirm. For [they] say peremptorily that the Pope cannot make bastar[ds] capable of any succession or heritage, nor

74
The civil and imperial law against bastards

of any [office] or magistracy. Neither can he give to them any power / to ordain and constitute any successors or heirs. And the civil and imperial law agreeth herein with the ecclesiastical law, for that law suffereth not bastards to inherit the patrimony and hereditary lands of their father, nor admitteth them to be capable of offices or dignities or titles without the special grace and dispensation of the prince. And the same law is in force in England, as I

Sir Edward Coke

have been informed by a very learned and signal judge of the laws of this land.

But some grave men are of opinion that these laws are too strict and too hard, and they hold it agreeable to reason and also to law – because law much affecteth and observeth reason – that bastards, being honest and worthy men, and the rather if they be allowed by their fathers, may be admitted to be partakers of such honours and dignities and titles and feuds and other ornaments and rewards of virtue as with other virtuous and worthy m[en.]

Of this indulgence or connivance we have had in England some

Dr [Stephen Gardiner,] Sir Thomas [Egerton, Chancellors of England]

ex[a]mples, and not long since. For two worthy and good men [flourishi]ng in this age, being bastards, were admitted to be the greatest officers, to wit, Chancellors of England. And the foresaid King Richard II in his charter of the legitimation of the Beauforts, insinuateth that men of desert, and avowed by their fathers, should be well esteemed and are fit to be advanced to honours and dignities and to possess feuds and signories, etc. And this King Richard and other kings of England, as also the kings of France, called and call the bastards of the princes of the blood cousins. And this is a great honour unto them. But yet it certifieth not their blood, nor inureth any title *to* the crown unto them. Neither doth it give any increment [or] advancement to their fortunes and estates, for they may be and are many times poor, notwithstanding [their cousinage to the king.] But to prevent that evil, this king [made the eldest son, John de Be]aufort, Earl of Somerset and Marquis of Dorset. And from them descended Henry, Duke of Somerset, f[ather natural] to Charles Somers[et,] Earl of Worcester by

[King Henry VIII,] **ut supra**. And it is w[orth the] noting that this Duke Hen[ry Somerset left the] faction of Lancas[ter and follo]wed King Edward IV.

[B]ut to leave these extravagant disputations, I will here [ex]hibit the true copy of the charter of the legitimation of [the] Beauforts and the confirmation thereof by Parliament, and [let] the gentle and learned Reader judge thereof. Only I prepare his way by a short advertisement, and necessary [in this cas]e.

First, then, the Reader must understand that in the Act of Parliament [there is a pream]ble or preface to the charter, and it was made by Dr Edmund [Stafford, brother of the Earl o]f Stafford, and Bishop of Exeter and Lord Chancellor of England, and in the [20th year of King Richard II.] This Lord Chancellor [intimateth that Pope Urbanus VI, at the earnest request of the king, vouchsafed to legitimate these Beauforts,] / the **74v** foresaid base sons and the daughter of the Duke of Guienne and of Lancaster. And that the king, also having power to legitimate and to enable bastards in the same kind and in as ample manner as the emperor hath or had (for so he professeth and avoweth in the Act) was pleased at the humble request and suit of the duke their father to make them not only legitimate but capable of lands, heritages, titles, honours, offices, dignities etc. And that this king, for the more authority hereof, craved the allowance and the favourable assent of the barons and lords of the Parliament and obtained it. And now I will transcribe hither the charter, as I have seen and read it in the archives and records kept in the Tower of London:

[Charta legitimationis spuriorum Joannis Ducis Lancastriae:

[Ricard]/us Dei gratia, rex Angliae et Franciae, Dominus **75v** **Hiberniae, [car]issimis consanguineis nostris, nobilibus viris Joanni de B[eaufort] m[iliti, Hen]rico de Beaufort clerico, Thomae domicello, et nobili mulieri Joannae [Bea]ufort domicella praecarissimi *avunculi nostri,** **[*patrui]** **nobilis viri Joannis duci[s Aqui]taniae et Lancastriae germanis natis, et ligeis nostris, salutem. [Nos] pro honore et meritis, etc., avunculi nostri congruum arbitramur [ut merit]orum suorum intuitu, vos qui magnae probitatis, ingenio, ac vitae, [ac morum hone]state fulgetis, et ex regali estis prosapia propagati, etc. Hinc e[st quo]d Joannis avunculi nostri genitoris vestri precibus inclinati vobiscu[m qui (ut] asseritur) defectum natalium patimini ut huiusmodi defectu et e[isdem qua]litates quascumque praesentibus, vos haberi volumus pro sufficientibus [ex]pressis non obstante. Ad quaecumque honores, dignitates, praeeminentias, [status,] gradus, et officia publica et privata, tam perpetua, quam temporalia, [atque] feudalia et nobilia quibuscumque nominibus nuncupentur, etiamsi du[catus,] principatus, comitatus, baroniae, vel alia feuda fuerint, etiamsi media[te] vel immediate a nobis dependeant, seu teneantur, praefici, promoveri, elig[i,]**

> **assumi, et admitti, illaque recipere, retinere, gerere, et exercere proinde li[bere] ac licite valeatis, ac si de legitimo thoro nati existeretis. [Quibuscumque statutis] seu consuetudinibus regni nostri Angliae in contrarium editis, seu [observatis quae hic] habemus pro totaliter expressis nequaquam obstantibus, de ple[nitudine nostrae reg]alis potestatis et de assensu Parliamenti nostri [tenore praesentium dispensamus, vosque et] quemlibet vestrum natalibus [restituimus et legitimamus. Die Februarii, Anno Regni 20, R. II]**

76 In this charter there be great graces and great honours and privileges conferred upon these Beauforts by the king. For here the king calleth them **consanguineos suos**. And he doth not only most graciously allow and confirm their legitimation, but also his making them (and by the help of the Parliament) capable of baronies, of earldoms, of principalities, and of all honours, titles and dignities. And he also enableth them to bear and to exercise all offices, public and private, temporary and perpetual, and lastly to take and to hold and to enjoy all feuds, as well noble as other, and all heritages and lands and signories hereditary, and to hold and to exercise and enjoy them as lawfully and as firmly and as rightfully as if they had been born in lawful matrimony. And these be as great honours and great privileges as may be given (at the least to a subject).

But they confer no royal interest nor any right or title to the crown, at the least [acco]rding to the observation and caution of these men which disallow the claim of the Beauforts and Somersets to the crown. For they say that to enable a man to have title to a sovereignty and to be an heir of a kingdom, there be higher and greater words required, and words of empire, of majesty and of sovereignty, and such as **regnum, summa potestas, corona, sceptrum, diadema, purpura, maiestas** and the like. But there be neither these words nor [an]y other importing sovereignty or empire or reign, nor any grant or permission to bear *arms* in this charter. And hereupon they conclude that without such words no title to the crown, nor sovereign quality, nor royal ensigns could pass to them.

To these objections are made these answers by the friends and favourers of th[e Somersets:] first, that whereas the opposers to the claim of the Beaufor[ts affirm] that there be no express or nuncu[p]ative words in the said charter to confer upon these Beaufort[s] a capacity [of] reign and of empire in this kingdom, the defendants for the Somersets *deny* that, and in their answer they say that there is a word in the charter which

Prin[cipatus]
Pri[nceps]

[com]prehendeth empire and reign and sovereignty, and that is **princi-[patus,]** and whereof the king and the Parliament make the Beauforts capable. And they *e*xplain, as th*e* scholars know, that **principatus** is the state of **princeps**, [the] title of the highest and most absolute sovereign prince. [For the Roman] emperors in their greatest height were called [**princeps**. Therefore **princeps** is thus defined:] **Princeps [est pen]es quem summa i[n**

76v **rempublicam potestas est, et qui primus omnium dominatur.]** / And **principatus** and **dominatus** are used as synonyms.

But the other adverse parties and opponents, replying, said that it was an error now to take **principatus** for **regnum** or for **supremus dominatus**, because that the word **principatus** in the age of King Richard II and long before, and ever since, hath been restrained to the estate of the primogenite and heir apparent, not only of kings, but also of dukes and marquises, as well feudal as sovereign. Furthermore it was objected by them that the king which made the charter was reckless and irregular, and so prodigal a distributor of all things, as well of lands as of honours and offices, and that he would give anything, although it were not to be given. So that he may be said to have be*en* rather a [dissipater than a] dispensator of honours and treasures, and such an one as the good Emperor Severus was.

But on the other side *they* say that the next king, namely Henry IV, who was a wise and a discreet and a wary prince, although he loved these Beauforts dearly (as being his natural brethren by the paternal side) and was willing to do them any honour or grace that might be lawfully done to them, yet he discovered plainly enough in a certain charter in which he entailed the crown to the heirs of his own body, and namely to his four sons and to t[hem] successively, and to the heirs of their bodies, that he reputed not the Somersets nor Beauforts to be Lancastr[ians, nor heirs of the crown] and of the kingdom of England. For there is not any one word to lead a remainder [thereof] to any of his said brothers the Beauforts, nor any one word [nor] mention of them.

[The charter of King Henry IV] for [entailing the crown]

For first he entaileth the crown and kingdom to his eldest son Henry, Prince of Wales, and after him to the heirs of his body. Then to Thomas of Lancaster, his second son, and to the heirs of his body. And thirdly to his third son, John of Lancaster, and to th[e] heirs of his body. And lastly to his fourth son, Humphrey, and to the heirs of his body. For still, and for every estate, the words are, **Post ipsum successive haeredibus suis de ipsius corpora legiti[me] procreandis.** And this is all. And this, though implicitly, is a plain and express exclusion of the Beauforts from the crown.

And this charter was confirmed by Act of Parliament held at Westminster by this King Henry IV upon the 22nd day of December, in the eighth year of his reign. And it was sealed with the seal, and upon the dexter side of the seal hung the [seals] of sundry lords spiritual, and upon the left side h*ung* the seals of the temporal lords and noble barons, the wi[tnesses thereof.] *And this* charter is now in the hands of Sir Robert Cotton, [where I have] seen and read it and transcribed these summa[ry notes from thence.]

77

Arms of bastar[ds] of the kings of England

And this is also here fitly to be noted, that the bastards of the kings of England bore not the arms of the kingdom, but they had other new arms devised for them, or else they were permitted to bear the arms of their mothers if they were gentlewomen and to whom the ensigns of gentility and nobility appertained. But if the bastards were tolerated to bear the arms of England, then they were diversified in a checking and debasing and rebating manner, and were not differenced with such honourable notes as the arms of the princely legitimate sons were, but with other differences which were marks of baseness, of rebatement and of obscurity and of novelty, as namely basters, bends sinister, bars, bordures, and such like marks, and in such manner as that they might be borne by any new gentleman, such as the learned call **filios terrae** and **novos homines** (and we vulgarly call them upstarts). But I will say no more of these things here now; besides, I have touched them already. I have written of them at large, and of all armorial signs, in the last five books of my **Baron**.

And as the Beauforts, alias Somersets, had never the surname of Plantagenet, nor yet of Lancaster, so they never bore the arms of England but d[ifferenced, as aforesaid.] Neither did or durst any of them assume or take these royal arms and royal surnames until Henry, Earl of Richmond vehemently aspiring to royalty, came, and albeit that he could not so well and so rightly bear the names of Beaufort or Somerset, be[ca]use he was a Tudor by his father, and so to be surnamed Tudor or some other Welsh surname, if there were any in his family; but by his mother's side he was descended from the Beauforts. For the Lady Margaret, Countess of Richmond, was the daughter and heir of Sir John de Beaufort, Duke of Somerset, and grandchild to John de Gaunt by Catharine, the wife of Sir Otes de Swinford. And this John de Beau[fort] was first Duke of Somerset, and created by King Henry V and his wife *Cathar*ine, Queen of England. He descended from the kings of France.

[The nobleness and family of the Earl of Richmond]

[Glover]

And I have [seen a] pedigree made for this earl since he was king, wherein he is [derived from] the ancient kings and princes of Great Britain, whose [princely posters being] chased out of the chief countries of Britain by the Saxons, they occupied Wales. / And I also acknowledge that he was near akin to Henry VI and that the king called him nephew, and that he called the king **avuculum nostrum** (instead of **patruum**): our uncle – as it is in the records of the Parliament of **anno** 1, Henry VII. And he was to King Henry VI **ex fratre nepos**, as Polydore writeth him.

[So] King Richard II called [John] of Gaunt '**avunculumnostrum**'. Records **in Turre.**

77v

[But this was] the fault of the [barbarous Latin clerks] not knowing [the difference between] **patruus** [and **avunculus**]

Polydore [Vergil] **Liber** 25

But he was not that king's nephew, that is as we, and erroneously, take it now: his germane younger brother's son; for then he had been a true masculine issue of the House of Lancaster and of Plantagenet, and of the royal house of England. But he was nephew to King Henry VI by his brother uterine, Edmund Tudor, Earl of Richmond, the son of Owen Tudor or Meriodoc and of the said Queen Catharine, daughter of Charles VI, King of France, and widow of Henry V, King of England. And this was well known in France, and he was in respect of his blood of France the better respected and the more honoured in France. But he was not content with that honour, but he would also be reputed to be a prince of the House of Lancaster, and so then of England, and to be a near kinsman to the crown. And he had much grace thereby.

[How the Earl of Richmond was of the House of Lancaster]

And this error passed so currently in France as that Monsieur Jean du Tillet, who was otherwise a very learned and faithful writer and an excellent herald, and the antiquary of France in his time, **ut supra**, was so far abused with the fame of this cousinage as that he hath committed this error to writing, and recorded in his book entitled **Le Recueil des Rangs**, etc., Part II. For there he writeth that John, Duke of Somerset, father of the foresaid Lady Margaret, Countess of Richmond, was the true and lawful son of John de Gaunt, Duke of Gui[enne] and of Lancaster, and begotten by him upon his first wife, and his right noble and virtuous wife, the Lady Blanche Plantagenet, daughter and heir of Henry and of the earldom of Lancaster.

But the noble and veritable historian Philip de Commynes, Lord of Argenton, had better intelligence of the pedigree of the Earl of Richmond and also of his title to the crown, and of either of which he conceived but slightly and lightly, as these his words show, albeit the earl was king when Commynes wrote this, viz.: **Il n'avait ni croix ni pi[lle] ni nul droit, comme je crois, à la couronne d'Angl[eterre.]**

But suppose that the Earl of Richmond had been one [of the lawfu]l progeny of the said Duke of Lancaster. Yet he could not rightfully and lawfully claim the crown of England] / nor make any title to the kingdom so 78
long as the royal family of York flourished and continued, because that Richard Plantagenet – Duke of York and King of England designate by Act of Parliament holden [in the] thirty-ninth year of King Henry VI, and to whom the titles of Prince of Wales, Duke of Cornwall, Earl of Chester, and Protector of England were given by the Three Estates in the same Parliament – descended from the daughter and heir of the second son of King Edward III (for as before, so still I leave the infant William of Hatfield out of the catalogue). And King Henry IV and his progeny descended from the third son of the said King Edward III, as it hath been here declared in the first book. And King Henry VI, being the best of the House of Lancaster then living, did acknowledge in the Parliament aforesaid that the title of Richard, Duke of York, was the only just and lawful title, and so consequently it was the true and next title, therefore better than of Lancaster or any other.

And all this was known well enough to the Earl of Richmond. And there was a time that he would have been content and glad with all his heart but to have possessed peaceably and *in* safety his earldom of Richmond and to have enjoyed the hon[ours and] dignities and signories thereof *with the* good grace of the sovereign. And he had reason, for it was a much better state and conditi*on tha*n that of a bandit or prisoner in a foreign country or a*ny*where else. [Besides that, the issue] of the two daughters of John, Duke of Lancaster, Philippa and Catharine, married to the kings of Portu[gal and of Castile, were to be preferred before any Beaufort or their heirs, if foreign titles be not excluded by Parliament.]

But after that Morton had infected his ears and *poi*soned his heart and his desires and affections with the ambitious aff*ectation and* aspiring to the crown and to the sovereignty, then nothing would *content* him but the crown, and his haste and impatience were such as that he m*ust* have and possess it forthwith, **quo iure quaque iniuria**. And he would imita*te the* insatiable ambitious thirst of Great Alexander, and therefore he would cut the s*ame* Gordian knot profanely and rudely, and not to regard to do it orderly and in due and convenient time, and time ordai*ned by God*. I make not doubt but that he was ordained to be king (as I intimated before,) *albe*it he ought by the laws of Christian religion to have attended God's leisure. *And it had been better for his* / honour and reputation in this world, and 79v
more for the safety of his soul in the next world.

But he followed the advice and counsel of that evil spirit transformed into an angel of light and wearing the habit of religion and of sanctity, and whose malice was so extreme toward King Richard as that nothing could appease it but the deturpation of the slaughter and the blood and the utter destruction of this prince. And that must not be delayed, but it must be performed and executed in all haste, albeit (as the Italians say proverbially) nothing is well done in haste. And according to the saying of Augustus Caesar, that which is well done enough is soon enough done.

Suetonius in **Augustus**

But Morton hastily prepared and raised great instruments for this monstrous and impious work, and he hastily brought and, as it were, he precipitated the earls of Oxford and of Richmond and of Pembroke and the Duke of

Buckingham and other men fitter for better employments, and he incited them to undertake this enterprise *and enter* into this conspiracy unduly and unseasonably.

And it was the greatest fault, and almost the only fault of this noble Earl of Richmond that he would hear evil counsels and too much follow them. And the reason was because they were given by such men whom he better loved, and of whose virtue and honesty and learning and prudence he had a much better opinion than there was cause. And such were Morton, Dudley, Empson, Bray, Urswick, Knevet, etc. And for that, his partiality and credulity, he beareth the blames of other men.

There be two extreme[es] in the case of the counsel of princes. The one is when the prince will consu[lt] with no man, nor hear the counsel of the wisest and best experienced men. And such a prince was Charles the Hardy, Duke of Burgun[dy,] who was so self-wise and so overweening of his own wit and judgem[ent] as that he thought no man to be so wise and so intelligent, and of which his madne[ss] there is the monument, **Carolus**
[Pontus Heuterus; John Meyerus] **Pugnax aliorum consilia, et rationes (ne dicam) sequi, vix audire volebat, ignominiae loco habens ab aliis discere et iudicavit se proprio cerebro omnia consilia habere recondita.**

[**Sententiae Arabicae**] But this is a better opinion, and it passeth for an oracle: **Vir optimus eget consilio**: the best man needeth counsel. But yet therefore the fault or extremity before mentioned is worse: that is to hear and follow evil counsels, and such especially as are given by men who are held to be envious, malicious, and wicked and impious persons, as much worse or most unhappy.

And such an one (if you will c[on]sider the testimonies and notes and censures which Mr More, [the old] servant of Bishop Morton, maketh of this said bishop his master) w[as] this Dr Morton. And because I will not be
[Dr Morton's character] his accus[er,] I will set down Morton's character as it was dra[wn and] portrayed by the said Sir Thomas More and by other.

80 I will begin with his studies of policy and with his natural inclination to
82 that kind of learning. / And first as concerning his skill in policy, Sir Thomas More declareth that in these words and shortly, **The Bishop (Morton) had gotten great experience in politic affairs and in worldly drifts**. And that is as much to say as that Dr Morton was a much better politician or Machiavellian than a divine or churchman. And according to the character, Dr J. Herd in his metrical history of England bringeth in the Bishop Morton speaking thus as an observer and worshipper of the pagan idol Fortune, and as a variable Proteus and Ambidexter, one while Yorkizing and another while Lancastrizing or Somersetizing, and in all Satanizing. And thus he brings him to describe himself and to characterize himself:

81 **Si fortuna meis favisset partibus olim**
Et gnato Henrici Sexti diadema dedisset,
Edwardi numquam venissem regis in aulam.
Sed quia supremo stetit hac sententia regi
Henrico auferre ac Edwardo reddere sceptrum,
Tanta meam numquam lusit dementia mentem
Ut sequerer partes regis vicit, atque sepulti
82 **Adversus vivum, etc.**

And this prelate used sp[eeches] to the same effect in his discourses with the Duke of Buckingham. And this is well said by a mere politician. But an ho[nest] man and a truehearted friend will love his friend or lord in adversity, and also when he is dead, as the divine Ariosto hath well observed, [and] maketh the descript[ion] of the one and the other in this elegant stanza:

Nessun può saper da chi sia amato [Ariosto, Canto 19]
quando felice in su la ruota siede;
però ch'ha i veri ed i finti amici a lato,
chi monstran tutti una medesima fede. 83
Se poi si cangia in tristo il lieto stato,
volta la turba adulatrice il piede,
e quel di cuor' ama riman' forte,
ed ama il suo amico dopo la morte.

Translated by me long before the translation of Sir John Harington was *pu*blished, and thus as follows:

No man ever whilst he was happy knew
Assuredly of whom he was beloved; 82v
For then he hath both feigned friends and true,
Whose faiths seem both alike till they be proved.
But he is left of all the flattering crew
When from his happy state he is removed;
But he who loves in heart remains still one,
And loves his friend when he is dead and gone.

But as they say in the proverb, the devil is good to somebody, and certainly this politic prelate was very kind and very friendly and faithful *and* firm to the rebels. And he took great pains for the advancing of their *cause* and for the seditious designs of the barons. And he crossed the seas betwixt the Earl of Richmond and these rebels and conspirators against King Richard; oftentimes and dangerously he adventured his liberty or his life for them. And all was for the love of the Earl of Richmond and of his mother the Countess of Richmond, and whom he visited often and observed, and with all devotion. And he seemed as their creature, for he had been the countess's chaplain, *a*s I have heard, and also the tutor of the earl her son when he was young.

And he was well re*w*arded for his love and service, *for t*he earl a*s soon as* he w*a*s king, made this man Archbishop *of* Canterbury and Lord Chancellor of England, and by the king's means [he] was also made Cardinal. And that was to be a better man [t]han the king himself, according to the order of Roman marshalling of states. For in the Pope's list of ranks [Ranks of the chief prelates] and of precedence the Pope hath the first place and the emperor the next, and next to him a cardinal and then a king.

And this doctor had other go*o*d politic gifts, and well worthy the 83v rewarding. And if they were not rewarded here in this world, there is no doubt but that they shall be considered and rewarded to their uttermost merit when every man shall receive his reward according to his worth: **Omnes enim non manifestari oportet ante tribunal Ch*risti, ut referat u*nusquisque propria corporis pr*o*ut gessit sive bonum sive malum**.

And that he was not only a seditious and treacherous man, but also a 85 covetous, bloody, cruel, and ambitious and a proud prelate. I will briefly

St Thomas in *Liber* Secundus** 4 art.20

here demonstrate. And first that he was treacherous and a traitor to the king his master, and his good master as long as he was true, that hath already been clearly demonstrated and proved by his many false and seditious practices and persuasions of disloyalty and rebellion to the Duke of Buckingham and to the earls of Oxford, Pembroke, Devon, Richmond, and to a great many other noble persons and worthy gentlemen of this land. And this crime of sedition and stirring of rebellion against the sovereign is not only a crime of **laese majesty**, but a deadly and damnable sin. Witness St Thomas Aquinas: **Seditio est semper de se peccatum mortale**. And certes, as I think, of all men, yea, even of all villains, a traitor is the wo[rst].

86

And as this was thus seditious and treacherous, so that he was as cru[el] and bloody, his many conspiracies and practices, not only against the life of King Richard, and the cruel counsel which he gave to put Edward Plantagenet, Earl of Warwick, to death, and also Perkin Warbeck (alias Richard, Duke of Yo[rk)], and his bloody thirsting after the destruction of all the princes of the House of York [are] great and pregnant testimonies thereof.

[Francis Godwin in **Catalogue Episcop-orum**]

[John Stow]

Now we will take a view of his covetous*ness*. And how covetous he was, these ex[amples] may serve to approve. Dr Godwin, now Bishop of Hereford, wri[teth] that when Dr Morton was Archbishop of Canterbury he exacted and extorted a much greater sum of money from the clergy of his dioces[e] than was ever before taken or extorted in that diocese. And moreover, he for his private commodity (which he chiefly sought) and for that purpose to bring certain leames to his own grounds about Wisbech, so weakened and shallo[wed] the fair River of Nine (which was before navigable and of much good public use) as that it hath since served to little good use. [He was also the deviser] and persuader of so great and so grievous a tax to be laid and levied upon the people as that it made th[em to rise in arms and rebellion.]

His pride and his ambition appear plainly in his affectation of the highest tithes, in his aspiring to the dignities and highest offices and great honour, as namely of the Chancellor of England, of the first archbishop of England, and of a cardinal. And this his pride was also observed by his servant More, and thus taxed by him. Bishop Morton's pride abused his wisdom, and it s[erved] his turn to his own deliverance and proper advancement and to the destruction [o]f the Duke of Buckingham. And his affection of the cardinal's hat and to be highest chief person in this kingdom be notable [tokens of his pride.]

I will not cloy and annoy this place with too much such noisome and fastigious matter; I will reserve the rest for other places. But by these it may sufficiently be seen how little credit there is to be given to his report and censu*re*. But by these it may sufficiently be seen how unworthy and how unfit he *w*as not only to give counsel to so good a prince as King Henry VII, but also to have the power to direct *and* [g]uide and rule him in anything.

[Queen Elizabeth]

And I say that the king his master was a good and also a wise prin*ce,* [and] he was so reputed of many men. And I will hold him to be so, the rather also because that the best p*rince or* [pri]ncess which ever reigned in this land was said to be so like to this king [her gr]andfather, as well in wit and in disposition as also in the favour and lineaments of body, as that [she was the lively and] perfect image of him. And now to return where we began, that how far off soever the [earl was from the titles and rights] of the crown when he first entered into his ambitious pr*actices of the crown* and of the sovereignty, yet I will avow and maintain [that after he was anointed and crowned king, he was the] *assur*ed and true proprietary of all the [rights and titles which carried the crown and kingdom, and whereof they depended.

[He got also the title of York by the marriage of the Lady Elizabeth] Plantagenet, eldest daughter of King Edward IV, and who was prince or **87v** head of the royal family of York and the first or chief Plantagenet. And the title of Lancaster instantly, and others, fell and escheated to the Earl of Richmond so soon as he was king, and the which before was in controversy and **in nubibus**, or in abeyance (as our lawyers say). For no man being a subject, how capital and chief a judge soever, and how great power of judicature soever he had, might presume to give a definitive sentence in any ambiguous and obscure cause or act of the king which was doubtful or uncertain. But the king himself only must give judgement in such cases. And this is an ancient and an authentic paragraph in the laws of England, as the very grave and learned judge Henry Bracton affirmeth and thus reporteth it: **De chartis regis et de factis regum non possunt Justitiarii disputare, nec si disputatio oriatur possunt eam interpretari: sed in dubiis et obscuris et ubi aliqua dictio contineat duos intellectus domini regis erit expectanda interpretatio et voluntas**, etc.

Bracton, **Lib**. 2, **Cap**. 16]

And the reason hereof is given in th[e] books of the civil and imperial laws, and peremptorily, viz: **Quia de principali iudicio non est disputandum**. And thus, and for these causes, that question and controversy whether these Beauforts or Somersets and their descendants were of the House of Lancaster and capable of the crown or no, it could not be decided nor determined until there w[ere] a judge who was also a king, and King of England. And Henry VII was both chief judge and also sov[ereign] lord and king of this land. And thereby he had full powe[r] and authority to determine this or any other ambiguous and doubtful [cause,] *and by* the virtue and power thereof, he adjudged and decreed to himself that the title of Lancaster, with all the royal a[ppurtenances] belonging *to it, was* his own and proper title. And accordingly he took the said title to himself, and the Pope confir[med it as] due and proper to him (and as you shall see anon). And then the writers of the stories said (as well English a[s French]), and m[ight truly] say that this King Henry VII was **de la ligne de L[ancastre,] et caput gentis regalis, et princeps [familiae Lancastrensis.**

[And the Chancellor Morton termed the marriage of this king and the Lady Elizabeth (and not improperly, but very fitly) the union of York and Lancaster. This was an eulogy very honourable and acceptable to the king, at the least in the beginning of] / his reign. But afterwards (as I have **88** observed) he had no great good liking of them, and which is more, he had none or very small affiance in those his titles now lately acquired of York and Lancaster, and much less of Somerset. He seemed tacitly to waive and (to wit) to quit them. For after that he had gotten the crown in the field and in victorious battle, he affected, and chiefly, so as it were, only the title of his sword. And he claimed the kingdom to be his by conquest and **de jure belli**. Because he would have this told, there were at his coronation proclamations made with these titles: **Henricus rex Angliae, jure divino**,

King Henry VII affected only [the] title **[de] jur[e] b[elli]**

jure humano, et jure belli, etc.

But the noble barons liked not this title **de jure belli**, nor would they allow it. But the king maintained and avowed that he might justly assume and bear it, and as a title and style due to h*im* [as] a conqueror, because he entered this land with hostile and foreign armies and fought for the crow[n] and won it. To this, the barons answered roundly and soundly that he was beholding to them for h[is] landing safely and for his victory, and that he could never have had that commodity of fair and prosperous descending upon the coasts of England, and much less to have marched in[to the] land and to have struck so much as one stroke for the crown and conquest of this re[alm without their favour and] permission.

For it was clear that without the love and help of the English nobles and people he had no hope [nor strength] but in his French soldiers; and they were not so many as the least legion of the Romans. By the testimony of the grave and honest French writers th[emselves, they] were **les plus méchants**, and no better than rogues and truhanes; that is, base men [and] men of no courage, and without sense of faith and of honour. And so that if ever they had la[nded, th]ey should have been so entertained by the valiant English as that *within* one hou*r they s*hould all have been cut into pieces and never more have seen the sun. And besides this, the King Richard and the ba[rons] *and* people would have conceived so mortal an hatred against the invader of this [kingdom] that they would never have left him nor the pursuit of him u[ntil they] had seen or wrought the death and destruction of him as of a most notorious traitor.

Wherefore the barons humbly prayed his grac[e to] consider these matters and to give to the noble barons and to the valiant loving people [their du]e, and duly and justly to ascribe his good success and his achieving of the crown to their *loyal* forces and not to the French ragamuffins nor to his Welsh sword, for by them *he s*hould never have been able to have won one foot of land in this kingdom. And th[at t]hence he attained to the crown by the favour and power of the *noble* and common English: he migh*t not be* said a conqueror of these people who entertained him with courtesy and safeguarded and *sustain*ed him with their forces and only put the crown upon his head.

[Seneca]

Moreover, the barons a[ssevered] that this King Henry was no conqueror; his achievement could not be called a conquest [or pu]rchase of the sword. Besides, they added that the names both of conqueror and of co[nquest were] very harsh and hateful words to all the English, and reputed as barbarous and heathenish and tyra[nnical titles.] And by good reason, for the work and end of them is to make all the people of the land sla[ves, to] possess all their goods and fortunes at their pleasures, and in brief to do anything; as the wise man said, **Quidquid victor audet, aut victus timet**. And hereof the examples of the conquering [Va]ndals, Longobards, Saxons, and Normans in Italy and Spain, in England, and lately the Spaniards in America, and many other cruel lords, estated only by their u[njust] *s*words, are not only very many, but also most hateful and detestable for their tyranny. *And for these* causes the barons would not endure the title **de jure belli**.

[An]no Domini 1486

[But the king changed not] his mind, and therefore he made means to the Pope to obtain of him [the ti]tle of Lancaster. But the king did not seek the titles d[irectly and desertly] *in his motion* and suit to the Pope, [but closely and cunningly. For the outside of his embassage was only for his marriage, fearing that therein he had committed incest, as he pretended, because the queen his wife was his kinswoman,] / **et quarto consanguinitatis, et forsan** **89v*** **affinitatis gradibus**. Pope Innocentius VIII granted this suit to the king in the first year of his reign. And afterwards, but on what occasion I know not, the king renewed this suit to Pope Alexander VI, who confirmed and ratified this pardon and dispensation made by his predecessor in the fourth year of the reign of this King Henry VII.

This Bull is in the hands of Sir Robert Cotton, and which I have seen.

90

[**An**]**no Domini** 1490

And it is observable that the Pope taketh not upon him herein to confer or to give any new titles to the king, but neither did [the] king pray the Pope by his letters to give to him these two titles, but his ambassador had that chiefly in his instructions. Therefore the Pope seemeth only to make a rehearsal of those titles as due and proper to him before. And so by the means of this device, the titles **de jure belli** and **de Lancastria** were not as any matters or proper subject of the Bull, but rather in respect of the desire which the Pope had to show the love and honour which he bore to the king, that he was pleased, **ex proprio et mero motu et certa [sc]ientia suis** to make an honourable memorial of all the royal and majestical titles which belonged to the king by right, and they are the more stately ornaments and precious embroideries of those his [gr]acious letters of apostolical indulgence granted / for the dispensation of the said marriage. And in this **89v*** style and in these words they are co[nveyed]:

[The Pope's charter] for [the title of Lancas]ter [and **de jure belli**;] and [for the dispensing of the king's incestuou]s [marri]age

Hic rex Angliae de domo Lancastriae originem trahens, et qui notorio jure et indubitato proximo successionis titulo et praelatorum et procerum Angliae electione et concessione, etc. Ac etiam de jure belli est rex Angliae. Afterward, for the more certain clearing, [repairing] and curing of all flaws and defects of titles, the Pope addeth the gracious clause, **Supplemusque omnes et singulos defectu[s,] tam juris quam facti, si qui intervenerint in regno dic[to]**. And then and there in the end this charter or Bull is entitle[d, and not in the front,] **Pagina confirmationis nostrae, approbationis, pronunci[a]tionis, constitutionis, declarationis, suppletionis, monitionis, requisitionis, prohibitionis, benedictionis, inhibitionis, et excommunicationis, et anathematiza[tio]nis in quoscumque qui praesumpserint infringere, ve[l] ausu temerario contravenire his litteris Apos[tolicis].** For all this must be thought and held to be don[e] **auctoritate Apostolica**: by the authority of the apostles St Peter and St Paul.

And thus you s[hall] also see how the king received of the Pope t*he confirmation of* these two noble titles, **de domo Lancastriae, [et de] jure belli**, [u]nasked, as it seemeth. For there appearet[h not any particular and express] suit made for them by the king, yet it [is very probable it was his suit underhand, because the] other things [are but slight and of necessity, nor obnoxious to any danger, when those two titles were the things he most aimed at.]

This king was not satisfied with those two titles, notwithstanding the **91** Pope's allowance and granting and authorizing of them, more than he was with his title of York and of Lancaster, as he discovered (and not obscurely) when he made very earnest request to all the estates of the kingdom assembled in the first court of Parliament which was summoned and held by him to give him an estate hereditary of the crown and kingdom of England with all the appurtenances, and to entail them to him and to the heirs of his body. And this great request and suit, and that suit of inestimable value, was granted unto him by the said high court of Parliament. And I will exhibit a copy of this gift as of a gift of a new title, and of the Act of Parliament conferring and confirming the same, when I come to relate and to rehearse the most noble and royal titles of our Sovereign Lord the King of Great Britain now reigning and flourishing.

And it were no hard piece of work to divine what the mislike of this King Henry VII was to the titles of York, of Lancaster, and of Beaufort or Somerset, and haply there is some discovery of them here already. But I must not confound this story with historologies, but rather, as we say in the proverb, with putting the cart before the horse preposterously and reporting matters out of their time and place. And I confess that this might be objected *ju*stly, were it not that I have no purpose to write the whole [st]ory of King Henry VII, but some parts thereof, and as they belong to this task. And therefore I must of necessity insert [su]ch matters of his story into this discourse as are proper *and* behoveful thereunto, and without the which the Reader shall want [kno]wledge of sundry things which much concern the credit, [honour,] and actions of this story of King Richard.

But now I *turn my* style again to the story of that King Richard, and according to the order [and affairs of] *these* times, I will proceed therein.
91v And therefore now it must be considered that *there* be near ten months passed since the Duke of Buckingham was suppressed, and since the Earl of Richmond was chased from Poole with the storm. And there we have left him all this while. And in the meantime I have reported what things of historical argument happened in this interim, and such as I have thought worth the writing, and with some arguments and discourses hereupon: and where they failed, I have entertained the time with other discourses, and not improper to the story of King Richard, and as I before promised.

The [second] invasion [of the] Earl of Richmond

And now I return to the affairs of that king. And wher*eas* it must be supposed that and understood that King Richard had intelligenc[e] that the Earl of Richmond was very busy and very diligent in France in making of his warlike preparations for his second invasion and second enterprise upon Eng*land*. And the king being careful to defend himself and to preserve his kingdom from invasion and from spoils and from bloody tumults and from much mischiefs and miseries as conspiracies and seditions and rebellion and war bring with them, wherefo*re* he caus[ed] a general levy of soldiers to be mad[e,] and armour and munition and other necessary things for th*e* war to be prepared and provided. And he gave order to have the havens and frontier places and towns to be reinforced and well guarded. And he had soon set all things in g*ood* readiness and in good abundance and in very serviceable good estate, saving only the faith and true hearts of a gr*eat* part of his subjects, as well nobles as *commons*, and this was his only want and defect. But *that was* a secret and hidden and [unsuspected] *defect, and* [could not provide against the evil of their hate and malice.]

92 And I must not omit to tell here how that the Earl of Richmond found it a more difficult work to obtain aid and succour in France now than he did before, and that by reason that all the labour and all the adventure of his first invasion and enterprise were lost and utterly frustrate, and his

adventurers and favourers not only much damaged, but also disc*ouraged*. For by the manner of his return into France, he distasted much his old and noble friend the Duke of Brittany. For the duke took it ill that he went to the French king and into France, albeit the earl could not otherwise do. For when he was driven from Poole, he was also driven upon the coast of Normandy. And being there, he came into the road at Dieppe, and there landed to refresh himself and his company. And from there he went to Rouen. And being then near to Paris, he thought it behoved him to see the king and to have some speech with him about his design and to pray his *assistance*.

And he came in very honourable and noble port, for (if Philip Commynes saith truly) that he was followed then with five hundred Englishmen, and he was entertained by the French king with much honourable courtesy. And he gave good audience to the earl, and who soon propounded the cause of his coming and his suit to the king. And the king liked well his enterprise, but he was loath to be party therein, because he was in good love and league with the King *o*f England, and also because he was loath to dispatch any [g]reat sums of money as were required in such a cause. *And* the king desired the earl to give him leave [to] pause and to consider and deliberat*e* of the matter.

And in the meantime, the earl (and as I related before) [behav]ed himself so well in the court of France as that [he con]ciliated the love and favour of the greatest persons, *gentlemen* and ladies. And amongst other, he became [very gracious] with the princely Lady [Anne de France, eldest sister to] King Charles VIII, and wife of Pierre de B[ourbon, Lord of Beaujeu, after Duke of Bourbon. But because it was] / his most stately seat and his most **92v** honourable signory, he would be called Monsieu de Beaujeu, and the duchess his wife was called Madame de Beaujeu. And this great *lady had so great* power over the king her brother in his minority as that her authority was greater than that of Lewis, [Duke of Orleans,] chief [prince of the blood; in envy or mis]like [whereof this duke took arm]s [and raised a civil war] in [France, as John Tillet] and [others write.]

And this most noble lady so much favoured the Earl of Richmond as that she ceased not to solicit and importune the king her brother, Charles VIII, until such time as he promised to give good assistance to the earl for the invading of England and for the recovery of the title and right and possession, *s*ceptre and diadem of his English progenitors, and for the seizing upon his royal patrimony and princely inheritance, and when the king forthwith commanded that there should be a good sum of money delivered to the e[arl, and] that there should forces be levied for this journey. And the forces were levied in Normandy, and to the number of 3,000 men. And they were odd fellows. For Philip Commynes saith that they were **trois mille hommes, les plus méchants que l'on pût trouver**. [Commynes,] p. 536

And whilst these forces were making ready, the earl, being desirous and careful to procure all the aid and help that he could, he resolved to go to his old noble friend the Duke of Brittany and to pray his assistance in this enterprise once again. And the duke hearkened favoura[bly] unto his suit and was minded to grant it. But when he propounded it to his council, his treasurer and chief counsellor, Peter de Landois, disliked the notion and dissuaded the duke from yielding thereunto. And for the reasons hereof, he told the duke that this enterprise, if it succeeded well, would prove very evil and unhappy to the duke.

'For', quoth he, 'the earl hath now obtained the favour and the assistance of Charles, the King of France, and he will hold him to be his best friend and ascribe all his good fortune unto him. And so you shall lose the earl and his love and confederation when he is king, and he will take part with the King of France against you if any jar[s] and wars should happen, and which the King Charles wisheth, because he hath a long time longed to possess this country and duchy of B[rittany,] and the which he cannot gain so long as [you] continue in the league and amity with the King of Eng[land.] But when that is broken, and the league and amity contracted firmly bet*ween* the king*s of* [France and England, how easy is it for the King of France to invade and swallow up both you and your dukedom?]

93 'Wherefore it shall be much more safe and more profitable to hold the earl fast whilst you have him here in your hands, for so you shall be assured to hold the King of England your fast and faithful friend. And if you will after deliver him to the King of England, you may set his ransom at what rate or price you will. For the king will think no sum too great for such a [purchase.] And so you may replenish your coffers with good store of treasure, and whereof there is now great want'.

Thus Monsieur Landois spake and delivered his opinion like a wise and an honest man. Albeit he loved the earl well, yet he well understood that he was bound to prefer the love and the good and safety of his master *to* those of any other man. And this counsel much prevailed with the duke, and it made him to alter his purpose. And he forthwith resolved to put a guard upon the earl and to keep *him* as his prisoner again.

But now, worthy Reader, mark now how still Fortune is propitious to her favourite *Earl* of Richmond. For whether it were by the secret advertisement and warning of some dear friend of his of the duke's council, or whether *it* were suggested to him by his good angel, sure it is that the earl came to knowledge, and by unknown means, or vehement suspicion of this treacherous plot of the duke before it could be put in operation. For it was not deter[mined] and resolved until it was night. And the execution was deferred until the morning, and that then there should be a guard set upon him. But in the meantime, and before midnight, the earl had prepared good means to fly, and he being accompanied with twelve gallant gentlemen, his followers and friends, and all well mounted upon good and swift horses, and he departed from Vannes and rode with such speed as that the earl was got out of Brittany and come into Anjou (a town of the French king's) before it was known to the duke that the earl was gone forth of his lodging.

From Anjou he went to the French court at Paris, and there [he] was very
94 welcome again, and still he thought and studied how he / might advance his cause and strengthen himself. And after that he obtained help [from the French kin]g, he thought it would also be very behoveful for him to use some mean[s to get the] Earl of Oxford out of prison of the Castle of Hammes in Fr[ance, whither he was co]mmitted long before by King Edward IV. And herein also he [followed the means and counsel of the Bishop] Morton, who had good quarter with the Earl of [Oxford and sometimes visited h]im [and acquainted him with the] plot of the Earl [of Richmond] *to*
93v *set him at* / liberty – because he was a great earl and a valiant gentleman

and a man of much power and very wise. And besides that, he hated King Edward IV and his children and also King Richard and all the House of York, and most mortally, and therefore *he would* be a sure and politic friend *when* he raised a force, if he could be drawn by the earl's means to like of his action of aspiring to the crown.

And hereupon the Earl of Richmond rode to Hammes, and then under the charge and government of Sir James Blount, and who entertained the earl with much honour and extraordinary and good respect. And the earl told him that he desired to see the Earl of Oxford. And forthwith Sir James conducted him to the earl's lodging, and the Earl of Richmond propounded his enterprise to the Earl of Oxford, and he liked it well and promised to give him all the help he could. And Oxford, having great [confidence] in the love and faith of the Captain of Calais, discovered the plot of Richmond to him, and he liked it so well that he turned traitor instantly and alterned to the Earl of Richmond. And the Earl of Oxford and James Blount went to Paris back again to the Earl of Richmond.

And by this time all his military provisions were ready. And whilst he was in the French [court,] he had a kind message from the Duke of Brittany, and with offer of auxiliary forces, the which the earl most gratefully accepted and prayed they might be sent to Harfleur, where his ships lay, and whither all his soldiers were to march, and whither all his necessaries and all his men and habiliments and instruments of w*ar were* to be conveyed. And in the end of July, 1485, he took his leave of the King of France and of his most noble and most favourable co*nfederate*, Madame de Beaujeu, and promising all humble and mos*t* faithful and thankful remembrance of the great l*ove* and graces of the king her brother and of her, and then departed from Paris and went into Normandy to the [port of] Ha[r]fleur, and where he met with 2,000 Bret[ons sent thither by the duke] most honourably.

But b[efore he came to Harfleur, he made some stay at Rouen, receiving advertisement] / which much troubled him and greatly distempered him, **95** and that was that the Lady Elizabeth, the eldest daughter of King Edward, should forthwith be married to King Richard; and to the end to seek by all means to prevent this match, he made the more haste to land in England, hoping that by the means and skill and arts and practice of his friends that treaty of marriage should be frustrated. Upon this marriage depended all the chief hope of the earl, and which of necessity must be effected, or else that his fairest and haply his best colour for title would fade and fail him. Yet if that should happen, he had so ready and so present a wit, and that he w*as* so good and provident (as aforesaid) as that he was upon any sudden chance instantly provided with counsels and resolutions for all fortunes. And thereupon he straight resolved that if he missed the marriage of the Lady Elizabeth he would marry her sister the Lady Cecily.

But ere he could do anything in these matters, the other plot and hope was also checked and crossed. For in the next packet which [c]ame out of England to him he was certified that the Lady [Ce]cily was newly married. But yet so quick and ready was his conceit *and* counsel and his resolution that by and by after the receiving of that advertisement, he left the purpose of that treaty, and he conferred ab*out it with* himself and his most wise and noble friends which were with him in Britanny ([th]ey were for the most part Welshmen). And one of them told that he knew *where* there was a very good wife for him, and with whom he should [no]t only receive a rich and large, bountiful portion, but also great *cel*ebrity of noble*s*, and with much [Polydore Vergil] esteemed allies and friends; and that this was a daughter of the foresaid Sir William Herbert, who was [a] gentleman of a noble family and had much noble alliance, and was a [chi]ef man in authority and power in the south parts of Wales (and as hath *been* before declared, **Liber I**), and whose elder daughter was not long [before] married to the Earl of Northumberland.

The Earl of Pembroke in[stan]tly embraced this motion and this alliance and sent to the Earl of [North]umberland, his new and secret friend, to solicit and to mediate his *alliance* with the younger sister of his wife the countess. And he required and *urged* him to be very careful and very earnest in this nuptial negotiation. *And the* Earl of Richmond made full accompt to be assured of the barons *and* of the best and greatest part of Wales, and easily by their means *to bear the ti*tle and possession of the principality of Wales. And th*is* [had been] a great fortune and an high advancement to a [banished poor earl.

[And] the better to confirm him in the hope and in the *expectation thereof*, **95v** [Dr Morgan,] a grave man [and a good] / politician advertised the Earl of Richmond that all the nobility and the people of Wales were exceedingly well affected to him and were all at his devotion and service. And therefore the doctor advised the earl, albeit he knew nothing of the earl's purpose to marry in Wales, yet for other good causes he counselled and advised the earl that he should descend in some part of Wales, and nowhere else, and he would land secretly. And thereupon the news was very acceptable and welcome to the earl, and whereas he had before been doubtful where to land, now he resolved to land in Wales.

And forthwith he put all necessary things aboard his ships, and he embarked his troops of soldiers at the port of Harfleur, and in the month of July, and then he weighed anchor and set sails. And he had a merry wind and a fair passage, and *with* which in seven days he arrived safely at Milford Haven in Pembrokeshire, his nat[ive] country. And there he was with all joy and courtesies and caresses received of his kinsfolks and friends and countrymen. And after he had reposed and ref[reshed] himself [and] his army a little while in that harbour, he marched to a [port] called Haverford-west, and where he was also very well entertai[ned.] For he was now come amongst his British or Welsh kinsfolks. And they bade him w*elcome, and very* kindly and very heartily welcome, and they did not use him and caress *him* favourably and h[onourably] only as their friend and countryman and kinsman, but also [as] a prince descended from the ancient kings and princes of Wal[es.]

96* And whilst he was in Wales, Sir Rice ap Thomas, Sir Water Herbert, Sir John Savage, Sir Gilbert Talbot, who disloyally drew his young nephew, the Earl of Salop, into this rebellion to the Earl of Richmond, brought or sent their forces and power to him, and in good plenty. And in brief, many Welsh and false knights and esquires and many perfidious and rebellious Englishmen of all qualities and inhabitants of the countries thereabout and near Wales came well armed and well resolved to fight for the earl and to make him king.

And the earl marched to Shrewsbury, where he found all pressed and ready at his service and commandment. And from thence he went to

Lichfield and had purpose to go to London if the [king had not stopped his way.] By that time, Sir Gi[lbert Talbot came with the forces of the Ea]rl of Salop, his nephew, to the earl, and anon [the] most ingrate and of all other the most perfidious baron of all, the [Lord] Stanley, and his brother Sir William, and the Earl of Oxford, and *m*any other had brought and joined their forces with the army *of* the earl. And then Sir Walter Hungerford and Sir Thomas [Bour]chier and divers other treacherously forsook the king and fled to *his* greatest enemy, the Earl of Richmond.

[Philip de Commynes saith that the Lord Stanley brought 26,000 men to the Earl of Richmond, his son-ally, but our stories say but 5,000 at the most.]

[T]he king, at that time when the earl landed and whilst he marched through Wales, lay [at] Nottingham, and he had spies upon the earl. And he presume*d* [he had a great] and a mighty army ready to encounter him. For the Earl of Northumberland and the Lord St[anley promised] to come to him [with all their powers, but unfaithfully] failed and forsook him. But there were many other valiant and most noble lords and knights, and which stood faithfully *by him*, as namely [John, Du]ke of Norfolk, Marshal of England, the Earl [of] Surrey, the Earl of Westmorland, and the Viscount [Lo]vell and others, etc.

The king came to Leicester, and the next day [bein]g Sunday, he rode out of the town in the evening *very* gallantly, wearing the royal crown upon his head, [and] accompanied with the said great lords aforesaid and with many other loyal barons and valiant and brave *knights* and gentlemen (for all had not bowed their knees *against him*) nor any loyal and true subject, as I may boldly and truly say. For all they which [came] with arms against the anointed and sacred king, and with purpose to depose *and be*reave him of the crown and of his life, who was [their so]vereign and liege lord and their lawful [anointed king,] were all rebels, and monstrous great *ones*.

Leices[trum inquit Rex] Ricardus, [cum maxima pom]pa, port[ans diadema in] capite. [Chronic]*le* **Croyla[ndensis.]**

For such bearers of arms [are not] to be called enemies, for that is too good a word for them, [as proper to the foreign adversary.] If the subjec*ts* [conspire against their sovereign and take arms against him, they ought to be called perduells, traitors, and rebels, and their wars] / and conflicts not to be termed wars, but seditious tumults and felonious outrages and rebellion[s,] and traitorous acts, and as the divine Plato said in the like case: **Bellum quod Graeci Graecis inferunt non est bellum sed seditio**. And the blood which they shed and the slaughters which they make in their seditions and rebellions are not to be said to be the good fortune of war and the honour of the victors, but the wilful murder and homicides perpetrated by traitorous parricides and by cruel assassins and unnatural murderers. For they kill their own kinsfolks, their own princes, and their own brothers, and their own friends and countrymen, and the lawful magistrates whom they ought to reverence and to preserve. And that these cruel and barbarously unnatural acts [are] **de Criminae Laesae Majestatis omnis, tam divinae quam humanae**: crimes of all treasons, as well against God as against men and against the king.

The diffe[rence between] enemies and rebels.

96v*

[B]ellum subditorum non est bellum sed [sedi]tio.

And this point of law and this doctrine politic would have been made manifest if watchful and circumspect prudence had so ordered and provided, *so that* all majesty had been drawn and stretched out, *and all* lawful arms and power of justice *had been* in readiness in those remote countries when these seditious persons arriv[ed] and when they marched toward their rendezvous, and that they had assaulted and charged those per*duells with force*, and lawful and more mighty arms, and had duly

97

suppressed them and had then apprehended their chief commanders into the presence of Justice. Then you should *have seen* her, or in her place her lieutenants, the learned and reverent *judges* of this kingdom, tell the proudest of them that they were felons, murderers *and* rebels. And then it would, and also plainly, have appeared who these men were, and what th*ey* were, who was their captain and what his title was, and they would have been taught that **Arma quibus lex non utitur, [legem] impugnant, et sicarii et latrones dicuntur, qui arma lege [non praeci]piente tractant**, as a good and a grave man hath truly pronounced.

[Joannes Sarisberiensis in **Policratico Lib**. VI]

But these troops of rebels were so much increased and grown that they were able to make their own way in despite of law *and of* royal faith and of justice. And in this proud and rebellious manner *they* passed boldly and safely to their rendezvous in Leicestershire. And there all these *traitors* were joined and united in one army, and all took part with the Earl of *Richmond*. And they yielded themselves and their arms and their faiths (if they had *any*) unto him and to his service and to the advancement of him and his cause. And they *met* their true and lawful sovereign there; they presumed to *give* [battle] to him.

And so (happily or unhappily) it fell out that [fortune] favoured them upon that day of battle. Therefore, they were afte[r re]puted and renowned
98 for brave captains and valiant, and therefore wo[rthy] / and happy conquerors. And some of them were honoured [with the] dignities and titles of barons and of earls. And some were made knights, and s*ome were* made bishops and archbishops, and others were made [great officers of the kingdom.] And success did honour and bless the enterpr[ise. And as it is
96v* well observed by a wise man,] / **Hon[esta quae]dam scelera successus facit.** And a[gain, **Prosperum ac fe]lix scelus virtus vocatu[r.]**

[Seneca in **Hippolito, Idem** in **Hercule Furente**]

99* [But when fortune is adverse to those gallants that they] / be overcome and taken, then they are the most wretched and most base, the most reprobate persons in the world, etc. Examples hereof we have infinite, both ancient and modern, as namely the Titans, Absalom, Eribastus, and Catilina, Spartacus, M. Cethegus, the Gracchi, Belisarius, Cario, etc., and m*any more*. And here at home, the fame and shame of the reason and fall of Sir John Oldcastle, Wyatt, Owen Glendower, and of the late earls of Westmorland and of Desmond, and many more, are me*ntioned in our stories*.

But to leave these examples and come to the relation of the affairs of those armies, now that these two armies, i.e., the army of the king and the army of the rebel Lancastrians, were now come to Redmore Heath and in the view the one of the other, and were approaching and disposed themselves to fight. And in the morning early, before the battle, there was some inference and consultation held in the tent of the king with those noble and principal gentlemen whom he best trusted. And it was there reported and affirmed that there was many of those principal men, and in whom the king was much affied, who were secretly fled to the earl and had forsaken the king, and would fail him when their faith came to trial and in the chief business; and those men following the example of Bourchier and of Savage and of other who had a little before revolted *f*rom the king. And some of them turned rebels even in the instant whilst the king armed himself and was ready to fight.

And it was also then and there discovered plainly that the Earl [of] Northumberland was turned Lancastrian, albeit he had faithfully p*romi*sed to assist and def*end th*e king, and not without good cause, for the king had a long time [be]en unto him a very kind and good noble friend in his private life, and since very gracious to him. And therefore he affied much in his fidelity and forces. But yet for all this, he fa*iled him*, and he *sec*retly and suddenly revolted to the earl's party, and therefore in the conflict he stood aloof as neutral.

And moreover, in the said consultation it was then also *r*emembered and urged that whereas the Lord Stanley, whom *t*he king very much loved and had much advanced and made him Constable of England, and who faithfully had promised to [bri]ng all his friends and forces to the king and to make [the] king more confident in him, had left his son, [Geo]rge Stanley prisoner or hostage with the king; yet [not]withstanding this, *he* left the king most *treacherously* [by the persu]asions and [subt]le seductions of his wife, the earl's mother. And this he proved true, for *he* [brough]t a great army to the earl, and the which consisted [of] 26 thousand men (if Philip de Commynes be not mistaken, for our own stories have but 5[000); and indeed it was a very great defection. For all the lords and all the people] were alienated from him, fled and revolted as suddenly as they came **101** swearing to him when they made him king, such was their perfidious inconstancy. And this happened by the few subtle and malicious persuasions and arts of Morton and of some few other the chief plotters of the rebellion.

And those are the doubts and mischiefs and treasons were declared and debated now; but it was too late. And therefore there remained none other matter for consultation or for counsel, but only to persuade the king to save himself suddenly by flight and to retire himself with all speed to some safe and strong and remote place, and but for a little while. For they told and assured him that if the camp of the enemies broke up and were once dissolved, which could not continue long, [i]t would never be reassembled nor brought together again. And they (*and* so the better to persuade and to encourage him to resolve to fly) had provided ready at the door of the general's tent a fair and a very swift and strong horse. And they offered and presented this horse to the king, and they de*s*ired and pray him earnestly to mount that good horse and to be gone with all speed. For they said that now otherwise the inevitable dangers and evil were so near as in a moment it would be too late to depart.

But this counsel w*as* very unpleasing and very distasteful to the king, for he scorned very much to [fly.] And the*n* his noble friends sought to terrify him and with these threats and frights of strange porte[nts and] prodigies which were seen and were for tokens of his great calamities *which would fa*ll upon him if he would not, whilst opportunity served, avoid them. And then also some *of* them repeated the rhyming prediction which was given to the Duke [of] Norfolk, and although it seemed trivial, yet it was very true and proph[etical:]

Jack of Norfolk, be not too bold,
For Dickon thy master is bought and sold.

And in brief, they told the king plainly and often that he was betrayed by som[e of] his chief friends, who were newly gone to the Lancastrians, and

had carried the g[reat] strength and power of his army with them. Wherefore again and again, and very earnes[tly,] they prayed him and urged him to be gone and instantly to take the commodity of that s[wift horse,] and if he thought best, to go into the north parts, where he had most friends and the *chief* persons and the most places at his devotion, and to remain there upon his gua[rd] but for a short time. For they told and assured him that the army of the enemy *could not* long continue, and their
102 victuals and money would soon be spent and *cut off*, / and by his better and more sharp sword.

But the king was so resolute, or rather so wilful and so obstinate, and even fatally, as that none of these counsels, nor persuasions, nor provident care, nor warnings, nor terrors, nor prodigies, nor prophecies, nor any vehement intimations of the great dangers and mischiefs present and imminent, could prevail with the king or induce him to put on a mind or purpose so base as to run away or to seek safety by his fligh*t*, and by such distance and absence to be secured until that viole*nt* tempest of the rebellious furors was overblown and passed. But this prince was so jealous of his honour and of the reputa[tion] of his valour, and so much scorned and abhorred the imputation *and* taint of cowardice and of fear, as that he resolved to adventure his fort[unes] *and* his life and his crown and all rather than by flight to save himself *or* to shun and avoid that present and dangerous conflict or battle with his traitorous enemies. [And,] as it were in defiance of fate and of fortune, he pronounced *and* protested solemnly and peremptorily that whatsoever should [be]tide him, he was constantly purposed to stay and to try and *a*bide the worst, so long as his life and his forces and his sword would maintain his resolution.

And this might seem to be a wi[lful and] desperate speech if he had not afterward by a particular action made demonstration of the hope – and of the great hope – which he had of victory and of good success in the battle of that day, and that he spake not these words aforesaid in despair either of his good fortune or *of* his good sword. And he built his hope upon this platform [or] plot, and the which, although it was very dangerous and difficult, yet it was bravely and valiantly and most nobly projected and also attempted, [which] was this: this brave prince, because he knew well that the Earl of Richmond [was] ambitious and appetent of renown and worldly glory; and that he *knew* also that he had small skill in military arts and in val*orous exer*cise and *prac*tice of arms; and that he was far inferior to him therein as in courage and contempt of peril; therefore the *king* [devised,] in the manner and lieu of a stratagem and of a peculiar and strange *device* [that as soon] as both the armies were appr[oached and ready to charge] the one the other, [he would] put [himself before the troops and make such signals as are usual for inviting the earl (being the Captain General of his forces)]
102v to come forth and to enter into single combat with him, etc., thus so to bring the earl to fight hand to hand with him, and nothing doubting of the victory, because he knew the earl's chivalry to be much inferior to his.

[Why King Richard wore the crown at Bosworth]

And the king, because he would be the better known, would when he made the challenge he had the royal crown of England upon his helmet, and that was the fairest and most *as*sured mark of a king which could be. And this was one of the causes why [King] Richard wore the crown in the day of the battle of Bosworth, but not the only cause, nor that which is brought and rendered b[y] Polydore Vergil: to wit, that King Richard wore the crown *up*on that day because he made account that that day should [ei]ther give end to his life and reign, or else beginning to his better reign. But this cannot be the reason thereof, and by reason that the king wore the royal ensign upon his head in the town of Leicester three days before. And he wore it when he departed from that town upon the Sunday before, and when he rode in great royal pomp and in martial magnificence toward Bosworth. Now these were no days of the trial of his fortune by battle. But doubtless the king chiefly wore [the] crown upon his head that all men might see and consider there the most notable foul fault of disloyalty; for the crown was a certain token of the royal majesty and of the sovereignty *of* him which weareth it. And that albeit the rebels had made and nominated another king, there attended upon hi*m, it was plain* that he had no crown nor might wear one, and so consequently he was no *king*. But that he himself which wore the crown and possessed it was the only and the true and lawful king, and that therefore all [true] and faithful subjects ought to obey and to follow and to serve him and [de]fend him according to the divine laws and for the obligation of their allegiance.

And thus much for his wearing of the crown. And to proceed with the matter of the combat: the king (according to this foresaid plot and purpose) as soon as the armies were confronted and preparing to fight, came forth, and with suc*h* signs of challenge to combat as aforesaid, summoned the earl to that single fight. And the ear[l] seemed gladly to accept the challenge, and pricked his [horse for]ward. And he came a good round pace, and very g[allantly and brav]ely, as if he had a full purpose to [fight, which is testified by a good author: **Comes Richmontiae directe super regem Ricardum processit**.] / But this career was but dissembled, and rather done for a train to draw on the king into his deadly snares, or else for that he liked not the furious approach of the ki[ng.] For suddenly the earl stopped, and withal he cunningly (and as mannerly as he could) he retired, and Mars became badly retr[ograde;] and he recovered by this means the vanguard of his battle. But King Richard pursued him so hastily and fiercely.

[Chronicle Croyland]

103

And the earl for his more safety put himself by the standard, and being the place of the most strength and security of the army. And thither also the king followed him and *made* his way through his enemy's troops with his sword, and cam[e] to the standard, and there with his own hands slew the stand[ard] bearer Sir William Brandon, father of Charles Brandon, [after]ward Duke of Suffolk. And he made accompt to have next despatched the earl. But the earl's men interposed themselves and [preserved him. Amongst them was] Sir John Cheyney, sometimes Master of King Edward's Horses. But the King Richard struck him [from his horse to] the earth.

And anon the king was environed with such multitudes [of] his rebellious enemies, and who all charged their weapons upon him. And they mangled and gored him extremely, and ga*ve* to him many cruel wounds. And they slew him upon the p[lain. And] thus Richard failed of his stratagem devised for this desperate[e plunge.] And the *r*eason was because it was his ill hap to meet with an [e]nemy or antagonist who loved no combats, nor would adven[ture his] person alone and hand to hand with his adversary. For if he had *so* done, then without doubt Richard, being so far superior *t*o Henry in the skill of arms and in chivalry, and also *in* courage and in hardiness, would have slain him in the combat, and not only so freed himself from his seditious practices, but also have brought an end to all other tumults [and] traitorous practices against himself.

And therefore the king's device *and* resolution in so desperate a case was commendable and politic and wise and very *hero*ical. For if that had well succeeded, he had made an end of all such quarre*ls, and* he should have enjoyed all peace and prosperity. For there was no ambitious person besid*es* who would trouble the king or the state as a proud affectator *of the crown*. Neither was there any man else whom the barons *and the people* loved as that they would adventure the*ir allegiance and their live*s for him. And so all

103v seditions, / conflicts, and troubles had been at an end.

But **non sic visum est superis**, and the king had ill fortune in his enterprise. And ill fortune is accounted a vice in military adventures. For in the wars, the fortune and success and event commend or condemn the *cou*nsel and the actor and the actions. And for this cause the king is reputed to be vicious and namely to be rash and to be obstinate and to be furious [and ov]erweening his own strength and courage, and of which *fa*ults more shall be said anon.

[But] to return to the matter of the battle and to conclude it. Both the battles at the instant joined, and their armies courageously en[countered.] And there was a cruel fight and much bloodshed on both sides. But the party of the earl was much stronger and more numerous, and therefore they prevailed and had the victory. And thus not only the king was lost and slain, but also very many of his most noble and most loyal servants and subjects were sorely wounded or slain outright in the field, or else, being taken, some of them were pu[t] into prisons. And as far as the battle was fought, th*e* Earl of Richmond was victor.

105*

Henry [of Richmond] crown[ed in the] fie[ld]

God gave [the crown] to Tedor, and so it [was] **θεοῦ δῶρον** *or The*odore: the gift [of God] to this earl so sur[named] Theodore

The crown which King Richard wore in the field was brought to the Earl of Richmond, and the Lord [Sta]nley, his father-allié, put it upon his head, [and] he was then forthwith hailed and styled Henry VII, King of England, etc. And this [was by the divine ordinance,] as the Prior of Croyland hath observed; and thus he writeth: **Ad postremum gloriosa victoria [Comiti] Richmondiae iam soli Regi una cum pretio[sissi]ma corona quam Ricardus Rex antea gest[avit] caelitus data est.** And so this gift of the crown and [his patern]al name Theodore may seem to be fatal and divinely due unto him, the on[e and the other be]ing **θεοῦ δῶρον**, that is, the gift of God.

[And th]us Henry, Earl of Richmond, son of Edmund ap Meredith [ap Tudor, alias] of Hadham, Earl of Richmond, and Mar[garet, daugh]ter and heir of John Beaufort, Duke [of Somerset, ob]tained to the crown of England [and the roy]al fortunes [of Richard, which he might have kept and

105v* enjoyed if] / life had been ordained for him, and if he had not omitted some

[Omissions and commissions of King Richard]

few good and needful businesses and committed some errors in that catastrophe of his reign. And his fault of omission (and a chief fault and error, and touched and observed before) was that he dealt not with the Marquess Dorset nor with the Earl of Devon, nor with his brother the Bishop of Exeter, nor with the Bishop of Ely, nor with the Lord Stanley and the rest of the chief conspirators and traitors who were in his power and a long time unarmed, as he did with the Duke of Buckingham or with the Lord

Hastings, as I urged in the former book. For if he had cut off their heads or but bestowed them in sure prisons, he had prevented their rebellions and his own overthrow and saved his own life and his crown and the st*ate*, and in this manner he having provided for his safety had done well, and that which was fit and convenient to be d*one* by a just and provident and a happy prince (**ut supra**, and as I said before). And this for the fault of omission.

And now for those of *com*mission, the which he committed upon the day of bat*tle*, and the faults which were his scorn and contempt of his [ene]my: his furious and rash pursuit of revenge, his surquidry and overweening of [Contempt] his own p[ower] and valour, the which are all unlucky and fa[tal] vices and haunt those men still and closely, **qui ferociter [ac] praepropere omnia** [Tacitus] **Historia,** **agentes contemnendis quam ca[ven]dis hostibus sunt meliores**, as Cornelius [**Lib.** 4] Tacitus, a grave man, hath well observed, and therewithal *soundly* taxeth sharply and shortly those faults of haste or rashness and of contempt. For [Rashness] the fault of temerit[y] or rashness alone had been too much. For it is both foolish and unlucky: **Temeritas praeterquam quod st[ulta] est etiam infelix.** *Livius*, **Lib.** 22 And therefore they are very carefully so shunned by a good captain. For as Augustus Ca[esar] observed, **Nihil minus perfecto duci quam [festi]natio et** [Suetonius] in **temeritas convenit**. **Augustus** For he which is [rash] and hasty in the affairs of war is apt [to fall] into the danger of all traps of treacheries *and en*gines. And by the testimony of the wise [and well-]experienced Polybius, **Temerit[as et** Polybius, **Lib.** 3] **impietas prae]ter rationem ad om[nes insidias et es]*c*[as obnoxia est.]**

[The fault of contempt aforesaid is in the same way of perdition. This was well known] / and reproved and taxed by Great Alexander in those his **106*** words: **Nil tuto in hoste dispicitur; quam spreveris valentiorem** Curtius, **Lib.** 5 **negligentia facis.** And the Christian philosopher had learned**, nihil est in bello perniciosius quam hostem quantumvis imbecillum contemnere**. Erasmus in **Epistolis** And this contempt and scorn is always accomplished with an overweening and pride of a man's own wit and power. And it is also a presage and foretoken of his ruin and overthrow, and even by the testimony of the Holy Ghost: **Comminutionem praecedit superbia, et ruinam elatio spiritus.** Proverbs, **Cap.** 16 And Strigelius, glosing upon this text, saith, **Superbiam comitatur error in consiliis, errorem infelicitas.**

The errors and the pains of this pride and contempt are prettily figured in the apologue of the Eag*le*, a proud and a scornful creature, and of the despised and poor and abject Scarabeius, or hornet. And thus the mythologers take it: the Eagle, holding the Scarab to be a base and contemptible *in*sect and of no power nor credit, used her proudly and *dis*dainfully, and did also to her some wrong. The Scarab *thereupon* took this so ill as that she resolved to be revenged of *th*e Eagle, and for the taking of this revenge she attended the time convenient, and that was when the Eagle did sit and lay her eggs. And when the time came, the Scarab *al*so watched the time when the Eagle would go out of *her* nest to prey and solace herself *after* her custom and kind. *An*d the times being come and fitly offering occasion of the *ta*king her revenge, the hornet climbed up into the *Ea*gle's nest and presently threw out the eggs down *to* the ground and broke them all to pieces. And then *she* sought out the Eagle's medicinal and precious *jewel, the* Aetites, or hatching stone, and she cast that away.

And thus this contemptible and vile animal took her *reve*nge upon the proud and scornful and mighty Eagle, the king *of* birds and the chief esquire of the God Jupiter. This *is only* a fable, and the moral is easy to be conceived by the *Rea*der. And shortly, it is a good warning for the *strong* and potent persons not to contemn nor scorn *their rivals*, how mean or how weak soever they *appear*.

106v* I have praised the resolution of King Richard which he made to single out the Earl of Richmond and to fight with him hand to hand, and called it a gallant and heroical and most noble resolution. And that it may be objected *that I* scoff at it afterwards and have reproved and taxed him for the attempt and act or enterprise (and I confess that I have said th*is, and both appro*ved him and condemned him), and the practice and execution of that re*proof* may be thought a levity in me: but yet I am not contrary to myself, but I still do and will still maintain the praise of his courage and resolution in that attempt, for I hold it *noble*. But I mislike his fortune and his judgement that he so unhappily made choice of a man which loved [no combats.] But otherwise I hold it not only noble and heroical, but also very proper to princes and *to this* prince, and even kind and also natural to this king, and to seek such encounters.

For I find in our stories that the royal Plantagenets have very often demanded and offered single combat to kings and princes being personally in their armies, and in the absence of the sovereigns to their chieftains or Captains General. As, *for* example, King William Conqueror challenged the combat of King Harold, and others did the *same*. [And] before, there was a combat fought betwixt King Edmund Ironside and Cnutus, the Danish king, for the [whole] k[ingdom] of [England.]And the kings Richard I and Edward I in Palestine against *the Turks* [ch]allenged the combat with some pagan princes. And King Edward III and Henry V sought and demanded the like combat with the kings of France.

[The challenge of James V, King of Scots, to Thomas, Duke of Norfolk]

And in the last age, the most valiant prince James V, King of Scotland, desired to fight in person with the Captain General of the King of England, namely Thomas, Lord Howard, Duke of Norfolk. And he gladly accepted the challenge. But the king required that the count[ry] or the lands which were then in controversy might be the [stake, and] to be **brabium victoris** (the prize of the victor), and which the gener[al could not grant,] because those lands were the inheritance of the king his master and not his, and therefore he had no right nor power to *make* those lands the wager and prize, as King James required. But the duke offered to pawn and to adventure better lands of his own upon the [combat.] But that offer was not accepted, and so the combat failed.

[But indeed the better end of those challenges and combats,] *and* their good judgement, proceedeth from the divine virtue, mercy, and piety. For the qua[rrel taketh end, and by that pious] and most noble [single adventure all] the innocent [blood of] both the [armies] is saved and [preserved from] shedding. And those provocations are also frequently occurrent in [the] ancient foreign stories and in the Latin and Greek and French and Italian and Spanish poesies. And it is reported in them and with many good words, that the kings and the generals have very often fought hand to hand in their battles.

Valiant and adventurous princes and great captains held it to be a great honour and most proper to them t*o be* matched and paired in arms with their equals and peers – that is, chieftains and chieftains, marshals with marshals, and dukes with dukes, and colonels *with* colonels, etc. And so kings desire to be encountered *with people* of their own singular and supereminent degr*ee and* like sovereign quality. For kings are p*eers of* none else, as our grave Bracton h*ath related. Thus also the Great Alexander did insinuate* / and acknowledge, being at the famous Olympic **agones** or 107 games, where he, being asked if he would contend in any of those noble and festival and ludicral conflicts and heroical exercises, he answered that he would gladly make one if there were any kings which would be his **antagonistes** and contend with him. But there were no kings – that is, no peers for the King Alexander.

Neither did this our King Richard meet with any of his peers nor with any of the heroical progeny of the foresaid antique princes, nor yet with any Plantagenets at Bosworth. For if he had there accepted, he should have sped better, or not so ill, for they would have come forth from their troops and willingly and fairly h[ave] encountered him singly, after the manner of other brave and courageous princes *with their* honourable and courteous enemies, and sought only honour and victory. And their manner was *to temper* their enmity and ill affections with noble caresses and honourable usage. And the example of this sat*isfied* men of invincible courage and most adventurous upon all danger. And this is very memorable in that royal family: that there was never any tainted of cowardice.

The va **** ch ****

But the manner of princes to combat and fight in their own persons is discontinued and lost long since, and they are now so f*ar* from hazarding their persons in singular fight as that they [t]hink not themselves safe anywhere in the army, no, not under the standard nor in the tents and trenches, nor in the midst of the main battle, but only at home and in their castles and palace or *court*.

P[rinces go not to the] c[amp]

And there is a late writer who ascribeth the beginning of this abstinence from arms and absence from the army of the great princes to Philip II, King of Spain. But he is therein deceived, for I say that I know the contrary and can refell that report by the testimony of most ancient stories of the kings of Syria and of Persia: to wit, that many of those kings did abstain from the wars and from the camp, as you may read in Herodotu[s, in Diodorus, in Trog]us Pom[peius, and the like. And I have also observed in t]he Roman stories written by Suetonius, Dion, Plutarch, Tacitus, and others that Augustus Caesar, **post adeptum [e]t firmatum imperium domi se cont[u]*n*[d]it, et bella [g]essit, proelia confecit, provincias invisit, rebelles con[tu]*n*dit, et gentes barbaras subegit per proconsules prae[to]res, per legatos**, etc.

And if King Richard had considered *tha*t the Earl of Richmond was wise and politic and [most apt] to follow great and safe examples, he would have had [little] or no hope that this earl his adversary would *ever* come to handstrokes with him. But notwithstand*ing, King* Richard being now grown desperate / *truste*d in the joining of the battle, and whereof he had little 104 cause to hope by *reason that* the forces of the adverse side were much greater and many more in number *than his own*, as hath been declared before. Yet he had and might have good hope [to overcome] the earl in single combat if he could have drawn him to have *fought with him in* person therein. For doubtless King Richard was the better horseman *and the better* soldier, and had much more skill and more courage and valour than the earl, and [as much] advantage of the earl in the monomachy as the earl had of him [in his multi]tudes of troops. And therefore in all reason Richard was the *indisputab*le victor in the combat, and so consequently of all his forces in the adverse host.

But yet suppose that he might *have received* deadly wounds in that single conflict, and at that instant when *he struck* and slew his enemy, and that they were both with mutual wounds *destroyed (and tha*t hath happened). Yet it would much have comforted and cont*ented him at the end* of his life that he had overthrown and destroyed his mortal *enemy:* ***Solamen*** **miseris socium est habuisse malorum**, as it was well sung of one. And by another, and as well said, **munu** *******************. *And in the m*anner of these old heroic and vindicative spirits, he would have comfort *of his victory* and honour and joy of his vengeance, and said with them, and with good contentment, and even with exultation, and in th*ese words*:

[*Vergil*] **numquam omnes hodie moriemur inulti**.

For men of so great and high courage esteemed the revenge of injuries and the rep*roof of dishonour* above life and all other worldly goods and blessings. And for these causes *the* king thirsted so vehemently after his revenge, and in the seeking thereof he dealt in *thi*s manner as is aforesaid, [**107v***] and so proudly and scornfully, / and thus desperately and most unhappily adventured hi*s* fortunes and his life and his crown and set them at a low rate for the reparation of his honour and good fame, much wounded and scandalized by his enemy, and for a revenge and punishment of him who had conspired his death and sought by all means to destroy him and his house.

But otherwise and at other time, this noble prince committe*d* not these errors. These his faults, rashness and contempt and overweening of his forces, were new faults in him, for in his former times, after the heat of his youth was p*ast and* he came to know a*nd* to understand the business of the world, he would do nothing either in civil or military affairs without good advisement and ripe deliberation, and he would wait and attend the best advantages and fairest opportunities.

But these new faults of the prince were ill-abod*ing* as they were new. And they were always fatal errors and unlucky faults, and sinister prognosti*cations* and foretokens of calamities and of great evil to come, *and as it is* observed by the learned, as well theologians as h*u*[ma]*n*ists, that when God is minded to scourge a state or king, a prince or any other great person, he taketh his understandi*ng* and discretion and counsel from him, or so darkenet[h and] obscureth those best and intellective facu[lties that he] can make no good nor [proper use of them, and so, when his divine will is purposed to change the families of kings, and as the potter in Jeremy to [**108***] break one] / jar and to make another, then also he taketh the counsel and understanding from the man whom he purposeth to throw down, and he [**[Hinc dici potest Rex a deo status]**] followeth false counsels and errors, as the apostle discovered: **Deus tradidit illum in reprobum sensum**.

And this was also observed by the wise heathens, and thus for example by one of them. First,

[**Lycurgus poeta**]
Iratus ad poenam si quis trahit deus.
Auferre mentem talibus primum solet,
Caliginemque offundit ut suas ruant

In clades, sibi quas noxiis
Averserunt ultro consiliis suis.

And another of them saith shortly and fully in the purpose:

Quos perdere instituit Jupiter,
illos dementat.

And thus hereof very divinely writeth another heathen man: **Mentem hominibus nonnumquam obscurat supera illa mens qua*e* cuiuscunque fortunam mutare constituit, consilia eius corrumpit.**

But we will cease to meddle further with these high and mystical judgements, and leave them with reverence to the secret and infinite and unsearchable wisdom of God. And we will proceed with the rest of the tragical story [o]f this unfortunate king, and whom punishments and miseries and wrongs and apprehensions left not in his death nor in his grave, and whereof I will bring some instances here, and for the clearer demonstration hereof.

First then, albeit he was slain and cruelly murdered, and *t*he quarrels and wars at end, and the Earl of Richmond king and quietly possessed of the crown and of all the royal *for*tunes of King Richard, yet then, and after all this, there *w*ere raised and maintained false slanders against *him* and against his true and faithful friends and constant *fo*llowers. And (which was worse) his [crue]l enemies made such haste to exercise their endless malice as that he was no sooner slain [but they fall upon his body,] being before all mangled and gashed with many *fatal* wounds and all dyed in his blood, and they stripped [his royal corse quite] naked, and then imitating the vultures [or wolves, tore and rent his flesh and carcase. Some trailed it on the ground, others pulled him by the beard and hairs and spurned and kicked him.

[Occidit in bello miseranda caede Ricardus, [Dr John Herd in
Crinibus attractus dum saeviit hostis amarus, etc.] **History Anglica**] **108v***

Those and such other be the words of his lamentable and miserable story, and then the carnifices, having not yet satisfied their inhumane eyes nor their malicious hearts with these cruelties and with the so miserable spectacles, they laid this prince's dead body upon a jade, as the butcher layeth a flayed calf when he carrieth him to the market, and so basely and reproachfully conveyed his body to Leicester. And in one word, they used this sacred cor*se* of a king so unreverently, so inhumanely, and so barbarously as is almost incredible. Neither shall I need to aggravate this so foul and so monstrous [a]n outrage and injury, and the which I may call an impious and sacrilegious injury, being done to the body of a sacred person and of an anointed king (as I said before), because it is so notoriously known in all parts, and so farforth as that it sticketh as a stigmatical brand of perpetual reproach and infamy to the cruel and barbarous actors and authors thereof, and much to *their shame*.

[Exer]cises *of cruelty* [upon the body of King Richard]

But how in a contrary wise a [strange prince, William the Conqueror, to his eternal honour, dea]lt with the body of King Harold, an usurper and his perfidious enemy, this *example* shows: and that he severely punished the barbarous [soldier which hacked the thigh of the dead king, and then with all courtesy caused the body to be delivered to his mother to be honourably buried as it should please her, which funeral was solemnly celebrated in his own monastery at Waltham, as Henry Huntingdon and Matthew Paris affirm.]

And at the same time also (and herebefore remembered), and upon cold blood and after the battle, many valiant and faithful subjects of King Richard were put to death at Leicester and elsewhere. And it was not raged enough yet, nor yet revenge nor vengeance enough was not yet taken, according to the minds and malice of his enemies. For in November following, there was a Parliament held, wherein the said King Richard was attainted [of a stran]ge crime, a crime which a king cannot commit against his subject, and name*ly* the king was attainted (and very strangely and injuriously) of High Treason, together with the other subjects. And they were men of great worth, and many of the*m* noblemen and nobly descended; and their titles in the story show them to be signal persons and faithful liegemen, for they are there called and entitled chief aiders and assistants of King Richard at the Battle of Bosworth:

[Noble persons a]ttain[ted by Parlia]ment, [**anno** 1, Henry] VII

As nam[ely] Sir John Howard, Duke of Norfolk and High Ma[rshal] and High Admiral of England (**ut supra**). And h*e* was also a most wise and a valiant and loyal knight, and of whom there is much honourable mention in th[e] stories of Philip de Commynes and of Enguerr[ant] de Monstrelet, and in many author[s as well] / foreign as domestical. And whereas some say that this Duke John retired himself from the court during the reign of King Richard, they err much therein, for it is certain that he was continually with this king, and ever very near unto him and in great credit with him, and seldom from the king but when he was employed in some great affairs of state. And Sir Thomas More confuteth their opinion plainly, for he affirmeth that the duke was one of the privyest to this prince's counsels and to his doings, even until his death.

109

Sir Thomas More

And Sir Thomas Howard, Earl of Surrey, and son and heir apparent of this duke, and a son worthy [so noble a father,] was al*so* in great favour and credit with King Richard. And he was a faithful and useful servant unto him. And he sped thereafter, for he was *with* the rest of King Richard's loyal servants attainted of High Treason [at] the foresaid Parliament. And as in like manner were Sir Francis Lovell, Viscount Lovell; Sir Walter Devereux, Lord Ferrers of Chartley; Sir [John] de la Zouche; Sir Robert Harington and James Harington; Richard Charleton; Richard Ratcliffe; William Berkeley; William Catesby; [Thomas Broughton]; John Buck; Humphrey Stafford; Thomas Stafford; Robert Middleto[n]; Robert Brakenbury; and John Kendall, Secretary to King Rich*ard*; and Walter Hopton; Geoffrey Saintgermain; Roger Wake; Thomas Pilkingto[n]; William Sapcote and William Brampton; and some heralds at arms and divers knights and gentlemen were then attainted of High Treason for the defending of their liege lord and sovereign.

[Parliament **anno** 1 Henry VII]

And it was enacted by Parliament that they should all stand disabled and forejudged of all manner of honour, estate, dignity, and pre-eminence, and should forfeit to the new king all their castles, manors, lordships, hundreds, franchises, liberties, advousons, privileges, nominations, presentations, tenements, rents, suits, reversions, portions, annuities, pensions, rights, hereditaments, goods, chattels, and debts. These be the words of the said Act of Parliament, and these very severe, and if **ius**, then **ius summum** and in all extremity.

And I would have been glad to have *include*d the noble name of Percy in this roll, and the which I have *observed* in many such rolls and records. And here it had been recorded if the [Earl of Nor]thumerland had been a true and grateful man. For *he had done good* service to King Richard, and he was much favoured, *as I sai*d before. And he came to Redmore He*ath, as the* / Prior of Croyland hath informed me, and you shall be partaker of 109v mine intelligence. And thus he writeth: **In eo loco ubi comes Northumbriae cum satis decenti ingentique milite stabat, nihil adversi, neque datis neque susceptis belli ictibus cernebatur**.

And here I cannot tell how his wisdom and judgement may be commended. For this his manner of standing still and neutrally could not be well taken of either of the generals, for the state of the victory stood in such ambiguity and doubt. For as he had falsely forsaken the one, and he seemed careless of helping and assisting the other, but yet he handled *the* matter so well as that he soon got in good favour and credit with King Henry VII. And he was serviceable and very officious to the king. But it succeeded ill. For he, to please and gratify the king, undertook to levy a hard and grievous tax upon the people of his country. They *t*ook such offence and indignation thereat, and grew into such hatred of him as that they (the *common people) met* him in great troups at a place near to York called Cocklodge, and set upon him and slew him there with some other of his friends.

But to return to the mention and memory of the faithful (but unfortunate) followers and friends of King Richard, and of whom many were slain in the battle and some fled, some were put to death. Yet they were all condemned in Parliament of High Treason, **ut supra**. The foresaid mos[t] valiant Sir John Howard, Duke of Norfolk, was slain in the battle, and (as it was thought) by John, Earl of Oxford. And the author of the story of Croyland seemeth to confirm this opinion, for thus he writeth: **Comes Oxoniae valentissimus miles in eam alam, ubi dux Norfolci[ae] constitutus erat in agro /de Redmore / tam Gallicorum tam Anglicorum militum comitatu stipatus tetendit**, etc.

[The Duke of Norfolk slain by the Earl of Oxford]

And there were then slain of King Richard's part the Lord Ferrers, Sir Richard Ratcliffe, Sir William Conyers, Sir Richard Clarendon, Sir Robert Brakenbury, and divers valiant and faithfu*l persons*. But Sir William Catesby and Sir John Buck and some other knights and men of *honour and* of good quality and of more stirring spirits, and the more witty and politic men, and not well affected to t*he* conqueror, as it was suspected, were beheaded at Leicester two days after the battle. And that was upon St Bartholemew's D[ay.] And it was another Bartlemy such as was in France in our time, when the great and cruel massacre of the Protestants was acted, and all such cruel and barbarous slaughters are now thereof St Barthelemies, and Bartelmies [simply, in a perpetual] stigma of that butchery.

A*nd there were some* which escaped that dismal day and *hid* themselves 110 until the storm of the bloody and cruel rage was overpassed. And here, before I go any farther, I must answer an objection which will be made by some against my saying that Thomas, Earl of Surrey was one of those which escaped out of the battle and saved his life by flight, because they hold an opinion (or error, as I think) that this earl submitted himself to the new king at Bosworth immediately after the overthrow. But this must not be believed of men of jud[ge]ment and who understand the state of those businesses.

[The Earl of Surrey escaped at Bosworth]

For this [is] certain, that the Earl of Richmond resolved most constantly and most cruelly to cut off all those noblemen and wor*thy* and wise men which had faithfully loved and served King Rich[ard, holding] them to be men most dangerous for his estate and to his safe possession of the cro*wn*. And therefore they were most feared and most hated of him. And [after] the Roman manner, he secretly proscribed them. And *these men* were *the* Duke of Norfolk, Thomas, Earl of Surrey, Francis, Viscount Lovell, Wal*ter* Ferrers of Chartley, Sir John de la Zouche, and Sir Humphrey *and* Sir Robert Stafford, brothers, Sir Robert and Sir James Har*ington*, Sir Thomas Broughton, Sir Richard Charleton, Sir Richard *Ratcliffe*, Sir Walter Conyers, Sir William Catesby, Sir John Buck, *William Berkeley*, Sir Robert Middleton, Sir Walter Hopton, Sir Robert Brak*enbury*, Sir Richard *Watkins*, Sir Geoffrey Saintgermain, Sir Rog*er Wake*, the Secretary Kendall, Thomas Pilkington, William Sapcote, *William Brampton*, Andrew Ratt, and some others whose names are partly in the roll[s] kept in the Chapel of the Convertites in Chancery Lane, and partly were omitted by the scribes.

And so many of these as could be taken or were not slain in the battle were beheaded the next day at Leicester most cruelly and most unjustly. And those of this list which fled and escaped that present scourge and violent and bloody fury of the execu*tion* escaped *and* survived, as namely the Viscount Lovell, and the two Staffords, and Sir T*homas Broughton, and the* said Thomas Howard, Earl of Surrey, and who, of all the rest, *if he* had been taken in battle, was so hateful and so much feared of *the Earl of* Richmond as that all the world could not have saved [his life], *and he must have joined those va*l*ian*t, brave prisoners who were executed at Leicester with all speed: **Quia** ***********************. [And therefore let] no man be so void of reason and sense to [think that he was taken or submitte]d himself at Bosworth. But [he did that some months after, at a

110v happier time, which I can prove by the testimony] / of an ancient and wise and veritable gentleman who was brought up from a child by this most noble Earl Thomas, and was ever with him until his old age, and was well acquainted with all his actions and his fortunes. Wherefore it must be understood both for [the] truth and for the just causes aforesaid that this earl fled from the [f]ield, and opportunely.

[Robert] Buck, the [grandfa]ther [of this Sir George Buc]k

But he could not post nor fly so fast not [f]ar as the rest, because he was sorely hurt and wounded in the fight. [But] he came by night to the house of a gentleman not far from Nottingham who [much loved] the earl and his father the duke and his noble family most dearly and faithfully. [There] he lay in all safety and secrecy until his wounds were cured. [And in] the meantime, that terrible Parliament held in November, and the attainder of all the *friend*s of King Richard, was ended, and all the punishments to the king's *con*tentment executed. And then, and soon after, followed a gracious [par]don of all the offenders and partakers in that cause and quarrel *of* King Richard. And now hereupon this earl, having good hope and not [on]ly of pardon (as the rest) but also of the recovery of the favour of the *n*ew king, and the rather because he knew that his offence in *t*he true and just understanding thereof was a small offence, or none at all, but rather an act of loyalty – wherefore he now was resolute to discover himself and to go [to] the king, and in all humility to present and to submit himself to His

111 Grace for / favour and pardon.

The king's choler was not yet allayed, nor his displeasure and indignation as yet passed over and worn out. But now he frowned and cast a stern look upon the [ea]rl, and uttered some sharp and rough words to him, and threatened to *cha*stise him severely for his bearing arms against him at Bosw*orth. And* the king commanded the earl to be arrested, to be carried to the Tower of London, and there to be imprisoned during the king's pleasure, or *rather during* his displeasure. And this displeasure dured and continued by the space and *time* of four years or thereabouts, from the first of th[is king unto the fourth year.

[The third year, the kin]g came to the Tower to meet Queen Elizabeth there, and to whom he was shortly to be married. And anon he called for the Earl of Surrey, and being *then in the Tower, and the* king seemed still to be angry with him. And he challenged him upon his [o]ld quarrel and charged him with his partaking with the late [u]surper and tyrant (for so he termed King Richard). But the [ear]l, being a man of good courage and wise and withal temperate, re[p]lied to the king (and yet in very humble and reverent manner) that he hoped that his highness would [not] always be displeased with him for an offence which [was of] that kind as that not only he, but also many thousand [good subj]ects took it to be no offence, but contrariwise, rather an action and an [effect of their] liege duties, and a just accomplishment of the obligation [and al]legiance to their king and sovereign. And therefore he humbly *prayed His Majesty to remit his* displeasure and to receive him to [his better opinion.

[The king (as suddenly moved with this reply) sternly demands if he would excuse his fault, or how he could expect his grace, having served an usurper and an unlawful king against him. The earl,] *in the* / like discreet **111v**
and reverent manner as before, replied and said, 'Sire, I beseech your Grace to consider that the prince whom I followed was as solemnly and lawfully and with all the general suffrage and with universal applause crowned *king of this* realm. And the ceremony was performed by all the great officers and peers of the realm, [both ecclesiasti]cal and lay. And he was my good and gracious master, and I held myself bound by the laws of God and nature and of this kingdom to obey and serve him faithfully. And I did never hold it my part or duty, nor fit for any good subject, to dispute or sift or question the title of the king, his liege lord, to the crown, but contrariwise to defend him and his crown with all his best means and fortunes and forces, and with the adventure and expense of my dearest blood, [and] saw no reason in honour nor in justice to be of any other opinion. Wherefore I confe*ss* I held him to be the true and lawful king and to wear the crown rightfully and lawfully. And I was then and ever shall be of the mind to serve and to love him with my heart who shall upon so good and honourable terms attain to the crown and wear it as he did. And I will live and die with him and in the defence of that cro[wn] wherever I shall find it, yea if it were set upon a stake', etc.

Thus the earl. And the king gave goo[d] ear unto his speech and marked it well, and also liked it, and better than he discovered at the instant. And soon after, *he be*came instantly gracious to the earl and pardoned his offence or error. *And he was* content now to acknowledge that the earl's answer was not only plain *but* discreet and very reasonable, and that he verily believed that the earl would be a very good and true and faithful servant to him who now had that imper*ial* crown of England, and would ever, as he said, keep it by God's grace. [This was the king's third y]ear. And in the beginning of the next, viz., **anno regni** 4, he set the earl at liberty and gave him good access to royal presence and well favoured him. And ere long he made the earl one of his privy counse[l,] and he made him lieutenant or governor of the north parts very soon after. And when there were wars to be made against the King of Scotland, he m[ade] the Earl of Surrey general of the army. Then (being captain and general) he overthrew the Scots.

But th[is was not when he took the king] at Flodden Field, for that was in the time of Henry VIII, and who at the earl's return received him very honourably and grac*iously*, and in reward of his many good services made him High Treasurer and High Marshal of Engla[nd.] Also, Henry VII restored him to his father's dukedom, being the inheritance of his gr[andmother] Mowbray. And in brief, both these kings, the father and the son, held him in great estimation and honour, and whereof he was very [worthy.] For he was so truly noble and so valiant and provident as that he crowned his actions with prosperous success and with immortal and glorious memory. For ve*rily*, fortune seemed to go hand in hand with him, and **paribus pa*ribus***, as the *Romans said*.

[Wherein] he resembled his most famous and very ancient progenitor
112 Heward[us,] / of whom it was doubted **utrum felicior an fortior esset**, so
Ingulfus fortunate and so heroical a knight he was. And sithence I have made this mention of this noble Hewardus, and also entitled him the progenitor and great ancestor of this great duke and of the noble Howards now flourishing, I will make it known unto the generous Reader what and who **this** Hewardus was, and that with as much brevity as I can. And not to the end to add any more greatness to the House of H*o*ward – for that were needless, in regard of their very m[any noble extracti]ons and propagations from the most noble families, and namely the Mowbrays of Warren, of d'Albeny, of Marshall, of Segraves, and with the princely Plantagenet of Brotherton, of Bigot, and with noble houses of Fitzalan, of Maltravers, of Buckingham, of Oxford, of Dacres; and besides, th[eir infinite alliances] and this cognation with all the most ancient noble families of the kingdom; and in rea*son* of their many hard and high and most famous exploits and achievements and great goo[d service] done to the king and to the kingdom. And for these causes, their honour is so great and so well kn*own* as needeth *not my blazon*.

Wherefore I have no [other scope] in this story of Hewardus but to restore them whom I take to b[e] their proper [and original] ancestor, as farforth as I shall be able. And as I have endeav*oured to do so for this family,* I shall be the rather pardoned because I have done the like honour and service to many other the most noble families *of this country* in my
113 **Commentaries in Librum Domus Dei** and in this story. / And I will follow Henry Huntington, Roger Hoveden, Matthew Paris, Matthew Florilegus, Anonymous, the writer of the ledger book [of the] monastery of Ely, Thomas Walsingham, and chiefly Ing[ulfus,] the Abbot of Croyland, who lived in his time and in his c[ountry, therefore] might best know him.

This Hewardus was the son of Leofric, a very noble, magnificent lord. And he was Lord of Burne in Lincolnshire, and of the c[ountry thereunto adjacent. And his moth]er was the Lady Edi*v*a, descended from the great
[Liber Eliensis] Oslac, a duke o[f the Easterlings in King Edgar's time. And I] find that there was a noble kinsman of his called [Heward.] This Heward was a tall

man and of goodly personage and of great strength and very valiant, and **nimium bellicosus**: much or too m[uch] affe[cted to] military enterprises. And to satisf*y* his desires, his natural inclination to martial enterprises, he se[rved in] the wars in Northumberland and in Cornwall and in Ireland. And when they were done, he went into the Lower Germany, and there he showed so great courage and valour as that he w[as] not only much esteemed there, but also much admired and reputed the *flower of honour*. And be[ing] in Flanders, and there being a time of cessation from arms, he fell in love with a fair lady called Turfrida, the daughter of a nobleman of Flanders. And he ma[rried her,] *and* they lived some years there together.

And whilst he was in these countries, Leofric his father died, and about that time William, Duke of Normandy, entered and conquered this kingdom. And Heward here being advertised that the conqueror had seized upon his lands and country and patrimony (and the which was in Holland and in the Marshland) and given them to the French count, the new Earl [of Holland,] Ivo Talbois, and that this count had handled very rudely the lady his mother, and thrust her out of her proper possessions and also out of her dower, Heward hasted into England and came into Lincolnshire. And he raised forces, and incontinently. And he went toward the new Earl of Holland, and he fought with him and overthrew him and took him prisoner, *and* held him in despite of the Conqueror until the earl had made *satisfactory recompense* for the wrongs which he had done in Heward's country, and that with a great sum of money.

[After that,] many barons spiritual and temporal and other good English, [bein]g chased out of their countries, were glad to fly to [the Isle of Ely,] as the place of most safety. They sent [to Heward] to come and take the charge [of all their forces and be their general.] *And he* [condescended, fought for them, and defended them. After, he built a castle there, called a long time after 'Heward's Castle'.] / As that he continued in the isle, the king was not 113v
able to take this isle, nor to subdue the barons, nor so much as offend the barons therein by all his forces. But in th[e meantime] the country of Heward was invaded and infested of the Normans, whereupon he left the Isle of Ely and returned home to defend his own country. And he so stoutly, also so politicly and victoriously demeaned himself there as that he did not only recover his own lands and large patrimony, but also he [brought] the Conqueror to such terms as that he was content to [receive him to his favour, which he enjoyed, and died] in good grace with him [and] was buried in the Abbey of Croyland.

And thus much for Heward. And now, as concerning his issue by his wife Turfrida. [Albeit there] is no mention made of any but of one daughter, named [also] Turfrida, who was married unto a nobleman called [Hugo] E*v*ermua, Lord of Deeping, yet there be divers reasons to in[duce many to] *have certif*ied that Heward had other children as well, if it be considered [how] strong and how lusty and how able a body he had. And also because there were [divers worthy persons which] bore his surname in that country a long time after him until the time [they left] that [country] to [inhabit their better heritage of acquists in other places.] *An*d therefore it is very probable that he had one natural [son a]t the least, and bearing his own name of Howard, and that next to [his noble father] *he* was the author [o]f this noble house of the Howards.

And let it not be thought any disparagement for a noble family to be raised from a [na]tural issue, considering that there have been and are infinite number of noble and princely families which are derived and propagated from bastards or natural sons. As for example, Aeneas and
[Homer, Livy] Romulus, the found[ers] of the best Roman families, were bastards, and Plutarch writeth that Theseus and Themistocles were bastards, and others say as much of Hercules and of many other noble and heroical persons. [The King of Spain descended from] Henry de Trastamara, base son of Alfonsus, the Justicer King of Castile. And some write that the ro[yal Stewarts of Scotland descend from a base son of Fleance.] And who hath not and doth not honour the princely race of William the Conqueror, who was the bastard son of Robert, the Duke of Normandy? And [there was never] a more noble nor a more valiant nor a more heroical man than Robert, Earl of Gloucester, bas[e son of King Henry I.] And the earls of Warren descended from Hamelin, a base son of Geoffrey Plantagenet, Earl of Anjou. And the noble Herberts are said to descend from a base son of King [Henry I.] And the earls and dukes of Somerset (which followed the Red Rose) were the offspring of the Beauforts, natura[l] sons of John of Gaunt. And I could come nearer to these tim[es, if I should no]t offend, but these examples may suffice to take away t[he jealousy] or imputation of blemish or dishonour from a bastardish or illegitimate original. [And this one example is above all, to wi]t that Jesus Christ, the greatest and most noble king, was content to descend from Ph[ares, a bastard.]

And now to show some other reasons why I hold these nob[le Howards] to be descended from Hewardus, or Herewardus (for [so some writers] call him – but Ingulfus, who best [knew him, calleth him always Hewardus). Both these names may signify in the Saxon or Old Dutch language a chief
114 captain of an army, whom the Romans call Imperator.] / And that the titles and names of great offices have given surnames to many noble families we have many examples, and particularly the Visconti of Milan, the Chamberlains of Normandy, the Stewards of Scotland, the Butlers of Ireland, and divers others who had their surnames from the offices of their ancestors or fathers.

And this is rather a good argument, and not only for their taking of the surname of Howard, but also [for the origin of that family] fro[m] Hewardus. For besides that (and before noted), to wit that the Ho[wards for many years and some] ages from the time of Howard dwelt in those countries of this heroical Hewardus, [as in] Holland and Marshland. And they continued there until they, acquiring more pleasan[t] possessions in Norfolk and in Suffolk by the marriages [of] the daughters and heirs of Fitton, of Tendring, o[f] Mowbray, of Tilney, etc., and then they left their old sea[t] of Howard in Holland and Marshland and came into Norfolk and into Suffolk and were lords sometimes of Sunninghill near Windsor. But their fairest patri[mony was in Norfolk and Suffolk.] And they have also borne this surname ever since, or with small interruption, [the old surname dis]continued, and have been lords and owners of some lands which belonged to the s[ame Hewardus.]

119 And I am of opinion if his arms could be found in any [charter, deed,] or monument of stone, metal, wood, or glass, and in all which there is n[o] doubt that his arms and gentilitious ensigns were imprint[ed or engraven] and to be seen if they were well and diligently sought, I say I make no dou*bt that the* arms of Heward and of the Howards would be found to be al[l one, and then they must needs be reconciled.] Then also there would be no question of his being the ancestor of the nob*le Howards*. For it is a certain and infallible principle not only in armory, *but* in the imperial laws that **identitas armorum et cognominis praesum[it iden]*ti*tatem familiae**.

And thus I have delivered mine opinion for the origin of the noble Howards or Hawards – for so they are for the most part written in stories, and He[reward] and Heward in charters and records, and which I have seen in the [cabinet] of my most noble good lord, my lord [William Howard]. / And if **114**
this be but a conjecture, yet conjectures made upon probable arguments and upon goo*d evidences and good* reasons usually pass for testimonies, as it is in the old leonine verse: **Qui bene coniectat, vates his optimus ex*s*tat**. And besides, I doubt not that our better learned heralds and diligent antiquaries (and whom it properly concerneth) can confirm all this which I have said with author*ity, and there be some of* them who agree with me and maintain this my assertion to be right.

And now to say something of the succession [and continuance] of this noble family of the Howards. It is most certainly and authentically to be proved that whilst they lived and dwelt in [th]ose frontier countries of Lincolnshire and of Norfolk (namely in *Holla*nd and Marshland), there were of them very worthy and signal and [honour]able persons. And amongst them in the time of King Edward I, [Sir William Howard,] *a good*ly and learned and honourable gentleman, was Chief Justice. And he [was grandfather to Sir John Howard, who] was Admiral of the North Fleet in th[e naval wars of King Edward III. His son Sir Robert Howard married the daughter of the Lo]/rd Scales. **117v**

Sir John Howard (who lived in the time of King Henry VI [and] died **anno** 16, Henry VI) had two wives: Margaret, daughter and [heir] of Sir John Plaiz, a knight of a noble family. And by her he had [Eliza]beth, an only daughter, and married to John de Vere, Earl of Oxford. *And to* him she brought a goodly part of the lands of Howard. And her [heirs were] married to Latimer and to Winkfield, very fruitful [families.]

The second wife of this Sir John Howard was the [daught]er of Sir William Tendring of Stoke Neyland in Suffolk, [by whom] he had his eldest son, Sir Robert Howard, who married [Margaret] Mowbray, daughter of a cadet of the house of Mowbray, and who became coheir with her sister, the La[dy Berkeley, to Thomas Mowbray, Duke of Nor]folk, dead in Venice and left his son John Howard [heir to H]oward and to Mowbray. And John Howard, the son of [John Howard, was] created Duke of Norfolk by King Richard III in the right of his mother Mowbray. *And* [he] married the daughter of the Lord Moleyns, and by her *he* [had] Thomas Howard, the first Howard Earl of Surrey. *And* [this] is he who survived the dangers and calamities of the Battle [of B]osworth and became afterward Duke of Norfolk and a *most* honourable and powerful peer of this realm, and from whom [all] the noble Howards now living are descended, and who, *as I* noted before, have matched with all the greatest and most *nob*le families of this kingdom.

And it is also most memorable [that] this most noble house of the Howards hath been so [hap]pily and so honourably fruitful as that it hath furnished [this] kingdom with four dukes and many earls and viscounts [and] barons, and with three High Treasurers, and with [six] High or Great Marshals of England, and with ten High [o]r Great Admirals, and with some honourable **Custodes** of the King's Privy Seal, and with sundry honourable Chamberlains of the King's House.

126 And here I may be called to account what au*thors* I have followed in this story of the noble Howards (besides the vulgar chroni*clers and the monk of Croy*land: in some things Philip Commynes, Inguer de Monstre*let, and other* French writers. I have also followed the memorials *set* up by the friars or monks of the monastery of Thet*ford* to the tomb of this great and first Thomas Ho*ward, Duke* of Norfolk. And other things I have declared from *the* report of my grandfather, who was brought up *by the* first Thomas, Duke of Norfolk and was with him *in all* his expeditions, and after his death held the *like* estimation with the duke his son.

118v And of this / most noble family there is yet one old and very heroical
[Sir Charles Howard] Howard living, [who ha]th with great honour and with great good fortune borne and ad*orne*d the high offices of Great or High Constable and of Lord Lieutenant [of Eng]land, and of Lord High Steward or Great Seneschal of the kingdom, *of* [High] Marshal and of High Admiral of England, and of Lord Chief Justicer [in eyre] of the better part of this kingdom. Besides that, he hath been Lord [Chambe]rlain of the royal house, and he hath also been very singularly happy in his *marti*al expeditions. And for example, he was famously and admirably victorious in the sundry marine battles and conflicts which were fought between him [and all] the naval powers of the King of Spain and of the Pope and of the princes [of I]taly, **Anno Domini** 1588. And he was also as fortunate in the siege and sack of [Cadiz, **An]no Domini** 1596. In these he had good success, *and* in other noble enterprises. And I speak not this by hearsay, but **ex certa scie[ntia, et visu pro]prio**: for I was both a spectator and an actor in them. And he is now th*e ol*dest captain and the most ancient counsellor of estate in Europ*e*.

120 *And* this is Sir Charles Howard of Effingham, Earl of Nottingham and High Admiral of England, and the most worth*y* grandchild of that most magnificent and most valorous Thomas, Lord Howard, Duke of Norfolk, and the which duke, for his better distinction and for his perpetual honour,
[Camden in **Octadinis**] is styled **Triumphator Scotorum** and of whom I can never speak honourably enough, and not only for his *v*ery many most noble acts and public honours, but also for his care in mine own particular obligation. Nor shall I ever be able to make sufficient testimony of my thankfulness for his great favours and many benefits bestowed upon mine ancestors and kinsfolks. And especially for the charitable and pious care which he had of the poor distressed orphans of Sir John Buck, my great grandfather, who by the fatal day of Bosworth lost not only his life, but also his fortunes and means, and the livelihood of home and est*ates*, and w*hich* was then in Yorkshire for the most part, where his ancestors had li*ved wor*shipfully and opulently even from the time of *King John*.

Egerton 162v-163 [And since I have made this grateful digression, let me crave the Reader's favourable opinion if I stray a little further to show some reason why that most honourable peer made such favourable declarations of his favour to that unfortunate Buck and to his children, nor let my pious remembrance of him and of his obscured family seem ostentation or vainglory, since in other histories and by others he is mentioned to be an intelligent, valiant, and faithful man, much favoured by the king his master and in good credit with him, bearing an ancient and hereditary love to the princely House of York, was also well descended and allied to many worthy ancient and noble families, by which means he came to be known to these noble Howards and much esteemed by them.

[And because I must add proofs to what I have said, I will begin with the testimony of the most learned Mr Camden Clarensius in his immortal [Camden in **Octadinis**] **Britannia**, who deriveth this Sir John Buck from] / Sir Walter de Buck, a 121 gentleman of Brabant and of Fland[ers.] And he and his ancestor had that surname of antiquity from the Castle de Buck in [Lisle, a] city and frontier town in Flanders, where [the ancient] earls were accustomed much to re[side.] And the ruins of the Castle de Buck were remaining in the time of [Lodovic Guicciardini in **Paesi Bassi**] Lodovic Guiccia[rdin]*i*. [For] he saith that he saw [the] carcase of that *castle*.

And this Walter Buck was a cadet of the House of Flander[s and was] employed by the prince then Duke of Brabant and Earl o[f Flanders] and sent to King John with auxiliary troops of soldiers. And Roger Wendover sai[th that this Walter Buck, and Gerard de Soceinni and] Godescalcus **venerunt in Angliam cum tribus legionibus Flandrensium et Breban-[tinorum militum**, etc.] And here he did good and valiant service to [the king,] as many of our historians report, as namely M. Paris, M. [Westminister,] Radulphus de Coggeshall, Thomas Walsingham, and others. And the king bountifully reward*ed* him for his good service against his rebel*lious subjects:* he gave lands to him in Yorkshire and in Northamptonshire.

And [he] found in Yorkshire (where he made his seat and abode) an ancient family of the surname of Buck, of Bucton in [the] Wapentake of [The ancientry of Buck] Buccross. And it seemed that that family had been *there* long, for the name is a Saxon or Dutch word and signifi[eth] a beech tree or a beechwood. And Walter contracted friendship and amity with this Yorkshire gentleman of his name, and also alliance. For he ma*rried* Ralph de Buck, his eldest son, to the daughter and heir of Gocelin[us] de Buck, who was grandchild to Radulfus de Buck, and who / was a part-founder and a benefactor to the 122 Abbey of Bridlington, as I have seen written in the charter of King Henry I, made for the foundation of that monastery.

And from this Sir [W]alter de Buck descended John Buck, knight, who married [a Strelley, and was so constant in his love that although] she died in his best age, yet he vowed never more to marry, and became a Knight of the Rhodes. And [his] arms are yet to be seen in the ruins of the [Hosp]ital of St John's near Smithfield and in the Church of All Ha[llows] in the [upper end of Lombard Street,] which was repaired and enlarged with [the stones brought] from that demolished [canopy. He lived **sub rege Edwardo, filio Regis Henrici**, as I have seen by the date of his deed in Herthill, **anno** 1, Edward I – **anno** 22, Edward I.

[And from this Knight of the Rhodes descended Sir John Buck, who for his] / too much forwardness and hardiness in th*e assaulting and* the charging 123 a fleet of Spaniards without the leave [of] his Commander in Chief, the Earl of Arundel, Lord Admiral, he was com[mitt]ed to the Tower. And this is testified in the records of the [Tower,] **anno** 13, Richard II. Laurence Buck, his [son, followe]d Edward Plantagenet, Duke of York, [and was a]t the battle of Agincourt with him, and *where* [this] duke was slain.

And John Buck, knight, [the son of this] Laurence, married a daughter and heir [of the noble] house of Staveley, and out of which house the barons [Parrs of Ke]ndal and Ross, and Queen Catharine, the last wife of [Henry] VIII, and the Lord Parr, Marquess of Northampton, and the [most noble] Herberts, Earls of Pembroke and of Montgomery, [are desce]nded. And those more ancient Bucks resided for [the mos]t part at West Stanton and Herthill in [Yorks]hire. And they took wives in divers worthy and ancient [families] of these parts, as namely of Strelley, or Stirley, of Woodhall, [of Th]orp, of Tilney (then of Lincolnshire), and of Saville, *and* [by] whom we have much noble and worthy kindred. *Yet the*re be but few of them that claim any kindred of us. *And th*at showeth that we flourish not nor are rich, *and* as it is in the Greek Comic:

[These Bucks] were all [soldiers, and so] were the rest [succeeding] *these*, for Robert [Buck, the son] of this unhappy [John Buck, fo]llowed Th[omas, Duke of Norfolk,] and was with [him at the battle] of Flodden. [And Robert Buck, my father, served King Henry VIII at the siege of Boulogne, and the Duke of Somerset, Lieutenant General of King Edward VI, at the battle of Musselburgh in Scotland. **Et nos militavimus et bella vid*imus*** G.B.]

τῶν εὐτυχούντων πάντες εἰσὶ συγγενεῖς.

fortunatorum omnes sunt *co*gnati.

But this is by the way. And I will only add that that [m]atch with Saville was the last marriage of mine ancestors [i]n Yorkshire. For John Buck, that unfortunate man, who, following constan[tly the House of] York, was sore hurt and wounded at the battle of Barnet. But he received a gr[eater] blow

123v and a deadlier wound, and that was for his service at Bosworth, / *as I have* intimated before, and for the which his head was cut off [a]t Leicester. And this John Buck married Margaret, the daughter of [H]enry Saville, and by whom he had [Ro]bert Buck, my grandfather, and most of his children, who were brought up into the south parts by [the] noble charity of the second Howard Duke of Norfolk, and where ever since we [have] remained under the comfortable and honourable wings [of the] most noble and magnificent Howards [and their p]osters. For these children of Sir John Buck *were left* young and in poor and miserable estate by [reason] of the confiscation of all the goods and lands of [their un]happy father by Act of Parliament, **anno** 1, Henry VII, **ut *supra***. / So that he might well say, as Iolaus said of Hera[clides's orphans,] **Ego illos filios servavi, et sub alis texi**:

126 [Euripides in tragedy **Heraclides**]

Those bairns I fostered and fed,
And over them my wings I spread.

But this noble duke did not only tender them in [their childhood,] but also provided well for them afterward and [bestowed the two] daughters in marriage, the one with the heir [of Bure, the] other with the heir of Fitzlewis, both of very worthy families. And from these matches div[ers honourable and] noble persons descended. The sons were one [a soldier, the] other a courtier, and the third a priest. A[fterward, the duke] placed Robert Buck, the eldest son, at Melford [Hall in Suffolk, a] rich and pleasant seat, and by his favour he [married into the] families of Higham and of Cotton, as also did [the Blounts of] Elwaston, the Talbots of Grafton, from whom the [barons of Mountjoy] and the Earl of Shrewsbury now *living is* [descended.] The duke also bestowed in marriage one of the d[aughters of this Buck with Frederick Tilney of Shelley Ha[ll in Suffolk,] a gentleman of a very ancient house, and h[is nearest kinsman by the duchess his mother's side.

123v [And I] have made a brief memorial of some of [my poor ancest]ors, and reason and duty also require *that I* should honour them from whom I have my being and my *source and* my pat[rimony and] mine interest in the

quality / gentle or noble (for all is one.) And this was wel[l and worthily 125
acknowledged by the great consula]r philosopher: **Parentes carissimos** [Cicero]
habere debemus, quod ab iis vita, patrimonium, libertas, civitas tradita est. And certes I think there is no gentleman (if he be not stupid or degenerate) but will take delight, also comfort, in the commemoration of the virtues and wor*ks* of their forefathers, and in the reporting or hearing of the commendations of those good men who brought or added honour or dignities or all to their families.

And this is not without warran[t,] for we have an express charge given to us from the most mighty *Judge and* from the best Lawmaker, and from the most severe exacter *of penalties and* of amends for the breach of His laws, that we must h[onour our f]athers and our mothers. And this is not to be understood only of [our parents **superstites** and living here with us, but of our forefathers also – that is, beyond our great grandfather (for we have no proper word for them above that degree but ‘antecessors’, **vulgo** ‘ancestors’, whom the Romans] called **maiores**) and of all our progenitors who departed [sooner or later] *from* this world and are (as we hope) in Paradise and **in region*e* vivorum.**

[For] the words **pater** and **mater** (as also **parens** and **parentes**) extend [very la]rgely, and reach even up to the highest ancestor. And the ancient Roman ju[riscon]sults deliver for an axiom in their law that **appellatione parentum [om]nes in infinitum maiores utriusque sexus significantur**. And this word **[pa]rentes** extendeth yet further, for it comprehendeth all our kinsfolk [and] all the cousins of our blood and lineage. And it is used in that sens[e by] Aelius Lampridus and by Julius Capitolinus and by other the best [wr]iters of the times of the declined empire, and as Isaac Casaubonus ha[th well] observed in his annotations upon these imperial historians.

Moreover, the [Itali]ans and the Spaniards and the Frenchmen, whose languages be for the [most part] **Romanzi** (that is, mongrel Latin and broken and corrupted R[oman] language) use **parenti**, **parentes** and **parens** for all their [kinsf]olks and gentilitious cousins. But we Englishmen (being [more pre]cise, and also more judicious) follow the more ancient and the more [eloqu]ent and more classic Latin writers and hold ‘parent’ strictly [to the] simple significance of **pater** and **mater**, and of the present and immediate [parents.] But the using of the word **parentes**, as these [imperial] historians, and as the Italians, Spaniards, and Frenchme[n use it, serveth] better for our purpose here. And I could be [content also to imitate] the pious gentlemen [of Italy, Spain, and France in their religious and charitable
endeavours to advance the joys and happiness] / of their parents defunct. 125v
And if I thought that any such good offices of charity and of devotion would do to those my **parentes** and forefathers any good, I would do them. But if it be in vain and a vanity so to do, yet it is the more venial vanity because it is an harmless and charitable and a gentle and a general vanity. And whether we will or no, we must all be content to say and to confess,
semel insanivimus omnes. Vergil in **Aegl** ***

*T*his cannot be but acceptable to all these generous persons who are *of noble mind.* And I would have those singular opiniasts which allow not these things nor anything but *relations of the living and in der*ision call these pious recordations the Legend of Lares and romances of shadows firs[t] to consider that the **genii** of men and the **umbrae** or ghosts of men deceased are as much on the other side delighted to behold and to speak with their friends yet **superstites**, and with their kinsfolk and children and progeny remaining upon the earth.

Circumstant animae dextra levaque frequentes:
nec venisse semel satis est, iuvat usque morari, etc.

This was the observation of that **pius** Aeneas when he went *to the* Elysian paradise and land of ghosts to speak with his good *father* Anchises, and who received him with great joy and gladness. [And] he was much delighted to talk with his son Aeneas, and told him fine tales and notable prophecies and good matters of stor*ies* because he would detain him in Elys*ium as* long as he could. And as the same author (viz., the divine *Vergil*) reporteth, Aeneas joyed as much to see his father's ghost and *have* speech and conference with him. And he was so desirous to *hold and* (as it were) to possess his father, as that he offered sundry t*imes to* take Anchises by the hand and desired that they join their right hands together. And he desired also to em*brace* and to accol his father Anchises, and as in these words *he* plainly declared:

Da iungere dextram,
da, genitor, teque amplexu ne subtrahe nostro.

126** And with this I will end this second book, the nex[t] task being to refell the slanders of King Richard, w[hich are] so many and so gross and false as I have not read [or heard] of any prince so impudently and foully injured – indeed [beyond] all comparison. And therefore I hope it will not displease [the] noble, pious, and just disposition if the next book purge [him] from the malice and venom of railing pasquil[lants and] libellers.

Explicit liber secundu[s]

THE THIRD BOOK OF THE HISTORY OF KING RICHARD THE THIRD 127

The Contents of this Third Book

The accusations and slanders of King Richard exam[ined, answered,] and refelled.

The malice of Dr Morton and of his [servant Sir] Thomas More against King Richard.

Their style and strange [arts of defaming him,] *and* their idle and frivolous exceptions and gross and foolish cavils taken against [King Richard for his] gestures, looks, teeth, birth, deformity, and his virtues depraved [and concluded.]

[**Utopia**.]

The deaths of King Henry VI and of his son Edward, Prince [of] Wales, and the actors therein.

How great the offence of killing of a king [is.]

Truly valiant men [hate] treacheries and treacherous and cowardly slaughters.

King Richard not deformed.

The sl[anders] of Clarence translated maliciously to King Richard.

The cause of Clar[ence's] execution.

How the sons of King Edward IV came to the[ir] deaths, and that thereof King Richard not guilty.

The story of Perkin Warbeck.

He is compared with Don Sebastian, King of Portugal.

Who are **Biothanati**.

Counterfeit princes detected.

False friends.

Young princes mar[vellously] preserved by Divine Providence.

Many strong arguments and testim[onies] for the assertion that Perkin Warbeck was Richard, Du[ke] of York.

His honourable entertainment with foreign people.

Vox [populi,] vox Dei.

Reasons why it is not credible that King Richard made away his *two* nephews.

Morton and More seem to excuse King Richard of their deaths.

The force of confession.

The cruelty of those of the faction of Somerset [o]r Lancaster.

Perkin imprisoned, tortured, and forced to accus[e and] belie himself.

The evil of torture.

The guilt of [at]tempting to escape out of prison.

What an escape is.

Heroum filii noxae.

The Earl of Oxford's persecutions of Perkin, and his [end.]

The base son of King Richard III, Captain of Calais, [secretly made] away.

The son of he Duke of Clarence put [to death for nothing.]

The [power of Furies,] De[mones, and Genii Apollonii Maiestas: **Quid tibi non vis, alteri ne feceris.]**

127v

THE HISTORY OF KING RICHARD III
THE THIRD BOOK

128 I intimated in the former books that some [politic] and malicious clerks, hating King Richard and seek[ing] to be gracious with his enemies, employed their w[its] and their pens to make King Richard odious and abhorre[d] and his memory infamous forever. That for this purpose they devised and divulged many scandalous reports, and made false accusations of him. And they made libels and railing p[am]phlets of him. And if haply they met with any of his [faults] (as they might doubtless, for there was never any man without fa[ults]), then, although these faults were small, and such unto which, or the like, even good men were obnoxious, they devise[d how they might] aug*ment* and amplify and aggravate them.

And so vehement and [constant] they were in their malicious prosecution thereof as that they did [not] only much defame and belie him in his lifetime, but so farforth as lay in them they persecuted even his shad[ow and] his ghost, and they scandalized extremely the memory of his fame and
129* name. / And they would not suffer him to rest in the general place of rest, and where all men rest and are at quiet – to wit, in his grave and sepulchre – but they molested and troubled his *mortal remains and exposed* them unto the wind and to the weather so that they did not on[ly,] according to the old
Erasmus [i]n **Chiliad**. proverb, and impiously, **Cum larvis luctari**; they st*rove* and they contended with his ghost and his immortal part, but also with his carcase and with [his ashes,] *and* barbarously, so that it cannot be said in the case of the king as it was wont,

[O]vid, **D[e Po]nt.**, **Lib**. 3

> **Pascitur in vivis livor, post fata quiescit,**
> **Tunc suus ex merito quemquem tuetur honos**.

But for these wrongs the times were most in fault, for then it w[as not] only tolerable and allowable to make and to publish such scandalous and infamous writings of him, but also it was meritorious and guerdonable. And on the contrary side to write well and honourably of him was an
T[erentius in **Adelphi**] offence. And these men had learned the rule of the comical [P]arasite and observed it: **Obsequium amicos, veritas odium [p]arit.**

And this malignant planet reigned a long time here. And it began *to give* [influence.] Name*ly, an*d now in a few words to particularize these writers and to make them known: Dr Morton, that politician, as before and often remembered. For he was the chief *instigator* and *prime* sub*mover* of a*ll these* trea*sonous* de*tractions* and the ringleader of these detractors and vitilitigators of King Richard. For he did not only bear malice and hatred to the princely family of York generally, [but m]ore particularly and more vehemently and more mortally toward King [R]ichard than to any other of them, as well because King Richard removed this prelate from the co[unsel table] *because of his* false heart, as also because this king [imprisoned] *this d*octor and Thomas Nandick of Cambridge, a notorious necromancer, and with other such to be attainted by Parliament of treacherous [p]ractices and of sorcery and of such peccadillos of the reprobate Portuguese as were [ne]xt in rank to **No creer in Dios**.

Libe[l of Dr Morton]

King Ri[chard had cause] to suspect [and punish sor]cery

For *t*his doctor, when the time served him to be revenged, took the advantage of the iniquous times, *and he* had it most proper and opportune for this revenge. And as is before intima*ted, he* was a good clerk and learned, and made his pen the weapon and instru[ment] of his malice and of his rancour and of his hatred. And for this purpose he made a book [in Latin] of King Richard and reported h*is acts and* chargeth him with many foul crimes, *and* aggravateth them. And on the other side, *he* extenua*teth* or suppresseth *a*ll his virtues and good parts.

And *this book of Dr* / Morton came after to the hands of Mr More, who had been the servant of Morton, and a man much renowned for his knowledge in poetry and in other good arts. But when he was young, and servant to Dr Morton, and also be*ing* a clerk to one of the sheriffs of London, and being then a man of small reputation, yet the[n] he was ambitious and desirous of preferment and of honour (as all the ingenious and best wits will for the most part), *and it well appea*red for a man of so mean fortune to have an aspiring mind and ambit[ion.] And for that purpose he must be provided with a good and fit viaticum of things. And he employed his wit and his best means and arts, and amongst them assentation and slander were of chief use.

129v*

[This boo]k [was lately In the hands of Roper of Eltham, as Sir Edward Hoby, who saw it, told me.]

And moreover, he was in two sciences or professions more dexterous and more skilful and more delighted than many other witty men, *to* wit, in the studies of the law and of the art of poetry. And by these two arts or professions he might be holpen much in writing fables or in doing of injuries. For lawyers have a privilege to tell false tales, or, in the plain English, to be for advantage. And I find such fortunes and false arts in one of the translations of Mr More thus warranted: **Ii qui cum usus postulat, et ad rem conducere vident, si mentiantur venia, immo laude plerique digni sunt**. And much more is to this purpose in those his transla*tions*. And poe*ts* as well as painters have **quidlibet audiendi aeqam potestatem**. And that Sir Thomas More was a good poet and much delighted with poetry and with quaint inventions, his many poems and epigrams yet extant testify; besi[des] the many petty comedies and interludes which he made and oftentimes acted in person with the rest of the actors (as his loving and familiar friend Erasmus reporteth). And to these hi*s* practices fantastical and his **Utopia** may be added.

[Amongst the dialogues of Lucian, Sir Thomas More made choice for h]is [transla]tion [of seven] only, [whereof three were **The Cyn]ic**, [**The Art of Necromancy**, and] this [of **Philopseude]s**, [or **Lover of Lies**.]

And this Mr More, having been a servant of Morton, and which is more, an understanding servant, knew that it was a chief duty of a servant **iurare in verba magistri, ut supra.** And therefore he had a care to *make* good and to confirm what his master had forged or hewed in his spiteful and slanderous anvil. And accordingly, he translated and interp*re*ted and glosed and altered his mas[ter's] book at his pleasure, and then he publish*ed it*.

[Juvenal]

And here that saying of King Dariu[s,] whch after became a proverb, hath place and use: **[Hoc] calceamentum confuit Histiaeus, in[duit autem Aristagor]as**. So Dr Morton, [acting the part of Histiaeus, made the book,

[Herodotus]

130* and Mr More, like Aristagoras, set it forth] / and added some things unto it.

And he had a purpose to write the whole story of King Richard III (as he himself intimateth in the title of his book), but it seemeth by his cold proceeding that that he grew out of liking of that melancholic and uncharitable work and weary of that base and detracting and scandalous style, and proper to the cynic of barking philosophers, who like cu*rs growl and snarl* and *detract and slander their betters*. And in truth it was more kind to such a maledicent mome as the deformed Thersites, who, as Homer writeth, was of such a railing disposition, and so immeasurably as that he reproached and reviled as kings and princes. And for these causes it is likely that Sir Thomas More left the story imperfect and defective, for otherwise he had time enough to have finished it. For he lived twenty-two [yea]rs after he undertook this work, and for the most part at his pleasure, [and] prosperously. For he began this work **Anno Domini** 1513, when he [was] Under-Sheriff, or clerk to one of the sheriffs of London, [and] in 1535 he died as he had lived, that is mocking and scoffing, [as Richard] Grafton reporteth.

But yet he was much favoured *of* fame and of the partial affection of men as that his vices were not only concealed and smothered, but also have greater [commendation] ascribed to him than there w*as* just cause. And for example, Mr M*ore was* [reputed a] great learned man, and also (and which
131 is much greater praise) that he was [a very holy man.] *But there is* / no just cause for either of these praises. For albeit it is [tr]ue that he well understood the Latin and Greek [la]nguages – [which was then held great learn]ing – but that was not enough to give to him the style of a great clerk. [Bu]t contrariwise, he was held to be a man of small [lear]ning by the profoundly learned men and by the great clerks, insomuch as he was
[Brixius **Antimoro**] censured by Germanus [B]rixius to be no better than **ineruditus** (that is [unlearned]).

[As] concerning his holiness, there were then many men more [ho]ly and more godly than he, and who never had the style *of* holy and of singularly godly men. And of the matter *there* writeth a plain man but a learned man, and one [that would flatter] nobody, and who better knew Sir Thomas
[Johannes Baleus, **De Scriptoribus Britanniae**, Century 8 **cap**. 69] More than these who since and [now have as]cribed so much learning and holiness to him:

[Hoc nos] probe novimus, qui eramus eidem Thomae [Moro viciniores,] quod pontificum et Pharisaeorum crudelitati [ex avaritia turpiter subser]-
130v* **viens, omni tyranno truculentior feroc[iebat.] / Immo insaniebat in eos qui aut Papae primatum, aut purgatorium, aut mortuorum invocationes, aut imaginum cultus, aut simile quid*d*am diabolicarum imposturarum negabant, a vivifica (licet) Dei veritat*e* edocti. Consentire porro noluit hic Harpagus, ut rex Christianus in suo regno primus esset: nec quod ei liceret cum Davide, Solomone, Josaphate, Ezechia et Josia, sacerdotes et Levitas, reiecta Romanensium Nembrothorum tyrannide, in proprio ord[i]nare dominio**, etc.

And doubtless this author had a*n* ill opinion of Sir Thomas More. For besides this his censure of *him*, he giveth to him the sole attribute and titles
132 of **te[nebrio**, of] **veritatis Evangeliae perversissimus / osor**, and of **obstinatus cacophanta**, [of **im]pudens Christi adversarius**. And then,

s]peaking of the end of Sir Thomas More, saith that **decollatus fuit in turre Londinensi, 6 die Julii, Anno Domini 1535. Capite ad magnum Lond[ini] pontem (ut proditoribus fieri solet) stipiti imposito, et nihilominus a papistis pro novo martyre colitur**. And thus he became a martyr, and this is his legend, according to Mr Baleus.

But there were other causes of his condemnation to death, as you shall see and know, and by his own testimony, having, as the pr*osecution declared*, judged himself by his own mouth. / For when he stood at the bar, **134** arraigned and to be tried for his offences, he confessed that there had been some exceptions taken at him because he seemed to uphold and maintain the Pope's supremacy in England. And that he said that he could not see **quomodo laicas, vel secularis homo poss[it vel] debeat esse caput status spiritualis aut ecclesiastici.** [But] he insinuated that this opinion was taken hold of and urged for a colour to supplant and to subvert him. And he affirmed that the chief ca[use] of the king's displeasure against him, and the greatest cause of *the* troubles and calamities whereunto he was fallen, was h[is with]standing the divorce between the king and Queen Cath[arine] of Castile, his wife, and his marriage with that most noble and fair Lady Anne Boleyn, Marquise of Pem[broke.]

And his own words spoken to the judges, according as they were taken and set down by hi[s dear] friend George Courinus in a short discourse [Courinus] which he wrote [of Sir] Thomas [More's] death, are these: **Non me fugit quamobrem [a] vobis condemnatus sim (videlicet) ob id, quod numquam volu[erim] assentire in negotium novi matrimonii regis**. And these words were uttered by Sir Thomas More after the sentence of his condemnation was pronounced, and that is a time when no evasions nor any subterfuges would be of any worth or benefit, and therefore they proceeded from his heart and conscience. And before this he wrote a long [letter to Mr Secretary Cromwell, which I have seen, wherein he protesteth] that he is not against the king, either for his second marriage nor for the church's primacy, but wish[eth good success to the king and those affairs, etc. Which words we]ll considered, it will plainly discover that Sir Thomas More, Lord Chancellor of England, was not so faithful and so stout a champ[ion] for the Pope and his sovereignty as many Romanists and his partial friends suppose.

Neither was he so good a Christian as they think he was. For I have seen [**In scriniis Domini** R. Cotton] amongst the multitude of writings concerning the strange conferences, counsels, and deliberations and resolutions had about the alteration of the religion and for the suppressing of all monasteries and religious houses, and too many churches, that he [made no opposition to] that sacrilegious plot and gave also his consent to the suppression and destruction thereof, and the which profane and barbarous work [the] king had never done nor put in practice if the Pope and his agents and his [instru]ments had not withstood that his second marriage – [which] error and insolency they have all since repented them, *but* too late. And of both these faults or crimes and *sacrileges* [the Lord Chan]cellor More was guilty, and so farforth as that he could [not defend his connivance] and consent [with any] arguments of wit or of policy.

But it was a happy turn for this kingdom that he was so by [j]ustice at that **134v** time taken away. For if he had lived and flourished and enjoyed his former credit and authority, England had been defrauded and deprived of the best queen that was, the sacred and worthily eternized Lady Elizabeth, late Queen of England. For she was a kingly queen, and a masculine dame. And she *was* wise and learned and temperate and chaste and frugal, and yet liberal and rich, and in a *manner* far exceeding these much renowned Amazons, Thalestria, *Pen*thesilea, Antianira, Hippolyta, and the rest, and also those *im*perial and monarchizing ladies Semiramis, Thomyris and *Artemis*ia, as that they were but May-ladies and maidens in comparison of her.

For she was ever dreadful to her foes, and always vict*orious* against her enemies, and a true **parens patriae** at home and everywhere and at all times. And she was *a m*artial and true heroical **virago**, which better deserved the honourable title of **mater castrorum** [tha]n Victoria Augusta did, and yet by the testimony of T*r*ebellius she was a wise and valorous and excellent woman. But *ye*t I say still that Queen Elizabeth surpassed them all. And in a word, *she* was the phoenix of her sex. And the variety of her noble acts and of her many arduous achievements and of her victories and of her w*ise* counsels and of her prudent policies is so great and so manifold and so exce[llent] with virtuous and good and pleasing matter as that the poets and romancers shall have no need to study for any new devices or delightful and artificial inventions to set them forth or to embellish the*ir* poesies of her, because this bringeth matter enough, and abundant of that kind.

But this place and the time will not serve to tell the least of her high praises and rare merits. And therefore I think it better to say little or nothing than not that which shall be worthy of her. And as for her early and cruel adversary [before she was in] **rerum natura**, Mr More, I have made bold to discover him and to pay him in his own coin and to paint him in his own colours. But yet I have not finished his character, but I will make it complete ere I finish this work. And in the meantime, if the Reader desire to know any more of this ungentle knight, I refer him to the ecclesiastical history of Mr John Foxe in the reign of King Henry VIII, and where you shall see him graphically described, and what a **morosus morus** he was.

And I shall leave his description and ret[urn] to his book, or to that his historical fragment, and wherein he took much pains to write the faults and false accusations and the evil fortunes of King Richard, and it was base and a bad subject and an incivil and inhuman ar*gume*nt. But yet his labours were well accept*ed*, especially in that time w*hen it was written*, and was
135 more safe / to rail at King Richard than to tell his virtues and to *praise him*
(**ut supra**). Therefore his writings were received plausibly and held as canonical and authentic, and not only by the readers of that time. But also annalists and chroniclers of this la[nd] *succe*eded him, or at the least of the weaker and more shallow sort, and who (**tamquam ignavum et servum pecus**) have followed him step by step and word by word, not having the judgement nor discret[ion to] consider his affections, nor his drifts, nor his arts, nor his placentine manners, nor his ends, nor to examine [the truth of] *th*e relations which he maketh, nor to search out the truth of his writings.

[But] yet I must confess that there may some excuse be made for these more simple scribblers or romancers, [if i]t be considered that the authors of that story, namely Morton and More, [were reputed] men not only of great learning and of much experience, and also of muc*h understanding* in civil and public affairs, and both men of great credit and authority in this realm *and* kingdom. And by these means, if they had been men free from malice on the one s*ide and ambition on the other, they* must have committed the accidents of these times and the *truth of events* and all historical matters growing in those times to writing, *especially those which pertained to* / King **135v** Richard and to the whole princely family of York, as I intimated be*fore*, partly for their own aim and worldly ends, and for the respect of their preferment and advancement (being men very *am*bitious and skilful and desirous to insinuate themselves into the favour of *gre*at ones of that state and to please the time, and to either of which King Richard was hateful.

And *by these* means, and by flattery and obsequious obs*erv*ation of humours and of affections, they gathered credit *and* promotion, *and in this busi*ness they turned their style upon King Richard and much wronged him, smothered and concealed his virtues *and the good* acts on the *one* side, and they aggravated and exaggerated his vices and offences maliciously and in all extremity, and these on the better side, and to curry the more favour, *and* extolled the acts of Richard's flourishing foes and magnified them much above the cause and above their desert. And to my seeming *Ammianus*, speaking of certain sycophants, saith that they **Id observantes conspiratione concordi, ut fingere*nt* vere supprimerent Caesar*em***, as these men dealt with King Richard.

And in this base kind, some tr[ivial] and clawing pamphleteers and some historical parasites ha*ve* dealt with the famous and most magnificent and very royal p[relate] (if prelates may be said to have the epithets of royal) and namely Thomas Wo[lsey,] Cardinal and Archbishop of York, who bore the mind of a grea*t* king, and he was a man without peer in his time. Yet they wronged him, for *they maliciousl*y extenuated his virtues and derogated from his *good parts*, and have depraved or suppressed m[any] excellent things in him. And they have detracted from the honou[rable] and immortal merit of many good and glorious and sumptuous works, and instead thereof, they have imputed to him many vic[es] and excesses whereof he was not guilty, and they have laid many crimes upon him which he never committed. And thus much in that high and *critical vein*.

And now I will return to the writers of the story of King Richard; and wh[o] so many of them have followed the foresaid Morton and Mor[e,] although haply they were honest men, yet because they were [of] small learning and of lesser judgement, and some of th*em* so simple and so credulous as th*at they* could swallow any gudgeon and never examine the [style or faith] of those aforesaid authors nor bring th[em to the touchstone of verity;] *but* / **136** contrarily they would believe anything and take any counterfeit and false coin of those crafty mintmasters for pure and current money.

And I advertise this by the way of caution, because they which read their books should be wel*l advised to consider* and examine what they read and make trial of such doubtful things as are written before they give credit unto them. And here also I signify to the*m of* those injurious writers, that by their leaves or without their leaves *I will reveal the* frauds of their faults, and I will lay op*en* their sland*erous* reports, and I will reprehend them and tax them for *their slanders*; and their false accusations and scandals and calumnies sha*ll receive* no better entertainment at mine hands than they deserve. And they must be content to *suffer the* same whip wherewith they have scourged others, and much better persons. And they must think and know that this *is a* just doom, and of the credit of an oracle, and recorded [**Iliad**, XX] by *the* ancient and most wise Homer: **Quale verbum dixisti, tale etiam audies**. It is just and due that they hear ill which speak ill, and [therefore it [Terentius in **Phormio**] must be said] to Sir Thomas More or to any of his followers, as the old Comedian said, **Quod ab ipso allatum est, id sibi [relatum esse putet**.]

137*
And men have / received and followed and passed for authentic many gross fables, and such other vain matters as all the world knoweth. And The ***** although Raphael Holinshed, Edward Hall, Richard Grafton, John Stow were honest men, yet they have incurred these faults, for they have followed the said Dr Morton and Mr More, and they have, without choice, transcribed the wh*ole* reports and speeces of these Antirichards into their stories and romances. And Polydore also so farforth may be numbered with them as he followeth Dr Morton's pamphlet. And in brief, the historians, chroniclers and romancers writing these matters are but the tru*m*peters and echoes of Morton and More.

Therefore, the Read[er] must read their writings warily, and consider what men th*ey be. For it* is a hard thing to find that prince's story truly and faithfully written, who was so hateful to the writers th*en; for when they w*rote they might write no better. And therefore, *th*ese reasons being considered, their writings must be *reg*arded and the authors censured accordingly. And neither they nor their **manes** must not *be* offended if their false accusations and crimina*ti*ons be laid open here, and if their *s*landers, and their railing discourses be reproved, and if they be taxed for their ill writings and find their scandals *an*d malicious style to be retorted upon themselves.

136
And now that these preparatives and advertisements be made for th[e facilitating of my] way to the answering and refelling and confuting of the said scandals and criminatio[ns, I will come to the su]bstance and the matter of them by sundry instances and exhibit [them faithfully] *to* the Reader, and with the answers thereunto. And I doubt not but that we shall discover strange and uncouth notions, and foul tokens of malevolence and of envy particularly in the enemies of King Richard, and re*veal such* conceits of railing and of malice, and such as very seldom or never fell unto the style or pen of *any dis*creet and ingenious or wise or indifferent or charitable writer.

For these [men by their malicious] alchemy will transmute virtues into vices. *And when it* so falleth necessarily into their discourse and pens they must make mention of King Richard's good parts and virtues, then their manner is either slightly and [scornfully] *to* overpass them, or else to **137v*** extenuate them and to pervert and t*o* / deprave them and to make gross and scandalous construction of any virtue or good part of his, and if they write of his faults and vices, they will aggravate them and make them more grievous and more heinous than they were, and suppose *every mole*hill to be a mountain.

And as concerning this, their first manner of their strange kind of cavilling and depraving of the come*ly and* good parts which was in the king, you shall see some examples in their words, and truly transcribed hither. It must be then understood that whereas, then, this king was ever and generally esteemed to be very courteous and affable, and that much to his honour, so far as these cavil[lers] could not deny it, but were forced to confess it. But they *maliciousl*y cracked the credit of that good eulogy and crashed it all to nought with this spiteful glose: viz., that his *courtesy was faul*ty and was a dissembling device to get the favours of men.

[The virtues of King Richard maliciously censured to be vices.]

When also they were driven to confe[ss] that he was liberal and had a mind to give boun[ti]fully, they perversely interpret this a subtle practice with large gifts and prodigality t[o] buy friendship. And he concealed his knowledge of his wrongs and slanders and bore them with patience and silence: they censured him for a secret and deep dissem[bling.] And as for his friendship and love, although there was never any m[an loved his friend] better nor more faithfully, yet they make it of no worth, or nought, for they say that to both fri[end] and foe he was much indifferent. And moreover, that he was held and reputed to be merciful and ready to forgive such as offended him, and in the high kinds of *offences*, and such offences as that of Fogg the attorney, who, not*with*standing he had made a libel of the king and count[er]feited his hand and seal, yet the king mercifully pardoned him and divers other the like. But these *cavillers* and hard and injurious censors term this clem*ency* and mercy to be a deceitfu[l clemency,] and to have been exercised and exhibited, and cunningly, to win [upon the good wills of the people.]

And they made other gross and ridiculous depravations [against his election. Though it was performed with all general good liking and suffrage, yet they shame not to say it was wrought] / by packing and **138*** practice, and slanderously and ridiculously they term it a mockish election. And many such malicious mockeries and apish and ridiculous depravations and perverse constructions they make of things which were in him good, and the which good men would convert to his praise and honour. But the scandals of this kind, as they are very frequently obvious in the writings of those and of such like malicious men, so are they of all other scan*dals* the most injurious and the most malicious. For by the very breath and poisoned speech of such perverse and envious persons, all the good works, and all the good words, and all the good gifts and good parts and vir*tues not only of King Richard bu*t also of any good man may be traduced and depraved, and all good things may receive false interpretations and foul constructions as of vices and of crimes. And all the good which is said or done by a man, yea, a good man, shall be censured to be *d*one out of dissimulation and hypocrisy.

A [strange kind of] cr[imination]

But [th]ese detractors are not satisfied with these kind of [ca]vils, for they rest not thus, but they taint and carp at and [re]proach this prince in a more subtle and more [cap]tious kind, and they find such strange faults in him as [e]ven Momus himself (the prince of carping and of railing *re*prehensions) would not have found and noted them. As for *ex*ample, these men make the casting of his eyes *and* the motions of his fingers and the manner of his pace and of his gait and his gesture and his other natural actions to be faults. I confess with Cicero that **status in[cessus, sessio accub*it*io,] vultus [occuli, manum motio**, have] a certain decorum belonging to them, but he maketh it no vice to err in them, nor that any error committed in them w[ere a vice] or a sin. [But it must be so] defined by the laws of [Utopia.]

[Cicero, **De Officiis**, **Lib**. 1]

[They can search yet nearer his soul, finding] *gr*eat faults and heinous crimes to the dreams *an*d visions and nocturnal phantasms of the prince, and hold them as not only fearful and pernicious [an]d terrible, but also as prodigious things. And yet I make no doubt *bu*t that they themselves, as well as I, find *that o*ther men, and good and virtuous persons, have had troublesome *and* terrible dreams and strange, frightful visions. Wherefore *doubt*less all these objections and exceptions are but frivolous *and* malicious curiosities, and mere ridiculous cavillers and [not] worth the answering. Neither had I meddled with them, but that it was and is fit that *these* sundry varieties of the malice of these men should *be rememb*ered in everything and in every kind, that as *well the inj*ustice and falsity as the grossness and ridiculousness *might bett*er appear, and that it might also *become apparent how that o*ther princes hath been *wronged.*

138v* *These* [calumniators and detractors,] if this prince had prevailed at Bosworth and flourished, would have highly extolled him and his virtues, and rather like to chemical imposters, have pretended to augment their golden value of his virtues and to multiply their precious essence with their glos*sing and* cogging *and* parasitism. And on the other side they would have concealed or extenuated his vices, his errors and faults. But such have been the practices of these men against this king after that great storm of calamities and adversities fell upon him, as that *they* either smothered and suppressed his virtues and good deeds and good parts, or else they extenuated and depraved them, and as I have often already intimated, and I may do again, for such re*quire many* confident affirmations. And in those adverse times of this king, they could find nothing to talk nor to write of him but vices *an*d faults, and they were studious to make their lucubration of that argument and to amplify and to aggravate his *faults, how trivial* and how light soever. Some, and almost all of these his faults were feigne*d* and falsely imputed to him.

But this is no new case, nor his case alone. Virtue in adversity hath ever been not only wrong*ed but also* accursed and oppressed, as very gravely hath been observed by the divine Philo, and in these few words: **Res praeclarae calumniis et rebus adversis solent obscurari et op[primi.]** And as the noble and pious Trojan told Achilles, it wa[s] very easy to detract much and rail [Homer, **Iliad** XX] without measu*re*, and **et navem centirerem conviciis onerari**: to lade a sh[ip] of a great burden with reproaches.

And of this kind of contumelies also, and those practised upon King Rich*ard*, I will bring some instances. As namely, these curious spy-fa[ults] impute as a great fault and a prodigious evil to King Richard that he was born with some teeth in his *mouth* – though I do not think that this prelate [King Richard not monstrous] or the lawyer ever spake with the duchess his mother or her midwife about this matter. And therefore I may doubt whether they had any certain intelligence here[of,] or whether they feigned it. But yet if it be a true tale, I am indifferent and I care not, for it importeth nothing. For there is no reason wh[y] those early or natalitious teeth should be turned t[o] his reproach, considering that there have been man[y] noble and good men who [Pliny, Livy, Valerius Maximus, Plutarch] have had teeth imputed as a fault [to] them. And namely Manius Curius (surnamed there[upon] Dentatus); and Gnaeus Papyrius Carbo, [King of the Epirots, a prince much renowned in the old stories for his prowess, **139*** victories, and virtues; and Monodas, son of] / Prusias, King of Bithinia, were born with an entire semicircular bone in their mouths instead of teeth.

And these early teeth were never objected to these men or to any other as matter of vice or crime.

[The Duchess of York died about the 11th of Henry VII at Berkhamsted, and was buried at Fotheringha]*y*[. John Stow.]

Then the pains which the duchess mother of this king felt in her travail of bringing him forth are ascribed by these cavillers to the wickedness and forwardness of this prince. And yet her pains were not extreme and intolerable, for then they would have killed her. Because *a*ccording to the principle of the best Stoic, Seneca, **quod ferri potest leve est, quod non ferri breve est**. But her pains and pangs were sufferable, for she overcame them and lived almost fifty years after his birth – when the pains of many childbearing ladies and of other women have been so extreme as that they have been mortal, and yet the children were never condemned as guilty of [murder,] but hel*d* for innocents.

Julia, the daughter of Julius Caesar and wife of the great Pompey, and Tulliosa, the [d]ear daughter of Marcus Cicero and wife of Dolabella, [and] Junia Claudilla, the empress and wife of Caius Caligula, [di]ed all of the difficulties and extreme pains of [the]ir childbearing and travails. And here in England, [Qu]een Elizabeth, the wife of Henry VII, died in childbed. And since that, Queen Jane, the *go*od mother of our most towardly and hopeful prince Edward VI, died in travail of his birth. And many [th]ousand women more have done the like, and yet their deaths, and much le[ss their pains,] were never laid nor im[puted to] the children born so painfully and so fatally.

King R[ichard not] deform[ed]

The next objection and exception which they take at King *R*ichard, and which is of more regard than these before *r*emembered, but yet not to be made nor to be regarded by wise and *l*earned and discreet persons, and that is the note of his deformity. For [they] / impute that to him as a great *and* 140 heinous crime. But because there be two kind of deformities, the one *of the* body and the other of the mind, and therefore distinction here were necessary*: th*us the deformities of the one are vicious and criminal, but *not* of the other. For the deformities of the mind, as namely heresy, sacrilege, *lec*hery, and the other such are sins and great crimes and faults of an heinous *nature, and* most foul and ugly deformities. But these calumniators have *not made* this distinction, for they disertly inveigh against the bodily deformities of King Richard, and when they *bring for*ward deformities and crimes, they name them plainly and in their proper terms.

But the case is not clear, for it is controverted whether the prince *was d*eformed of body or no. And some say peremptorily that he was *not deform*ed. One of these is the honest John Stow, who could not flatter and *speak dishonest*ly, and who was a man very diligent and much inquisitive to un*cover* all things concerning the affairs or words or persons of princes. And he was very curious in [his] description of their forms, their favours, and of all *the lin*eaments of their bodies. And he by all his labour and search could not find any not[es of such] deformities in *the person* of King Richard, albeit he had made great inquisition to know the *certa*inty thereof, as he himself told me. And further, he said that he had spoken with old and grave men who had often seen King Richard, *and th*at they affirmed that he was not deformed, but of person *and bo*dily shape comely enough, but they said that he was very low of stat*ure*.

*And th*is is also the same deformity and no other which other men have

observed in the p[rince,] amongst them Archibald Quhitlaw, the ambassador of the King of [Sco]tland unto the King Richard, who said in his description of this king that he had **corpus [exigu]um**. And to my seeming, Philip de Commyes and the Prior of [Croy]land, who had seen and known this prince and king, seem to clear [him im]plicitly of this note of deformity. For in their many mentions and [dis]courses of him, they never directly nor indirectly nor covertly nor aptly ever insinuate any deformity of body in him, and the which they would not have concealed if any such thing had been. And this same Mr Stow told me also [that John] Rous, who knew
139v* King Richard and wrote much of him and well described him, / noteth not any deformity in him nor a*ny* fault in his lineaments. And I myself have seen sundry picture[s of this king, but could never] discover any deformity in them. I have observed his warlike face, or crabbed [visage, as Sir Thomas More termeth it.]

And also maketh much against this objection that this Richard, of all the
[**Rotuli in Anno** 2, Richard II]*I* ch[ildren] of the Duke of York, is said to be the most like [in] stature and in favour and in shape to his father; albeit the duke his father were not tall, yet *he* [was] of good and comely feature. Moreover, it cannot be [thought] that Dr Shaw would openly in the pu[lpit at St Paul's Cross,] when King Richard was [Protector and there present with many hundreds of people who had before seen the king and knew him well and might then take their full view
142 of him and amend] / their knowledge – I say it cannot be that this divine doctor would have made this fair description, and not only of the mind of this prince but also of his person, if he had been a man deformed. And these be his words:**The Lord Protector is a very noble prince, and the special pattern of knightly prowess. And he as well in all princely behaviour, as in the lineaments and in favo[ur] of his visage, representeth the very face of the noble duke his father. [This is] the father's own figure, this is his own countenance, the very sure [and] undoubted image and the plain express likeness of that noble Duke of York.** Thus Dr Shaw in his sermon at St Paul's Cross. And he was Dean of St Paul's and a [grave] and a lear[ned man.]

141 [Sir] Thomas [Mo]re **a[pud** Hardying] *and* *Graf*[ton]
Sir Thomas More himself, speaking of the supposed def[or]mities of King Richard, doth not affirm that certainly he was deformed, but that he rather took it to be but a false [s]peech. For he saith that King Richard was deformed, as th[e] fame ran, and as men of hatred to him reputed or im*puted*. And thus **habemus rerum confitentem**. So that I rather think th*at* [this] adversary of King Richard, after his usual manner of translat[ing] *the* faults and vices of other men to the prince (and as it shall plainly app*ear by* his manner hereafter) hath here transferred a deformity of hi[s o]wn to King Richard. And that is where he reporteth that King Rich*ard h*ad one shoulder higher than another; and falsely as it hath appeared [by] the former testimonies and arguments. But it is certain that Mr [Mo]re had this deformity. For it is plainly affirmed *of M*r More *by* his friend who wrote the life of this Mr More in Latin and was as much *in* his favour as he could, that Sir Thomas More had one shoulder higher th[an the other.] So that to conclude, I see no cause, the arguments *and* proofs and testimonies of King Richard's clearness from deformities being so fa*r* manif*est*, [why there s]hould any apology be made for him in that behalf.

But suppose and admit that this prince were deformed of body. [Yet] this is no discreet nor just objection, nor hath any analogy with piety or humanity, but it savoureth strongly *and manifes*tly of cavil and of malice, and partly of superstition, and of trivial vulgar fancies and false *crimin*ations. For without doubt, a man deformed of body may, not*withstanding* that, be wise and valiant and learned and liberal and bountiful *and magnificen*t and temperate and religious and pious, and be in every good part *sufficient* and absolute, as all men know.

And if examples thereof be *required, Epi*ctetes / was reputed and 142v
adjudged the most wise of all Greece, yet he was a man in face and in bodily lineaments vicious and deformed. And although Sergius Galba was ill-faced and ill-favoured and crookbacked, yet he was so wise and so valiant a man and so expert *and* excellent a captain as that the Romans, even those of the greatest *judgement* and of the greatest authority, preferred him in the election of their new emperor before all the fair and handsome and personable *gen*tlemen of the whole empire. And these men, whatsoever their *outwar*d appearance was, yet they were well known to *have* had beautiful insides. And these be the true and necessary beauties, [as] sins and vices be the worst deformities of the internal parts.

[Socrates, Aesopus, Epictetus, Galba, a great and excellent captain of the Romans]

And to come nearer home, there have been here in this land, as well in the present age as in the more ancient times, men deformed in bodies and ill-favoured in visage. But those vices of nature were no blemishes unto them, because they were of those kind of deformed who (as I said even *now*) were wise and valiant, magnificent and magnanimous and virtuous and liberal and learned and pious and religious men, etc., and in so good and great measure as that few or none of the most fa*ir* and goodly and comely personages might be compared to them for their virtues and rare gifts of mind. And whatsome*ver* the outward appearance of such men was, yet all w*ise* and discreet persons, knowing that some men, albeit deformed in body, and yet that they had good internal bea*u*ties and virtuous minds, hold them worthy to be esteemed and honoured.

But not to spend any time more in the answer and confutation of so idle and foolish and ridiculous objection or imputation as this, I dare boldly say and *affirm as the* final conclusion of this argument or disputation that without a*ny* doubt men of deformed bodies may *ha*ve very beautiful minds,
and may have lesser and fewer vices than the fair and *com*ely persons. / And 143*
therefore defor*mit*ies of the body, where the mind is fair and beau*ti*ful, ought not to be objected, and much less upbraided, nor held as things of shame *or* offence and as crimes.

But we will leave these mali*cious slanders and th*ose slight and peevish cavils, for they are but *tr*ivial and ridiculous calumnies of envious detractors and of idle sycophants, and are here at the ful*l confuted*. Now we will go to the great and more heinous offences *wh*erewith the adversaries *of* King Richard charged him.

The first of King Richard's great and more heinous crimes is said to be 144
the murder of King Henry VI. And he were very much to be condemned if it could be proved against him. For this prince was not only a good prince, but also a sacred and an anointed person – that is, so much privileged and, as [the learne]d say, so sacrosanct, and as no man by the express and strict interdict of Almighty God might lay violent hands upon him, or so much as unreverently or rudely touch him, and much less to kill him. Wherefore

[Whether King Richard were guilty of the death of King Henry VI or not]

the murder of a king anointed is so foul and so extremely atrocious a crime
as that *the* perpetrator is worthy of the most sharp and most shameful
punishments which may be devised.

And this King Henry, although he were of an usurper's line, yet he was
so virtuous, so pious, and so religious a man as that he was sty*led* and
entitled by these grave and good men which knew him. **Sanctus rex,**
[Polydore Vergil] **[sanctus] Henricus, et rex sanctissimus**, etc. Of this prince Richard thought
well, and was never said to bear any evil affection towards him, and *as* [the]
adversaries of King Richard (though obscurely) insinuate, as none of them
imputeth the plotting and contriving of this murder to [him,] but disertly
and only to the King Edward.

But I must co*nfess that* some of his accusers say that the said king his
brother persuad*ed and* commanded this his brother the Duke of
Gloucester to execute the said murd[er.] But the request or tax and work be
so foul and so bas*e* as that it is not credible that they were even moved or
p[ropounded] to the Prince Richard. For first there is not any honourable
145 and truly n[oble and] *valorou/*s person (and such as King Edward was),
who would require so vile, so dishonoura*ble* [and hate]ful a piece of work to
be done by a prince and by his own brother. And next it is not to be
belie[ved that] the duke his brother, being a man of most honourable and
noble and pious disposition, w[ould endu]re to hear such a villainous and
nefarious motion made to him, and much less entertain th*e motion* thereof.
For such foul murders and treacherous assassinates be no offices nor
act*ions fo*r any heroical and honest and truly noble persons. Wherefore
Quintus Curtius reporteth *that the* murder of the noble Clitus was held the
more heinous and more odious because th*e king* was the executioner and did
the office of a hangman and of a villain: **Detestabile carnificis ministerium
occupaverat rex**. For it is the **mestier** and the proper office of a ruffian and
villain and of an **assassino**, as the Italians call them, to murder men cruelly
and barb*arously and to* kill them secretly and treacherously.

And Sir Thomas More himself is of opinion that King Edward would
appoint th[at butcherly office rather to any other than] to his brother. Thus
More. But he useth so much to speak ironically and in jest as that it is hard
to *impute so* foul and so base and treacherous a design to a prince and to a
man of equal blood and royal [lin]eage to himself, if it be considered that
the king had plenty and great ch[oice] *for* [such] employments, and who had
been bred in his long and cruel civil war[s,] *and who would* make no
conscience of shedding any human blood, and were to b*e led by the rewar*d
and good look of the king, and who, as they knew, also was *tender of the*
146* *honour of himself* / and his dearest brother.

Besides, there is no man of any brave, noble courage and of the true and
right noble and generous spirit, and truly valiant, or if he have any religion,
who will ever plot or conspire, and much less act the secret and treacherous
murder of any man, and above all other men, of a king anointed of God.
******su-** And to this purpose also make these *strong and* inseparable principles in
******k.** philosophy and in nature and in humanity, viz. Πάνδειvον φονικόν:
******chther** **omne timendum est cruentum**. Or, as some say, **Omnis tim*ens* est homicida**:
****** Axio*mata*** that is, every coward is bloody and *cruel; and* **omnis vir fortis odit insidiosas**
***P*olit.** **homicidias et caedes insidiosas**: that every truly valiant man hateth to shed
blood secretly and by treachery *a*nd treason.

And there is no writer, either friend or foe of King Richa*rd*, who doth not confess and testify that he was a most valiant and *most* courageous prince, and one that feared nothing. And therefore he was obnoxious to treacherous effects *and* base practices of cowards. And besides all this, this duke is not *charged* [direc]tly by any creditable writer of that time to have committed *that act.* Ne[ither is it discovered by th]em who murdered King Henry VI. Because, [being the actor is so] concealed, it were no hard matter to acquit also King Edward, *who was as* noble and as magnanimous and as heroical *and judicia*l as any hath been a long time.

But I fear it *w*ill be harder to acquit him than the duke his *bro*ther. And the Prior of Croyland maketh it the more suspiciou[s, because he] giveth the [ti]tle of **tyrannus**, i.e., tyrant, to him who was [the] actor in this murder of King Henry. And the proper int*erpretation* of **tyrannus** is **rex, id est** 'king'. And whoever is **rex** is **tyrannus**, [according] to the genuine and ancient signification of **tyrannus**. For anciently and properly amongst the Gr[eeks, **τ]ύραννος** was used for a king simply, were [he] good or bad. And when this murder was committed, [R]ichard was Duke of Gloucester, *a su*bject and not a king. And there was not any king then in England *but* these kings Henry VI and Edward IV.

*But I sha*ll argue this question no further, but I will bring some authorities and only offer the words of the authors to the consideration of the judicious Reader and leave the [gloss to him:] **Hoc tempore inventum est corpus [Regis Henrici Sexti] exanime in turre Londiniarum. [Parcat Deus et spatium] paenitentiae, ei donet [quicumque sacrilegas manus in Christum domini ausus immittere, unde et agens Tyranni et patiens gloriosi martiris titulum mereatur**. Thus he, and this is] / that maketh against King Edward. [Chronicle Croyland] **146v***

And that this *is* but a doubtful and but a suspicious accusation, and it may be answered and refelled by good authority. There be some grave men of opinion that this King Henry was not slain nor murdered, but that he died of natural sickness and of extreme infirmity of body. And certainly he was a weak man, and sick in body and also in mind. And at the least seven years before his death, **Rex Henricus 6 ab annis iam multis ex accidente sibi aegritudine quandam animi incurrerat infirmitatem, et sic aeger corpore et impos mentis permansit diutius**. And then this infirm state of his body being consid[ered,] it is very p[robable] that he died of infirmity and [g]riefs, and lesser cause of sorrow than he had might soon and easily shorten the life of him and of a stronger man than he. But certes his griefs and cares were great, and extreme*ly* great, and not tolerable, especially to so weak a heart and so weak a mind and so weak a body as h*is* were. **Idem** Croyland

For the great grief and care which he took f*or* the loss of his crown and of his liberty (he be[ing] then a prisoner); and of all his friends and for[ces] which were then overthrown in the battle of Te[wkes]bury; and above all evils, the greatest evil happened unto him, for th*at was* where his only and most dear son, [the] prince, was murdered, and which was a killing c[are] alone. And therefore it is very probable that *he* [under] these many and very heavy occasions of grief came to his death, and not by the sword and by violence. And this opinion and report is also received and alleged by a learned and discreet gentlem[an] who wrote in this age of this matter, and in these words: **This accusation (of the murder of K[ing] Henry VI) hath no other proof but the malicio[us] affirmation of one man. For many other** [Anonymous MS.]

[Rex Henry] VI in custodia [ut alii refe-] runt gladio, [ut alii m]aerore deperiit. [Johannes Meyerus,] **Annal. Flandr**. [**Lib.** 17]

men more truly did suppose that he died of mer[e] grief and of melancholy when he heard th[e] overthrow of his cause and of his fr*iends* and of the slaughter of the prince his son. [Thus he.] And Johannes Meyerus, a good historian, saith that it was reported King Henry VI died [of grief and thought.] And doubtless from that one man whom the English gentleman meaneth, the which one was the malicious Morton, the **malus genius** of Richard, all the other [succeeding] writers have sucked this slanderou*s tale of the* death of King Henry VI.

[The slaughter of the prince, son of Henry VI]

Concerning this slaughter [of the prince, the only son of this King Henry VI] here menti[oned, it is noted his death is not effected out of pretended malice or premeditated treachery; and so it cannot be called wilful]
148* murder, because his slaughter *was* [casual] and sudden, and occasioned at the instant [by his] own fault and by his insolence and [proud speech. For] when the king demanded of him why he invaded his kingdom and for what cause he raised tumults and bore arms against him in the field, the prince proudly answered that he did that which he ought and might do and tha*t* he took arms for the defence and preservation of the right of the crown and of the kingdom belonging rightfully to the king his father an[d] to his heirs.

[Holinshed in Henry VI]

The king, being much moved a[nd] put into a choler and wrath with this peremptory and proud [an]swer, replied and said to the prince that he *nev*er had any right to the crown, and that the *prince* lied. And the king might well so say, because [th]e crown was entailed to his father, Richard, [Du]ke of York, and to his heirs by Act of Parliament [aft]er the death or deposing or resignation of King [Hen]ry VI. Besides that, King Henry IV, grandfather to King Henry VI, was but [an usurper.] But the prince still maintained his [asse]rtion boldly and stoutly, and whereat the king, *bein*g moved, struck the prince with his fist (*and he*, as some say, was armed with a gauntlet of [i]ron). And then instantly the noblemen attending *up*on the king – and by name George, Duke of Clarence, the Marquess of Dorset, and the Lord Hastings [and] others – drew their swords and instantly struck [the] prince and killed him.

[Polydore Vergil, **Lib**. 24]

And whereas it is said by the [adversaries] of the Duke of *Gloucester* [that only he] slew this prince with his sword, the contrary hereof is true. For I
147 have read [in] a faithful manuscript chronicle written of those / [tim]es that the Duke of Gloucester only, of all those great persons, stood still and drew [not] his sword. And for this his forbearance there may divers good reasons be [give]n. And first that it grew out of the mere conscience of honour and out of this *heroi*cal and truly noble detestation of base murders. And secondly because there [was] no need of any more swords, there being too many already drawn. For where *there* was need of his sword to defend the king his brother, there was no man's sword [more] ready. And chiefly, he abstained to be a fellow homicide in this *act in* regard of this prince's wife, who (as Johannes Meyerus saith) was in [the room with him, and] was near akin to the Duchess of York, his mother, and whom also *he loved* very [affe]ctionately, though secretly. But he professed to love the prince, and her for his sake only, like a lover *of chivalry, and he* spoke as he soon after showed, for he married this widow.

[Chronicis in quarto MS. apud Dom. Rob. Cotton]

Anna u[xor Ed]wardi, f[ilii Regis] Hen. VI [capta] est cum [marito.] Johannes M[eierus in **Annal. Flandr. Lib**. 17]

*And besi*des all these reasons, a charitable man would rather think *that* [this noble duke] had forborne to be a partisan in that *he* [bore such a sense of noble actions in his bosom;] which maketh somewhat more to the purpose *when* [that misliking the obscure and mean burial] of the corpse of K*ing* [Henry VI, this prince's father, he caused his corpse to be taken from Chertsey and to be honourably conveyed to the royal and stately chapel of Windsor, ordained for kings. And therefore with these reasons our charity may excuse and acquit him of] *the* / slaughter *of this* King *Henry* VI and of his son. **148v***

[Richard not guilty of the death of the Duke of Clarence]

And now we will exa*mine another* crime of King Richard *III*. Sir Thomas More writeth [that some] suspected that duke to be a pr[acticer] and [procurer of th]e death and *of the* execution of his b[rothe]r, the Duke of Clarence. But yet notwithstanding this su[spicion,] this author [confesseth] that it was commonly said [that] Richard [opposed hi]mself against those so unnatural proceedings of [th]e king, and resisted them both privately and openly. But I will make it better appear and more p[lain]ly by and by that Richard was not any whit guilty thereof. For the [truth is] it was a doom whereof the king had [immov]ably a[nd] inexorably resolved, and that the execution of the [punishment was justly and] necessarily [inflict]ed [upon] the Duke of Clarence. For as I declared in the tenth chapter of the third book of my **Baron** and here in this story, *the* Duke of Clarence had committed many and great tre[asons,] and by his much ingratitude and continual perfidiousness had so ex[tremely] provoked the wrath and hatred and indignation of [the] king his *brother* against him as that no man had hope to gain any [grace] for him. Neither durst any of his friends move th[e] king for it nor speak for him. And this did the [king] afterwards acknowledge, and with much discontent, when his wrath was over, and had remorse of his brother's blood. And then he *repented*, and he was grieved that nobody would make s*o bold* to save the duke his brother's life. And he declared his grief in these few words: **O infelicem frat[rem,] pro cuius salute nemo homo rogavit**.

[Polydore Vergil]

Polydore [Vergi]l

These word*s* are reported by Polydore, but not rightly understood by him, [as] you shall see by the sequel by and by. And *you shall* see these foresaid railers detected of another false a[ccusa]tion. And I think best first *to* relate that, and this *it is*. They affi[rm] that Richard, Duke of Gloucester raised a sland[erous] report of the birth of the king his brother and [gave] it out that he was not the son of Richard, D[uke of] York, but of another man who had secret familiarity with the Lady Cecily, th*e Duchess of York*, his mother (and whom hereby *she bore a* son) and the*se corrupt chroniclers so affirm,* [making this slander one special matter of Dr Shaw's sermon, that he should say in the pulpit that King Edward was a bastard, and that the duchess his mother had wanton familiarity with a certain gentleman.

[Errors of Dr Shaw]

[There is none but will say this loose and foul language deserved] *to* / be blamed, and the rather because it is certain that *he ha*d not any inf*ormation* from the Lord Protector for that speech nor for some other. But he excee*ded* his commission and spake according to his own conceit, and according to such false intelligence as he had, and as I will prove. And for example, this d*octor* in that sermon called the gentlewoman to whom it was said that King Ed[ward] was betrothed before his marriage with the Lady Gray by the name of Elizabeth Lucy; whereas it is certain that her name was Elean[or Butler,] alias Talbot, and so called by King Richard, and so written in the record[s and] all authentic writings. And whereof more in the fourth book. **149**

[That the Duke of Gloucester raised not the slander of his mother's whoredom nor his brother's bastardy.]

That King Richard willed not this preacher to say that his brother King E*dward* was a bastard, there be many good and irrefutable reasons, and besides, testimonies of great credit. And first it may be thoug[ht King Ri]chard was not so gross and so blockish and insensible as to lay an [imputation of] whoredom upon his mother, and a virtuous and honourable [lady,] about the begetting of the king his brother, because it laid also an asper[sion of] shame and of bastardy upon himself. For if his mother did offend [in] the getting of one child, she might as well be dishonest and offen[d in] like manner in the begetting of the rest. And besides, it is a good pre*su*mption that this prince raised not this defamation upon his mother, and in the most scan*dalous and* injurious and unnatural kind, because he was never noted to be *used or* accustomed to speak foul and reproachful words of any man, *and* much less of ladies, and therefore in no wise to slander and defame his *ow*n mother, and so great and noble a lady.

And if these arguments will not *ser*ve to acquit King Richard of the raising of this slander (albeit they be *ver*y strong and efficacious), yet I shall make it out of doubt by credible *te*stimonies. It is affirmed by Sir Thomas More and by Richard Grafton and by Mr [Ha]ll that King Richard was much displeased with Dr Shaw when he heard *th*at he had laid so foul a blot and stain upon the honour of his most *d*ear and virtuous mother. And this was also affirmed by the Duke of Buckingham [in] his speech with the Lord Mayor of London, and the which was in these words: *he said* that Dr Shaw had committed a foul fault and had incurred the [great d]ispleasure of the noble Protector for speaking so dishonourably and *slander*ously of the duchess his mother in the pulpit at St Paul's Cross; [and that] he was able to say upon his own knowledge he had done [wrong to] the Protector therein, in regard that it was certain that [the Protecto]r reverently, and as nature required, bore a true and [filial love] to the duchess his mother.

And lastly, and which chiefly *puts all doubt from the* question, it was proved and it is test[ified upon record that George, Duke of Clarence, who bore extreme hatred and malice to the king his brother, raised this slander, not Richard. For he, most of all men, loved and honoured his brother King

150*

Edward,] / and *he fai*thfully adhered always to him and took his part against all his *ene*mies (as I have said before), and still followed and *accom*panied him in all fortunes, good and bad, and as well *in exi*le and in foreign countries as at home, and in the war *as* in *p*eace. And when the Duke of Clarence, the other *brother* of the king, and the Marquess Dorset, his wife's son, *and his* much professed friend and best servant, the *mighty* Earl of Warwick, and when almost all his friends *deserted him*, yet Richard of Gloucester never forsook *him, and did* partake with the fortunes of this king, *and what*soever they were.

Richa*rd*, *Duke of Gloucester*, his love *for his brother* Edwar*d*

[**Lib**. MS **in quarto apud D**. Rob. Cotton]

And in their most calamities, and when [King Henry VI had overthrown King Edward in a battle, recovered the kingdom and made King Edward to be proclaimed an usurper, yet Richard stuck still unto him, and so far as that he was] *exiled* /

150v*

and proclaimed traitor for him. And when the Queen Margaret besieged the city of Gloucester with the king's power of Henry VI her husband, the [citizen]s defied the queen and resisted her army and told her that it was the Duke [of] Gloucester's town, who was with the king and for the king, and [they] would hold it for him, and most *peremptorily* and briefly.

Anno 10 Edward IV

Chroni*cle* Croyland

And certainly he was very just and faithful and constant to his friends; and of his faithful *service* and firm loyalty a gentle overture in his poesy or motto, and which was *this*: **Loyaulte me lie**, and the which I have seen written [w]ith his own hand, and subscribed 'Richard Glouceste[r']. *A*nd to be brief, it is manifest that he ever kept good *q*uarter with his brother King Edward and was al*ways in* amity and friendship with him, and *always* very obsequious to him. Therefore I say and conclude that Duke Richard co*uld* not and would not be the author of these foul scan*dals* against *his mother*.

[Loyalty bindeth me]

[But if you] will hear the truth, then I must tell you that these scandals of whoredom [were] devised and broached by the Duke of Cla[rence,] who a long time bore a hollow heart toward the [king.] And there were many jars and piques between [the] king and him. And certainly Clarence gave to the k[ing] just cause to hate him very much. For Clarence loved the king's enemi*es* better than the king, and cared not how little *he* was with the king or to his court: **Visus est Dux Clarentiae magis ac magis a regis praesentia se subtrahere, in consilio vix verbum proferre, neq[ue] libenter bibere aut manducare in domo regis.**

After this the Duke of Clarence confederated [with] the Earl of Warwick his father **allié,** and then the k[ing's] false vassal. And they went into Fr[ance,] and there solicited the French king for forces [to] be brought into England against the king. [And he and] the earl brought them in and brought them against [the] king, and fought with the king his brother and [overthrew] him, and then so fiercely pursued his victory [that] the king was fain to fly out of the land, *as I* related in the thirteenth chapter of the Third Book of the **Baron**.

[Father **allié,] quod vulgo [et corrupte** 'f]ather-in-[law' **dicitur**]

And seeking and studyin[g how] he might utterly supplant and r*emove* [the king his brother,] / Clarence had falsely and untruly published that the K[ing] Edward was a bastard, and not legitimate to reign, and that he himself was therefore the true and lawful heir of the kingdom, and that the regality and the crown of England belonged only to him and to his heirs. And these be the very words of the record. And now we see plainly who raised that slander of the bastardy of King Edward and the whoredom of his mother, and how slanderously and injuriously Dr Morton and his followers deal, which ascribe it to King Richard, and falsely. And by the premises also it is manifest that the king had just and very important cause to rid Clarenc[e] out of the way and to be inexorable in the suit for his [par]don (**ut supra**).

151*

[In Parliament, **anno** 17 Edward IV, John Stow **vidit et legit**]

And here was a bitter proof of [the] old proverb, to wit, **fratrum inter se irae acer[bissi]mae sunt**. For all the favour which Clarence could at [his en]d obtain was to choose what death he would die. [And h]e, loving malmsey, desired (as Jean de Serres reporteth) to be choked with it. [Thus you may see] that the Duke of Gloucester was not guilty of the death of the Duke of *Clarence*, [but] it pro*ceeded from* [the king's] *deep* and imp[lacable] displ[easure] conceiv*ed of his brother* for [his malice and treasons that cut him off.] *And* the king *had so great fear* of him [that he never thought] himself [secure until he] was dea[d. Witness Polydore] Vergil: [**Edwardus rex,] post morte*m* [fratris se a] cunctis t[imeri animad]vertit, et i[pse iam timebat] neminem**, etc.

[Erasmus, **Chiliad**.]

[Jean de Serres, **Invent**.]

*And n*ow I will take another accusation to task, and *which was a v*ery heinous crime in itself. But for aught [I] can see, it is rather suspicious and ambiguous [than c]lear and proved against Richard III. But [be it] as it may be, I will set down truly what [I fin]d written of it and in good authors and in good books *and as* well printed as written. [And I will give the accusers free liberty to] *a*ccuse and to indict him and to give all the evidence which they can give against *him*, [and where their] memories fail in any of these things I will help them to make the supply. In this fair manner they shall be dealt with here.

Who [made away] the sons [of] Edward [IV]

The case is the conspiracy and treasonable slaughter or murder of the two young princes, the sons of King Edward, *n*amely Edward V, the king in hope, and Richard [of S]hrewsbury, Duke of York and Norfolk, his younger brother. *And King Richard is* accused and condemned for the death and murder of them. *And in* this manner and form the accusation is made, and *name*ly *his* accusers say that King Richard, being desirous to rid his two nephews out of the world, first employed [a tr]usty servant, John Green, to Sir Robert Bra[kenbury,] the Lieutenant Constable of the Tower, [about the] *e*ffecting and executing of this murder; and by reason that the plot took no effect, because Brakenb*ury misliked of* [it,] the Protector [suborned four] desperate and reprobate villains, and [John Dig]hton, Miles Forrest, James Tyrell [and William Slater to undertake it.] And [the] accusers affirm boldly that these **sicarios** [did] *and* [the] manner thereof was [by smothering the noble children in their beds, which done they made a deep hole in the ground at the foot of the stairs of their lodging **151v*** and there] *the*/y buried them, and very secretly, and laid a heap of stones upon the grave after the ancient manner of **tumulus testis** mentioned in the burial of Rachel, but not to fair and famous end. (Ge*nesis* **Cap**. *35*)

Thus the murder is reported by some of the accusers, but some others vary from them and say that these young princes were embarked [in] a ship at Tower wharf, and that they were conveyed from hence into the seas, and so cast into the deeps and drowned. But some others say that [they] were not drowned, but were set safe on shore beyond the seas.

Here it is manifest that these accusers (like to the false *ju*dges in their accusation of Susanna) differ much in their tales, and in very many and material points. And these differences or contradictions shake the credit of the whole accusation and make it very suspicious and uncertain, and so farforth as that no just and learned and religious judge would condemn [any upon such false suggestions and contradictions.] For here the one accuser giveth the lie to [the] other, and to my seeming also it is likely so to fall ou*t in* the end that they must be content to share the lie *among* them.

For it will by arguments and by authorities *be* demonstrated here that **152** neither both these pr*inces* were buried in the Tower, / nor both conveyed into foreign countries by sea. And then it must needs follow that they could not b*oth be smothered* and buried in the Tower and also be cast into the seas. And here it is worthy [the noting how] *these methods* and forms are opposite and, as it were, **ex diametro**, the one repugnant to the [other,] and *as our author for*getteth, **argumentum bicorne**, and a dangerous dilemma and needeth a g*ood so*phister to solve it and also to salve it. For indeed it is against the art *of sophistry* and logic. For the professors thereof hold peremptorily that two c*ontraries* in one subject may not stand, because there is but one *truth*. And yet there be many contraries in this report.

For some say tha*t they* were shipped alive and conveyed over the seas: **In**

vulgus [fama] valuit filios Edwardi regis aliquo terrarum partem migress[e, atque] ita superstites esse. Thus Polydore. Dr Morton and Sir Thomas More agree in [one] place with this place of Polydore. The man (they say) commonly call[ed Perkin] Warbeck was as well with the princes as with the peo[ple, English] and foreign, held to be the younger son of King Edward IV, and a[gain they say] that the deaths of the young King Edward and of his brother Richard h[ad come so] far in question as that some are yet in doubt whether they [were destroyed] in the days of King Richard or no. Here you see that it w[as held and believed that] th[ey] were living after the death of King Richard. And then those ta*les of their* burying and drowning must needs be lies.

[Polydore V]ergil, [**Lib.** 26]
[Dr M]orton; [Sir Thomas] More

And as the act [of their death is thus] uncertainly disputed, so the manner of it is also controv[erted. For Sir Thomas] / More affirmeth, as before **152v** related, that they [were smothered] in their beds and in their sleep. But Polydore saith [peremptorily] it was never known of what kind of death these two *princes* died. And another author, *an* ancient and a reverend man, *the Prior of* Croyland, agreeth with him and thus writeth: **[Vulgatum est] regis Edwardi pueros concessisse in fata, sed q[uo genere] interitus ignoratur**.

[Prio]r [of Croylan]d

And one reason thereof may be be*cause that* they who held Perkin Warbeck and / Richard, Duke of York, to be one give another a[ccount] **153** and of the manner thereof, for they say that he was [hanged] after King Richard's death, and at Tyburn, **anno** 15, Henry [VII. Again,] if it had been certain and undoubted that these four assassi[ns] had murdered these two young princes, then it had bee[n] known certainly the place and the time and the manner of *their death, by* the due examination of those villains who were al*ive* [long after this] murder was said to be done by them, and went up and [down freely and] securely everywhere and every day. And therefore there can be n[o excuse] for this neglect of the examination of them, and much less [for the suffer]ing such fellows to go unpunished and to live at liberty. *And I urge* the Reader to mark and well consider this, for this manner of dealing *hath* much to make for the clearing of King Richard from having suborned **sicarios** to murder his foresaid nephews. And whereof more shall *be* said anon.

And as for the burying of their bodies in the To[wer,] if that be brought in question, certes then the affirmative w[ould] be much more hard to be proved than the negative or contrary. For this is clearly true, that there was much and diligent search made for their bodies in the Tower. And all these places were opene[d] and digged where it was said or supposed their bodies were laid. But they could never be found by any search. And then it was said that a certain priest took up these bodies and buried them in another and **154** so secret a plac[e] *that* it could never be found out. And hereunto, and with decorum, and for the more credit of this ass[ertion, they might have ad]ded that this burial by the priest was made **sub sigillo confessionis**, and which may not [be] revealed.

[More, Holinshed, Grafton, Hall, Stow]

But Sir Thomas More and the rest, seeing the absurdities and contrarieties of these op[inions,] and as a man puzzled and distracted with the variety and uncertainty of them, concludeth *that* the said princely bodies were cast God wot where, and in another place he saith [that it] could never come to light what became of the bodies of these two princes. And

Holin[shed] and Hall and Grafton and the rest confess that the very truth hereof was never known.

And [questionless the] princes were not buried in the Tower nor drowned in the seas. Wherefore there must some [better] enquiry and some better search be made for the discovery of this dark mystery. And f*or* [the body of
153 one of them and the finding it] / there is good hope and possibility. For it hath been averred and testified by sundry grave and discreet and credible men, and such as knew the young [Duke of] York, that he was preserved and saved and conveyed secretly into a foreign [c]ountry, and was alive many years after the time of [this] imaginary murder, and as it shall be largely and with good argument *and* testimonies declared and demonstrated ere long.

And rath*er first* I will speak a word or twain of his elder [brother, and] *make* [the] best [enq]uiry and the best conjectures that we can to know what became of him. [It is first said the Lord Protector before his coronation]
153v *had them / mur*dered, and cruelly and treacherously, in the Tower. But this report *is* [false.] For there may certain proofs be made that not *only* the younger brother, but also that Edward, the elder brother, *was* living in the month of February following the death [of the king thei]r father, and which was ten months after. For [King Edward died in April] before. [And this] is plain in the records of the Parliament of **anno** 1 of [Richard III,] where there is mention made of this prince, and as then living. [And Sir Thomas More] *in one* place confesseth that they were living long after that time aforesaid. [But I think the elder] brother Edward died [of sick]ness and of infirmity (for he was weak and very sickly, as also w[as his br]other, and as the queen their mother intimated in her speech to the [Card]inal Bourchier). And their sisters also were but of a weak constitution as their short live[s showed.]

And it is likely also that he died in the To[wer, and so]me men in these days are the rather brought to think that this young king died [in] the Tower because there were certain bones, like to the bones of a chi[ld, fo]und lately in a high and desolate turret in the Tower. And they suppose that *these* bones were the bones of one of these young princes. But others are of opinion *tha*t this was the carcase and bones of an ape which was kept in the [To]wer and that in his old age had either chose that place to die in or else h*ad* clambered up thither, according to the light and idle manner of those wanton animals, and after, being desirious to go down, and looking downward, and seeing th[e] way to be very steep and deep and the precipice to be very terrible to behold, he durst n[ot] adventure to descend, but for fear stayed and starved there. And although this ape were soon missed and being sought for, yet he could not be found, by reason that that turret being reckoned but as a wast and damned place for the height and uneasy access thereunto, nobody in many years went up to it.

But it is all one for this question and disputation wh[ether] that was the carcase of an ape or of a child, and whether this young pr[ince] died in the Tower or no. But wheresoever he died, I verily think that he died of a natural sickn[ess] and of infirmity. And that is as probable as the death of his cousin germ[ane,] Edward, Prince of Wales, son and heir of King Richard, and who was sai[d] to die of a natural infirmity.

And there be many causes and reasons why they should both die of one kind of death and at one time. For they were like and very even parallels

almost in all things, as *that they* were both of one constitution, both of one age, and bo*th alike in* bodily constitution and in one like corporal h[abitude. And to make this p*a*rity the more complete and general, they were both of one forename and surname, of one quality and fortune, and] *there is little doubt* / but that they were (or might very probably be) both of 156
the [same] studies, of the same affections, of the same passions, and of the like common distemperatures, and so consequently subject to the like and [to the same infirmities.] And to these may also be added equal and common constellations and [the same] compatient and commorient fates and times. And then there is [reason] and natural cause that they should both die of the like disease[s and na]tural infirmities.

And then they could not be said to be **βιο[θάνατοι]** – that is, men taken away by violence, secret or overt. [I say] *this* because the adversaries of King Richard will needs have it [suspected] that this *Edward*, the eldest son of King Edward IV, died a violent death, *and* because also it may be as well suspected that the other Prince Edward, son of King Richard, and being in the like danger of secret vi[olence] and for the same cause as his cousin was, died of violence.

I will say therefore th*ese things and* will still b*e of the* opinion that the deaths of them both were alike and that the same dis*ease* or destiny predominated over the lives of both. But then it never may be granted that King Richard made away the one of these princes, because one of them was his only and most dear son, and all the hope of his succession and of his future being. Neither may I be brought to believe that King Richard would treacherously make away Edward, the other prince, who was his nephew, and whom he did not only love most dearly, but also gladly took him for his king and sovereign lo[rd,] and observed and served him with all reverence and obsequious duties, *and* as I have fully demonstrated in the former books. Besides that, he being king and by just and true title, and so taken of all his subjects, and that on the other this his nephew and his brother were reputed illegitimate, and so declared and pronounced by the spiritual forecourts and by the high court of Parliament, he had no cause to doubt or fear that the lif*e* of his nephews, being bastards, could do him any hurt or any ways endanger his estate and title.

For we see by infinit[e] examples and continual experience that there is no danger nor / evil dreaded nor doubted in the claim of any of the bastards of 160
[sovereign princes.] And for the more credit of this assertion, let any m*an* [peruse the historie]s and chronicles of France, and he shall not find any re[lation of any attempt or] enterprise made by any royal [bastards upon the crown and kingdom.] Neither shall he [find any such thing] in [the histories of Spain, the ambit of one only royal bastard excepted: Don Enriq, Earl of Trastamara, who was drawn into that action by the violent rages of the people and by the persuasions of the revolted estates of Castile to put down a monster of sovereignty, the hateful tyrant Don Pedro el Cruel.

[Neither have I read of any bastards of the kings of England who have made any public sign of their aspiring. And therefore Henry II was secure of Robert, Earl of Glou]/cester, base son to King Henry [I. And we find not 157
that] King Richard I ever suspected his base brothe[r, Geoffrey Plan]tagenet, of any affectation of royal state. And the like [may] be said of the security of the three kings of the House of Lancaster, and albeit their

158 father and forefather, John of Gaunt, / Duke of Lancaster, left many base children, and gallant and [aspiring enough,] the Beauforts or Somersets, and those very fertile and faithful. Th[ese kings never suspected] or feared any treacherous and proud aspiring in any of these bastards or of their noble posters. [Neither] Henry VII nor Henry VIII ever suspected [Arthur Plantagenet] *of such ambi*tions and so highly aspiring practice. And why then should this [Richard III, who] was as wise and as courageous and as secure and as c[onfident] *and as* kind and as pious as any of the kings his pr[ogenitors, be] *more* [afraid of] *bastards* than they (I speak as they were then taken and adjudged), or be more c[ruel and bloody-minded than they, having then no cause to fear]? And that these two *princes* should be destroyed by him for fear, and by him who *s*****************************.

This is somewhat for King Richard, and very considerable. But there be ma[ny] argumenets and reasons besides, and which is more, many and *various* testimonies and authorities that this king made not away his nephews. And amongst *these arguments*, and a good one, and affirmed by Sir Thomas More [and others, our] best chroniclers: to wit, that it was doubtful whether these tw[o] brothers were taken away in King Richard's time or no. And again that [one of them] was living many years after the death of King Richard. [And what can be said] more for the acquitting of King Richard?

And I like better this opinion, because it maketh mention of [the sur]vivance but of one of them. Neither do the best [stories] make mention of the transportation of more than one of th[em into] Flanders. Neither had they reason so to do otherwise, for surely the [elder] brother died before, and in manner as hath been before decla*red and* discussed even now. And it shall be sufficient for the clea[ring] of King Richard of this conspiracy and treachery if one of them su[r]vived him more or less time. And now we will see h*ow* that may be proved and sufficiently warranted, And because it will be the more apparent and conspicuous in the true and simple relation of the story of this one brother, and the rather because every story is full of repor[ts] of him and few or none of his brother, albeit that some write tha*t* [Holinshed, Polydore] [the]y were both secretly taken out of the Tower and both set a*float in* [a ship] and conveyed together over the seas. But because I [find no mention] of the being of the elder brother in Flanders, but [very frequent mention of the younger] brother's being there and of his other adventures and travails, I will let th[e elder brother, Edward, rest, and speak of his] brother's [transport]ation and [the rest of his actions and life.

[And because the question may be who sent him away, I will first resolve that. We must know then this prudent and honourable care of sending away
158v this younger brother is ascribed to that worth]/y and faithful knight Sir Robert Brakenbury, Lieutenant of the *Tower*. [Others] say it was the good device of the queen his mother. And it may be [well ascribed to her.] And there is no doubt but that there were other grave and well-[affected friends, as shall appear, and not obscurely. And it is the more credible the qu]een was a dealer therein, because in the story of Sir Thomas More [it is affirmed] she was before suspected to have in purpose to take her son *out of the* sanctuary at Westminster and to send him out of the land. [It is also intima]ted there and in the other stories that this plot of the conveying [out

o]f the realm was objected to the queen by some of the lords. [And the] Cardinal Bourchier, Archbishop of Canterbury, told the *queen* [the] chief reason why the Lord Protector and the other nobles were so [earnest to have] young Richard sent to his brother, being then in the Tower, was because [they had a strong] suspicion and fear that she would send him out of the realm.

And now *by these* premises it hath been made plain enough that the younger son of King *Edward* was conveyed into a foreign land by sea, and that foreign country was Flanders, as all the sto[ries testify,] *and* that he was recommended by those his most dear and careful [friends to] the safe and courteous and secret custody of an honest and worthy gentleman [of Warbeck,] a town in Flanders, and where this Richard had good education. And he was still, and a long [time, kept close,] first because these friends durst not trust the king his uncle with that counsel and cau*se*, [nor let him know] where his nephew Richard was. And there may the more credit [be given to] that report of these matters because it agreeth well with that which was made thereof [by Duke Richard,] or Perkin Warbeck himself (for so now he was called or [nicknamed) unto the] most noble and prudent prince, James IV, King of Scotland. And the which [was th]at he, after the death of [Grafton] his brother, was preserved by the favour of God and by the means of a good man, and so good and charitable a man as Josada, who saved the little prince Joas from the bloody practice of Queen Athalia. *And he* said then that for his more safety he was sent out of England *into Flanders, and took shi*p into a foreign country, etc. Thus he.

And thus obscurely and [un]known this young duke lived until King Richard was dead. And then the Earl of [Rich]mond being come to England and being a great enemy to the House of York, [the young duke was st]ill kept unknown. But then *some* careful friends of Duke Richard, for the more safety of him, thought best to put him into the *stu*dy and tutelage of Charles, Duke of Burgundy and of the Lady Margaret, the duchess, aunt [to this prince,] and a kind lady. And these his friends took the example hereof from the Duchess of Yor[k, who, upo]n like fears on the one side and upon like hopes of security on the *other*, [sent her two] younger sons, George and Richard, to the same d[uchess, and her own daughter,] their good and most loving sister, as hath been *before related*.

[The duchess] *was* [very gracious and *observa*nt of this young duke, [to let] *him* [have all princely and virtuous education in Tournay, in Andwerp,] / and after in the court of the Duke of Burgundy, as he had [been 161 in Warbeck, etc.] and [the greater] care taken of his safety because the Duchess of Burgu[ndy] was as jealous of King Henry VII as the queen widow [was of King] Richard III. And she heard that king had ma[ny ears] and had many and long and strong hands, and could find out such as they would and reach them anywhere. Besides, she knew the king's ha[tred] of the House of York to be such as that he would use any means to have and to possess this young [duke.] Therefore she would not yet have the name and the quality of [the young] prince to be known, as well for the reasons aforesaid as / because he was not yet of years and of strength and of 162 knowledge ripe enough to undertake the enterprise for the recovery or gaining of a [kingdom,] *and* the crown and kingdom of England. And besides that, the times and opportunities for such were not yet ready nor propi[tious for such] business.

It must *be* expected that there should be tumults and mutinies and seditions and also rebellious factions in England, and whereof their king was great and pregnant, because the government of the realm of *England was very* grievous to the subjects by reason of his covetousness and of his actions and of some acts of cruelty and tyranny. And for the which grievances it was not long ere there were sundry rebellions in the north and in the west count[ries or other parts of the kingdom. And not long after also (which ma]de well for these purposes), great unkindness and enmities fe*ll* betwixt King Henry VII and Charles, the French king, by the fault of our king. For he so far provoked the French [king that he passed] into [France with a great army,] *and* he besieged Boulogne by land and by sea. And the quarrel (and as I noted [before) made well for this purpose and was of good] use for the plots of the Duchess of Burgundy and for the advance[ment of the D]uke of York, as you shall better understand anon.

And in the meantime, the duchess was very careful that her princely nephew *s*hould have education. And to the end that he might know and be acqua[inted too with foreig]n princes and with their courts and governments, she sent him into France and unto [Portug]al and unto other places, and where he was honourably entertained, and like a prince. [And in the] meantime the English noblemen and gentlemen which were privy to the conveyance of Prince Richard (as I intimated before), and who knew where he lurked or lay close, [finding good] opportunity to help him to his right sent Sir Rob[ert Clifford and Sir William Barley] into Flanders to the Duke of York to [give him a visit and acquaint him what] potent [friends he had ready to assist and aid him. For there had been some counterfeits, which
162v by private encouragement had taken upon t]/hem to be Edward, Earl of Warwick and Richard, Duke of York. *And they instructed* those gentle knights their messengers in that charge to [examine those secret] marks of this Richard and to look diligently that he *was not* an imposter and a counterfeit. And this was a fit charge to those gentlemen, for they knew the young duke even from [his cra]dle.

And they went to him and viewed and considered him well and warily, and they had secret markings. *And* they found that by his face and countenance and other [lineaments,] and by all tokens before known to them that he was [the young]er son of King Edward. And they observed a princely [grace and] behaviour in him, and which *was* a good token of his princely birth. And he could readily account very *accurately for* [many thin]gs he had heard or seen whilst he was in England, and some [things that had been done and spoken very] privately. And besides this he spake English very perfectly, [and be]tter than Dutch or Wallonish. And hereupon Sir Robert [Cli]fford and the rest were so confident in their certain plain discovery and knowledge of the young prince as that they wrote to the Lord Fitzwalter and to Sir Simon Montfort and other the better and more faithful friends of the duke they were not *in doubt* [in their opinion] *of his being a* gentleman, and his *being* in good health and a princely spirit. And his most noble behaviour, and such as became the son of a king, bewrayed well that he was no counterfeit. And that besides all this, he had all the marks and tokens of the young Duke of York, and was certainly the second son of King Edward. This they affirmed **ex certa scientia et supra vi[sum corporis.]**

But now it happened that one of the said counterfeits began to be stirring, and it happened there was a bruit that some noblemen and other principal persons, well affected to Edward, Earl of Warwick and in hope to get him out of the Tower, and in purpose to make him king, and who, as it seemed, had no certain intelligence of the state and condition of Richard, Duke of York, and therefore they, desiring to set up the Earl of Warwick *by and* by, they got / a handsome young fellow and like to the said earl, and whose 163* name was Lambert Simnel of Lancashire. And he was bred in the University of Oxford and was instructed in the royal genealogy. And he was taught to say th[at] he was the son of the Duke of Clarence, an*d* other particularities of that kind fit for him *to* know. And he was maintained and abetted [by the] Viscount Lovell and by the Earl [of Lincoln, Sir] Thomas Broughton, [and Sir Simon Priest, etc., and was presented to the Duke and Duchess of Burgundy, who honourably entertained him.] *And he was entreated* / and 164* much made of, and as the son of the Duke of Cla*rence*.

And in Flanders he drew to him Martin Swartz, [a great] captain, to assist him. And he came with forces into Ireland, where he was received [as the] Earl of Warwick and as a prince of Englan[d.] From thence he came into England and was [well] received here of many. But this deceit was soon discovered, [and in excuse thereof it was] said that [the intent] of those lords was but to use this Lam*bert* as the [counterfeit] of the Earl of Warwick and for colour of their [practice] whilst they could get the said Earl Edward of Warwick out of the Tower and ma[ke] him king (as their purpose was, and as I noted before). And this Lamb*ert* was soon found to be a counterfeit. And all this while Richard, Duke of York, lurked *in hiding*.

And it is a very easy thing to discover an imposter of that kind, and such a counterfeit prince as this Lambert was, as by many examples it is manifest: although he deceive many men, yet there be some who know him so well that will not be delu*ded*, as there was a Ψeudo-Agrippa in the time of Tiberius, who was soon found to be Clemens, the servant of Agrippa, and very like to Agrippa. And there was a Ψeudo-Nero in Otho's time, whom some took to be Nero revived, [but] he was also soon unmasked. And [V]*e*[lleius Paterculus telleth us of a certain ambitious counterfeit in Macedonia who called himself Philip and would be reputed the next heir of the crown, but was discovered and nicknamed Ψeudo-Philippus]. And in the reign of Commodus there was one pretended to be Sextus Condianus, the son of Maximus. And many such impostures are obvious in old stories, and they were still easily detected and convicted and in sharp manner, according to their demerits. And many such counterfeit princes and per*sons* [ha]ve been discovered here in this our kingdom, and the reports whereof are everywhere obvious in our stories and chronicles. And by reason of th*ese examples there was much doub*t and jealousy had of this Richard (alias Perkin) and of his fame and of the truth of his *birth and report* thereof when he first came to be heard of.

[Dion, Tacitus, Suetonius] [Counterfeit princes]

[It is written by some of the old historians that King Harold was not slain at the battle of Hastings by the Conqueror,] but h[e survived and went to Jerusa]lem, 165 [etc. But it not importeth whe]ther [he were the true Harold or] Ψeu[do-Harold, because he never cam[e to claim anything in] *this* kingd[om.]

I will intermit therefore a while the continuate narration of his acts and story until I have made [a brief disgression] in answer to these jealousies and suspicions which were had of him. [For] those jealousies and doubts, as afterward it was found, proceeded not from the detection [of any] frauds or dissimulations of Richard, but from the late abuse and impostures of this said Lambert and of the shoemaker's son, who both *passed* for the Earl of

Warwick, son of the Duke of Clarence. And the people had thus been before illuded and abused by th[ose Ψeudo-Clarences,] so that they feared that everyone th*at* [assumed the name of greatness] *was a* counterfeit. [In regard whereof, many shrunk in their opinion of this Perkin or Richard, **164v*** and many others, suspecting their belief] *who had* / considered better of this matter and taken good and full *note of* him, well informed themselves of his true condition and estate. Then the[y were very careful,] and curiously they looked upon him. And after that the *more they searched and they* pried into him, the more certain they grew and the better, the more they were per[suaded] that he was the second son of King Edward IV. And this knowledge ripely and *timely* came, for **Tarda solet magnis rebus inesse fides.**

Ovid in **Epistul.** 16

There were some men of harder belief, and *so jea*lous as that *they* [o]bjected first that it was not possible that this [young duke] should be conveyed out of the Tower, nor next that he could not be so secretly preserved anywhere. This objection was held by the wiser to be very weak and of *little credit*, and by many reasons and examples. And it only *betrayeth* and showeth little reading and knowledge in histories. And at the observation of *the clai*mant thus argued and pleaded: there be, said they, *examples* in the ancient histories, both Greek and Latin, many reports and many relations of many nob[le] children, the deaths and destruction of whom hav*e* been plotted and determined by tyrants and by other cruel persons and thought to have been accomplished, and yet those child*ren* have escaped those [deaths] and bloody plots and have been secretly and safely preserved, a[s Livy and Diodorus witness in some, and others in many,] *by the grat*eful providence of good men. And many of them have been preserved by the divine ordinanc*e*.

[Noble chidren destinated to be slain divinely preserved]

As for example, Herodotus and Trog*us* write that King Astyages most unnaturally purposed and resolved to destroy his young n*ephew and* gave charge to Harpagus, his noble servant, to slay this innocent infant Cyrus. But *he*, *abhorring* this act, conveyed the child away, and he was secretly preserved, and so safely as that he came afterward to *be a* grandfather and to be king of the Medians and of the Persians. Likewise, King Amulius in Italy willed that Romulus and Remus (being then infants) should be made aw*ay*. But the compassionate Faustulus saved them and brought them up unknown. In like manner the death of the famous and great Queen Semiramis, when sh*e* was a child, was decreed. But yet she was *pre*served in a secret and remote place until that tyrannou*s king was dead*. *And in* the Holy Scripture it is recorded that Joas was saved from slaughter by the good *Josada and preserved* six years, *and Joas* became *king six* years *after* this *experience, according to Holy Scripture*. But of all the examples of this kind, *the story* of Moses is the most signal and the most strange and the most authen*tic*, for as it is recorded in the Book of God. And there it is *recorded that* he being an infant was desperately and cruelly e*xposed to* the mercy of the unmerciful eleme*nts* and to the most dangerous water, the River of Nilus.

[And this Perkin himself, in his own behalf, when such objections were made against him, did allege to James, King of Scoland, the history of Joas mentioned in the Book of Kings, and that most signal one of Moses, by **166** which it is made possible for this] / child Richard, the young Duke of

York, to escape his *death*, being practised and destinate by man, and to be *pre*served safely and secretly in a remote place. This noble child so escaped, and so was kept and *preserved* [beyond the] seas, and in the towns of Warbeck, of Tour[nay,] Antwerp and elsewhere, and until there was a fit time for his revealing and for the making of h*is identity and* his quality and his titles known, and according to the *considerati*ons and reasons before delivered.

And although he *was* an unknown and concealed person, yet he was honoura[bly] kept and entertained, and by the said duchess his aunt, [sister germane] to his father King Edward IV. And which lady, being wise, after good deliberation and consideration had of *the c*ertain quality and condition of the young lord, and well assured that he was the second son of the king her brother, she entertained him as a prince and as her nephew. And he was not only honourably entert*ained* by her, but also by all the chief nobility of those parts, and much honoured by them, and in testimony of the good and certain opinion they had of being a son of England and an heir of the House of York, they gave, or rather rendered to him the noble and gentilitious ensign and title of La Rose Blanche: the White Rose, being [the] proper and ancient device of the House of York. And in *re*gard of his princely condition, there was a guard *of honour*, a gallant guard of soldiers and armed men [to a]ttend and to defend him. And he was much esteemed and favoured [by] *other* princes, as namely by the Archduke Maximilian, King [of the Roma]ns, and by Philip his son, Duke of Burgundy, and [by Charles, the] French king, and by the kings of Portugal *and Scotland* and [by the nobles] of Ireland and by other many *noble princes*. / And they **169*** promised to give good assistance in his enterprise.

[The practices of Henry VII with the Duke of Burgundy]

But as soon as King Henry heard these news and well apprehended the dang[er,] he [bestir]*red* himself so dexterously and so diligently, and he was so vigilant and so provident as that he found means to alter and to check and finally to *quench the* good affection and gracious inclination of the foreign princes and lords towards this young duke, and to make them to ab*andon him*. And first, and to *this* end, he sent Dr William Warham (after Archbishop of Canterbury) [and] Sir Edward Poynings, a grave and worthy knight, to [the] said princes and lords of Burgundy, etc., and to inform them that *they were misin*formed and were abused. For the king affirmed peremp[torily] that [he w]hom they took to be the son of King Edward [was merely a counterfeit and the son] of a Fleming and of a base fellow, and the[refore requests they would no further countenance him nor so much wrong their wisdoms and nobleness to give him any hope of succour.] *And they received this* / **169v*** message so well as that they obtained of [Philip,] Duke of Burgundy (for Maximilian his father was before returned into Austria), that Perkin should have no grace *nor succour* nor help in his dominions by any of his [subjects.] But he excepted the widow Duchess of Burgundy, the [aunt of Richard,] and whom as he had no power to command, because she had all [jus]tice and consideration in those great and large signories whereof her dowry was composed. And the duke's [Council also] assured the king's ambassadors that no lords in their provinces should [as]sist Perkin nor any of his complices, for the [honour and] love which the duke and they bore to the King of England, and for the desire which the duke their *mast*er had to be in peace and amity with the King of England,

*and concluded a*new the ancient and reciprocal league which had been between England and Burgundy. [T]hus the king supplanted Richard of York in the countries *under authority of the D*uke of Burgundy.

But I can say little of the hope of help which he *was promis*ed by the voyage into Portugal, where albeit he was well and honourably received, yet by reason of the far distance of the country it ma*y be gues*sed that he built little upon the aid of the King of Portugal. But he ret*urn*ed, for he understood that he had many great friends in England and also in Ireland, and that they desired much to see him and to have him to be their king. And
168 hereupon he sailed with a pretty fleet into Ireland, / and there he [w]as very welcome therefore, and received as the younger son of King Edward IV. [Some of the] Geraldines and other great lords in Ireland purposed to make him their king. But [whilst] this matter was there treated, King Henry sent Dr Henry Dean, Abbot of Llanthony, and a w[ise, able] man, into Ireland. And he made him Chancellor of Ireland, and he sent also with him the foresaid Sir Edward Po[ynings,] *and he* gave them so good instruction as that anon the reb*els persuaded* Perkin he could do no good with the Irish. And he resolved to return home.

[The means used by Henry VII to prevent the practice of Perkin in Ireland]

But in the *mean*time, whilst he was in Ireland, he was informed and
169v assured that King James of Scotla[nd] / wished well unto him and had a good opinion of his cause, and would help him to his right by all means. This news was most welc*ome* to Perkin, and he forthwith went into Scotland, and he found his entertainment there answerable to the adver*sity* which he had before. For the king did not only receive him honourably, but also yielded to him his title and style of Duke of York, and promised to give him strong footing in England. And he called him cousin, and to make him yet *more* akin or nearer allied to him, he bestowed in marriage upon him the most noble and fair lady Catharine Gordon, his ne[ar] kinswoman, and daughter of Alexander, Earl [of] Huntley. And further also, he forthwith raised forces to hel*p him* to recover his right in Engla*nd*.

[This lady was so ra]rely [fair and so lovely that King Henry VII wondered at her beauty and was enamoured of h]er, and so [sent her to London to be safely kept till his return out of the West Countries where he was then and first saw her. Robert Grafton]

[When King Henry heard this, he was more perplexed than before,
170 knowing King James to be a wise and a valiant] / prince, and that he would not easily be gu*lled or* abused by any counterfeits or imposters. And [true it is] that King James was very precise and curious in the discerning of *impostures and* would not accept Perk*in* [till] he was clearly ascertained that he was the true son [of Edward IV.] *And he became a* friend unto him, and the rather also because there was then *some contention*, and between King Henry and King J*ames, and who bore* him little good will; by reason whereof, King James was *the enemy of King Henry*, and therefore would be apt *to give* grace and aid to Perkin. All this was well understood. But yet he was *so circumspect* and so provident as that he thought that there might practice be brought to pass to bring King James out of his good opinion *and* liking of [Perkin, and alienate him, as] he had done with other princes in the same cause.

[The practice of Henry VII with the King of Scots and of Castile, to get or supplant Perkin]

And for this cause he wrote to the King James, and he persuaded and informed him th*at he should* abandon his enemy, who was a counterfeit, etc., and that *he* would requite the king's courtesy and favour in anything he could, and he also made great offers of rich rewards. But all could not prevail with King James, for besides that he stood *in* [ill affection to Henry VII,] he would n[ot] dishonourably leave and abandon a distressed prince flying to him for succour, and much less delive[r him] to King Henry, being Perkin'*s* mortal enemy, and to be slain and destroyed by h*im*.

This answer was very unpleasant and distasteful to King Henry. But he, being a man that could suddenly apprehend all occasions and all adva[ntages,] and could readily find means of help and remedy for his evils, called to mind that there was great love and friendship betwixt King James and Ferdinand, King of Castile, and who was a prince worthy to be beloved and honoured, for he was one of the most worthy princes then living. And as it also happened then (and happily) there was good intelligence and amity betwixt King Henry and King Ferdinand, insomuch as there was a motion or treaty of marriage to be made betwixt Arthur, the Prince of Wales, and Catharine, daughter of the King Ferdinand. And it [wa]s mutually well liked and embraced.

Therefore, King Henry [des]patched in post a wise and worthy gentleman toward [Casti]le, and gave him instructions (besides his letters) to advertis*e the* King of Castile of that which had passed between [the King of Scot]land and him, and how unkindly King James answered *him*, [and so to urge] Ferdinand to use his power and credit [with King James] *to* del[ive]r Perkin to him or *dismiss him*. [King Ferdinand undertakes this, sends Don Pedro [Don Pedro Ayala] Ayala, not one Peter Hiales nor Peter Hailes, as our vulgar stories have,] / *an* **170v** obscure man, but a signal gentleman [of a ver]y noble house, and a wise and learned man, [as he well declare]d himself to be in this employment; *for he so* well acquitted himself therein as that he obtained [of King J]ames his faithful promise forthwith to dismiss [Perkin] *and* quite to leave him to himself and to his fortunes. [Yet] *he* would by no means deliver him to the King of England. For he held that were barbarously and impiously to *violate the* law of hospitality and to betray his friend and his noble guest to his *certain de*struction. And yet this king, according to his promise, [comma]nded Perkin to depart out of his country. And [thu]s again King Henry overreached Perkin with his arms and *his* policy, and, **virtute vel dolo**, supplanted him everywhere.

And now Perkin was driven of force to return into Ireland for his convenient repassage unto his friends. And being arrived there he was again well entertained as a prince of England. And whilst he was in Ireland and practising for the domin*ion*, Charles the French king sent to him two gentlemen, Loys de Lucques and Estienne Friant, earnestly to request Ha[ll] in H[enry VII] Perkin to come into France to him, as to one who was and would be his best friend, and that he would take his part and assist him to recover the kingdom of England, his inheritance. And this offer was made then unfeignedly and from his heart. And the reason was because the King of England and he were fallen out (as I declared before), *and there was* great feud. And the King of England threatened to invade France with a mighty army, and [both of them prep]ared forces to fight.

And Perkin hasted into France, and the king received him with great honour, and as a great prince, and appointed a guard to attend upon him, the captain whereof was Monsieur Congresalle. And this was another thorn in King Henry's eye. And on better advisement, fearing that he should take more hurt than good by force, therefore he began to think of accord and peace, and made his desire thereof and also very fair conditions to be propounded to the French king, who soon and willingly hearkened thereunto. And there was friendship made and a league concluded *be*twixt these kings.

And anon the French king looked stra*ngely upon* Perkin and was alienated suddenly from him. And Perkin, not liking that, [suspecting King Charles might upon some capitulation of the new league deliver him to the King of England, therefore he secretly made from Paris to his aunt of Burgundy again, to whom he as was before very welcome. She encouraged
171 him afresh to pursue his design.] / And although Perkin was thus dishonourably left and forsa[ken,] *and although he might* have been much discouraged and dejected, but yet all his spirits nor all *his daring was not quenched*, presuming that he had many and good and great friends in his *party*, and who favoured his right and title and wished him *well* and would afford their best means for the accomplishment *of his designs*.

[And he makes another voyage] into Ireland, but albeit and as in like manner the Irishmen had promised to him [all assistance,] *by the king's* means they fell from him and failed him. I have d*isclosed that* they were so hardly and secretly curbed by the care and wisdom of [the king's officers.] And then from Ireland he sailed into England, and he *landed* [at Bodmin] in Cornwall. And the Cornishmen and other western men [received him very] gladly and honourably and were willing and ready to assist him. And they *proclaimed* him King of England and of France, etc., and by the title of King of England, etc., as he was before proclaimed in the [north parts o]f England and by the counsel and countenance of the King of Sc[otland.

[And now] Perkin marched into Devonshire, and he came to Exeter and [lay siege to it,] *and not*withstanding so many great foreign and domestical friends had forsak*en him*, he had above five thousand men in his train and army. But yet the king's army was at hand and much stronger. And not to be cha*rged*, he was fo[rced to leave the] siege and to seek to save himself. And now these few followers which were left, seeing his weakness of forces
172 and fearing the great and many mischiefs, and *seeing* / the great forces of [t]he king which were approached unto them, they fled from Perkin. And he being thus abandoned resolved instantly to save [h]imself by flight, and being well mounted and accompanied with [some forty or fifty] gallant and resolute gentlemen, he posted toward the Abbey of [Be]aulieu in Hampshire and he arrived safely there. And he [en]tered the monastery and took the sanctuary and claimed the holy privilege *and pro*tection of the place. And the king's forces pursuing him [foun]d where he was, and came to the Abbey and would have *taken* Perkin away perforce. But the abbot and the religious [persons] would by no means endure that there should be any violent and impious *threat* to be offered [against their holy privilege.] Whereof the king being advertised sent his messenger*s with* [proffers of favour] and mercy to Perkin, and to promise to him [such hon]ours and dignities [and revenues as should be grateful to him. Upon which fair conditions and protestations Perkin yields himself up.]

175v *And the king k*ept him in the court as a noble person and used him very bount[ifully.] But his kindness lasted not long. For [the king's jealousy tor]mented him much, as that afterwhile he abated his favour [and bounty toward him] *the*n and there, and whereby he was restrained of much of that liberty *which he had at* his first coming. Whereupon he grew malcontent and *despairing* of his safety. And thereupon soon after, he passing [by the

[Perkin's entertainment in the court]

monastery] at Sheen, he entered it suddenly and gave his guard the slip, [claiming the privilege of] that holy house, and the which was granted to him. And so he was then rid of his keepers and of his fea*rs*. *When the king* heard this, he sent again messengers and mediators to *go and* persuade him to return to the court, and with great and large [promi]ses of honours and of advancement, as before. But Perkin [durst] not trust the king, because he had broken such promises before.

And then the king dealt with the [pri]or to deliver Perkin to him. But he was a good and pitiful man and would not yield to del*iver his* prisoner or guest unless the king would promise to [use] him favourably. And the king made faithful promise *to do this*, and Perkin was again delivered to him. But as soon as he had him in his hands, he sent *him* to the Tower, and where he was hardly used, and much *lament*ed therewith the care and misery of his imprisonment *and* grief, and insomuch as he would curse his princely *state with* groans and oftentimes deep sighs, and would desire and wish that he rather had been the son of a peasant than of a king or of any Plantagenet. And indeed everyone could tell he fared t[he] worse for his name, for it was **173**** observed then there were three m[en] who were most feared of the king, therefore most hated by him: Edward Plantagenet, Earl of Warwick, Perkin Warbeck (alias Rich[ard] Plantagenet) and Edmund de la Pole, son of King Edward's sis[ter,] all of the family of York. But the king feared Perkin much [more] than the other twain, being of a more ambitious and active spir[it] and more sensible of his wrongs than they. Therefore he took mu*ch* more care and employed more counsel and treasure in the seeking [and] suppressing him, and answerably aggravated his miseries and dis[graces,] which now began to exceed. For now he was not only sharply rest[rained] in the Tower, but the fame was that the question, or **Gehenne**, was given him. Sometimes he was taken forth of the Tower and [carried in the] most ignominious manner abroad and set in a pillory, [otherwhile in] the stocks. / But he was not yet *arrived* at the worst of his entertainment in **175v** the Tower, for anon some wise and eloquent and treacherous orators were sent to him to persuade him to [submi]t himself to the king and to crave his pardon and to confess his fault and to renounce his blood and his birth and his title and to take the name of Perkin Warbeck, that of a poor Dutchman, upon him, and they *mi*ght the more colourably do it, because he was brought up in the Lower Germany. But he utterly refused to slander or to belie himself, and in no case to abuse and to defa*ce his* lineage.

But when the king saw that he could not be [wrought] to this recantation by fair means nor by any cunning persua*sion or an*y flattering devices, then his durance was made much more hard, [and now he was] lodged and more hardly and poorly fed and worse clad, [until at length] he [by mi]series and by torments and other [extremities was forced to say anything and content to unsay what the king would have him.] / And then (after that he was **176** taken from the *Tower and* by these cruel me*thods tortured, he* made a recantation and a renunciati*on* and of his princely name of Plan*tagenet*, [and] *of his* parentage, and of his title to the *crown, and* he confessed and professed himself to be but a mean *and base* son of Warbeck and some *lowborn woman*. And he *confessed* himself to be very base and mean, as you may see at large in the chron*icles* of Grafton and of Edward Hall, etc.

And he was constrained to sign this confession, and this being done, he brought by officers unto the more public places of London and West[minster,] *and as before* related, there he was used like a base malefactor and he was se*nt* to the pillory; and now he was prepared and accommodated to speak anything basely. And then he was commanded to read *and to* pronounce with a loud voice the writing cont*aining the* foresaid recantation and renunciation. And he obeyed and rea*d it*, as that *he persuaded* the multitude to think he was so mean and so base a man as he professed.

*And it sou*nded so basely and so vilely in the ears of the people standing about him and giving cre*dence to th*at vile and base matter which was delivered by him and of himself, as it had *been* [current.] *And* immediately **varium et mutabile vulgus** changed their opinion of Perkin and of his princely birth and quality and said that now *he was ignoble* in that he was but a counterfeit *a*nd an imposter and a base and ignoble fellow and a forei*gner and a* poor Fleming. *Nor was it* suspected, or at the least at that time or a good while after, that this was a forced and co*unterfeit* confession drawn from him by threats and by terrors and torture; for that *many of* them which had heard thereof had not the wit and reason *to co*nceive and to consider that racks and torments [will] make a man say anything, and belie himself, a*nd* [falsely accus]e any other man (although he be a good *and just man). And in* testimony hereof there be many exa[mples of m]en who in [torture have not only] *been brought* / to accuse *their* fellow thieves, but [other, and falsely.

[The force and mischief of torture]

176v

[Of tortures I have written at large in the 13th Book of my **Baron Cap**. 16]

[Seneca telleth of a man who, being suspected of theft, was enforced by torture to confess the theft and his fellow thieves. But having none, he a]ccused the good and just Cato, to the end to avoid the tortures. [Which is worse, it] maketh men not only to slander other men, but also by false oaths to blaspheme Almighty God. Wherefore [St Augustine] enveigheth sharply against this cruel [use of torture,] and amongst many other faults which he findeth [in it, this is] one: **Tortus si diutius nolit sustinere tor[menta, quod n]on commisit, se commississe dicit**. And this the pri*soner does* because he may the sooner come to exchange those [torments with] death, and the which is much less painful and less grievous.

August*ine*, **De Civitat*e* Dei, Lib**. 19

And by *these* **Gehennes** and cruel means of expression of confession, *this Rich*ard (alias Perkin), not able to endure the question, confessed and professed anything [which] was required of him and slandered and belied hims[elf and hi]s princely parentage, and the which to do, although *it wa*s a great fault, yet it was the more excusable and *ve*nial in him because he was young and ignorant [and could not yet] be confirmed in any brave and firm resolutions of princely ambit and of religion, and the worse also by reason of his long imprisonment and great t[rouble,] besides that he had no friends *to* advise and to counsel him, nor so much as in charity to comfort him. But he was a miserable and desperate and a forlorn man and feared so to be forever. And at th*is point* hereunto I may add that if learned and grave men, and me[n of gra]ce, [ha]ving large and great talents of spirit and of science, have for fear of such pu[nish]ment denied some chief points of Christian faith and have been accused fo[r the torture sake] (and whereof there is testimony in the ecclesiastical stories) then may th[is] young and unlearned man Perkin be allowed and excused in tortures to renounce earthly and worldly things.

But because *the means* and effects of torture are always evil, therefore not *only* the doctors of the civil law, but also of theolog[y,] / and the best of 177 them, condemn and abhor tortures. And they have good warrant, and drawn [from the ex]ample of our Lord Jesus Christ, who, notwithstanding that he certainly knew the c*are of his c*elestial father to be infinite, and his faith and his love toward him most constant and *firm, yet* in the extremity of his tortures and torment charged his father imp*licitly with* ******p and with inconstancy, and, as it were, dishonourable revolt.

[The French call torture **la Gehenne**]

[There is yet a]nother mischief of torture, and it is **Arc[anum Gehenne**, a secret of torture, or of hell. That is when the prison]er's body by extreme torment [is brought into any mortal state or symptom of death, or made incurable and deadly. Then to avoid the imputation of murder, the prisoner by a short and private process is condemned of some capital crime and presently executed whilst there is yet some life in him. And to that censure Perkin at last came.] *This* / ignominious degradation, and (as it were) the 178 utter *denial of all honour* and dignities, wrought such effects in the commo*n people* that in a moment they reputed him to be a counterfeit. And yet this was not sufficient to satisfy *the king*, nor to secure and void *him* of jealo*usy*, nor anything else but the shedding of his life and his blood, and the dea[th] of Perkin. And that could not be brought to *bear* by course of law, nor by the hand of [justice,] because Perkin had not been attainte[d nor] condemned of any capital crime. [But] after that scruple or obstacle had been a little considered, th[ere] was soon found out a way to take that away [and ma]tter enough to make him guilty of a capital offence.

And for this purpose it was devised and resolved that there should a practice of escape be offered to him. And be[c]ause the case of Edward Plantagenet, Earl of Warwick, was the like unto this, as well because he was not attainted of any cri*me as that* his death was as much desired as that of Perkin, and that his guilt was as little or less, [therefore he must also desire] to escape. There wanted nothing of their slaughter but matters of capital guilt. Therefore, these false friends and treacherous instruments were now sent and willed to propound the same practice of escape to the said Perkin and the Earl of Warwick. [And some say] the innocent Earl of War[wick at his] arraignment was charged with the persuading of his cousin Perkin to make an escape. *And he was an* innocent young man and gladly hearkened to that [mo]tion and plot of their escape, prizing liberty above all things, and ex*pecte*d nothing but death or miserable captivity continual and most woeful.

[York and Warwick parallels]

And [soon after], both these young men, and cousins, and *innocent, as the* world thought, were accused [as guilty of practice and conspiracy] to steal out of the Tow[er, and were for the same arraigned and condemned to die, but great difference put in their process and execution. For the Earl of Warwick was] / tried by his noble peers, and he had th[e suppliance of a 179 noble] and an honourable place, to wit, in the [Tower of London.] But Perkin (alias Richard) was tried [by a common jury, who] are men many times of little honesty. *And* [his punishment] *was that* which they call a dog's destiny (that *is, hanging*). And he suffered it in the most infamous pl[ace, Tyburn.] *And the* extremity of his punishment answered well with the hatred which was borne to him. And he was in this base and vile manner proceeded *against so it might* be thought that he was a base fellow, and *as if* the name or nickname of Perkin Warbeck [was] supposed to have utterly disnobled him and (as [it were]) divested him of all noble blood and of titles of honour. But it serve[d best for a cloak] against that purple shower which fell at the fall of this miserable prince.

But yet [methinks] in consideration that the capital crimes of young Clarence and of Richard [were alike and] the same, and their quality of much equality, it ha[d been more] honourable to have made them both to pass the same fi[le] *and* justicing sword. But I rather think that the [Earl of Warwick] had been brought to as shameful a death as Perkin, if the [wit and malice of the cruel Car]dinal could by any trick or device have brought him to be reputed a counterfeit and a base *person*. [But all men knew] *this earl* was no counterfeit, no more than was King Richard nor his son nor the de la Poles. Yet *their fates were all* alike, and all passed one purgatory. And therefore it was all one to be fi*ctitious* or a true prince. And this Edward of Warwick was not only a tr[ue] prince of the royal blood of England, but he was also an honest man, *free from a*ll evil desires and evil practice. Yet he was restrained [of his liberty,] and [for the] most part of his life a prisoner, from the time of the attainder of his father until he [suffered.] And he was as innoc*ent* as the lamb which was wont to be sacrificed. And this was after they had [survived King Richard] their uncle [about fifteen years.] And *the survival* of one of them was a sure and happy means to clear the king from the slander of this murder.

And these were the ends of these two noble plants of the roya*l* Genest, and of the House of York. And they may well be said to be parallels, but not after the manner of Mr T.G., but after Plutarch's manner. For they were bo*th eq*ual in blood and in time, and partakers of the same and of the like ill for*tunes* and like calamities. And they were both held in jealousy for one strange *reason*, and both arraigned and both condemned and both put to death *for a crime* which is disputable and *held by some to be no fault* at all.

[Now let us bring their fault (if it were one) to the test and better opinion
179v of the more grave and learned ju]/dges of the best *laws*, and whereby we shall come to know certainly [of wha]t kind their fault *is* called in our law.
[Of escapes] [And first] I will advertise that I have observed that some hold an escape to be but an [error, a natural dislike of bondage, or a forfeit] of simplicity. And they hold also that it proceedeth from a [natural and very toler]able desire of liberty. And these opinions may [also] be good and right, and at the least in the cause [of these two p]rinces, and they may also the better be received and enter*tained* [if it be we]ll considered and weighed that this plot of [these two] cousins for escape was not projected by themselves, but it was cunningly and treacherously [propounded] by proper instruments of such frauds and deceits unto them (being silly and simple and inexperienced *young me*n), and to the end to entangle them in the snares *of* [some c]apital offence, and so consequently of death, and of [which kin]d of offences they stood clear before, or not accused, and were not obnoxious *to the penalties* of them, by reason that they had never been [in]dicted nor attainted of any capital crime. *And the r*eason thereof must be because they were guiltless *or in*nocent persons, as all men would think.

And I confess that here I say very much more than I would have said if the most p*rofound judges and o*ther our historians had not said as much.

For they all agree in opinion *and they* say and affirm that the king / could 182* not take away [the lives] of Perkin Warbeck nor of the Earl of [Warwick] until the practice of their escape wa[s laid to] *their charge*, and that they were also found guilty ther[eof] and condemned for it. Ergo, then, they were [not traitors] before, neither was Perkin a counterfeit now to be thought, but [a prince of the] blood and claiming the crown. Otherwise, as he was Perkin of Flanders and a base fellow, *he* was a most culpable [and] notorious traitor, and there needed no e*xcuse* to be sought to put him to death, because treas*on is of* all the greatest offence. But surely if he were [not a traitor, it was] as great as tyranny to make of an innocent man and of a g[uiltless] captive a traitor or a felon, and that by trains and [acts to] *make him* guilty and attainted of a crime which was not any offence or cri*me or semblance* of a crime.

For a man without offence *may* desire and seek freedom and de*sire to be* out of bondage and out of the miserable and hate*ful* state of captivity. And an innocent and a tru[e man] may purpose and intend that act of es[cape, [Escape, what] also] commit it, and yet be still an honest man and a faithful subject and a true ma*n* to God *and* to his country. For nature and reason teach an[d] allow all men to eschew injuries and oppression a[nd] to avoid and also to hate captivity and servitude, and to love and seek liberty and security above all other *things*. Bes[ides,] this practice of these young men to escape [was] found (as Polydore well observed) **crimen alie[num]** and not **crimen proprium**. And then how much [greater was the wrong] and cruelty to chastise, and much more to take [away their lives] *for the o*ffence of another man.

But [however i]/t may be laid upon them, yet it was nothing [but a desire 183v of] liberty and of deliverance out of the hard captivity [in which they were *restrain*ed for small or no offence. The civil law holdeth a suspicion [of flight or escape to be no crime: **su]spicio fugae, quia non solet detrimentum Reipub*licae* adferre, non censetur crimen**. [So Ulpian. And by the laws of England, if a prisoner] do escape who is not imprisoned for felony nor for [treason,] but for some other less fault, and which is called trespass, then according to the old [law of England,] Escape **non adiudicabitur versus eum** [Justice Stanford in **qui [commissus e]st prisone pro transgressione**: i.e., escape shall not be **Pleas de la Corone**, adjudged for felony or other crime in one who is committed for a tres[pass. **Lib**. 1, **Cap**. 26, 27] For the offence of escape is made in] common law to be of the same guilt and nature [with] the crime whereof the prisoner is attainted *and judged* guilty. For certainly neither Edward, Earl of Warwick, and Richard (alias Perkin) [were attainted] for any felony or treason or other capital offence committed by *them and law*fully proved against them,

And therefore the desire to *es*cape is no offence, and according to that, the French word **eschapp*er*** *is interprete*d 'to be free', and the Frenchmen translate **eschappé** into Latin **salvus**. For a man, especially an innocent man, and guiltless *of* felony or treason, to seek to be at liberty and to be safe, and *for deli*very of bonds and the fear of an unjust death is a very small and a very venial *offence*, and much more if it be **crimen alienum**. But be whose or what it will, it was but t*he natural desire for liberty*. And therefore it was not the law, but the will – and the wicked will – of the princes' enemies which cut off their l*ives*. Pleading for those two young men will now do them no good, and therefore I will say no more but **requiescat**

in pace, as also their persecutors *may say.*

As soon as these noble Richard and Edward were cut off, some of those treacherous varlets which were the instruments *for* betraying and drawing
184 them into this snare *or* n[et,] as [W]/alter Blewyt and Thomas Astwood, servants to the L[ieuten]ant of the Tower, were sent soon after them in post to Elysium by the w*ay* of Tyburn, beca[use] they should tell no tales.

And thus much for the his[toric]al relation of the life, adventures, actions, and *attempt*s of Richard, the younger Duke of York. And for the true
185 *report thereof* / there cannot be produced greater testimonies than these faithful [witnesses] of all conditions and estates. And they all maintained at the last g[asp that Perkin was the true Duke of York,] and whose testimonies shall follow by and by.

Before *that, however*, [give me but leave on the way] to answer a calumny brought against this duke who was called in scorn Perkin Warbeck. [A new writer] affirmeth that this Prince Richard was a counterfeit and an imposter. And therefore he would have it thought he knew much, and especially matters of [histories] as of other countries and nations, and would not have *himself thought ignorant* of any of them. And yet he shows himself pl*ainly ignorant in* stories, as well of Don Sebastian of Portugal as this of Perkin Warbeck, and that in a pamphlet or b*ook* to have discovered his knowledge of the story of this p*rince*. The title and the subject thereof is **The History of P[erkin Warbeck**.]

In this book he spendeth all his skill and wits and his labour [to prove him] *to* be a counterfeit prince, and to make him as a parallel in adv[erse fortune and supposed base quality] to this great Don Sebastian, late King of Portugal, whom also he terms [an imposter. And to arrive] to this extraordinary knowledge he would have us think that he took much pains in perusing and sifting [of authors; and indeed I think he did sift them.]

[Whether Don Sebastian of Portugal were a counterfeit or no]

And yet I will not deny but that these two may be *compared* as well for their fortunes as also for their true and proper qua[lities.] They were both the sons of kings, and both unhappy and miserable *men*, [but] no counterfeits – and as it hath well appeared here already for the *one, and* Perkin, and as it shall appear reasonably well for the other by and by, and by the leave of th*is* gentleman, and who will find that he understood not rightly either the story or the prince.

But as concerning his ignorance in the case of Don Sebastian, [it may be tolerated,] because the Spaniards, when he was in Spain, disguised the certain rep*ort* and concealed the truth thereof from him; for they are close and wary and [most politic,] and will give many gudgeons to tramontane travellers. Bu*t there is no* excuse to be made for this ignorance, being a professor of such knowledge of the public and common stories o*f this* country. At the least for *a* professor to profess such ignorance therein is a gross and a silly blindness, and worse than **caecutire in sole**, as the pr*overb* is.

But mark the strange power of verity, and ever to be reverenced. For she from this wi*tness* hath drawn and, as it were, extorted such a confession of the right of this pr*ince that ma*tter could not be more thereof, nor more could not be said of them who have earnestly ass*isted him* and most endeavoured to deliver him from the scandals put upon him. For he saith that Richard, Duke of York, and Perkin Warbeck were both one man.

And because you shall see that I do to him no wrong, *h*ear his own words; **186** and these they be: **Whether I name *Peter, or Perkin*, or Warbeck, or Prince Richard, or Richard, Duke *of* York, or King Richard the Fourth, all is one man, and all had *one en*d.** Thus he, and thus (and unwillingly, as it seemeth) he confess*eth and consorte*th with and agrees with the advocates for the right of Duke Richard, and he is on our side most *when* he pretendeth to be against us.

*In t*he comparing Perkin and Don Sebastian together, he argueth and censureth and he conclu*deth* both counterfeits. Yet I doubt not but to give him such better [reaso]ns of Don Sebastian as that he shall also change his opinion in that matter and conclude the contr*ary of* him after the manner which he said of Perkin, viz., that whether *he saith Don Seba*stian the counterfeit or Don Sebastian late king, all is one. And because this may seem to be a digression, and will then require to be sh*own to be one* of the many reasons and arguments which I have for this prince, [I will urge some reaons] such as I think may serve sufficiently *at* the least to prove that Don Sebastian was [no Ψeudo-Sebastian, nor a false kin]g.

It must then be prem[ised that Don Sebastian, King of Portugal,] / was **186v** overthrown in a very fierce and bloody battle [in the fields of Alcaz]ar by the King of Morocco, and where it was thought that he was [slain. But] he escaped the fatal edge of the sword and fled [secretly, travestite, or disguised.] And travelling in that manner through many [parts of Afr]ica and of Asia, *he* spent therein by the space almost of thirty years, and in the which he suffered much care and lived in captivity and in muc*h* [misery. But a]t the last, by the favour of God, he escaped and came [into Europe, with] purpose to have gone into Portugal and to have taken again his kingdom.

And as he passed on his way, *he* [came] to Venice, and there he discovered himself and craved a[id of the Venetian] state to assist him for the recovery of his kingdom and the crown of Portugal. And the Venetian state entertained him w*ell and honourab*ly, and as a prince distressed, and gave him good words. But they durst not give h[im] *an*y aid or lend any forces for fear of giving offence to the King of [Spain.] But yet the chief senators, and a great many of the wisest, and gentlemen of the signory, made no doubt of his truth and of his title. And amo[ngst them] Signor Lorenzo Justiniano, a gentleman of the senatorius order, and [a very] wise and grave gentleman, was appointed by the state of Venice to [be a] commissioner with other worthy and wise gentlemen to hear and to examine th[e cause] of Don Sebastian. And they took much pains for the searching and finding *out* the truth of this cause. And the Signor Justiniano, being here [not] long since Ambassador Ligier for the Signory of Venice a*verred* and protested solemnly that he and all the other honourable and grave [commissioners] were clear and very confident that this Sebastian (whom G. saith was a counterfeit) was certainly, and without all qu[estion he was] *the* true Don Sebastian, late King of Portugal. But not[withstanding] all this their knowledge, yet, and as I said even now, the Venetians durst not, *because of* the King of Spain, lend any succours. **[Hic legatus haec domino Baroni Darce]*ii* [retulit]**

And then he p*urposed to* try some other great lords and princes of Italy, and he solicited them, but they all *for the same* cause as aforesaid estranged them/selves from him and withheld their helping hands. Whereupon **187** Sebastian was counselled to leave Italy and go into [Fr]ance, in regard there was a king who favoured right and feared *no*body. And he took Florence in his way and entered the city disguised [in] the habit of a friar. But yet by some who were set as spies at Venice by Ferdinando, the Grand [Duke of Tuscany, to follow] and to observe him, he was discovered and made known to Ferdinando, this Grand Duke, who, to curry [favo]ur with the King of Spain, Philip II, and for some other weighty, commo[dious] *and formida*ble [consi]derations, delivered Sebastian to the governor of [Orbatella,] a Spanish port in Tuscany, and he sent him by sea to the [Count de] Lemos, Viceroy of Naples, and from thence he was con[veyed into Spain.] And there for a while his entertainment was [no better than in the galleys. And what othe]r entertainment he had I know not, [but the fame went certainly that he was secretly] made away since Philip III [was king.

[But the said Viceroy of Naples confessed to a friend of his that he verily
187v believed] / his said prisoner was the true Sebastian, [King of Portugal, and] was induced to be of the opinion by [the strange testimonies and many] strange and peculiar marks which [some honou]rable Portugueses – and the which were all *well acquainted with him – did find* [about the body of] this Sebastian. And this also is a good argument: *that* [the French king,] Henry IV, was by good information persuaded that this was the true King
[Henry IV] Sebastian. For when [the news was] *brou*ght to him that the Duke of Florence had sent [this Sebastian to] the King of Spain, he was much moved and troubled and offended, *and he* called for the queen and told her what an ill deed [her uncle] had done, and used these very words: **Votre oncle a [fait u]n acte forte indigne de sa personne**.

189 [And much more] / might be said in the behalf of this Don Sebastian if the place w*ould permit*. [But this] may serve for sufficient intelligence and instructions for the gent*leman to* recant his errors, which made him injuriously to call Don Sebastian *and* Perkin Warbeck imposters and counterfeits, lest these and such errors be *the work of* a counterfeit historian. And the causes neither of the one nor of *the other are* to be liked any whit the worse for erroneous or hard and rash censure *in his work*, as I noted before.

And thus do men experienced in the affairs of state and of policy who think their titles and claim to be s*light*ed because that they were slightly or inconstantly or perfidiously used by some princes of *better claim*; that the end and scope of all which these princes do is their own good, and to serve their *own* turns. And it is a very rare thing to find in any story the example of a [prince bei]ng seized and possessed of any signory or principality, how
188 unlawfully or how wrongfully [soever,] who hath res/igned or rendered them or any of them willingly and quietly to the true heir *and own*er and *the* right proprietary thereof. And the reason is because that for the covetousness and the oppres*sion* of usurpers and of raptors and of tyrants, and their extreme thirst after the p*ossessi*ons and sovereignties and signories of other men are as insatiable *as* hell, and the which (as they say) will never be filled nor satisfied. And the*ir* greediness is fed with a violent and fanatical imagination that the *confines* and limits of their signories and principalities are never large enough ext*ended* so long as their neighbours have any land. And such were th*ey* who were Giants – that is men mighty and impious, such as would do any*thing. And such ambi*tious men desire to

extend the bounds of their domin*ions*, and for the force and reputation of great martial men and of conquerors. And that which these men *seek is solely their own gain*.

But it is a much more dishonourable act in a prince *to seize by* force or by 190
fraud the signories or territories or principa*lities from his cousins* or brothers or fathers and parents or *children, men stronger than* all heirs, but weaker than those Giants, and whom the laws of nature and *of nations exhort* to defend and to protect, as they are *the rightful* possessions and hereditary signories *of these men*. And such disseisins are mere avarice and of extreme injury, and **latronum praed*ae***, and are no*t only illegal* acts, but also impious and damnable *sins*.

And of such kind of men there be many *examples*, as well divine as profane, and none mo*re famous than* that of King Herodes, who, albeit he kn*ew the* blessed saviour and eternal and universal lord *was the true* and most rightful and lawful heir of the kingdo*m of the Jews*, and the which right was publicly *under* his hand, yet that subtle and false and covetous fox t*he usurper* was so far from restoring that kingdom to the true p*roprietary*, Jesus Christ, as that he sought and desired much rather to see him *perish and* to be cruelly and shamefully crucified. And by this e*xample* we see that the vassal renounced and dissseised his lieg*e*. And it was a great treason.

But yet *in* the world it is thought to be a much more heinous crime *for* the son to disseise his father and hold and usurp his signories and kingdom. And yet in this land it hath been seen that the so[n] hath taken the kingdom from his father and would not render [it again] to him, but rather sought to
bring his father to his end. The *signal* persons were Kings Edward II and [Edward II **et**
Edward III, and much after the same manner, Henry, Duke of Lancaster Edward III]
(after he had gotten the kingdom wrongfully) held it by force and by tort, and would not resig[n it] to the true heir thereof, namely to King Richard II, nor after his death to the Earl of March, although he knew [t]hese men to be no counterfeits nor imposters.

Neither was Edward, Earl of [W]arwick a counterfeit, but an undoubted Plantagenet and an heir [of] the House of York without all question. Yet King Henry VII would not *give up* the royal throne nor resign the sceptre
unto him. But / I wish that there had *been done no* more than the detaining 192v
of his royal heritage from him. *And* [all the injury] *which* were done him is not by the unjust disposition of the king, but [by the cruel] and evil counsel of his Cardinal favourite, and who *wanted the* blood of the young earl spilled, and then finding and seeing that [he could not prevail] with the king to have his way by law, yet he brought it to pass by another Machiavellian advice which he gave [to Ferdinand, King of Ca]stile, and the which was that he should not yield to con[clude the treaty of the mar]riage between Prince Arthur and his daughter [until] this earl and also Perkin were [taken away.] King Ferdinando followed his advice and advised and admonished the *king* for his own safety and security, as also for the more assured *safety* [of his son] and of his wife and of their issue, that these dangerous [impediments mi]ght be removed out of the way and out of the world. And this suit [took hol]d, and they were both dispatched and put to death and were *removed that* all might sing his **nunc dimittis**. For he desired to see the ruin and utter destruction of the House of York. *And he* died soon after execution of these two young princ*es*.

I might add hereunto for further example of the resolute and o*bstinate and envious* withholding of lands and signories and principalities by *foreign* princes from the true heirs and rightful lords and owners thereof, as namely the French kings, who certainly knew that *the king*s of England were and are the true heirs and just lords of Nor*mandy, of* Aquitaine, of Poitou, etc. Yet they would never restore these lands and provinces to our kings.

Moreover, he who [hath r]ead the book of Sir Edward Hoby entitled **La Anatomia de [Espagna**, and] some foreign writers, hath seen and understood that the kings of Spain unjustly detain [sundry] signories and principalities from the true and lawful heirs and just prop*rietors* thereof. And many more such examples of such wrongful rapines and tyrannical usu*rpers* might be brought here, but I like not to lay any imputations *of scandal* or infamy upon princes. And besides, such relations are occ*ursive everywhere* to the studious in ancient and modern stories. Wherefore I *keep silence* for all that I have read and heard of many oppressed princ*es who* demanded and claimed signories and principalit*ies from their true* heirs and proprietaries, but I *c*ould *relate much more*.

193 And therefore I dare not give any *com*fort to Don Sebastian. And in [brief, it is not possible] to persuade a king or prince who *is possessed* of any principality or signory, and althoug*h without* justice, to believe or to confess that another *is the* true lord and proprietary thereof and [hath a better] title or better right than he. And that is *a* maxim of nature and of *nations*, that possession or seisin of land is be*tter than any* titles. But if the wrong done by another such usurping *or* disseising lord be put to this former usurper and *detainer* and false possessor (and the possessor **male fidei**, as the [Imperial] jurisconsults will term him), then he will not st*ick* to say that such an usurping and rapinous prince d[oth] wrong, and that he unjustly occupieth and possesseth th*e* lands of another man. And hereof we have seen s*ome* examples in the very case and story of Perkin herebefore related.

But enough of this matter. And now we will [ex]hibit the catalogue of
194 witnesses or martyrs before promised. / And although the arguments and the *testimo*nies here already brought be *enough* for the proof and warrant of his *being* the son of King Edward, and there needeth no mor*e*, and yet, because *there be* plenty of proofs, and that according to the *ancient* principle, **abundans cautela non *nocet*;** *I* will add hereunto the names and testi*monies of* men, some noble and very signal person[s and] worthy and honest and well-understanding, *and who* maintained this duke's birth and title very st*rongly*. And some of them confirmed their testimonies *with t*heir bloods and lives given in witness of their *kno*wledge and belief in the premises. And they shall be as **testes** and witnesses *summoned.*

And I have made mention before of the testimony of Sir Robert Clifford, a knight of [a] noble house, namely of the barons Cliffords. I will [proceed
[More, Holinshed, Stow, Gainsford] with that whic]h is the more remarkable here in him because he was of a family *whic*h had long hated the family of York, *eve*r since the battle of Wakefield, and when and where [they] resolved upon such deadly enmity against that princely house *t*hat they vowed never to be reconciled nor satisfied *so* long as anyone of that family was remaining alive. But it happened happily that this un[charit]able vow was broken, and the Cliffords became again [followe]rs of the House of York, and this Robert

Clifford [serving] King Edward very near, and in good credit, [and] *su*ch as he had good and certain means to know [the king's son]s and to have special marks of them. *And he stated* as is aforesaid and certified that Perkin was [certainly the younger son] of King Edward IV, **ut supra**, and [though there was much wrought to change him in this opinion and alienate him from the prince, yet his knowledge stood upon such certainty that he confir]/med the 194v opinions and beliefs of many *who had been willing to recei*ve him and to learn by all *those many wise and sig*nal persons, and who for the most part [served] *the king and knew* the younger son of King Edward IV *and* were privy to the conveyance away *from England.*

And a chief among these *was the* Baron Fitzwalter, who maintained this [Perkin the] true Duke of York most constantly, and even [unto death.] Likewise Sir William Stanley was a*n a*ffecter of this Duke of York, albeit he was Lord [Chamberla]in to the King Henry VII and in great favour with him. And he *so mu*ch loved this king being Earl of Richmond that h*e for*sook his good and gracious lord and sovereign King Richard and preferred the advancement of the earl to the crown before his faith and allegiance to the king his master. And he died in the maintenance of the right of Richard, Duke of York. Likewise Sir George Neville, brother to the Earl of Westmorland, and Sir Simon Montfort and many other were confident and avowed th*at* Perkin was Richard, Duke of York. So did Sir William Da[ubeney,] father to the Lord Daubeney, Sir Thomas Thwaites, Sir Robert Ratcl[iffe] of the house of the Baron Fitzwalter, Sir John Taylor, Sir Thomas Challo[ner,] Thomas Bagnol, and many other gentlemen of quality and of good credit. And all these maintained that Perkin was the son of King Edward IV. There were also sundry prelates and priests, very learned and grave, and who had been chaplains to the king his father, or otherwise occasioned [to] attend in the court, as namely Dr Rocheford, Dr Poynes, Dr Su[tton,] Dr Worsley, Dean of St Paul's, and Dr Leyburn and Dr Lessey, and many o[ther] learned professors of divinity and intelligent clerks who would [not] endure to hear that he who was called Perkin was a counter*feit*, but that he was Richard, Duke of York.

More, Holinshed, Stow, Grafton, Hall, Gainsford

[**Idem auctores**]

And some of the nob[les] and more signal persons before named, viz., the Lord Fitzwalter, the noble progenitor of the earls of Sussex, and Sir William Stanley, Lord Chamberlai*n, and* [Sir Si]/mon de Montfort, Sir Robert Ratcliffe, 196* Sir [William] Daubeney and others could not be brought, [neither by] fair offers or with sharp cruel words or threats, to *change* [their] opinions and to recant t*heir beliefs*, [but in the affirmation thereof, as martyrs of state, confirmed their testimonies and liege faith with their bloods. In the same faith, the king's Serjeant Ferior, for the knowledge he had of Richard (alias Perkin), leaving the king's service, was executed as a traitor. Likewise, one Edwards, who had served this Duke Richard and afterwards the queen, his sister, in the place of a yeoman, was cut in pieces for the same cause, as also was Corbet, Sir Quentin Betts and Gage, gentlemen of good worth. And two hundred more at least were put to death in sundry cities and towns, particularly in Kent, Essex, Suffolk, Norfolk and about London for their confidence and opinion in this prince.

[And there were some great men, though they made no profession of their opinions and certain knowledge of this prince, yet they could whisper it one to another, which likewise in general words passed by all our better writers.]

198* [Holinshed, Grafton, Hall, Stow] And in brief he was held *in all* places to be the Duke of York and the son of [King] Edward, and as Holinshed and Grafton and *Hall and* Stow write. Not only the meaner sort of *the* people of England, but also the nobles b*elieved* all that was said of him, although he were called Perkin Warbeck. But if you suspect any favourable or partial dealing in these author*s* before cited (and for the which I know no reason, *for they were* not anything beholding to this young prince) you shall hear the same testimony and to the same effect given by the enemies both of King Richard [and of this Duke] Richard, and the which, doubtless, verity drew and ex*tor*ted from them.

And that is Sir Thomas Mo[re aft]er Dr Morton, and thus he writeth: **[The**
[John Morton, Thomas More] **man commonl]y called Perkin [Warbeck was as well with the princes as with the people held to be the younger son of King Edward IV.** And
197 Richard Grafton affirme]/th this. In Flanders, saith he, [and most of all, here in] England, it was received [for an undoubted truth,] not only of the people but also of [the nobles, that Per]kin was the son of King Edward IV. [And they all swore and] affirmed this to be true. Thus this hones*t author*.
[Mr William Camden] [I have also heard a] very grave and well-learned and well-experienced [writer say] there were many wise and grave and great persons [of good intelligen]ce who lived in that time and near unto it, and who affirmed [confidently this] Perkin was the second son of King Edward, *and that not*
199 *only the nobility* / but also that the people took Perkin for the certain Duke of *York*, and so consequently for the next and true heir of the crown.

And *this is firm testi*mony and proof that King Richard killed not both the brothers, *since one was alive* long after he was dead. And he had no [reason to kill the one an spa]re the other, being both of equal blood and titles. [Neither indeed was there ever any proofs made by testimony,
200 argument,] / by presumption, nor by reason of honour or of poli[cy that he was or could be] the perpetrator of this crime. But there *were* [many to the] contr[ary,] and arguments and testimonies brought here to prove that *he* loved those his nephews very dearly; and that he was full of their health and welfare and prosperity; and that he *cared for* them and kept them in safety so long as he could preserve *their* safety and life; and that he served the young king very obsequi*ously* and reverently and loyally; and that he was very loving and kind to the *sisters* of the young king, albeit they were to succeed their brothers *in the* inheritance of the kingdom before him (if they were legitimate).

And he kept not only *alive his* nephew, the Earl of Warwick, Edward Plantagenet, son of his elder brother George, Duke of Clarence, but also in safety and in pleasure, and was pleased that he should live in a stately and delightful house of his own. But if this Prince Richard had been ambitious and treacherous, he would rather have made that earl away, because his title was to take place before his own title, if his blood and title had not been corrupted and attainted by his father's attainder for treason.

In regard thereof, this good King Richard, when his own and only dear son died (and very immaturely), he then forthwith caused his other nephew John de la Pole, eldest son of the [Du]ke of Suffolk and of the duchess his sister, and then the next lawful [hei]r of the crown, to be proclaimed heir apparent (as hath *been* aforesaid, **Liber I**). And all this well showeth and testifieth that *the* king loved his princely kinsfolks and favoured the true and just and next title to the [crow]n in whomsoever it was.

But other men regarded [not] these rights so much, as the unhappy sequel showed, for they which *were* princes of the blood royal and the nearest to the crown [were soon]er or later rid out of the world, and violently. And [it is most probable that] they which were the plotters and practicers of [the death of the princes of] the House of York before made away were [as likely to dispatch the] rest afterward. And these evil a*ctions*, [without any great straining, might be imputed to the Lancastrian faction, instigated by the counsel and malice of that mortal enemy to the House of York, the Cardinal.

[For the clear proof hereof, the] *destruc*/tion of King Richard and of his **201v** son were *contrived by him, and not only of* his son, but also of the *Earl of Warwick* and of the rest of the princes *of the House of York. And what was prac*tised and acted herein may be imputed to these *ill-affected Lancastrians* [and to Morto]n. And there was necessity, though [an impious necessity, that the Lancastrians must act this.] For unless all these princes of [York, especially the males, were taken away, no other] titular lords or pretenders could be kings of this *land by any* colour of right nor by any other [means, unless he] *could* have married a daughter, and the eldest daughter, of [King Edward IV.

[And although] the deaths, and also the manners and kinds of the making away of the sons of King Edward are held by our writers [uncertain and obs]cure, yet it is manifest [at least for the general m]anner of their deaths. It may be affirmed that they were made away either by [the public or] by the private sword. And by the public sword, that is [the sword of justice and o]f battle or war, King Richard and the children of the Duke of [Clarence and the Duke] of Suffolk were dispatched. And to these some add [Perkin Warbeck.] And by the private sword (that is by secret [slaughters and close treachery,] which the Romans called **insidiae** and **dolus**, by smothering, by strangling, by poison, by sorcery and the like) [so passed] the eldest sons of King Edward and of King Richard and also [King Edward] himself, if he died of poison, as some credible authors [say;] *and that will be else*where argued here.

Public sword, private swor[d]

Sorcery and [the acts of treachery]

And that this private and treacherous sword was exercised [a]gainst this family of York there is not only conjecture for it, but good [testimony,] and also records. For I have read in an old manuscript book [it] was held for certain that Dr Morton and a certain countess, [conspirin]g the deaths of the sons of King Edward and some other, resolved that *these treach*eries should be executed by poison and by sorcery. And in the Parliament [of **anno** 1] Richard III there were taken and accused of sorcery and such [other devilish] practices Dr Lewis, Dr Morton, William Knevet of Buckingham, [the Countess of Richmond, and Thomas Nandick of Cambridge, conjurer, and others.

[There] was then also an earl accused of this crime of sorcery and other such hellish [and devi]lish arts. And I call them devilish arts because they were devised and always practised by the devil and his ministers and instruments. And I make no doubt but that whosever they *were* which gave counsel to shed the innocent blood of our English Abel, Ed*ward Planta*genet, Earl of Warwick, had their instructions from some infernal spirits, and th*at the* devil dealt with them, or they with the devil. And this is canonical. F*or it is revealed by* the Holy Ghost that the devil is a

murderer, and the murderers' fa*ther; and they obey* him and observe him, even as the dutiful child obeyeth his natural fath*er. And the* father doth not only will and command his child*ren* ********************************
****

203 **imperii infernalis**, and the which many t*imes are* so sore as that they may not be tou*ched; yet I would* touch them, but yet tenderly and softl*y*. And *I would not have* ventured had I not been bound by my solemn profession and in the *name of honour* to maintain the truth, and as well for the *regard which* I bear to all truth, as also for the special love and *duty which I bear* to the House of York, and the *which persuades* me to tell the truth for them and to do *them justice*.

And for this cause, I have laboured to purge and clean*se King Richard* in sundry foul crimes laid to his charge, but falsely, *and as* hath been made apparent here before. And especially my care hath *been to* redeem him from that most infamous and ugly scandal of the murder *of his* princely nephews, and for all the which crimes he hath been *a*ttainted, and ever without proofs and lawf*ul evidence*, and ever unheard. And therefore there may doubt be justly *cast upon* the justice of those processes.

And whereas *he is* accused and charged with the murder *of his* nephews, and falsely (as it hath been prov*ed), I* marvel why that they, holding Richard to be so politic and so pr[ovident] *and wise* as they acknowledge him to be, should not suggest and add tha*t he was t*he murderer of his nieces, the sisters of these princes. For as it was to no purpos*e to* make away the one brother and not the other, so it would not serve his turn [to rid] away the brothers if he spared the sisters. Wherefore certainly it behoved
202* *him* to have made away / all the other female chil*dren of Edward* IV, because the women of the blood [royal of England] are also capable of the crown [and have their] turn royal before any collateral [males.]

[Reasons why King Richard would not destroy his nephews]

He must also have destroyed the ch[ildren of his elder] brother George, Duke of Clarence, [Edward] Plantagenet, Earl of Warwick, and [the Lady Marga]ret his sister, after Countess of Salisb[ury, for they,] without their father's attainder and the [corruption] of their blood thereby, the which might easi[ly have been salved] by Parliament – for the lords pitied them, as also did the *people, who* respected no*t their* defects much – and that being then obtained, then those children of the *Duke of* Clarence had priority of blood, and a preced[ence] and pre-eminence of right and title to the crown before the said Richard the Protector.

And moreover, [I would know the reason] why King Richard might not endure the lives of [h]is nephews, being held to be illegitimate and so adjudged by [Parliament,] as well [as] the kings Henry VII and Henry VIII endured Arthur [P]lantagenet, the bastard of the same King Edward (and before noted), their **natales** and cases being alike *i*n manner *as I* intimated before. But more probably it might be supposed *the work of Henry VII* and of the cruel Cardinal: he who put to death the said innocent Edward, Earl of *W*arwick (not having committed any crime against the king or the people) did also by the same counsel, and of the same **malus genius**, take away the title of the foresaid Richard, Duke of York, and both for an imaginary fault, **et falso damnati crimine mortis** (at the least if Perkin and Richard of York were *on*e, and as all the world thought and said.)

And Sir Thomas More or Dr Morton or both (who shamed to *sp*eak anything in favour of King Richard) yet they *co*nfess (being doubtless enforced and adjured by verity) that there was no *cer*tainty of the deaths of the two brothers, nor of the *circumstanc*es thereof, nor that they were killed in the reign *of* King Richard III, and in these words. And although I have cited *this before*, I will again, *for it is true that* ***repetere frequen*ter pulchra**, and that such repetitions press and require more earnestly the credit *of the Reader:* ***The deaths* and final infortunes of the young King Edward *and his brother* have come so far in question that *some remai*n yet in doubt whether they were destroyed *in the days of* King Richard or no**. Thus they say, *and it must be believed* as well because they lived in those times as because they speak ***ex propria scientia***.

But against *this they speak* / in another place and contrary to their 202v* former *saying. And thus we find* them often contrary to themselves. And *this deprives them of their repu*tation, or in any man *the im*putation of a veritable writer. *And it must* proceed not only from their *malice, but* also from ill memory, and whereunto all these *writers are ob*noxious who are delighted with telling *falsehoods and* in reporting of leasings and fables. And *a wise p*hilosopher adviseth such men to have *a ca*re to preserve and to strengthen their memo*ries. And he* holdeth peremptorily that **oportet mendacem esse memorem**. Aristotle

*And the*se authors, Morton and More, write in one *place th*e contrary to that which they said in another. *For they* sa*y* in one place, as I have cited it before, that it was held in doubt whe*ther they were murdered. But they* say afterward that Tyrell and Dighton, being examined, confessed plainly and certainly the murder of the two princely brothers, the sons of King Edward IV, and all the man[ner] of it. These be contrarieties. And by these con*tra*rieties their speech falleth into another argument bicorne or crocodilites, a*nd* bringeth much disadvantage to their cause and scandal to their greatest friends. In this their revealing of the[se men,] there is secretly and implicitly intimated their fault was not then to be [punished,] and as it will appear plainly if it be cons[idered.] And it is clear that the confession of a man is the greatest evide[nce] and testimony which can be given against him, for th*at* he judgeth and condemneth himself. And there*fore* this axiom of the law, viz., **Confessi pro damnatis habent*ur***. And it is a strong axiom in the civil law, and as *well* in other laws.

And then in regard that the confession of [those was such as that] it might not be disclosed nor the crime called in question and to justice, but left unpunished (as the said authors confess), then it was but a counterfeit confession. And these writers there had in mine opinion [done] better to have concealed the report of that confession than to have revealed and published it, for thereby they raise suspicion [of the] falsity thereof, or else of consciousness and of privity of some gr[eat] ones (and before insinuated, and chiefly Cardinal Morton) in lying, and an imputation of injustice a*nd* connivance upon the chief presidents of judgement and upon the rest of honourable justices. [Other grea]t ones [privy to the] deaths [of the princes, especially of King Edward's sons]

Here I may note also that this fault and error of these writers is the *result of their own ill will to which they give the* chiefest and cunningest scope, or of some sinister stratagem *of their patrons*. For if it were true that Tyrell 205 and [Dighton, Forrest and Slater] confessed the murder and the act and [manner, and King Richard being dead, who was said to suborn and protect them] during his life, as it might be thought, and no longer, for *after his death he could not, then* [necessarily, and especially in] so heinous and so bloody a crime *and* [an act of so high a nature, of due] course of law and justice, the punishment [should have been] extremely inflicted by his successors and the rather *because we must else suppose that they were* murdered *after* Richard's death. But being for some [strange causes deferred, and after a while omitted and pardoned,] it may be [thought such] strange clemency and impunity [proceeded from some] singular and high indulgence, and from som*e* good will and favour borne by the great *ones* towards the person*s who confessed* and were accused or accusable by the confessants afore*said*. By this me*ans*, for the great favour borne to them, might the capital magistrate or prince *not* have brought in question, and much less to have the persons chastis*ed* condignly for this offence.

Or else it will be thought that the report and dispersion by secret fame and rumours of these examina[tions and] confessions about the murder of the two young princes were but buzzes and quaint devices and counterfeit *practices* to amu[se the] people and to entertain them with the expectation of some jus[tice] to be done after in convenient time upon the guilty and grievous offenders therein. But this justice was deferred so long as that the tr*aitors lived*.

But this is to be understood after the death of King Richard. For all that [was done before was th]at he was made the only author and contriver of that horrible crime, and the rest of the sicaries were in peace and safety and
205v at liberty. *And it is not a new* / policy to make an innocent *man* culpable, but it is an old and stale *stratagem* and court juggling. And amongst other, I have *good example* thereof in the story of Great Alexander. There was in the court of this king [a great] man, and so great in favour and honour of the [nobles and] of the people as that the king grew jealous [and fearful of his] *virtue* and his greatness and his popularity. And he would *study how to* put him down, or at the least to much abate his *honour* and his credit, and, if it were possible, to bring him [to] contempt, into utter disgrace.

But he could find no col[our nor] fit means for the effecting hereof, because that *gr*eat man was in great favour with the people, and he was so honourable and so virtuous as that there was no crime noted in him. And therefore the king's jealous[y] and fear troubled and perplexed him the more. And he, being des*irous* to be holpen by some advice herein, imparted his care and [unbosoms himself to the] counse[l and care of his] most crafty and trusty counsellor, who was call*ed* Medius, and of his country, as I think. And he asked him [to] advise and how he could devise to abate the greatness of that great man and bring him into disesteem and to make him contemptible and hated of the people, in respect that he was so good and so virtuous a p*erson*.

'O sire', quoth Medius, 'let not that trouble you. This is easy enough to be done, and by this means: we will have him to be accus[ed] of some grievous crime (though falsely), and we will find means to have him to be pronounced and declared culpable and guilty of that feigned crime. And it shall be so formally and firmly done as that the infamous note and the b[rand] of that scandal or crime shall ever remain upon hi[m'.] And he uttered that sentence in these terms, though diverse, but th[e same in effect]:

Medea[tur licet vulneri qui morsus aut dolatus [est, reman]ebit tamen cicatrix.

And it is very true and [approved by an ancien]t Christian [poet thus:

[Paulum distare vid*en*tur [Ausonius]
suspectus vereque re*us*:
The guilty and the suspected innocent
In man's opinion are little different.]

And there is nothing worse, *nor* [a more dangerous destiny,] nor a more fatal to greatness *in a* prince than to be brought *into the* [contempt] of the people. For, according to [the doctrine of the great] master of policy, **odium et contemptus** be the two evils [which overthrow] kings and kingdoms. And they proceed, the one, to wit, cont[empt, proceeding from vanity and dissoluteness] of the prince; and the other [from this opinion] which the people have *of* those and of his other vices and tyranny. And then he must neither reign nor live any longer, but must instantly perish. For as the old and wise Ennius said, and which sentence is attes*ted* to the credit of an oracle with the most wise Cicero, **Quem oderunt perisse expetunt**.

206 | Aristotle in **Politics** | [Ennius **apud** Ciceronem, **Offic., Lib**. 2] [**Perisse prisce pro perire**]

And to conclude this disputation, all this was practised by the Lancastrians and executed upon the fortune, fame and sacred person of King Richard. And it may here out of the proceedings in [t]his cause against this prince be gathered that he was not held by the good men and best and wisest to be guilty of this bloody crime, nor that the same cunning **translatio criminis** could not take any hold of him in their judgement nor in equity of wisdom and of [r]eason. But rather, and according to these judgements, this translation reflected and returned upon these magistrates who suffered the confessed cri*mi*nals to pass with impunity. And surely that layeth a scandal upon them, and it tacitly accuseth *them* of some secret guiltiness, **ut supra**. For otherwise, *the rulers* and chief magistrates neither tolerate nor acquit nor *pardon* such heinous offences.

Neither is it probable [that] the Earl of Richmond, when he was possessed [of this kingdom (for he was a wise and] religious prince), [and all] justice in his hand and in his [power, was of opinion that King Richard was guilty of the murder or subornation of these felons] / to perpetrate that treason, [nor yet that he thoug]ht [them] the actors and executioner*s of the* murder of the two sons of King Edward IV (and as it hath been before urged), beause those men were not apprehended *and brought* to justice, nor yet so much as restrai*ned of their li*berties. But contrariwise, they were suffered to go up and down and at their pleasure and in peace *with imp*unity until they came to die their own na[tur]al death. And this is affirmed by Sir Thomas More and *by* Raphael Holinshed and by John Stow and others. But Tyrell may be excepted in one respect, because he died not his natural death but a violent death. But yet that was not inflicted upon him for the murder of the two young princes, but for other treason long afterward committed by him, and against King Henry himself. Moreover, John Green, who was said to be a party in the practice of this foul treason against the young princ*es*, was never called in question.

206v

But to conclude, if all the accusations against these cutthroats had been known true and plain without sophistication, and to have been taken **bona fide**, then doubtless the king himself (who was reputed a good and godly and a wise prince) would have had that due care to have done right to justice and to honour and to the laws divine and human, as that he would have provided and commanded that men gui*lty* of so horrible crimes should have had not only *the* pun*ishment* which the law ordinarily ordaineth and usually inf*licteth* upon traitors, but also he would have caused *exqu*isite torments to have been added to their executions, and given in the most public and frequent place of their *performance*, that their terrible sufferings might be *the more grievous to them*selves and terrible [to the people and to the times.]

207 *And* / plainly there was *no reason why* King Richard should take away the lives of *his two nephews, since they were allowed* to be bastards, and then and before that King Richard was avowed generally to be the true and *lawful heir*, and as hath before been often and at lar*ge related. And he had* much more reason to preserve them, being so near kinsmen.

But I cannot say so much in the behalf of any [of the Lancastrian faction, for there] was a necessity for them, if they would [have a king of that family] (as the Cardinal and some others did) to take those princes aforesaid away, as so to *destroy not only* King [Richard] *and* [his son,] but also all the legitimate issue of Lan[caster; for all those were before any of the house of Beauf]ort in the true order of the succession in the kingdom. And they stood in the *way, as* [also] did the lawful progeny of Brotherton, of Woodst[ock, of both the] Clarences, of Gloucester. But they feared few or n[one of those] titular lords, for they were modest men and affected *not the* [sovereignty,] but were content with their own private and safe [fate and feudal estates.

[B]ut all was one with the *amb*itious and malicious Lancastrians, and whose malice *was* so [vehement that they regarded no title, how juster or better soever. For besides the death of King Edward IV and his two sons, of King Richard and his son, the Prince of Wales, there was afterward, and as occasion served, the Earl of Warwick, the Duke of Suffolk, and others both male and female of that princely family laid in their urns. And it must be so, else there could be no place upon the royal throne for the Beauforts and Somersets, their turn, if any, being last, the kings of Portugal and of Castile and others being before them, if not excluded by Act of Parliament.]

208 *And Richard was accounted a go*od and *faithful man all* his life, and was reput*ed a* virtuous prince and a *wise, and his law and govern*ment were of the best and without *stain*. Hereunto, he was most unhappily and *falsely slandered* by disloyal practice. Why th*en do they say* that he was only a wicked man and a pa*rricide a* sho*rt* time and (as it were) the moment of his corona*tion and* inauguration? But that cannot be, neither, for *his nephews* were both living after his coronation and after his pro*gress to the* north, and also after his Parliament which he had after *his* progress. And it is clearly and certainly to be proved that the prin*ces* lived *during* his reign and royal government. And the most chron*iclers and histor*ians write that very many men confidently affirm *that these* two princely brothers were alive many years after th*e death of King* Richard.

Why then, it is not likely that *he* killed or murdered his nephews in his lifetime, but that he committ*ed that murder* after that he himse*lf was deceased* and dead and laid in his grave to rest. And this tale *is as likely* and as credible as that which is told in the anthology of a certain stepmother being dead and entombed slew *as many of her* stepchildren as touched or approached her tom*b*. But this is an invention of a poet and may be allow*ed. But* I hope our adversaries and anti-Richards, though *they be insolent* and impudent, yet they will not so grossly *abuse* their writings and their names with such false and absurd fictions, and so to make King Richard an assassin after *his death*. Well then, the case *proves* plainly that there is no time of Richard's *life when he* should kill his nephews, and that after that he coul*d not*.

Now I will add to this tragedy *of these* Plantagenets *one act more, and of* 209* *the* Earl of Oxford, and worthy to be well regar*ded* [for example's sake,] besides that here it also may make [somewhat for the cause] and for the innocency of the two young men, *Edward, Earl of Warwick, and Richard, Duke of York. And* this it is. [T]he Earl of Oxford, Sir John de Vere, w*ho was m*uch affected and devoted to this King Henry VII, *as we* have seen here by some good instances, was a great ene[my to] this Richard, alias Perkin, and I think the only [en]emy which he had of the greater nobility. And wheth[er his] evil will grew out of incredulity, or were it out of malice, *or becaus*e he hated King Edward and all the House of *Y*ork; or else because he applied himself very obsequiously [to o]bserve and to humour the king then reigning in everything – but [I] cannot determine whether of these. But this is certain, [th]at he was so vehement a persecutor of Perkin as that he and t[he Cardinal were] said to be the chief persuaders and procurers of *the* more hasty dispatching of Perkin out of the way *and* of his destruction. And this earl also [pronounced the] cruel [sentence against the] Earl of Warwick, son of the Duke of Clarence (for he was High Judge or Constable in that a*ction*), [whose dealing thus in those matters] *was much* misliked.

[The Earl of Oxenford persecutor of Perkin]

And this dealing with them being reported, and near to Heveningham Castle, [t]he chief seat of the earl, it came to the ears of an [old] hermit who lived in the woods near to Heveningham [Cas]tle, and who was held to be a very good and devout [and] holy man. And this man as soon as he heard this *new*s was much troubled and grieved afterward, because he much [loved the ancient and noble family of Oxenford. And in] much anguish of spirit, he said the earl and his house would repent and rue this [guilt] and bloody pursuit of these innocent princes. And for the events of [which prophecy] this hath been observed, viz.: that not [long after, the earl] was arrested for a small offence, [and so small that no man thought] that a man of [his merit and credit with the king could be called in question. He was fined also £30,000, the which in those days was a kingly sum. After this he lived many years in great discontent, and died without issue or any child la]/wfully begotten by him. 210

[The Earl John died **anno** 4, HenryVIII, 1512]

[**Dominus**] *de* [Arundel, **viva voce**]

And in much [shorter time than his] life's time, that great and stately [earldom of Oxenford, with the] very opulent and princely patri[mony, was dissipated] and wasted, and it was very suddenly *and swiftly u*sed and consumed, and **como sal en agua**, [as the Spaniar]ds say in the refrain. But not by the fault *of the earl t*hen lord thereof, but rather by the fate of the *divine or*dinance. For certainly the earl was *a dev*out and a magnificent and a very learned and religious [nobleman,] and so worthy in every way, as I have heard some grave and [di]screet and honourable persons (who knew this earl from his y*outh* and could very well judge of the hopefulness and the *spring*times of young men) say and affirm that he was much more like to raise and to acquire and to establish a new earldom than to decay *and* waste and lose an old earldom. And in a word, he was a *Vere* in deed as in name, **vere nobilis**. For he was v*erily* and truly noble and a most noble Vere.

209v*

[The mathematicians that calculated the nativity of this Earl Edward told the earl his father that the earldom would fall in the son's time]

And I speak *that* which I know, for he vouchsafed me his familiar a*cquaintance*. And whereas I call his earldom a stately [earldom] / and a princely patrimony, I do *so after the te*stimony of that aforesaid most noble and late Earl of Oxford, who, being pleased to do me the honour to come to my lodging at Hampton Co*ur*t, there he told me that after he was come to the possession [of it,] there were certain rich and *prosperous men* who desired to farm a part of his earldom, who offered to pay him yearly the *sum of two* thousand pounds, and to leave to his use and [occupation all] castles and manor houses and wont*ed places* of residences of the ancient earls, with *all* the parks and woods or forests. And all the *de*mesne lands thereunto adjacent and appertaining *to* this surplusage might doubtless be of mor*e w*orth, being brought to a yearly value or *re*venue, than are sundry earldoms in this age.

An*d* this earldom was wasted and almost all dilapidated and spoiled, and the castles and manors pulled do[wn,] and the chapel wherein this Earl John de Vere was entombed and where all the sepulchres and goodly monuments of his ancestors were erecte*d were* all defaced and demolished and razed to the ground, and the bones of the ancient earls we*re* left under the open air and in the fields, and all [which happened] within less than threescore years after the death of the said Earl John.

It *is a warning not to lift* a finger in the shedding of innocent blood, nor to wrong nor to oppress, much less to destroy princes nor the children of princ*es* and of heroical persons. And thereof we are wa*rned* to take heed by an ancient oracle or sacred proverb *in* this heroical hemistich:

'Ανδρῶν ἡρώων πήματα τέκνα

Heroum proles est perniciosa vivorum.

That is to say, children of heroical *lineage*, of princes or (as we say) those of the *blood royal*, are dangerous and mischievous th*ings when* they be outraged.

212*

[Grafton **et** Chronic. MS. **in quarto apud** Mr Robert Cotton]

[Bastard of King Richard]

[Thomas Gainsford]

It happened about the same time that these unhappy gentlemen [su]ffered there was a base son of King Richard III [ma]de away, and secretly, having been kept long before [in] prison. And the occasion whereof (as it seemeth) was [to] prevent a practice of certain Irishmen of the wes[t an]d south parts of Ireland who sought and atte[mpted] to get him into their hands, and with a purpose to [ma]ke him their chief or prince, for they would *have been* glad of any noble gentleman of the house of York, wer[e he legitimate or natural, for] the love which they bore to Richard, Duke of York, *w*ho was sometimes their very honourable and good [an]d magnificent governor or viceroy (**id est**, king's deputy).

[Why the public] jus-[tice] de[ferred the death of these men]

And thus much b[riefly of that.] *N*ext, I will only endeavour to resolve a doubtful question which is or might be demanded or enquired what the reason should be why the king deferred [so] long the death and execution of those Plantagenets [an]d took so long deliberation about that matter, considering *th*at he was resolved to do it, and that there was no *ma*n could impeach him nor withstand the act. For there was there not any man who had po*wer, or who*m he had cause to fear, because he was a sovereign and not a subject, nor *obnoxious* to any human power or authority. Therefore these doubts *and dan*gers and difficulties which were (if any were) *must doubt*less be understood to be scruples of *conscience* and conflicts of the mind, the which are of all oth*er scruples the most troub*lesome and full of cares and of vexation, *and so power*ful as that they will curb the *highest* designs *by the force of their truth and are obno*/xious to any human power and higher authority. 212*

There be some reasons brought by some men why the king deferred *the* execution of Perkin so long, but they are not all worth the reciting But [the] chiefest of them is (viz.) that because Perkin was an alien and born out of the *ki*ng's dominions, and in the allegiance of a foreign prince, that therefore he could not be condemned nor executed for felony nor for treason by our la[ws.] But this is a fiction and an idle evasion. For we have many examples in our stories wherein we find that the natural subjects of the kings of France and of Scotland and of the princes of Germany and of Italy and of the kings of Spain and of Portugal have had judgement and execution by our laws for felonies and for treasons: as namely, [Peter de Gaveston, a Fren]chman, and Sir Andrew Harclay, a Scot, and now lately Dr Lopez, a Portug[uese. T]herefore certainly there was no cause nor worldly nor civil respect why King Henry should so long, [so doubtfully, and, as it were, timorously,] defer the arraignments and executions of these men.

[Then it must be some other cause, and not most unlikely some inward awe and secret and concealed scruples] *of the king*. / They are also so forcible and powerful as that they *can* resist and check and cross and crush the designs and plots *and* practices of the greatest men, of the most mighty *m*en in the world. And the heathen people called *th*ese scruples Eumenides and Erinyes, which as they said and believed haunted and frighted *and* terrified those men who had devised and [practised some] murder or other most wicked [act.] *And h*ereupon it was that the poet said well, **[Patiturque tuos mens saucia] manes**.

211v

[Daemones, Genii]

212v

Claudian

And they also [assign to every man his pr]otecting spirit, whom [the Greeks called **Daemo]nes**, and Latins **Genios**. And *they affirm that some*times when the genius of him against [whom the mis]chief is plotted is more strong and more [active than the] genius of that man who is the plotter and prac*tiser*, the practice hardly or never prevaileth. And [for example,] *when the* feud and irreconcileable enmity was between Octavianus [Caesar and Marcus Antoni]us, and that Antony could not prevail by any practice or in an[y] a[ttempt against Oct]avian, he consulted with soothsayers who told him that the reason thereof [was] that the ge[nius of O]ctavian was too mighty and too strong for his genius, and that it held his geni[us in awe.]

And good authors likewise write that the great philosopher [Apollo]nius had such a secret protection, and so strong as that alb[eit] Domitian the Emperor, hating him much, would fain have taken [his life from him, yet he had not the power to do it;] and Suid[as] addeth that this philosopher in the confidence of this his protect*ive* genius, when he departed from this emperor, uttered this verse:

[Philostratus in **Vita Apollonii**]

οὐ μέν με κτενέεις, ἐπεὶ οὔτοι μόρσιμός εἰμι.
Me non occides, quia fataliter protectus sum.

And this is that which Flavius Vopiscus called **maiestatem Apollonii**, as I [guess.]

The professors of Christian and the best religion agree with these heathen in the effects of such secret and sacred protectors, but not in the cause of them, for those whom the heathen theologers called **Δαίμονες**, Daemons and **Genios**, the Christian theologers called angels and *archangels, and* so like, and that there be of them good and bad. And they also hold and teach, and that by the best warrant, *that* Almighty God giveth charge to His angels to guard and protect the *good* and godly persons in all places and in all needs, and to defend them from their enemies and from the practices and snares of Satan. And they hold also that the eternal God hath given such power *to his* angels as the heathens believed that the Eumenides or F*ates* and the **mali genii** had, and that He useth their ministry for *chastizing* the wicked and ungodly persons and for the affrighting and tormenting of the minds and consciences of the rep*robates, and to* hold them in such imperious awe as
213 that *they refrain from evil deeds. For otherwise* / by the craft of Satan's *spirit his* malice secretly breaketh through ************ and worketh mischief against that *reprobate*, and also useth his devilish mischief to *make him cease to be* in awe of any other angels or divine powers and *cast* away all fears of God and of divine justice as vain, *and as a* miserable captive to proceed with his impious design and *will. And by* these means this evil angel bringeth his misera*ble* client *from that whi*ch bringeth all security and good success and happi*ness and* fear of God, and which preserveth a man from sin and *from evi*l acts. For that fear is a curious and a severe censor of all crimes *for the* faithful and pious to know: that it is **horrendum incider*e in* manus Dei,** and that **Deus est terribilis.** But to the ungod*ly and* the reprobate this fear is unknown or at least of no account, although there be *no other fe*ar profitable or of any worth or good use, for (as it was *di*vinely said by a holy man) **Nullus est dolor utilis nisi pe*ccati* nullus metus nisi Dei**. But the wicked are *subject to an un*happy fear and entertain other fears – desperate fears and base, vain and idle fears – *and as* the prophet said, **Timent ubi non est timor**, and they fear to *cross* and *to o*ffend the Devil and loss of his favour, and therefore to preserve that their b*ondage they do* his unjust and hellish hests and his wicked will *and pr*actise and execute these wicked things and impieties whereunto *the Devil* hath tempted and drawn them in longer or in shorter time.

[But] those philosophical and theological arguments may seem [to b]e parerga or not grateful to some, and therefore I will leave them, returning to my *mai*n argument, and that was the purgation of King Richard of the
214 crimes and of the / other scandalous matters imputed to him, and chiefly for the deaths of his *n*ephews, and for the which much hath already been said, and enough. And therefore at length upon the allegate and probate matters passed, it may be concluded that King Richard was no more guilty of their deaths than he *was o*f those of his two brothers, King Edward and Clarence, nor of his own legiti*mate and* base sons. And he had been sure enough to have been made the plotter and author of the deaths of the children of the Duke of Clar[ence, the Earl Edward] *and* the Countess Margaret, and of Edmund de la Pole and of the oth[ers,] notwithstanding the falsehood thereof, *ha*d not the parachronism have been to[o gross, he being dead before.

[But] as the good antiquary and diligent searcher [of] *kno*wledge of the obscure and *hi*dden things appertaining to our story, and by name Mr John Stow, when I pressed much to know and *under*stand the certainty of this murder of the *sons* of King Edward IV and what he [thought] of it, and what proofs thereof he had found in his [various and m]anifold readings, his answer was this, and as peremptory as sho*rt*, that it was never [pr]oved by any true evidence nor by credible testimony, nor by [prob]able suspicions, nor so much as by the oaths [o]f the knights of the post, nor yet by any fine fiction or ar*gument* or poetry, that King Richard killed his nephews or was guilty of the practice thereof. **215v***

And whereas Mr Stow addeth fiction and poetry to the proofs, he alluded (as I conceived) to the poetical disposition of Sir Thomas More, because he was a poet and wrote *a poetical boo*k, to wit, **Utopia** is a fable. And whereby it seemeth that he could *better indite and that he* had more felicity and facility in ficti*ons and in counterfei*t histories and fables than in historical *narratives and* true *r*elations (**ut supra**). And he first published this *story of this murder.* / [And Sir Thomas More, being puzzled with his equivocations, **Egerton 237v-238v** and that it never could come to light what became of the bodies of these two princes – Grafton, Hall, Holinshed and Stow agreeing in this report that the very truth hereof was utterly unknown. And they say well, for it is not possible it could never be known that they could be both murdered in the Tower and buried there, or both have sunk in the deeps if it be considered one of them survived until the fourteenth or fifteenth year of King Henry VII. Therefore their contradiction is, as the comedian said,

[Quod dictum est indictum est, [Terentius in
Quod modo erat ratum irr]*i*[tum est. **Phormio**]

[Besides, if Perkin were not the second son of King Edward, he must be nothing. For the Flemish, French and Wallons acknowledge no such noble young man to have been bred in Warbeck or in Tournay, but make honourable mention of a young son of the King of England who was brought to the Duchess of Burgundy, his aunt, being then in Flanders, and how he was in France and in other kingdoms.

[We will therefore close this book with his own affirmation and protestation to King James of Scotland, to whom he avowed that he was conveyed, being young, into a strange and foreign country and preserved secretly by Divine Providence, as young Joas was.

[Explicit Liber III]

216

THE FOURTH BO[OK OF THE HISTORY] OF KING R[ICHARD THE THIRD]

The Contents

THE FOURTH BO[OK OF THE HISTORY] OF KING RI[CHARD III] 216v

[It hath been declared] at large and often before that the [title King] Richard had to the crown accrued and [fell to him by the illegiti]mate birth, or bastardy, of the children [of King Edwa]rd IV, and by the attainder of the [Duke of C]larence, and which was accompanied with the corruption of his blood and [forf]eiture of his title in him and in his heirs, [of which there] was no question. But of the forfeiture and [dis]heritage of the sons of King Edward IV, th[ere hath b]een much question, and the true ca[use thereof hath no]t nor cannot be well known without th*e* [true] report made of the sundry loves, wooing[s, especially con]tracts and marriages of the king their father.

Therefore I must crave leave to unfold and to relate these. I shall not need [to intimate how amorous] *he* was, and wanton, for that is well known. Yet it shall not be amiss [to say something] *here*, and how that he had many m[istresses,] or **amasias**, and who were kept in severa[l] houses and very honourably entertained, after the [manner] of the seraglios of the great [Turks.] And amongst these dainty and dear damoiselles and loose and b*eautiful ladies,* the [most fa]mous were Catharine de Claringdon, Elizabe[th W]*ay*[te] (alias Lucy), Joanne Shore, the foresaid La[dy Eleanor] Talbot and others.

[How extreme his desires were, y]ou [may see in the speec]h [of the] Duke of [Buckingham] set [down by Sir] Thomas More

And it is worth the remembering amon[gst such matters as these that there] was another fair woman very dear unto him, and *whom he* [suspected] to be false, and therefore the king caused her to be *chastened*, and he gave her warning of his suspicion *of* her error by a quaint device. And for this purpose *he had* [a symbolical figure] made, much after the manner [of the trivial ierogliffs used in France and called **rebus de Picardy**, *and pro/vided* a fair and rich jewel as a love token, and therein the device or 217 **rebus** was a falcon encom[passed] with a fetterlock. And the mott hereof was **[au fa]ulcon serrure.** And what the meaning hereof [was I] will forbear to tell in plain terms for offending modest ears. But I will [intimate the dev]ice lieth in the ambiguity and double sense of falcon, which, being wh[ole signifieth the hawk c]alled a falcon. But the word being divided into two words hath an [obscene] signification; [and by this means] ‘falcon’ [becometh] aequ[ivole.] And the king afterward liked this device of the *falcon and fetter*lock so well as that he caused it to be [carved and painted in many] of his royal works, and yet to be seen, [at Fotheringhay and elsewhere.

[But though the king’s jealousy was thus particular to her, his affection was as general to others, being a frank gamester, and one that would cast at

218v* all fairly set. Yet above all for a ti]me [he] loved the Lady [Eleanor Talbot,] a very fair and noble lady, [daughter of John Talbot,] Earl of Shrewsbury, and [her mother was] the Lady Catharine Stafford, [daughter of [Philip Commynes in Lud. XI, **Cap**. 112 **et** 132] Hum]phrey Stafford, Duke of Buckingham. [And this Lady E]leanor was the widow of Thomas, [Lord Butler,] Baron of Sudeley. And the king's [affection] *was so strong, and* he was so fervent and vehemen[t, and also at] that time so honest toward her as th[at he mad]e choice of her for his wife. And he was f*irmly and* [sole]mnly contracted and also married to [her by] a reverend prelate, namely Dr Thomas [Stillington, Bishop of B]ath, a grave and learned man and a counsellor of state, and much favour[ed] by the king, and often employed in great affairs (as I have partly int*imated* before). And this matter is witnessed by our Eng[lish] stories, and also by the honourabl[e] and veritable [histo]rian Philip de Commynes, and in these word[s:]

L'Évêque **de Bath (lequel avait** été **conseiller du Roi Edouard) disait que ledit Roi avait [promis] foi de marriage à une dame d'Angleterre, et qu'il avait nommée, et que le Roi avait fait la p[romesse] entre les mains du dit** Évêque**: et dit a[ussi] cet** Évêque **qu'il avait après** épou**[sé] et [n'y avait q[ue lui et eux deux.** That is summarily in English thus: The Bishop of Bath, a Privy Counsellor of [King] Edward, said that the king had plighted [his] faith to marry a lady of England, w[hom] the bishop named */*viz., the Lady Ele[anor] Talbot,*/* and that this contract was made [in the] hands of the bishop. And he said that afte[rward] he married them, and no persons being presen[t but] they twain and he. And he said also th*at* [the king] charged him very strictly that he shou*ld not* reveal this secret marriage to any man [living.] And this contract and marriage are related in the Act [of Parliament] aforesaid, and where it is di[sertly called a former marriage. And the king had a child by this lady.

[But too soon growing out of liking of her, he entertained others into the **219*** bosom of his pleasure.] / And not long after, the [fame filled] the court of a very fair and [excellent lady living] in the court of France with th[e Queen Charlotte, wife] of King Lewis XI and s[ister to this lady, whose] name was Bona. And she was the d[aughter of Lewis, Duke] of Savoy. And the king, being very *affectionate*, also so covetous of fair women, fell [straight in love] with the fame of this Lady Bona and w[as so strangely and suddenly engaged in the report of her beauty that he was] desirous to have her to his wife. And [he despatch]ed an ambassador speedily into Fran[ce to treat about this] business. And he committed the treaty a[bout this allian]ce to [The great Earl of Warwick] the great and renowned earl, and t*o* h[is best] friend and most faithful subject, namely Ric[hard N]eville, Earl of Warwick and of Salisbury, an[d Captain of Calais, who, wi]th much good liking and a*ll* alacrity undertook this *w*ooing business and went into France in very [honoura]ble and magnificent manner. And there he propounded *the k*ing's suit to the French king and to the queen, as [the] fittest mediators in this behalf. And he [presen]ted the most loving and honourable offer of the king and *his* love and affection and devotion to the Lady [Bona.] And to be brief, this earl ambassador [express]ed himself so wisely and so honourably and so [magn]ificently in this negotiation as that he brought [it to] the wished effect, and that he did effect with the more faci[lity] *because* he *was* a man of great estimation for his valour and [wisdo]m and other heroical virtues, as well in France as [in all] parts of Europe. And having happily accomplished *this nup*tial expedition, he took his leave of the [king an]d queen and of the lady bride and the rest of France and came *home again a pro*ud man, thinking that he should be very [welcom]e home *to* the king, having so well and so speedily *done for the ki*ng the great business wherein he was *employed*.

The [Lady Bona] was af[terwards mar]ried to [Don Galeazo] Sforza, Duke of [Milan.] El. Reusuer[q]

But when he came to the court, he [found an alterat]ion of the affections and also [the countenance of the king.] And the reason was *that* [the king had suddenly wooed and wedded another lady, the Lady Elizabeth Gray, relict of Sir John Gray, daughter of Sir Richard Woodville and of Jacquetta, sometime Duchess of Bedford and daughter of the Earl of St Pol. The] / late husband of this Lady [Gray was a knight of Gr]ooby, but he became a ve[ry vehement Lancastrian,] falsely revolting from the House [of York, and therefore] was hateful to those of that [family, also to the] Earl of Warwick as to the other fo[llowers thereof. He] was slain at the battle of [Barnet. And of] this lady and of her husband Philip de [Commynes writeth] some words which I shall not or will [not under]stand. I will set down here [the sentence] and leave the interpretation of it to [the more] skilful Reader. These be the words: **[Et depu]is ledit Roi Edouard épousa la fi[lle d']un Chevalier d'Angleterre, femme ve[uve,] qui avait deux fils et aussi pour amourettes**.

219v*

[Philip de Commynes, **Cap.** 112]

[But] neither the despised state of widowhood of this lady nor [the meanness] of her quality and conditions, nor the [earnest] dissuasions of the duchess mother of th*is king* [and] best friends could make him withdraw his af[fection] from her, so exceedingly and so deeply he was s[urprised] with her beauties. But yet if he could ha[ve enjoyed] her sweet embraces otherwise, he woul*d* [not] have married her. But she was so witt*y and* so wise a gentlewoman, and had so good c[ounsel] given by the well-experienced lady, [the] duchess her mother, as that she withstood *the* king's temptations and lustful batteries as a*n* immovable rock, or as an unassault*able* or impregnable citadel. And she vowed *and* protested that she would never yield to [any] dishonourable parley or unchaste motion, although it stood upo*n the* safety of her life.

Then the king told *her* that he perceived that she would not *resist* whilst they were married; and then she [implored] and humbly prayed his grace not to thin[k her so] exorbitantly and so vainly am[bitious as] *that* she would [wish herself a queen or to have the hope and presumption to be anything higher than what she was, his poor and humble vassal.] *And on the* other / side, she said that she *was not of so* dishonest and so foul a mind [as to violate] her chastity or lose her hono*ur* [or be the] mistress of the greatest king.

220*

And then the king (when he [perceived there was no other remedy)] told her that he was willing [to marry] her, and notwithstanding his inequali[ty. For] *he* esteemed her love and her beauties and [her virtues] so rare and so precious as that in reg*ard of these he thou*ght her in birth and in fortunes and *in powers as no*ble and as worthy and as great *as the* greatest king in Christendom. *And he* [d]id not long deliberate of the tying of th*e matri*monial knot, nor deferred the accomplish*ment* any longer than there was necessity; but *so* suddenly and hastily (and haply with more haste *than* good speed) he was married unto her without *the ch*arity of any counsellor, kinsman, baron *or any* friend whatsoever.

This [marriage] was [in the forest] of Wychwood.

And there was so much haste made *that* the much approved ceremony of the banns' [asking] was pretermitted, and such was the want [of reve]rend bishops then as that he was fain to [take an] ordinary priest to marry him. And that was *done* in a chamber instead of a church, and in [a lod]ge or forest-house instead of a palace, and nobody present but the duchess and her company, *and tha*t few of them. And where he first saw *this fa*ir widow, and by chance, there at the next [interv]iew he married her, and by ill chance and *unhappi*ly, and much to his dishonour and disparagement, [and as] much to the offence and dislike of the barons *of the* kingdom, and who took double offence at *this marr*iage. The one offence was because he matched so *unworthily* and so unequally to his estate, and *also that* he married without privity of them *and without obtaining their* [con]sent, and the which they assevered [the king ought to have done, by their ancient and privileged honours. But it much exasperated their dislikes when they

220v*

considered the great unequality between her conditio]/n and the regal condition [and the Imperial Maje]sty of England, as also *that she was the wid*ow – that is the reliquies and *the leavings* [of another ma]n, and that of a poor knight *and of a* false and mortal enemy.

[L'indignité de] ce mar[iage du roi Edouard] avec [une simple gentille] femme dé[plaisait ta]nt au co]mte de War[wick et aux princi]paux seigneurs [d'Angleterre, et off]ensa telle[ment le Roi L]ouis XI, qu'[ils faisaient la con-f]édération con[tre le Roi E]douard, etc. [Jean du Tillet,] pt. 2.

But yet [above all, the Earl of Warwi]ck was much more offended, and by *much mo*re scandalized than all the other *barons, and besi*des that he was as farforth wronged *in the common* case of the noble barons as any *of them*, he besides held himself much d*isgr*aced in France for the matter of *the* king's light and loose dealing with the Lad[y Bo]na and her princely friends, and to whom *and to* her friends the earl had engaged his *honour* for the king's due performance of the espous*al, and* he had mediated and laboured at his great *trouble* and great charge and brought to fair eff[ect.] Also of such covenants as being authorized by t[he king's] commission he had made and undertaken *the* foresaid treaty of the marriage with the said L*ady* Bona of Savoy, and the which he had so lately *done* in his embassage in France. And he was als*o* aggrieved and troubled with the affront and s[corn] offered to the French princes by this levity [and] rashness of the king, and whereof he kn[ew] that the French king and the queen and t*he* other princely friends of the fair virgin *and* noble espouse would be very sensible [and] apt by occasion to revenge it.

And for these *slights* and disgracious usage, the Earl of Wa[rwick] forsook the king and renounced *his* love and allegiance unto him and would nev*er more* come to him, but soon after took arms against him. And of this hasty and so much d*istasted* match and marriage, and of the offences th*at followed*, and of the many evils thereof ensuing, [you shall hear] the grave and judicious historian P[olydore] make report and also censure:

[Polydore, **Lib**. 24]

[Rex Edwardus, mutate consilio de ducend]*e* [in uxorem Bona, filia Ducis Sabandiae, Elizabetham, viduam Johannis Gray militis, in matrimonium duxit, et de eo matrimonio mulieris humilitatem, non modo necessarios

221*

principes, verum etiam Ricardum Widdeuillum,] / patrem mulieris celat; qua [causa cognita cuncti pro]tinus mirari, principes [fremere passimque voces emittere] indignationis, et regem no[n ex sua dignitate fecisse,] easque nuptias ei crimini [dare, et dedecori] assignare, quod caeco amore n[on ratione ductus esset,] sed inde initium profectum est [simultatis ortae inter] regem Edwardum et Ricardum co[mitatem Warwici,] etc.

Thus Polydore the Italian. But [if you will not] give credit unto him (for indeed ma[ny are jealous of him,] and yet in my opinion not for any *or many* just causes), then you shall hear a[n Eng]lishman and a prelate, and living [in those tim]es report the same matter, and in this manner: **[Edward]us rex fretus propria electione [cuius]dam militis relictam nomine Elizabeth, [inconsu]ltis regni proceribus clandestino sibi desti[navi]t matrimonio: postea ipsam in reginam co[ronar]i fecit. Quod quidem regni optimates aegre [tuler]unt, quia de tam mediocri stirpe feminam [procre]atam ad regni consortium secum praepropere [sublim]aret.**

[Kings must not marry the daughters of their vassals]

And thus you see how this lustful [king] lost his honour and his reputation and very many *and* very great and best friends by this mean and *bas*e marriage, and he had much trouble afterwards; [ye]t he escaped well that he had no more real and present [feeling] of the error and ill of this his strange marriage. And *this* king was the first king of England who [ever] debased himself and so disparaged his royal [blood] and sovereign majesty in the alliance and mixture *of it* with *a* private and mean family and with *the da*ughter of his vassal, and she also a poor *widow*, and of a man who hated the king and his *family,* ***u*t supra**. Therefore all circumstances consi*dered. this* marriage was a dishonourable and a rash *contract* and a perilous act.

I have read [in the story of Arag]on of a king who was not only *dishonoured but also* [deposed] for marrying of the daughter [of his subject. And King Edward fared not much better, for soon after he was deprived of this kingdom and expulsed. But being a man that in his troubles was industrious and diligent, of invincible courage, he happily recovered] the kingdom again; but [never the honour and friends] and reputation **221v***
which he lost, [which he might have prevented, and all th]e miseries and calamities which [overtook him in h]is issue and in his friends.

But if he would have been ruled [by the duchess his] mother, he had prevented all *these miseries and* calamities. For she, having secret [advertisement of] this love of the king to Lady Gray, *as I said b*efore, and having much misliking of *it, persuad*ed him from it, and she bestowed all the *fine tou*ches and all the art which she had, *and she* used also her authority of a mother to [dehort hi]m from that lust and to leave the said Lady [Gray and] to return again to the Lady Eleanor Tal[bot, his] former love and wife, or at least his contra[cted] spouse. And further, and most earnestly, she *exhorted* and charged him upon her blessing and upon h*is love* to God and to Christian religion to finish and [consummate] with public ceremonies of matrimony that his contra*ct* with the Lady Elizabeth Talbot, alias Butle*r*.

And because the arguing and discoursing and disputing of this qu*estion* **222**
concerning the king's marriage aforesaid between the duch*ess his* mother and him is very witty and *wis*e and full of weighty *argu*ments, I think it good to transcribe it hither, and as I have gathered *it* [out] of the stories and chronicles of Sir Thomas More and of the rest of our English [writers.] And I will follow them faithfully so long as they err not in the m*att*er nor write false and incongruous English.

First then *I will relate, as I have* done here before, that the king's mother, bein[g much troubled with] his purpose and resolution to mar*ry the Lady Gray,* [with a strong hope to dissuade him, came to him thus:

'[My liege lord and my dear son, it is very commonly reported you are

[The speech of the Duchess of York to King Edward IV]

purposed to marry the Lady Gray, a widow and a mean gentlewoman, which you cannot but conceive will redound to your disparagement and dishonour. All the wise, great and noblest persons of your kingdom think it far more to the advantage of your honour, profit and safety to seek the
223 alliance of a noble progeny, and rather in] / a foreign country than in your own realm, [as well in regard] *that* thereupon dependeth great strength to your estate [and] great possibility of increase of your possessions, as also [(if well considered)] *that* [you may] not safely marry any other than the Lady Bona, the Earl of Warwick having proceeded in the motion [so far, w]ho (as it is likely) will not take it well if all his [troublesome and costly n]egotiation should be in such wise frustrate, and his appointments [deluded]'.

*M*oreover, she told him that it was not princely for a king to m[arry his ow]n subject, at the least no great and important occasion lea[ding him the]reunto, nor possessions or other commodities depending thereup[on. 'B]ut it would be in the same kind as if a rich man should [marry his] maid if and only for a little wanton dotage upon her person, [in which kin]d of marriages many men commend more the maid's fortune [t]han the master's discretion. And yet for all that, there was more honesty in such a marriage than there was honour in the marriage which you affect and seek, for so much as there is not great difference between a rich merchant and his own maid as is between the king and the widow Gray. And in whose person, albeit there is nothing to be misliked, yet there is nothing [s]o excellent in her but that it may be found in divers other women, yes, much better than she, and more meetly and more agreeable to your state – and those also virgins, and who are of a much more honourable [estimation] *and e*state and condition than widows.

'Wherefore the only widowhood [o]f Elizabeth Gray (though she were in all other things convenient *and fi*t for you) yet that alone should suffice fully', in the opinion of *his* lady mother, 'to make you to refrain and abstain from that *match*, especially you being a king, and because it is an unfitting *matter and a* great blemish and a high disparagement to the sacred ma[jesty of a prince (who] ought as nigh to approach the priesthood [in pureness and cleanness as he do]th in dignity). And that is not [to be defiled with bigamy in his first marriage'.

[Thus far the king could have attention to hear the duchess, but being
223v extremely far g]/one in love, or rather *in lust,* [he] was resolute to marry her, [and to that purpose framed his answer] *unto the duc*hess his mother, partly in [earnest and partly in play,] as one that wist and well *knew that* [he was out of the check and rule of a mother.] And albeit he would have been *glad of her satis*faction and contentment, yet he was *fixed in his own* mind to proceed in these espousals and *took she it well or otherwise.* Yet reverently and in good *part he* [thus replied] to his mother's speech, and as followeth:

[The answer of King Edward IV to the Duchess of York, his mother]

'[Madam,] although marriage, being a spiritual thing, [ought rather to be m]ade according to the will and ordinance of [Almighty God, whe]re he by his grace inclineth either parties to [love mutually] and virtuously (and as I trust and hope that God doth [work in our] cause), and not for the regard of any temporal a[dvantage, ye]t natheless, this marriage, as it seemeth to me, and bein[g consi]dered even after the worldly accompt, is not unprofitable, nor [I re]ckon not the amity and alliance of any earthly nati[on or foreign pr]ince so necessary for me as the friendship and love of mine [own subjects,] and who, as I hope, will bear to me so much the [more l]ove and favour because I disdain not to marry with a w[oman of my ow]n land.

'And yet if foreign alliance were thought so requ[isite, I cou]ld find the means to enter therein much better by other [of my] kin, and where all parties would be content, than to ma[rry myself] to one whom I should haply never love, and for the possi[bility of] more possessions lose the fruit and pleasure of this which I ha[ve alr]eady, For small pleasure taketh a man of all that ever he [hath] beside if he be wived against his appetite. And I doubt not but there be (as you, Madam, say) other women which be in every [point] comparable to the Lady Gray. And therefore I let not other [men] to wed them. No more, then, is it reason that any man mislike *for me to* marry where it liketh me.

'And I doubt not that my cous[in of] Warwick neither loveth me so little as to grudge at that [which I] love, nor is so unreasonable to look that I in choice of a [wife shou]ld rather be ruled by his eye than by mine own. For th[at were] as though I were a ward, and were bound to ma[rry by the appointment] of a guardian. But I would not be *bound* [with] *such* [servile and hard condition] as that I should [not be king.

'[As for the possibility you urge of more inheritance by new affinity in strange lands, that is not always certain. But contrariwise,] / that is often 224
the occasion [of more trouble than profit. Besides, we] have already a title and sei[sin so good and great as may suffice] to be gotten and to be kept [by one man and in one man's days.]

'And whereas you object [that the Lady Gray hath been a wife and is now a widow, and hath] already children, why, by God['s blessed Lady, I that am a bachelor] have some children too, and so for [our better comfort] *each of us* hath a proof that neither of us is [like to be barren. And I trust in] God that she shall bring forth [a young prince, and your pretty son,] who shall be pleasing and acceptable to [you.

'[For the bigamy] which is objected, let the bishop hardly lay it [in my way when I come t]o take orders of priesthood. For I con[fess I understand] bigamy is forbidden to a priest, but I never wi[st it yet] was forbidden to a prince. And therefore, good Madam, I [pray you be c]ontent, and not to trouble yourself nor me any furth[er.]' And here the king ended his speech and answer to the duchess.

But she was nothing content nor satisfied. And therefore [she must urge] one point and one objection more, and which she thought to be the g*reatest of* all other. And that was his contract with Dame Elizabeth [Lucy, and his having had a child by he]r. So, as the duchess said, he was bound in discharge of her conscience to cha[rge him with t]hat act, and by means whereof he was her husband before [God.] And Mr More and Grafton and Stow and the rest say that the king denied that contract or betrothing to Mistress Lucy. And the foresaid authors may and ought to retract that which they hav[e written therein.] For the truth is he was never contra[cted to] her, but he loved her well, and she was his witty concubine, *for she* was a wanton wench, and willing and ready to yield herself to [the] king and to his pleasures without any conditions or capitulations. And she herself never said *tha*t the king was betrothed unto her, but only that he would speak

[very] kind and sweet language unto her. And who knoweth not that **credula** [Ovid] **res a[mor est**.] And it is also true that the king [had] a child by her, and that child was the bastard Arthur, and [called c]ommonly (but unduly) Arthur Plantagenet. And he was afterward [made Viscou]nt Lisle by Henry VIII.

But in this relation the [historians] have much and foully erred. *For they* have not only corrupted the story, b[ut have injured the Duchess] of York *and mu*ch detracted from he[r judgement and knowledge in those matters and from the tenor of her former speech. For they make her to charge the [Elizabeth Lucy] king that he was contracted to Elizabeth Lucy, who was of birth and quality much meaner than the Lady Gray, whom she conceived so basely of, as her **224v** speech implies. For Elizabeth Lucy was the dau]/ghter of one Wayte of South[ampton, a mean gentleman, if he w]ere one. And she was the wife [of one Lucy, as mean a man as] Wayte. And it is true that the [king kept her as his concub]ine, and she was one of these *who were known by* peculiar epithets. And this Mistress Lucy was *his witty concubine*, for difference called by the *king. And* she was the mother of the bastard Arturus. [For] the confession which the said writers [say she made and] protestation that she was never [assured] *to the king* [they impor]t nothing, and therefore [I] doubt that they were ever exacted [from her.]

But if you will truly understand th[e story and salve the errors] of the said writers, then you must know [for certain that the] lady to whom King [Lady Eleanor Talbot] Edward was first betr[othed and also married] (**ut supra**, as it was affirmed and whereof more anon) was [the Lady Eleanor] Talbot. And she was the daughter of a great pe[er of this realm, a man of most noble and illustrious fam]ily, and of the rank and quality of princes (*for the hera*lds say that earls be princes). And her father was [the Earl of] Shrewsbury, and a man very highly honoured and of great authority. And she is also called in authentic writ[ings the Lady] Butler, and that was because she was then the widow [of] Lord Butler, Baron of Sudeley, and as hath been here before declared. And she was a very fai[r and vir]tuous lady. And the king was much in love with her, but h[e could] not prevail in his wanton and luxurious attempts until he promised her [marriage and] was not [only contrac]ted to her, but also married (and the which shall be better demonstr*ated*) [and] had a child by her.

And this is that noble lady (and not Elizabeth Lucy) to whom the duchess *said the* king was contracted, and for the which she so wisely and so *earnestly* [presse]d *and ex*horted and urged her son to take and to hold and to avow the said Lady Talb*ot his* true and lawful wife, and none other. And here to note, **obiter**, this [king's breach with] this lady was the cause that the subtle widow would not for any promises or solemn p[rotestations from him yield] of her dainty person to his burning appetite and venerous amplexes until he had married her, [for she had learned **credulitas damno** [Ovid] **solet esse puellis**. And therefore] neither good counsel nor motherly authority nor religion nor threatened *war* and imminent dangers could dissuade or deter him from his purpo*s*e: his affections or lust were so excessively fervent and so vehement and so violent that there was *no rem*edy but he must needs wed and bed, and in all haste, the said Lady Gray, and that in so sudde*n and strange* and disparageous and clandestine and obscure manner as aforesaid.

And when that news was told to the Lady [Eleanor But]ler, she was greatly grieved, and she lived a melancholic and heavy and solitary life ever aft[er, and how sh]e died is not certainly known, but it is out of doubt that the king [killed her no]t with kindness. But he exceeded in all manner of kindness and of care*ful love* to [his new] wife and queen, the Lady Gray. And many years following, he fully satisfied and satiated him*self with the* [joys and pl]easures which he conceived to be in her, and he bega*t* [many children] *upon her*.

And yet afterward that precontract stuck in his cons[cience after a time and much perplexed him, labouring by all occasions to suppress it. And it so much and nearly touched him that he held them not his friends nor good subjects which mentioned it. And this was the cause of his displeasure against his ancient chaplain Dr] / Stillington, Bishop of Bath, a[lthough he **225** did but what he was bound to do] in conscience before God and by his [duty to the kingdom.]

But [it is not known] *to every*body how and to whom he first discovered this m[arriage, nor everywhere] *set* down, but this is the opinion thereof *which some men hold of the matter*, and this it is. That after the Lady [Eleanor, being much] troubled in her mind with this wrong and d[ishonour done her by the king, he]r heart was so full of the grief *that she was rea*dy to burst, and that she could no longer conceal *it*, she revealed her marriage [to a lady] who was her sister, or, as some say, her [mother, the Countess of Shrew]sbury, or to both. And her mother told it to the earl her husband herewith. *And* [he acquaints it to his noblest] and wisest and nearest friends. And they were all much offended and scand*alized with this* affront and wrong.

And because they would be better *and more firmly* resolved herein, they thought it fit to talk with Dr [Stillington, who] *knew the truth of the* matter, and they so did. And he confessed and affirmed that the king and th[e Lady Elea]nor were contracted and married by him. And hereupon [they] *said* to the bishop that, he being a man of holy orders and [a bishop,] also a privy counsellor to the king, it behoved him in [his duty to God and to the king to admonish the king of this fault and to advise him better to considerati[on of the wr]ong which he had done to the Lady Eleanor and to her [noble] lineage and family, and to take some course to salve it and to redress and make satisfac[tion.]

The bishop liked w[ell the proposition, but durst not deal with the king] in this matter and manner, but yet he promised that he w[ould use some means whereby it might] be imparted to the king. And then he acquainted the Duke of [Gloucester] therewith, [who was most inward and gra]cious with the king of all other. And hereof thus writeth Philip de [Commynes:] [Philip de Commynes] **Cet l'Évêque de Bath mit en avant à [ce Duc d]e Cloucester que ledit Roi Edouard** était **fort amoureux [d'une] dame d'Angleterre et lui promit de l'epouser, pourvu [qu'il couch]**ât **avec elle. Elle s'y consentit et dit cet Évêque [qu'il les] avait épousés, et n'y avait que lui et eux deux, ut supra.**

[And the Duke] of Gloucester dealt with the king about this business, but he could do no good. [For all the effect] hereof was nought, and that was that the king grew exceedingly wroth [with the Bishop of] Bath for revealing their marriage, and checked and rated *the bishop*, and bitterly, and charged him that he had betrayed [his children,] *and said that* he would make him repent his trea*chery and* [put him from] the coun[s]el [table and

225v commit]*ted* him to *pri*/son, where he lay a long time [in much sorrow] and misery, and at the *last* [the king made him glad to] redeem these bonds of imprisonment *for his* garrulity at a heavy fine. And this [is testified by]
[1620] Francis Godwin, now Bishop of Hereford, [in his **Catalogus] Episcoporum**. And hereof also this *same* noble Frenchman, Philip [de Commynes, thus writeth:] **Le roi Edouard désappointa l'**[Évêque**, et le] tint en prison, et le rançonna d'une bonne [somme d'ar]gent.** But this was injustice, for the bishop [not deserving to] be punished in this case because he was [bound
[How King Edward died] i]n conscience to reveal this former marriag[e.]

Not long after, King Edward died, and it was [held] doubtful upon what
226 disease or evil he came t*o it.* / Polydore Vergil saith he died of a disease
[Polydore, **Lib**. 24] u[tterly] unknown to all the physicians, which showeth some that there was some *foul play*, and that may be understood to be either poison or sorcery. Who were the dealers in th[ese arts I have show]ed before. And the author of the **History of Brittany** [in] plain terms saith that the king was killed by
[**Lib.** 4 **en Hist. de Bretagne**] poison as the report in France was: **Aucuns disaient que le [Roi] d'Angleterre avait été empoisonné [au mois d'avril en l'an 1483**.]

227 And Enguerant de Monstrelet [writeth that some said] / he died of an
[Monstrelet, pt. 3 **de ses Chroniques**] apoplexy, and that some other said that he was poisoned in wine of Creu w[hich King Lewis XI sent him.] And Philip de Commynes seemeth to be of the same opinion, for he saith that **[Aucuns] disent que le roi Edouard mourut d'un catarrhe**: some say [that King] Edward died of a catarrh. For so they say in France when a grea[t man] is made away by poison. And of such a venomous catarrh died the young King Edward [the sixth.] And in this sense the French king Henry III *died of a* catarrh. And I came to understand it upon this occasion: it *fell th*en unhappily that when I was in France and in the *court, there was* news brought that the Lady Mary Queen *of Scots w*as beheaded in England, and at *the arrival of this news they said that she had died of a catarrh*.

[But to whose hand King Edward IV had his is not told. This is certain: he
228 was generally beloved of all his subjects, e]/xcepting [those of the Lancastrian faction, who in their hearts ha]ted him and wished his death and the short *lives of* [all the Pl]antagenets, and especially those of the royal family of [York.] *And the*y made quick and round riddance ere it was long time. *And* the King Edward acted the first part of this truculent tragedy, and *then* his sons stayed not long after him in this world And King Richard and his son bled out mo*re in the next a*cts, and they were succeeded in that bloody protasis by Edward Plantagenet, *Earl of* Warwick, and by Perkin Warbeck and by the Countess of Salisbury, by the de la Poles and others. And the daughters of King Edward were but short live*d. And it* was a long tragedy, for it was in acting forty years at the leas*t. And it* was well performed, for there were none then left which had any parts to play *on tha*t dismal stage. But these be harsh and distasteful matters, and *I w*ill speak no more of them, but I will proceed.

[As soon as] King Edward was dead, the silence broke. And now there was not only [general muttering] of the king's marriage, but also loud and common and public inveighing [against it.] And now all tongues were loose and at liberty, and pardons were hoped [for all offences.] And then the
229 general voice / and common opinion was that this ma[rriage was] *contracted invalid*ly and that the children were illegitim[ate (in plainer

[Dr Morton, Sir Thomas More, Grafton, Holinshed, Stow]

terms,] that they were bastards.) And Dr [Morton affirmeth the] Duke of Buckingham and other noble [lords saw and read certain] authentic instruments made and signed by [learned doctors] and proctors and notaries with the depositions of [sundry] credible persons, importing and testifying that th[e children] of King Edward IV were bastards. Moreover, [the city] of London was possessed with this base opinion, and the *p*reachers also, and namely Dr Shaw and Friar Pynk [and others] declared in their pulpits and pronounced them illegitimate, and that they were **spuria vitulamina** – bastard [branches – and might take no r]oot. And likewise the people of the north parts *made* known that they held these children *to be ba*stards in their supplicatory scroll, [before m]entioned. And finally the court of Parliament declared, *pronoun*ced, adjudged and decreed both the marriage and the children to be unlawful, as I have related, and at large, before.

230*

How King Edward might have pre[vented] all the afte[r evils]

[But there] was a means and an opportunity, and [which lasted] some years, and if it had then and timely been *taken*, whereby King Edward might have salved [that fault] and might have anteverted and made [frustrate a]ll future claims and repaired and *salved all flaw*s and defects of titles and have avoided all quarrels and [questions which after arose upon] the foresaid precontract. [He might] also have taken away and cleared [the error and inconvenience of the postcontract and later marriage, from whence grew the imputation of bastards to his children, and so have avoided all ensuing mischiefs and calamities.

230v*

[For if first he had procured a divorce of the first contract or marria]/ge with the Lady Eleanor fro[m the Pope, who was then held] to have all the power of [heaven and earth] *and to be* able to confirm or ensure and to d*ivorce or unbind*. [Or if after] the second marriage, and while he *was king*, *which was the best part* of fourteen years, he had either [by his own prov]ident care and due consideration, or by the good counsel [of his best friends] and counsellors craved [the Pope's] pardon for his breach of the pre[contract with] the Lady Eleaor Talbot, and next his Ap[ostolical B]ull of dispensation for his postcontract (or m[atrimony] superinducted as they call it) – and which suits mig[ht] have been obtained at Rome for money.

And the*reafter*, these suits being obtained, to have summoned a [Parliament,] and therein to have desired and required the Th[ree Estates] of the kingdom to have ratified and confirmed [the Bulls] containing the pardon and disp*ensation or* approbation of the said marriage with the Lad[y Gray,] and the legitimation of his children. And *after these things were* obtained of Parliament, to accept and *declare* and pronounce and establish those things *as* [lawful] by Act of Parliament according to the indulge[nce] *of the* Pope (which was then held a most sacred and [inviolable] thing). And lastly to have declared and prono[unced] and decreed in Parliament that the said childr[en of this] king, being thus now made legitimate, were [ca]pable of all honours and dignities and of a[ll estates,] public and private, whereof the king was [possessed] and seized, or which were anyways appertaining and proper to [the king] of England and of France.

I say if he had done thus, [he had] *accommo*dated and compassed all errors and defects and had prevented all the succeeding dangers of claims and practices and had forestalled and *secured that the*n no claims nor titles of any ambitious, presumptuous and inju*rious upstart could be o*f any force

or regard; and all might have been obtained and *performed* by the king living, he having then so great *authority and* power in this kingdom, and so
Egerton 259 good *favour* with the popes. / [And this course was by another opportunely thought on.

[But it may be thought the judgement of God, hanging over the king's head for his many and great offences, captivated and took his understanding and provident care from him. For his sins were not only his adulteries and fornications, those in the height and excess, but he was burthened with the crying sin of bloodshed. Yet Polydore Vergil imputeth his greatest guilt to the violating his faith and solemn vow to God and to the holy clergy when he was suffered to enter York upon condition he should demand nor seek anything but his dukedom of York. And these indeed are the just causes of God's punishments against men. And many times He is pleased to leave them so blinded and secure in their sensualities and sins that they have no sense or power to see or *prevent* the mischiefs that stand at their doors.]

231 And whereby the children of King Edw*ard were* pronounced illegitimate and made incapable *of the crown*, which, or the like Parliamentary power, also *could* have made them legitimate (as I *intima*ted). And these great and high and difficult wor[ks are indeed] *the provi*nce of the great and transcendent po*wer of Par*liament. And those courts are well worthy to have *such cred*it and authority if they be assembled and used [and held] as they ought to be. For the court of *Parliament* is or should be a general assembly of all the most [noble] *and m*ost honourable and most just, the most godly, and the *most* [rel]igious persons of the kingdom, as well laical as [eccle]siastical. And by the many good and wholesome laws *which were* made in that Parliament of **anno** 1 **Rege Ricardi**, the second marriage of King Edward was adjudged [unlaw]ful. And the aims of that Parliament were for the most part repealed and abrogated [afterward.] And yet it appeareth plainly en[ough that t]he general judges and the lawmakers of that Parliament were [wise] *and* just and good and godly men, and that their laws were good and jus[t,] and therefore whatsoever [was adjud]ged and decreed then by them was to be received as *j*ust *and* authentic and inviolable, how roughly soever it was afterward h[andled.]

And in the case of [the disa]bling of the sons of King Edward, there is least cause [to suspect] them because the cause was so new and plain and so notoriously [known th]at no man might be ignorant therein. [Therefore to hav]e given any other judgement in the cause [but according] to the evidence and proofs, it might justly have been censured an ac[t of error and ignorance, or partiality and inju]stice. If it be objected that [the case was o]bscure and doubtful, [that cannot be. For the Estates had all substantial and ready means to inform themselves] of the truth, and whereby they [might be satisfied and cleared of all doubts. For all the witnesses and
233v* dealers in that cause, and such per]/sons as were privy and [acquainted with] *those* businesses were then living, [and they must and would] have truly and certainly informed the [court of Parliament] *and* delivered to them the state *of the matter there*unto lawfully required and called and swor*n to* it.

[For the special and reverend] care which the court of Parliament hath [is the advancing of justice] and truth. [And therefore] all subjects by nature or gr[ace are bou]nd by the duty of their allegiance to give rev*erend* credit to Parliaments and to believe in their a[uthority] and power as the ancient pagans did in ora[cles.] *And* further also, we must confidently hold and belie[ve] the [high] and transcendent quality and virtue of tha[t court] to be such as the Papists held the power o[f the] Pope: that is, to have all power and [authority,] and that they can do anything [but err.] 234

But this must be understood of the courts of Parliame*nt* assembled and holden by such wise and good and just and godly men as aforesaid. For if th*e* court be pestered with ignorant, corrupt, unjust and irreligious persons, then it is **thronus anomiae et consilia impiorum** and ***la* chapelle de mal conseil**, and the tribunal of tyranny and consistory of corruption. And the laws which are then made are naught, and taint and not to be kept nor observed. And in s*uch* cases if the next or another court of Parliament, good and godly men shall decree to revoke and to annul the evil and unjust laws made by such unjust and unworthy men, their proceedings and acts are good, just, honourable and pious. Otherwise, and generally, to repeal and abrogate the acts of a good Parl*iament is a* violent and a giantlike and an unjust work, and *it is gener*ally taxed, **Clavum cl*avo pellere.*** And no Erasmus, **Proverbs** question, to repeal or abrogate a good and just law made in Parliament is a wrong and scandal to that general counsel and to the universal wisdom, providence, justice and piety of the kingdom, which at the best is but an intestine war of civil dissention.

[And there be examples of such] / Parliaments here in Eng[land, 235 wherein many acts firmly made] were repealed and rescind[ed,] *and* [sometimes the whole Parliament] abrogated. But these tr*ibunals and* manner of proceedings were but in time of the greater [seditions and factious tumults,] and in the times of the civil or un[natural wars, when] injustice and wrong and oppression overra*n* [all.] *And* [some] of these irregular and evil *bodies have nicknam*es as stigmas left upon them, [as the Parlia]ment of Wonders, the Black Parlia[ment, the Bloody Parliam]ent, etc. And none was worthier of an evil name than that Parliament [which condem]ned to confiscation and destruction a gr[eat] many [churches and re]ligious houses erected and dedicated to the service of God.

And so great were the evils and mischief th*ey pronounc*ed and decreed as it may well be doubted whether *the Holy* Ghost were in the midst of that synod or court or no. *And it* is great presumption that the deviser and giver of ancient and most pernicious *co*unsel, viz., Satan, was there. For he hath also his synods, and he requireth his or*ators to* persuade *th*e spoil and the destruction of all the houses of God and of his *ministers. And* he hateth piety, faith and charity and verity and would fain *abolis*h them. But God giveth such an invincible strength *to veri*ty above the rest as that she is champion able enough to defen*d them, and she* overcometh Satan in the end with all his hosts of lies and of sin. *And truthfulness* hath only these great and all victorious eulogies, viz.: **Magna et prae omnibus fortior, super omnibus *est* Veritas. Magna est Veritas, et praevalet.** *And also, in* ***quo inest omnis cum subtilitas disserendi tum veritatis iudicandi.*** But these 235v judgements be but opinions *fit only for* ***consilia impiorum*** **et thronus** Cicero **iniquitatis**. And I have already spoken abundantly and generally of *this matter in the* ********B*ook of my **Baron**.

Therefore I will speak *briefly, and as I reck*on is fit and proper to the place and *give examples of Parliaments* of that kind. And amongst them *I* *will say some*thing of the Parliament holden **ann[o** 1 Henry VII, wherein the]re be Acts enough to frustrate and to enervate [and dissolve] and abrogate itself, as by examples and parag[raphs of that] Parliament I will plainly demonstrate and prove *beyo*nd affection. First then, whereas there is an Act for [attaint]ing the true and lawful king of this land, namely R[ichard] III, of High Treason, and that for his bearing of arms ag[ainst the Earl of] Richmond, fal*sely in r*ebellion proceeding from Milford Haven into Leicestershire, entitled the Sovereign Lord. For when he came on land to fight [the] battle, he was then no king nor sovereign, which can *any way be* proved. But the truth is, the earl was then in the time aforesa*id*, or oug[ht to have been,] a vassal and a liege subject of King Richard, the true [king] and only sovereign lord of the realm and of the people *as long* as he lived.

Therefore it is plain that in this paragraph there be th[rice] *mon*strous gross faults and falsehoods. For first it is certain that Richard was [during his reign] a sove[reign: therefore] he was no subject. Secondly, there was no enemy in the field [who was] then a sovereign, but all were vassals of the crown and king of England. And to conclude upon these two f*irst* arguments, Richard, being a king and a sovereign, and no subject, could [not] be adjudged a traitor, nor justly and lawfully be attainted of [High Treason,] because there was no man in those armies but he was the humble and loyal vassal of him, the said King Richard. And *this is to turn* all things topsy-turvey and very preposterously to set f*irst the subject above the sover*eign and the malefactor above the magistrate. In one word it is to rever*e the* subject and the disloyal and rebelling and seditious *traitor when* he committeth the **crimen** of **laesae m*aiestatis*** *and violates the sacred ma*jesty of the k*ing*.

236 *However,* / as I *intimated, King Richard was attainted,* with all the rest of the true and c[onstant subjects of the king that bare arms] in the field and battle [at Bosworth] *and risked* their fortunes and their pers*ons to defend* their sovereign lord, and of *right as they were* bound to do. All these men *were for this* service done to their sovereign accus*ed of* High Treason, and their goods and lands confis[cate.] And this must needs be a great *scandal* in this Parliament.

One Thomas Nan[dick, a necromancer, havin]g been with other his consorts justly condemned to di[e for necr]omancy and sorcery, was in this Parliament [pardoned the horrible things] which he had committed by his art. But it seemeth that [he had not then left the] *practice of sorcer*y and of conjurations (or rather adjurations), because he [hath in that Act of Parliament still the style of] conjurer, viz.: Thomas Nandick of Cambrid[ge, Conjurer and Necromancer, which h]ad been a fitter title for his gibbet than for his pardon, and to be sent and dispatched by the post of Newgate, albeit he ha[d not by his sorcery or] enchantments hurt or destroyed any human and Christian creature, but [for his abjura]tion of Almighty God. And the opinion of a great and a lear[ned and religious doctor, **Magos et] incantores** (saith he) **hominum genus dignum quod vel ob [solam Dei O.M. abjurationem] capitali supplicio afficiatur**. And other such matters t[here be in that Parliament] which detract and derogate much from their credit and authority thereof. But I will *hol*d my promise.

And now I will return to King Richard and bestow some *time in the*
237* *defend*/ing and clearing of him of one offence more, [or rathe]r of an error,

[The treaty of marriage between King Richard and his niece, the Lady Elizabeth Plantagenet]

[Dr Morton, Sir Thomas More, and their followers]

for it was no worse at the worst (although made a very heinous crime). And that was also about *a m*arriage matter. For his adversaries devise and derive this new crime [from] the treaty which King Richard had about the marriage [of the] Lady Elizabeth Plantagenet, his niece, and whereof [I ma]de some mention in the beginning. And his old adversaries *bla*me this king very much for this suit or attempt thereof, *and they* censure it to be a thing not only most detestable *but also mu*ch more cruel and abominable to be put in execution. *And they* add hereunto that all men, and the maiden *mo*st of all, detested this unlawful copulation; *and that* he made away the queen his wife to [make way for this marr]iage; and that he propounde[d not the treaty of marriage until the queen his wife was dead.

[That there was such a motion for the marriage of this lady to this king is true, and which is more, and most] / certain it [was entertained] a good while and well liked by the k[ing and his friends, also by the Lady Elizabeth and the] queen her mother. And indeed, [the treaty of this] match was so acceptable [unto the queen, concern]ing very much comfort and [happiness therein, that] she presently sent into France [to her son, the Marquess of D]orset (who was there with [the Earl of Richmond, prac]tising treason with him against [the king), and requires] him earnestly to leave that earl and his treacher*ous* pract*ices* [and come] home, and she assured him that he should be wel[come to the king], *and be pardon*ed by him, and also advanced so great*ly that his* fortunes should be much mended. 237v*

And in further token of [her liking to] th[is match, she sent the Lady Eliza]beth her daughter to the court to attend upon the quee[n, that she might be,] and by that means, more in the eye and in the heart of King Richard. And at Christmas follow[ing, the Queen Blanche, for the better] colour for the sending of her eldest daughter to the court, she *also* [se]nt her other four daughters to the court, and where they we[re all re]ceived with the most honourabl[e] courtesies and the best welcome that could be given, [and with] great feast and revelling during all the Chris[tmas,] the which the king then kept in Westminister Hall. [And t]he queen regnant entertained also the young ladies with all h*er* courtesies and gracious caresses, and espec[ially] the Lady Elizabeth, whom she used with so much famili[arity] and kindness as if she had been her own sister, and ca*used* her to wear robes and apparel and attire of the same *pattern* and the same colour and of the same fashions which she herse*lf wore*.

But the queen had small joy and little pleasure in these festiv[al and] pompous times, because she was sick and was much in languor and [sorrow] for the death of the prince, her dear and only son, and the which *grieved her sorely*. But albeit this counterfeit wooing of the king was kept very close, yet the curious and w*aver*ing enemies of the king, and who were devoted to the Ea[rl of] Richmond, began to suspect that the king had a purpose *to* marry the Lady Elizabeth and so to prevent and to bereave the earl *not* only of her marriage, but also of his best and chiefest ho[pe,] *which* was to attain the crown by her title. And therefore these [mal]*con*tent and seditious lords and other murmured and [muttered] very much and very broadly against the motion and suspic*ion* of this marriage of the Lady Elizabeth with the *King Richard*. Thereupon the treaty of this marriage was carrie[d more closely] and more coldly also on the king's part.

And in [April follow]ing, the young Prince of Wales, son *of King* 238*

Richard, died, *as ha*th been before related, as also *hath the effect of it*. [All this while, neither the queen widow nor her daughter were altered or estranged, but continued constant in their desire and expectation] *and* pursuit of this marriag[e. Only there was objection made by the ladies against the] king for having a w[ife, as though she living, he could not marry another] at once, not considering [it was usual not only with kings] but also with private me[n to put away one wife and] take another, and not only for ad[ultery and treason] *but for* other lighter crimes as, for exampl*e*, [the Romans might repud]iate their wives for conversing [with men which were not of] their kindred, or for g[oing to see play]s and to behold Circensian spectacles where their [husbands] *were* [not with them,] or if the wife were an unquiet [woman, or curst of her tongue,] *or,* as we say, an arrant shrew, her husband might p*roperly put her away*.

[J]ustus [V]ulteius [in] **Jurispru[den]-tia Rom.**

And King [Henry VIII put away two] wives, Queen Catharine of Castile and Qu[een Anne of Clev]e, for none of these crimes, but one becau[se she was] *too ugly* and too old and not pleasing to him, and the other [because she] was not fruitful or not wanton enough. And som[etimes men] have put away their wives because they were sluts [or] *had* unsavoury and unwholesome breaths, or else for some infec[tious disea]se. Yet none of these repudiators took away the lives of their wives, nor needed *to do so,* because it was lawful for both of them to marry when they wou[ld. And] the Pope Clement VII so ratified the divorce of King [Henr]y VIII against Catharine of Castile, as he defied all laws, [div]ine as human, which should contradict and impugn his p[ower and dispe]nsation, and in these words: **Non obstante iure divino [nec] humano, nec quibuscumque constitutionibus repugnatibus [aut in] contrarium editis.**

[Bulla Pope Clementis VIII, **apud D**. Robert Cotton]

[And t]his manner of putting away of wives which their husbands [like] not was very ancient and in common use amongst *the* Israelites and the Jews and the select people of *God. An*d there is a law of divorces and of repudiations c*ompos*ed by Moses. And there was also a formal bill or [libel m]ade for the separation and divorcing of the man and [wife,] and it was in this tenor, as Andreas Osiander, a learned man, [wh]o thus translated it out of Hebrew into Latin affirmeth, *and the which*, *b*ecause it is rare and proper to this argument, I have *transcribed it* hither, and thus it is:

[Osiander in **Annotations in IV Ebr., Harmonius Evangelic.]**

[Die] tertia Hebdomadis 29 die mensis [Octobris, anno ab orbe condito, 43]49 . . . . Ego Joa[chim cognominatus N. filius Nathanis, qui consisto hodie in urbe N. in regno N. te, N. uxorem meam cognominatam N. filiam N. quae fuisti uxor mea antehac, nunc demisi et liberavi et repudiavi te tibi, ut sis tui iuris, et domina animae tuae, et ad abeundum ut ducaris abs quolibet viro quem volueris, et ne vir quisquam prohibeat quo minus sis in manu tua ex hoc di]/e et in aeternum. Et [ecce permissa es unicuique viro. Et hic esto t]ibi a me datus libellus [repudii, et epistola dimissoria et instr]umentum libertatis, iuxta [legem Moses et Israelis.

238v*

[But to pro]ceed and to relate the answer which was [made in the name of the king to the Lady Elizabeth,] *to* wit, concerning the life or death of the Queen Anne. And the *queen*'s life, which was very near at an end, would be no impediment of any [long continuance, she being a very weak] woman and in a consumption and [past hope of recovery,] *t*hat according to the opinion of her physicians, she could not live much [past the middle of Februar]y next following. And they guessed *not* [much amiss, for the]

[The credit of the Duke of Norfolk with King Richard and with the Lady Elizabeth, and her letter to him]

queen died in the next month, viz., M[arch. But when the mid]st and more days of February were gone, [the Lady Eli]zabeth, being very desirous to be marri*ed, and growing n*ot only impatient of delays, but also suspicious of the [success,] wrote a letter to *Sir John* Howard, Duke of Norfolk, intimating first therein that [he was the] one in whom she most [affied,] because she knew the king her father much lov[ed him,] and that he was a very faithful servant unto him and to [the king his brother then reign]ing, and very loving and serviceable to King Edward's children.

*Fir*st she thanked him for his many courtesies and friendly [offices, an]d then she prayed him as before to be a mediator for her to the k*ing* in the cause of [the marriage], who, as she wrote, was her only joy and maker in [this] world, and that she was his in heart and in thoughts, in [body] and in all. And then she intimated that the better half of Fe[bruary] was past, and that she feared the queen would nev[er die.] And all these be her own words, written with her own hand, and this is the sum of [her] letter, whereof I have seen the autograph or original d[raft] under her [own] hand, and by the special and honourable favour of the mos[t noble] and first count of the realm, and the chief of his family, Sir Thomas Howard, and Baron Howard, etc., Earl of Arundel and of Surrey, and the immediate and lineal [heir] / of this Sir John Howard, Baron Howard, Mowbray, and Duke of Norfolk, etc. 239 And albeit he be young and in his flourishing age, yet for his courage and much knowledge and ripe judgement, he is capable of any h*ard* employment, and ready to undertake and to embrace any noble act*ions*. And he keepeth that princely letter in his rich and magnificent cabinet, among precious jewels and rare monuments.

[The cabinet of the Earl of Arundel, now Earl of Surrey too]

And by this letter it may [be] observed that this young lady was inexpert in worldly affairs, and hereby igno[rant that a man] having a wife living might marry another and suffer her to live. *But she* understood and wrote like to herself, that is to say like to a *young* maiden, and as having heard nothing of repudiations and *divorces, s*he seemeth to say as the young and fa*ir ones think.* / But I have here sh*own that she could have been* married to 240* the king and the que*en have remained alive if he had wished* and had any hearty desire to proceed or purpose *to marry her.* [But the truth is, the king] had no mind nor inten[t in his heart to make her his wife from] the beginning, but in policy he entertained [this treaty,] and as it plainly [appeared afterward, when the queen his wife was dead,] and that he had then all fit op[portunity] *and* commod*ity* [to marry her, no let nor impediment being, but so strong in absolute power] that it was not in the power of *any man to* [debar] that alliance.

[Chronic. Croylan.]

Yet he took her *not, although he pretended desire* to marry her, but for the said other causes. And *he* made open protestation in the Great [Hall at St John's near] Smithfield before all the Knights of Ma[lta and a great asse]mblance of noblemen and of gentlemen, [the Lord Mayo]r and aldermen also, and many citizens being [likewise pre]sent, that he had no purpose nor desire nor intent [to marry the] Lady Elizabeth. And he protested, **Quod ea res, [viz. volu]ntas contrahendi matrimonium cum consanguin[ea germ]ana sua, numquam ei venerat in mentem**. For [so it is testi]fied by the Prior of Croyland.

But it may not be [deni]ed but that he made love to this lady and pretended [to marr]y her, and obtained both the good will of the lady [and] of the queen her mother, as hath been before showed. But this love was made [in] policy and cunningly, and that was to draw her to him that thereby he migh*t* [divert her affection] from the Earl of [Richm]ond (**ut supra**), to whom Morton and the seditious barons had promised *her*, and upon which marriage and by the title thereof dependi*ng, the* earl's hope of the crown also and chiefly depended. And th*us saith* [a good auth]or: **[Non** [Chronic. Croyland] **a]liter videbat Ricardus Rex regnum sibi confirmari neque spem competitoris sui auferri posse, nisi in matrimonio [cum dic]ta Elizabetha contrahendo, /vel simulando/**.

And as I verily believe *and apprehe*nd, the king had no other end in wooing of the Lady *Eliza*beth but to prevent the earl and to frustrate [those hopes of] his fortunes which he had by her – so I think verily – nor that the king *had this* same will or purpose by treachery to make a[way] the queen his wife. And I am the rather of this opinion, and have before proved, that he ever hated base and secret acts *and treac*hery, and besides [The queen died the 16th March, 1484] that he was always so [affectionate and kind that] he was rather ta*ken to be* [uxorious than otherwise, and at her death expressed it in his heavy mourning, causing very magnificent exequies to be prepared for her, [Prior Croyland] interring her **non cum minore honore quam reginam decuit**, as the Prior of Croyland testifieth.]

240v* *Now for the opinion of his* / adversaries, viz., that *the Lady Elizabeth detested* this unlawful copulation, [that you may see appears a false suggestion, the contrary being proved by] her own letter, before cited. And *this affirm*ation, to say that this marriage was a [detestable and cruel thing is a vain and ignorant affirmation] because she was so near akin to him, whereas [m]arriages between uncles and [nieces have been very frequent and allow]ed in other countries, and by the Church. And in our [times, the daughter and heir] of the Duke of Infantasgo in [Spain was married to his brother, Duke Alonso de Mendoza. [And more recently the Earl] of Miranda married his brot[her's daughter. In the] house of Austria, marriages of [this kind have been] rife and usual and thought [lawful and] honourable when the Pope hath dispensed [with them. For] they say in Spain, **Que el padre san[to quiere, Dios l]oquiere.**

And now lastly I will say one word *concerning* the queen, wife of King Richard, although it be almost *the last*. And whereas it is affirmed also by the adversari*es that* King Richard made away his wife to marry this *Lady* Elizabeth Plantagenet, I have demonstrated already this also to be as false *by arguments* and proofs. I desire therefore the worthy Reader to review and consider what *I have said before*. But the king cleared himself of the imputation of seeking of that marr*iage by swearing on his hono*ur (which is a great oath) and by his neglect when his w[ife was] dead and he free, and that then her life could be *no* hindrance to his second marriage, yet he pursued *not this* cause, nor had any desire to marry her. And thirdly, this is a good *i*mputation or accusation, to wit all his accusers charge him not with the practice of the death of *the* queen his wife directly and disertly, but [Sir Thomas More; Holinshed] doubtfully and in this [manner]: **the [queen] (howsoever it fortuned) departed out of this life the 16th of March in the Lent season**. And this rather maketh to clear him of these a*ccusations than accuseth him*.

But albeit he were a good and loving husband to his wife, yet I say *not* that he always lived continently and with[out wrong] to her bed, because I find that he had some [bastards,] and two of them I have mentioned before, here *in this work*. [Yet] haply he had them in his youth, and before his m[arriage, and then the] fault was the less.

And thus much for the many injurious censures and sha*meful slanders* made of King Richard by his quadrupla[tors,] and whose brains doubtless were very fertile of inventions and very ingenious in such *false and evil* slanders and foul *detractions, and which* should *not be believed*. [So that all King Richard's guilt is but suspicion. And suspicion is] / in la[w no more **241** guilt or culpableness than imagination] or the *accusations whi*ch are weak be*cause they are* false *And they are not to be belie*ved, nor *are they credited by the learne*d judges, because *they have not been pr*oved to them certain by idoneou*s* proofs.

[Suspicio est opinio male ex levibus signis.] *S.* [Thomas Aquinas.] **[Suspicio est actus, per quem indubitationem trahimur**. Prateius.]

[For] suspicion, although it many tim[es lay a great blame] upon a man ([for men hold him to be guilty] whom they suspect to be guilty, althou[gh the suspicion be false and] injurious), but it is not held in the law to be a crime: and [in regard] that suspicion supposeth many tim[es] *men* [to be g]uilty and culpable of crimes whereof they are n[ot. So that an innoce]nt may as easily be condemned as a malefactor, [being an evil grow]n from the error of men. Wherefore mere suspicion of itself bring[eth no sentence against any man by the laws natural or moral, civil or divine.] And therefore the wise and just judges and magistrates requ*ire strong* evidence of the accuser, or else they pronounce the *accuser guilty* of condemnation, and the execution of the same punishm*ent is decreed against him for being an* accuser and not being furnished, which is due by law to him who is guilty of the offence or crime which is laid by the *accuser to the* innocent man's charge.

And after this manner proceed the *learned* judges of the imperial and civil laws, and by good right, *accor*ding to that wise sentence of the old Mimographus, **Suspicio [grave est homin]ibus malum**. And therefore the Divine Chrystostom admonisheth [that **Suspicio t]ollenda est, non inferenda**. And he tacitly giveth another reason [in another] place where he saith that [a] good man hardly suspecteth [another man to be] evil, and an evil man scarcely ever supposeth any man [to be good. He fur]ther amplifieth and exemplifieth this argument: an adulterer (sai[th he) or fornicator thinketh o]ther men to be such as he is. And the proud man thinketh *that all men are prou*d, and the murderer thinketh that all men [are murderers.

[And born under the like influence were they that] raised this suspici[on upon King Richard. But it had been more credit to have observed the rules and counsel of this divine epigram:

[Culpare in quoquam, quae non sunt nota malignum est, **[Anthologia Sacra]**
Praesertim si quae cognita sint] ***bona*** **[sunt.**
Non pateant faciles duris rumorib]/us aure[s; **241v**
Quae nescire iuvat credere n]on libe[at;
Linquantur secreta deo] ***cui*** **quicquid [apertum est;**
Inspicit et nullis] indiget indicibus.

And this is the sense in English:

[Accuse no] man of faults to thee unknown,
And much less him from whom good fruits h[ave grown.]
Lend not thine ears to scandalous repo[rts.]
Believe not that which known nought t[hee imports.]

Leave secret things to God, who knows [all hearts,]
And hath no need of the promoter's arts.

[promotor's = dilator's]

*B*ut to be short, I confess that the best were never to be suspe[cted of any crime:] **Felicio innocentia est citra suspicionem**, as Sen[eca said well.] And as Julius Caesar, who had many excellent observations, was [wont to say,] that **Vir bonus [tam suspicione] quam crimine carere oportet**: that a good man must be as [well without] suspicion as without crime. But yet let no [man] presume of his righteousness and of his integrity and of his innocency but that h[e may] *be* suspected of some crime, and by some malicious or env[ious] *persons, and conde*mned for it, although he never committed it. For such per[sons, like to the **polypus**,] will take any colour and make any show of crime serve their [turn].

[Suetonius]

But it shall be well for a Christian man, and it shall savour of more charity (and which is *grateful* to Almighty God, who only knoweth the secret soul*s of men, not to credit the* suspicion of his neighbour, nor to suppose and report none other men *guilty of* crimes according to their opinion or ill affection, and whereof they *have no knowledge*. For suspicion is for the most part an erroneous and an injurious and an unchari*table opinion, and oftenti*mes it wrongeth and condemneth an innoce*nt man and even after death when he cannot be woun*ded any more.

THE [FIFTH BOOK] OF THE HISTORY [OF KING] RICHARD THE III 242

The Arg*ument*

Herein is discussed what a [tyrant is,] and how a tyrant and King Richard diff[er.]
[The destruction of the Plantagenets.]
[The daughter]*s* of King Edward, how bestowed.
Death of the queen their mo[ther.]
The sundry virtues of this King Richard III.
[The eulogy of the three brothers, King Edward IV,] George and Richard III.
The magnificent, public and charitable b[uildings] and other good works of King Richard [III; his good laws and other good works.]
That to die in the [wars is no dishonour, but an] honour.
The age of King Richard III.
Artes r[egiae, crimen regale.]
His comparison with other kings accounted good, but worse than he.
All the Pla*ntagenets put to death by his successors*.
[The] character of King James; his gracious demeanour t[owards his cousins.]
[A character and eulogy of King Richard] III.
The title of the Norman race and of [York] defended.
The sundry titles of King James.
The wedding ring of England, **lapis regno fatali[s.]**
King Richard's sepulchre and epitaph.
The author's scope, peroration, **et votum**.

THE FIFTH BOOK

That I have examined and sifted and tried and found guilty and false *the accusers of King Richard will be now apparent. And the greatest of them* **243*** *was Sir Thomas More, whose chief studies were philosophy and law.* / But yet besides *these studies and* delights and other and studious *activities* he was much transp*orted by and much* addicted to poetry, *as I intimated* before. And it appeareth *so by this* pamphlet, for many of these accusa*tions* are but fables and fictions and poetical in*ventions. B*esides he had much intelligence with the *kingdom* of Utopia, and perhaps many of those imaginary *accusations were* advertisements from that strange and uncouth land, *or* some of them might be suggested to him in his dream*s and* visions by his worser genius. But I doubt that those *excus*es will neither salve his credit nor make amends to *the* extremely wrong and slandered King Richard. *And* yet this good knight hath so many good friends as well *abroa*d as at home, as that they will excuse him for any *faults* and cover the multitude of them with their love and *partia*lity.

What a ty[rant is]

But I like the plain and honest dealing of *John S*tow better, who affirmeth confidently that those greatest *crimes*, as namely the slaughter of his nephews, etc., were *never* proved against him, neither by witness and lawful evidence *no*r so much as by the oaths of the knights of the post.

Now that I *have refuted* the particular and special and more spite*ful scan*dals and accusations of King Richard, I *will say* some things in the interpretation and declamation of a vocable or term of *s*candal cast upon him, and which comprehendeth all scandals *and accusation*s and all impieties whatsoever. And that is the word 'tyrant', or an evil king. **Tyrannus est qui** [Aristotle in **Ethics**] **[suis propriis commodis stud]et et publicis adversatur**. [And again, [**Idem**] **Tyrannus est qui dominatu crudeliter abutitur**. And the Holy Ghost [**Proverbs**. Cap. 19] resembleth a tyrant to a roaring lion, bent upon spoil and bloody cruelty. **243v*** A tyrant is] / *by P*lato termed a wolf, and [by another wise man compared *Plato in* ***Republic*** t]o a dragon, who becometh [not a dragon until he hath eaten] and devoured many ser[pents, of which conceits t]his epigram was framed and wittily:

> **[Post plures colu]ber serpentes Draco fit esos,**
> **[Gustata hum]ana fitque homo carne lupus.**
> [The dragon which doth many serpents eat
>   Becomes a dragon of huge shape and strength.
> And so the man which makes man's flesh his meat
>   Transformed is unto a wolf at length.]

*And so much for these re*semblances. For the tyrant *lives on hu*man blood.

[Philosophu]*s* [Anonymus apud Plutarchum]

And another wise sa[ying of a philoso]pher dissenteth not far from hence, *who, when he was as*ked what beast was of all the most perni[cious] *and* heinous, he answered that of all tame beasts [the flatt]erer or parasite was the most hurtful, and of [all wil]d beasts the tyrant was the most cruel and pernicious. *For the* tyrant forbeareth not for any respect, nor maketh a *gentle* conscience to do any ill, but he is delighted in oppressi[ons,] *in* wrongs, in exactions, in robberies, in sacrileges, in [bloodshed,] in murder, in adultery, in incest, in rapes, in r[iot,] in gluttony, in prodigality and lavishness, and in a[ll manner] of excesses. These be his arts of reigning, and these [be his] virtues. For as for the true virtues and the pro*fessors* thereof, he hateth them.

[Lucan]
[Seneca, **Hercule Furente**]
[Demosthenes]

Invident [tyranni] claris, fortesque trucidant, as saith one. And another saith, **Tyr[annus miserum vetat perire, faelicem iubet**. And he exalte*th* and advanceth the persons most contaminate therewith. *And* it was truly said of the famous orator of Athens, **[Libe]ralitas tyranni nihil aliud est quam translatio pe[cuniarum] a iustis dominis ad alienos idque indignos.**

And the tyrant's t[hirst] *for* gold, and his covetousness, is so great and so *unquenchable*, and all for the serving of his inordinate lusts and prodigal humours, *and it is* so extreme; and for his foolish and monstrous largitions and inordinate lusts and those of his truhanes and parasites, bestowed upon *spoil*ers which are so excessively costly and wasteful as *to consume all his substance.*

[Claudian, **In Rufin]***um*

[Non Tartesiacis illum satiaret harenis tempestas pretiosa Tagi, non stagna rubentis aurea Pactoli; totumque exhauserit Hermum, ardebit maiore siti, etc.

[Juvenal, Satire IV]

> **[Quidquid conspicuum pulchrumque est aequore toto**
> **Res fisci est, etc**.]

244*

And in brief, a tyrant *is one who embraces both with* heart and wit *oppression and avarice*. [And] this [may serve] here for the descript*ion and qualification* of tyranny, and the which *I have made* to the end that it may be the *pattern of such actions* and by the comparing of them *with the actions* of this King Richard (and the which shall here follow), *it shall be m*anifest that he was very *susceptible to the virtues and not* obnoxious to the vices. And I *doubt he can in any wise* justly be called a tyran*t; for he* had many virtues and qualities, and he was *noble and generous*, which I will declare more at large, and offer *evidence thereof, after* that I have compared some of the acts of a tyrant *and the acts of* King Richard together, of the same subject, but contrary in their *effects*.

[King Richard no tyrant]
[In Parliament **anno** 1 Richard III]
[The Duke of Buckingham said that the name of 'benevolence' as it was taken in the time of King Edward IV signified that every man should pay not what he of his own good

First then, whereas the [tyra]nt imposeth many and grievous taxes and tribut*es upon h*is subjects, this King Richard took away such grie[vances.] And *there had been ena*cted by Act of Parliament a hateful tax, but disguised with the [name of] 'benevolence'. *And he relea*sed his subjects of the burden thereof, and forebore a*lso to levy any* new tax or charge upon them. Se*co*ndly, tyrants do not only pill and poll their people *and ta*ke their goods from them, but also they spoil and [rob] churches and churchmen and take from them holy things *d*edicated to God. But King Richard contrariwise [did m]any good things as well for the good of the people and for the public *bene*fit, as also for the promoting and advancing of the [servic]e of God and for the maintenance of his ministers the [churc]hmen, as shall be more particularly demonstrated in the *list of his achievements*. And this showed will list, but what the king of his] g[ood will list to take. Duke Buckingham **apud** Thomas More.]

[Sir Thomas More]

that he was a bountiful and pious princ*e*. [B]ut **Tyrannum pium esse non est facile**, as Sophocles [well obs]erved. Nor may he be happy or blessed, for the oracle pronounced **portae feli[citatis] ad tyran[nidem clausae**.]

Item: Tyrants be cruel and bloody. But [this king,] even by the testimony of his enemies, was very [merciful] and mild. For they say that he was of himself [very gentle] – these be their own words. Therefore, where *there are* [tyrannica]l acts objected to him, they must be under*stood to be* [done by other m]en or by their practices and [ill persuasions, or else before he was king. And what he did then was not or could not be properly called tyranny.

244v*

[And amongst those acts] done by him whilst [he was king,] *there are many not tyrannical when considered* properly. The beheading [of Henry Stafford, Duke of Buckingham,] is held to be one, and [the chiefest. Yet that act, the cau]se and just motives of the duke's cutting *off* [being considered, it cannot be censu]red tyranny, but due and [necessary justice. For if the king had] not put down that duke, [the duke would have put] *him* down, and he would have usurped [the throne royal] and seized upon the principate, if his p*ower and force could* have reached so far, and if w*ith arms he could have achieved the* sovereignty. And I have also *recounted* what and how gr*eat his offe*nces were, and deserving justly to *be punished by this ho*nest and most mild and gracious king.

I have s*een accounts wherei*n King Richard is reported to have used [tyranny] against his nephew Edward, Earl of Warw[ick,] *so*n to George, Duke of Clarence. It is true that [he sent him] to Sheriff Hutton, a goodly and pleasant house of h[is own in] Yorkshire, and where this young lord had libert[y, large diet,] air, pleasure enough, and lived in safety there. Therefore, if that [were imprisonment,] it [were **prison**] **curtois**, as J. Froissart says. But yet this must be no les[s than] tyranny, according to the judgement and style and charity of Sir Thomas More. *But* Henry VII, as soon as he had got the crown at Bosworth, instantly sent for t[his young prince,] and afterward cut off this prince's head, and for *nothing*, as you have heard before. But Sir Thomas More could no*t say th*/at this was an act of tyranny in that prince.

245

[King James]

[**Comes** Arundel, **viva voce**]

But let h*is acc*omplices make as light of it as they will, yet I dare boldly *say th*ere is a prince within the British world who would not have done *the* like cruel act to have gained thereby the whole empire and mona*rchy* of Europe. And I have reason to be of this opinion, and first because I know [he hath protested against that particular act and held it] in detestation. And secondly because the time by experience hath made it known that he destroyeth no regal titul[ars,] albeit there were some noble person[s in] one of the kingdoms who pretended title to the crown thereof by r*ight*, being descended from some kings of that country, yet this most magnanimous and gracious and pious prince was so far fr[om] seeking the destruction of any such aspirer, or so mu[ch as the] restraining them, as that he suffered them to live at [liberty] and to possess and enjoy quietly all their honours and p[ossessions] in safety and in peace. And the king might safely a*llow them with* security, for he knew that his title [was good, and so strong that he needed] *not* [fear] *a*ny m[eaner titles.

[Yet now his title and right is better than it was, for he is the true and next heir of King Edward III, of all his crowns and kingdoms; so hath he also a title to the crown of Scotland by him, and even that old title of the Balliols.

For Edward Balliol, King of Scotland, surrendered all his right and title to King Edward III)] / in Roxburgh: **Ed[wardus Balliol, Rex] Scotiae [regnum et coronam Scotiae] transtulit in [Edwardum Regem Angliae litteris suis patentibus] et authenticis inde confec[tis anno regni sui 33, anno Domini 1356**.] And thus King Edward III, besides [his most ancient titles from King Arthur and from] some of the Sax-Angle kings, hi[s title **de jure belli et de jure gladiis** came also by transaction] and [by purchase] (for he paid a great sum of m[oney to the said King Edward Balliol) and by] lawful surrender, to be the more abso[lute and rightful King of Scotland than before.] *And this prince* and king, my master, possesseth *by right* the many and all the royal titles of *all the per*sons descended from the princes of Scotland.

246
Thomas [Walsi]ngham

And when I consider his majesty's justice, so *full of clemency* and magnanimity it maketh me to be of opini*on that if the* young Clarence, Edward Plantagenet, had been his *subject*, being as he was a man peaceable and loyal, that *the* king would not only have pardoned and redeemed his *life,* and *removed* the duke his father's fault and attainder, but also would have restored *to him* the dukedom of Clarence and his other paternal signories and *honours*.

[But to] return to King Richard and to answer some more of the objections *made a*gainst him, and who is reputed a tyrant for punishing of [Jane S]hore, a common and notorious adulteress. And as the Duke of [Buckingh]am, who knew her very well, censured her, a vile and an *abomin*able strumpet. And she deserved so justly to be punished, *and* the punishment which was inflicted upon her was rather [favour]able than severe, and savoured more of clemency than of rigour [or t]yranny. For by the sacred and most authentic law, such offen*ders w*ere to be punished with death. And in this punishment the king showed not obscurely that *he hate*d and abhorred whoredom and adultery, and whereof also he [made an]other famous overture when he declared by public [proclamatio]n the foul incontinency and palliardise of Thomas Gray, Marquess of Dorset, [in these w]ords: **Thomas Gray, late Marquess of Dorset, [not fearing G]od nor regarding the peril of his soul, hath devoured and [deflower]ed many maidens, widows and wives, and holding t[he unshameful and mischievous] w[oma]n Shore's wife, in adultery.**

[Jane Shore]

[Then the death, the execution of William Colingbourne is censured another tyranny, because (as some trivial romancers chant) he was hanged for making a satirical or railing rhyme, when the truth is he was arraigned] *for* some treasons or *libels* [and] condemned of High [Treason, as it may be yet seen in the record.] And so then this execu[tion was an act of justice, not of] tyranny.

248*
[A]nonymus [Juris pe]ritus in [Ap]ologia *th*is Richard III.

[Moreover, **Tyrannus est res inimica civibus,] / legibus contraria**, as De[mosthenes well observed. But King] Richard was very loving [and gracious to his people, and caref]ul to have the laws duly [observed. And his ma]king many very good laws [was no small argument of that and his love to] law and to justice, and whereof mo*re will be said anon*.

246v

[It is observed too that tyrants contemn good counsel and advice] / but rather con*sult only their own wills*. [For they] *have too* good an opinion of [their own wisdoms, and] *are* [obstinate to d]etermine all matters by themselves [without co]nsultation or taking advice. [And these phila]*u*[tists are] called by the Greeks **ἰδιοβουλε]ῦ[ται** – self counsellors. And they say

247v
[Axiomata Politica cap. 219]

that they are **natura [plerumque occ]ulti et insidiosi, et arte et astu ea tegere [et dissimul]are conantur quae agunt, non communi***c***[antes] quicquid de suis consiliis aut rebus cum aliis, [nec a]b aliis consilium petentes, neque admittentes, sed [tant]um sua consilia sequuntur**. And herein [they err] much. This sentence well showeth, and which is equal to an oracle:

[**Sententia Arabica**]

Opti[mus v]ir eget consilio. And in brief, this other is an axiom of [a] grave

[Erasmus in **Epistolis**]

and great Christian clerk: **Nullo consilio qui[cquam m]agnae rei aggredi tyrannicum est.**

And now to show that [King] Richard was not obnoxious to this fault, but contrariwis*e, he* would do nothing of importance without advice and counse[l of] the wisest and most noble and most expert counsellors. And if in [m]atters of consultation he had declared and delivered his opinion and his judgement as it were resolutely and confidentl[y,] yet then his manner was (as even his adversaries confess) to say in the end and conclusion of his

[Sir Thomas More]

speech, 'My lords, this is my mind, but if any of you know or perceive anything else to be better, I shall be ready to change mine opinion, for I am not wedded to mine own will'.

[Caligula spent 236 million of crowns in less than a year.] [Suetonius] [Nero said that there was no use of money but for riot and prodigal expenses.]

Now lastly, largition and excessive expenses and prodiga*lity* [have been] thought vices proper to tyrants, and the rather be[cause those tyrants] of the Roman Empire (and whose excesses were so extr[eme that they were call]ed **m[o]nstra et prodigia et l[ues] imperii, pes[tes reipublicae,** etc.) were observed to be great prodigals and acolasts in all excess, as Caligula, Nero, Vitellius, Domitian, Commodus, Alagabalus, Caracalla, etc. But King Richard was

248*

held to be as frugal as might stand with the honour of a prince.] / And lastly, and in a word, this king was *not giv*en to prodigality, nor to palliardise, nor to riots, nor to gluttony, [which be] vices following many tyrants. But he was mo[derate a]nd temperate in all his actions and in all his appetite[s, whic]h is by his enemies confessed, and therefore it needeth [no] *m*ore *gl*osses.

And thus ye see by that these many acts and notions of *tyra*nt and of tyranny that both the one and the other were unjustly imputed *to* King Richard, because they are not to be found in him. *B*ut I think it had been better for him that he had [been] a tyrant for a while and to have used some tyranny or cruelty for a *time*, [for that had been the preserv]ing of his life and of his kingdom in the other *while. But he did not so because of his dis*like of tyranny and his little skill therein, and so little as that knowing not

[King Richard in this was like Julius Caesar, who, knowing by certain intelligence the conspiracy and conspirators against his life, also the time and place of execution, yet he seemed to slight and not regard it.]

even so much as a stage player: for he can put on the tyrant suddenly and act that part cunningly. *And* certainly the ignorance of King Richard in the tyrant's part, or his neglect the*rein to act it accor*dingly in due and needful and fit times, was the *cause o*f his ruin and utter overthrow. For if he had *been a tyr*ant or could have played the tyrant when *he ought*, [Bishop Mo]rton, the Marquess of Dorset, and the Earl of Devon and his [brother the bishop,] the Lord Talbot and the Lord Stanley [and his brother) Sir William Stanley, with his wife [the Countes of Ri]chmond, and Hungerford and Giles [Daubeney, Reyno]ld Bray and Parson Urswick, [Dr Lewis and the rest, had met their dooms ere their practices had took head, he having sufficient notice and intelligence of all their plots and

248v*

agitations;] *and had he dealt with them as with the* / Duke of Buckingham *he would have been secure, a*nd the success thereof *in their removal* might for many years have so *assured him as to give him as much* happiness as any other *prince. But his cle*mency bred his bane, [not his cr]uelty or tyranny, for that at *least* [had been] his best safeguard and protection.

But this King Richard is also from this violent in*terlude shown to be* a wise prince, and namely for *the love he showed his* people *and the care he took to man*age all his studies for the ad*vancement of* some fit and prosperous estate of the king*dom and the peo*ple, and to order his reign and government, which *was all his care* after the *rebellion, with* clemency and with equity, and to make his *magnanimity and justice* examples to others. And he was resolved to love and honour the clergy and *to revere the* holy church. And when he had made all the good to appear by long e*ffort, he* supposed and presumed th*at their hatred, by h*is good life and good endeavours would abate and q*ualify* the malice of his enemies and reconcile and d*eliver* them and their love to him. And he had good reason to presume and *expect that it would*. But the malice and *long enmity* of the factious and seditious persons *was* grown so great *and to* such extremity, and the traitors so obstinately resolved to r*evolt*, and *neither goo*d example nor good deserts nor fear nor force might prevail nor pres*erve him from th*ese plots.

And although this general revolt and rebellion was sudden, the king was not altogether secur*e in his* cause, nor negligent and careless [of the] manner to encounter and to prevent these mischiefs [and] treasons when hatched. Nor had the conspirators so farfo*rth suc*ceeded nor so prevailed if Sir Ralph Ashton had [diligently] and faithfully discharged the trust and service committed to him when the king made him Vice-*Constabl*[e of England] by letters patents and gave to him the authority [and power] of the office of the High Constable of Engla[nd, or rather] more and greater, and he gave him full [power] *and* authority to attach any person suspect[ed or guilty] of treason, and to examine him *and* [imprison and proceed to justice at his discretion. But it appeareth not that Sir Ralph made proper use of his] commission, or did [any service according] to his charge. Fo[r all the conspirators] *went up and* down freely and [enjoyed themselves and liberty] until they joined [with the Earl of Richmond,] *and they* had such success and victory as hath *been recounted here before, and* as all the world knoweth an*d acknowledgeth to be true*.

*Vice-Co*nstabular *office*

[**Rotul. in domo Conversorum, anno** 1 Richard III]

249*

The virtues and properties of a good king are wisdom, justice, fortitude, bounty, [magnificence,] temperance and piety. And I do[ubt not] to find here that these royal virtues, and proper to *sovereignty, were in the heart* and mind of this *defamed* King Richard and by him put in practice and in execution in the *government of his kingdom*. But also that they were fairly *applied. And there is no doub*t that he was endowed with wisdom and *prude*nce and skill, especially in those arts which he more properly professed, the *conduct and dealing* in politic affairs, that mad*e itself mani*fest in the judgement and pr[udence] in the wise and provident managing and order*ing* not only of his own private affairs, but [als]o in the administration and government of [the p]ublic business and affairs of state, and in the m[ilitary] *counse*l when he was a subject, as afterward when he was a *sov*ereign and a king. And I shall not need to demons*trate* this assertion with testimonies and autho*rities*, because his adversaries and calumniators [confes]s that he was a very wise and a prudent and [politi]c and an heroical prince.

[King Richard's virtues]

And moreover, this wisdom, together with his justice, appeared very

[Justice Shelley commendeth the laws of King Richard III to

Cardinal Wolsey. **Vide** John Stow, in Henry VIII, p. 882]

plainly and beautifully in the good] laws which he caused to be *made* and *in their number* and quality. He made so many as ever *did any king* whose reign was so short. And *this* [hath been acknowledg]ed and also honourably [predicated by our reverend and most learned professors of the laws. For his farther knowledge and love of justice there can be no fairer argument than]

249v*

Chron[icle] MS. **[in quarto] apud** R. Cotton

his desire and [custom to sit in court of justice] and to hear the [causes of his subjects with an] *in*different ear, and [distributing justice] *equally* to all men. And when [he made his progress in]to Yorkshire, and being [informed there were some] extortioners and other foul and notorious [offenders apprehended and] not tried, he caused *the punishment* due by law to be inflic*ted on them*. Before this, he gave strict [charge and command]ment to the judges and justicers and [to all officer]s of justice, as well of the greater a*s of the lesser* nobility, to do justice to all men indifferen*tly in the* circuits and in their courts and counties, and in every place of jurisdiction and through t*he r*ealm.

And as concerning his clemency and his gentlene*ss and* mercy I have spoken already, and some things *have I said of his* piety, and more anon.

The fortitude and magnanimity of this prince, [though] he was but of small and low body, yet they were [so great] and so famous as they need no testimony and [precony.] *The princi*pal reason hereof was *that* he was from his youth bred in arms and in [martial] actions, and (as I have related before) he was a*n* actor in many conflicts and in many battles, as in the battles of Barnet, of Exham, of Donca[ster,] the second of St Albans, of Tewkesbury, etc. And he *so* valiantly and so skilfully bore himself in a*ll these martial* and warlike affairs as that he won the *honour* and high reputation of an excellent soldier and of a *valiant cap*tain. And being made general of the king's [armies into] Scotland, he prevailed happily in this e[xpedition,] and particularly recovered that famous [and strong] frontier town of Berwick, th*e* [which King Henry VI] had so [weakly let go. And in this you shall hear the eulogy of his adversary, one that was loath to speak much in his favour, yet occasion forced him to speak his knowledge, though coldly

251*

and sparingly, who of his valour,] / magn[animity and bounty] *thus* writeth, **King Richar[d was no ill captain in the war.] He had sundry victories [and sometimes overthrows, but] never by his own default, [for want of hardiness or poli]tic order.** [Whereunto he addeth, concerning his bounty,] **Free [was he called of dispense, and libera]l somewhat above his [power**. These be the words o]f More, or of Morton, f[or their books are all one.

[Dr Mo]r[ton] [Sir Thomas More]

[To which I w]ill add one more such eulogy or testi*mony,* [above all] for credit and authority, and [recorded in Act of Parliament, and it was addressed to him [in the name of] the whole high court of Parliament, in these words. **We consider your great wit, pruden[ce, justic]e and courage, and we know by experience th[e memora]ble and laudable acts done by you in divers [battles] for the salvation and defence of the realm.**

[In Parliament **anno** *1* [Richard III]

[Her]e followeth another memorable and general testimony of the su*ndry* endowments and virtues of this prince, and it is the more to be [regard]ed because it was made and propounded by one which had known [him from] his youth and had held much and long familiarity [with him, which was] the foresaid Duke of Buckingham, who, after that Richard was made king and that this duke was become ill affected and malcontent [for his] repulses which he suffered in his suits (as declared), yet notwithstanding he acknowledged and confessed to Bishop Morton in private speeches between

[Morton, More, **apud**] John Stow, p. 77[4]

them that he thought King Richard from his first knowledge even until that time a man clear without dissimulation, tractable and without injury, and that for these [respects, and love] of King Richard's good disposition, he was [very desirous to] advance him, and laboured earnestly to make him [protector. The]se be the words of Dr Morton, and [reported by Sir Thomas More. T]herefore, whatsoe[ver the duke said after in reproach of the king, it may justly be thought to proceed from spleen and malice.

[**Eloquentia principibus maximo ornamento**, Cicero **De Finibus, Lib.** 4]

[And there is to this another commendation added, and that is of his eloquence and pithy, witty, pleasing] speech and the which, [though it be no royal virtue, yet it is an] ornament to [the greatest] princes, [and a gift] commendable and [gracious in any. You] / shall hear this eulogy of their eloquence delivered by [the Prior of Croyland, who, rep]eating the debating of a [controversy bet]ween the two brothe[rs, George, Duke of Clarence, and this] Richard, Duke of Glo[ucester] *in the* [council] *cha*mber before the king th[eir brother, sitting] then in his chair of estate. T*hus he saith* of the eloquent and grave arguing *of* these two brothers: **[Pos]t suscitatas inter duces fratres discordias, [tot u]trimque rationes acutissime all]*e*[gatae sunt in prae[sentia r]egis (sedentis pro tribunal in Camera Consilii) [quod] omnes circumstantes, etiam periti legum eam [rationis] abundantiam ipsis principibus in suis prop[riis causis] adesse mirabantur,** etc. And this author, then speaking of the excellent wit an[d] of the rare gifts of all the three brothe[rs] maketh this honourable precony th[ereof:] **Hi tres germani, rex et duo duces, tam ex[cellenti] ingenio valebant, ut si discordare non vo[luissent] funiculus ille triplex difficillime rumpere[tur.]**

251v*

[The praise of the three princely brothers]

[The good works of King Richard]

And now I will derive some testimonies of th[is king's] virtues from his good works and from his h*onourable* and charitable and magnificent and profitable and pious *and* religious works and monuments. And as for [example]:

[John Stow, **Annal**.]

This King Richard founded a collegiat[e church of] priests at Middleham in Yorkshire.

Item: He founded another college of p[riests in London in] Tower Street, near [to the church called Our Lady of Barking.]

Item: [He built a goodly church or chapel in Towton in Yorkshire, a monument of his thankfulness to Almighty God for the happy and great victory the king his brother had upon the partisans of the family] / of Lancaster and [the son of Henry VI, who] before slew Ric[hard, Duke of York, king designate and] father of the two k[ings] *Edward IV and Richard III.*

252*

[Poly]dore, [**Lib.** 25]

Item: King Richard *III* [founded a college in York] convenient for the enterta[inment of a hundred priests.]

[King Richard loved not Wychwood for his brother's unhappy marriage]

Item: [For] the good and benefit[t of the people of Oxfordshire and the] places adjacent, he [deforested a great part of the fo]rest of Wychwood and [other vast woods between] Woodstock and Bristow.

Item: [He] built the high stone tower at W[estminster, and it i]s a work of good use yet to this day. [And when he] had repaired and fortified the Castle of Carlisle, he fou[nded and built the Castle of Penrith in Cumberland.]

Item: [He] manumissed many bondmen.

Item: [Fo]r the better encouragement of the Aesterling [Haunces,] and because their trade was beneficial and [profita]ble to this kingdom, he granted to them som[e good pri]ivileges (as Polydore Vergil writeth.)

[In Rotul. in Domo Conversorum, anno 1 R III]

Item: [H]e also first founded the College and Society of [Hera]lds, and made them a corporation, and as the words in the ch[arter are, he ordained **it ut sint in perpetuum corpus corporatum in re et nomine, habeantur successionem perpetuam**, etc. In which all men may see] a good and commendable testimony of his love to [honour] and of his noble care, and for the conservation *of the m*onuments of nobility and of chivalry and of honour [and gentry.] And this college is of good and honourable and very necessary use for the continuance and preservation of *the ensi*gns and arms of nobility, and of all generous *and gentle persons*, and well-deserving and ennobled for their virtue. And this king established *this* [cor]poration by his royal charter and placed the heralds [in an anci]ent fair house which was called York Inn, some[times] after commonly called Coleharbour, and situate upon the Thames. [And he orda]ined and established four Kings at Arms, and by these names and titles: [John Writh, Garter; Thomas Holme, C]larensius; John Moore, Norway and Richard Champney, Gloucester. And for Wa[les I have a charter wherewith the k]ing created first [Rich]ard Champney, Esquire, King at [Arms by the title and name of Gloucester, dated in the mon]th of March, when the charter [of the foundation was granted.

[And he further established that these four Kings of Arms and the rest of the heralds, who are in the charter called **Heraldi et Prosecutores, sive Pursueandi**, should lodge, live an common together in that house] *with* [the rolls, monuments and writings appertaining to the art of heraldry] *and*

252v*

of armory. And *he gave* [also certain lands and t]enements for the perpetual maintaining of a chap]lain or chantry priest [to say and sing divine serv]ice every day [and to pray for the] *prosper*ity of the king and [queen and] *for the pr*ince their son, and *for* [their souls when t]hey were dead. La[stly, he gave sundry] good privileges an[d immunities to the said] corporation and coll*ege, and this* same charter [was] kept continually in the office of the he*ralds* [unt]il within these few years. But now it is no *longer*

[Mr R]*alph* [Brooke, York Herald at Arms]

there, but I know where it is and I have seen it. And the lack of it [importeth nothing, being] the duplicate of it is in records [in the archives] and [the Convert] House, now called the Rolls. And this charter was confirmed [by the Parliament and dated **ii die Martii,] anno regni primo, apud Westminster.** Barowe. [And underneath was written, **Per breve de privato sigillo, de datu praedicta auctoritate Parliamenti**.]

And moreo[ver,] *King* Richard III built or repaired some parts [of the] Tower of London toward the Thames, and in memory *and* token thereof there be yet his arms, impal[ed with] those of the queen, standing upon the ar[ch adjo]ining to the sluice gate.

Lastly, this king began many other good wor[ks] *which* miscarried by his untimely death as Polydore *Vergil* [thus] witnesseth: **Ricardus tertius multa opera p[ublica] et privata inchoavit, quae, immatura mo[rte prae]reptus, non perfecit**. And these good, magnific*ent works* be not the [acts] of the minds of tyrants nor of any wicked princes, *but of virtuous* and religious princes, as all indifferent and sensible men will judge and confess. [And Polydore] Vergil (being neither of the House [of York] nor of Lancaster, but only an honest man) write[th in the] same book much in the commendation of his [piety and] of his charitable disposition, and whereunto for brevity I [refer the readers and put it to their indifferent judgements.] I would desire these men which give to this King Richard III the *name of tyrant to judge* [how many good kings have exceeded him in such good, charitable and magnificent deeds in their much longer and prosperous time of government, being in quiet possession, too, of their crowns and kingdoms.]

And though I have given testimony / and proof of the v*irtue and piety* of 253* this prince, yet th*ere is* [one thing more,] the which I may not omi*t* [of him, promised before,] *and the good* will therein showed ca*ndour and truth and is* a corollary of the honour[s and commendation made by a stranger, and one that had] sometimes more caus[e to dislik]e him than to lo[ve him; for King Richard, not long] before, and oftentimes, had [st]*r*[uck upon his friends and made] spoils in his country. [Therefore it can be thought no flattery or partiality in him] *that he* hath spok*en and sai*d favourably of this kingdom, but *true report*.

And the man by nation was a Scot, and *he spoke truly* and out of his good knowledge, and for the *Scots were* thought not apt to give to Englishmen more *pra*ise than was due. This man also was a wise man and well [experien]ced and acquainted with the affairs of state of [divers] countries, and knew the princes and chief persons [in them,] by reason he had been employed to foreign prince[s] *in servin*g his master , James IV, King of Scotland. [And] *he* [knew] King Richard well, and the Duke of [York, hi]s father, and was with him in Ireland when [he was] Lieutenant of that kingdom. And above this, *he was* a priest and a spiritual man: that is a special p*rofessor of* truth. And he was of the king's Privy [Counci]l and Chief Secretary and one of the [honourab]le commissioners which were sent by King James *of Scot*land into England to King Richard [III to t]reat of the making and concluding of a [p]eace and of making and contracting [a mar]riage betwixt James the prince, eldest [son o]f the king, and the Lady Anne, daughter [of John de] la Pole, Duke of Suffolk, as hath been *related*.

[An]d this worthy prelate, and by name [Archibald Quh]itlaw, being to make the oration [for the] more solemn proposition of the[ir legation before the king, and publicly, amongst other things, his illustrations gave much to the praise of military art and chivalry, still reflecting the period of that praise and honour to the king.] *And the speeches of this counsellor are* good and exact *and made by a* worthy and *pious man. And I / have thought* 253v* good *to collect these, and* also *the* speeches of the king *in reply to this oration,* and to present them *to the judgement of the R*eader. And here these follow:

> **[Serenissime Princeps: Una me res consolat]ur, et iuvat tua scilicet in [omni virtute genere celeberrim]a fama per omnem orbis terraru[m ambitum disseminata,] tuae etiam innatae benignitatis cl[arissima prae]stansque humanitas, tua mansuetudo, libera[litas, fides, su]mma iustitia, incredibilis animi magnitudo, tua [non humana sed] paene divina sapientia, quibus te non modo s[ingulis] facilem verum vulgo et popularibus affabilem pr[aebes, et] quibus virtutibus, altaque prudentia, cuncta et pron[unciata] et dicta in meliora commutas.**
>
> **Serenissimus Princeps, Rex Scotorum, dominus me[us,**

[Pacem et uxore neptem Regis petiti]

qui te] alto amore prosequitur desiderat, tuam [ami]citiam et affinitatem affectat super captum [cogitationis] meae. Si quid a me erratum erit, tuis id divinis vir[tutibus,] quibus commercium cum caelestibus numinibus et [societatem,] contraxeris, tribuendum putato. Faciem tuam summo imperio et principatu dig[nam inspicio,] quam moralis et heroica virtus illustrat: de [te dici] praedicerique potest quod Thebanum principi [inclutissi]mo Statius poeta his verbis attribuit:

[Ricardo fu]it [statura parva]

Numquam tantum animum natura minori
corpore, nec tantas nisa est includere vir[es.]
Major in exiguo regnabat corpora virtu[s.]

In te enim sunt rei militaris virtus, peritia, [felicitas et] auctoritas, quae omnia in optimo exercitu[s principe Cicero] requirit. In te, Serenissime P[rinceps, praeclari regis,] et [imperatori praecepta ita concurrunt, ut nihil ad tuam bellicam aut domesticam virtutem cuiusquam oratoris verbis apponi possit. Tu igitur, Serenissime Domine et Princeps, de ineunda inter te et nostrum principem caritate et amicitia sic age, ut Angli et Scoti dilectionis respectu nullum penitus discrimen habeatur, sed in unum amoris et benevolentiae vinculum] / videantur esse conn[exi. Sic innumerabiles commoditates ex tui et] nostri populi dilect[ionis unione dulci, connubio, matrimonio, et] affinitate, consurg[ent.]

254*

In freta dum fluvii cu[rrent dum montibus imbres,]
sint arati convexa, polus [dum sidera pascet,
dum iug]a montis aper fl[uvios dum piscis amabit,
dumque] Thymo pascentur [apes dum rore cicadae,
semper ho]nos nomenque tuum laud[esque manebunt.]

[Thus t]his grave and learned and ing[enious Scottishman] *has giv*en noble testimonies of the good parts *of King* Richard, and to the shame and reproach of *all those* men which contrariwise have raised so *many scandals* and reproachful tales and taxes *of him*. *And thes*e have not been satisfied to traduce and depra*ve the* actions of his life, but have also found a *way* how to put in practice and to exercise their *malice* upon him after his death, as I partly showed before, *and which I shall a* little amplify here. For these spiteful persons, and in the same kind *and manner*, retrieved another crime and the *punishm*ent thereof in his death and after his death. *And that is* when they make the catastrophe or last [tragical] act of his life, and the manner of his cruel slaughter *to be a m*anifest declaration of the divine wrath, enkindled [for] his offences and tyrannies and against his sins, and to be as a present purgatory *or incor*poral chastisement for them. And therefore they inchantally infer that in due *recompens*e of those his manifold and excessive *crimes* God brought him to that just, miserable and *tragical* end at Bosworth.

[To be slain in the wars is no evil or unhappy death]

These speeches and *censures*, *a*lthough they be sharp and peremptory *and un*christianlike, yet they might be tolerated *in certain per*sons, viz., in superstitious clerks and [in women,] *and such as there* be who are enemies to [fighting and bloodshed.] But if the [malice of Bishop Morton and

Chancellor More (although they were men of the long robe) had not much blinded their knowledge in these affairs, considering with whom they conversed] / and where they [most lived, they could not have been 254v* ign]orant that for a [martial and heroical person to die] in a battle and [war, and fighting valiantly for his country] and for his life and [friends was always held] to be a glorious bidding [farewell to the world.

[And what simple man knowe]th not that infinite [numbers of virtuous and most noble] *and* very honourable [captains have been slain] in the wars? And in brief, Lampridius [affirmed that all the best men have died by violent deaths. And no prince nor other heroical] person could adventure his *life* [in a better] quarrel than King Richard did, *who undertook* to fight for his crown and kingd[om and all] his happy worldly fortunes and al*l his subjects*. [He was also,] according to the charge of his high **justitiaria**, and his office and sovereign ob[ligation, t]o take vengeance upon murderers and rebels and trai[tors,] *who* are hateful to God and to all good men.

[Optimos quosque violenta morte consumptos esse ostendit. Lampridius in **Alexandro Sev.]**

Wherefore there must some better consideratio[n] *be made* of the cause of the prince's slaughter and bloody death, for *he may* not be said to have been punished as a tyra*nt, for he* was no tyrant, as I demonstrated bef*ore*, but a good king, and did no act of a ty*rant all* the time of his reign. Neither may it be said that he *was dishonoured by* the battle, because that is an honourable death, **ut supra**. And it [hath] been seen very often in this world that [God hath taken] away good and godly and just princes in the field and [elsewhere] for *the transgressions* and iniquities of the people, and whom Go*d deems* in His divine judgement to be utterly unwort*hy of a* good and virtuous king. And being minded to punish them, *He* suffereth them *to fall* into the hands of a prince who will mo*rtify and* punish them and scourge them with rods for their wickedness and for their ingrat*efulness*.

And hereof we have many examples, as *well in* Holy Scripture as also in sundry te*stimonies,* as namely of King Josiah and great and *horrible crimes* of Ti*berius* the Emperor. And here in *England*, ************************,

[Therefore I see no reason why the cause of King Richard's death should not be favourably interpreted, or at the least held in an indifferent scale until it be safe to enquire further after it. And he that owes him no malice (all things considered with charity and justice) will confess] *that he* / was a 255* good king and *that he died in a* just quarrel, and in the *battle of Bosworth*, 22 August, **Anno Domini** *1485*, [when he] had reigned two years and five m[onths, account]ing his protectorship, which is a king*ship*, [abou]t the thirty-seventh year of his age, and he *might have live*d as many more years by the cours*e of na*ture, and haply for the great good of the *kingdom*, if it had stood with divine providence.

[Las]tly I will crave leave to tell them who [cen]sure the lives of men by the manners of *their* [dea]th that many of the enemies of King [Richar]d had worse deaths, having their [throat]s cut by the reprobate and most vile crea*ture*, the hangman, as namely the Duke of *Bucking*ham, Sir William Stanley and Sir *Thomas* More himself, and many others. [And th]ere is no man who in *him* hath any Christian [charity] or but a reasonable pittance or portion [of humani]ty who will judge a man's life by his [death, con]sidering that very many good and [holy men,] even the best men, have suffered the *most* [shameful] deaths. Witness the most *virtuous man* that ever was, our blessed S*aviour, who suffered crucifixion*.

[And although this prince was not so superlative to assume the name of
255v* holy or best, you see him a wise, magnificent,] / and a valiant man, *and a* [just,] bountiful, [and temperate;] *and* an eloquent *and magnanimous and* pious prince; and *a benefactor to the holy* church and to this *realm*. [Yet] for all this, it ha[th] been his [fortun]e to be aspersed and fouled *and* to fall into this *malice of those who have* been ill-affected *towards him* and who have bee*n ready* to plunge and *vilify* his fame and good name and *noble* memory in their blackest and Stygi*an r*eproaches and calumnies, and in th*is mali*gn and injurious kind they have r*ailed* more vehemently and more despitefully *against t*his king than against any other, albeit [many] of those kings were not endowed w*ith* good parts and with so many virtues as he, *but* rather and contrariwise were more vic*ious and* more blameworthy than he, and com[mitted more public] evil and more crimes than he; and th*is is* manifest and well proved, and wherea*s* [his] crimes are for the most part but suspected *but* never proved and made known, as I *have* intimated and approved in several passages of this *work* and confuted the accusations.

And the gre[atest] fault whereof he is suspected or con*victed* and
256* presumptively accused / is for [the re]moving the Prince Edward out of his way. And yet that fault hath be[en] *freely* and usually committed by many other prin*ces,* [and yet] they are thought brave and magn*animous and* glorious princes. For the [ambitious great ones who desire sovereignty and affect empire, having means and power to advance] *and to ac*/complish and attain to th[eir designs], *spare not* brother or sister no[r nephew] *nor* [niece,] nor any person if he ha*th a kingdom* before him, or else after the *kingdom is in* his possession. And in this r*egard ambition impels* them to *repudia*te faith and *justice for the possession of a* kingdom.

And *they have a* [rule for i]t and this it is:

[Euripides in **Phoenisses**]

[Εἴπε]ρ [γὰρ] ἀδικεῖν χρή, τυραν[νίδος πέρι]
Κ[άλλι]στ[ον] ἀδικεῖν, τὸ ἀλλὰ εὐσ[εβεῖν χρεών.

Th]us verbatim in Latin:

[si iniu]ste agere oportet, pro tyrannide (aut re[gno) pulch]errimum est iniuste agere, in aliis pietatem [col]*e*[re] expedit. [But Juliu]s Caesar, having long in purpose to make use [of this doctr]ine, translated it better to his purpose, and in this manner, as Cicero relates: **[Si viola]ndum est ius, regnandi gratia [violan]dum est; aliis rebus pietatem colas.** And thus in English:

[Cicero, **Lib**. 3. **De Officiis, et** Suetonius **in Julio**]

[If right fo]r aught may ere be violate,
[It must] be only for a sovereign state.

[And Antonius Car]acalla alleged this text for the justifying [the killing] of Geta, his brother and his colleague and partner of [empire with him.]

Euripides is the most ancient recorder of this sentence, but the [au]thor is more ancient than Euripides , or than he [whom he maketh to spea]k this speech, namely Eteocles, and is [even as an]cient as Lucifer. But this ambitious Eteocles, [affecting] the kingdom of Thebes, usurped this sentence [and put it] in practice, and as many other aspirers have [done.] *An*d the said Julius Caesar had it often in his [mouth, and] gave such authority to it as both his acts [and also Cicer]o and Suetonius witness. And he held *murder in such c*ase but one and a chief of these arts which are called
[**Vide Lib.** 1] **artes imperandi** or **artes regiae**. [And if it be an offence,] it is a princely

offence. It is **crimen sacrum** [**vel crimen regale**, or **crimen**] **sacri ambitio**. And it is so highly privile[ged that it is not punishable by] human laws, at the [least if that imperial axiom be infallible: **Princeps est solutus legibus** [Ulpian] – which some great clerks approve, or else the reign of princes is miserable, as it was told to King Atreus: **Ubicumque tantum honesta dominanti licent, precario regnatur**. [Seneca in **Thyeste**] And Polyneices, the brother of Eteocles, was of the same religion, for he said a kingdom could not be bought at too high a rate; that he would give the lives of his best friends and] / burn his nearest kinsfolks, [his wife and all his riches for a kingdom.] 256v*

[**Imperium quolibet pretio emptum vili tamen constat. Polyneices apud Euripidem in Thebaide.**]

And besides the *case of these Thebans and of* Julius Caesar, *there might many other example*s of this proud principle afore*mentioned be added* out of foreign stories [Greek and Latin] *and others*, frequent mention of [such offences] *and of such* causes and motives as before *were seen in these examples,* and her*e also we find* unjust ass*aults upon the* rightful heirs, but [by men who had better wits, higher] courages, prouder hearts and sha[rper swords than those princes which] had the true and bes[t titles.] *And they appli*ed their haughty and *proud hearts to all* perils and obtained the garland, a*nd they usurp*ed the kingdom or principality *which they had conquer*ed and had won by force or fraud. And they and their post[ers] reigned *over their* princely purchases, and happily, and they have been accounted [lawful and] worthy princes.

But I will leave these fo[reign and] exotic precedents, and I will bring d[omestical] examples, and those of English princes (because the prese[nt cause and question] *requires them*) and who, h[aving no] better titles than their swords and their ambition ga*ve them,* have imitated these foreign *princes* in their affectation of sovereignty and of *ambi*tion, and with as good success as they.

[King Henry I] And I will begin with King Henry [I,] the good clerk and learned prince, but a*s* [covetous] and as ambitious as any ignorant *and unlearned* and bad *commoner, though* of good letters. And he was not content to usurp here in [this kingdom] of England the right and privilege of the *inheritance* and of the primogeniture of his eldest brother, [Robert Courtheuse, but also by force took the D[uchy] of Normandy from him, and to make his [injuries] the more complete and his crime m*ore* [monstrous,] he put his brother in the Castle of G[loucester and] kept him there in hard and cruel durance and put out his eyes [and with tyrannies] wearied and tired and [consumed him till he died most miserably.

[King John] [King John is likewise by general voice charged with the murder of Arthur Plantagenet, the son of his eldest brother, and so the next prince in right of blood to succeed King Richard I,] *and* / 257* so got wrongfully the possessi*on of the crown*.

[King Edward III] Item: It is written [that King Edward] III was not only pri[vy and consenting to the deposing] of the king his fathe[r, a king anointed, but also] to his massacre. And because [Edmund Plantagenet, Earl of Kent, Protector, and his uncle, moved him to restore the crown to his] father, King Edward [II, he called him traitor and cut off his head at Winchester.

[Now King Henry IV caused Richard II,] his king, another anointed [king, to be cruelly] butchered at Pom[fret; and this was] **scelera sceleribus tueri**. [Seneca, **De Clementia**]

[King] Edward IV is accuse[d of the murder and death of the king St

[King Edward IV] Harry, and of the Princ]e of Wales, his son, **ut supra**.

[King Henry VII] *And in order the*reof King Henry VII is next, and he m[ust have a] place in this catalogue, alth[ough] a very good king. But he was not innocent [nor guilt]less of that **crimen sacrum vel regale**, which adventureth to *destroy princes with better titles*. For he, as you [hear]d before, cut off the head of Edward [Plantagenet, Earl of Warwick, an innocent: **Edwardum filium** [**Gul.** Camden in **Britan. et Cornav**.] **ducis Cl]arensi purum et [in]*s*[ontem] in [suam et suorum securi]ta[tem capite plexit.]** H[e was the] son and heir [of the D]uke of Clarence, and then the chief of the House of [York (un]less Perkin Warbeck may be taken [for Richard,] Duke of York, as he must.) And then he must be the *first princ*e of the blood royal of England, and *heir ap*parent of the crown. But all is one. For by the malice of the [Cardinal instigating the king, they were both dispatch]ed, as hath been before declared. And it hath been all one with them whether they [had been] both counterfeits and impos[ters or true princes] of the blood royal. For princes acknowledge no man to have a better title than [their own,] if they be in poss[ession. And I] do verily believe that if this King [Henry VII had confessed or] certainly known that Perkin had *been* [the second] son of King Edward IV (as he [knew hims]elf to be the grandchild of that [famous Owen] Tudor) yet he would not have [resigne]d the crown and sceptre, [so dear and sweet an enchantment is in the name, much more in the possession of empire. But he left not thus, nor was secure of his estate whilst he lived, therefore proceeded to subtle and sharp forms
258 of policy to establish his own and prevent] *the urging by others* / of all claims, beca*use his own was weak*.

[Grafton, Holinshed] [Amongst other, his practice] with Philip of Austria, [Duke of Burgundy, King of Castile and of A]ragon is very mem[orable. This Prince Philip was [**Historia de**] Ç[urita et Garib]*ay* by cross fortune] put into the king's hands *who* [out of Flanders took shipping at Sluis,] purposed *and* resolved to go [into Spain with the queen his wife. And passing by the coasts] of England, he w[as by a tempest forced, for his safety, to put into] the port of Weym[outh in Dorsetshire. And the queen being ill and distempere]d much with the stor[m, he was compelled to make some stay] *at* Weymouth for the refreshing *of his company*.

[In the meantime,] Sir John Carew and Sir Thomas [Trenchard, principal men and magist]rates of those parts, gave advertisement to the king *of the arrival of the s*aid duke and of the queen his wife in th*e port of Weymouth*. The king was glad of this news, and he straight pu[rposed to make good us]e of this their misadventure, and he forthwith sent to those [knights] *and commanded* them first to give all honourable entertainment to the du*ke and his wife* and to all his train, and next that they should not suffer [them depart] until he had seen and saluted them.

The duke, as soon [as his queen] *w*as well and all his company well refreshed, thanked these knights [for the honourable] courtesies which they had done to him, and told them that he *would se*t sail and be going on his journey into Spain. And he bid them *farewell*. [But] they earnestly desired him to stay, because they were advised *by* [the king] *t*hat he greatly desired to see him and the queen. This motion [was distasteful] to the duke, and he pressed much to depart with their favour, but [there was no] remedy but he must stay, and also ride to Windsor, where the [king would me]et him and bid him most heartily and royally welcome.

And thither th[e duke went,] much against his will (for this entreaty was somewhat imperious) [and there] *the king* received him and the queen in all magnificent and princely manner. *And* [the king propou]nded a suit to the duke, and that was that he would deliver [into his hands] Edmund de la Pole, a pretender of title to the crown of England, [and] disloyal to him, and who was then lurking in the duke's [dominions.] This suit seemed strange and unreasonable to the duke, and therefore *he would fain be requesting* the king not to desire such a dishonourable thing of him. And the *deed was not only a base* and a reproachful thing for him to do, but also a dero[gation from all princely] prerogative and privilege of his sovereignty, whereby he as other [princes had power to receive and] to protect such distressed noble persons [as did appeal to their] faith and [tui]tion and that to perform this requ*irement* was [to violate **ius gentium et sacro sanct]*a*[m hospitii fidem**. For to deliver any oppressed by fortune, malice or envy, and flying under another prince's wings for favour and protection, was to betray them into the hands of their enemies and utter ruin.]

*And the king so wrought that thus shou*ld be betrayed the noble **258v**
gentleman Edmund de la Pole and that in this ma*nner* his patron and defender should *be the oc*casion and instrument *of his death. And* the duke pleaded for his *safety and his life. But this* was all in vain, for no argu*ment was* of any weight. *But for*thwith *he must deliver up* Edmund de la Po*le, or he must stay here* still. When the duke s*aw* [the obstinate resolution of the king,] *and discov*ered in what danger *he was and into what* [extreme disadvantag]es *he* was fallen, he told the king th*at* [if he would accept and perform some] honourable [condi]tions which he would offer, that then h[e would take order to send] *Edmund* de la Pole hence to him into England. And the [conditions were that the] king should not use the young gentleman rigorously, *and that he was no*t to lay any punishment upon him, and in no case to p[ut him to dea]th. The king promised solemnly, and bound himself in a[ll the strait bonds of honour and of religion to observe those con*ditions and* covenants aforesaid.

And the duke sent this noble and unhappy de la Pole [into England,] and the king received him and committed him to the Tower. But when he lay a-dying, he finely frustrated his prom*ise* to the Duke of Burgundy by a kind of sophistical equivocation: for his part, he would keep his promise and not put Edmund de la Pole to death, [but by a mental reservation desti]nated de la Pole to death And that was when he was dead, the prince his son and heir should cut off the head of this [young man.] *And o*f this business and butchery he gave charge to the said prince, and the prince fulfilled his fath[er's charge so soon as] he was king. But this could not be without taint of dishonour and of perfidious*ness in the* king the father, nor of tyranny in the king the son.

The son held himself both ac[quitted and also] warranted by the example of King Solomon, the son [of] David, who was made the instrument of such a subtle and perfidious s[laughter.] And David also helped himself by the
virtue of equivoca[tion, which ought not to be follo]/wed by any Christian **259**
prince. For this was a sin, and [sins are to be] shunned and not to be imitated.

[But let us] look a little further into the miserable estate of those *of* [the family d]e la Pole, descended from the royal Plantagenets of [York.] *And* (as it seemeth) this Prince Henry VII was not willingly and malicious*ly, as i*t were, [their **malus genius**,] as it may appear by this example. The eldest brother of these de la Poles, [John de la Pole, heir to the Duke of Suffolk, and the h]ead of this noble family, was slain cas[ually in the battle of Stoke, being fought for this king. This is he who, being nearest kinsman to King Richard III, was proclaimed heir apparent. And the sister of these princely **259v** de la Poles, the Lady Catharine, was kept close prison]/er in [the Tower until grief and sorrow set both her soul and body at liberty.

[Grafton] [Nor is it much from this purpose to note that] the chief Plantagenets, [namely the children of King Edward IV, were littl]e regarded or favoured th[en. For the Lady] Bridget was thrust into [a nunnery at Dartford, [Polydore, **Lib.** 4] chiefly, as it was] thought, because she might [live sterile and die without issue. Th]e Lady Cecily was [worse] bestowed, for she was [married to a base fellow,] that so her iss[ue might be ignoble and contemptible, and her] wrong therein [was the greater, in regard she might have been matched according to her] degree and quality. And [the King of Scotland] *sought her to be the* wife of the Prince James, his [son. The French king Lewis also demande]d her for the spouse of the Dauph[in, Charles of France.

[Although the Lady Anne and the Lady Catharine were well married, that may not be alleged here, for they were bestowed in the time of Richard III, the one to the Lord Howard, after the Duke of Norfolk, the other to the Earl of Devon. Robert Glover.]

[It was observed too] that this king was but an unkind and s[evere husband to the Lady El]izabeth, the queen his wife. And they all had b[ut short lives. It is] reported in our stories that he picked a quarrel [with the Queen Dow]ager, his mother-**alliée**, for an old and a venial er[ror,] and because she delivered her son Richard to the Lord Pro[tector. And for t]his there was a sentence of confiscation of all her goods, [chattels and revenues,] and she was confined as a prisoner to Berm[ondsey Abbey,] and where she lived, and not long, but very sorrowfully and *full* of care and [Grafton, Gainsford] grief.

And the bastard of Gloucester was sud[denly and secretly] made away about the time that Perkin and young Clar[ence suffered.]

[Thomas Gainsford] And therefore, to my seeing, it was well observed and s*aid* [by a lear]ned gentleman, and yet living, that it was a fatal time to them, for it rid them *and deprived* them of their liberties and also of their fortunes and of the*ir lives*. And this prince showed himself to be of the House [of Lancaster] in nothing so much as in his hatred and cruel dealing *with the members* of the House of York and with their kinsfolks and best friends. And when he was gone and had bidden farewell to the [glories of this] world and to the policies and practices thereof, and so could *unburden his* heart, then came [Joel, **Cap**. I] his heir and supplied his room and office. And th[en **Residuum lo]custae bruchus comedit, et residuum br[uchi comedit rubigo.** For he utterly] con*founded and* [made an end of the remainder of the House of York, and **260** besides the putting] / to death of the for[esaid Edmund de la Pole, he caused] the Lady Margaret [Plantagenet, Countess of Salisbury, and the daughter] and heir of th*e* [Duke of Clarence, to be attainted of treason] by [**Dominus** Johannes, Baron Lumley, **viva voce**] Act of P[arliament, and contrary to justice to be condemned unheard.] And *she* was dragged [to the block very barba]rously, and being th*en* [above three-score years of age, **anno** 33 Henry VIII.

[And] Sir Henry Pole, her [eldest son, was also soon after] put to death. And her [son Reynold Pole was attainted o]f treason with her, but no m*ore harm befell him, bec*ause, as it seemeth, it was *forbidden of God, and* Divine Providence so safeguarded him [that he was] conveyed secretly and suddenly out of the king[dom, and wen]t [highly renowned for his le]arning and for his piety and for his other truly noble and t*ruly* [Christian] virtues. But all they could not have saved his life *if he had* not fled hence.

Item: Richard Pole, anoth[er son of] this Countess of Salisbury, was fain to fly [and live a]s a banished man in foreign countries, and with good [reputati]on until he was slain at the battle of Pavia. *And by tha*t honourable dispatch he escaped the English hangman's ha*nds*. [And this was the last act of the] catastrophe of the violent and turbulent trag[edy of York.]

And to conclude, these great wrongs and bloody prose*cutions* were not crimes of suspicion only, as these *of King* Richard's were. But these cruel acts were and are most *widely* known, and were very manifest and clear. And **vel*ut* quod non fuit dictum et scriptum calum*nia*e gratia et privil*egii***. *But we* must be wary and sparing in the relation of matters of this kind, because they are not everywhere agreeable and current and plausible generally, as also because I had no purpo*se to condemn* the faults of any princes. Neither have I so done but where the defence of *King Richard and* the necessity of the cause drew me into it and extracted such a style and *relation of the* crimes of *princes who destroyed those with better titles than themselves*.

[Nor is it strange, nor by me only noted, that] / King Henry VII [had his] **262v*** faults as well as oth[er princes.] Yet I aver still *that he was a* [good] *and a* wise and a provident and a [religious prince,] and further also that he was the restorer of the ancient lin[e of the British] kings to their reign and kingdom, *and that he* was the nephew of King Henry [VI] by his grandmother, Queen Catharine, [widow of] King Henry V and mother of King He[nry VI and of his brother uterine, Edmu]nd Tudor, Earl of Richmond, the father of this King Henry VII. [And so he] was nephew also to Charles VII, King [of France.] and that by the Pope's grant and prerogative royal, he was an [offspring of] the House of Lancaster. And besides, I [will ever] say (and to his greatest honour) that h[e was the most] happy grandfather of as noble, as [wise, virtuous, h]/appy and as victorious **263** a queen as ever lived and reigned in the [world.]

And lastly, and to declare myself more plainly, I [do not mislike] his having of he crown and his possession of the kingdom, as I have said before that it was foretold by a d*ivine* prophet that the Earl of Richmond should be king. And I hold also that he was ordained from above to *be the* sovereign of this land. But (and as I said, **Liber** II) I utterly mislike *that he would not* tarry the Lord's leisure and receive a kingdom *in His time*; and that would have been *time enough*.

[To hasten, then, to the conclusion, I will only by the way, for my promise's sake, say something in answer to the imputation of some defect or break in the titles of the Normans and the princes] / of York, a[lthough **264*** there is no need in that] behalf; and *yet there has* been some d[efect supposed and insinuated covertly] by our vulgar [historians] (as I *said before)*. And [I will in brief deliver mine] opinion thereof.

[The sundry titles of King James to the crown of England]

And the*refore* [first it must] be supposed that if there happened *a weakness and a blemish* by the err[or of the marriage of King Ed]ward, whereby that title was held to be impaired, [that w]eakness and that blemish had no force nor faith but fo*r a short time, and it* was made good and sound again as soon as K[ing Richard bega]n to reign. And afterward it was so well [cured and] reinforced by the most mighty power of sundry Parliam[ents that it was] made as strong and firm as ever it was. And the [holy aids of the dis]pensations and confirmations apostolical [of those t]imes were sacred and very authentic, and so that by these *it was* fully restored and reinforced even, and borne of *King Henry even as not havi*ng been broken by mischance and cunning, *and by th*e setters' hands hath been made as *firm and as strong and* as sound – yea, and more strong and more sound than it was before.

And besides, and if need were w[ithout that], this *mighty* prince now happily and gloriously [reigning h]ath of other titles and rights rich [varieties and] more than **funiculus triplex**, and some [more ancient] and some more authentic and more just, and therefore mor[e assured and secure and] more prosperous hopes *tha*n that Norman title for which was a violent acquis[t] *and* cruel *pur*chase made by blood, and [so consequently n]one of the best, as it was well conceived [by that great Mac]edon when he said, **[Non est diuturna possessio] in quam gladio inducimur**.

Alexander **apud** Curtius, **Lib**. 8]

[Neither would it avail in this behalf to cite or avouch the donation of this kingdom which the Confessor is said to have made to William the Conqueror, being to no purpose, because that great gift or legacy was disclaimed and disavowed by the barons of this land and found to be void and of no force. But yet time now and prescription have also made that title good and authentic, for prescription hath power to ratify and confirm not only the titles of princes, but also of private men.

[Prescription]

264v*

[Yet as I said even now, our sovereign hath better] / and [more noble titles. For first, he is immediate,] true and sol[e lawful heir of King Egbert, who] first gave the name [of England to this land and] was absolute lord of it. [And from him, by the] *great* and glorious kings Edgar, E[dmund, Athelstan, Alfred] and many other rightfully good kings, as well [Saxons and An]gles as Anglo-Saxons, the right and title [of this king]dom was duly descended and devolved to Edmund Ironside, Kin[g of England,] who was father to the most noble Cliton, [Edward surnamed] Exul, whose fair daughter and heir, [and a holy lady,] the Princess Margaret of England [was married] to Malcolm Canmore, King of Scotla[nd, from] which ancient, princely and blessed allia[nce the king] our sovereign lord is certainly and [directly descended,] and is their true and only heir to their right[s and] t[itles, which were without flaw.]

[Clito: prince of the blood]

Likewise the most ancient and famous [title and right] of the antique kings of Britain are in King Jam*es*, [being the] next heir to our late British king [Henry Tudor,] whose genealogy I have seen derived [from the ancient] king of Britain, Coëlus and from Cad*wallader*, *the* last king of Britain, and from diverse [other British] princes. And this Henry Tudor, or t[he Seventh,] would have all the titles of this king[dom confirmed] to him by the strongest and greatest [authority, procured] to have them decreed to him and to his issue and settled *and* [established in himself] and in his royal issue and his posterities forever by [Act] of Parliament, and in [this] man[ner and words:

Egerton 305v-307v

[To the pleasure of Almighty God, and for the wealth and prosperity and surety of this realm of England, to the singular comfort of all the subjects

of the same, and in avoiding of all ambiguities and questions, be it ordained, established and enacted by the authority of this present Parliament that the inheritance of the crown of the realm of England and also of France, with all the preeminences and dignities royal to the same appertaining, and all other signories to the king belonging beyond the seas, with the appurtenances thereunto in any wise due or appertaining, to be, rest, remain and abide in the most royal person of our Sovereign Lord King Henry VII and in the heirs of his body lawfully begotten or coming perpetually with the Grace of God, and so to endure, and in none other.

[**Anno** 1, Henry VII in Parliament in November]

[Thus this Act, which is also another title of our king, heir to Henry VII. And this Act was renewed firmly and fully established for our sovereign lord King James, **anno regni primo**. But yet King Henry VII, not contented with all these titles, obtained of the Pope another title, **jure belli (ut supra).** And so this great king had all the titles and rights which ever were appertaining to this kingdom and to the empire of Britain. For as we see here, he hath not only the titles of the ancient kings of Britain, of the Saxon and Anglo-Saxon kings and of the Norman race, but also the titles and rights of the royal families of York and Lancaster and of Wales, etc.

[The wedding ring of England]

[Edmerus Alvredus d'Rivallis]

[He hath in possession also those singular and particular monuments of empire and reign, by some called **fata regni,** and **instrumenta et monumenta regno et imperio destinata.** The one of these being the ring of the holy King Edward, the son of King Ethelred, which was consecrate and extraordinarily blessed by St John Baptist in Palestine and sent back to the king, as old writers affirm. Which ring hath been carefully and religiously kept in the Abbey of Westminster, being, as they say, the ring which the Archbishop of Canterbury is accustomed at the inauguration and consecration of the kings to put upon their finger, called, in our stories, the wedding ring of England.

[The other monument of British empire is the marble stone whereupon Jacob laid his head when he had those celestial and mystical visions mentioned in Holy Writ, which stone was brought out of Palestine into Ireland, and from thence carried into Scotland by King Kenneth, after translated to the city of Scone and used for the chair wherein the kings sat at their coronation. And out of Scotland it was brought by Edward I into England, which is witnessed by the best historians of Scotland and England:

[Hector Boethius, **Lib.** 14, **et** George Buchan]*an*

[Cathedram marmoream regibus Scotorum fatalem (in qua insidentes Scotorum reges coronari consuerant).

[Rex Edwardus primus e Scona Londinum transtulit, in Westmonasterio, ubi hodie visitur, deposuit.

[Guil. Camden]

[It is set and borne in a chair of wood and for a perpetual honour. This is written upon a table hanging in the chapel at Westminster:

[Si quid habeat veri vel chronica cana fides ve,
Clauditur hac Cathedra nobilis ille lapis;
Ad caput eximius Jacob, quondam Patriarcha,
Quem posuit cernens numina mirapoli,
Quem tulit ex Scotis Edwardus primus, etc.

[And George Buchanas said that the people are persuaded that in this stone, whch he calleth **lapidem marmoream rudem**, the fate of the kingdom is contained, and that **fatum regni** is thus understood, viz., that what king of Scotland soever is lord of that stone and sovereignly possessed thereof

[**In hoc lapide fatum regni Scotiae continetur**. George Buchanan]

shall be king and reign in that country where he findeth that stone, which is told in a prophetical distich:

[Ni fallat fatum Scotus quocunque locatum
Inveniet lapidem regnare tenetur ibidem.

[**Scotus: rex Scotus, ut Anglus, Gallus, Hispanus Dominus, etc. Pro Rex Angliae, Galliae, Hispaniae,** etc.]

[Which prophecy was accomplished in King James when he came first into England. For his titles were not only **funiculus triplex (qui difficile rumpitur)** but also **funiculus multiplex, qui numquam rumpitur**. And this large and spacious divinely established reign from him shall be, according to the saying of the heavenly messenger, **regnum perpetuum et cuius non est finis**. Amen.]

Why King Richard lost the kingdom:

265* **** that imp*erial justice a*nd exe*rcise performed by* God, whe*n presump*tive men thr*ough abusing* of His justi*ce caused Him* to put down *their impious power* which hath high offen*ces done unto Him, and hath* still gone on in their wicked *ways. And for* example, the crown of Israel was taken *from Solomon for hi*s disobedience and for the favour borne by *him* to idolators, and the kingdom was transla*ted to another* family. And as the wise men directly said, ***Regnum a g*ente in gentem transfertur propter iniustitias *et iniurias e*t dolos**, etc.: God translateth a kingdom *from one nati*on to another nation, and from one family to *another fami*ly, and from one people to another people fit for *rule over them* and at such time as He is resolved to be revenged thereof (**ut supra**).

And this was the cause (as Gildas the wise Briton *saith*) *that* the Saxons and other barbarians *were commanded* by God to conquer and to destroy the *native Bri*tons. And afterward, when the Saxons, and *in the dar*kling age of their monarchy, *were* as foully polluted with all sin as the old Britons were, and worse, then and thereby *they provoked* the wrath and vengeance of God to come with *more force an*d more fury against them. And Henry *Huntingdon sai*th that God gave the English nation *to be conquered an*d to be spoiled and to be destroyed by the *French* nation for their manifold and enor*mous cruel*ty. And in testimony hereof, [W]illiam Malmesbury writeth [it was declared in the time of] Edward the Confessor and pronounced [as by a voice from Heaven] that neither the princes, [nobles, prelates, priests nor people of England were the ministers or servants of God, but of the devil. And therefore King William I, though in his pride and jollity he would pretend he came to the kingdom by right of title and blood and by heritage and gift of the King Confessor, and power of the sword, yet when he came to shake hands with death and was **articulis morti**, he disclaimed

[Malmesbury, **De Gestis Anglorum**]

265v* t]/he titles [and disliked that] of the swor[d, confessing it was] *by* [the providence of God] *and by th*e means [of His favour only,] saying **Non e[nim tantum decus** (viz.) **regni Angliae heredita]rio iure possed[i, sed di]*r*[o conflictu, et multa effu]sione humani cru[oris, etc. Diadema regale,] quod nullus predecessorum [meorum gestavit] adeptus sum, quod divina sol[ummodo gratia mihi] non ius hereditarium contulit.**

[**Liber Abbat St Stephani**]

An*d this* [was well said, f]or doubtless God sent him hither for two [causes: the] one, to be a scourge to the sinful Saxons and to e[xtirpate them] and their generations, and the other cause *was* [God's] gracious purpose to advance this prince [to the crown of England] and to plant his

[The causes of alterations of kingdoms]

family and nation in th[is kingdom.] These two be the chief ends of the alteration [of estates] and of the translation of kingdoms which t[he learned observe.]

And to be brief, Polydore (who was a g[ood divine)] in this present case of the rejected and [detected children] of King Edward bringeth the same r[easons and] causes aforesaid, and thus he delivereth: **[Illud] fortasse istis duobus innocentibus puer[is contigit,] quod Edwardus eorum pater neglect[ae religionis] crimen subiisset per sanctissimum insiu[randum violatum] qui ad portas urbis Eboraci aliud [mente aliud] verbis promissum fecit et postea [per Ducis Clarentiae] fratris necem, /et regis Henrici, et fi[lii eius caedes, et pro] violatione sponsalium cum Domina Alien[ora, etc./ magnae] se suosque apud Deum poena obligass[et.**

[And here these words **apud Deum** – that is 'with Go]d' – give fit occasion and good reason to make [the true and better interpretation of the letter 'G', which was so terrible to King Edward by reason of the prophecy that 'G' should be the destruction of the kingdom. For by this it may appear it was not meant (as some men sillily expound) by 'George', much less 'Gloucester'. But doubtless that fatal and terrible letter 'G' was to be understood of God, and for and of His divine vengeance.

[And now we are come to the last act of this tragical story to see the place where, after all the malicious eyes were satiated in beholding those barbarous cruelties done unto the body of this dead prince, they gave his royal corpse a bed of earth, which was done by commandment and order of King Henry VII, and honourably in the chief church in Leicester, called St Mary's, belonging to the order and society of the Greyfriars. And the king also, soon after, caused a fair tomb of mingled colour, marble adorned with his image, to be erected upon the monument. There was also an epitaph made for him, whereof I have seen the copy in a recorded manuscript book chained to a table in a chamber in the Guildhall of London, which here (the faults and corruptions being amended) followeth, together with the title thereunto prefixed as I found it: **Egerton 308-309v**

[Epitaphium Regis Ricardi Tertii, Sepulti apud Leicestriam, iussu et sumptibus Sancti Regis Henrici Septimi

Hic ego quem vario tellus sub marmore claudit
Tertius a iusta voce Ricardus eram.
Tutor eram patriae patruus pro iure nepotis,
Dirupta tenui regna Britanna fide;
Sexaginta dies binis dumtaxat ademptis [(A) **Annos** 2 **et** 52 **dies**]
Aestatesque tuli tunc mea sceptra duas.
Fortiter in bello certans desertus ab Anglis,
Rex Henrice tibi Septime succubui.
At sumptu pius ipse tuo sic ossa decoras
Regem olimque facis regis honore coli.
Quattuor exceptis iam tantum quinque bis annis [(B) **Anno Domini** 148]*5*
Acta trecenta quidem lustra salutis erant,
Anteque septembris undena luce Kalendas [(C) 1 **die** 22 **Augusti**]

**Red]d[ideram rubrae iura petita rosae.
At mea, quisquis eris, propter commissa precare,
Sit minor ut precibus poena levata tuis.**

**Deo O. M. Trino
et Uni sit laus
et Gloria aeterna
Amen.**

**[Epigramma in tres Ricardos Angliae Reges,
ex vet. lib. MS. transcriptum:**

**Tres sunt Ricardi quorum fortuna erat aequa,
In tribus ast aliis sua cuius propria sors est.
Nam concors horum finis sine posteritate
Corporis atque rapax vitae modus, et violentus
Interitus fuerat sed major gloria primi,
Proelia qui terra sancta gerit, et redeuntem
Tela Balistarum feriunt apud extera regna.
Alter depositus regno quum carcere clausus
Mensibus extiterat certis, famae velle perire
Elegit potius quam famae probra videre.
Tertius exhausto satis amplo divitiarum
Edwardi cumulo proscribens auxiliares,
Henrici partes post annos denique binos,
Suscepti regni bello confectus eisdem
Mundanam vitam tum perdidit atque coronam,
Anno milleno, centum quater, octavageno
Adiunctis quinque et cum lux sextilis adesset
Undena duplex, dentes apri stupuerunt,
Et vindex albae Rosa rubra refloret in orbe.]**

TEXTUAL NOTES

Abbreviations used in these notes:

T	British Library MS. Cotton Tiberius E.X
T*	scribal hand in Cotton Tiberius E.X
Ted	George Buck, Esq's alterations in T
E	British Library MS. Egerton 2216
M	Bodleian MS. Malone 1
F	Fisher MS., University of Toronto
P	printed edition by George Buck, Esq., 1646
***	lacuna in MS.
[ ]	portions crossed out in MS.
\ /	addition above the line in MS.
{ }	one word written on top of another in MS.
italics	conjectural emendations by current editor

Where a reading is not followed by indication of source, the emendation is mine. Where the reading is clear and indisputable there has been no point in giving the copies' variants. When dealing with copies' variants I have listed them in order of composition, unless adopting a reading from one of them. When more than one copy shows the same reading, the spelling I have given in these notes is of the earliest composed. I have cited P only (1) where its readings have been of assistance in establishing a reading, (2) where the extreme nature of its divergence probably indicates considerable difficulty in reading the original.

Numbers heading notes refer to page and line numbers in the text.

1 T contains no title page. A crossed-out draft in Buc's hand used for the back of an insertion in *Comm.* (Bod. MS. Eng. Misc. B. 106, f. 3^{v}, shown on Plate IV) is a complete draft for it. T f. 171^{v}, a discard, is the (incomplete) remains of a draft of the title page, showing vestiges of this same wording. Wording is confirmed by Malone's title page, which differs only by saying 'written by Geo: Buck, Esq*uire*'. Egerton calls it 'The History off Richard the Third'.

3-5 All non-conjectural emendations are from M, the only copy representing any part of this section, though its dedication is to a potential patron of the Editor.

Book I

17/43-18/37 This material, of which there is no representation in T, would have been approximately equivalent to one normal leaf in that MS. I have thus assumed that a leaf is missing from T at this point and have filled the gap from E.

20/3rd mar. n. Howard] Haward EMF.

23/15 of them] of him T.

23/2nd mar. n. Polydore] Pollydor MF / Pollyder E.

23/23 of honour and of piety] of pietye, and hono*u*r EMF.

26/40 politicians] crossed out in T; revision above line is lost / politicians EMF.

27/34 acknowledge] crossed out in T, perhaps in error.
27/36 Catesby] crossed out in T, probably replaced in lost section / Catesby EMF.
29/20 were] not in T but should have been added as part of above-line revision in Buc's 'erasure hand'.
33/1st mar. n. 1340] 1440 EMF.
35/23-24 afresh troubled with this news] This sentence is in a state of incomplete revision and has been adjusted as well as possible to make sense. Copies have a different grammatical construction.
37/26-39/23 A leaf is evidently missing from T here and has been supplied from E.
38/42 filium] filiam EMF.
39/4 to him] [to him] E / *omit* MF
42/7-42 This section is in a chaotic state of partial revision. I have revived some crossed out words and deleted some not crossed out to render it coherent and intelligible.
42/18 repositum] repostiu*m* T. Buc seem to have intended to cross the 't' in a hurried revision and accidentally crossed the 'i', also smearing the word.
42/38 reprehended] seemed to reprehend TedEMF.
43/23 The sentence beginning here is preceded in T by '\scrupules/ vaynly suspicious termed', whose purport is lost since the Editor has made drastic revisions to this part of T, crossing out the second half of f. 32v and the first three quarters of f. 33 when writing a new version in the margin.
46/3 regimine] Regimen EMF.
46/5 Marmoream] P / Marmoreu*m* EMF.
46/15 ut] P / Et EMF.
46/2nd mar. n. Dobuni] dolucus E / dobuc*us* M / dobic*us* F.
48/26 and most extraordinary rich and gallant] [and most extraordinary rich, and gallant] \in [and bra] that dayes brauery/ E / in that dayes brauery MF / carrying the splendour of that dayes Brauery P.
56/5 seu] se TEMF.
56/7 remot*am*] TEMFP omit mark over 'a' to expand to 'remotam'.
59/28 Bohun] MF / Bohum E.
61/25 to assist him] [to assist hym] the like E.
61/26-63/4 This section is confused, difficult to read and in a state of incomplete revision. I have made minor deletions of uncrossed out words and reintroduced words crossed out to make it coherent.

Book II
69/16 Hereupon he] Hereupon wh*ic*h he T.
76/21 troisième] F / troisiesme EM.
76/22 quelle] qui EMF; concession] P / concessois E / concesso$\left\{{i \atop r}\right\}$s M / concessors F.
77/1st mar. n. This note I have taken from an earlier version of this p., f. 69v.
78/3rd mar. n. Stephen] P / Hen: E / Ste: M / Steven F.
79/25 spuriorum] P / spurios EMF.
79/mar. n. patrui] substitutes in text l. 30 for 'avunculi' P / patrai EF / [patrai] avinculi M.
82/49 pille] pilla EMF / pile P.
83/28-29 This passage is confused, damaged, and crossed out, probably by George Buck, Esq. The author is not in the habit of deleting passages derogatory to Henry VII, and when he repeats this information in Book V (see above, text, p. 213) he refers to having spoken of it in Book II. George Buck, Esq., on the other hand, is in the habit of deleting material derogatory to Henry VII, and either crossed it out for this reason or the author crossed it out intending to rewrite or transfer it (a mark shaped like a theta suggests a possible intention to transfer it).
85/9 però ch'] 'per' is on f. 83, which was originally pasted at the bottom of f. 82.
86/9 and 1st mar. n. The words 'peccatum mortale' and the marginal note are taken from f. 86, of which f. 85 has rewritten a portion.
86/38 pride] MF / price E.
87/40 and not improperly] P / [and] not improperly E / not improperly MF.
90/22 that there be near] that be near T / there bee neere Ted.
91/40 the earl] [the Earle] \him/ E / him MF.
94/43 brought or sent] and brought or sent T*.
95/2nd mar. n. Chronicle] Chronije E / Chronice M / Croni F (page trimmed) / Chron. P.
95/4th mar. n. Copies include a note before this one: 'Arma subditorum rebellorum non bellum sed seditio', probably an accidental duplication derived from an attempt to improve the sense, of which no trace appears in T.

99/27 processit] MF / possessit E.

99/27-28 but dissembled . . . train] but a dissembled . . . train T / but a dissembled, [& rather don for a] trayn Ted.

100/10-11 as that] yt that T.

101/4th mar. n. Livi*us*] Lini*us* EF / Lineus M.

101/23 escas] estas EM / astus F.

101/28 imbecillum] MF / in becillum T*E.

102/6-103/6 This scribal folio is extremely confused with authorial revisions.

103/38 contundit] contudit M / conludit E / condudit F.

104/36 humanists] Ha**mists T* / Hamanists EF / Hamamists M.

104/2nd mar. n. status] M / *omit* E / latus F.

105/2 Aver*t*erunt] averserunt T*.

105/25-26 It is clear from the partial revisions by the Editor in T that he intended to turn all verbs into the present tense. He has succeeded only in producing a mixture of past and present. I have followed the structure indicated by T in giving all these verbs in the past tense.

108/25 And] [And] E / *omit* MF / And P.

110/48 Edi*v*a] Edina TEMFP.

111/42 E*v*ermua] Enermua TEMFP.

113/6 iden*ti*tatem] >tatem T / Identatem E / Identotem MF.

113/13. exstat] extat T.

113/10-27 Certain short sections of this folio have been crossed out by the author. They are reinstated here, following the practice of EMF, because the construction requires them.

114/6-14 This paragraph fits nowhere else in the text. This folio is in the hand of the Editor and probably rewrites an authorial draft now lost.

114/45 King John] These words are retrieved from an earlier draft of this page, f. 118^{v}.

114/46-115/9 Evidently a short section is missing from T here. I have supplied the gap from E.

115/14 Guicciardin*i*] Guiccia*** T / Guiccardjn E / Gui$\left\{{cc \atop rr}\right\}$ardine M / Guirrardine F / Guicciardine P.

115/2nd mar. n. Guicciardini] Giucardjn E / Giuccardin M / Giurcardin F / Guicci P.

115/3rd mar. n. MFP / *omit* E.

115/41 Lombard] Lumbard TEMFP.

116/14 συγγενεῖς] συγγενες T.

116/1st mar. n. Thomas, Duke] Tho: 1 Du: EMF ('1' is probably misreading of the 's' of 'Thos.'); at the battle of Musselburgh] MF / & ye Batell of Musselborough E; militavimus] F / meletavimus E / melitavimus M ; vidimus] videmus EMF.

116/30-47 This page is in the hand of the Editor, probably a rewriting of an authorial draft now lost.

116/43-44 the Earl of Shrewsbury now living] [that bee the erle of the erles] and the late erle of Shrewsbury now ****** Editorial hand in T. The whole page (f. 126) is in the Editor's hand, presumably a rewriting of a page of the original. He revises as he goes, seeming to alter the sense of the original. I have emended the passage so it accords with what seems Buc's intention: to refer to a contemporary earl of Shrewsbury.

117/15 antecessors] Antecessours P / Antocesors EMF.

Book III

119/44 alteri ne feceris] P / alteri [non] feceris E / alteri feceris MF.

121/4th mar. n. Philopseudes] Philopseude EMF.

122/41 Quid*d*am] corrected from 'quidam' T (scribal).

123/21 Courinus] MP / Corvinus T. The author has marked this name with a cross before and an asterisk after, possibly pointing to a marginal note giving the correct spelling.

123/2nd mar. EP / *omit* MF.

124/14 T*r*ebellius] Tebellius T.

125/20 Caesar*em*] Caesaris T.

125/40-126/1 This portion is crossed out in T, certainly by the Editor, though some lighter strokes below his crossings out might indicate authorial deletion as well. The material is in some respects duplicated in the scribal f. 137 and possibly the author decided to discard this version of it. The copies have rejected f. 137^{v} and used only f. 136. Because of the uncertainty and because this material is not necessarily exclusive but can be seen as reinforcing, I have retained both folios in full.

127/45-49 This sentence is a late addition by the author in T which continues down the margin of the page saying 'never ha***** very of******* moreover'. It is impossible to fit these fragments into the reconstruction.

127/46 accubitio] accubatio EMF / occubatio P.

128/47-49 In T this section, at the bottom of a page, is badly burnt and reads 'and Cn. Papyrius Carbo, two most *********** most honorable Romans, \& who/ were bornne ********************s the vertuous and **********'. This is too seriously damaged to be reconstructed, and a corresponding passage from E has been substituted which seems to represent a later authorial version, since it contains more additional factual information than the Editor is in the habit of adding.

129/1st mar. n. Fotheringhay] Fotheringham EMF / Totheringham P.

130/1st mar. n. Richard III] R. 2. EF / missing in M.

130/28 This is] M / whoe is EF. M's version is closer to More's wording.

130/2nd mar. n. Hardyng and Grafton] Hardington EMF / Harlington P. In the process of copying the scribe has evidently left out the first part of the name that follows 'Hardyng'.

131/18 This sentence is directly followed in T by the passage below, p. 131, ll. 34-35 ('men of . . . comely persons'), which I have transferred from this place to that for the sake of organization. Buc never completed his revision: having apparently concluded his argument here, he decides to continue it, making the conclusion – which he has failed to delete – inappropriate at this point. He has then failed to finish organizing the conclusion at the later, appropriate point.

131/34-35 See note 131/18 above. The conclusion has been shifted here from that point to replace a partly obliterated and incompletely composed similar statement appearing here.

132/46 πάνδεινον] πανδειλον T (f. 146*).

133/16 τύραννος] τοραννος EMF.

133/25 martiris] FP / marticis EM.

133/26 titulum] P, titulam EMF; mereatur] mereantur EMFP.

135/3 Chertsey] FP / Che]r{t/l}sey M / Chelsey E.

137/1st mar. n. me] men EMFP.

137/48 timebat] MP / tinebat EF.

139/16 an] his T.

145/33 Velleius] Vallei*us* E / valler*us* M / Valeius F / Valerius P.

146/28 Trog*us*] Trogas T*.

148/4-5 This passage is in a confused state of partial revision.

149/2 Perkin's] Perkin T.

149/25 But] but would M / [but] \yet/ E / Yet FP

151/17-30 This folio is in the hand of George Buck, Esq. All of it may be the Editor's reworking of what still appears in T, but in case some of it represents authorial work now lost I have included that part of it not represented elsewhere so explicitly.

153/25-38 T is very confused here from incomplete revision and crossing out by author and Editor. I have made some minor changes through deletion of uncrossed out material, reinstatement of crossed out material, and rearrangement of word order.

155/2nd mar. n. 26.27] M / 29.26 E / 26.29 F.

157/2nd mar. n. Darceii] Darcey F / [Darey] Darcy M / Darey E.

161/50 in general words passed] [in generall words passed] is confessed E / in generall words is confessed MP / in generall words [passed,] is confessed F.

166/1-6 This section is badly damaged and the version in EMF paraphrases and alters word order. In restoring it I have had to guess at the order the author intended.

166/6 after] Ted.

167/1st mar. n. Ausonius] MF / Ausonus E.

167/5 *reus*] reas EMF /rei P.

169/38 the which] [the] which E / which MF.

169/3rd mar. n. Dominus de Arun.] Dominus de Arundell P / Do*mi*nus dr Aran E / Do*minus* Dr. Arun: M / Do*mi*nus Dr. Annn. F

169/41 his] MFP / this E.

170/11 *two*] 12^{mli} EMF / some 12,000 pounds P.

171/36 At this point the hand changes from scribal to authorial.

171/49 κτενέεις] κτανεεις T; μόρσιμος] μορισμος T.

173, f. 215v* The first part of this folio is in a state of incomplete revision and cannot be reconstructed. Hence I have had to omit it. It reads:

*******e paynes, and Care to demonstrate his yong **********cause it was so lowe ********** but otherwis ********d as little labour and care in the refelling & an********f the rest, as well for the reasons before declared as also becaus the greate accusation*n* *********nne lawfull & good euidence proved; but its concern ****************ed & ***roached by ye Calumnie or slander of them who haply were guilty of ********* and afterward it was ************d broached and nourished by lyeing fame & by the Fame & by the ma********ue; and other ******** faction or the Credulous people: But certanne grounde or proofe therof was **********

173/25 indictum] P / indicte EMF.
173/26 irritum] P / irratum MF / arratum E.

Book IV

174/2 the Third] the III EMF.
174/39 the late] whole line crossed out in E, missing MF.
175/18 W*ay*te] Wyat EMF / Wiatt P.
176/12 English] MFP / Englished E.
176/41 a*ll* alacrity] a allacritie T.
177/44 her virtues] MF / hertues E.
178/42 ducende] ducenda EMFP.
180/12 deluded] The copies' wording is clearly a revision which repeats some of the wording that survives in T. Since this whole section is very close to More's wording, I have taken this emendation from More (p. 62).
180/36 have attention to hear] [haue] \with/ attention [to] heare E / with attention hear MFP.
180/38 his] MF / this E.
186/5-34 There is evidently a fragmental page missing from T here. I have supplied the gap from E.
187/2 and to believe] MF / *omit* E.
187/15 men] [men] vniust & vnworthy law T. This passage is in a state of incomplete revision.
188/10-11 ought to have been] MF.
188/40 which] FP / [which] that E / [that] w*hi*ch M.
189/1st mar. n. Plantagenet] MFP / *omit* E.
189/29 honourable] EMFP / honourably T.
190/41 ex] Ea EMF / ito P.
190/42 repudii] P / repudis EMF; dimissoria] MP /dimistoria E /demissoria F.
192/19 minore] emendation taken from Crowland Chronicle, p. 174 / immorte EMFP; reginam] P / regmani EF / regimani M; decuit] deciat EMF / dicunt P.
193/1st mar. n. S. B.] EMF / B: P.
193/41 bona] P / boreas E / borea MF. [In EMF this passage occurs near the end of Book V. Ed. replaces it here with an attack on the stage.]
193/43 nescire] P / nescere EMF.
193/44 cui] qui EFP / que M.
194/2 promoter's] promoters P / promooters T / dilators EM / Promotors (with 'dilators' as marginal gloss) F. T has starred 'promooters' so must have a similar marginal note.

Book V

196/28-29 Reconstruction here combines the remaining text of Tib. with the shortened revision of it in the copies, rearranging material from copies so as to preserve logic.
196/32 Draco] P / Drago EMF.
196/35-38 This translation may have appeared in a burnt away margin of T; there is no place for it in the body of the text. Since there is no trace of it remaining in T one cannot say whether it is the work of author or Editor. It is a form Buc uses elsewhere in his short translations, and its simplicity and unpretentiousness point to him.
197/1st mar. n. Philosophu*s*] Philosophu*m* EMF.
197/16 pecuniarum] P / pecunieru*m* EMF.

197/ 5th mar. n. In Ruffin*um*] in Ruff E / in Ruffin M / in Ruffen F / in Ruff. P.

197/23 Tartesiacis] correction from Claudian's original / Tertessiaris EMF / Tartessiaris P.

197/27 Res fisci est, etc.] P / Res fisci est et terrebrionu*m* &c. EMF.

199/42-45 Emendations have been taken from M and F, since they do not alter the construction of the original, whereas E does.

199/49 phila*u*tists] philantists EMF / Plaintiffs P.

199/50 ἰδιοβουλεῦται] ἰδιοβουλενται. EMFP.

201/31-33 The transitional section in T here is too badly burnt to be reconstructed and has been crossed out, apparently by the author, who seems not to have written a substitute for it. The Editor substitutes in the copies a transition of his own.

202/3rd mar. n. Morton] MP / Mooton EF.

203/17 allegatae] P / allogatae T* / allogate EMF.

203/36 son] sonnes EMF.

204/5 perpetuam] P / perpetuum EMF.

204/2nd mar. n. Ralph] Robert EMF.

205/44 cl[arissima] clarissima P (confirmed by MS Cotton Vespasian C. XVI, f. 75) / carissima EMF.

205/47 praebes] P / praebos E / probo M / praebo F.

206/1 prosequitur] P / prosequart T* / prosequar te EMF; et desiderat] te desiderat T*EMFP.

206/8 dici] P / deci EMF.

206/19 nostrum] FP / nostram EM.

206/20 amicitia] MFP / amicita E.

206/21 respectu] P / respectis EMF; nullum] P / nullam EMF.

206/22 unum] P / unam EMF; benevolentiae] P / benevolentia EMF.

206/26 fluvii] P / flauij T*EMF.

206/28 amabit] P / amubit EMF.

206/30 manebunt] P / manebant EMF.

207/mar. n. consumptos] P / consumptus EMF; ostendit] (original quotation) / affaris E / affarit M / afferit F / affirmat P.

207, f. 255 The first few lines of this folio are too badly damaged to be reconstructed or placed in the existing context: 'et multiplicuntur ******** noe reason but th******* might be more fauor ********** full and in suspense ********** neither is it safe to en************ God **** forbidden vs to *********** matters whereof *******bly it only to himself *********.

207/36 1485] 1493 EMFP.

208/28 Εἴπερ / Εἴπες EMF.

208/29 Καλλιστον / from Euripides / Ναλλίsον E / Ναλλίρον MF.

208/32 colere] colore EMFP.

209/6 precario] (from Seneca) precacirio EF / precaririo M.

210/7 insontem] (from Camden) infontem EMF / infantem P.

210/14 had been] F / had bee EM.

210/25 Austria] Austriche EMF / Austrich P.

210/35 Trenchard] P / Treachard EMF.

211/13 sanct*a*m] sanctum EMFP.

212/11 Dartford] P / Datford EMF.

212/42 and the] and then EMF.

212/47 soon after put to death] MF / put to death soon after E.

213/33 wise, virtuous, happy] wise, virtuous [happie], fortunate E.

213/40 receive] receiveth T. I cannot reconstruct the passage so as to make this form fit. The whole section is in a state of partial revision, badly burnt and crossed out by the Editor.

214/22-23 void and] [void and] E / a void and MF.

214/30 Athelstan] P / Athelston EMF.

214/49-216/10 A leaf is evidently missing from T at this point.

215/4th mar. n. Lib. 14] MF / lib. 4 EP.

216/42 diro] dico EMF.

216/43 multa] multam EMF.

217/20-218/28 This section is missing in T.

217/20 And now we are come] MF / [And nowe] wee are \nowe/ come E.

217/36 iusta] P / iustae EMF.
217/37 nepotis] Nepotis P / Nepotem EMF.
217/38 Britanna] EMP / Britannia F.
217/39 binis] P / binius EMF.
217/43 decoras] taken from another copy of epitaph, B.L. MS. Add. 45131, f. 10[v] / diceras EMF / dicaras P.
217/2nd mar. n. 1485] 1484 EMFP.
218/1 reddideram] redideram EMFP.
218/15 terra sancta] terrae sanctae EMF / terrarum P.
218/25 milleno] P / millerio EMF.
218/26 Adiunctis] MP / Advinctis EF.

GENERAL NOTES

When referring to Buc's sources I have where possible used the edition, sometimes the copy that Buc used. Where this could not be determined or was difficult to come by I have used either an edition to which Buc could have had easy access (if one was available) or the standard – or a good – edition or reprint.

It must be understood throughout that Buc usually does not quote precisely from the sources cited: his tendency is to paraphrase. I have not given the original version in every case where deviation occurs but have done so where the alterations are either very drastic or materially affect the sense.

I have in brackets throughout given translations of foreign quotations and expressions not translated in the text itself. Those from the second continuation of the Crowland Chronicle are given, except where stated, in the translation by editors Nicholas Pronay and John Cox. Domenico Mancini's treatise of 1483 now appears in two editions, by C.A.J. Armstrong, *The Usurpation of Richard III* (1969) and Annette Carson *de occupatione regni Anglie* (2021), page references being given as (Arm: nn, Car: nn). Those from Camden's *Britannia* are from the 1610 translation by Philemon Holland. I acknowledge with gratitude the considerable assistance of Dr John Blundell, Editor, Thesaurus Linguae Latinae, Munich for help with mediaeval and even some classical Latin; and for help with some abstruse mediaeval French passages Professor Maureen Boulton, University of Notre Dame. I have not translated biblical passages, which are mainly decorative, assuming readers will have easy access to a version of the source.

BOOK I

1. The first quotation, a translation of Plato, *De Legibus*, V, 730, is correctly documented [He should be honoured who does no harm, but he is more worthy of honour who refrains from opening a way for other people to do it]. The second quotation I have been unable to locate in St Ambrose's *De Officiis Ministrorum*, though certain passages resemble it [Anyone who does not, if he can, expel injury from his environs is as guilty as the person who introduces it].

3/1-6. Born in 1585, Thomas Howard, well known as a patron of scholars and artists (see p. 210 of Kevin Sharpe, 'The Earl of Arundel, His Circle and the Opposition to the Duke of Buckingham, 1618-1628', in *Faction in Parliament: Essays on Early Stuart History*, ed. Kevin Sharpe, Oxford, 1978, pp. 209-44). Educated at Westminister and Trinity, Cambridge, he was created Knight of the Garter in 1611, a member of the Privy Council in 1616 and in 1621 officially made Earl Marshal after acting in the post in commission with others. He died in

1646. A scholar and avid antiquarian collector, he possessed family papers and relics. He numbered among his friends Cotton, Camden, Spelman and Selden. He was interested in acting and performed in court masques. He and Buc shared a passion for ancestry: 'In his will, he desired that a history might be written of his "noble auncesters, whereby their good memory may be preserved, and those that shall succeede may bee invited to bee virtuous, or at least ashamed to bee vitious"'. (Mary F.S. Hervey, *The Life, Correspondence and Collections of Thomas Howard, Earl of Arundel,* Cambridge, 1921, p. 137). Lord Maltravers was not his title but that of his eldest son. Buc was listing it among all the other Howard family titles.

3/14. Buc is probably referring here to Sir William Cornwallis's essay entitled in its earliest extant version *The Encomium of Richard the Third*, cited again on text pp. 133f and 199. He was clearly using a later version of the work. Its later versions conclude, 'yet for all this knowe I hold this but as a Paradoxe' (p. 32). For discussion of this defence and Buc's indebtedness to it, see above, pp. cxxii-cxxv.

3/mar. n. I have been unable to trace and hence to complete this quotation, which suffers from burning in the manuscript, or to locate an author called Johannes Veteranus.

3/25-29. Richard III created John Howard first Duke of Norfolk and his son Thomas Earl of Surrey on 28 June, 1483, a few days before his coronation, in which Norfolk bore the crown and Surrey the sword of state (see *The Coronation of Richard III: the Extant Documents*, ed. Anne F. Sutton and P.W. Hammond, Gloucester, 1983, *passim*). Norfolk was granted the offices of Earl Marshal and High Steward of England, the former, the traditional Mowbray office, in right of his Mowbray mother. He was King's Justicer and Commissioner of Array in East Anglia. One of the chief commanders at Bosworth, as was his son Surrey, he died fighting for Richard, despite the famous warning pinned to his tent, according to Hall (see text, p. 97 and note thereto). Surrey became a military hero under Henry VII and Henry VIII without compromising his loyalty to Richard III: see Camden *Remaines*, 1614, p. 283 (also in 1605 edition, p. 217. All future references are from the 1614 edition unless otherwise indicated). See below 109/26-43 for the full quotation from Camden.

3/34-36. Buc discourses further on the history of the Howard family, text, pp. 110-4.

4/9-13. In text, pp. 114 and 116, Buc acknowledges his gratitude to the Howards for their aid to his ancestors, as he had in *Comm.*, f. 453.

4/29. Buc uses 'story' throughout this work in the sense of 'history'. For a discussion of Buc's historiographical methods, see Introduction, Chapter VII.

4/47-49. Buc is probably referring to Grafton. The controversy between Grafton and Stow, discussed in the Introduction to Stow's *Survey of London*, ed, Charles Lethbridge Kingsford (Oxford, 1908) and in F.J. Levy, *Tudor Historical Thought* (San Marino, 1967), p. 188, was based to a great extent on Stow's objections to Grafton's lack of documentation. For a discussion of the technical ideals of the antiquaries in Buc's time, see Introduction, Chapter III.

4/50-5/4. For a discussion of popular literature see above, pp. cxlii-cxliv.

5/5-7. [Buc's version translates: 'testimonies and examples drawn from ancient memorials and monuments tend to have special authority']: This is Cicero, *In*

Verrinem II, 3, 209, slightly paraphrased.

5/18-19. Vergil, *Eclogue* VI, 3-4 [When I was singing of kings and battles, Cynthius tugged my ear and advised me: Tityrus, a shepherd's job is to feed his sheep].

6/5. For a discussion of Buc's *Baron*, no longer extant, see above, pp. xliii-xlvi. The tendency of some of Buc's digressions to grow to proportions exceeding the work intended to contain them can be seen in *The History* in the extensiveness of his discussion of 'Plantagenet' in Book I and that on Perkin Warbeck in Book III.

6/14-15. Charles Yarnold in Egerton 2218, f. 50 identifies the 'worshipful shallow magistrate' as Thomas Gainsford, author of *The True and Wonderfull History of Perkin Warbeck* (London, 1618). But since Gainsford's active life was spent in Ireland, and Buc's references to him in other places are not so discourteous, this is not plausible. I cannot identify the person Buc refers to here.

6/1st mar. n. [A public person is the prince or magistrate who presides over a republic or part of it] Hermannus Vulteius, *Jurisprudentia Romana* (Marburg, 1602), I, xiii, 64.

6/2nd mar. n. [The blessed kingdom of the holy King James]

6/39. For Morton's possible contribution to Ricardian historiography, see above, pp. cxxii-cxxv; also see Introduction to William Cornwallis, The *Encomium of Richard the Third,* with introd. by J.A. Ramsden and A.N. Kincaid, ed. A.N. Kincaid (London, 1977). The 'apes' are those historians who incorporate More's writing into their own: Grafton, Stow, Hall and Holinshed.

7/1. propria mercedem [just reward].

7/1-2. Corinthians 5:10.

7/8-9. I can locate no specific source for this axiom.

7/11-12. Plato, *Philebus* 59e-60a, *Gorgias* 498e, *Laws* 754c and 956e.

7/22-25. This could again refer to Grafton.

7/26-28. Authors commonly made lists of their sources at the beginnings or ends of their works. Hall and Holinshed list theirs at the beginning, and there is also some marginal documentation in Holinshed. Grafton does not document at all. Stow lists his sources at the beginning and documents fairly thoroughly in the margins, though not as thoroughly as does Buc.

7/35-36. See above, Introduction, Ch. III for a discussion of antiquaries. William Camden, educated at Winchester and Oxford and for some time schoolmaster at Westminster, became Clarenceux Herald in 1597. He was an indefatigable and highly respected antiquary, travelling throughout the country to do research for his *Britannia*, first published in 1586, and *Remaines*, first published in 1605. He possessed, through purchase, some of Leland's and Stow's collections of manuscript material, including historical observations, records, and chronicles. Ralph Brooke, York Herald, was a vehement critic of Camden's *Britannia*. Possibly his animosity arose from Camden's appointment above him as well as from Camden's errors in genealogical matters. Brooke's criticism forced Camden to closer examination and documentation of sources. It is interesting that both men were willing to assist Buc in his research, and that he was able to ignore their differences and consider them both his friends. He cites them both in the *Commentary* also.

Sir Robert Cotton, the greatest collector of his time, was a former pupil of Camden's, whose library he ultimately inherited. The original manuscript of Buc's *History* also ended up in his collection. As will be seen often in these notes and Buc's own marginal notes, Buc made considerable use of Cotton's extensive manuscript collections. An interesting exchange between Buc and Cotton is cited above, p. lvi.

7/42. Desiderius Erasmus, *Adagiorum Chileades* (Basle, 1536), p. 557 [The doors of the Muses are always open].

8/12. For dating of this work, see above, p. cl.

BOOK I

9. Buc follows his outline quite closely in Book I. He deviates only in that though Richard's lineage and family are discussed first, his 'birth, education, and tirociny' come not until after a long digression, 'The antiquity of surnames'; 'The quality and title of the Beauforts . . .' are discussed not here but in Book II; 'King Richard demandeth a tribute of France' follows 'His careful and godly charge . . . for the administration of Justice'; and the two topics 'He holdeth a parliament . . .' and 'Morton . . . attainted of treason . . . and the king declared . . . heir to the crown' are reversed.

10/3. Richard of York, described here as the fourth duke, was actually the third. The first Duke of York was Edmund of Langley, 5th son of Edward III. Edmund's older son, Edward, inherited the title as second Duke of York and died childless in 1415, a hero of Agincourt. His younger brother Richard of Conisbrough, Earl of Cambridge did not inherit having been executed for treason against Henry V a few months earlier. Because he was not attainted, his son Richard, whom Buc describes here as King of England designate, succeeded as third duke at the age of about four.

Some doubt surrounds the birth of Richard of Conisbrough, son of Isabel of Castile: he 'may have been the product of his mother's illicit liaison with John Holland, earl of Huntingdon' (G.L. Harriss, 'Richard [Richard of Conisbrough], earl of Cambridge', *ODNB*. See also T.B. Pugh, *Henry V and the Southampton Plot of 1415* [Stroud], 1988, pp. 90f). Though he did not provide Conisbrough with land or livelihood or mention him in his will, the Duke of York evidently accepted him as his son. If he were illegitimate this might explain the failure to match the Y-chromosome of his grandson, Richard III with that of some of Edward III's modern-day descendants. It would not have affected Richard's right to the throne, since this right came not from Richard of Conisbrough but from the latter's wife, Lady Anne Mortimer, heiress to Edward III through a line senior to her husband's: he was (nominally) descended from the 5th son, but Anne was descended from the 3rd son Lionel, Duke of Clarence. (Buc called Clarence the 2nd son, leaving out of account William of Hatfield, the actual 2nd son, who died the year he was born. For ease of reference, Edward III's 2nd and 6th sons have been omitted from this book's simplified Family Tree.)

10/4-5. Parliament had proclaimed Richard, Duke of York Heir Apparent to the throne in recognition of the Yorkist claim's superiority over the Lancastrian. Henry VI's son Edward was to be passed over. See *PROME* XII, ed. Anne Curry and Rosemary Horrox, Parliament of Oct. 1460, 1 Edward IV, p. 524.

10/31-11/17. For a previous example in Buc's work of his admiration for Henry II, see above, pp. xxxii-xxxiv, the discussion of *Daphnis*. There also he speaks of the extent of Henry's empire, quoting at length from Du Haillan, Newburgh, Giraldus, and Salisbury, and referring also to De la Hay, Fabyan, Stow and Camden.

10/34-37. [Queen of the English . . . Son of the Emperor . . . of the short cloak]

11/1-2. Camden, *Britannia*, 1607 (all future references are to this edition unless stated), p. 119 (trans. Philemon Holland, London, 1610, pp. 164-6) discusses the fluctuations in priority of the terms duke and count at various times during the Roman empire and after it ceased in England, when the terms were, by the time of William the Conqueror, interchangeable. In *A Collection of Curious Discourses*, ed. Thomas Hearne (London, 1773), I, 177-86 are several discourses on etymology and on dignity and antiquity of dukes in England. All mention the interchangeable use of the terms 'Dux' and 'Comes' in the time of Edward the Confessor and William I.

11/2nd mar. n. Buc evidently means this documentation to apply to the whole of his information on Henry II, not simply to the title 'Regum Britanniae Maximus' [Greatest of the Kings of Britain], which in *Daphnis* (sigs. C and C2) he twice documents explicitly as coming from Salisbury. Giraldus Cambrensis, *Topographia Hibernica* in *Opera*, ed. James F. Dimock, R.S. 21 (London, 1861-91), V, 189ff, gives these limits to Henry's empire, but not this particular epithet, though his praise is lavish. Johannes Sarisberiensis [John of Salisbury], *Policraticus*, ed. Clement C.J. Webb (Oxford, 1909), II, 49, 614b, calls Henry 'rex optimus apud Britannias' [best king in Britain] and 'maximus regum Britanniae' [greatest of the kings of Britain] (II, 424, 822a): William of Newbergh, *Historia Regum Anglicarum* in *Chronicles of the Reigns of Stephen, Henry II, and Richard I*, ed. Richard Howlett, R.S. 82 (London, 1884-5), I, 278, says, 'inclitus ille rex Henricus, inter reges orbis terrarium nominatissimus, et nulli eorum vel amplitudine opum, vel felicitate successuum' [that famous King Henry, among the kings of the earth most famous, and inferior to none of them in the greatness of his wealth or happiness of his successes].

11/25-16/11. The origin of the name 'Plantagenet' is still uncertain, but there is agreement that it was the personal nickname of Geoffrey of Anjou, father of Henry II, though he never used it officially. Camden in *Remaines,* p. 107f says, 'I know not why any should thinke *Plantagenet* to be the surname of the royall house of *England*, albeit in late yeares many haue so accounted it'. In *ODNB* under Henry II Thomas K. Keefe says, 'Geoffrey's sobriquet, which is attested by several contemporary sources, has been plausibly but not certainly ascribed to his wearing a sprig of broom, *Planta genista*, in his helmet. But its attribution as a surname to all the kings of England descended from him until 1485, though undeniably a genealogical convenience, is factually unwarranted.' The name was not used after Geoffrey until Richard, Duke of York adopted it as a surname:

> 'Après lui le surnom disparaît. Henri II est appelé "fitz Empress". Aucun membre de la famille ne porta plus ce nom-même au XIIIe siècle, quand la mode fut aux sobriquets, –jusqu'à Richard d'York qui, en 1460, voulut,

par ce nom, marquer la superiorité de sa maison sur celle des Lancastre' [After him the surname disappeared, Henry II being called FitzEmpress. No member of the family bore this surname in the 13th century, when sobriquets were the fashion, until Richard of York, who, in 1460, wanted with this name to signal the superiority of his house to that of Lancaster] (Josèphe Chartrou, *L'Anjou de 1109 à 1151 – Foulque de Jerusalem et Geoffroi Plantagenet*, Paris, n.d., p. 84).

11/31-32. For discussion of Buc's *Commentary* see above, pp. xxxvii-xlii.

11/40-41. Sir William Dethick succeeded his father, Sir Gilbert, in the office of Garter Principal King of Arms. He was a member of the original Society of Antiquaries, which often held meetings at his house (Linda Van Norden, *The Elizabethan College of Antiquaries,* unpublished doctoral dissertation, University of California at Los Angeles, 1946, p. 306). He became involved in an internal squabble in the College of Arms which has biased evidence of his character and attainments and makes it difficult to assess them. In 1606 he was brought before the Earl Marshal's court for abuse of his office through embezzling books and falsifying pedigrees. This case seems to have arisen from the interest of Sir William Segar in obtaining Dethick's office and from the king's wish to confer it on Segar, previously Norroy Herald. Records of the proceedings exist in B.L. Additional, ff. 291v-296, Harl. 1453, ff. 31v-71, and Cotton Vespasian C.XIV, f. 96. According to Dethick's own explanation in Cotton Vesp. C. XIV, f. 96, the accusations were stirred up by his jealous associates who had removed and hidden the books.

Anthony Richard Wagner's description of the College of Arms at the end of the sixteenth and beginning of the seventeenth century (*The Records and Collections of the College of Arms,* London, 1952 pp. 9-13) accounts to some extent for the internal disputes and accusations. The library was built up gradually and passed on by heralds to their successors. Some books were privately owned, some belonged to the College, and for some the ownership was uncertain. In 1568 the Earl Marshal, Thomas Howard, Duke of Norfolk, established rules for the College, including incorporation of the library. Further reform came in 1597 when Camden was made Clarenceux. Wagner thinks the accusations against Dethick may have manifested resistance against the Earl Marshal's imposition of rules and the heralds' insistence on continuing to regard as private property what had to belong to the College for it to function effectively as a corporation. Brooke, provoked by the promotion of Camden, seems to have added fuel to the fire with 'A Catalogue of a fewe Arms and Crestes as hath byn given by William Derick [*sic*] . . . with some note of other his abuses maynteyned and lyked of by some his followers new elected Officers of Armes which haue byn Brokers for the same' (B.L. MS. Harl. 1453, f. 31v).

Buc's description of Dethick does not accord with the accusations of dishonest and incompetent practice and unpleasant behaviour. One might interpret this as an example of his tendency, also manifested in this *History*, to see the best in people and it may perhaps be his intention here to mount a defence. In any case,

Dethick seems to have retained a library of some sort, probably partly furnished from the collection left him by his father, who had instituted the College's library. That Buc praises his library is not evidence of his embezzling from the College, for the private collecting activities of his contemporary antiquaries were considerable. However, the ethics of collecting to which these men adhered were not always strictly scrupulous by modern standards.

For additional information on Dethick's character see Introduction, pp. xl-l and Katherine Duncan-Jones, *Shakespeare, an Ungentle Life* (London, 2010), pp. 114-8, where he is depicted as notoriously quarrelsome and violent and having a tendency to issue questionable arms. However, Brooke's biography in *ODNB* may lead one to believe that many of the slurs on Dethick's character may be ascribed to Brooke, who appears to have been perhaps a rather nasty piece of work himself.

12/5. Jean Nicot, *Thresor de la Langue* (Paris, 1606), p. 602 'Toutesfois le sotbriquet (comme le vocable de foy le monstre) est vne adiection populaire au nom d'aucun, faicte par accident, & tendant à gosserie [However, the nickname (as the phrase 'to show loyalty' demonstrates), is a popular addition to a name, created by accident and tending toward silliness].

12/10-23. A longer collection of surnames with their etymologies appears in Camden, *Remaines,* pp. 115-211.

12/2nd mar. n. Roger de Hoveden, *Chronica*, ed. William Stubbs, R.S. 51 (London, 1868-9), II, 300f. 'Rievall' refers to Ailredus, Abbot of Rievaulx, who wrote an historical work of which there are several manuscript copies in the Cotton collection. In the volume Buc used (Julius A.XI) it was bound with a history of Henry II's reign by an unnamed Benedictine abbot, and it is this history, not Ailred's, that Buc cites. He confused the two because the Benedictine's history, beginning f. 29, follows, both in the volume and chronology, directly after Ailred's. The hand, to an eye not carefully trained in palaeography, appears the same, and only close examination reveals that these are two separate works. The Benedictine history is edited by William Stubbs as *The Chronicle of the Reigns of Henry II and Richard I*, 2 vols., R.S. 49 (London, 1867). There are several mentions of the projected crusade: Henry in 1172 when formally absolving himself of Becket's murder swears to go on a pilgriage to Jerusalem the following summer (I, 32).

13/29-48. Claude Paradin, *Alliances Genealogiques des Rois et Princes de Gaule* ([Geneva], 1606), p. 176: Fulke had his stepson (not nephew) Drogo drowned in a bath by his nurse. To avoid the burden of guilt in old age,

> S'en alla donques en Ierusalem, suyui de deux seruiteurs: &, y entrant, s'accoustra en criminal, &, comme vn condamné, se mit vne corde au col, &, se faisant trainer par l'un de ses gents, se faisoit aussi (ce pendant) fouetter par l'autre sans cesse auec des verges: & ainsi, arriuant au lieu de S. Sepulchre, se print à crier, disant: Recoy, mon Dieu & Seigneur, ton miserable Fouques fugitive & parjure.

[He went then to Jerusalem, followed by two servants, and, entering there, accoutred as a criminal and a condemned man, placed a cord about his neck and having himself led by one of his men, made the other whip him with switches without stopping, and then, arriving at the Holy Sepulchre, he began to shout, saying, Receive, my God and Lord, your miserable Fulke, fugitive and perjurer.]

Bernard de Girard, Seigneur du Haillan, *L'Histoire de France* ([Paris], 1577), p. 342, whom Paradin uses as a source, copying from him the quotation cited above, says it was not known what crimes Fulke had committed. Paradin does not mention his defrauding a church. It is Du Haillan who notes that Fulke lived afterwards in the regard of all men (p. 342). More recently, Joseph Chartrou says of this episode that Fulke, 'par manière de pénitence, se faisait flageller nu dans le rues de Jérusalem' (p. 78) [in manner of penitence had himself flagellated naked through the streets of Jerusalem]. Fulke seems to have been, like Geoffrey Plantagenet, a colourful and charismatic figure. Calmette, *Le Moyen Age* (Paris, 1948), p. 164 calls him 'le premier des grandes comtes' [the first of the grand counts].

13/33-34. Du Haillan, p. 552, says mistakenly that he was the son of Geoffrey Martel, who was in fact his son. Grisegonelle was the third count of Anjou (see P. Marchegay and A. Salmon, *Chroniques des Comtes d'Anjou*, Paris, 1871, p. lxvii).

13/34-36. Geoffrey 'Plantagenet' was the fifth count of Anjou after Fulke, but removed from him by only four generations (Paradin, pp. 176-88).

14/1st mar. n. Zosimus, *Historia Nova*, II, xxix.

14/45-46. See above, n. 13/29-48.

15/27. For 'the hieroglyphical learning', see below, n. 175/24-33.

15/30. Vergil, *Georgics*, II, 434 [the humble broom plant].

15/39. It is evidently from Fuchs, *De Historia Stirpium Commentarij Insignes* (London, 1551*)*, p. 218 that Buc derives this quotation (which comes from Pliny, *Historia Naturalis*, XXIV, xl), since the spelling follows Fuchs's version (p. 219), which gives 'Genista tusa cu*m* ax ungia, genus dolentia sanat' [Broom pounded with axle grease cures pain in the knee]. Pliny gives 'axungia' as one word. Buc substitutes 'etc.' for 'ax ungia' because he does not understand it.

15/40-41. Fuchs, p. 219, comments on the purgative value of the plant.

16/5. Strabo, *Geography*, XVI, ii, 36.

16/2nd mar. n. Du Haillan, p. 553: 'Ce qui fait que plusieurs croient, que pour ceste grand & humble reparacio*n*, Dieu voulut que son peche fut entierement celé' [Many believe that after this great and humble repentance God wanted his sin to be entirely erased]. He says Fulke's descendants were kings of Jerusalem and England. Buc adds France, Ireland and Scotland.

16/31-48. Robert Glover, Somerset Herald, one of the original members of the Society of Antiquaries, was highly regarded by Buc and Camden. *The Catalogue of Honour*, ed. Thomas Milles (London, 1610) is a genealogical work which begins with a discussion of English ranks and ceremonies and continues to show the genealogy of all the noble families in England. It was compiled and published after Glover's death by his nephew Thomas Milles with the help of Camden and Cotton. There were editions in 1610 and 1616, the latter using the Crowland Chronicle as a source. Glover reproduces original documents, a practice Buc follows in reproducing the order for the creation of Vice Constable (text, p. 55f).

The name Plantagenet appears occasionally in Glover. It does not appear in Jean du Tillet, *Recueil des Roys de France* (Paris, 1602), in Du Haillan or in Jean de la Haye, *Les Memoires et Recherches de France, et de la Gaulle Acquitanique* (Paris, 1581). Paradin, p. 28, mentions the name Geoffrey Plantagenet. Camden's only references occur in *Britannia*, p. 217 and *Remaines*, pp. 107f. The latter states that there is no reason to consider it a royal surname. This collection of references illustrates the type of inaccurate recollection of which Buc was sometimes guilty when relying entirely on memory. Glover is the only source which completely fits his description. Buc owned a copy of Glover, which has changed hands within the past c. twenty years, but I have been unable to locate its present whereabouts.

16/49-17/1. Camden, *Remaines,* p. 107.

17/13-14. According to Paradin (p. 168), the counts of Anjou were descended from Robert, Prince of Saxony, who in 870 was created the first count of Anjou.

17/20 Ovid, *Metamorphoses*, XIII, 147: [He was divine through both parents].

17/1st mar. n. [God, that is King]

17/22-23. Richard was born at Fotheringhay (William Worcester, *Annales Rerum Anglicarum* in *Letters and Papers Illustrative of the Wars of the English in France*, ed. Joseph Stevenson, R.S. 22, London, 1864, II, ii, [771]). The suggestion of Berkhamsted comes from John Stow, *The Annales of England*, London, 1601, p. 766: 'King Richard the third, borne at Fodringhay, some say at Barckhamstede'. All future references to Stow's *Annales* are from this edition unless otherwise noted.

17/25-27. Richard III was born in 1452, Edward IV in 1442. There were twelve children, nine surviving infancy, seven born between the two kings. This information comes from William Worcester, who gives names, dates and places of birth for the Duke of York's children. The name of the one child he neglects to mention is listed in a contemporary rhyme quoted by Augustine Vincent in *A Discouerie of Errours in the First Edition of the Catalogue of Nobility, Published by Raphe Brooke, Yorke Herald, 1619* (London, 1622), pp. 622f.

17/28. Edward IV died at 40, not 41.

17/34. Richard was not brought up at Middleham until after his father's death, when he resided for some time in the northern household of the Earl of Warwick in the later 1460s.

17/37. The battle of Wakefield occurred in 1460, not 1461.

17/44-45. Clarence and Gloucester were welcomed by Duke Philip of Burgundy, father of Charles the Bold. In 1468, after his father's death, Charles married Richard's older sister Margaret, not his aunt. Buc seems to be confusing this with the occasion of Richard's second exile in Burgundy, in company with his brother King Edward, who in 1470 was driven from his country by Warwick and Clarence. In text, p. 143, Buc mentions that Margaret of Burgundy gave Perkin Warbeck as warm a welcome as she had given Clarence and Gloucester many years earlier. There, however, he seems to realize that Margaret was Richard's sister and Perkin's (nominal) aunt. The error of assuming Margaret was aunt rather than sister to Edward IV and his brothers appears also in Shakespeare's 3 *Henry VI*, II, ii, 144.

18/8-16. George and Richard were made Knights of the Bath 27 June 1461 and created respectively Duke of Clarence (28 June) and Duke of Gloucester (1 November), then Knights of the Garter. Edward granted the honour of Richmond to Richard then transferred it to Clarence. There is no record that Edward IV ever deprived Henry Tudor of the title, though it was assumed by Clarence under Henry VI's readeption (1470-1). Richard was made High Admiral[*], 1462, High Constable[*], 1469, Warden of the West Marches, 1470, Great Chamberlain[*], 1471 (surrendered to Clarence in 1472 and reappointed in 1478). Carlisle was not at that time an earldom, but in 1483, as a reward for his actions against the Scots and to assist him in protecting the border, Richard was granted the Wardenship of the West Marches and 'the castell, cite, towne and lordshipp of Carlile and the feeferme of the same' for term of life and successively thereafter to his male heirs (*PROME*, XIV, 425, ed. Rosemary Horrox, Edward IV, Jan. 1483). [*] = Great Officers of State.

18/15. See text, p. 20, 5th mar. n. for documentation of this manuscript, which seems no longer extant.

18/19-24. Buc is in error. Clarence and Isabel were married without the king's consent in Calais in 1469, during the rising of Clarence and Warwick against Edward IV. Richard and Anne were married after Warwick's death, at some time between June 1472 and April 1473. In 'The Marriage of Lady Anne Neville and Richard Duke of Gloucester', *Ricardian Bulletin* (December 2016), 46-52, Annette Carson and Marie Barnfield give evidence for the second half of January or early February 1473 being the most logical time for the marriage to have taken place. Richard and Anne both stood to gain from it, Richard by becoming joint heir of the Warwick estates and Anne in that he was the only man powerful enough to enforce against Clarence her claims to her inheritance (see T.B. Pugh, 'The Marcher Lords of Glamorgan and Morgannwg, 1317-1485', *Glamorgan County History*, III, Cardiff, 1971, p. 200).

It was long thought that no dispensation for this marriage was extant, but one has fairly recently been discovered: see Peter D. Clarke, 'English Royal Marriages and the Papal Penitentiary', *EHR* CXX (2005), 1013-29, citing ASV, PA, Reg. 20, f. 481. This dispensed with the the relationship (known as 'affinity') between Richard and Anne in the third and fourth degrees. This referred to the 'relationship' between Richard and the son of Henry VI, Anne's first husband, a less significant matter than the blood relationship between Richard and Anne themselves. It is highly unlikely that this secondary dispensation would have been sought or granted without the more important one having been granted first. See Marie Barnfield, 'Diriment Impediments, Dispensations and Divorce: Richard III and Matrimony', in *The Ricardian*, XVII, 2007, 92, which shows that dispensing with the affinity due to Anne's former marriage 'implies that the impediments of consanguinity had already been absolved'; supported by H.A. Kelly, 'Incest and Richard III, Bigamy and Edward IV', *Ricardian Bulletin* (Spring 2007), 28.

Michael Hicks, however, had built a character assessment of Richard as abnormally selfish on the assumption that he had not bothered to obtain a dispensation for his marriage (*Richard III and His Rivals*, London, 1991: that no dispensation, he claims categorically, 'was ever obtained denotes either an extraordinary carelessness inconceivable in a man of such remarkable foresight or indifference to the fate of his heirs . . . whose interests were subordinated to an unusual extent to his own' (pp. 278f). When a dispensation was discovered implying a previous one, Hicks claimed that the couple needed yet *another* dispensation of the 'relationship' created by two brothers (Richard and Clarence) marrying two sisters (Anne and Isabel). He has continued to hold onto his theory of the marriage's invalidity despite the statement of ecclesiastical historian H.A. Kelly, in 'Incest and Richard III', 28, that 'there was no prohibition against double marriages, two brothers marrying two sisters. . . The law of affinity only prohibited *one* brother from successively marrying two sisters or two cousins'. This was confirmed in an e-mail (25 June 2016) to Annette Carson from Richard Helmholz, professor of law whose specialism is the mediaeval period and author of 'The Sons of Edward IV: a Canonical Assessment of the Claim that they were Illegitimate' in *Richard III: Loyalty, Lordship and Law* (London, 2000), pp. 106-20. Despite all this, the alleged prohibition against two brothers marrying two sisters has been stated as fact yet again by Chris Skidmore in a recently published biography, *Richard III* (London, 2017), p. 74. For him this constituted affinity in the third and fourth degrees, which was so extremely prohibited that Richard's applying for a dispensation required unusual chutzpah.

Hicks has also held onto claims that Richard was a 'serial incestor' (a term he invented in *Anne Neville, Queen to Richard III,* Stroud, 2006, resurfacing in *The Family of Richard III*, Stroud, 2015), though Richard never remarried. Possibly his attachment to it is due to his pride in having invented it, or it may be that he thinks undermining Richard's marriage to Anne will somehow support the rumour that he planned to marry his niece. (Peter D. Clarke says of this, 'it is difficult to attach much credence to rumours that he was planning to marry her himself', p. 1025.) This progresses to Richard's (apparently consciously) acting throughout the five hundred years between then and now 'to conceal the nullity of his first marriage, the invalidity of Anne's coronation and of Edward's investiture, and the illegitimacy of his son and heir' (*The Family of Richard III*, p. 56) – subtly implying that Richard's claiming his brother's children were illegitimate because of his invalid marriage was the height of hypocrisy. But Clarke had pointed out in his article of ten years before (p. 1026),

> Richard III based his claim to the English throne on the apparent irregularity of his brother's marriage, hence it is all the more surprising that historians have assumed that Richard married without a dispensation, thereby exposing his own heirs to similar challenges. Historians thus neglect at their peril the penitentiary records as sources for mediaeval political history.

This is an immensely complex area, perhaps best left to experts in mediaeval ecclesiastical law like Clarke, Kelly and Helmholz to explain. It is perhaps not surprising that Hicks has been unable to comprehend it despite repeated explanation. As for the scholarship involved in such a quest, it is well to remember what a minute number of documents survive from Richard's day to the present and that a document from the period being no longer extant in no way implies that it never existed. (It may of course still exist, the object of miscataloguing.)

18/28. Halsted I, 231 calls Buc's remark that Anne was 'the better woman' a 'quaint expresssion' suggesting 'superiority, either in mind or person'. It is nothing of the kind but refers to her social position as widow of the Prince of Wales.

18/30-31. There is no evidence that Richard loved Anne, but none that he did not, though tales were introduced into the Tudor histories that he planned to poison her to marry his niece Elizabeth of York (see text, pp. 73 and 192). He refuted the existing rumour of his marriage plan, according to *The Crowland Chronicle Continuations, 1459-1486*, ed Nicholas Pronay and John Cox, [Gloucester, 1986], pp. 174-5, not saying, as several historians seem to think, that he had changed his mind, but that 'such a thing had never entered his mind' ('ea res numquam venerat in mentem suam'). All three brothers showed inclination to marry within the kingdom, and Edward, at least, married for love. Polydore Vergil (*Anglica Historia*, 2nd ed., Basle, 1555, p. 557: this will be the edition referred to hereafter unless noted) claims that Richard killed Anne with cruelty by forsaking her bed in her last illness, by complaining of her barrenness and rumouring her death. But since he was responsible for the kingdom it seems unavoidable that he should have felt duty bound to avoid contagion, particularly since he presumably did this on medical advice, as Crowland seems to suggest (pp. 174f). He may have made known his fears of her death to members of the Council. Polydore, p. 557, says he confided in Archbishop Rotherham about her barrenness. These matters concerned the safety of the throne and kingdom.

18/32. For the creation of Richard's son as Prince of Wales, see text pp. 48 and 51 and notes thereto.

18/34-45. For the character and actions of the Duke of Clarence, see below, nn. 135/7 and 136/48.

18/36-37. Stow (*Annales*, pp. 716f) was the first to discover and print the record of Clarence's indictment, in which he is accused of stating that Edward IV was illegitimate. He documents this information from 'Tower Records'. The accusation appears in R.E. Horrox, ed., 'Edward IV: Parliament of Edward IV, Text and Translation', in *PROME* XIV, 402, Appendix, n. 1.

19/16-18. The first battle of St Albans took place in 1455, the second in 1461, Blore Heath in 1459 and Mortimer's Cross in 1461. Richard was too young to have fought in any of these, and during the last was in Utrecht with his mother and brother George. Bearing a commission of array, he joined the king at Pontefract in 1464 (Paul Murray Kendall, *Richard III*, New York, 1955, p. 56), but the battle of Hexham in the same year was fought by Lord Montagu's forces. Near Doncaster in 1470 Edward IV and his supporters, Richard among them, were routed and fled to Holland. At the same time Clarence was supporting Warwick and Henry VI. At Tewkesbury in 1471 Richard commanded the vanguard, particularly distinguishing himself. Shakespeare also makes Richard fight at Mortimer's Cross as well as at Barnet and Tewkesbury.

19/27–20/12. In *Comm.*, Buc cites Camden and Glover as his sources regarding Fauconberg. Here he seems to be using Polydore, pp. 530f or the English historians who translate him. The chroniclers' accounts are variable and inaccurate. Warwick placed his cousin Thomas Neville, Lord Fauconberg ('the Bastard of Fauconberg') in command of a fleet to guard the Channel against Edward IV's adherents. However, according to Hall and Grafton, he fell into poverty after Warwick's death and 'robbed both on the sea & the lande, aswel his enemyes as also his frendes' (Edward Hall, *Chronicle*, ed. Henry Ellis, London, 1809, p. 302. References henceforth will be to this edition), then gathered a force against London, ostensibly to release Henry VI, but actually to rob and spoil. Stow, *Annales*, p. 706f adds that the Bastard withdrew to Sandwich after being beaten off by the Londoners and there sued for pardon, which Richard was sent to bestow. Later he was taken by Richard at Southampton and beheaded at Middleham. *Paston Letters and Papers of the Fifteenth Century*, 3 vols., ed. Norman Davis (Oxford, 2004), give the date of execution as 27 Sept. 1471 (II, 432f). An editorial note on this page corrects the date to 22 September.

Raphael Holinshed's account (*Holinshed's Chronicles of England, Scotland, and Ireland*, 6 vols., London, 1807-8, III, 321ff), based on *Historie of the Arrivall of Edward IV* (ed. John Bruce, Cam. Soc. 1st ser. 1, London, 1838), pp. 33-8, is the most detailed. The dates of Fauconberg's movements are confirmed by J.R. Scott in 'Letters Respecting Fauconberge's Kentish Rising in 1471', *Archaeologia Cantiana* XI (1877), 359-64, on the basis of original letters: he wrote to the Council (8 May) asking permission to land, supposing Warwick and the Prince of Wales still alive. The Council refused, telling him of Edward IV's victory. He attacked the Kentish coast on 12 May. Edward sent men against him. From 16 to 18 May, he lurked around London, fleeing when he heard of Edward's approach. He was captured by Richard, pardoned on 10 June, going north with Richard who was appointed the king's lieutenant-general to fight against James, King of Scotland. But he fled, was recaptured and put to death at Middleham (Cora L. Scofield, *The Life and Reign of Edward the Fourth*, London, 1967, II, 1f), his head being sent to London as the Paston extract indicates. It was at this time counted as treason to renege on a pardon for treason (Carson, *Richard Duke of Gloucester as Lord Protector and High Constable of England*, Horstead, 2015, p. 30).

20/15-16. Richard was appointed Warden of the West Marches in 1470 on the defection of Warwick, who held it previously (*Rot. Scot.* ii, 423-4). Henry Percy, Earl of Northumberland, was Warden of the East Marches (*Rot. Scot.* ii, 422, this and the previous reference cited in R.L. Storey, 'The Wardens of the Marches of England towards Scotland, 1377-1489', *EHR* LXXII, 1957, 614f). Storey elsewhere describes this charge thus: 'For the society of the English border counties, the local lord commanded more respect than *the* distant king' and says that Richard's Council of the North, a model for the Tudor version of it, was effective in providing swift redress of grievances ('The North of England' in *Fifteenth Century England*, ed. S.B. Crimes, C.D. Ross and R.A. Griffiths, 2nd ed., Stroud, 1997, p. 132). It met quarterly to examine complaints and examine actions against the peace (F.W. Brooks, *The Council of the North*, Historical Association Pamphlet 25, London, 1953). To determine the nature and scope of his responsibilities it is useful to look at the articles for his nephew John, Earl of Lincoln, whom as king he appointed to lead the Council. These encompass examining bills and complaints, dealing with riots, and organizational matters (Harl. 433, f. 264^{v}; cited in edition by Rosemary Horrox and Peter Hammond,

British Library Harleian Manuscript 433, Gloucester, 1982, III, 107f).

20/16-17. See n. 18/8-16 above for discussion of this appointment. The earldom of Carlisle did not come into being until the seventeenth century, and that Buc's friend Lord William Howard of Naworth, who was to be the founder of the line of earls of Carisle, had his seat there was probably the cause of Buc's eagerness to find a precedent in Richard. Buc qualifies this appointment below, ll. 38-43.

20/18. Yorkshire cannot be called Richard's native place, since he was born in Fotheringhay Castle in Northants. However, he almost certainly spent a period of his childhood here some time between 1465 and 1469 in Warwick's household, possibly at Middleham Castle, with which after his marriage and the birth of his son he was very closely associated. See A.J. Pollard, *The Middleham Connection: Richard III and Richmondshire 1471-1485* (Middleham, 1983). Pollard in 'North, South and Richard III', *Richard III, Crown and People*, ed. J. Petre, (Gloucester, 1985), pp. 349-55, notes that Sir George Buc's ancestors being largely from the North may have bolstered his sympathy with Richard.

20/22. Ovid, *Ex Ponto*, I, iii, 35-6 [Our native land alone sweetly delights us all]. All editions read 'ducit' (leads) where Buc has 'mulcet'.

20/25-21/1. A.J. Pollard assesses this government in *Middleham Connection*, p. 20: 'he revealed in these years [from 1471] an almost charismatic quality of leadership' and brought to the North 'a degree of harmony and unity for Yorkshire society which had been noticeably lacking in the preceding decades'. For a detailed account of Richard's northern government see Brooks, *Council of the North*, and Charles Ross, *Richard III* (Berkeley, 1981), pp. 199-203. The day to day relations of the Council of York with Richard can be seen in *The York House Books, 1461-1490*, ed. Lorraine Attreed, 2 vols. (Stroud, 1991). He made several visits to the city when Duke of Gloucester, and the Council expresses thanks to him for his good lordship (I, 250). On 15 June 1483 they raised 'CC horsemen defensibly arayed' to go to London to support him on the basis 'that the qwhen and hyr adherauntes intendyth to (destrew) hys gude grace and odir of the blod riall' (I, 284). On his first visit after becoming king he attended a Creed Play staged for him (I, 292f). At the time of 'Buckingham's rebellion' he sent to the city, which responded by sending soldiers (II, 713).

At his death local loyalty went so deep that the Council recorded profound grief: 'King Richard late mercifully reigning upon us was . . . piteously slane and murdred to the grete hevynesse of this cite . . .' (Attreed, I, 368f). David Palliser, 'Richard III and York', in *Richard III and the North* (Hull, 1986) says, 'The outbursts of feeling in the corporation minutes over the death of Richard and revering his memory are unprecedented in fifteenth-century council minutes.' (p. 72). He goes on to say (pp. 72f) that the York City Council firmly rejected Henry VII's nominees for office in 1485-6. Two months after Bosworth that Council mentions 'the moost famous prince of blissed memory, King Richard, late decesid' (quoted Palliser, p. 59 from *Richard III and the City of York*, compiled with an introduction by R. Freeman and E. White, York City Archives, 1983, doc. 8). Robert Davies, *Extracts from the Municipal Records of the City of York during the Reigns of Edward IV, Edward V and Richard III* (London, 1843), pp. 220-3, mentions a dispute as late as 1491 when an insult to Richard by one northerner to another was met with a threat of violence. Francis Drake in *Eboracum*, London, 1736, p. 124 comments on this posthumous loyalty to Richard and difficulty it caused for Henry: 'It is plain that Richard, represented as a monster of mankind by most, was not so esteemed in his life time in these northern parts'. Henry VII, he goes on, 'must know that neither his title, nor his family, were recognized, or respected, in these northern parts'. A.J. Pollard, 'The Richmondshire Community of Gentry during the Wars of the Roses', in *Patronage, Pedigree and Power*, p. 56), says after the death of Richard members of the gentry around Middleham, found the loss of their privileges 'too great, and they joined Lords Lovell and Scrope in raising rebellion in 1486 and 1487'.

Around the time Buc was writing his defence Francis Bacon speaks of Henry 'being truly informed that the northern parts were not only affectionate to the house of York, but particularly had been devoted to King Richard the Third . . .' (Francis Bacon, *History of the Reign of Henry VII*, ed. James Spedding, Robert Leslie Ellis, and Douglas Denon Heath, *The Works of Francis Bacon,* VI, London, 1938, p. 43). The North proved rebellious and refused to pay taxes: 'the old humour of those [North] countries, where the memory of King Richard was so strong that it lay like lees in the bottom of mens hearts: and if the vessel was but stirred it would come up' (Bacon, p. 88). Indeed a later biographer of Henry VII, Thomas Penn (*Winter King; the Dawn of Tudor England*, London, 2012, p. 132), says the murder of the Earl of Northumberland, while his retainers stood by, was assumed to be revenge for his failure to join with Richard at Bosworth (p. 132).

Several references in *Letters and Papers, Foreign and Domestic, of the Reign of Henry VIII*, ed. J.S. Brewer, 2nd ed. (London, 1920), especially I, pt. ii, nos. 2382 and 2913) show that Richard's northern government was still held up as a model in Henry VIII's time. A.J. Pollard, in 'North, South and Richard III', speaking of the lingering effect on his reputation of his work in the North, notes, 'That there was a strand of antagonistic feeling towards the north and northerners among southern opinion in the late fifteenth century can be readily demonstrated' (p. 349). As is seen above, northerners tended to praise Richard and to be loyal to him even after his death, whereas southerners, such as the author of the Crowland Chronicle and the Londoners who gave information to Mancini disliked and disapproved of him. To this Pollard plausibly attributes the fact that there are still two versions of Richard – 'a noble Richard and a monstrous Richard' – due not so much to Tudor propaganda as to division between north and south. Pollard in 'The Tyranny of Richard III', *Journal of Medieval History*, III (1977), 147-65, Keith Dockray in 'Richard III and the Yorkshire Gentry', *Richard III: Loyalty, Lordship and Law*, pp. 38-57, and Rosemary Horrox in *Richard III: a Study of Service* (Cambridge, 1989), *passim*, postulate that Richard's 'plantation' of northerners to fill gaps in southern leadership left by 'Buckingham's rebellion' was a major source of the hostility against him, which culminated in his defeat at Bosworth. 'This action transgressed', Pollard says, 'the unwritten rule that the rule of the counties lay in the hands of their native elites'. Thus Richard came to be regarded as a tyrant in the south, but not in the north (p. 147).

20/35. Camden, *Britannia*, p. 639 in 'Cumberland'.

20/35-37. William Hutchinson in *The History of the County of Cumberland*

(Carlisle, 1794), I, 317, says that Richard resided at Penrith to set up opposition to the Scots. He built new towers and strengthened the whole structure. Penrith is inland, not a port. See also n. 203/46-47 below.

20/3rd mar. n. William Howard of Naworth, born in 1563, was an uncle of Thomas Arundel, to whom Buc's *History* is dedicated. He was, according to Hervey, p. 138, known for his upright character and intellectual interests. A noted antiquary, he numbered Cotton, Camden and Spelman among his friends. In *Comm.* Buc often cites him, as here, as a *viva voce* source and refers to documents in his collection.

20/4th mar. n. [Count, that is President]

20/39-42. See n. 18/8-16 above.

20/5th mar. n. This manuscript (or these manuscripts) to which Buc makes six references in *The History* is (are) no longer extant. In the early Cotton catalogues are listed several chronicle histories which can no longer be traced and probably perished in the fire of 1731. For further discussion of this/these manuscripts, see Introduction, pp. lvii-lviii and cxxxi-cxxxii.

20/45-46. For the co-operation between Richard and Northumberland as rulers of the North during Edward IV's lifetime see Charles Ross, *Richard III* (Berkeley, 1981), pp. 199-230.

20/49-50. There is no evidence that Richard desired greater power before the death of Edward IV. After Clarence's death, says Mancini (Arm: 62-65, Car: 44-5)

> In provincia sua se continebat. Suos officiis et iusticia sibi devincire studebat. Alienos clara fama morum et studiorum suorum ad sui amorem non mediocriter alliciebat. In militia ita clarus erat, ut quicquid arduum et cum periculo pro regno gerendum esset, eius consilio et ductui committeretur. Iis artibus Ricardus populorum benivolentiam sibi quesivit . . .

[He kept himself within his own lands and set out to acquire the loyalty of his people through favours and justice. The good reputation of his private life and public activities powerfully attracted the esteem of strangers. Such was his renown in warfare, that whenever a difficult and dangerous policy had to be undertaken, it would be entrusted to his discretion and his generalship. By these arts Richard acquired the favour of the people . . .]

21/13-16. Polydore, p. 538, states that Edward IV's grievance against the Scots was a raid on his territories which ignored the truce between the two countries. Buc seems to have misunderstood his source or to have treated it too curiously, for Polydore had said just previous to this that King Louis of France refused to pay tribute, and this breach of promise led King James III (not James IV as Buc states, p. 22, l. 33 and p. 205, l. 21), an ally of France, to break his treaty with England.

21/21-26. Albany went to France in 1479 and returned in 1482 in response to Edward's solicitations. Edward was to promote Albany as claimant to the Scottish throne in return for securing Berwick and breaking off Scots alliances with France (Ross, *Edward IV*, London, 1974, p. 287).

21/27-48. See *Foedera*, ed. Thomas Rymer (Farnborough, 1967) V, Pt. 3, 104f [XII, 115f] for the appointment of Richard to defend the north of England against the Scots in May 1480. (For *Foedera* the book and page numbers for the London 1741 edition will hereafter be given in brackets after the citation.) Two months later Edward issued a Commission of Array to him, in company with the Earl of Northumberland, and others.

21/32-33. Polydore, p. 538, 'Hoc feliciter expedito negotio . . .' [Having happily settled this business . . .].

21/34-22/34. Buc has confused the account of this campaign by indicating that the Castle of Berwick fell with the town. There were two excursions to Berwick, the town falling in the first, the castle in the second. Richard's journey to Edinburgh intervening. A detailed account of the campaign is given by Scofield, II, 302-49 and Ross, *Edward IV*, pp. 287ff.

21/46-47. Sir Edward Woodville was not Lord Rivers. It was Queen Elizabeth's oldest brother, Anthony Woodville, who held that title.

22/10-11. Crowland, p, 148f: 'Nam sine ulla resistentia cum universo exercitu veniens usque Edinburgam, ditissimum oppidum dimittens incolume, rediit per Berwicum, villa namque ipsa in primo patriae introitu capta fuit: ac castrum quod diutius tenuit, tandem non sine caede et sanguine in Anglicorum potestatem venit' [Thus, having got as far as Edinburgh with the whole army without meeting any resistance, he let that very wealthy town escape unharmed and returned through Berwick; the town there had been captured at the outset of the invasion and the castle, which held out longer, finally fell into English hands though not without slaughter and bloodshed].

22/11-12. Hall, p. 336: 'kyng Edward . . . muche com*m*ended bothe his valiaunt manhode, and also his prudent pollicie . . .' Crowland's (pp. 148f) seems a more mingled tribute: 'Doluit Rex Edwardus frivolum tantarum exitum expensarum tametsi dolorem ipsum tantisper alleviaverit recuperatio, Berwici supradicti' [King Edward grieved at the frivolous expenditure of so much money although the recapture of Berwick alleviated his grief for a time].

22/32-34. Richard III's peace with Scotland was concluded in 1484. See text, pp. 57f and 205.

22/38-40. Polydore, p. 538; Holinshed, III, 350-4; Hall, p. 330-6; Stow, *Annales*, p. 719f; Richard Grafton, *Grafton's Chronicle; or, History of England*, 2 vols. (London, 1809), II, 71-7.

23/6. See text, p. 163 and below n. to p. 184/21-2. The suggestion there is of Edward IV dying by poison. This is amplified on p. 184. Polydore, p. 538 and Hall, p. 341 mention this rumour. For a speculative consideration of one possibility of this see Annette Carson, *Richard III: The Maligned King* (Stroud, 2013), pp. 15-20, 32f, and 40f, citing R.E. Collins, 'The Death of Edward IV' in J. Dening, *Secret History* (Brandon, 1996). See also below, n. to p. 184/10-17 and 3rd mar. n.

23/9 Richard was no longer in Scotland when Edward died, but in Yorkshire (David Baldwin, *Richard III*, Stroud, 2013, p. 94).

23/11–16. Several sources report these letters both to and from Richard after the death of Edward IV, although none of the letters survives. Mancini (Arm: 70-2, Car: 50-1) heard that the late king's friend and chamberlain William, Lord Hastings, in the throes of a deadly feud with the queen's party, wrote to Richard due to his affinity with him. Mancini also details Richard's letters to the Council, the contents of which seem to have been made publicly known since he records a generally approving reaction in London. The Crowland writer, pp. 154f, makes it appear that Hastings was in communication with Richard and the Duke of Buckingham since he seemed to predict the size of their expected retinues. Polydore, pp. 539f, says Hastings sent to Richard in Yorkshire to tell him of the king's death and to urge him to come to London 'ad rerum omnium cura*m* suscipiendu*m*' [to assume responsibility for everything].

The final will of Edward IV does not survive. His will of 1475 is extant and is transcribed in *Excerpta Historica* (London, 1831), pp. 366-79. Buc accepts Polydore's statement (p. 539) that the king had committed to Richard his wife, children, goods, and everything he had. The Crowland Chronicle (pp. 152f) states that Edward added codicils on his deathbed but does not indicate their content. It records (pp. 156f) that Richard's appointment as protector mirrored the constitutional precedent of sixty years earlier when Humphrey, Duke of Gloucester was appointed Protector of the Realm during Henry VI's minority. In her study of Richard's role as protector in 1483, Annette Carson traces the history of the three protectorates necessitated during the reign of Henry VI (*Richard Duke of Gloucester as Protector and Constable*, pp. 13-22), and argues that as a doctor of law (whether civil or canon is uncertain) the chronicle's author would have known that upon Henry V's death his codicil naming Humphrey as Regent of England was rejected by the King's Council and Parliament on the grounds that he could not rule from beyond the grave. Instead, the Council appointed itself to govern under Parliament and created for Humphrey a new office whose role was to safeguard the security of the kingdom. As confirmed by Parliament, the full title which would apply to Humphrey (in lieu of his brother John, who was not in England) was Regni Anglie et Ecclesie Anglicane Protector et Defensor ac Consiliarius Principalis domini Regis [Protector and Defender of the Realm and Church in England and Principal Councillor of the lord King] (Carson, p. 16, *Rot. Parl.* iv, 174-5). This act appears in *PROME*, X, ed. Anne Curry, Nov. 1422, Parl. 1, Henry VI. The care of the underage king himself was placed *not* in the hands the protector but consigned to a group nominated separately (Carson, pp. 14, 16).

Thus when the King's Council formally appointed Richard Lord Protector of the Realm upon his arrival in London in early May the office implied no responsibility for the wife or children of Edward IV (his goods were already sequestered by his executors). Polydore merely followed the assumptions of earlier chroniclers that Edward IV's will made Richard guardian of his children, something for which we have no evidence, e.g. Mancini (Arm: 70-1, Car: 42-3); John Rous, *Historia Regum Angliae*, 2nd ed., Oxford, 1745, p. 213; Bernard André, *Historia Regis Henrici Septimi*, in *Memorials of King Henry the Seventh*, ed. Gairdner, R.S. 10, London, 1858, p.23). The office of Protector of the Realm being unique to England, all foreign reporters (Mancini, André, Polydore, etc.) mistakenly assumed it was equivalent to the office of Regent with which they were familiar and thus carried wardship of the heir to the throne as well (see Carson, *Richard Duke of Gloucester as Protector and Constable*, p. 55). It seems still to be a general assumption that Richard was protector of Edward's sons. This error has resurfaced again in Chris Skidmore's biography, p. 6 (Richard was 'entrusted as the new king's Protector').

This confusion may also arise because of the draft *pronunciatio* prepared to be given by Edward V's Lord Chancellor, Dr John Russell, at the opening of his post-coronation Parliament, setting out the Council's policy for the administration during the young king's minority. Formulated during the protectorate, it rhetorically denigrates the queen's party and proposes Richard as custodian of both the realm and the minor king (printed in pp. xxxix-lxiii in *Grants, etc., from the Crown during the Reign of Edward the Fifth*, Cam. Soc, 1st ser. 60, London, 1854). This provision did not, of course, come to pass, nor was the speech given, owing to Edward V's deposition.

23/16-17 and 2nd mar. n. Polydore Vergil, p. 539 [he made a will, designating his sons heirs, whom he committed to the guardianship of his brother Richard, Duke of Gloucester].

23/22-26. Davies, *York Records*, 143f, n., states that there is no evidence of this visit by Richard to York. However, Crowland mentions (p. 154f) that Richard made all the nobility of the North swear an oath of fealty to Edward V, first taking the oath himself.

23/41–24/5. Records show that at least as early as 23 May leading members of the King's Council, including the Dukes of Gloucester and Buckingham and the Archbishops of Canterbury and York, made overtures to the Queen Mother to quit sanctuary with her family, saying they were willing to swear an oath, whose terms were read publicly in the City of London Council. These, however, were rebuffed (LMA COL/CC/01/01/009: Journal 9, Court of Common Council, City of London Corporation, transcribed by Carson in *Richard Duke of Gloucester as Protector and Constable*, p. 67). The Tudor chroniclers who follow Thomas More's pathetic account of the Duke of York's removal from sanctuary, *The History of King Richard III*, ed. Richard S. Sylvester, *The Complete Works of St Thomas More*, II, New Haven, 1963) ascribe it entirely to Richard's desire to have both boys in his power so that he could usurp the throne without leaving the Woodville party a prop. The Woodvilles in retaining the Duke of York had, according to More, this specific aim: Rotherham, delivering the Great Seal to Elizabeth Woodville, says, 'if thei crowne any other kinge then your sonne, whome they nowe haue with them, we shal on the morowe crowne his brother whome you haue here with you' (p. 22). However, if Richard was scheming as alleged, he had evidently forgotten the boys' several sisters, who remained with their mother. His opponents were well aware of the opportunity this presented, and during his reign a plot was hatched to send some of the daughters abroad so that the crown might one day return to the 'rightful heirs' (Crowland, pp. 162f). Charles T. Wood, 'The Deposition of Edward V', *Traditio*, 31 (1975), 262f, emphasizes the impossibility of conducting a coronation when division threatened, with the king's mother and brother (the next heir) still claiming sanctuary. That Bourchier was sent by decision of the Council is confirmed by Mancini (Arm: 88f, Car: 62-3) and Crowland (pp. 158f). The latter source confirms that the duke's removal from sanctuary probably occurred on 16 June, after the execution of Hastings: not *before*, as Buc says, following the multiplicity of sources which make this mistake derived from Mancini.

24/9-10. The Tower was not at that time a prison, but London's principal royal palace, garrison, and sanctuary. The repository of the royal treasure and state mint, it was the strongest and safest place in the kingdom. Edward IV used it as a palace, and it was the customary lodging of kings before their coronation. According to Crowland, pp. 156f, Edward's transfer to the Tower was by decision of the King's Council.

24/25-26. Philippe de Commynes, *Mémoires*, ed. Josephe Calmette (Paris, 1924-5), II, 305 [The Duke of Gloucester did homage to his nephew as to his king and sovereign lord].

24/26-28. More's statement, p. 24, is that 'the Duke of Gloucester bare him in open sighte so reuerentelye to the Prince, with all semblance of lowlinesse'.

24/37. The prior of the Crowland Abbey was responsible for the first continuation, not the second. Who wrote the second continuation is not known, though there are now many theories. It was for a long time assumed to be John Russell, Bishop of Lincoln (see Alison Hanham, *Richard III and His Early Historians*, Oxford, 1975, pp. 74-97). Pronay and Cox in their edition (Introduction, pp. 78-96) favour Dr Henry Sharp, while David Baldwin suggests John Gunthorpe in *Elizabeth Woodville* (Stroud, 2002), pp. 162-66. Henry Kelly has settled on Richard Lavender in 'The Last Chroniclers of Croyland', *The Ricardian*, VII (1985), 142-77, while Michael Hicks suggests Richard Langport in 'The Second Anonymous Continuation of the Crowland Abbey Chronicle 1459-88 Revisited', *English Historical Review*, CXXII (2007), 349-70. Hanham in 'The Mysterious Affair at Crowland Abbey' suggests these searches for someone on the outside are a red herring and that the author must have been a monk within the monastery (*The Ricardian*, XVII, 2008, pp. 1-20).

24/38-40. Richard [did not put off or refuse to offer to his nephew, the king, any of the reverence required of a subject such as bared head, bent knee, or any other posture]. This passage (Crowland, pp. 156f), actually starts by saying that Richard was leader of the plot to separate the new king from his mother's relations and supporters but *despite this* showed him signs of duty.

24/42-25/11. See text, pp. 39-45 for an extended version of this solicitation, for which Buc's source is More's *Richard III*.

25/39-27/14. Edward IV died leaving factions behind him. Mancini (whose work was not known to Buc) describes how his elevation of his wife's family had created resentment among the old high nobility (Arm: 68f, Car: 44-5). There have been studies of the Woodvilles and their power, making clear the sense of danger this posed: Michael Hicks regards Edward as extremely unwise in promoting his wife's family to a situation of such power and influence ('The Changing Role of the Wydevilles in Yorkist Politics to 1483', in *Patronage, Pedigree and Power*, pp. 60-86). E.W. Ives, 'Andrew Dymmock and the Papers of Earl Rivers, 1482-1483', *BIHR*, XLI (1966), pp. 216-25 demonstrates how Earl Rivers was an inveterate plotter.

Arrangements were made for Richard to rendezvous at Northampton with Rivers, who was in command of Edward V's 2,000-man army escorting him from Ludlow to London. Consequent upon the attempt by Rivers to frustrate Richard's rendezvous with the king, arrests were made among Edward V's entourage by

Richard exercising powers over military arrays as High Constable. Earl Rivers, Sir Richard Gray and Sir Thomas Vaughan were sent north into custody, the army was dismissed, and the king's escort to London taken on by Gloucester. The Woodville contingent in the capital attempted to raise forces before their arrival, but Mancini reports hostility to them (Arm: 78f, Car: 54-7). The queen took some members of her family into the sanctuary at Westminster Abbey, including her son the Marquess of Dorset. Meanwhile her brother Sir Edward Woodville had emptied the state treasury raising soldiers and a fleet (see *Financial Memoranda of the Reign of Edward V: Longleat Miscellaneous Manuscript Book II,* ed. Rosemary Horrox, Camden Fourth Series Miscellany XXIX, vol. 34, Royal Historical Society, London, 1987, pp. 212f). He then absconded with two ships and £10,250 in gold coin, eventually placing the ships and over £10,000 of state funds at the service of Henry Tudor in Brittany. The queen and her family were now set against the government (see below, 26/47-48). Rivers, Gray and Vaughan were tried at Pontefract by the court of the Earl of Northumberland and executed on 25 June (Rous, p. 213). See Carson, *Richard Duke of Gloucester as Protector and Constable*, pp. 61-7 and 75-6 for a study of Richard's powers to arrest and try (in the Constable's Court) persons caught plotting rebellion, and to sentence without appeal. Some writers complain that he failed to gain authorization from the Council to execute these men, though the Council had no such authority; the conditions of the High Constable's appointment make quite clear that there is no necessity for this formality. Even so, it appears that in this instance the offenders were given a trial presided over by Northumberland.

26/2nd mar. n. The title given More's work here suggests that Buc is referring to its representation in one of the chronicles which have chapters divided by regnal names (Hall, Grafton, Stow, Holinshed). All these authors insert More's work *verbatim* into their composite histories. What More says (p. 14) is that the queen surrounded the prince with her own kin, 'whereby her bloode mighte of youth be rooted in the princes fauor'. He has Richard then object that it was 'vnto vs no litle ieopardy, to suffer our wel proued euil willers, to grow in ouergret authoritie with the prince in youth, namely which is lighte of beliefe and sone perswaded'. If the Woodvilles bring the prince to London with great force they will antagonize the old nobility, 'And thus should all the reame fall on a rore' (p. 16).

26/27–32. More, pp. 10f states that there was dissention between the queen's kindred and Lord Hastings (not between the queen's kindred and the king's blood), which Edward IV tried to reconcile on his deathbed. However, both More and Mancini assume that Richard, before the Woodvilles' attempted coup, harboured resentment of them based on the fate of Clarence. More also states the contrary, i.e. that Richard was secretly not displeased at Clarence's fate. No historical evidence exists for either argument. Richard had spent most of the preceding ten years occupied in the North of England, which left him little opportunity or reason to carry on feuds with Edward IV's courtiers.

26/47–48. More, p. 19: 'they [Gloucester and Buckingham] sayde that the Lorde Marques hadde entered into the Tower of London, and thence taken out the kinges Tresor, and sent menne to the sea. All whiche thinge these Dukes wiste well were done for good purposes and necessari by the whole counsaile at London . . .' Mancini reports a division of the late king's treasure among the Queen Mother, Dorset, and Sir Edward Woodville (Arm: 80f, Car: 56-7). Armstrong, p. 119f, considered this evidence against the Woodvilles, though he felt that putting the fleet to sea was a legitimate strategic measure. However, he was unaware of the evidence, published after his edition of Mancini, in Horrox, 'Financial Memoranda', which showed the Woodvilles' actions as ruinous for an already heavily indebted treasury (Car: p. 99). The Queen persistently refused the solicitations of prominent Council members to leave sanctuary (see above, 23/41–24/5). The Council ordered the fleet to return and disband or be proclaimed enemies of the state, but its Woodville commanders refused (Mancini, Arm: 84-7, Car: 58-61). By the end of May Dorset and Edward Woodville had absconded with money and ships.

26/49-27/1. More, p. 24:

> such of the Dukes seruantes as rode with the cartes of theyr stuffe that were taken (among whiche stuffe no meruayle thoughe somme were harneys . . .) they shewed vnto the people al the waye as they wente: loe here bee the barelles of harneys that this traitours had priuelye conuayd in theyr carryage to destroye the noble lordes with all.

27/15-28/12. More is Buc's source for Hastings's death, the events surrounding which are obscure. More's account is somewhat fanciful, since it has Richard send Catesby to Hastings sounding out whether he will support Richard as potential king. Bearing in mind the difference in their social status, this is not dissimilar to More's scene-setting on the privy for Richard to ask a page to recommend someone to kill the sons of Edward IV. Polydore's version is much more matter-of-fact and observes, according to his usual fashion of ascribing misfortune to divine punishment, that this was Hastings's divinely appointed fate for being one of those who were said to have slain Henry VI's son Edward at Tewkesbury. Mancini (Arm: 90f, Car: 62-5) is the only contemporary account that gives details of the incident, mentioning Richard's public proclamation of an armed attack initiated by Hastings, but claims Richard made it up.

The Cely letters contain a hastily written report of the rumours circulating in the wake of Hastings's death (*The Cely Letters*, *1472-1488*, EETS, London, 1975, pp. 185 and 285-7). The rumours are that the Bishop of Ely is dead, Richard may be in danger, there are fears that the king (Edward V) may be dead and fears for his brother. Editor Alison Hanham interprets this report as written immediately after Hastings's execution and in a note on p. 287 suggests it might reflect rumours put about by Richard's party to suggest 'that Hastings and his companions had taken part in a widespread conspiracy to destroy the protector's party and to seize the persons of the king and his brother'. Records show other co-conspirators were rounded up but only Hastings was executed, the swiftness of which suggests that Richard was acting in his capacity as High Constable, empanelling a summary tribunal to deal with the discovery of an act of treason. See A.F. Sutton, 'The Admiralty and Constableship of England in the Later Fifteenth Century' in *Courts of Chivalry and Admiralty in Late Medieval Europe*, Musson and Ramsay, eds

(2018), p. 205. In such circumstances, during a period when no anointed king wore the crown, the crime would have consisted of conspiring to kill the chief councillor of the ruling government, who also held state offices placing him in charge of the forces constituted to protect the country: thus a treasonous attempt to overthrow the government. An anonymous London citizen summarizes the event: 'ther was divers [*i*]magenyd the deyth of the duke of Glocester, and hit was asspiyed and the Lord Hastinges was takyn in the Towur and byhedyd forthwith, the xiij day of une Anno 1483', transcribed from College of Arms MS. 2M6 by Richard Firth Green in 'Historical Notes of a London Citizen, 1483-1488', *EHR*, XCVI (1981), 588.

One can only speculate on Hastings's motive if he did plan armed action. Much is made by some chroniclers of a supposed (though unlikely) friendship with Richard, now disappointed as Buckingham gained the ascendant, meaning that he feared and resented loss of his former power while lacking the protection of Edward IV. Chris Skidmore suggests, p. 172, he may have been drawn by Mistress Shore to lean toward [his previous enemies] the Woodvilles.

27/22-27. More, p. 46. 'And vndoubtedly the protectour loued him wel, & loth was to haue loste him, sauing for fere lest his life shoulde haue quailed their purpose'. He of course means this ironically.

28/13-16. The defence on grounds of reasons of state Buc probably drew from the whole of Cornwallis's essay, which instead of clearing Richard of the crimes attributed to him grants their existence but finds roundabout ways of justifying them. Cornwallis uses this defence to exculpate Richard when speaking of the alleged destruction of the Edward IV's sons: 'sutch is the difference, betwene the thought*es*, the actions, the dispositions of Princes, and Subiect*es*, that I houlde no Subiecte sufficiantly Iudiciall to Censure them: theire Courses soe vnlike, that what is meete and expedient in a Prince in a lower fortune is vtterly vnmeete, vnexpedient' (p. 19).

28/17. Ogygus, according to the *Oxford Classical Dictionary*, 2nd ed. (Oxford, 1970), p. 748, was 'a primeval king . . . The first Deluge was in his time'. Buc is saying 'since the flood'. Camden also uses the expression.

28/24-25. [To have obtained an ancient kingdom by stealth and fraud is a form of sovereignty]: this is a paraphrase of Seneca, *Thyestes*, 222-24.

28/27-28. Seneca, *Thyestes*, 312-13 [If no one teaches you the ways of fraud and wickedness, kingship will teach them]. Buc, probably quoting from memory, has given the line division incorrectly.

28/39-40. [The way to power is to put up with rivals and suppress adversaries]; *Axiomata Politica* seems no longer extant. It was originally part of Cotton's collection and was evidently a compendium of political maxims. Buc also quotes from it once in the *Commentary*. For further discussion, see above, see pp. cxxviii-cxxxii .

28/40-50. Aristotle, *Politics*, III, viii, 5.

29/24-44. The idea that Richard should be taxed for not killing those he should have destroyed instead of those he was alleged to have killed is derived from Cornwallis, who cites his lenity to the Countess of Richmond and to Stanley, pp. 26-8:

> for though he Cutt of the head of a mighty Conspirator [Buckingham], yet he suffred the Conspiracye to take soe deepe Roote, that, in the end it cutt of his glorey, and ouer shaddowed his greatness . . . would a cruell bloodthirsty Prince haue done so . . .
>
> ....
>
> what Prince could haue done lesse, nay what Kinge would not haue done more, since both the effecte, and the precedent ffeare, are both such inward tormenters, as hard it is to determine w*hi*ch is moste greeuious, soe opposite, soe contrarye to the nature of a prince: beinge borne not to feare, but to be ffeared; that it is most naturall, and most iuste to remoue sutch a teror.

29/29-36. Dr John Morton, Bishop of Ely, according to More who grew up in his household, roused Buckingham to rebellion against Richard (pp. 90-3), then fled to Flanders to aid Henry Tudor. Richard had committed Morton to Buckingham's custody after arresting him as an accomplice of Hastings. He granted him a general pardon in December, 1484 (Harl. 433, f. 89, Horrox and Hammond edition, I, 243). **Christopher Urswick**, an agent of Morton's who bore his messages to Henry Tudor, became chaplain to Henry VII and might have informed More's *Richard III* (Sylvester, Introduction to More, p. lxviii). **Peter Courtenay**, Bishop of Exeter, and his cousin Edward, Earl of Devon, after the failure of 'Buckingham's rebellion' fled to Brittany and joined with Richmond. They were thereupon attainted by Richard. Elizabeth Woodville's son **Thomas, Marquess of Dorset**, who had taken sanctuary after the failure of the Woodville cause and had gone into hiding, also joined in plotting for the rebellion and fled to Brittany after its failure. He was associated with the Courtenays in the attainder, but after Richard had persuaded Elizabeth Woodville to come out of sanctuary in 1484 she wrote to Dorset urging him to return to England and make peace with Richard. This was discovered by Henry's men and he was brought back to Tudor's party. Nevertheless, Richard seems to have trusted in Dorset's good faith, for he omitted his name from his June 1485 proclamation against the rebels, though he had previously included it. Perhaps he had reason for his trust, for the Marquess was imprisoned briefly by Henry VII on his accession. **John de Vere, Earl of Oxford** was an enemy of the house of York, rebelling against Edward IV, who had executed his brother and father, then against Richard III. He aided the rebellion of Warwick and Clarence, taking part in the battle of Barnet, from which he fled. Taken by Edward IV in 1473, he was imprisoned in the castle of Hammes. Richard III made generous provision for his wife (Harl. 433, f. 53[v]). Oxford, having won over his custodian, **Sir James Blount**, escaped from Hammes to join Henry Tudor's expedition and became commander of a large force against Richard at Bosworth. **Walter Hungerford** was attained for his part in 'Buckingham's rebellion', but was pardoned by Richard only to join Henry Tudor at Bosworth. **Sir John Fortescue** was Porter of the Town of Calais and assisted Blount in releasing the Earl of Oxford. He had accompanied Blount on 6 July 1483, on a commission from the French king for the purpose of renewing the treaty between

England and France (*Foedera*, V, Pt. 3, 134f [XII, 1]. On 20 September 1485 Henry VII granted Fortescue the office of Chief Butler of England (*Pat. Rolls*, 1485-1491, p. 8). **Sir Thomas Bourchier** left Brackenbury's contingent along with Hungerford to support Tudor at Bosworth. **Sir John Savage**, **Sir Brian Sandford,** and **Sir Simon Digby** defected from Richard the night before the battle (Polydore, p. 562). **Dr John Morgan** and **Rice (Rhys) ap Thomas** held positions in Wales, the latter being a prominent military leader. They secretly entered Henry's service and assisted him on his landing in Wales. Kendall (*Richard III*, p. 414) suggests that **Sir Gilbert Talbot** deserted for personal causes: his 15 year old nephew, **George, 4th Earl of Shrewsbury** was married to Hastings's daughter, and Richard's revelation of Edward IV's precontract with Lady Eleanor Talbot 'had exposed to the world the shame of his kinswoman' (see p. 256). The earl himself is not known to have deserted. Kendall, p. 569n, mentions his presence on Richard's side at Bosworth (documented from B.L. MS. Harl. 452) and his capture afterwards by Henry, but feels the evidence is inconclusive. Horrox, however, considers it likely that he supported Richard (*Study of Servic*e, p. 224). But see also below, nn. 94/42-3 and 95/2-3. **Reginald Bray** was an instrument of the Countess of Richmond, employed carrying messages for her and acting as her agent in organizing the Kentish leaders associated with 'Buckingham's rebellion'. He was pardoned by Richard but continued secretly to assist Henry Tudor. **Dr Lewis** was a physician in the entourage of the Countess of Richmond employed in carrying messages between her and Elizabeth Woodville. By **Poins**, Buc may refer to Sir Robert Poins, knighted in the field by Henry VII, a member of Henry VII's council and of Henry's forces at Taunton against Perkin Warbeck. But the similarity of this name and that of the much more prominent Sir Edward Poynings in the chronicles suggests he might have confused the two. Poynings escaped to Brittany after 'Buckingham's rebellion' and aided Henry Tudor. Stow (*Annales*, p. 787) notes that knights made by Henry in the field included **Sir John Mortimer** and Sir Robert Poins. By **'young Stanley'**, Buc meant either Sir William Stanley or George, Lord Strange, son of Thomas, Lord Stanley, probably the former. Sir William was directly responsible for Richard's death at Bosworth, holding neutral until the last moment. Having thrown in his lot with Tudor, though nominally loyal to Richard, he was, like his brother, a timeserver, waiting to see how the battle went before acting. When Richard broke from his host to attempt a daring cavalry charge upon Henry and those immediately surrounding him, he rode across Sir William's flank. Sir William cut the king off from his army and descended upon him. Lord Strange, caught deserting, was held during the preparations for the battle as hostage for his father's loyalty. When Lord Stanley continued to refuse Richard's orders to join him in the battle, Richard declared Strange's life forfeit, but the sentence was delayed until after the battle, and Strange, though Crowland reports (p. 177f-8) that he revealed his family's impending treachery, survived to become the subject of Henry Tudor, as did his father and uncle. Most of the supporters in this list can be found in *Pat. Rolls* as recipients of grants and offices under Henry VII.

30/10. *boutefou* = firebrand.

30/23-27. Morton, when he saw that the rebellion was doomed to failure, after stopping briefly at Ely fled not to France but to Flanders and from there communicated with Henry Tudor, forwarding his aims.

30/22. 'Brecknock' is now Brecon.

31/9-38. In this account of Henry's early years Buc mainly follows Polydore, who probably derived the information from Henry himself, as do the other Tudor chroniclers and recent historians. (Scofield II, 19 and 172f and Chrimes, *Henry VII*, London, 1972, pp. 15ff).

Buc has either been careless with his sources or has confused them, or both. Some alterations seem accidental, others designed for effect. He distorts the facts regarding Pembroke's efforts to rescue Henry Tudor: Tudor was in Pembroke, not Raglan Castle, and Pembroke was coming from Tewkesbury, though he had previously been in France. Sir William Herbert had died in 1469. Buc deviates from Polydore to return to his old authority Glover (see below, n. 32, 2nd mar. n.) in the motivation he gives Duke Francis for retaining the Tudors, and places Edward IV's first embassy somewhat later than Francis's private decision to keep them under guard. He adds an extra embassy from Edward by splitting into two parts the one which followed the French peace. The confusion probably arose from the mention of Stillington by the chroniclers (Hall, p. 322, Grafton, Stow, and Holinshed) but not by Polydore. Buc gives the date of the Stillington embassy as 1480, however (text, p. 35), while the chronicles give it as 10 Edward IV (1476). Buc's descriptions of events and motivations are more detailed than Polydore's, and he increases the dramatic effect by reversing the roles of Henry, Landois (whose name is more often given now as 'Landais', 'Landois' being the mediaeval French version) and Chenlet (not 'Chandait', as Buc has it, perhaps confusing him with Philibert de Chandée, who later commanded Henry's Norman recruits) and inventing a scene of indirect discourse. He has compressed into one negotiation Hutton's embassy before Henry's first invasion, which was rejected, and the second, after Henry's return to Brittany, which was accepted, though he escaped.

31/15-18. This is actually Grafton's statement in his continuation to *The Chronicle of John Hardyng*, ed. Henry Ellis (London, 1812), p. 463.

31/33-40. Henry was four years old when he was committed to the custody of Lord Herbert. He was born in January 1457 and captured by Herbert in September 1461.

31/34-37. Commynes, II, 233: 'le1quel m'a autresfoiz compté, peu avant qu'il partist de ce royaulme, que, depuis l'aage de cinq ans, il avoit esté gardé comme fugitif ou en prison' [who once told me shortly before he left this country that since the age of five he had been kept as a fugitive or in prison].

31/42-43 and 32/1st mar. n. An example of incorrect recollection. Stow merely says (*Annales*, p. 707), in an entry under the year 1472, that Pembroke and Richmond fled to Brittany.

32/34-37. [Several of the lords of England who were on the side of King Henry VI fled across the sea out of the realm, and among others the fleeing Earl of Pembroke saved a young prince of England named Henry, Earl of Richmond] Alain Bouchard, *Les Grandes Cronicques de Bretaigne* (n.p., [1517 – publication date given in Buc's hand in Bodleian copy], f. cxcix. The Bodleian copy has an

'X' in the margin at this point. That the quotation suffers virtually no alteration except in spelling probably indicates that Buc was copying directly from the book, which he evidently owned, in process of writing at least an early draft.

32/3rd mar. n. According to Glover, p. 609, John the Valiant, Duke of Brittany and Earl of Montfort and fourth Earl of Richmond (1339?-1399), was the last to hold both titles. This is confirmed by Michael Jones in *ODNB*.

33/13-15. Commynes, II, p. 234 [The duke treated them kindly for prisoners].

33/15-16. [Courteous imprisonment]

33/26-29. [Because of Henry, Earl of Richmond, he did not dare swerve from his friendship with Britain] Johannes Meyer, *Annales Flandriae in Annales, sive Historiae Rerum Belgicarum* (Frankfurt, 1580), Ch. 17, p. 418. Buc's references vary his first name from Johannes to Jacobus. At this point the Editor (his great-nephew George Buck) or his scribe misreads 'Meyerus' as 'Neyerus' and it appears thus in all the manuscript copies and the printed edition.

33/32-33. Commynes, II, 234.

33/48. The word 'politician' was frequently used in a derogatory sense during the late sixteenth and early seventeenth centuries, for example, in *1 Henry IV*, I, iii, Hotspur's reference to the king, "I am whipped and scourged with rods, / Nettled and stung with pismires when I hear / Of this vile politician Bolingbroke'.

34/7-10. Ennius, in Cicero, *De Officiis*, II, vii: 'Quem metuunt oderunt; quem quisque odit perisse expetit'. This is given in Cicero as a single verse line.

35/7-14. Since Polydore gives no dates, it is impossible to say exactly when Edward's overtures were made.

35/1st mar. n. The justification for this statement is probably the passage quoted in text, p. 32 from Bouchard, f. cxcix.

37/35-36. Commynes, II, 233 says around fifteen years, not twelve: 'Ce conte de Richemont avoit esté quinze ans ou environ prisonnier en Bretaigne' [This Earl of Richmond was for around fifteen years a prisoner in Brittany].

37/39. Lucan, *De Bello Civile*, III, 448 [fortune aids many noxious people].

38/1st mar. n. The reference is evidently to Seleucus I. Confusion may have resulted from the fact that this ruler was killed by Ptolemy 'Ceraunus', so called from the Greek for thunderbolt (Gnaeus Trogus Pompeius, *Historiae Philippicae* XVII). The second epithet Lucretius applied to Scipio in *De Rerum Natura*, III, 1034: 'Scipiadas, belli fulmen, Carthaginis horror' [Scipio, thunderbolt of war, terror of the Carthaginians].

38/16-17. Henry the Saint is Henry VI, for whose canonization Henry VII applied (Polydore, p. 532). Thomas Penn in his recent biography of Henry VII, speaks of Henry VI's 'helpless diffidence – which Henry VII was now reinventing as a saintlike passivity . . .' (p. 180). The prophecy appears in Polydore, p. 522: 'Iste nempe iste est, cui nos ac nostri aduersarij rerum possessione cedemus' [This surely, this is he to whom we and our adversaries shall yield possession].

38-46. B.P. Wolffe and Charles T. Wood ('The Deposition of Edward IV') have stressed that knowledge of later events must not make us too ready, as were the Tudor chroniclers, to see in events preceding the deposition a carefully planned scheme by Richard to take the throne: self protection and desire to extend his protectorship after the coronation would have been his first considerations. But that he should eventually seek the throne was logical: although there was 'a strong predilection' for primogeniture, Richard, Duke of York in being named heir to the throne had bypassed Henry VI's son; Edward IV twice took the throne from Henry VI; and the Duke of Clarence tried to take it from Edward IV.

> usurpation by the strongest and ablest male member of the larger royal family became almost the norm. From 1399 special 'inauguration ceremonies', by which the king performed every kind of royal act prior to his coronation, were designed to convert usurpation into valid authority. The office of king was a very exacting one. Its holder had to be physically tough, able to win battles and campaigns, with a commanding presence and integrity; able to inspire loyalty, service and confidence.
> (Wolffe, *Yorkist and Early Tudor Government*, London, 1960, p. 6)

Because no law governed succession, the strongest claimant could make his own case. First Clarence attempted to seize the throne by circulating a story that Edward IV was a bastard and not fit to reign. (*PROME*, ed. Rosemary Horrox, XIV, Appendix, p. 402, from TNA C49/40). Richard's claim relied equally on bastardy, this time of the assumed heirs by primogeniture. Both brothers thus attempted to maintain the Yorkist platform of legitimism by which their father had claimed the throne. Richard then had his election by the Three Estates ratified by Parliament, thus making his title doubly sure according to public authority. (S.B. Chrimes, *English Constitutional Ideas in the Fifteenth Century*, Cambridge, 1936 *passim*; Wood, *passim*). The formal steps Richard took in his accession closely followed his brother's precedent, according to C.A.J. Armstrong, 'Inauguration Ceremonies of the Yorkist Kings and Their Title to the Throne', *Transactions of the Royal Historical Society*, 4th ser., XXX (1948), 51-73: (1) popular petition, (2) formal protest, (3) political sermon at Paul's Cross, (4) the people's assent to his accession, (5) the act of sitting in the King's Bench, (6) addressing the judges, and making a symbolic gesture of pardon all followed Edward's pattern. Wood stresses the importance to Richard's claim of its ratification by Parliament.

As the most powerful and experienced magnate in England it would have been surprising had the assumption of the throne not been a possibility Richard considered. But the question is whether he did so only when pushed to the limit by danger to himself and to government stability or whether it was the result of pure ambition, or a combination of the two, and it seems unlikely anyone will ever know for certain. These two sides have been argued for centuries, and conclusions expressed with the goal posts set in different places. Annette Carson expresses most clearly the arguments for his being compelled to assume the crown because of Woodville pursuit of power (see *The Maligned King,* Chs. 3-6, for a clear and readable overview, also *Richard Duke of Gloucester as Protector and Constable*, the first detailed and comprehensive study of the powers of the two offices Richard held). A.J. Pollard in *Richard III and the Princes in the Tower*, Stroud, 1991, pp. 90-106, presents the opposing argument, that Richard usurped the throne from pure ambition, having planned it from the start, though, he points out, 'We tend to favour a conspiratorial theory of the past, where often a "cock-up" theory might be more applicable. Did Richard III mastermind a brilliantly conceived *coup d'état*? Or did it all happen in confusion, ignorance and fear?' (p. 101).

38/42. Genesis 21:10.

38/5th mar. n. Buc's disclaimer of responsibility resembles Cornwallis's closely (see above, n. 3/14). It is interesting that at this late date Buc should feel compelled to protect himself against the charge of attacking the Tudors. Indeed nearly twenty years later his plagiarizing great-nephew considerably watered down the original work's attacks on the Tudors before publication of a shortened version of it as his own. Since James I was descended from Edward IV's daughter, the allegation of illegitimacy could not be expected to please him. For Buc's general attitude toward James and the Tudors, see above, pp. cxlv-cxlviii.

38/47-39/6. For the statement regarding the general consent to Richard's title, Buc is relying entirely on *Titulus Regius* (*PROME*, Richard III: Jan. 1484, XV, 14-17), which he takes at face value, and on his reading of More, which disregards the irony. Rosemary Horrox in 'Richard III and London' (*The Ricardian*, VI, 1984, 322-29) suggests that everyone acquiesced because his accession seemed likeliest to preserve the status quo (p. 325), noting that the London chroniclers writing under Henry VII would have had to be silent about any general sense of support (p. 324). She points out that 'the Woodvilles remaining in the city attempted to whip up armed resistance, and their failure must reflect the attitude of the city as well as that of the political establishment' (p. 325). The evidence of the only two contemporary sources, Mancini and Crowland, is that the measures taken by Richard leading to his assumption of the throne had the full assent of the King's Council, who had already formulated the speech to Parliament to be given by the Lord Chancellor, Dr John Russell, proposing that Richard continue as Protector, while denigrating his opponents, the Woodvilles (*Grants, etc. from the Crown,* pp. xxxix-xlviii). The Three Estates then petitioned him to take the throne. In addition, there was a remarkably full attendance at his coronation. The troops he had sent for from the North were still in progress of being mustered, so he had no army at his disposal and no other means to force these magnates to side with him. As Buc says, if Richard schemed the taking of the crown, the great men of the realm were complicit (text, p. 45).

39-45. This account is taken, with some liberties, from More, pp. 73-80; Holinshed, III,, 390-6; Grafton, II, 107-112; Stow, *Annales*, pp. 758-65; and Hall, pp. 369-74. The reference to Morton as the first of the chroniclers follows the assumption, discussed above pp. cxxii-cxxiii and cxlvi that Morton was the author of a pamphlet which formed the basis of More's work on Richard. See also A.N. Kincaid, 'Sir Edward Hoby and "K. Richard": Shakespeare Play or Morton Tract?', *Notes and Queries*, XXVIII (1981), 124-6. And see Daniel Kinney in his edition of Thomas More's Latin text, *Historia Richardi Tertii*, Introduction, pp. cxxxvif, where he says Hoby

> may well have examined a Latin tract very similar to More's English history around 1595 and . . . have heard from its owner, More's grandson Thomas Roper, that it was not More's work but Morton's. . . . We may trust

> Hoby's conceivably eyewitness-account of the manuscript without accepting his hearsay account of its provenance according to More's grandson Roper, who may . . . have gotten two manuscripts confused or else made far too much of an old family rumor that More's work was based on a document by Morton. . . . [W]e can safely assume that the Latin history is More's, whether or not he had access to any notes about Richard by Morton.

39/21-22. Richard's descent into the Great Chamber is an addition of Buc's. More, whose account he follows in this scene, has Richard listen to Buckingham's address from a balcony of Baynard's Castle. Buc obviously has his own dramatic image, for he sees Richard sitting down when he enters the chamber and standing to answer Buckingham's address. See Baker, pp. 336f for analysis of Buc's use of his version of these events to erase from the Tudor story 'any traces of the discreditable origins of the Act of Settlement'.

39/37-40/40. The speech Buc has Buckingham address to Richard is an abbreviated version of Buckingham's earlier oration to the Mayor and citizens, pp. 72-4. He presumably makes this substitution because the former speech is more detailed and, being in direct discourse, more dramatic. He substitutes Lady Eleanor Butler for More's incorrect citation of Elizabeth Lucy as Edward's first wife.

39/43-49. During Richard, Duke of Gloucester's protectorate, at some time before early June 1483, the news came to light that when Edward IV secretly married Elizabeth Woodville in 1464 he was already secretly married to the still living Lady Eleanor Talbot, widow of Sir Thomas Butler and daughter of the 'Great Talbot', the Earl of Shrewsbury. She is identified in Crowland (p. 160) and *PROME*, Richard III: Jan. 1484, XV, 15. Commynes attributes the revelation to Robert Stillington, Bishop of Bath and Wells and Edward's former Lord Chancellor, who conducted the marriage and confirmed that it had been consummated (II, Bk. V, ch. 20, p. 232 and Bk. VI, ch. 8, p. 305). H.A. Kelly, 'The Case against Edward IV's Marriage and Offspring: Secrecy; Witchcraft; Secrecy; Precontract', *The Ricardian*, XI, 1998, 327, states: '"Precontract" . . . means *previous marriage*, when alleged as a challenge to a subsequent marriage'. He repeats this in *Ricardian Bulletin,* Spring 2007, p. 30: 'a precontract was a "previous marriage to someone else"'. This is a corrective to the common assumption that the term referred merely to a betrothal. (Curiously, Chris Skidmore's new book ignores all the learned articles on the technicalities of Edward's marriage and reverts to the old assumption that a precontract was a betrothal.)

A letter written by Simon Stallworth, a member of Chancellor John Russell's staff, reported on 9 June that 'My lord Protector, my lord of Bukyngham with all othyr lordys, as well temporale as spirituale, were at Westm. in *th*e councel chamber from x to ij, but ther was none *th*at spake with *th*e Qwene. *Th*er is gret besyness ageyns *th*e coronacion . . .'. (letter 330, *The Stonor Letters and Papers*, 1290-1483, ed. Charles Lethbridge Kingsford, Cam. Soc., 3rd ser. 29 and 30, London, 1919), II, 160. By 17 June the council had decided to postpone Edward

V's coronation to 9 November. This can only have been to give them time to consider the new evidence of the heir apparent's illegitimacy.

On 26 June a petition was presented to Gloucester 'on the behalve and in the name of the thre estates of this reame of England' (*PROME*, Richard III: Jan. 1484, XV, pp, 13f) urging him to accept the crown. Richard III's Act of Succession, passed in January 1484, recorded the words of the petition and confirmed that Edward IV's Woodville offspring had been rendered illegitimate due to their father's marriage with Elizabeth Woodville being both bigamous and secret. It also stated that the court of Parliament carried such authority that 'the manifestacion and declaracion of any trueth or right made by the thre estates of this realm assembled in parliament . . . maketh, before all other thynges, moost feith \and certaynte/' (*PROME*, Richard III: Jan. 1484, XXV, 17). Historians' opinions are divided on the precontract. Ross considered it a political invention (*Richard III*, pp. 89f), while Gairdner (surprisingly) had maintained there were insufficient grounds for this view (*Richard III*, p. 91). Hanham, *Early Historians*, claims the Crowland Chronicle 'makes it clear that the petition referring to Edward's alleged marriage with Eleanor Butler was fraudulent' (p. 97), but all it makes clear is that the author of it thought it fraudulent. For the position in canon law see Helmholz. For the authority of Parliament see Chrimes, *English Constitutional Ideas*, p. 22.

39/4th mar. n. Richard's Act of Succession (*Titulus Regius*) was repealed by Henry VII and ordered to be destroyed. William Campbell says of this:

> This hatred of the rival House is the key to very much of his future action as king. He never seemed to be weary of branding the names of Yorkists, and their supporters, with the gravest charges of rebelliousness and want of patriotism, and . . . the name of the late king is never mentioned by him without the favorite iteration of 'king in dede, but not in right'. The state scriveners seem to have received a standing order to introduce this hateful formula to every paper connected with Richard's name, however insignificant. . . . He must have perceived that the 'fiery Richard' . . . would have been a formidable rival to him in the memory of the nation.
>
> *Materials for a History of the Reign of Henry VII* (London: 1873, 1877), I, xiii-xiv.

This is Henry VII's order to destroy the Titulus Regius, registered in Parliament:

> The kyng, at the speciall instance, desire and prayer of the lordes spirituall and temporall and the comons . . . woll it be ordeyned, stablisshed and enacted, . . . that the seid bill, acte and ratificacion, . . . for the false and cedicious ymagynacion and untrouth therof, be voide, adnulled, repelled, irrite and of non effecte nor force. And that it be ordeyned by the seid auctorite that the seid byll be cancelled, destrued and that the seid acte, recorde and enrollyng shalbe taken and avoided oute of the rolle and

> recordes of the seid parlement of the seid late kyng, and brent and utterly destroyed. And . . . that every persone havyng any copy or remembrauncez of the seid bill or acte brynge unto the chauncellor of Englond . . . the same copies and remembrauncez, or otherwise utterly destrue theym, afore the fest of Ester next commyng, upon payne of emprisonement . . . so that all thynges seid and remembred in the seid bill and acte therof may be for ever out of remembraunce and forgete.
> *PROME,* Henry VII, Nov. 1485, XV, 134.

Buc and his fellow antiquaries saw a copy from Parliament Rolls in the late sixteenth century and were thus aware that More's *Richard III* was incorrect in naming the lady of the precontract 'Elizabeth Lucy'. *Titulus Regius* (XV, 15) and Crowland, pp. 160f both cite Eleanor Butler (née Talbot) as the woman to whom Edward was precontracted. More and his imitators who reproduce the account of Edward's marriage call the woman Elizabeth Lucy, one of Edward's early mistresses (though probably her name was not Elizabeth), who for a long time was thought to have been the mother of his illegitimate son Arthur Wayte, later Lord Lisle, an identification Buc accepts. Edward does appear to have had a mistress surnamed Lucy in his bachelor days and seems to have had a child with her, a daughter. It appears that she had no connections to the Wayte family and also that Arthur Wayte was born much too late for a bachelor liaison to have resulted in his birth. Thus two mistresses seem to have been conflated. See Marie Barnfield and Stephen Lark, 'The Paternity of Lady Lumley, Some New Evidence', *The Ricardian*, XXVI (2016), 113-20, and Erratum, XXVII (2017), 223.

The inquisition in which 'Elizabeth Lucy' denies she was ever contracted to Edward is an invention of More's (More, p. 65). The whole affair is minimized as a desperate measure on the part of the king's mother to stop the Woodville match by arguing that Edward was Dame Lucy's husband before God because he had got her with child (pp. 64f):

> *By reson of which wordes, such obstacle was made in the mater,* that either y[e] Bishoppes durst not, or the king would not, procede to the solempnisacion of this weding, til these same wer clerely purged, & the trouth wel & openly testified. Whereupon dame Elysabeth Lucy was sent for. And albeit y[t] she was by y[e] kinges mother & many other put in good comfort, to affirme that she was ensured vnto y[e] king: yet when she was solempnely sworne to say the trouth, she confessed that they were neuer ensured.

Two purposes were thereby served: the precontract basis of Richard's claim was shown to be without foundation, and Arthur Plantagenet, thought to be her son, was, rather than the children of Edward IV, proven illegitimate, thus without claim to the throne. Buc was the first author to use the Crowland Chronicle, which gives the correct name of the woman to whom Edward was precontracted.

Helmholz examines the legal aspects of the precontract in 'The Sons of Edward

IV' and concludes that the determination that the princes were illegitimate was legally valid. He advises historians 'to avoid rejecting out of hand the claim of illegitimacy put onto the Rolls of Parliament', saying that the tendency to reject it 'is more a product of modern habits of thought than it is the result of study of the law applicable at the time. . . . Under that law the Parliamentary claim stated a legitimate cause of action' (p. 120).

It may be interesting to note that Buc's dedicatee, the Earl of Arundel, was married to Alethea Talbot, a descendant of the same family as Eleanor, Edward IV's first wife.

41/17-42/1. This speech is constructed, using much of More's phraseology, from More's report of Richard's reply (pp. 78ff).

42/18. [stored deep in the mind]

43/8. [last farewell]

43/9-44. This second attempt is Buc's own addition, as is the Lord Mayor's speech. Buc's version of Buckingham's final speech is expanded from More's text, and in it he deviates further from More's wording than he has in previous portions of the account.

43/50-44/3. More, p. 79: 'These wordes muche moued the protectoure, whiche els as euery manne may witte, would neuer of likelyhoode haue inclyned therunto'. More, of course, meant this to be ironic. But the protestations attributed to Richard would in fact have been, as More has the populace assume, a matter or form. His father's formal protestations when granted the Protectorship under Henry VI may be seen in *PROME* XII, ed. Anne Curry and Rosemary Horrox, Henry VI: Mar., 1453, 259f.

44/1-2. More means this ironically.

44/8. [evil genius]

44/9. The reference to the Earl of Richmond is Buc's interpretation of More's words, p. 79: 'If he woulde geue them a resolute aunswere to the contrarye, whyche they woulde bee lothe to heare, than muste they needes seke and shold not faile to fynd some other noble manne that woulde'.

44/17. This speech is very much expanded and inflated in style from the speech More gives to Richard, pp. 79f.

44/49-45/2. If Richard had lived long enough it is possible he might have renewed the war with France. He had stood out strongly against his brother Edward in the latter's decision to accept a peace and take his army home in 1475. In using the war with France as part of his platform, he would have been following the precedent of his father, who adopted the name 'Plantagenet' on the surrender of Maine and Anjou. Montague Rhodes James, *A Descriptive Catalogue of the Manuscripts in the Library of Lambeth Palace* (Cambridge, 1930-2), no. 506, registers a book, William Worcester's *Collections on Normandy*, which includes a prefatory letter addressed by Worcester's son to Edward IV. However, it appears to have been originally addressed to Richard III and the name altered by erasure. It mentions the king's (presumably Richard's) intention to war with France. Queen Isabella wrote to Richard on his accession to propose alliance against France but although he responded with friendship, he did not mention France (*Letters and Papers Illustrative of the Reigns of Richard III and Henry VII*, ed. James Gairdner,

R.S. 24 (London, 1861-3, I. 31-51.)

45/12. [let there be reverence in the speech]

45/14. [or both]

45/19-20. Richard's claim was ratified in Parliament on 23 January 1484 (*PROME,* Richard III: Jan. 1484, XIV, 14-17). This is one of several examples of Buc's upholding the authority of Parliament, an important contemporary problem. Like Buc more than three hundred years before, William Huse Dunham and Charles T. Wood in 'The Right to Rule England', *American Historical Review*, LXXXI (1976), 738-61 stress the importance of the proceedings surrounding Richard's accession in exalting Parliamentary authority (*passim*). They go so far as to say, 'No king of England did so much – on paper – as did Richard III to raise parliament's position in the frame of government' (p.758): his need to have his election ratified showed that its 'authority now derived from that of the kingdom; and hence that in politics, if not in law, that body had become transcendent' (p. 761). David Weil Baker discusses this justification of Parliament by Camden, Buc and Speed and the concomitant attempt to improve Richard III's reputation as an important aspect of seventeenth century antiquarianism (see above, p. xlviii).

45/26-30. This suggestion of a petition sent from the North during the protectorate originates with Crowland (pp. 160f: 'Divulgatum enim tunc erat quod rotulus iste in partibus borealibus . . . conceptus fuit' [It was put about that this roll orriginated in the North . . .]. The extant evidence of Richard's dealing with the North is in the form of urgent letters, one on 10 June to the City of York (Davies, pp. 148-50). He gives as his motive for these requests the plots of 'the Quiene, hir blode adherent*es* and affinitie, which have entended, and daly doith intend, to murder and utt*er*ly destroy us & our co^u^syn the duc of Bukkyngham, and the old royall blode of this realme' (Davies, p. 149). Rumours of intimidating numbers of men were soon circulating, although the force when it arrived was in the region of only 4,000 and did not reach London until around 4 July. Richard's letters could not have produced troops in the capital before the end of June at the earliest, i.e. a week after the scheduled coronation and Parliament (22/25 June), by which time large numbers of magnates with their retinues were expected to be present (Mancini, Arm: 94–5, Car: 66-7). Horrox in *Study of Service*, p. 130 points out that 'The northern reinforcements were not a private army but summoned to aid the protector against insurrection'. It is in this context that Richard's alleged intentions of using troops to intimidate the London populace during a takeover need to be considered.

45/40-46 and mar. n. For a similar disclaimer by the author, see text p. 38, 5th mar. n. Cornwallis feels a similar fear in setting forth so unpopular an opinion and one which challenges the claim of the ruling house: '. . . I neuer had taken sutch paines to defend his Innocency, nor in some Iudgement*es* to Indainger my owne' (p. 29).

45/47-46/1. That Richard took possession of the marble seat in Westminster Hall on 26 June is attested by Crowland, pp.158f, More, p. 82, and confirmed by a document of 28 June in Harl. 433, f. 238 (see below n. 46/3-16). Armstrong's n. 100 to Mancini, p. 97, dates the assembly petitioning Richard to take the throne 25 June and the beginning of his reign 26 June. Since this seat was the official chair of the king in his role as dispenser of justice, it was probably at this time that Richard, as More relates (p. 81), lectured his officers on justice and administration of the law and pardoned John Fogg. It has been noted above how this ceremony followed precedents in previous coronations (n. to pp. 38-46, above).

46/3-16. Crowland, p. 158-61: The translation given here is of the excerpt as it stands in the Chronicle: [Richard, the protector, claimed for himself the government of the kingdom with the name and title of king; and on the same day in the great hall of Westminster he thrust himself into the marble chair. The pretext of this intrusion and for taking possession in this way was contained in a certain parchment roll, that King Edward's sons were bastards, by submitting that he had been precontracted to a certain Lady Eleanor Boteler before he married Queen Elizabeth, and, further, that the blood of his other brother, George, duke of Clarence, had been attainted so that, at the time, no certain and uncorrupt blood of the lineage of Richard, duke of York, was to be found except in the person of the said Richard, duke of Gloucester. At the end of this roll, therefore, on behalf of the lords and commonalty of the kingdom, he was besought to assume his lawful rights]. Buc makes some changes, both to clarify and to soften the attitude to Richard (changing 'intrusit' to 'immisit' in l. 3). Buc interestingly seems to approve the assumption that the petition came from the North (see n. 45/30, above).

Because we no longer have the manuscript Buc used, we cannot tell to what extent the differences between his and the above version are the result of his making changes to reduce derogatory implications for Richard. That he can be seen throughout this work to do this on occasion where it is more possible to check suggests the alterations are his. However, his addition of 'et tum mox omnibus proceribus tam laicis quam ecclesiasticis et ceteris assidentibus et astanti us' [and then soon by all the nobility, lay and clerical and others seated and standing] seems too long to be accounted for by deliberate rewriting (for which, anyway, there seems insufficient motive) and may have been in the manuscript he used. There is evidence of its accuracy in Harl. 433, f. 238, which calls the attention of the king's officers in Calais to Richard's accession:

> Whose sure & true title is evidently shewed & declared in a bille of peticione whiche the lordes spirtuelx & temporelx and the commons of this land / solemplye porrected unto the kinges highnes at London, the xxvj[ti] day of Juyne Whereupon the kinges said highnes notably assisted by welle nere alle the lordes spirituelle & temporelle of this Royaulme went the same day unto his palais of Westminstre / and there in suche Roialle honorable appareilled within the gret halle there toke possessione / and declared his mynde that the same day he wold begyne to Reigne upon his people /
>
> (Harl. 433, Horrox and Hammond ed., III, 29.)

46/22-50/36. Detailed records of Richard's coronation, based on all available contemporary sources, are set forth in Sutton and Hammond, *The Coronation.*

46/30-31. Camden, *Britannia*, p. 261 [He was most worthy to reign, and to have been numbered not among bad but among good princes for his wisdom] Holland trans., p. 371. See Introduction, p. cx for erroneous assertions that this quotation did not exist in Camden.

46/42-43. Howard was knighted at Towton, 29 March 1461, by Edward IV and created Lord Howard before 4 March 1470, when he is first documented as 'lord Howard', CSP, 1467-1474, p. 204.

46/47-48. Buc refers to Thomas of Brotherton (b. 1300), fifth son of Edward I.

46/50-47/2. I have not located this precise copy of the warrant. For notice of other copies, see below, n. 57/27-30.

47/6-7. Kendall, *Richard III*, p. 551n compiled evidence to show that Stanley was released almost immediately. It is possible that he was never formally arrested or perhaps only briefly kept under observation. Richard allowed him to carry the mace of High Constable at his coronation (*Coronation*, p. 249 attributes this honour to Richard's need for Stanley's support; see also pp. 37, 276, 399). He also carried the king's sword (*Coronation*, p. 217, which is identified as a particular honour, p. 249). He was steward at the banquet afterwards (p. 45): *Coronation*, p. 259, n. 36 says 'It seems that Surrey was . . . Steward of the Household at the time of the coronation. He certainly was later'. This is the office Stanley had held under Edward IV. His appointment after the death of the Duke of Buckingham, who held it previously, to the Constableship for life at the annual fee of £100 is given in *Pat. Rolls* (1476-85), p. 367, 18 Nov. 1483.

47/10-11. This reference is not in More. Buc has failed to note where the More section copied *verbatim* into the chronicles ends.

47/15–18. Rotherham was Archbishop of York, not Canterbury. In the panic of Elizabeth Woodville's retreat into sanctuary at Westminster prior to Richard's arrival with the king, More (p. 22) describes Rotherham rashly (and illegally) handing her the Great Seal and later, regretting his foolishness, retrieving it. He remained a member of the protectorate Council but lost his position as Chancellor, which was given to Dr John Russell, Bishop of Lincoln (More, p. 25, Mancini, Arm: 84f, Car: 58-9). Rotherham was one of the conspirators arrested on 13 June, along with Hastings and Morton, among the ringleaders mentioned by Mancini as having met together in each other's houses (Arm: 90f, Car: 62-3). His collusion with the Woodvilles is beyond question and his offences, admitted by all authorities, considerable, yet Richard soon released him and he was present at the investiture of Richard's son as Prince of Wales on 8 September 1483.

47/19. The 'old Order' is that of the Garter, established under Edward III. The 'new Order' is that of the Bath, which took on its name and procedure at the coronation of Henry IV.

47/23-33. All existing representations of this list, printed or in manuscript, are in the order Buc follows. B.L. MS. Harl. 1386, ff. 16-16^{v} and 2115, f. 124 (the latter is printed in *Excerpta Historica*, p. 384), as well as College of Arms I.18, seem to be copies of the manuscript source, probably once in the College of Arms, from which Grafton took his account of Richard's coronation. **Henry Neville**: the son and heir to the Lord Abergavenny was actually George Neville. The name is given in Grafton, II, 113 and Holinshed, III, 298 and in the manuscripts listed above as Sir Henry 'Aburgauennie', 'Burgany' or 'Burgaveny'. Buc's form may indicate that he used another manuscript in addition to the chronicles. **Henry Baynton**: this name is given in Grafton, II, 113, as 'Banington'; in Holinshed, III, 398 and in Harl. 1386 as 'Babington', and in Harl. 2115 and Coll. of Arms I, 18 as 'barington'. **Breus of Clifton** (corrected to 'Jarvis' in Additional and 'Gervoise' in the printed version of the *History* edited by Buc's great-nephew). All printed sources except Grafton give this name as 'Gervais of Clifton', Harl. 1386 gives 'Jervis', but it is difficult to read, and Harl 2115 and Coll. Arms I.18 give 'denys', which is equally difficult to read. **Thomas of Vernon**: printed sources give this as 'Vrmon', Harl. 1386 as 'Vrmonde', and Harl. 2115 and Coll. Arms I.18 as 'Ormond'. Buc first wrote 'Vermon', probably trying to make sense of 'Vrmon', and replaced it, through inaccurate guesswork, with 'Vernon'.

47/47-49. Richard became king in the 22nd, not the 25th year of Louis XI, who succeeded in 1461. The dates 19 and 20 June given by Grafton are incorrect. See nn. 45/47-46/1 and 46/3-16 above.

48/1st mar. n. More mentions the coronation on p. 82, but gives no detail. Buc follows Grafton, II, 113-16 in very close paraphrase. The first appearance of this description was on pp. 516-18 of Grafton's continuation of Hardyng, the source of all the chroniclers' accounts of the coronation. Hall, pp. 375-6 follows Grafton. Then Polydore, p. 546, who is normally Grafton's main source where More is not, gives no detail. Crowland, p. 158f, gives no detail, stating only that Richard took the chair in Westminster on 26 June and was crowned on 6 July. Holinshed, III, pp. 397-400, follows Grafton's account with a few omissions which Buc does not share. Stow's account, *Annales*, p. 766f, ends after the description of the events of 6 July. Buc's deviations from Grafton are minor: Buc's 'Archbishop Cardinal' is merely 'the Byshop' in Grafton II, 116. Of those attending on the king at the coronation, Grafton (II, 113-15) gives a complete list. Their number, which Buc rounds off to eighty, is seventy-seven.

The Coronation does not mention 19 and 20 June as significant dates in Richard's bid for the crown. The petition to accept it was presented to him on 26 June, after which he was escorted to the Palace of Westminster. On 4 July the king and queen progressed to the Tower, possibly attended by pageantry, it is uncertain whether by land or water. On 5 July Richard created Knights of the Bath, then rode from the Tower with his queen, processing to Westminster where they spent the night before the coronation. The details Buc gives are similar to those given in Sutton and Hammond's *Coronation,* apart from the fact that there it is assumed more likely the king was anointed and crowned first, then the queen.

48/2nd mar. n. There is no such reference in Enguerran de Monstrelet, *Chroniques* (Paris, 1595). Buc several times makes the mistake of citing references to Howard in Monstrelet. There is a reference in Commynes, II, 241.

48/10-11. Richard created his son Edward Prince of Wales on 28 June 1483 (Harl. 433, Horrox and Hammond edition, I, 81f. The investiture occurred on 8 September the same year. Annette Carson and Marie Barnfield ('Edward of Middleham's Birth', *Ricardian Bulletin*, Sept., 2016, 51-3) establish Edward's birth year as 1476, which would make him seven at the time of this creation. The incorrect dating here comes from Grafton, II, 113.

48/18-20. See nn. 47/6-7 and 47/15-18.

48/33-34. The list given in B.L. MS. Add. 6113, f. 19, as printed in *Coronation*, pp. 270-74, mentions 3 dukes, 32 earls, 87 knights, and 16 Knights of the Bath. But we have no way of knowing whether all these were in the procession or whether this was the total at the coronation.

The proclamation against Buckingham on 23 October 1483 (*Foedera*, V, Pt. 3, 138 [XII, 204]) gives more detail of Richard's judicial policy during and soon after his coronation:

> Forasmuch as the King . . . remembryng his solempne Profession which he made at the tyme of his Coronation to Mercy and Justice, and folowyng the same in dede; first beganne at Mercy in yevyng unto all maner Personnes his Full and Generall Pardon, trustyng therby to have caused all his Subgettes to have be surely Determyned unto hym according to the Duety of their Ligeance; and eft son his Grace, in his owne Person, as is well knowen, hath dressed himselfe to divers Parties of this Reame for the indifferent Admynystracion of Justice to every Person, havyng full Confidence and Trust that all Oppressours and Extortioners of his Subjectes, orible Adultres and Bawdes, provokyng the high Indignation and Displeasure of God, shuld have be reconsiled and reduced to the wey of Trouth and Vertue, with the abiding in good Disposition.

50/3. Here and on p. 57, l. 5, Buc erroneously gives Sir Robert Percy's name as 'Thomas'.

50/mar. n. This is not in More. It appears in Hall, p. 376 and Holinshed, III, 400. Spiritual lords and religious worship are not mentioned.

50/45-51/6. [Sitting on high, with such speeches he addressed his ministers of law and justice: Moses, persuasive in counsel, with his father-in-law Jethro, because he could not compound the strife of the people alone, established among the people prefects and tribunes. Thus with me when the tremendous cares of rule oppress me, the uncomfortable reward of great responsibilities. And the first among you must contain wicked rebellion, weigh cases with equal justice, not spurning the citizen who is wretched because of poverty; prayers do not secure the orphan against the winds; finally generosity, lest injustice corrupt you, etc.] This poem is extant in manuscript, with the author's corrections, in B.L. MS. Cotton Julius C.II, ff. 97-263: 'Historia Anglicana Heroico Carmine co*n*scripta authore Joanne Herdo medicinae doctore' ['English History in Heroic Song written by author John Herd, doctor of medicine']. It was no doubt part of Cotton's collection when Buc used it. This section appears on f. 182 at the beginning of 'Historia Richardi tertij'. The first line Buc gives does not exist in the original, but only a suggestion of it in the words, 'In solioque sedet'. In l. 7 the original has 'Sed' where Buc's Editor (his great-nephew) gives 'Et', and the words 'a vobis' are substituted by Buc for something completely illegible in the original. Buc evidently copied the passage with the work in front of him, since he follows it so closely.

51/7-52/3. See Rhoda Edwards, *Itinerary of Richard III* (London, 1983), which gives Richard's whole four-month itinerary with maps. Buc varies slightly, for example reversing Woodstock and Oxford. Rous says the progress was accompanied 'clamore populi' [with popular acclaim] (p. 216), and Dr Thomas Langton, Bishop of St David's, who accompanied Richard on his progress, wrote in a private letter,

> He contents the people wher he goys best that ever did prince; for many a poor man that hath suffred wrong many days have be relevyd and helped by hym and his commands in his progresse. And in many grete citeis and townis wer grete summis of mony gif hym which he hath refusyd. On my trouth I lykyd never the condicions of ony prince so wel as his: God hathe sent hym to us for the wele of us al.
> *Christ Church Letters*, ed. J.B. Sheppard, Cam. Soc., 2nd Ser. 19
> (London, 1877), p. 46.

51/12-13. The fresh air and green woods and red and fallow deer are an example of seventeenth-century embellishment. They have no origin in Buc's sources.

51/15-16. On 22 July, the founder of Magdalen College, William Wayneflete, Bishop of Winchester, came to receive King Richard. On 24 July he was received by the Chancellor (Lionel Woodville, Bishop of Salisbury, no longer in sanctuary), the Regents, and the Founder and brought to Magdalen, where he spent the night. On 25 July two disputations were presented before the king, in which William Grocyn participated, and Richard rewarded the disputants (William Dunn Macray, *A Register of the Members of St. Mary Magdalen College, Oxford*, new ser. I, London, 1894, pp. 11f).

51/17-21. This information about Gloucester comes from *Arrivall,* p. 26f by way of Holinshed, III, 317, who probably draws it from Polydore, p. 529f. Queen Margaret's forces on the way to Gloucester were prevented from entering by Edward IV's messengers. The story is repeated, text, p. 136.

51/26-30. This ceremony, according to the chronicles and to Rous (p. 217), was not a second coronation, but rather the investiture of Richard's son Edward as Prince of Wales amid great splendour and acclamation (see above n. 48/10-11). Only Crowland (pp. 160f) speaks of it as a second coronation, presumably ironically. Davies (p. 287) pointed out that neither in Rotherham's papers in the York Episcopal registry nor in the archives of the corporation of York can be found any reference to a second coronation, as there surely would have been had one occurred. All chronicle accounts derive from Polydore, pp. 546ff.

51/31-34. Crowland, p. 160f, considerably paraphrased for brevity and clarity [There on the day appointed for the repetition of his crowning in the metropolitan church, he presented his only son, Edward, whom that same day he had created Prince of Wales with the insignia of the golden wand and the wreath; and he arranged splendid and highly expensive feasts and entertainments . . .]. The Crowland passage continues that this was intended to attract people's affection.

51/38-40. The York House Books record for 2 September 1483 that 'it was agreid that the Creid play shall be playd afore our suffreyn lord the kyng of Sunday next cumyng, apon the cost of the most onest men of every parish in thys cite'

(Attreed, I, 292). Four days later it was agreed that all the aldermen should appear with the mayor 'to atend apon the kynges gude grace to morou at seyng of the Creid play' (Attreed, I, 293). Hall says, 'the citezens receyued hym with great pompe and triumphe, according to ye qualities of their educacion and quantitie of there substaunce and habilitie, and made diuers daies playes and pageantes in token of ioy and solace'. This is not in More but derives from Polydore, p. 546: 'aliquot dies gaudium publice celebrarunt' [they celebrated publicly some days of rejoicing].

51/40-41. John (not Richard) of Gloucester was not created Captain of Calais until 11 March 1485 (*Foedera*, V, Pt. 3, 162 [XII, 265f]). Buc's wording is ambiguous: it is not quite clear whether he is saying Richard created him Captain of Calais in York or at some time in the future. If the former, a source for the error of placing the creation at York is Robert Fabyan, *The New Chronicles of England and France*, repr. from Pynson's edition of 1516, ed. Henry Ellis, London, 1811, p. 670 (Buc's 'As some say' refers only to this source). For the error in the name of the boy no source can be traced. Fabyan gives no name, and Buc probably guessed that he was named for his father. It appears nowhere that Buc knows of the second reputed illegitimate son, the bricklayer of Eastwell, known as 'Richard Plantagenet', whose romantic story is told in Francis Peck, *Desiderata Curiosa* (London, 1732), II, 13-15 and who received some attention from the late David Baldwin in *The Lost Prince* (Stroud, 2007).

51/45-48. Fabyan, p. 670; Richard 'in shorte processe folowynge [the coronation], rode northwarde to pacyfie that countre, and to redresse certayne riottes there lately done'. The executions of rebels are mentioned in Stow, *Annales,* p. 767, Hall, p. 376 and Holinshed, III, 400.

51/50. Vergil, *Aeneid* XI, 97-98 [I say hello forever. . . and forever farewell].

52/4-39. Buc's information on Richard's dealings with the French king comes from Commynes, II, 305, who states that Richard wanted Louis' friendship and probably the continuance of the pension, 'mais le roy ne voulut respondre à ses lettres ne oyr le messaige et l'estima trēs cruel et mauvais . . .' [but the king did not want to respond to these letters or hear the message and regarded him as very cruel and evil]. Hall, who follows Commynes here, may have been Buc's immediate source. He says (p. 376) that soon after Richard's coronation 'he sent a solempne Ambassade to Lewes the Frenche kynge, to conclude a league and amitie with hym, trustynge to obtayne the tribute whiche kynge Edwarde his brother had before out of Fraunce, but the Frenche kyng so abhorred hym and his crueltie, that he would neither se nor heare his Ambassadors, and so in vayne they returned'.

The communication between the two kings took place not after but before and during Richard's progress. The existing documents contradict Commynes's assertions about Louis' refusal to communicate with Richard. *Foedera* V, Pt. 3, 134f [XII, 195f], reproduces a commission of 16 July for renewing the treaty. In Harl. 433, f. 236^v^, there is a brief letter from Louis, dated 21 July, acknowledging the favourable reception of Richard's letters and his news (presumably his assumption of the crown) and desiring his friendship. Richard responded on 18 August from Leicester that he intended to keep the truce concluded with Louis by his brother for its stipulated term. However, he mentions that his merchants have been harassed by Frenchmen and asks what Louis intends to do about it (Harl. 433, f. 237v). These letters are in the Horrox and Hammond ed. of Harl. 433, II, 26-28. There seem to have been no communications directly relating to the tribute. Louis died on 30 August 1483. On 21 March 1484 (*Foedera* V, Pt. 3, 145 [XII, 223f]. Richard sent a commission for renewal of the treaty to Charles VIII, and on 13 September (*Foedera*, V, Pt. 3, 150 [XII, 235]) he granted a safe conduct to messengers from Charles. No other communications are preserved.

52/9-10. Commynes, II, 303-4, II, 303-4, 'et se doubtoit bien d'avoir perdu sa pension que le roy luy donnoit, ou tribute que l'appelloyent les Angloys . . . .' [And he imagined he had lost his pension which the king paid him, or tribute as the English called it']. Also, II, 231, 'luy fut rompue la pension qu'il prenoit de nous qu'il apelloit tribute, mais ce n'estoit ne l'ung ne l'autre . . . ' [The payment he took from us was interrupted, which he called a tax or tribute, but it was neither one nor the other].

52/1st mar. n. Jean du Tillet, *Recueil des Roys, Traictez*, p. 248 (this book is divided into two parts separately numbered, 'Recueil des Traictez d'Entre les Roys de France et d'Angeterre' [Collection of the Treaties between the Kings of France and England] 'Recueil des Roys de France, Leurs Couronne et Maison' [Collection of the Kings of France, their Crown and House], henceforth distinguished as *Traictez* and *Roys*: 'septante-cinq mille escus, vallans chacun escu trente-trois sols, que ledit Roy Louys promit payer audit Roy Edouart pour les frais e son armée' [seventy-five thousand ecus, each ecu worth thirty-three sols, which the said King Louis promised to pay the said King Edward for his expenses and his army]. This was evidently a lump sum, the annual pension being referred to as 'pension annuelle de cinquante mille escus . . .' [annual pension of fifty thousand écus]. B.L. MS. Add. 6297, ff. 108v-109v, is a copy of a letter, dated 29 August 1475, in which the French king promised to make an annual payment to Edward IV of '50 Thousand Scutes of Gold every Scute being of the Value of three & thirty great Blancs', half at Michaelmas, half at Easter.

52/27-30. *Ibid.*, 'Constituta nonnullis magnatibus Anglicis annua vectigalia multi auri' [For quite a few English magnates there was a large annual honorarium of gold].

52/30-35. Rotherham was Bishop of Lincoln before his translation to the archbishopric of York. It is interesting that of this list so many ultimately betrayed Richard: Dorset, Hastings, Rotherham, Cheyney, Morton (Master of the Rolls), and St Leger ('Mr Challoner' is a misreading or mishearing by Commynes of Thomas St Leger). Perhaps in their connection with France lies a partial explanation of their betrayal. Blount, Fortescue, and Talbot, who became traitors at Bosworth, were also sent at one time as ambassadors to France. It was primarily due to the wooing of the French king that Warwick was led to break with Edward IV, who favoured a Burgundian over a French alliance. Cornwallis, with the anti-French prejudice of his time, thinks that Hastings's connections with France made him untrustworthy: 'could Hastinges be inocent whom Philippe Commin*n*s reporteth to be a Pentioner of the ffrench king Lewis the 11th the onlye subtile Prince of that time & he of all others that moste affected Tirranie, and was naturally the mortall and most vndermininge enimie of this kingdom' (p. 10).

52/40-42. All Monstrelet says is 'passerent la mer d'Anglettere pour venir en France par deuers le Roy, le Seigneur Hauart, vn Prothonotaire, & autres Ambassadeurs Anglois, pour le fait de l'entretenement de la trefue d'ẽtre le Roy, & le Roy d'Angleterre' (*Chroniques*, f. 71 of segment after vol. 3 called 'Autres Nouvelles Chroniques') [Lord Howard, a prothonotary, and other English ambassadors passed over the sea from England to come to France to the king for maintenance of the truce between the king and king of England].

52/44-46. See above, 46/42-43. John Howard's installation as Knight of the Bath is not recorded in extant documents. He received his barony before 4 March 1470 (*CPR*, 1467-77, p. 204).

52/4th mar. n. Du Tillet, *Traictez*, p. 248 says Howard and Cheyney stayed as hostages until Edward returned home with most of his army.

52/46-50. Commynes, II, Bks. IV-VI, *passim*, writes of Howard's prominent part in arranging this peace. The amount is noted in II, 242. J.R. Lander, 'Council, Administration and Councillors, 1461-1485', *BIHR* XXXII (1959), 161 observes, 'The fact that a newly created peer (Howard) and a mere knight [Montgomery] got more than a bishop-chancellor and the chamberlain [Hastings] twice as much, seems to lend credibility to the figures as an index of Louis' estimate of their influence with the king'.

52/50-53/1. Alain Bouchard, *Les Grandes Croniques de Bretagne*, n.p., [1517], f. cxcix: 'le conte de Vuaruich qui tant auoit au roy de france couste a entretrenir' [The Earl of Warwick who had cost the King of France so much to entertain]. Warwick received this pension from Louis in the 1460s. Buc has placed an 'X' opposite the information in his own copy.

53/5-6. See above, text, p. 44, ll. 49-50.

53/14-16. See above, n. 52/4-39.

53/17-23. See Harl. 433, f. 308v (Horrox and Hammond, III, 190) for Richard's promise to Elizabeth Woodville, made in a public ceremony on 1 March 1484, that her daughters would be assured of their lives, protection, freedom, provision for marriage to gentlemen and an annual income of 200 marks, and granting the former queen an annual income of 700 marks to be paid three times annually. He also promises not to believe anyone who speaks ill of them without allowing them to defend themselves. On the basis, evidently, of her trust in his good faith, Elizabeth sent to her son Dorset urging him to return and make peace with Richard. That the daughters were well treated may be attested by the fact that according to Crowland, pp. 179f, Elizabeth, the eldest, was given apparel similar to the queen's at the Christmas celebrations of 1484. Elizabeth Woodville seems not to have been easily won, for Crowland, pp. 170f, says that she gave in only after frequent intercession and threats.

53/25. The information on the magnificence of Richard's Christmas celebrations in 1484 is derived from Crowland, pp. 174f.

53/28-30. See text pp. 197 and 203f.

53/32-47. See text, p. 176f and notes thereto.

53/33-4. See above, n. 39/43-49, for legal definition of 'precontract' (previous marriage to someone else).

53/42-43. *PROME*: Richard III: Jan. 1484, XIV, 14 cites this as a petition of the Three Estates, not of the Northern people. Buc is relying on Crowland's incorrect assumption (pp. 160f) that the petition was concocted in the North (see above, p. 46, l. 8 and n. 45/26-30.

53/48-54/3. See n. 45/19-20.

54/4-25. During Edward IV's reign, the honour of Richmond was in gift of the crown and was given to Clarence on the readeption of Henry VI but reverted to the crown on Clarence's death. Henry had an hereditary claim to it from his father, Edmund Tudor, to whom it had been granted in 1452 by his half-brother Henry VI, but he was deprived of it by Edward IV. Mention was made in Richard's Parliament of Henry Tudor's conspiracy and his landing at Plymouth. Henry and his uncle Jasper Tudor were attainted (XV, 28), and his mother, the Countess of Richmond's land holdings were conveyed to her husband, Thomas, Lord Stanley (XV, 36). Henry was in Brittany, not, as Buc says, in France at the time. No mention is made of his Lancastrian claim or marriage plans. The Pope had no power to confer or confirm titles.

54/31-41. *PROME*, Richard III: Jan. 1484, XV, 24 lists these, among others, as being attainted for treason in 'Buckingham's rebellion'. Morton, Knevet, John Rush, and 'Thomas Nandik late of Cambrige, nigromansier' (p. 24) are said to have conspired with Buckingham at Brecon on 18 October and, among other things, persuaded Henry and Jasper Tudor to bring a foreign army and navy to attack England, landing at Plymouth on 28 October (p. 25). Risings in Kent, 18-25 October, are mentioned, in connection with which most of the other participants were attainted. In *Pat. Rolls* we find every one of these rewarded by Henry VII, who reversed their attainders in his first Parliament (*PROME*, Nov. 1485, XV, 102; and see n. 188/34-40 below). Agnes Ethel Conway, 'The Maidstone Sector of Buckingham's Rebellion', *Archaeologia Cantiana*, XXXVII (1925), 97-119, studies the Kentish participants in the rebellion. The Woodville seat was at Maidstone, and 'the outstanding rebels were relations or connections by marriage of the Woodvilles, the Hautes, and the Guildfords. Some others seem to have been friends of Bishop Morton . . .' (p. 106). **John Guildford** was a friend of Rivers. He was sent to Newgate for one month. **Sir Thomas Lewkenor,** father or uncle of the Thomas Lewkenor who was made Knight of the Bath at Richard's coronation and who remained faithful to Richard, was pardoned. **Thomas Fiennes** of Hurstmonceux was pardoned. **Nicholas Gainsford**, who already had a history of rebellion under Edward IV, was pardoned. That **Sir George Brown**, husband of **Edward Poynings**'s mother, was executed indicates that he was probably the leader of this sector. **Sir John Fogg**, husband of Alice Haute, a cousin of Elizabeth Woodville, was pardoned. **John Darrell** was nephew to Guildford. **William Clifford** is unidentified but is probably one of the Cliffords related by marriage to Guildford.

54/33-34. 'Thomas Morton' is obviously an error for John Morton. Buc was probably thinking of More.

54/45-48. *PROME,* Richard III: Jan. 1484, XV, 17. Buc paraphrases slightly.

54/50-55/11. The *Titulus Regius* incorporated in the Parliament Rolls is intended to represent the petition presented to Richard before his accession and thus merely proves that the sons of Edward IV were living at the time Richard was formally petitioned to be king, not that they were still living at the time of the Parliament. Those at the Parliament evidently had no reliable knowledge of whether they were at that time alive or dead; no contemporary source mentions anything but rumours of their death. As for Buc's statement that their lives could not prejudice him, this is an argument which has from his time to the present day been naively put forward by Richard's defenders. That summer's rebellion, being an attempt to free the sons of Edward V, showed that they posed a threat to his security, since they could still be used as a rallying point. Crowland Chronicle (pp. 162f) reports that following Richard's accession a number of rebel plots existed on both sides of the Channel aimed at replacing him with Edward V. The Woodvilles seem to have been preparing and financing a full-scale rebellion. By August the exiled Tudor camp in Brittany had been enlisted by Edward Woodville, and financial and logistical support for an invasion of England had been secured from Francis II of Brittany. By mid-September the Duke of Buckingham had joined the Woodville rebellion, persuaded by Bishop Morton to oppose the king. Thus, until the rumour was spread in September that the sons of Edward IV were dead, the rebel consortium had been setting them up to contest the throne.

In other instances of one king deposing another, Henry IV found it necessary after imprisoning Richard II to have him put to death because of plots, uprisings and pretenders. Edward IV, after the Bastard of Fauconberg's uprising, saw the death of Henry VI as unavoidable. Henry VII, pursued by pretender after pretender, seized the opportunity to dispose of Clarence's son Warwick on a trumped-up charge of conspiracy with Perkin Warbeck. This is not proof that Richard had either of the princes killed. There is no evidence either way. But the argument that he had no reason to desire their removal ignores the insecurity of kingship in this period and the fact that rebellion was being mounted in Edward V's name which could have led to civil war. David Baldwin in *Richard III*, p. 118 says that 'while he could be ruthless no one has suggested that he could be also stupid. Had he killed the princes he would have been assured of opprobrium, and this would not have improved his tenure of the crown. Keeping them alive in hiding kept his enemies from using them'.

55/14-15. Text, pp. 74-82 and 141f.

55/23. [in an inner chamber]

55/29-30. Buc's source for the oath sworn to support Richard's son is Crowland, pp. 170f. There was at the time no legal practice governing succession, and Richard, like Henry IV and Edward IV before him, was making special provision to try to ensure the crown to his own issue.

55/36-56/36. J.G. Bellamy, 'Justice under the Yorkist Kings', *American Journal of Legal History*, IX (1965), 141: 'It was the practice in the Yorkist period for the king to appoint a constable whenever a rebellion was thought to be imminent. His special function was to administer summary justice on those traitors who had been taken in arms'. Annette Carson has published the first detailed study of the office in Yorkist hands: *Richard Duke of Gloucester as Protector and Constable*. It also had particular interest to Buc, whose sole surviving contribution to the collection of documents pertaining to the Society of Antiquaries concerns the office of Constable (see above, p. xlvi). The appointment was necessitated by the fact that Buckingham, who was High Constable, had become a major rebel. Ashton therefore was called upon to preside at Buckingham's trial and sentence him. After Buckingham's execution Stanley was appointed High Constable. There is no evidence of Ashton's inefficiency. On 29 April 1485 he was reappointed Vice Constable, 'De Fidelitate, Circumspectione, & Industria . . .' [for fidelity, circumspection and industry] (*Foedera*, V, Pt. 3, 163 [XII, 168f). Carson, 'Notes towards the Definition of a Tyrant', *Ricardian Bulletin* (Dec. 2013), pp. 43-5, demolishes legends of Ashton's particular cruelty.

55/47-56/21. [The king to his beloved and loyal Ralph Ashton, greetings. Know that we, fully confident in your loyalty, circumspection, and probity, have assigned, deputed and ordained you for this time only as our Viceconstable of England, giving and granting to you by tenor of this our commission general authority and special mandate to hear and examine and proceed against whatever persons are suspected of crimes against our royal majesty, both by way of hearing and examination of witnesses and otherwise as may seem better to you, through your office, mere or promoted, and also in those cases by judging or passing sentence according to the requirements of the situation and the deserts of the offenders without the noise and customary form of trial, any appeal whatever being excluded, whenever it may seem good to you to proceed and to judge and put into final effect, further with all clauses, words and special terms required by law or custom for the execution of this our mandate and our authority, all of which we have also here expressed, taking with you some trustworthy notary who may write down each particular together with other things which in or concerning the matters above mentioned shall seem necessary or in any way requisite; commanding and firmly enjoining on you that, leaving aside all other things whatever, you shall give attention as often and whenever it shall be necessary to the matters aforesaid and shall hear and examine the aforementioned cases and proceed in the same and judge them and put into final effect as aforesaid. Furthermore, we give firmly in command to all and every one of those concerned in this part that they shall obey, assist and help you in carrying out the aforementioned with diligence in all things. Whereof, etc., witness the king at Coventry on 24th October in the first year of his reign. By the king himself orally.]

Buc's reference in the margin is correct, and miniscule deviation from the version given in *Foedera* V, Pt. 3, 138 [XII, 205] suggests that it was copied directly from the document with care by someone other than Buc, who gave it to him, and he inserted it directly into his manuscript. This italic appears nowhere else in the work.

56/43-57/10. (All information in this note is from *Pat. Rolls* unless otherwise indicated.) The Constableship was granted to Buckingham on 15 July. Lord Howard was created Marshal 28 June 1483 and the office made hereditary. He was created Admiral of England, Ireland, and Aquitaine on 25 July 1483. The Lord Chancellor was **John Russell**, Bishop of Lincoln, but no record of his creation can be found, though he is often mentioned in that capacity. From numerous references in Harl. 433 we know that Russell possessed the Great Seal, which only the Chancellor was allowed. Francis, Viscount Lovell, was the King's

Chamberlain (i.e., Chamberlain of the King's Household). **Sir John Wood** was progressing toward his office through the reigns of Edward IV, when he was Under-Sheriff, and Edward V, when he was Treasurer of the Exchequer, to which office Richard III reappointed him. Evidently he died, for on 6 December 1484, **John Tuchet**, Lord Audley, was named Treasurer. On 22 September 1483, **Dr Thomas Barowe** was appointed Keeper of the Rolls. There is no evidence that Henry VII kept him on in this office. **John Kendall** is frequently mentioned in *Pat. Rolls* and in the records of the city of York as the king's Secretary, but his appointment is not recorded. In March 1484, **William Hopton** is mentioned as deceased, without indication of his office. He is referred to as Treasurer in Grafton's coronation record (II, 116), and *Coronation*, p. 358, confirms him as Treasurer of Richard's Household on evidence of TNA E404/78, f. 22, a post in which he served at the Coronation, as documented from Add. 6113, f. 22. Buc gives Percy's name incorrectly, following Grafton. The Controller was **Robert Percy**, who was, along with Lovell, one of Richard's youthful companions in Warwick's household. His appointment is not recorded, but he is mentioned in *Pat. Rolls* as Controller of the Household. There is no mention to be found of John Buck's office. That he held a post in Richard's household is suggested by his position directly after John Kendall in the list of Henry VII's Bosworth attainders (*Rot. Parl.*, VI, 276). See above, pp. xvii-xviii and cxxvi for Buc's research methods on this point. There is a reference of 16 July 1483 to **John Gunthorp**, 'whom the king appointed keeper of the privy seal . . . on 27 June last'. **William Hussey**, or Huse, Chief Justice of the King's Bench under Edward IV and Edward V, was confirmed by Richard on 26 June 1483. **Thomas Tremayle** (not Tremain, as Buc has it), **Roger Townsend**, and **John Vavasour** also began their careers as Sergeants at Law under Edward IV. They received their grants of office from Richard III on 27 June 1483. **Morgan Kidwelly** was appointed Attorney General by Edward V and the appointment was renewed by Richard. For the appointment of **John of Gloucester** as Captain of Calais, see above, n. 51/40-41. A number of those officers were kept on by Henry VII: Hussey, Russell (as Controller of the Privy Seal), and Audeley; Tremayle, Vavasour, and Townsend became justices; Barowe was pardoned and given a prebendary; Gunthorpe is mentioned only as 'clerk'; and **Thomas Fitzwilliam** became Mayor of London. No appointments for him are listed, since his offices were bestowed locally, not royally.

57/11-16. *Foedera*, V, Pt. 3, 155 [XII, 246f].

57/19-22. See above n. to 52/4-39 for the negotiations with France. The only negotiations between Richard and Denmark occur in connection with the treaty with Scotland mentioned directly below. Hall, p. 400 gives as Article XIII of that treaty an agreement that the allies of each party should be entitled to be included in the league. Charles VIII of France and John, King of Denmark and Norway are listed as the special confederates of the Scots. The treaty is printed in one of its original Latin forms in *Foedera*, V, Pt. 3, 157 [XII, 252]. Buc may be referring to this treaty when speaking of Richard's relations with Denmark, or he may be referring in error to the negotiations of 1476 when the King of Denmark sent an embassy asking Edward IV for a new treaty and redress for grievances (*Foedera*, V, Pt. 3, 70f [XII, 27].

57/27-30 and 5th mar. n. In this treaty (*Foedera*, V, Pt. 3, 149 [XII, 234]) 'Argyle' is given as 'Ergile'. Buc has omitted one of the commissioners, Laurence, Lord Oliphant. It is clear from the form of Buc's representation that in listing the items and ambassadors involved in this treaty he was not using the manuscript printed by Hall in English and later in *Foedera* in Latin, but probably B.L. Cotton Caligula B.V, ff. 151-2, in which similar mistakes are made: the name of Colin, Earl of Argyle, is given as 'Coly Erle of Erguile', William, Earl of Nottingham's name as 'John', and places for the Christian names of Strange and Powys are left blank. (Strange's name was George, Lord Powys's John.)

57/31-41. For Quhitlaw's address see text, pp. 205f and note thereto.

58/13-15. Glover, p. 539, lists under John de la Pole, Earl of Suffolk and Elizabeth, daughter of Richard, Duke of York, '*Anne*, a Nunne at *Syon*'.

58/24-25. *Foedera*, V, Pt. 3, 158 [XII, 255] and 160 [XII, 260].

58/28-31. Commynes, II, 305 suggests that Richard's communication with Louis was for the purpose of exacting tribute, but there is no evidence of this in the messages themselves (see n. 52/4-39 above). Richard attempted to establish a truce with France in 1484 after Charles VIII's accession, without success.

58/32-33. Text, pp. 189-92.

58/43-46. Text, pp. 203f.

59/13-15. Matthew 21:9, John 19:6 and 19:15.

59/21-60/14. Buc gives this account in *Comm*., ff. 128f as well, citing Glover as his main source. In the earlier work he is slightly more detailed, since genealogy is his subject there. Richard did not deny the Herefordshire lands to Buckingham but granted them provisionally on the assumption that Parliament would confirm the grant (Harl. 433, ff. 107v-108; II, 2f Horrox and Hammond edition). Buckingham's power was already immense, similar to that Richard held in the North after the Scottish campaign. He had the supervision and array of Shropshire, Hereford, Somerset, Dorset and Wiltshire, was Chief Justice, Chamberlain, Supervisor, and Governor of the whole of Wales, and Constable, Steward, and Receiver of several important Welsh castles and lordships, with power to appoint officers therein. His rebellion, therefore, cannot be attributed to dissatisfaction at not being granted lands and power – this is a fiction derived from More and Polydore – but more likely to his possessing too much already. He also had a claim to the throne.

Richard's supposed retort to Buckingham when he asked for the restoration of the lands is from Polydore, p. 549: 'Num Henrice dux, uis tibi id ius Henrici quarti uindicare, quo ille perperam regnum occuparet, atque ita ad illud uiam patefacere?'

60/2. Buc gives 'Mary' erroneously for Eleanor.

60/20-22. More (p. 44) is the inventor of the story that Richard and Buckingham had formed an agreement, on the latter's promising to aid Richard's elevation to the throne, that Buckingham's daughter would marry Richard's son. It recalls the agreement between Queen Margaret and Warwick that the Kingmaker's daughter was to marry the heir to the throne as a reward for the restoration of Henry VI.

60-64. Buc is combining with some difficulty the conversations between Morton and Buckingham as reported by More and by Hall. More breaks off, and

Hall (pp. 383-90), continuing this conversation, is obviously inventing to fill a gap. More for his part of the conversation might have had the direct authority of Morton, and he is probably right in attributing the duke's rebellion to Morton's persuasion. Buc observes this in his notes to his copy of Godwin: in the margin opposite the entry for Morton, p. 117, he says 'Morton made this duke a traytor & other good men he did to harm Witness S. Tho Mor'. Buc has somewhat confused Hall's account, which allows for little wavering on Buckingham's part. The alterations may result from clumsiness in combining the More and Hall sections, but more likely they are intended to show Morton more clearly as the instigator, corrupter and manipulator. And Buc may also have been attempting to add tension and vividness by portraying Buckingham's changes of emotion.

61/2nd mar. n. More, p. 91, says Morton devised this marriage and does not mention the agency of Elizabeth Woodville.

63/1st mar. n. [Noblemen are the hope of the wretched]: this sounds Senecan but does not appear in either *Declamationes* or *De Clementia*.

63/38-45. primus motor [prime mover], primus molitor [chief builder], malus genius [evil genius].

63/48-64/38. Kendall, *Richard III*, pp. 314, notes that the story of Buckingham's meeting with the Countess of Richmond is improbable: it is likely she was in London, busy with her own plots, while Buckingham left Richard at Gloucester and went to Brecon. Bridgnorth, where they were supposed to have met, was northwest of Buckingham's route. (However, Conway notes, p. 103, the countess had a residence near Brecon.)

64/1st mar. n. Glover lists Margaret, Countess of Richmond, on p. 399 and Buckingham's mother on p. 401. Their fathers were brothers, though Glover confuses this issue by calling Edmund, Duke of Somerset nephew instead of grandson to John of Gaunt.

64/49-65/1. *Paston Letters*. II, 442f is a letter of 10 October from Norfolk to Paston urging him to come with men at arms to London, since the Kentishmen are in arms and planning to rob the city. Richard heard of the insurrection two days later at Lincoln. A letter of 13 October from Richard to the Council of Southampton shows the nature of his preparation. He states that Buckingham has turned traitor 'and entendith thutter distruccion of us, you, and alle othre our trewe suggiettes that have taken oure part . . .' He urges them 'that with as many as ye may reise and make in defensible array on horsback ye do sende to be with us at our Citie of Coventre the xxij day of this present moneth withouten faile . . .' ('The Manuscripts of the Corporations of Southampton and King's Lynn', Historical MSS Commission, 11th Report, Appendix, pt. iii, 1887, p. 103). On 18 October, Edward Plumpton writes to Sir Robert Plumpton:

> People in this country be so trobled, in such comandment as they have in the Kynges name and otherwyse, marvellously, that they know not what to doe. My lord Strayng goeth forth from Lathum upon munday next with x m. men. . . . The Duke of Buck: has so mony men, as yt is sayd here, that he is able to goe where he wyll; but I trust he shalbe right withstanded and all his mallice: and

els were great pytty. Messengers commyth dayly both from the Kings grace and the Duke, into this country. *Plumpton Correspondence*, ed. Thomas Stapleton, Cam. Soc., 1st ser. no. 4 (London, 1839), pp. 44f.

65/2nd mar. n. Polydore, p. 552. The reference to Lib. 25 is correct.

65/3rd mar. n. The source of this misinformation is Hall, p. 395, whose whole account is a blatant fabrication for the purpose of creating a crude moral exemplum. Banister's Christian name, given by Hall as Humphrey (the error originated with Polydore, p. 552) was Ralph. The subsequent fate of his family is outlined as follows: his first son went mad, his daughter contracted leprosy, his second son grew deformed, his third son drowned, and he himself was tried for murder in old age. After this follows the statement about his reward from Richard: 'And as for his thousand pound kyng Richard gaue him not one farthing, saying that he which would be vntrew to so good a master would be false to al other, howbeit some saie y^t^ he had a smal office or a ferme to stoppe his mouthe with al'. In fact both Harl. 433 (f. 133), Horrox and Hammond edition, II, 58f, and *Pat. Rolls*, p. 482 (15 Aug. 1484) record grants to 'our wellbeloved servaunt Rauff Banaster' for help in taking the rebels. Fabyan, p. 670, and *The Great Chronicle of London*, ed. A. H. Thomas and I. D. Thornley (London, 1938) p. 235 give no first name for Banister, and in addition to the £1000 reward he was given they mention land worth £100 annually granted to him and to his heirs in perpetuity, reward for bringing in Buckingham.

65/29. Buckingham's execution occurred the first year of Richard III, 2 November 1483.

65/33-35. More, p. 90-3. For notice of the flight of the conspirators in 'Buckingham's rebellion', see above, n. 29/29-36.

BOOK II

66-67. Buc follows his outline somewhat less closely than he does for Book I and is more digressive within certain areas. 'The Prince Edward and Queen Anne die . . .' follows 'The Earl of Richmond . . . came first to Poole . . . and secondly to Milford . . .'. The nobility of King Henry VII' is in the right place, but 'He affied not much in the titles of York and Lancaster' is not discussed until after 'The prerogative of the king in judgements and controversies' then it is followed by 'His aptness for diverse wives'. 'The titles of King Henry VII' and 'Kings go not now to the wars' are reversed. 'His goodness to the children orphans of Sir John Buck' precedes 'Walter de Buck and his progeny'.

66/4 [with good omens]

66/19. [by right of war and of the house of Lancaster]

68/7. Euripides, *Heraclides,* 866.

68/11. [Fortune is generous with adversity but grudging with prosperity] Valerius Maximus VII, introduction, somewhat altered.

68/12-13. This sentence is a close paraphrase of Hesiod, *Works and Days*, I, 825.

68/24-25. [Fortune is more effective in the short term, virtue in the long term]

68/34-37. Polydore and the English chroniclers do not make one of the two invasions by Henry Tudor. Only Fabyan (p. 672) may be said to do so, for he mentions only the second invasion. Stow, *Annales* (p, 779), mentions the first, but does not allow that Tudor's party landed in England, saying they sailed away without setting foot on land, when, after their ships had been scattered by storm, they saw the army on the shore. Polydore (*The Anglica Historia of Polydore Vergil*, ed. Denys Hay, Cam. Soc. 74, London 1950, p. 53), Grafton and Holinshed say the storm occurred before Tudor sent his scouts ashore, and when their report made him suspect a ruse he set sail. He stopped in Normandy, and planning to proceed to Brittany, sent ambassadors seeking safe conduct of Charles VIII, who sent money as well.

69/9. Evidence is lacking that Stanley was complicit in 'Buckingham's rebellion' or involved with Henry Tudor's schemes this early, though he might have been secretly involved through his wife, the Countess of Richmond.

69/40-42. Commynes, II, 306: Henry was 'reins estimé. Sauf que sa personne estoit et est honneste' [Henry was of little esteem, except that his person was and is presentable].

69/42-43. Vergil, *Aeneid*, V, 344.

70/21-23. Bouchard, f. ccviii [At the service of the Earl of Richmond were three large ships of Brittany, full of men, arms, etc., which put to sea].

70/32-45. This information is from Polydore, p. 553.

71/24-27. The accounts given by Polydore, p. 551, and his followers say that when Richard heard of the invasion he was unprepared and did not know where to meet the enemy. His plan was to pretend that he had heard nothing until he had raised an army. Nothing is said of a 'secret friend', who seems to be Buc's invention and is reminiscent of a secret friend of Dorset whom Buc mentions above, text, p. 27. For neither is there any evidence in Buc's sources, but in both cases it is a likely assumption.

72/20-23. More says nothing about Henry VII except that Morton arranged for his support by Buckingham and his marriage with Elizabeth of York (p. 91). Buc follows Polydore, pp. 548-53 very closely in this section. The invasions are mentioned by Commynes, I, 54; Grafton, II, 128-57; Stow, *Annales,* pp. 775-9 and 783-8; Hall, pp. 383-98 and 402-21; Holinshed, III, 410-79, and Du Tillet, *Traictez*, p. 251.

73/12-15. The prince died at Middleham Castle on a date about which there has been much speculation. Crowland, p. 170, says Richard heard of it before his departure from Nottingham (27 April 1484), and recent research suggests a date around Easter, which fell on 18 April. See Annette Carson's website for her research on the date of his death: http://www.annettecarson.co.uk/357052362. From available evidence it seems Edward's age at death was about seven and three-quarters. It is no longer thought that the tomb at Sheriff Hutton is his, and it is now assumed he was buried at or near Middleham as indicated by Rous.

73/18-19. Crowland, p. 170f, 'Videsses . . . patrem & matrem . . . prae subitis doloribus pene insanire' [You might have seen his father and mother almost grow insane for the sudden grief].

73/26-27. Seneca, *De Consolatione ad Marciam*, XIV, 3, '. . . tam cito dolorem vicit quam omnia solebat' [as quickly he conquered grief as he tended to do everything].

73/29-30. Crowland, p. 170 [King Richard nevertheless found time for the defence of his territories].

73/31-35. Queen Anne died 16 March 1485, nearly a year after her son, following a long illness.

74/3-8. There is no reliable evidence of Richard's ever having officially nominated an heir, but all sources except Rous say that Lincoln was nominated. Rous (p. 218) notes that Warwick was proclaimed heir 'in Richard III curia regali' after the death of Richard's son and was served after the king and queen at table, but that afterwards Lincoln was preferred. It may be worth noting that Rous had particular interest in the earls of Warwick. Kendall states that after a four month delay following his wife's death, Richard appointed Lincoln Lieutenant of Ireland, the usual post for the heir apparent of the house of York (*Richard III*, p. 349). Lincoln was also made head of the Council of the North, which Richard founded (Brooks, pp. 11f; Kendall, *Richard III*, p. 377). Warwick's youth, even assuming a reversal of his father's attainder, would have been a risk to Richard's establishing a strong succession. Besides, recalling the chaotic situation in which he found himself on the death of his brother, he is not likely to have preferred a child. John de la Pole, Earl of Lincoln, his sister's son, was a man of proven ability. Still, Ross, *Richard III*, states that 'there is no direct evidence whatever to support the claim made by several modern scholars that he was publicly recognized as heir to the throne . . . ', p. 158.

74/17-18. [head and prince of the house of Lancaster]

74/19. [a member of that family]

74/39-40. Filii populi [sons of the people]; liberi vulgo quaesiti [commonly known as far-fetched children]; sine patre [without a father].

74/42-3. Salisbury, *Letters*, ed. W.J. Millor and H.E. Butler, revised by C.N.L. Brooke (London, 1955), I, 230: 'liberi qui ex dampnato et illicito coitu . . . sunt, ab omni prorsus haereditatis beneficio excluduntur, eosque nec iura ciuilia nec leges, agnoscunt canonumque adeo improbat vigor . . .' [children who are from a damned and illicit connection are absolutely excluded from all benefit of inheritance and neither civil right nor laws recognize them, and force of canon law excludes them]

74/45. 'Otho Swinford' = Sir Hugh Swynford.

75/3. [concubine]

75/8-16. Four children were born to John of Gaunt and Katherine Swynford (née Roët) between 1372 and 1377, before the death of Gaunt's second wife and his marriage to Swynford. 'They were given the dynastic name of Beaufort, a lost French lordship of the duke's . . .' (Simon Walker, 'John, duke of Aquitaine and duke of Lancaster, styled king of Castile and León (1340–1399)', *ODNB*). The name was not discarded by John, Duke of Somerset, but persisted until the natural son of Henry Beaufort, Duke of Somerset, who became Earl of Worcester under Henry VIII, took Somerset as a surname (see text, p. 78).

75/1st mar. n. Thomas Walsingham, *Historia Anglicana*, ed. Henry Thomas Riley, R.S. 28 (London, 1863-64), II, 219.

75/19-21. John of Gaunt had three years more to live. He married Katherine

Swynford in 1396 and died in 1399.

75/2nd mar. n. For this charter see text, pp. 79f.

75/30. [nor those who were descended from them]

75/31-36. Buc refers to his discussion in Book I, above. See also n. 16/31-48.

75/36-41. Members of the royal house belonging to these families are given the surname Plantagenet by Glover, *passim*.

75/42-43. John of Gaunt's daughter Philippa married King John of Portugal in 1387. After the death of Henry VI the royal house of Portugal became the senior heirs of Lancaster.

75/4th mar. n. For Buc's account of the Cadiz expedition, see Stow, *Annales* (1601), Pppp3-Pppp8 and Bod. MS. Eng. lett. b. 27, ff. 106-9.

76/7-8. Henry Fitzroy, Duke of Richmond, was the natural son of Henry VIII. William de Longuespée was the natural son of Henry II. Sir Roger Clarendon was reputedly the natural son of the Black Prince. **76/20-23.** Du Tillet, *Roys*, p. 207. This is nearly an exact quotation [The third line is barred entirely as bastards not only from the crown but also from admission to the surname of France, which concession is permitted to bastards of the king].

76/26-45. Hamelin Plantagenet, illegitimate son of Henry II's father Geoffrey of Anjou, married Isabel, daughter of William de Warenne, third Earl of Surrey, and in her right succeeded to the title as fifth Earl of Surrey, Camden, *Britannia* in 'Surrey', p. 217:

> Verùm vltimus solam filiam suscepit, quae primò Guilielmum Stephani Regis filium, & postea Hamelinum Galfredi *Plantageneti* Comitis Andegauensis nothum, maritos eodem titulo adornauit. Priore autem marito sine prole defuncto, Hamelinus Guilielmum Surriae Comitem ex ea genuit, cuius posteri, ascito *Warrennorum* nomine, eundem titulum gesserunt . . .

[His sonne . . . had issue, a daughter onely, who adorned first *William,* King *Stephens* sonne, and afterward *Hamelin* the base sonne of *Gefferey Plantagenet* Earle of *Aniou*, both her husbands, with the same title. But whereas her former husband died without issue, *William* her son by *Hamelin* was Earle of Surrie, whose posterity assuming unto them the name of *Warrens* bare the same title] (Holland trans., p. 304).

Arthur Agard in his discourse for the Society of Antiquaries, 'Of the Antiquity of Arms in England', 2 Nov. 1598, gives a different explanation from Buc's of Hamelin's bearing his wife's name:

> And of what great accompte, the same Normans and other Angevyns made of theyre armes of antiquytie appeareth in a role of the pedegre of the howse of earle Warren, which is in the Q. Majesty's threasaurye, wherein it is said that Hamelinus, brother to kinge H. 2d. after he had maryed Isabell, the daughter and onely heyre of the sayd howse of Warren, *assumpsit arma Uxoris suae, et arma patris sui dimisit & heredes sui post ipsum*, [assumed the arms of his wife and laid down the arms of his father as

> did his heirs] esteminge yt greatter honor to carye the auncyent armes of his wiffes auncestors, then his fathers, which was a straunger.
> (Hearne, *Curious Discourses*, I, 175)

Buc is under the delusion which he exhibits above, text, pp. 11-16, that Plantagenet was 'the royal surname' before Richard, Duke of York's time. It was not really a surname at all but a nickname. That a bastard's son should prefer his mother's native surname, when he acquired with it an earldom, to his grandfather's foreign nickname is not surprising.

76/34-35. These two John de Warrens became earls of Surrey in 1240 and 1304.

76/46-47. Arthur Plantagenet, Viscount Lisle, was the illegitimate son of Edward IV. See above 39/4th mar. n. Since 'Plantagenet' as a royal surname had originated with his grandfather, Richard, Duke of York, and since another family, associating itself with the house of Lancaster and never having borne the surname 'Plantagenet', now held the throne, it was suitable for a bastard to bear it.

77/1st mar. n. Psalms, 136:9, Vulgate; King James version gives it in 137:9.

77/6-7 and 2nd mar. n. Gainsford, p. 111: 'For it was a dangerous time for any Plantagenet to live in . . .'

77/11-15. Camden's genealogical collections in B.L. MS. Cotton Julius F. XI indicate that Hamelin's grandson was styled 'Joannes Plantagenett' (f. 42). During the genealogy craze under Elizabeth there was considerable heraldic fabrication arising either from false evidence or from family tradition being the only available evidence (Wagner, p. 16). Forged documents in Latin, Old English, and Old French were readily accepted by the heralds (J. Horace Round, *Family Origins*, London, 1930, p. 5), since the sciences of palaeography and philology were not yet well developed. Possibly the heralds shared actively in the fabrication of these documents. According to Michael MacLagan ('Genealogy and Heraldry in the Sixteenth and Seventeenth Centuries', *English Historical Scholarship*, ed. Levi Fox, London, 1956, p. 42), there were layman 'herald painters' who sold fabricated arms and pedigrees.

77/15-21. Hamelin's arms, according to English heraldry, appear in the sixth quarter of the coat of arms which formed part of the accusation against the poet Earl of Surrey, executed in 1547, as drawn by Dethick in B.L. MS. Harl. 1453, f. 69. They contain the arms of Anjou, the gold fleurs-de-lis borne by the later earls. The ancient Angevin earls (pre-fourteenth century) bore, as Buc says, a scarboucle.

77/33-35. In the National Archive Museum (Museum Catalogue, No. 8, TNA register no. E42/244) can be seen a seal of John de Warenne, Earl of Surrey and Strathern, from the year 1346. Though worn and broken, it seems to show a military scarf tied at the base of the shield.

78/14-15. Miles [knight], Clericus [priest], Domicellus [son of a nobleman] and Domicella [lady].

78/19-27 and 2nd mar. n. Although this is a *viva voce* reference, it is confirmed in Sir Edward Coke's published work. See *The First Part of the Institutes of the Laws of England*, ed. Francis Hargrave and Charles Butler (London, 1794), III. References to bastardy occur in Book II, sec. 188, n. 189 and Book III, sec. 400,

n. 180. The latter says 'the pope cannot legitimate in temporals'.

78/3rd mar. n. Buc mentions these two cases in the *Commentary* as well. For Gardiner he derives his information from Glover and Godwin, saying that he was the son of Lionel Woodville, Bishop of Salisbury, who married his mistress to a gardener in his employ (*Comm.*, f. 83v). Of Egerton he says, '& what hath it prejudiced Tho. Egerton . . . in his preferment to be a bastard? He having attained to the first place of . . . honor in this kingdome, & to bee made a pere of the realm?' (*Comm.*, f. 18v). Stephen Gardiner (1483-1555) was Bishop of Winchester and became Lord Chancellor in 1553. The story, which first appeared in the early seventeenth century, that he was the Bishop of Salisbury's illegitimate son, seems discredited by lack of reference to it by enemies during his lifetime. Sir Thomas Egerton (1540?-1617) was Lord Keeper and Master of the Rolls under Elizabeth and rose to be Baron Ellesmere and Lord Chancellor in 1603. He had a substantial library and was a friend of Buc, whom he assisted in the lawsuit over the Tilney inheritance (see above, p. xx), in gratitude for which Buc sent him an inscribed copy of *Daphnis* (see Eccles, pp. 455f).

79/1-3. Somerset did not follow Edward IV very long. A Lancastrian leader, he surrendered to and was pardoned by Edward in 1463 but deserted him later the same year. He was defeated, captured and beheaded at Hexham in 1464.

79/25-80/10. *PROME*, Richard II: Feb. 1397, ed. Chris Given-Wilson, VII, 322f; *Foedera*, III, Pt. 3, 126. [VII, 849f]. [Document of legitimation of the bastards of John, Duke of Lancaster. Richard, by the grace of God, king of England and France, lord of Ireland, greets his dearest cousins, the nobleman John de Beaufort knight, Henry de Beaufort, cleric, Thomas, nobleman, and our dear noblewoman Joan Beaufort, children of our dearest uncle ["patrui" in margin = paternal] John, Duke of Aquitaine and Lancaster, and our subjects. We, for the honour and merit, etc., of our uncle, judge agreeable to the merits, great probity of character and life and the natural honesty with which you shine, and that you are sprung from royal lineage, inclining to the prayers of our uncle, your father, who (as asserted), your defect of birth laid open, notwithstanding this defect and whatever qualities by these presents we wish to be held by suffient expressions of no effect. Whatever honours, dignities, preeminences, estates, degrees and public and private offices both perpetual and temporal, both feudal and noble, called by whatever name, such as duchies, lordships, earldoms, baronies, or other fiefs they might be, either held or depending on us mediately or not mediately, preferred, promoted, elected, assumed, or admitted, to receive, retain, bear and exercise freely and lawfully and as if you were born legitimately. Whatever statutes or customs of our kingdom of England state or observe to the contrary, we hold entirely of no force, by the fullness of our royal power and by the assent of our Parliament we dispense by these presents, and restore to legitimacy you and whoever is born of you. Day of February, 20th year, R.II] That Buc differs from some wording in the *PROME* version probably represents his attempts to clarify.

80/9-10. 'nono die Februarii' [9 February], says *Foedera* (see previous note).

80/13. [his cousins]

80/23-33. Buc had clearly not seen a copy containing the interlineation 'excepta dignitate regali' inserted in Henry IV's 1407 exemplification of this charter (see

Excerpta Historica, pp. 152ff and Patent Rolls, 20 Richard II, p. 2. No. 6). Although *Excerpta Historica* suggests that Henry IV could not legally interpolate a Parliamentary statute, Kendall says, 'Whether, in the light of present-day constitutional studies, he had the right so to alter an act of Parliament matters little; most people of the fifteenth century took it for granted that the legitimating patent barred the Beauforts from the throne' (*Richard III*, p. 185), and Mortimer Levine, 'Richard III – Usurper or Lawful King?' *Speculum*, XXXIV (1959), 391n., says: 'Though J.D. Mackie (*The Early Tudors,* Oxford, 1952, p. 48, n.1) may be correct in maintaining that Henry's addition could not avail against the act confirming Richard's patent, it is questionable that Richard's legitimation could extend to the crown in the case of bastards born while their parents' lawful spouses were living'. Buc, apparently unaware of the interpolation, makes this assumption. More recently Michael K. Jones and Malcolm G. Underwood (*The King's Mother*, Cambridge, 1992, pp. 22-4) assert that the language of the Act itself conferred no such rights as those excepted in the interlineation. In any case, no one challenged it, and Henry VII ignored it.

80/28-29 [kingdom, highest power, crown sceptre, diadem, purple, majesty]

80/45-46 [Prince is the highest power in the state, and chief ruler above all]

80/46-48 Vulteius, I, xii, p. 62: 'Princeps est potestas summam in Republica autoritatem imperium obtinens, superioritatem vocant, frequentius majestatem' [The prince holds the highest authority in the Republic, called supremacy, more often majesty]. This is the closest precept to this reference that I was able to locate in the work. Buc may have paraphrased it from memory.

81/1st mar. n. *PROME*, ed. Chris Given-Wilson, Henry IV: Oct. 1399, VIII, 33. Henry IV's oldest son Henry was appointed Prince of Wales, Duke of Cornwall, and Earl of Chester and the king seeks that the lords and commons assent to his being heir to the crown. They agreed.

81/26-27. [After him successively to the heirs of his body legitimately procreated]

81/29-47. Francis Thynne, Lancaster Herald, in a discourse for the Society of Antiquaries on 'The Duty and Office of an Herald of Arms' given in 1605, notes that by English law bastards cannot bear arms because they cannot inherit, having no blood interest; for 'they are not any man's children but *filii populi, & concepti ex prohibito coitu*' [children of the people, and conceived by a prohibited connection]. The custom of nations, however, allows for a bastard who bears his father's name to carry his father's arms with a 'difference' (Hearne, *Curious Discourses*, I, 140). The currency of the term 'filii terrae' [sons of the earth] is attested by Erasmus's listing it in *Chiliades*, p. 292. 'Novi homines' [new men] is still reasonably current, though it has developed a different connotation.

82/2nd mar. n. Glover, p. 398.

82/15-18. Since Henry's title was virtually nonexistent, he reinforced it with mythical rights of inheritance. Welsh nationalism came to his aid with the prophecy of Cadwallader, last of the 'British kings', that the 'British' would one day reign again in England. During the plans for Henry's conquest, Welsh bards spread prophecies of British supremacy and Richmond's future success (see Introduction to *The Poetical Works of Lewis Glyn Cothi*, Oxford, 1837, p. xxxiv) and urged the people to regain their rights under a saviour descended from Brut and Cadwallader (see W. Garmon Jones, 'Welsh Nationalism and Henry Tudor', *The Transactions of the Honourable Society of Cymmrodorion*, 1917-18, pp. 1-59). Associated with these prophecies and the revival at Henry's accession of the 'British History' was the cult of King Arthur. Henry included in his arms quarterings for Brut and Arthur as well as England and France and adopted the red dragon as his badge (see T.D. Kendrick, *British Antiquity*, London, 1950, p. 35). He arranged for his first son to be born at Winchester and named him Arthur as if in fulfilment of this prophecy. Pageants associated the new prince with the legendary kings (see Thomas Sharp, *A Dissertation on the Pageants or Dramatic Mysteries Anciently Performed at Coventry*, Coventry, 1825, p. 155, and *Great Chronicle,* pp. 297f). The Welsh prophecies and Arthurianism seem to have waned when there was no longer great need for them (see Josephine Waters Bennett, *The Evolution of the 'Faerie Queene'*, Chicago, 1942, p. 68). Sydney Anglo claims that the emphasis on British descent was not much exploited after Henry's accession ('The *British History* in Early Tudor Propaganda', *Bulletin of the John Rylands Library*, XLIV, 1961, pp. 17-48) until Elizabethan nationalism revived the cult of Arthur and inspired poets with the theme (see Charles Bowie Millican, *Spenser and the Table Round*, Cambridge, Mass., 1932).

82/21-22 and 3rd mar. n. See charter, text, pp. 79f.

82/22. [nephew by his brother] Henry VI's widowed mother, Katherine de Valois, married Owen Tudor. Their son, Edmund Tudor, was Henry VI's half-brother and Henry VII's father. So Henry VI was Henry VII's half-uncle on his mother's side.

82/35-44. Du Tillet, *Traictez*, p. 7.

82/40-50. Commynes, II, 306 [He had not a penny to his name, or vestige of any right, as I believe, to the crown of England].

83/5-9. *PROME*, ed. Anne Curry and Rosemary Horrox, Henry VI: Oct. 1460, XII, 522-25.

83/32. [by whatever right and whatever wrong]

83/46.-47 and mar. n. The Latin expression is 'festina lente' [hurry slowly]. Suetonius gives it in Greek in Augustus XXV, 4, *Vita Caesarum,* directly after the quotation from this work on p. 101/19-20.

84/8-9. Edmund Dudley and Sir Richard Empson were lawyers, members of Henry VII's council and rigorous tax collectors for the king. Popular hatred forced Henry VIII on his accession to have them executed on a charge of treason. They are mentioned in Polydore (pp. 613 and 620) and all his usual English followers. There is no indication that they caused any difficulties for Richard III. Buc probably introduces them because they were hated men who rose under Henry VII. For the others in this list, see above, n. 29/29-36.

84/1st mar. n. and 84/16-19. This quotation I have been unable to find in either Pontus Heuterus, *Rerum Burgundicarum* (Antwerp, 1584), whose Book V covers Charles of Burgundy, or in Meyer, whose Book XVII deals with the Burgundians [Charles the Bold did not want to hear the advice of others or – I hesitate to say – follow reasons, thinking it ignominious to learn from others, and judged everything himself in private by his own cogitations].

84/20-21 and 2nd mar. n. [The best man needs advice]: I have been unable to find this source, though there are extant works with similar titles. The quotation – which seems proverbial – is repeated on p. 200, l. 6 with the same citation.

84/34-35. More, p. 91, 'Thys man . . . hadde gotten by great experience . . . a depe insighte in politike worldli driftes'.

84/43-50. Herd, ff. 188v-189. This is an exact copy [If fortune had supported me and given the crown to a descendant of Henry VI, I never would have joined the council of King Edward. But when the decision stood with the supreme king to take away the sceptre from Henry and return it to Edward, I would never have been so crazy as to follow the party of the vanquished and support the dead against the living].

85/7-14 and 1st mar. n. Ariosto, *Orlando Furioso*, XIX, i. There are a few alterations in Buc's copy: 'Nessun' for 'Alcun non'; 'chi' (l. 4) for 'che' and 'amico' for 'Signor'. The first two are grammatical improvements. The last is an adaptation to Buc's sense. In the manuscript he wrote 'signor' first, then crossed it out and substituted 'amico'. Buc's translation is plodding and awkward, in part because he is following the rhyme scheme of the original, for which Italian is much better equipped than English.

85/36-39. Morton became Archbishop of Canterbury in 1486, Lord Chancellor in 1487, and Cardinal in 1493.

85/46-48. II Corinthians, 5:10.

86/1st mar. n. and **86/9**. Thomas Aquinas, *Summa Theologia*, pt. IIaIIae, quest. XLII, art. 2. Buc's 'art. 20' is a slip for '2', perhaps because he misread his own notes. The section discusses the problem and comes to this conclusion [Sedition is always in itself a mortal sin].

86/3rd mar. n. Stow, *Annales*, pp, 801f.

86/33-38. More states, p. 91, that Morton held these offices but does not consider them evidence of ambition: 'he . . . went to Rome neuer minding more to medle wt the world til ye noble prince Henry ye .vii. gate him home again, made him archbishop of Canturburye & chaunceller of England wherunto ye Pope ioined thonor of Cardinal'. Of his pride More says precisely the opposite of what Buc reports: 'Whose wisedom abused his pride to his owne deliueraunce & the dukes destruccion' (p. 90).

86/18-27 and 2nd mar. n. On p. 117, Godwin says that Morton, with the Pope's authority, forced the clergy to contribute towards his translation and that 'of his owne Dioces onely (which is one of the least in England) he receaued 354 pound'. He does not say specifically that this was a greater sum than ever before exacted. And on p. 221 he says,

> At wisbich castell likewise all the building of brick was of his charge. As also ye leame that he caused to be made for more conuenient cariage to his towne, which they say serueth now to smale purpose, and many complaine that the course of the riuer Nine into the sea by Clowcrosse is very much hindred thereby.

Godwin became Bishop of Hereford in 1617. The river Nine is now called 'Nene'.

87/12. in nubibus [cloudy].

87/19-22 and 1st mar. n. [About the writings of a king and the deeds of kings, justices cannot dispute, nor if a dispute should arise can it be interpreted: but in doubts and obscurities and when any edict contains two senses, interpretation can be expected at the will of our lord the king] Henricus de Bracton, *De Legibus et Consuetudinibus Angliae*, 6 vols., ed. Sir Travers Twiss, R.S. 70 (London, 1878), I, 268.

87/24-25. [Because the judgement of the prince is indisputable]

87/37-38. [Of the line of Lancaster, and head of the royal house, and prince of the family of Lancaster]

87/39-41. Chrimes, *Henry VII*, says that Polydore claims the plan for Henry to marry Elizabeth was worked out between Margaret Beaufort and Elizabeth Woodville, and that he probably got this from Henry himself. Polydore, pp. 549 and 550f gives two stories of the origin of the idea, one by Buckingham, the other by Margaret Beaufort. More has Morton originate the marriage (p. 91) but does not call it a union of York and Lancaster. Hall expands this remark, saying Morton's service to Henry Tudor consisted in 'Fyrste deuisyng the mariage betwene the lady Elizabeth daughter to kynge Edwarde the fourth by the whiche his faithfull and true seruice declared to bothe his maisters at once, was an infinite benefite to the realme, by the coniunction of the bloudes of Lancaster and Yorke . . .' (pp. 382f). Buc in his copy of Godwin, p. 221, has made a marginal note opposite the remark that Morton promoted the match and union of the houses: 'of this Morton & of his co*n*iunction vide Philip. Com.' Commynes says nothing about it; nor does Buc, probably having checked in the interim, refer to him at this point in the *History*.

87/50-88/1. [Henry king of England by divine right, by human law and by right of war]

88/2-48. These remarks seem to be expanded from a statement in Crowland, pp. 194f:

> In hoc Parliamento confirmatum est Regnum domino Regi, tanquam sibi debitum non ex uno sed ex multis titulis, ut non tam sanguinis quam victoriae bellicae conquaestusque jure rectissime populo Anglicano praesidere credatur. Fuerunt qui consultius aestimabant, verba ejusmodi silentio potius quam edicto committi; eo potissime, quod in isto eodem Parliamento tractatum est, atque per Regem assensum, super matrimonio dominae Elizabeth primogenitae Regis Edwardi: in cujus persona visum omnibus erat posse suppleri, quicquid aliunde ipsi Regi deesse de titulo videbatur.

[In this Parliament the king's royal authority was confirmed as due to him not by one but by many titles, so that he may be considered to rule rightfully over the English people not only by right of blood but of victory in battle and of conquest. There were those who, more wisely, thought that such words should rather have been kept silent than committed to proclamation, particularly because, in that same Parliament, and with the king's consent, there was discussion about the marriage to the lady Elizabeth, King Edward's eldest daughter, in whose person, it seemed to all, could be found whatever was missing in the king's title elsewhere.]

88/15-16. See below, p. 91 for full quotation.

88/42 and 1st mar. n. [Whatever the victor dares or the vanquished fears] Seneca, *Troades*, 586.

89/4-5. [and in the fourth degree of consanguinity, and perhaps in the ranks of affinity]

89/6-9. Pope Alexander's Bull of 1494, confirming Pope Innocent's of 1486, appears in B.L. MS. Cotton Cleopatra E.III, f. 147 and was printed several times by de Worde and Pynson. See E. Gordon Duff, *Fifteenth Century English Books* (Oxford, 1917), nos. 228-30. Duff assumes that the reissue was due to the uprisings connected with Perkin Warbeck. It is perhaps this Bull rather than Pope Innocent's to which the marginal note refers.

89/18. [from his own mere motion and from his certain knowledge]

89/24-37. [This king of England having his origin in the house of Lancaster, who by well-known right and indubitable succession to the title and by election and grant of the prelates and nobles, etc. And also by right of war is king of England. . . . And we supply each and all defects, as of law and of deed, if any intervene in speaking of the kingdom. . . . The pages of our confirmation, approbation, pronouncement, institution, declaration, making good, advice, requisition, prohibition, inhibition, benediction, and restraint, excommunication and anathematization against whoever should in whatever way presume to infringe, or dares by any means to contravene these Apostolical letters . . . by Apostolical authority.]

This Bull is printed in *Materials*, ed. Campbell, I, 392-8. Text, p. 89, ll. 4-5 [and in the fourth degree of consanguinity, and perhaps in the scale of affinities] is an exact quotation. Text, p. 89, ll. 24-26 is from the following (p. 393):

> Henricus rex praefatus, quanquam non modo jure belli ac notorio et indubitato proximo successionis titulo, verum etiam omnium prelatorum, procerum, magnatum, nobilium, totiusque ejusdem regni Angliae plebis electione et voto necnon decreto statuto et ordinatione ipsius Anglae regni trium statuum in ipsorum conventu, Parliamento nuncupato . . .

[Henry, the foresaid king, who not only by right of war and by famous and undoubted proximity to the title, indeed by election of all the prelates, princes, magnates, nobles, and by election and vote of all of the people of England not without statutory decree and by order of the kingdom of England itself in conclave, by pronouncement of Parliament].

89/48-90/7. This hereditary title can be seen in *PROME,* Henry VII: Nov. 1485, XV, p 97. Buc quotes it below, with stylistic paraphrasing only, text, pp. 214-15.

90/31-94/8. For the outline of the story of Henry Tudor's second invasion preparations, Buc has followed Polydore, pp. 553-61, with information added from Commynes and Tillet. He seems to have invented Landois's speeches.

91/11-12. Commynes, II, 234.

91/43. Commynes, II, 306. [three thousand men, the most wretched that could be found].

91/48-92/40. Richard sent to the Duke of Brittany offering him the revenue of the earldom of Richmond in return for the surrender of Henry (E.F. Jacob, *The Fifteenth Century*, 1399-1485, Oxford, 1961, p. 628). The message was received during the duke's illness by Landois, whose interest was in money and increasing his own influence. Henry was warned by Morton through Urswick, who then went on to procure a safe conduct to France for Henry and his followers (Polydore, p. 555). Negotiations between Richard and Brittany are recorded in *Foedera*, V, Pt. 3, 147 [XII, 226f] and 148 [229] and *Pat. Rolls* (1476-1485), pp. 517 and 547.

94/mar. n. Polydore, p. 559.

94/18. That Buc used Polydore as his source in this section we can tell from his reference to Dr Morgan ('Johannes Morganus', Polydore, p. 560), whom his followers turn into 'Morgan Kidwelly' (Hall, p. 410, Grafton, II, 147, Holinshed, III, 434).

94/19-48. For the important part played by the Welsh in Henry's rise to the throne, see Howell T. Evans, *Wales and the Wars of the Roses* (Cambridge, 1915).

94/39-40. See n. 82/15-18, above.

94/42-43 and **95/2-3**. Although his uncle Gilbert Talbot followed Tudor and brought most of the family's retainers, George, Earl of Shrewsbury, reputedly fought for Richard. See above, n. 29/29-26.

95/1st mar. n. Commynes, II, 306: 'se vint joindre son beau pére le seigneur de Stanlay avec bien XXV mil Angloys' [there came to his aid his father-in-law, Stanley, with at least 25,000 English']. The sixteenth-century editions of Commynes give the number as 26,000. Such a large number is most unlikely. Polydore, p. 563 and most of his followers say Lord Stanley had a goodly company and Sir William Stanley 3,000 (Holinshed, III, 435, says almost 5,000). Ross conjectures (*The Wars of the Roses*, London, 1976, p. 139) that 20,000-25,000 men were involved in the battle on both sides.

95/12-13. Northumberland, whose power in the North was overshadowed only by Richard's, had once before played the game of neutrality, not stirring to strike for either Henry VI or Edward IV in 1471. According to accounts from Hall (p. 429) onwards, he made no move during the battle and afterwards was captured but soon restored to favour. An article by Anthony Goodman and Angus Mackay, 'A Castilian Report on English Affairs, 1486', *EHR*, LXXXVIII (January, 1973), 92-9, throws light on Northumberland's behaviour at Bosworth. According to a contemporary account of Mosén Diego de Valera, Northumberland committed himself to Henry before the battle but was afterwards arrested on information that he planned to replace Henry as king with Edward, Earl of Warwick; he remained imprisoned until Warwick was in custody. Valera, contrary to the common report of Northumberland's neutrality during the battle, says that he marched before Richard's vanguard, turned his back to Henry's and began fighting along with it. But, Goodman and Mackay suggest, the chroniclers concealed his assistance because of Tudor reluctance to be indebted to Percy influence. It is perhaps significant in this context that all Buc's great-nephew's copies of Sir George's work omit the reference to Northumberland that appears in the original (text, p. 106f).

Stanley had a history of waiting to see which side was winning before joining battle. At Blore Heath in 1459, he was summoned several times and when he came did not engage in the fighting. For this he was attainted by Henry VI. *Paston Letters*, II, 432f, report that after the Welles uprising Clarence and Warwick hoped for his aid. At the readeption Stanley joined Henry VI, then reappeared at Edward's side after the latter had regained the throne. His behaviour while Richard and the Woodvilles were battling for control was so ambiguous that we are still in doubt as to whether or not he was arrested at the Tower council. If so, he was very soon released. Before Bosworth he was making promises to both Richard and Henry. He was also making excuses to both for not presenting his forces in overt support of either side. Lord Stanley's presence at Bosworth is doubtful, but his brother Sir William Stanley participated in the battle. He was reported to have held aloof until the opportunity arose to take Richard by surprise at the height of his mounted charge at Henry. Seeing the king's flank exposed, William Stanley and his 3,000 men attacked and overwhelmed him. (Polydore, p. 563). David Horsfall, *Richard III* (London, 2015, p. 238), points out that unreliability of armies was a problem throughout the period and that Edward IV had been much more 'comprehensively abandoned'.

The site of the battlefield was 'lost' for centuries. Recent archaeology has recovered it. See Glenn Foard and Anne Curry, *Bosworth 1485, a Battlefield Rediscovered*, Oxford 2013 for an account of the fascinating archaeology.

95/2nd mar. n. [(King Richard) left Leicester with great pomp, wearing the diadem on his head. . .] Crowland, p. 178.

95/19-20 and **98/46-99/18.** Armstrong, 'Inauguration Ceremonies', pp. 70f, discusses the revival by Yorkist monarchs of a much earlier custom, crown wearing outside Parliament, a practice indulged in by Edward IV and Richard III when their authority was not in danger as well as when it was, 'to stabilize by an appeal to the visual senses, social conditions which had become dangerously fluid. . . . At a crown-wearing the identity between the person and the office of the king could be intuitively perceived, because the formal and actual seat of authority was unmistakably apparent'.

95/33-34. Plato, *Republic*, V, xvi, C [War which Greeks instigate against Greeks is not war but sedition]. Also quoted in Erasmus, *Institutio Principis Christiani.*

96/1st mar. n. Salisbury, *Policraticus*, '. . . in veterum scriptis sicarii dicuntur et latrones quicumque lege non praecipiente arma tractant. Arma namque, quibus lex non utitur, legem impugnant' (600b) [. . . in the writings of the ancients the names of assassins and bandits are given to all those who make use of weapons without the direction of the law; for weapons which are not employed legally attack the law].

96/26 and 2nd mar. n. [Any crime that proves successful becomes honest] Seneca, *Hippolytus*, 598.

96/27 and 3rd mar. n. [A prosperous and successful crime is called a virtue] Seneca, *Herculens Furens*, 251-2.

96/34-35. Sir Thomas Wyatt the younger, son of the poet, led a Kentish rebellion against Queen Mary in 1554. He was beheaded, drawn and quartered. **Sir John Oldcastle**, a Lollard conspirator against Henry V, was executed in 1417. **Owen Glendower** led the Welsh sector of rebellion against Henry IV. **Charles**

Neville Earl of Westmorland, co-leader of a rebellion against Queen Elizabeth in favour of Mary, Queen of Scots, was attainted in 1571 and died in 1601. Gerald Fitzjames, Earl of Desmond, rebelled in Ireland against Elizabeth in 1579, was attainted in 1582, and slain in 1583.

96/47. Polydore, pp. 561ff and all his followers say that Sir Walter Hungerford and Sir Thomas Bourchier and others joined Henry Tudor between Lichfield and Tamworth, and on the evening of the same day, Sir John Savage, Sir Brian Sanford, Sir Simon Digby and others, having left Richard, came to him.

97/17-18. See above, n. 95/1st mar. n.

97/25-38. This story was related first, cited as popular report, by Polydore (p. 564), and copied by his followers. It is corroborated by Valera, who says that Salaçar, a Spaniard in Richard's service, urged Richard to seek personal safety. Richard refused, saying, 'Salazar, God forbid I yield one step. This day I will die as king or win'. (E.M. Nokes and G. Wheeler, 'A Castilian Report of the Battle of Bosworth', *The Ricardian*, II, 1972, 2.) He then put on his crown and mail and fought with such strength and courage that those who were with him fought hard by his example.

97/47-48. First reported by Hall, p. 419. This rhyme 'one wrote on his gate' to warn Norfolk to refrain from the field.

98/39-45 and **99/20-32.** Polydore, p. 563, speaks of combat between Richard and Henry in much more general terms than do his followers: 'Sensit contra se Henricus Ricardum ire, & quia omnis spes salutis in armis erat, se certamini auidè offert. . . . Sustinuit tamen Henricus impetum diutius, quàm etiam eius milites putarent, qui uictoriam iam penè desperaba*n*t' [Henry decided to attack Richard, and because all hope of safety was in arms, he eagerly offered battle. Still Henry kept up the attack for a long time, more even than his soldiers expected, who almost despaired of victory]. Hall (p. 418) turns this into personal combat: 'Therle of Richmonde perceyued wel the king furiusly commyng toward him, and by cause the hole hope of his welth and purpose was to be determined by battaill, he gladly proffered to encountre with him body to body and man to man'.

99/1. Polydore, p. 564.

99/26-27 and mar. n. [The earl of Richmond advanced directly upon King Richard] 'Comes Richmundiae cum militibus suis directe super regem Richardum processit' is what Crowland actually says, p. 180. This does not refer to single combat. Buc (or the version he is using) omits the words 'cum militibus suis' [with his troops] after 'Richmundiae'.

100/13. [the gods thought otherwise]: "sic visum superis" is in Ovid, *Metamorphosis*, I, 54. It appears subsequently in collections of proverbs, like Erasmus's *Chileades*. Buc has merely made the positive expression negative.

100/22-24. Richard's force appeared larger to begin with, but betrayal by the Stanleys, the non-participation of Northumberland, and the defection of the Welsh during the battle (see Cothi, p. xxxvi) meant that Henry's forces ultimately outnumbered Richard's. The Tudor historians stress that Henry's army was small in comparison with Richard's (it was if we count only the forces he brought to England), because if the number is small, the victory seems more attributable to God's favour: 'Non in multitudine bellantium sed in Dei manu consistit victoria'

[Not in size of host but in God's hand lies the victory], says André, p. 27.

100/29-31. Polydore, p. 564, is the first to report that Lord Stanley crowned Henry in the field, and all his followers copy this report, so it became a myth, but is unlikely to be more than that.

100/32-35. [In the end a glorious victory was granted by heaven to the earl of Richmond, now sole king, together with the priceless crown which King Richard had previously worn] Crowland, pp. 180f. Buc only very slightly paraphrased it.

100/47-48. The Earl of Devon and the Bishop of Exeter were not brothers but cousins. This is an error Shakespeare adopts in *Richard III* (IV, iv, ll. 500-1), deriving it from Hall.

101/12-13 and 2nd mar. n. [Those who fiercely and quickly despise instead of fearing the enemy fare better]: Buc here paraphrases Tacitus, *Historiae*, IV, lxxi.

101/17 and 4th mar. n. [Rashness, which is first of all stupid, is also ineffectual] Livy, *Ab Urbe Condita*, XXII, xxxviii, 12, paraphrased.

101/19-20 and 5th mar. n. [(He judged) nothing less perfect in a leader than haste and rashness] Suetonius, *Augustus*, XXV, 4.

101/22-23 and 6th mar. n. [Choosing rashness and impiety over reason leaves one open to all traps and snares]: Paraphrased from the Greek of Polybius, *Historiae*, III, lxxxi, 9.

101/26-27 and 7th mar. n. [Nothing about the enemy is safe to underrate; those whom you scorn you make more valiant by ignoring them] Quintus Curtius, *Historiarum Alexandri Magni*, VI, iii, 11.

101/27-28 and 8th mar. n. [Nothing is more ruinous in war than to dismiss the enemy as incompetent]: I have been unable to trace this quotation.

101/9th mar. n. Proverbs 16:18.

101/33-34. [In council error accompanies pride, unhappiness accompanies error]: this remark is not in Strigelius's gloss, *Salmonis Libri Tres*, n.p. 1565, though there is a somewhat similar remark there.

101/36-102/2. This is an Aesopian fable given in Erasmus, *Chileades,* 777, under the title 'Scarabeus aquilam quaerit' [The beetle seeks the eagle].

102/29-39. The King of Scots requested single combat with Surrey for the town of Berwick and the fishgarths on the Western Marches. Surrey replied that

> he thanked hys grace that he wolde put hym to so moche honour, that he being a kyng anointed wolde fighte hande to hande wyth so poore a man as he, howbeit he seid, he wolde nat deceyve hys grace, for he seid though he wanne hym in batayle, he quas never the nerer to Berwicke nor to Fyshgarthis, for he had no such commyssyon so to do.
> (Surrey's epitaph in Thomas Martin, *The History of the Town of Thetford,* London, 1779, Appendix, p. 46).

The chroniclers repeat the story.

103/4-5. There are several references in Bracton to the concept of the king being without peer: Vol. I, p. 38, Vol. II, p. 172, Vol. VI, p. 248.

103/5-11. Plutarch, *Moralia*, 179 D.

103/36-39. [after he had held onto the sovereignty and consolidated it he stayed at home and waged war, concluded battles, invaded provinces, beat rebels, and subjected barbarian peoples through proconsuls, governors, through deputies, etc.] Suetonius, *Augustus* XX, says that Augustus conducted only two foreign wars in person, and his others were conducted by generals, though he was often present or nearby. The reference in Dion Cassius is *History of Rome*, LIII, 4. I can find no reference in Plutarch incorporating this information. Tacitus, *Annales*, I, ii, says something similar in sense but not in expression.

104/9-10. This quotation is most familiar from Marlowe's *Doctor Faustus*, II i, which does not include 'est' [It is a comfort to those in misery to have had companionship in suffering]. John D. Jump, editor of the Revels edition of *Faustus* (London, 1962), p. 42, says it occurs in other period works and has been traced back to Seneca's *De Consolatione ad Polybium*, xii, 2, which does express the same general idea, that it is consoling to share misery.

104/15 [Not unavenged shall we all die today] Vergil, *Aeneid*, II, 670.

104/2nd mar. n. [Here I am using 'god' to stand for 'king']

104/41-42. Jeremiah 18:3-4.

104/44-45. Romans 1:28 slightly paraphrased.

104/48-105/2. [If some angry god drags people to punishment, first he usually deprives them of their good sense and pours darkness over them so that they may rush to their ruin, to which they have turned of their own accord, by their own ill counsel.] Buc says this is translated from Lycurgus (author of *Against Leocrates*), but I have not found it there. The verse breaks down in the third line, between which and the fourth line Buc makes no division, and appears to end in two lines of inferior verse. I am grateful to John Blundell for locating something similar as an anonymous fragment in Nauck, *Tragicorum Graecorum Fragmenta*, second edition 1889, Adespota fr. 296 on page 896. Probably a fair number of Buc's Latin decorative remarks came from commonplace books. One was taught in school to keep them in mind to use when required.

105/4-5. [Whom Jupiter chooses to destroy he makes mad] translation of Euripides, Fragment inc. B. xxv.

105/6-8. [The mind of men is sometimes darkened by that higher mind which, whenever it determines to change someone's fortunes, corrupts his counsels]. I have not been able to trace this to an author.

105/22-25. Hall, p. 421, whose description is an elaboration of Fabyan's (p. 673), says:

> his bodye was naked and despoyled to the skyne, and nothyge left aboue hym not so muche as a clowte to couer hys pryue members, and was trussed behynde a pursuiuant of armes called blaunche senglier or whyte bore, lyke a hogge or a calfe, the hed and armes hangynge on the one side of the horse, and the legges on the other syde, and all by sprynceled with myre and bloude . . .

Crowland says that Richard's body, treated with many indignities and not enough humanity, a rope about his neck, was carried to Leicester (pp. 182f). It was suggested by Philippa Langley in a lecture as part of the Middleham Festival in July 2016 that the display of his body, taken to Leicester slung face-down over a horse, would have accentuated one of the effects of scoliosis visible only when bent forward, i.e. that the lateral twist of the spine can cause the shoulder-blade or ribs on one side to protrude. This, laid bare for the first time, may have been what gave rise to the hunchback legend (see Appendix, p. 355).

105/1st mar. n. [Thus fell Richard in battle, in miserable slaughter, cruelly dragged by the hair by the cruel enemy] Herd, f. 186v.

105/34-36. When his skeleton was discovered in 2013 it appeared that some of the wounds were humiliation wounds bestowed after death.

105/43-50. Henry of Huntingdon, *The History of the English*, ed. Thomas Arnold, R.S. 74 (London, 1879). Though Huntingdon's history includes this period, he does not relate this in detail. It is contained in Matthew Paris, *Chronica Majora*, ed. Henry Richards Luard, R.S. 57 (London, 1872-83), I, 542.

106/1-3, 107/32-36 and 108/16-17. Polydore and his followers speak of these executions after the battle, mentioning only Catesby by name. Since Buc mentions only Catesby and his own ancestor, it is clear that he had no source other than the chroniclers and family tradition regarding his great-grandfather. Polydore says (p. 564), 'Bidue post Lecestriae Gulielmus Chatysby leguleius, cum paucis suis socijs supplicio afficitur' [Two days after at Leicester William Catesby, lawyer, with a few of his companions, was put to death].

106/5-108/15. The attainder of Richard's followers, which would have been illegal had not Henry purposely misdated his reign as beginning the day before the battle, appears in *PROME*, Henry VII: Nov. 1485, XV, 108. Buc's list agrees with it, with very little deviation. The Act of Attainder given in *PROME* does not include Thomas Broughton, who was attainted later in connection with Lincoln's uprising, or Sir William Conyers, or Thomas Stafford, who ought to have been included since he is listed by Polydore (p. 564) and his followers as one of Richard's party who escaped after the battle (in Buc's second list, 'Robert' is probably an error for 'Thomas' Stafford). Only one Herald at Arms, Richard Watkins, is mentioned as such in the *PROME* list. Where in text, p. 106, l. 45 Buc says 'suits', the *PROME* list says 'services'. Buc's wording here seems more likely. *Plumpton Correspondence*, Letter X of 13 December 1485 contains a similar list, also leaving out Conyers and Thomas Stafford. The attainders were passed, it says, 'Howbeit, ther was many gentlemen agaynst it, but it wold not be, for yt was the Kinges pleasure' (pp. 48f).

106/16-17. Commynes, II, Book IV, *passim*. Monstrelet gives one mention: see above, n. 52/40-42.

106/18-23. The idea that Norfolk retired from court during Richard III's reign seems to have come from Surrey's epitaph 'they both [Norfolk and Surrey] servyd . . . kynge Richard truly as hys subgettis duryng hys lyffe, lieng at home in their owne cowntrys, and kepyng honorabyl howses' (Martin, Appendix, p. 44). Melvin J. Tucker, *The Life of Thomas Howard, Earl of Surrey and Second Duke of Norfolk, 1443-1524* (London, 1964), pp. 44ff shows that the epitaph is misleading in suggesting that they stayed at home and ignored Richard's reliance upon them. Both were often with him, Surrey as Steward in constant attendance. Norfolk was Admiral of England, Ireland and Aquitaine and had power of array in thirteen shires. Their military, Parliamentary, and ambassadorial activities were numerous and important.

106/23-25. This statement is not in More as we now have his text, but seems to have been in an earlier draft which is represented in Grafton and Hall's inclusions of More's *Richard III* in their works (see Sylvester, Appendix, in More, pp. 273f). Hall speaks of Thomas, son to the Lord Howard, 'which lord was one of the priueyest of the lord protectors counsaill and dooyng' (p. 361). Whereas the More passage seems to refer to Surrey, Buc takes it as referring to Norfolk.

106/47. [if law, then the highest law]

107/4-7. Crowland Chronicle, p. 180 (with omission only of filler word 'vero') [In the place where the earl of Northumberland stood, however, with a fairly large and well-equipped force, there was no contest against the enemy and no blows given or received in battle, p. 181].

107/25-29. Crowland, p. 180. Buc has misread 'magno' as 'in agro' and explained it in brackets as the field of Redmore (the brackets appear in the original manuscript. I have slanted them to avoid the assumption that they enclose a portion from Egerton). Buc has made some cuts [the earl of Oxford . . . a very valiant knight, with a large force of French as well as English troops, took up his position opposite the wing where the duke of Norfolk was stationed, p. 181].

107/43-110/1. Fabyan (p. 673) says that Surrey was taken in the field. Polydore (p. 564) and his followers state that Surrey submitted and was taken prisoner in the field and held a long time. Hall adds he was last restored '& for his trueth and fidelity after promoted to high honors offices & dignites' (Hall, p. 419). A fuller account is given on Surrey's probably autobiographical epitaph (Martin, Appendix, pp. 44f): he went to Bosworth with Richard, was wounded, taken in the field, and imprisoned in the Tower. During Lincoln's rebellion he refused the Lieutenant of the Tower's offer of keys to liberate himself, saying that he would wait until the king who had committed him released him, and

> after that for the true and feithful service that the seid kynge Henry herd of hym doon to hys other prince; and also that he sawe himself, he dide on Bosworth feld, and for the great prayse and truth that he herd of him whills he was prisoner, and that he wold nat, thoughe he had libertie, come oute of the tower at the erl of Lincolns feld, he toke hym out to hys presence, and to be about hys owne person . . .

Buc is in the habit of supplying circumstantial detail to add narrative interest, so its presence cannot serve as evidence of the story's reliability. But because of his grandfather's intimate connection with Surrey, his account should not be dismissed. Either the story of the chroniclers and the memorial was invented to add greater glory to the Tudors or the story Buc heard was invented to add greater glory to the Howards. Surrey's attainder was removed in 1489 as the first item of the Parliament of that year (*PROME*, ed. Rosemary Horrox, Henry VII: Jan. 1489, XVI, p. 11).

109/9-10. Henry married Elizabeth in 1486 and had her crowned in 1487.

109/26-43. Camden in *Remaines*, p. 283 (p. 217 in 1605 edition), gives this story a pro-Parliamentary twist:

> When *Richard* the third was slaine at *Bosworth*, and with

> him *Iohn Howard* Duke of *Norffolke*, King *Henry* the seauenth demaunded of *Thomas Howard* Earle of *Surrey* the Dukes sonne and heire then taken prisoner, how he durst beare Armes in the behalfe of that tyranne *Richard.* He answered; *He was my crowned King, and if the Parlamentary authority of England set the Crowne vpon a stocke, I will fight for that stocke. And as I fought then for him, I will fight for you, when you are established by the said authority.* And so hee did for his sonne King *Henry* the eight at *Floddon* field.

The source is given as 'Anonymous'. Buc retells the story at greater length, substituting all the 'great officers and peers men of the realm' (p. 109) for a direct mention of Parliament by name, but whether Camden borrowed from Buc or Buc from Camden or both used the same source is not known. Philippa Langley, in an e-mail to me (16/01/2017), suggested that Henry's reason for executing Sir John Buck, Buc's great-grandfather, who was a Howard adherent, directly after the battle may have been as a warning to Surrey, and that it clearly worked. Sir John Buck's attainder is recorded in *PROME,* Henry VII: Nov. 1485, XV, 108.

110/10-11. Surrey was made High Treasurer in 1501 under Henry VII and restored to the dukedom of Norfolk under Henry VIII in 1514, not, as Buc says, under Henry VII. Buc is correct in stating that he was made Earl Marshal under Henry VIII (1510).

110/18. [side by side]

110/20-113/39. The name might be Scandinavian, from an original 'Hereward'. This assumption led to the genealogical conjecture current among the heralds in Buc's time that the Howards were descended from Hereward the Wake. But more likely it comes from 'Heyward', a warden of barns (Gerald Brenan and Edward Phillips Stratham, *The House of Howard*, 2 vols., London, 1907, I, 3f). Camden in *Remaines*, p. 131 gives the name's variants in Domesday Book as 'Hereward, Howard, Heward', citing them among names derived from Christian names. William Dugdale was unable to trace the family beyond Edward I's time and mentions that some trace it to Hereward, but he cannot support this theory since he notes that Crowland mentions as Hereward's sole issue a daughter (*Baronage of England*, London, 1676, II, 265). Nor does Henry Howard of Corby (*Indications of Memorials . . . of the Howard Family*, Corby Castle, 1834) try to trace them further back.

Buc gives a similar account of the family's origins in *Comm.*, using all the sources he cites here apart from Matthew of Westminster. For more recent history he seems to have used the Rolls and the private collection of the Lord Admiral. *Comm.*'s account contains more direct quotation from Crowland, whereas the *History* paraphrases the same material. *Comm.*'s information on Hereward is substantially the same, but Buc in that work is more explicit in attempting to derive the Howards from Hereward by logic: the Howards might have sprung 'from a Heward or Hereward in Marshland who liued about the tyme of the Conq.' (*Comm.* f. 18), since there was a Fulco *filius Hewardi* living under William II or Henry I, and this man's family possessed lands in Marshland very early. The same error in reading 'Edina' for 'Ediva' appears in *Comm.*, but there is no mention of her ill treatment or of Tailbois's ransom. The interchangeable spellings are documented in *Comm.* as they are here from records found by St Low Kniveton and from the papers in Lord William Howard's possession: 'my L. W. Howard of Naworth shewed me out of an ancient deed made by the sayd Hereward his ancestor, & who is called in one place Hereward & in another Heward . . .' (ff. 18f). For the interpretation of the name as 'leader of the army' he cites Camden's *Remaines*, and for recent history Nicholas Charles's researches in the archives. As here, he argues that bastard stock is not dishonourable, giving as examples William the Conqueror, King Arthur, the Bastard of Orleans, the Bastard of Burgundy, Alexander the Great (according to Plutarch), and Jesus Christ (*Comm.*, f. 18^{v}). Some of the recent details differ in the two accounts. Both fail to distinguish John Howard who lived under Henry VI from his sons John and Robert, who, by predeceasing him, made the John who was to become Duke of Norfolk heir to his grandfather, not his father. Because of the numerous tipped in pages in the section of *Comm.* which describes the origins and history of the Howards, it may be surmised that Buc was actively working on this genealogy quite late in the course of *Comm.*'s composition, around 1614. He had mentioned the Howards' derivation before that only once, in *Daphnis* (sig. E3^{v}), saying that they sprang from Edward I's son Thomas of Brotherton. By the time of writing the *History*, he has managed to sort out some of his evidence and fill in some gaps.

110/20. Crowland, in *Rerum Anglicarum Scriptorum Veterum*, ed. William Fulman], (Oxford, 1684), I, 67 [whether he could be happier or stronger].

110/41-45. Huntingdon, p. 205; Hoveden, I, 125f; Matthew Paris, II, 7; Matthew of Westminster, *Flores Historiarum*, ed. Luard, R.S. 95 (London, 1890), II, 5f; and Walsingham, *Ypodigma Neustriae*, ed. Riley, R.S. 28/7 (London, 1876), p. 72, all tell the same story of Hereward's defence of Ely. *Liber Eliensis*, ed. E.O. Blake, Cam. Soc., 3rd ser. 92 (London, 1962), pp. 173-92, of which there were manuscript copies in Cotton's library, gives a detailed description of Hereward's defence of Ely. But most of Buc's material seems to come from Crowland, Fulman ed., I, 67-71 or from a ms. fairly similar to it.

110/44-46. Crowland, Fulman ed., I, 67. Hereward's father is described as a great benefactor of the monastery; his wife had died an inmate there four years before; his daughter still lived nearby and had just married Evermue, also a friend the monastery.

110/50-111/2. All sources stress Hereward's strength and vigour. Crowland, Fulman ed., I, 67 says he was a youth of tremendous strength, tall, a most handsome young man, but too bellicose.

111/13-18. Crowland, Fulman ed., I, 70 says only that Hereward's lands were given to certain Normans. That this meant Tailbois is suggested by a later remark (p. 71) that Tailbois ruled all the surrounding country.

111/19-23. Crowland is not clear as to whether Hereward took Tailbois or Thorold, Abbot of Burgh (Peterborough) prisoner. Without much doubt Thorold is meant and Buc has misinterpreted. Also, Buc has confused Ingulph's sequence of events: first Hereward returned and drove out his mother's persecutors (p. 70). Nothing is said of taking the new earl prisoner, nor is the earl identified. Next he defended Ely (p. 71), during the siege of which he defeated Tailbois (p. 125). Next Tailbois egged Thorold on against Hereward, who captured the abbot and released him for ransom.

111/24-29. This information is from Paris, II, 7.

111/40-41. Crowland, Fulman ed., I, 67. See n. 110/44-46 above.

112/mar. n. There is a general reference to Aeneas's birth in *Iliad* II, 819-21. In several places it is stated that he was son to Venus and Anchises, but legitimacy is not mentioned (though one might perhaps entertain doubts on the legitimacy of a connection between a mortal and a god). Livy speaks of Romulus and Remus's birth, *Ab Urbe Condita*, I, iv.

112/6-7. Plutarch, *Lives*, in 'Theseus', 3-4 and 'Themistocles', 1.

112/30-33. In *Comm.* (ff. 161ff) Buc gives more examples of surnames derived from offices.

113/6. I cannot trace the origin of this axiom [identity of arms and cognomen presumes identity of family].

113/13. [Who makes the best conjecture appears the best prophet] I cannot trace the origin of this verse.

113/34-41. This passage, in an incomplete state of revision, makes more sense if we read below in 113/39-40, 'John Howard, the son of Robert Howard', which is what Buc meant to say. Robert Howard, the father of Richard III's follower Sir John Howard, was the younger son of a John Howard who had a son John by his first wife. Robert died in England, but his father John died on a pilgrimage (see Brenan, I, 10-12).

113/35. Stoke Neyland = Stoke by Nayland.

114/6-14. Commynes, II, 242 and Book IV, *passim.* Monstrelet gives only one mention: see above, n. 52/40-42. The memorial on Surrey's tomb at Thetford is printed in Martin, Appendix, pp. 43-9.

114/26-30. See n. 75/4th mar. n., above.

114/2nd mar. n. Camden in 'Iceni' (Norfolk), not 'Ottadini'(Northumberland), p. 352, tells how Henry VIII honoured Howard for the victory at Flodden, but this particular title is not mentioned. Buc makes a correct reference to 'Ottadini' in his next note.

114/37-116/47 For a discussion of Buc's ancestry as given in *History* and *Comm.*, see above, pp. xv-xvii.

115/7-13 and 1st mar. n. Camden in 'Ottadini', p. 668:

> Rutarios vocauit haec aetas exteros illos & praedatorios milites quos è Belgio & aliunde in subsidium Regis Joannis Falcasius de *Brent*, & Walterus *Buc* adduxerunt, *Brent* homo efferatus tandem regno eiectus. *Buc* verò sedatior cùm strenuam operam regni nauasset, possesssiones in agro Eboracensi & Northantonensi à Rege accepit, eiusque posteri ibidem floruerunt vsque ad Ioannem *Buc* proscriptum sub Henrico Septimo. Cuius pronepos est à Georgius *Buc* vir literatè doctus Eques auratu & à regijs spectaculis, qui (iuuat enim profiteri per quos profeci) multa in historijs oberuauit, & candidè

> impertijt.
> [That age called forraine and willing souldiours, *Rutars* whom Falques de *Brent* and Walter *Buc* brought out of the Low Countries and from other parts to aide King Iohn. *Brent* a wilde madbraine, was at length banished out of the Realme: but *Buc* a more staied man after hee had done the King stout service, had given unto him by the King, possessions in Yorke-shire and Northamptoushire: and his race flourished there, untill that Iohn *Buc* was attainted under King Henry the Seventh, whose great grand-son is Sir George *Buc* knight, a man well learned, of great reading, and Master of the Kings Revells; who (for I take pleasure to professe by whom I haue profited) hath observed many things in historie, and gently imparted the same to me [p. 812].

Camden may well have got this information from Buc.

115/13-14 and 2nd mar. n. Ludovico Guicciardini, *Descrittione di Tutti i Paesi Bassi* (Antwerp, 1581), p. 432: 'vi si veggono ancora le reliquie dell'antico castello di Buck, doue fu la prima dimora di quegli Signor, che alla guardi di Fiandra, per i Re Franzesi dimorauano' [You come next to the remains of the ancient castle of Buck, the first dwelling of those gentlemen who stayed there as guards of Flanders for the French king].

115/19-20. Roger de Wendover, *Flores Historiarum*, ed. Henry G. Hewlett, R.S. 84 (London, 1886-9), II, 147 [They came to England with three legions of soldiers from Flanders and Brabant].

115/21-22. Paris II, 622, 636 and 645. Radulphus de Coggeshall, *Chronicon Anglicanum*, ed. Joseph Stevenson, R.S. 66 (London, 1875), pp. 177f. Matthew of Westminster, II, 155. Coggeshall's and Westminster's comments on Walter Buck are unfavourable and are given as evidence of King John's tyranny in hiring foreign mercenaries in 1215. Wendover in a later passage than the one Buc cites is not favourable either, saying that Walter Buc with his Brabantians seized people from all the churches and tortured them cruelly until they paid a hefty ransom (p. 171). Paris follows Wendover and emphasizes Walter Buck's atrocities. Walsingham does not speak of Walter Buck by name but briefly mentions the Flemish mercenaries (*Ypodigma*, p. 133).

115/33-35. This charter, B.L. MS. Cotton Augustus II, 56, is printed in Dugdale, *Monasticon Anglicanum* (London, 1830), VI, pt. i, pp. 285, no. I. A charter of the Abbey's foundation dating from around 1130, it lists the contributions of the founders, among them 'Radulf*us* buhc. & Gozelin*us* fili*us* ei*us*' [Ralph Buc and Gocelinus his son] who gave four bovates of land each, the former in Grendale, the latter in Bucton. Buc mentions this charter in *Comm.*, noting that it is in Cotton's collection. There he follows it in describing Gocelinus as the son of Radulphus rather than the grandson (*Comm.*, f. 451v).

115/43 and **116/8.** Herthill is now spelt 'Harthill'.

115/45-49. *Pat. Rolls* (5 Nov. 1389), 146, 'Discharge of Richard, Earl of Arundel and Surrey, admiral of England' from a bond to keep safe Sir John Buke, 'a prisoner of war lately captured at sea' and not to ransom him without licence from the king or Council, on which assurance Buke was delivered from the Tower and was in Arundel's custody until his death in October, 1389. Buc notes in Cotton Cleo. D IV, f. 182v Stow's notice, based on the Rolls in the Tower, that John Buck was liberated by Arundel in the thirteenth year of Richard II.

116/14. [All the fortunate are related] from Menander, *Γνῶαι Μονόστιχοι* [One-line maxims], 748.

116/2nd mar. n. Euripides, *Heracleides*, 10-11.

116/43-44. George Talbot (1545-1630) became Earl of Shrewsbury in 1618.

117/2-3 and 1st mar. n. [We ought to hold parents very dear, since from them we get life, inheritance, freedom, citizenship] Cicero, *Oratio cum Senatui Gratias Egit*, I, 2.

117/20-22. [The term 'parentes' signifies ancestors back to infinity and of either sex]; Ulpian, *Digest*, II, iv, 4: 'parentum hic utriusque sexus accipe: sed an in infinitum, quaeritur. Quidam parentem usque ad tritavum appellari aiunt, superiores maiores dici' [take 'parentes' as meaning either sex, but it is questionable whether this is to infinity. They allow the appellation up to grandparents, but I say it applies to ancestors further back].

117/24-27. *Historiae Augustae Scriptores*, ed. Isaac Casaubonus (Paris, 1603), p. 479. This annotation is actually made on a section by Trebellius.

117/45 and 2nd mar. n. [We have all been insane at some point]: a proverbial remark, not in Vergil. Buc prefaces it with metrical markings: / - - / - /. The dactyl probably suggested Vergil to Buc, and on the next page he does quote Vergil. '*Aegl.*' is perhaps an odd stab at "Eclogues'.

118/4-5. Vergil, *Aeneid*, VI, 486-7. [The spirits stand around on his right and his left, and it is not enough to have come up once: it helps to linger.] Buc reads 'venisse' (to have come) for the original's 'vidisse' (to have seen).

118/18-19. *Ibid.*, ll. 697-8 [Give me, father, give me your hand, do not draw back from my embrace].

BOOK III

119. The initial heading is really a general description of the whole of Book III, just as 'The story of Perkin Warbeck' is a general description of a major part of it. The rest are really subheadings under these two. Buc follows his outline – except that 'King Richard not deformed' should follow '*Utopia*' – until he begins to discuss Perkin Warbeck, when his organization goes awry. All the topics listed are covered, but not in the order given, and sometimes more than once. Indeed, the repetition is so considerable that most of Book III's final third could be discarded without much loss.

119/39. See text, p. 170, l. 29 and note thereto for this quotation.

119/43-44. Matthew 7:12 and Luke 6:31.

120/17-22. Richard's body was carried naked and 'unreuerently' (Fabyan, p. 671) to Leicester, covered with a mean black cloth from the waist down and displayed for about three days, presumably on the day of battle and two thereafter. Valera says three days (Goodman and Mackay, p. 92), Polydore, p. 565, says two: 'bidue post terra huma*tur*' [two days later interred in earth]. He was buried by the

Grey Friars. 'Petit' Salazar, who took part in the battle on King Richard's side, gives this account: Henry VII 'ordered the dead king to be placed in a little hermitage near the place of battle, and had him covered from the waist downward with a black rag of poor quality, ordering him to be exposed there for three days to the universal gaze' (trans. by Nokes and Wheeler, 'A Spanish Account', p. 2). Fabyan, p. 673 says he was 'with lytel reuerence buryed'. Ten years after Bosworth Henry VII erected a tomb in the Greyfriars priory church: Holinshed speaks of an effigy of alabaster, 'doing that honour to his enimie, vpon a princelie regard and pitifull zeale, which king Richard (mooued of an hypocriticall shew of counterfeit pitie) did to king Henrie the sixt, whom he had first cruellie murthered' (III, 447). This is confirmed by the epitaph below, pp. 217f, as well as by Henry VII's privy purse expenses in *Excerpta Historica*, recording a disbursal in 1495 'To James Keyley for King Richard tombe, £10.1s' (p. 105). Around the time Buc was writing, William Burton, *The Description of Leicester Shire* (London, [1622]), p. 163 mentions this monument: 'Within the town was an house of *Franciscan* or *Grey Freirs*, . . . whether (after *Bosworth* field) the dead body of K. *Richard* the third (naked, trussed behind a Purseuant of Arms, all dashed with mire and bloud) was brought, and there homely buried; where afterward King Henry the 7. (out of a royall disposition) erected for him a faire Alabaster Monument, with his picture cut out, and made thereon'.

Many, including Kendall and Ross, believed that at the dissolution of the monasteries Richard's remains were thrown into the Soar, but this myth was finally put to rest by the discovery of his bones in 2012. See Philippa Langley and Michael Jones, *The King's Grave: The Search for Richard III,* London, 2013 and A.J. Carson et al, *Finding Richard III: The Official Account of Research*, Horstead, 2014. See below regarding Richard's epitaph note to 217/33-218/7.

120/1st mar. n. Erasmus, *Chiliades*, p. 81.

120/23-4 and 2nd mar. n. [Envy that feeds on the living, is silent when life has ended] Ovid, *Amores*, I, xv, 39. Buc's citation of author is correct, but not of the work. The several uses of 'livor' in *Ex Ponto* III probably led his memory astray.

120/30 and 3nd mar. n. [Envy brings friends, the truth brings hatred]: as in the previous reference, Buc's citation of the author is correct, but not of the work. The quotation is from Terence, *Andria*, I, 68.

120/25-30. This is the first statement of 'Ricardian historiography', the first recognition that the historical view of Richard was prejudiced by Tudor bias and the necessity for Tudor historians to foster it.

121/6. [Not believe in God]

121-122. For a discussion of the Morton book, see above, pp. cxxii-cxxv.

121/17-25. More was a page in Morton's household c. 1490-92. He was an Under-Sheriff between 1510 and 1518. He can hardly have been described as ambitious and seeking preferment at the age of twelve, when, in any case, his family was of sufficient standing to place him in the household of the Archbishop of Canterbury and Lord Chancellor. The office of Under-Sheriff was, R.W. Chambers tells us (*Thomas More*, London, 1935, p. 103), an important one, and More prospered in it. He was not lacking in professional preferment nor unknown in humanist circles.

For discussions of More's *Richard III's* genre and purpose, see Sylvester's introduction to his edition of it. The work was written when, Sylvester says, 'More was at the height of his powers' (More, Introduction, p. lxxx) both in the legal profession and in literature; Kincaid, 'The Dramatic Structure of More's *History of King Richard III*', *Studies in English Literature* XII (1972), 223-42 (also anthologized in *Essential Articles for the Study of Thomas More*, Hamden, CT., 1977 and in *More*, vol. 1, *Great Political Thinkers* 6, Elgar Reference Collection, Cheltenham 1997); Hanham, *Early Historians,* pp. 153-90; Elizabeth Story Donno, 'Thomas More and Richard III', *Renaissance Quarterly*, XXXV (1982), 402-47; Dan Breen, 'Thomas More's "History of Richard III": Genre, Humanism, and Moral Education', *Studies in Philology* CVII (2010), 468-92; the introduction to George M. Logan's edition of More, *The History of King Richard the Third* (Bloomington: 2005); and the introduction to *Historia Richardi Tertii.*

121/3rd mar. n. See above, p. cxxii.

121/4th mar. n and 32-4. [Those who, when the need arises and they see that it is conducive to the purpose, are worthy of pardon if they lie, or rather – most of them – of praise] More, translating Lucian's 'Philopseudes', *The Translations of Lucian*, ed. Craig R. Thompson, *Complete Works of St Thomas More*, III (New Haven, 1974), p. 45. More translated four, not seven dialogues. His attitude to this one, which he considers of moral value in ridiculing the love of lying, is seen in his dedicatory epistle, pp. 4-7.

121/35. [Whatever you like hearing has equal power] I have been unable to locate a source for this remark, which sounds axiomatic.

121/38-40. Erasmus, *Opus Epistolarum Des. Erasmi Roterodami*, ed. P.S. Allen (Oxford, 1904-58), IV, 16 to Ulrich Hutten: 'Adolescens comoediolas et scripsit et egit' [As a youth, he wrote little comedies and performed them]. Buc would have had access to this letter, appended as a 'Vita' of More to his *Latin Works* (Basle, 1563). There is a fuller account of More as improviser in William Roper, *The Lyfe of Sir Thomas Moore, Knighte*, ed. Elsie Vaughan Hitchcock, EETS, orig. ser. 197 (London, 1933), p. 5.

121/44-5 and 5th mar. n. [to swear to his master's sayings] This is not Juvenal but Horace, *Epistulae*, I, i, 14.

121/47. More did not publish his book on Richard III, which he laid aside unfinished, in both English and Latin versions. The English version was first published by Richard Grafton in 1543, unattributed, as an adjunct to Hardyng. It was published under More's name in 1557 by his nephew William Rastell. It seems to have circulated little during his lifetime, for it is first heard of in 1538, after his death.

121/49-50. Herodotus, *Histories*, VI, i [Histiaeus made the shoe, but Aristagoras put it on].

122/2-10. Unknown to himself, Buc is helping to disseminate contemporary slander against More which is comparable in origin and falsity to the slanders of Richard III which he is so ardent to dispel in the name of charity and justice. He was the victim of current Protestant writing on More after his death, just as he objects that the chroniclers were victims of the writing on Richard after his.

122/4. It seems likely that William Rastell gave the book this title when he published it after More's death.

122/8. The word 'kind' is used here to mean 'natural'.

122/9-11. *Iliad*, II, 212-14.

122/15. See the section on dating the work in Sylvester, Introduction to More, pp. lxiii-liv.

122/16-18. Hall, pp. 817f reports More's jests on the scaffold with a tone of enmity and contempt. Grafton, II, 454, merely reports the incident with no critical tone.

122/1st mar. n. Germanus Brixius (Germain Brie), *Antimorus* (Basle, 1519). This work and the aspersions it cast upon More's literary style were part of a literary quarrel which had developed from a political argument between the two men. For an account of it see Chambers, pp. 190ff. The poems that sparked and fed the controversy are found in *The Latin Epigrams of Thomas More*, ed. Leicester Bradner and Charles Arthur Lynch (Chicago, 1953).

122/2nd mar. n. and 37-45. John Bale, *Scriptorum Illustrium Maiores Brytanniae* (Basle, [1557-9], pp. 655f. Buc repeats, to some extent in paraphrase, almost the whole of Bale's account. [This we know well, we who were closer to the same Thomas More: that in his base subservience to the cruelty of high priests and Pharisees, motivated by greed he raged more fiercely than any tyrant. Nay, he raved against those who denied either the primacy of the pope, or Purgatory, or invocations of the dead, or the adoration of images, or any such devilish impostures, though they are instructed in the quickening truth of God. Further, this Harpagus would not agree that a Christian king should be the first in his realm, nor that he should be permitted, along with David, Solomon, Jehoshaphat, Hezechiah and Josiah, to reject the tyranny of the Romish Nimrods and control the priests and Levites in his own realm,]

122/49-50. [Haunter of shade, most perverted hater of scriptural truth, obstinate false prophet, impudent adversary of Christ]

123/1-4. [He was beheaded in the Tower of London, 6 July, A.D. 1535. His head was fixed to the great bridge of London (as the custom is with traitors), and despite this he was venerated by the papists as a new martyr]

123/12-13. [by what means a layman or secular man could or should to be the head of a spiritual state or church]

123/1st mar. n. G. Courinus Nucerinus in 'Epistola de Morte D. Thomae Mori', printed as a supplement in Thomas More, *Latin Works* (Basle, 1563), pp. 511-30. Reynolds, pp. 2-8, says that Courinus was an amanuensis to Erasmus and probably not the author of the document. First published in 1535 with a different heading, it is the main source of information on More's trial and is known as 'The Paris News Letter'. Several manuscript copies exist in the Bibliothèque Nationale. Quite likely the original author was Philip Montanus, Erasmus's friend and fellow scholar, who sent it to Erasmus, and Erasmus had it prepared for publication by Courinus. Buc's suggestion that Courinus was More's 'dear friend' was natural, since he clearly assumed Courinus was the author. An accessible version appears in Nicholas Harpsfield, *The Life and Death of Sr Thomas Moore, Knight, Sometimes Lord Chancellor of England*, ed. Elsie Vaughan Hitchcock (London, 1932), Appendix II, pp. 258.

123/22-24. [The reason why you condemn me does not escape me: it is (clearly) that I would never assent to the business of the king's new marriage]

123/28-31. The letter from More to Cromwell is in B.L. MS. Cotton Cleopatra E. VI, ff. 144-53. More states that he has kept aloof from arguments and meddling in both considerations as too high for his learning. He is sorry the king 'shold reken in me eny man*er* of obstinate harte agaynst his pleasure in eny thing that ever I sayed or did concernyng his great mater of his mariage or concernyng the prymatie of the pope'. He had never in his writings or speeches 'advaunced greatly the popes authoritie', and he himself had had doubts on the question of whether it was divinely established until convinced that it was by the king's own book (*Assertio Septem Sacramentorum*, which Henry wrote in 1521 and for which the pope granted him the title 'Defender of the Faith'), and by other learned works that he would be in peril of his soul if he did not believe this doctrine. As for the king's marriage, now that it is accomplished and Anne Boleyn anointed queen, he wishes them both 'long to lyve & well'. This letter was printed in More, *Workes* (London, 1557), pp. 1424-28. Buc could have seen it either there or in the Cotton manuscript. In the modern edition of More's letters, *The Correspondence of Sir Thomas More*, ed. Elizabeth Frances Rogers (Princeton, 1947), it appears on pp. 492-501.

123/36-41. There is no extant evidence in the present Cotton collection or elsewhere that More in any way assisted in or assented to the suppression of religious houses.

124/11-42. parens patriae [parent of her country]; mater castrorum [mother of the camp]; rerum natura [the nature of things]; morosus morus [peevish fool]; tamquam . . . pecus [like a lazy and servile herd]. The closest suggestion I can find for a source of the last is Horace, *Epistolae*, I, xix, 19: 'o imitatores, servum pecus' [O, imitators, slavish herd].

124/13-15. Trebellius Pollio, *Triginta Tyranni*, XXXI, in *Historiae Augustae Scriptores* (London, 1583).

124/30-32. John Foxe, *The Ecclesiasticall Historie, Containing the Acts and Monuments of Martyrs* (London, 1583) II, 1008f and 1068f. Buc seems to have followed Foxe's attitudes to More on various points. For example, on p. 1008 Utopia is spoken of as an actual place, 'from whence . . . can come no fittons but all fine Poetrie'. And again on pp. 1009 and 1013 he refers to More's 'licentia*m* poeticam' [poetic licence]. On More's fanciful writings he bases the supposition that More must of necessity be considered dishonest: 'If M. More had neuer made fictions in hys writinges beside, or had neuer broken the head of veritie, in so many places of hys bookes as I could shewe hym, then might this argument goe for somewhat . . . hee hath crackt his credite so often, and may alwayes be bankrout . . .' (p. 1009). Concerning More's 'Holiness', Foxe notes 'a bitter persecuter he was of good men, and a wretched enemie against the truth of the Gospel', and that he 'wilfully stoode in the Popes quarell against his owne prince . . .' (p. 1069).

125/19-20. [Maintaining concord in conspiracy, they really planned to put down Caesar] Ammianus, *Historia*, XIV, 6, with one very minor variant.

125/22-23. Polydore and Hall are vehemently hostile to Wolsey. Cavendish's life of Wolsey, written in 1534-8, not published until 1641 but circulated in manuscript and used by Stow, Holinshed, and Speed, is sympathetic and temperate. Written under Mary, it tries to correct what the author probably thought the result of Protestant propaganda in previous reigns and seems to intend direct contradiction of Hall (see Sylvester, Introduction to his edition of George Cavendish, *The Life and Death of Cardinal Wolsey*, EETS 243, London, 1959). Although Stow and Speed use Cavendish for information, their attitude remains essentially that of Hall, on whose account they primarily base their own. Holinshed is more sympathetic.

126/4-5. Homer, *Iliad*, XX, 250 [The sort of words you have spoken are the sort you will hear].

126/7 and 2nd mar. n. *Phormio* 21 [He should think himself paid back for what he started].

126/10-17. All these authors have used More's narrative *verbatim* for their section on Edward V and the first part of Richard III's reign, interpolating only Grafton's description of Richard's coronation: Hall, pp. 342-79; Grafton, II, 79-123; Stow, *Annales*, pp. 722-73; Holinshed, III, 360-96 and 400f.

126/13. In coining the word 'Antirichards' Buc seems to be associating Richard with Christ, as he has done in his Biblical reference, text, p. 59. Rous, whom Buc seems not to have read, calls Richard an Antichrist (p. 218).

126/23. [shades (ghosts)]

126/37-45. Cornwallis, p. 13: 'this worthey, his princely ornament, some Calumniators haue sought in him to deface, alledginge that his liberalitye to some p*ro*ceeded from his extortion from others . . .'

126/46-127/12.

More, p. 8:

> Free was hee called of dyspence, and sommewhat aboue hys power liberall, with large giftes hee get him vnstedfaste frendeshippe, for whiche hee was fain to pil and spoyle in other places, and get him stedfast hatred. Hee was close and secrete, a deepe dissimuler, lowlye of counteynaunce, arrogant of heart, outwardly coumpinable where he inwardely hated, not letting to kisse whome he thoughte to kyll: dispitious and cruell, not for euill will alway, but ofter for ambicion, and either for the suretie or encrease of his estate. Frende and foo was muche what indifferent, where his aduantage grew, he spared no mans deathe, whose life withstoode his purpose.

There is no evidence of Richard's having wasted money, indeed he found it necessary to subsidize Edward V. Having inherited an already impecunious treasury depleted by the Woodvilles, he ran short due to a rebellion so closely following his accession. He dealt with this by taking out loans from his subjects rather than taxing them. He compromised his popularity among southerners by 'planting' northerners on southern estates confiscated for treason (see Horrox, *Study of Service*, *passim*).

127/13-20. Cornwallis, p. 22:

> beinge desirous to reconcile him selfe to all sutch as held them selues offended (as before he had done with ffog a meane Attorney who had highly offended him) he laboured to winne the one sorte with benefit*es* & gift*es* and freely pardoned the others misbehauiours & offences: he had noe cause to feare fogg, therfore ffeare was not the cause, noe it was a worthie, a kingely, humilitye, that would rather abate his greatnesse then haue it Stained w*i*th the blood of soe meane a vassall for a crime comitted againste him selfe: yet was he guiltye of Counterfaitinge his roiall hande and signet & of a moste vntrue & infamous libell . . .

More, pp. 81f:

> And fynally to thentent that no man shoulde hate hym for feare, and that his deceitful clemency mighte geat him the good wyll of the people, when he had declared the dyscomoditie of discorde, and the commodyties of concorde and vnitie, he made an open proclamacion, that he did put oute of his minde all enymities, and that he there did openly pardon all offences committed against him. And to the entente y[t] he might shew a proofe thereof, he commaunded that one Fogge whom he had long deadly hated, shold be brought than before him. Who being brought oute of the saintuary . . . in the sight of the people, he tooke him by the hand. Whiche thyng the common people reioysed at and praised, but wise men tooke it for a vanitye. In his returne homewarde, whom so euer he met he saluted. For a minde that knoweth it self giltye, is in a maner deiected to a seruile flattery.

Polydore ascribes Richard's generosity to a politic move to win friends and to guilty conscience (p. 548).

127/24. More, p. 82: 'When he hadde begonne his reygne the twenty sixth daye of Iune, after this mockishe eleccion, than was he Crowned the sixte day of Iuly'.

127/43-45. More (p. 87) with marginal title, *'The out & inward troubles of tyrauntes'*, says:

> . . . I haue heard by credible report of such as wer secrete w[t] his chamberers, that after this abhominable deede done, he neuer hadde quiet in his minde, hee neuer thought himself sure. Where he went abrode, his eyen whirled about, his body priuily fenced, his hand euer on his dager, his countenance and maner like one alway ready to strike againe, he toke ill rest a nightes, lay long wakyng and musing, sore weried with care & watch, rather slumbred then slept, troubled wyth feareful dreames, sodainly sommetyme sterte vp, leape out of his bed & runne about the chamber.

Polydore (p. 565) mentions Richard's biting his lip and his habit of unsheathing his dagger and sheathing it again. He may have been More's source for this.

127/45-46 and 3rd mar. n. [standing or walking, sitting or reclining, expression of eye or motion of hand] Cicero, *De Officiis* 1, xxxv, 128. He says each of these has a decorum.

127/48-49. See n. 124/30-32, above.

127/50. Crowland, p. 181f merely reports the dream as current rumour and says that Richard regarded it as a presage. Polydore (p. 562), followed by Hall, Grafton, Holinshed, and ultimately Shakespeare ('I have not that alacrity of spirit / Nor cheer of mind that I was wont to have', *Richard III*, V, 3), draws a moral from it. In the words of Hall, p. 414:

> The fame went that he had the same night a dreadful & a terrible dreame, for it semed to hym beynge aslepe y[t] he sawe diuerse ymages lyke terrible deuelles whiche pulled and haled hym, not sufferynge hym to take any quyet or rest. The which straunge vision not so sodeinly strake his heart with a sodeyne feare, but it stuffed his hed and troubled his mynde with many dreadfull and busy Imaginacions. For incontynent after, his heart beynge almost damped, he prognosticated before the doubtful chaunce of the battaile to come, not vsynge the alacrite and myrth of mynde and of countenaunce as he was accustomed to do before he came toward the battaile. And least that it might be suspected that he was abasshed for feare of his enemyes, and for that cause looked so piteously, he recyted and declared to hys famylyer ffrendes in the morenynge hys wonderfull visyon and terrible dreame. But I thynke this was no dreame, but a punccion and pricke of his synfull conscience, for the conscience is so muche more charged and aggrauate as the offence is greater & more heynous in degre, whiche prycke of conscience although it strike not all waye, at the last daie of extreme life is wont to shewe and represent to vs our faultes and offences and the paynes and punishementes which hang ouer our heddes for the com*m*yttyng of thesame.

Cornwallis presents a corrective (p. 29):

> It is affirmed that the night before the daie of battell, he dreamed a most dreadfull & horible dreame, w*hi*ch by our Croniclers ys Interpreted to be a testemonie of his wicked and Tirranous life, did not Caesar before he attayned the Empire, dreame that he knew his owne mother Carnally. had not both Dion, & Brutus the figures of horible spirit*es* rep*re*sented vnto them the night before theire end? yet these weare accounted good men, and Louers and Protectours of theire Country: and because Kinge Richard dreamed w*i*th some terrour, must his life of necessity be euell?

128/31-32. This idea is expressed in Philo, *On Abraham*, 264 [Noble deeds in adversity are wont to be obscured and oppressed by calumnies].

128/1st mar. n. *Iliad*, XX, 246-7.

128/38-41. Rous is the first writer to mention Richard's being born with teeth, p. 215. More adopts it with a caveat (see below, quotation in n. 129/3-5). Cornwallis, p. 3 answers: 'His beinge toothed as soone as borne, me seemes rather a blessinge, then anie imputation, as beinge a prognostication of his future worth, since it was an extraordinarie and noe vnproffitable marke, for nurses houlde the cominge out of Childrens teeth to be verie painefull'. It is a not uncommon medical phenomenon. But, as Buc points out, the people who report these things are hardly likely to have spoken to the midwife.

128/46-50 and 3rd mar. n. Pliny, *Natural History*, VII, xvi, 68f notes that Carbo and Curius were born with teeth, and the son of Prusius (not named) was born with a bone instead. Although Valerius Maximus, Livy and Plutarch all mention Curius, and Plutarch and Livy mention Carbo as well, these anatomical details appear in none of them. Livy in Book XI gives Curius the epithet 'Dentatus'. L. Domitius Brusonius, *Rerum Memorabilium* (Frankfurt, 1600), III, ii, 290, says that Prusia, son of the Bythinian king Prusia, had a single bone of length equivalent to that of top teeth.

129/3-5. Richard's mother's travail at his birth is another invention by Rous, enlarged on by More. Both associate it with the teeth and hair story to suggest Richard's unnatural origin. Rous says Richard was two years in his mother's womb. More writes (p. 7) that he was

> from afore his birth, euer frowarde. It is for trouth reported, that the Duches his mother had so muche a doe in her trauaile, that shee coulde not bee deliuered of hym vncutte: and that hee came into the worlde with the feete forwarde . . . and (as the fame runneth) also not vntothed, whither men of hatred reporte aboue the trouthe, or elles that nature chaunged her course in hys beginninge, which in the course of his lyfe many thinges vnnaturallye committed.

Shakespeare goes to the other extreme and has him born prematurely (*Richard III*, I, i, 20). Cornwallis, p. 3, says, 'why should not the same Axiome be a motiue to Cleare this wronged Prince, whose Accusers lay to his Charge, the anguish his mother felt, when he came in to the worlde, then w*hi*ch accusation what can be more friuolouse, it beinge a punishment hereditarie to all woemen from the firste'.

129/1st mar. n. Stow, *Annales*, p. 801.

129/7-8. I have not found this in Seneca. It sounds, from its rhyme, proverbial [What can be borne is trivial, what cannot be borne is brief].

129/23-131/38. Cornwllis, pp. 3f:

> but he was Crookebacked, lame, ill fauored, I might impute that fault to Nature, but that I thinke it rather her bountie, for she beinge wholy intentiue to his minde neclected his forme, soe that shee infused a straight minde in a Crooked bodie, wherin she shewed her carefull

> prouidence, for often times the care to keepe those p*ar*tes well formed, withdrawes mens mindes from better actions, and drownes them in effeminate Curiositye, his lamenes turned to his glorye, for w*i*th those vnp*er*fect limms, he p*er*formed actions moste p*er*fectly valiant . . .

129/37. That Richard was physically deformed has been an essential component of his portrayal as evil, the popular assumption being that physical deformity betokens an equally twisted mind (see below, Appendix). Though no one – even among those hostile to him - records any deformity during his lifetime, his literary, pictorial and stage persona afterwards has been, at very least, of a hunchback with a withered arm, both More's invention. It was found on discovery of his skeleton in 2012 that he had neither a hunchback nor a withered arm, but that he did have scoliosis, a disorder curving the spine (laterally) to a greater or lesser degree. This would have shortened his normal height and led to his right shoulder being slightly raised but clearly, since no one noticed it, it had no noticeable effect when he was clothed, apart from what contemporaries noticed: he was short. The final diagnosis, by Jo Appleby, Piers D. Mitchell, *et al.*, 'The Scoliosis of Richard III, Last Plantagenet King of England: Diagnosis and Clinical Significance' (*The Lancet*, CCCLXXXIV. 31 May 2014), p. 1944, is that the scoliosis was of adolescent onset and that

> physical disfigurement from Richard's scoliosis was probably slight since he had a well balanced curve. His trunk would have been short relative to the length of his limbs, and his right shoulder a little higher than the left. However, a good tailor and custom-made armour could have minimised the visual impact of this. A curve of 70–90° would not have caused impaired exercise tolerance from reduced lung capacity, and we identified no evidence that Richard would have walked with an overt limp, because the leg bones are symmetric and well formed.

The article is accompanied by a picture of a model of his spine based on examination of the individual vertebrae. This is not remotely as dramatically curved as the popular photograph of his posed skeleton laid out by the University of Leicester for tabloids and television which, when I showed a slide of it in a talk, caused a doctor in the audience with a speciality in scoliosis to advise that so extreme a curve would have prevented its sufferer entirely from functioning.

Scoliosis is a not at all uncommon condition shared by many people, some of them famous (Usain Bolt, for example, whose scoliosis has not proved an impediment to his being a leading athlete). Henry Tudor adopted as part of his platform the 'unkingliness' of Richard's physique, viz. Dafydd Llwyd ap Llewelyn ap Gruffudd's focus on his size, comparing him with his brother Edward: 'little R. is killed . . . it is odious to see a pale leg . . . , instead of a mighty thigh' (trans. printed in Pamela Tudor-Craig, *Richard III*, London, 1973, the catalogue for the National Portrait Gallery exhibition of portraits of Richard III). This grew in time into the excesses of describing him as a hunchback with a withered arm. A literal withered arm (deformed since birth) was invented by More, probably elaborating on Polydore Vergil's metaphorical remark that he was under such stress that his strength was fading, his breath short, and he was growing emaciated, as evidence of which he showed his arm at the Tower council. Then gradually other oddities crept in: Richard Baker makes him, in addition to everything else, splay-footed and goggle-eyed (*A Chronicle of the Kings of England*, London, 1643, p. 137). Being goggle-eyed is another mediaeval mark of an evil soul. As x-rays show, portraits of him were later doctored to narrow his eyes, clench his mouth and raise one of his shoulders. Alterations to the Royal Collection portrait after its creation included extending the right shoulder to create the impression of a hunched back. Tudor-Craig (p. 91) describes how in x-rays one of the Society of Antiquaries' portraits was seen to have been 'radically altered' to accord the subject's appearance with the traditional humped back and withered arm. The discovery and study of his skeleton showed clearly and definitively that he had neither. See Appendix, pp. 354-6.

Silesian knight Niclas von Popplau, who was very much impressed with him, describes him in a way which accords well with his bones: 'three fingers taller than I, but a bit slimmer and not as thickset as I am, and much more lightly built: he has quite slender arms and thighs, and also a great heart' (trans. from mediaeval German by Livia Visser-Fuchs, '"He hardly touched his food, but talked with me all the time": What Niclas von Popplau Really Wrote about Richard III', *The Ricardian*, XI, (1999). Von Popplau was evidently a short, chunky man.

130/9-11. Although Rous introduces into his *Historia* the report of Richard having one shoulder higher than the other, he mentions no deformity. There is no indication of deformity in the picture which he drew in the Warwick Roll. It is likely that he knew Richard's appearance well at first-hand (see Kendrick, pp. 18f). In Buc's time the manuscript of Rous's *Historia* was in the Cotton collection, but Buc does not seem to have read it.

130/13-14. More, p. 7, describes Richard as being 'hard fauoured of visage, and suche as is in states called warlye, in other menne otherwise'. Some versions of his portraits from the seventeenth century show this sort of face (see Tudor-Craig, nos. 35 and 37).

130/1st mar. n. All the Editor's copies erroneously read 'Richard II'. This reference appears in *PROME,* Richard III: Jan. 1484, XV, 16. It does not say specifically that Richard was the most like to Richard, Duke of York, but only that he is his 'undoubted son and heire'. The sermon is reputed to have said he looked like his father (More, p. 67).

130/25-30. This is from More, p. 67f, with the most minor alterations.

130/31-32. Dr Shaw, or Shaa, was not Dean but a canon of St Paul's, an office he held from 1477 until his death in 1484 (A.B. Emden, *A Biographical Register of the University of Cambridge to 1500*, Cambridge, 1963, p. 520).

130/2nd mar. n. More in Grafton's continuation of Hardyng, p. 469 and Grafton, II, 81, '. . . whither menne of hatred reporte aboue the trouthe' (More, p. 7). This is actually said in relation to the rumour that Richard was born with teeth. More does not qualify his reference to Richard's deformity, saying that he was 'little of stature, ill featured of limmes, croke backed, his left shoulder much higher than his right' (p. 7).

130/37. [we have confuted the matter]

130/44-46. Erasmus, *Opus Epistolarum*, IV, 14: 'Dexter humerus paulo videtur eminentior laeuo' [his right shoulder looked a little higher than his left]. More had a motive for making Richard's left shoulder the higher, contrary to both his own physique and the real Richard's appearance: the left ('sinister') was the devil's side.

131/21-38. See Appendix for mediaeval as well as more recent views of deformity.

131/44-134/8. All contemporary accounts of Henry VI's death suggest either that he died of natural causes or that Edward IV was responsible, depending on whether their bias is Yorkist or Lancastrian. Fauconberg's rising would have shown Edward the danger of letting Henry VI remain alive, and his exhibiting the body confirms that Henry's existence was a threat to him. Edward would have followed Henry IV, who had Richard II put to death secretly and countered rumours that he was still alive by exhibiting the body. Richard III followed Henry V, 'atoning' for his brother's crime as Henry V 'atoned' for his father's by giving the body a noble burial. Abroad there was no question as to the murderer's identity. *Calendar of State Papers, Milan*, I, ed. Allen B. Hinds, London, 1912, says quite bluntly, 'King Edward has not chosen to have the custody of King Henry any longer . . . as he has caused King Henry to be secretly assassinated in the Tower . . . (p. 157).

The deed was later attributed to Richard. The only corroboration Tudor authors might claim for this attribution is the dubious account dated to 1484 formerly misattributed to John Warkworth (see article on him by Edward Donald Kennedy in *ODNB*), *A Chronicle of the First Thirteen Years of the Reign of King Edward the Fourth*, ed. J.O. Halliwell, Cam. Soc. X, London, 1939, p. 21, which mentions that Richard, among many others, accompanied Edward to the Tower on the night Henry was killed. No account mentions Richard's complicity as a fact: each includes some qualifying remark. Dafydd Llwyd in his poem celebrating Bosworth and in praise of Henry Tudor (Tudor-Craig, p. 95) seems to have originated the story, saying Richard, who killed 'the saint' Henry, has now himself been killed. There is a tradition that Llwyd was Henry Tudor's host when he stayed in Wales on the way to Bosworth (see R.A. Griffiths and R.S. Thomas, *The Making of the Tudor Dynasty*, Stroud, 1985, p. 145), and it is not impossible that he drew the focus on Richard's physique and the story of his killing Henry VI from Tudor. He also suggests that if Richard killed Edward IV's sons his own death is justified, citing a parallel with Herod, which parallels Henry's allusion to 'shedyng of infantes blode' (see *PROME*, XV, 107, Henry VII: 1; *vide infra*, Appendix). The first English writer to mention Richard's killing Henry is Rous, who says Richard killed him through intermediaries or, many believe, with his own hand (p. 215). Commynes speaks uncertainly: 'si je n'ay ouy mentir, incontinent après ceste battaille le duc de Clocestre, frère dudit Edouard, lequel depuis a esté roy Richard, tua de sa main ou feït tuer en sa presence, en quelque lieu à part, ce bon homme le roy Henry' (I, 215f) [if I have not heard lies, immediately after this battle the Duke of Gloucester, brother of the said Edward, who afterwards was King Richard, killed this good King Henry with his hand or had him killed in his presence].

André remarks that Richard killed Henry, 'si vera est fama' [if the rumour is true] (p. 19), but says he was sent by Edward to do so (p. 23). Fabyan and the *Great Chronicle* are equally uncertain. 'Of ye deth of this prynce dyuerse tales were tolde: but the moost com*m*on fame wente, that he was stykked with a dagger, by the handes of the duke of Glouceter . . .' (Fabyan, p. 662); *The Great Chronicle* says. 'the comen ffame then went, that The duke of Glowcetyr was nott all Gyltlees' (p. 220). More says, 'He slewe with his owne handes king Henry the sixt, being prisoner in the Tower, as menne constantly saye' (p. 8). Polydore's wording is 'Hu*n*c, ut fama co*n*stans est, Ricardus Glocestriae dux gladio percussit, quo ita Edouardus rex eius frater omni hostili metu liberaretur' (p. 532) [As the constant report is, Richard, Duke of Gloucester struck him with a sword, whereby King Edward, his brother, was liberated from fear of all hostility]. The succeeding authors copy More and Polydore, though Holinshed notices the writers who say the king died of melancholy (III, 324). In Shakespeare Richard's killing Henry VI is no longer a doubtful event but dramatic fact (3 *Henry VI*, V, vi). But whoever killed him, the responsibility for the deed must lie at King Edward's door.

A violent death was suggested by the apparent matting with blood of the little remaining hair, states W.H. St John Hope, 'The Discovery of the Remains of King Henry VI in St. George's Chapel, Windsor Castle', *Archaeologia*, LXII (1911), 533-42.

132/6-7 and 1st mar. n. [Holy king, holy Henry, and most sacred king] Polydore does not refer to Henry VI by these epithets but does call him 'uir bonus, gratus, pius, modestus, sapiens [a man good, pleasant, pious, modest, wise], and says that Henry VII 'cu*m* inter diuos referendu*m* . . . curare coepit' [began to see to it that he should be reckoned among the gods] p. 532).

132/22-26. [I shall say nothing, at this time, about the discovery of King Henry's lifeless body in the Tower of London: may God have mercy upon and give time for repentance to him, whoever it might be, who dared to lay sacrilegious hands on the Lord's Anointed! And so, let the doer merit the title of tyrant and the victim that of glorious martyr] Crowland, pp. 128-30, which Buc amends very slightly to fit his sentence structure. H.T. Riley, nineteenth-century translator of the Crowland Chronicle (*Ingulph's Chronicle of the Abbey of Croyland with the Continuations by Peter of Bois and Anonymous Writers*, London, 1834), p. 468, says, 'This appears to be a hint of Edward's complicity'. The chronicler had reason to conceal Edward's name since he was father of Henry VII's intended queen, something which, in Tudor times, had made placing the blame on Richard politic. Writing, as is now thought, shortly after Bosworth, he shows close knowledge of the rebels' plans and would have known that the princess Elizabeth was destined for Henry. He also would probably have heard any suggestions of Richard's complicity in Henry VI's death, and his not mentioning this suggests there were none.

133/32-34. [King Henry VI, by reason of the infirmity he suffered, which weakened his mind, remained thus sick in body and feeble-minded for many years]. Crowland Chronicle, Fulman ed., I, 532.

133/3rd mar. n. Cornwallis, pp. 6f:

> The death of Henry the sixt in the Tower can noe way

> belonge to him, since the same reason that cleareth his brother acquiteth him, he beinge able if desiringe his death to haue effected it by a more vnworthey hand. And in deede this accusac*i*on hath no other proffe, but a malicyous affyrmac*i*on, for many more truly did suppose that he dyed of meere melancholy & grief when he had hard of the ou*er*throw of his frend*es* & slaughter of his sonne.

(Cornwallis does not, in any extant manuscript, refer specifically to a malicious affirmation of one man, though this may be implied.) By 'others', Cornwallis, refers to *The Arrivall*, p. 38: 'not havyng afore that, knowledge of the saide matars, he toke it in so great despite, ire, and indignation, that, of pure displeasure, and melancholy, he dyed the .xxiij. day of the monithe of May'. This account appears to have been concocted for Yorkist benefit: Henry's death is post-dated so as not to coincide with Edward's presence in London. That the news of Tewkesbury should have taken nineteen days to reach him is not credible.

134/1st mar. n. [King Henry VI died in custody, some say by the sword, some say from grief]; Meyer, p. 403: 'Henricus Rex Londini in custodia, vt alij moerore, vt alij Glocestrij gladio deperijt'. The original mentions Gloucester as wielder of the sword that killed Henry.

134/5-8. This theory has been pursued by Zeeveld and by Kincaid and Ramsden in the introduction to Cornwallis. Most likely the reference is to More. See Hanham, review of Kincaid and Ramsden, *The Ricardian*, IV (1978), 24.

134/9-135/6. No contemporary or near-contemporary suggests that Richard killed the Prince of Wales. Contemporary accounts agree that he was killed in battle (see Kendall, *Richard III*, p. 528), and these leave no room for doubt. The accretions of the stories against Richard are easy to see: Fabyan (p. 662) and the *Great Chronicle* (p. 218) say the prince was taken after the battle and brought before King Edward, who questioned him, eliciting an unpalatable answer, upon which the king struck him with his gauntlet and the king's servants slew him. Polydore follows this version, substituting for the servants the names of Clarence, Gloucester and Hastings (p. 530). Hall (p. 301) adds Dorset. More does not even mention the incident. That Richard is now thought of as the sole 'murderer' is probably attributable to his confession in the wooing scene of Shakespeare's *Richard III* (I, ii), where the stakes are set higher against his wooing Lady Anne successfully by portraying him not only as the slayer of her father-in-law but also of her husband. Since this is one of the most famous scenes in Shakespeare, one forgets the same author's 3 *Henry VI*, V, v, which shows the prince being stabbed by Edward, Clarence and Gloucester, and *Richard III*, I, iv, where Clarence, describing his dream, says the prince's ghost accused him of stabbing him.

134/3rd mar. n. Holinshed, III, 320: 'At which words king Edward said nothing'. Polydore, Hall and Grafton say the same.

134/4th mar. n. Polydore, p. 530. He does not mention Dorset as one of the slayers, as his successors do, but does mention Richard.

134/5th mar. n. See above, n. 20/5th mar. n.

134/6th mar. n. [Anne, wife of Edward, son of King Henry VI was captured with her husband']; Meyer, p. 403: 'Est qui Annam Principis vxorem vna cum marito captam tradit'. Neither this nor Buc's paraphrase of it actually says she was in the room at the time.

135/7-137/48. More is the first to suggest Richard's complicity in Clarence's death, though Rous (p. 215) and Polydore (p. 537), who, like all historians before Stow were at a loss to account for it, mention that the 'G' prophecy came true in Richard's 'usurpation'. Contemporary sources, foreign and native, say only that Edward had his brother put to death for treason, and this is confirmed by his indictment, first discovered by Stow and reported in the 1592 edition of his *Annales* (London, 1592), p. 708 (see also *PROME*, XIV, 402, Appendix, n. 1). Crowland's report, which reads like that of an eye-witness, makes clear that the sentencing and execution were conducted by form of law. The execution was not public, but there seems to have been no expectation that it should be. Relations between Clarence and Edward had been so threatening for many years that it is perhaps a wonder the king did not deal with his brother sooner. Clarence had fomented rebellions, connived and fought with Edward's enemies, tried to make himself king, publicly impugned the king's justice, and spread rumours derogatory to Edward, all of which were treasonous activities. See Ross, *Edward IV*, pp. 116-244 *passim* and 441f.

135/7-13. More, p. 8: 'Somme wise menne also weene, that his drifte couertly conuayde, lacked not in helping furth his brother of Clarence to his death: whiche hee resisted openly, howbeit somewhat (as menne demed) more faintly then he y[t] wer hartely minded to his welth'. Richard's opposition also appears in Mancini (Arm: 62-3, Car: 44-5), who ascribes it to inability to dissemble, as opposed to More's accusation of dissimulation. In Harl. 433, f. 265v is yet another suggestion that Richard was incensed at his brother's death and blamed the Woodvilles (Horrox and Hammond ed., III, 108).

135/2nd mar. n. Polydore, p. 537 reports several causes of enmity between the brothers. But the remark opposite which this note appears is better illustrated by Crowland, p. 144: 'nemo arguit contra ducem, nisi Rex; nemo respondit regi, nisi dux' [No-one argued against the duke except the king: no-one answered the king except the duke].

135/27-28 and 3rd mar. n. [O unhappy brother, whom no man sought to save] Polydore, p. 537.

135/32-136/32. Armstrong says, "One result of the xenophobia prevalent in England during the latter middle ages was that a member of the royal house born abroad was liable to be called a changeling or a bastard by his enemies' (in Mancini, p. 109). Lander observes that 'Accusations of bastardy were . . . part of the common stock of political smears in the fifteenth century and should not be taken too seriously' (p. 26n). *PROME*, Richard III: Jan. 1484, XV. p. 16, makes a point of Richard's being born in England, 'by reason wherof . . . al the thre estatis of the lande have . . . more certayn knowlage of youre byrth and filiacion'. Richard did not originate the story of Edward's bastardy. Warwick spread this rumour in France in 1469 (J. Calmette and G. Périnelle, *Louis XI et l'Angleterre*, Paris, 1930, 'Pièces Justificatives', no. 30, pp. 306f). Commynes reports that Louis XI heard in his presence how in 1475 Charles of Burgundy called Edward 'Blayborgne, filz d'un archer' [Blayborne, son of an archer] (II, 50). Clarence used Edward's supposed illegitimacy in his campaign for kingship (see above, n. 135/7-137/48). Edward's debasing marriage lent fuel to the story, for Mancini relates that the Duchess of York was so upset that she offered to prove Edward was illegitimate and hence not fit to reign (Arm: 60f, Car: 42-3), though Mancini later deplores the effrontery of preachers who he claims were suborned to make the same allegations (Car: p. 111). See 179/28-180/12 below.

Gladys Jenkins, 'Ways and Means in Elizabethan Propaganda', *History*, new ser, XXVI (1941), 108 notes the importance of the pulpit as a means of communication and its use in politics. The Paul's Cross sermon 'was delivered every Sunday at the cross outside the cathedral, and to it came not only the ordinary citizens, but also notables of the city and court'. This sermon, which set forth Richard's right, again followed the precedent of his brother Edward IV, who had had the Bishop of Exeter preach a sermon at Paul's Cross setting forth evidence for his title to the throne, then rode in procession to Westminster Hall, where he took possession of the royal seat. Neither Crowland nor Rous mentions Shaa's sermon. Fabyan takes it as a matter of course in the succession of political events.

135/46. See above, 39/4th mar. n., also text p. 176 and notes thereto.

136/17-28. More, p. 73, does not say directly that Richard was displeased but rather has Buckingham refer to the illegitimacy by *praeteritio*:

> . . . other thinges, which the said worshipful doctor rather signified then fully explaned, & which thynges shal not be spoken for me as ye thing wherin euery man forbereth to say that he knoweth in auoidinge dyspleasure of my noble lord protectour, bearinge as nature requireth a filial reuerence to the duches his mother . . .

Hall, p. 371 and Grafton, II, 109 repeat More, as do Holinshed and Stow.

136/4th mar. n. This story is not in Crowland Chronicle. See above 51/17-21.

137/15-17. [It was noticed that the duke was gradually withdrawing more and more from the king's presence, hardly uttering a word in council, not eating and drinking in the king's residence] Crowland, pp. 142f.

137/3rd mar. n. Stow, *Annales*, 1592, p. 716. See *PROME*, XIV, 402, Appendix, n. 1: 'He also said that the king was a bastard, not fit to reign'.

137/4th mar. n. [hostilities between brothers are intensely bitter] Erasmus, *Chiliades*, p. 80.

137/5th mar. n. Jean de Serres, *Inventaire General de l'Histoire de France* (Paris, 1600), II, 215: 'Mais à la priere de leur commune mere, Edouard moderant la sentence, luy donna l'option de tel gêre de mort qu'il voudroit élire & suiuant ce pouuoir, il voulut mourir dans vne pipe de maluaisie'. [But at the prayer of their common mother, Edward moderated the sentence, giving him the option of choosing his means of death, and following this permission, he wanted to die in a butt of malmsey.] This manner of death is also reported in Mancini (Arm: 62-3, Car: 44-5), Commynes, I, 53, Fabyan (p. 666) and the *Great Chronicle* (p. 226).

137/46-48. [King Edward, after the death of his brother, turned away from all fear. and now feared no one] Polydore, p. 537.

137-173. All that can be said about the death of the so-called 'Princes in the Tower' is that no one to date has managed to find out how or when they died and probably no one ever will. There is consequently no sense in blaming one person or another. As A.J. Pollard says in *Richard III and the Princes*, p. 120, 'Many versions were offered.... Since no official enquiry was conducted or pronouncement made, before or after the accession of Henry VII rumour ran rife and spread throughout Europe. . . . But no one really knew what happened to them'. He cites similarity with the story of the Babes in the Wood as a suggestion of a literary inspiration behind More's tale. We can certainly say More's circumstantial story is completely incredible and quite likely was meant to be. Having said there are many stories about it, he first departs from all likelihood by having a page offer a reference for a potential murderer while Richard is sitting on the privy. And at the end he states equally implausibly that one of the murderers is still walking about freely. This was the story copied by Hall, Grafton, Stow and Holinshed.

After Buc's death the discovery of the 'bones of the princes' was believed because they were supposedly found precisely where More said they were buried. But More says that *after* the initial burial under a stair foot they were removed by an unnamed priest and buried somewhere else, no one knows where (p. 86). Or in an alternative version that the priest put them in a coffin, which he consigned to the Thames (from Hardyng text, see More, note, p. 86). Clearly expecting them never to be found, More explained why they *could* never be found, since the unnamed priest had taken the secret to his grave. His brother-in-law John Rastell, in *The Pastime of People* (reprint of 1529 ed., London, 1811), p. 292f, seems to be sending this whole situation up, citing every possible diverse theory of what might have happened to them.

Survival of one of them is not implausible, otherwise Perkin Warbeck would have had no following. Nor is the suggestion that they died of the sweating sickness: made in an article by John A.H. Wylie, 'The Princes in the Tower, 1483 – Death from Natural Causes', *The Ricardian*, VI (1985), 178-182. Interestingly, College of Arms MS 2M6 records a rumour: 'this yer [before the end of October 1483] . . . Kyng Edward the iiij sonys, wer put to deyth in the Towur of London be the vise of the duke of Buckingham' (Green, 'Historical Notes', 588).

138/24 and 2nd mar. n. [tumulus testis = mound as witness] Genesis, 35:19-20.

138/31-32. Apocrypha, story of Susanna, Daniel 13.

138/50-139/10. [in vulgus fama valeret filios Edouardi regis aliquo terrarum secreto migrasse atque ita superstites esse: common fame went that the sons of King Edward had secretly travelled to another land and thus survived] Polydore, p. 569. More, p. 82:

> Whose death and final infortune hathe natheles so far comen in question, that some remain yet in doubt, whither they wer in his dayes destroyed or no . . . Perken Warbecke, by many folkes malice, and mooe folkes foly, so long space abusyng the worlde, was aswel with princes as ye porer people, reputed and taken for the yonger of those two . . .

139/15-16. Polydore, p. 547, 'se quo genere pueri affecti fuerint, non plane liquet' [By what sort the boys were afflicted is not clear].

139/17-19. [Among the common people the fame went that the sons of King Edward had yielded to fate, but by what kind of death was unknown]; Crowland, p. 162f, actually says, 'vulgatum est dictos Regis Edwardi quo genere violanti interitus ignoratur decessisse in fatu' [a rumour arose that King Edward's sons, by some unknown manner of violent destruction, had met their fate]. Buc's version is closer to Mancini's comment of 1483, which also leaves the possibility of natural death open: 'suspitio foret esse sublatum. An autem sublatus sit, et quo genere mortis nihil adhuc compertum habeo' [there was suspicion that he had been taken by death. Whether, however, he has been taken by death, and by what manner of death, so far I have not at all ascertained] (Arm: 92-3, Car: 64-5). We have no possible way of knowing whether 'violenti' was or was not present in the text of Crowland that Buc used, since, though it is missing in all copies of Buc's manuscript, in Cotton Tiberius everything between 'sed q' and 'interitus' is burnt away, and there could conceivably have been space for the word there. Or the omission might have resulted from assimilation to the similarly worded quotation from Polydore, p. 547, given above, n. to p. 139/15-16. One cannot ever make a case against Buc's accuracy on the basis of the copies, though on p. vi, n. 1 of his Introduction to the 1646 reprint by George Buck Jr., A.R. Myers tries to. See above, pp. cx-cxi.

139/25-31. More, p. 87; Holinshed, III, 402; Grafton, II, 118; Hall, p. 178; Stow, *Annales*, p. 769. Buc here includes Sir James Tyrell among those alleged assassins never examined or punished for this reputed crime because he knows that Tyrell was executed in 1502 on a charge of treason against Henry VII. More (pp. 86f) originated the story (subsequently widely accepted) that Tyrell confessed to killing the sons of Edward IV:

> at such tyme as syr James Tirell was in the Tower, for Treason committed agaynste the moste famous prince king Henry the seuenth, bothe Dighton and he were examined, & confessed the murther in maner aboue written, but wither the bodies were remoued thei could nothing tel
>
> ....
>
> Miles Forest at sainct Martens pecemele rotted away. Dighton in dede yet walketh on a liue in good possibilitie to bee *hanged* ere he dye. But sir Iames Tirel dyed at Tower hill, beheaded for treason.

Buc deals with More's accusation on 165/24ff. He gives the real facts surrounding Tyrell's execution on 167/41-44.

139/46-140/2. More, p. 86: 'thei say that a prieste of syr Robert Brakenbury toke vp the bodyes again, and secretely entered them in such place, as by the occasion of his deathe, whiche onely knew it could neuer synce come to light . . .' This is echoed by Grafton, II, 118, Hall, p. 378, Holinshed, III, 402 and Stow, *Annales*, p. 769. The words emphasized here are underlined in the original MS.

140/16-21. See above, n. 54/50-55/11 for discussion of Buc's argument that the sons of Edward IV were living in February 1484.

140/24-27. More, p. 35.

140/26-27. The relatively early deaths of Edward IV's daughters may be attributable to tuberculosis, which was evidently the cause of Anne, Countess of Surrey's death and the death in childhood or infancy of all her children (Brenan and Stratham, I, 122). Elizabeth, wife of Henry VII, was born in 1466 and died in 1503; Cecily, born in 1468, died in 1507; Margaret was born and died in 1472; Anne was born in 1475 and died in 1521; Catherine, born in 1479, died in 1511; Bridget, born in 1480, died in 1517; and Mary was born and died in 1482.

140/28-42. Tiberius. f. 153^{v}, Buc's original page on which he describes the ape's discovery, is Plate I, above.

There have been many cases of bones being dug up in the Tower and supposed to be the missing princes. The most famous were discovered by workmen in 1674 ten feet under the stairs outside the White Tower and in 1678 placed in an urn in Westminster Abbey, where they still reside, under Charles II's assumption (or perhaps decision) that they were those of the princes. See Carson, *Maligned King*, Chapter 10, especially p. 213, which clarifies the impossibility of a secret burial at a depth of 10 feet, whether under a staircase or beside it: 'The obvious deduction is that they were already there before the structures were unknowingly built over them'.

In addition to Buc's report in 1619 of a discovery of possibly an ape's bones in a turret, his friend the herald Ralph Brooke reported a discovery of two child skeletons in 1622 (see *A Catalogue and Succession of the Kings, Princes, Dukes, Marquesses, Earles, and Viscounts of this Realme of England*). Brooke states that the princes were murdered in the Tower, and in the 1619 edition of his work that it was not to this day known where they were buried (p. 267). But in the 1622 edition he says it was 'not known vntill of late, when as their dead carcases were there found, vnder a heape of stones and rubbish' (p. 33). So between Buc's mention of the ape and Brooke's second version there evidently was a discovery of bones in the Tower which were thought to be those of Edward IV's sons. Again in 1647 a discovery dating to around forty years earlier was recorded on a flyleaf in a copy of More's *Richard III*: when a wall was taken down a small room was revealed containing a table on which lay the bones of two children around age 6-8, too young for the princes. This discovery is cited in Lawrence E. Tanner and William Wright, 'Recent Investigations Regarding the Fate of the Princes in the Tower', *Archaeologia*, LXXXIV, 1935, 1-26.

The next discovery came in 1674 and is the one which, having the stamp of Charles II, has come to be thought of as the *real* bones. Between discovery and inurnment, however, some of the bones had been damaged, lost, given away, replaced by animal bones, and it is not at all certain to what extent those bones found in 1674 were the same ones placed in Westminster Abbey in 1678. See CP XII, 32-9, Appendix J for discussion of whether the remains found in 1674 were or were not those of the princes and whether they were murdered by authority of Richard III or Henry VII, saying that the Tudor story of the murder 'deserves little credit'. If More's story is true, 'the bones of the two children excavated under a staircase in the Tower in 1674 and alleged to be the remains of the two princes could not have been those of Edward and Richard' (X11/2). Appendix J (XII/2 p.

32) discusses the likelihood of their being killed (1) under Richard, (2) under Henry.

The report of an examination of them in 1933 by Tanner and Wright makes it clear that these researchers started with an assumption of the date of burial as 1483 and that the bones in the urn represented were Edward IV's two sons (there was no way of telling how many individuals the bones represented), actually referring to them as 'Edward' and 'Richard' throughout. The ages were judged to agree with those of the brothers, and a stain on one of the skulls was interpreted (though later recanted) as suggesting possible suffocation. But neither date of death nor sex nor familial relationship could be determined at the time.

Dr Richard Lyne-Pirkis in a talk for the Richard III Society in 1964 pointed out that in light of more recent research we can no longer, as Tanner and Wright did, determine age from eruption of teeth, from appearance of ossification centres, or from joining of the epiphyses, which were the evidences on which the 1933 investigation entirely relied. His conclusion was that the bones belonged to children of different ages, perhaps roughly aged seven or eight and fifteen or sixteen. He notes that the skull of the elder shows signs of osteomyelitis, a very painful and potentially fatal disease, which, according to Annette Carson, *Maligned King*, pp. 218ff, could not have escaped notice in Edward V's lifetime. Dr W.M. Krogman, quoted in Kendall, *Richard III,* p. 577n, demolished the theory that the stain was caused by suffocation. It is unlikely that more information will emerge until they are examined again, and more sophisticated testing applied. Their place of burial, in view of More's statement that a priest reburied them and told no one where, does not, as most people seem to assume, 'prove' that these are the bones of the princes, but in fact indicates the opposite. Nor does any evidence of any sort prove Richard III responsible for their death.

Helen Maurer, in a pair of articles, 'Bones in the Tower: a Discussion of Time, Place and Circumstances', *The Ricardian*, Part 1: (1990), VIII, pp. 474-93, Part 2 (1991), IX, pp. 2-22, carefully studies the reports of all major finds of 'the princes bones', and how the political circumstances of the periods when they were found conditioned how they were received. Philip Schwyzer in *Shakespeare and the Remains of Richard III* (Oxford, 2013) catalogues these several discoveries in the Tower of 'the princes' prior to the one under Charles II and stresses that Prof. Wright's findings were as much due to More and Shakespeare as to the bones. 'The skeletons which so gratifyingly came to light – again and again – in the seventeenth century, did so in response to expectations and desires provoked by an early-sixteenth-century text . . . [T]he long dead are the fruits of human desire' (p. 51f). As to the actual fate of Edward IV's sons, this is a question that may yet be resolved by the diligent but unglamorous methods of historical research.

140/41. 'Wast' was in Buc's time a normal spelling of 'waste' (see Harold Jenkins, note to *Hamlet*, I, ii, l. 198, Arden ed., London, 1982). See glossary for meaning.

141/2-3. Edward V was born 2 or 3 November, 1470. Annette Carson and Marie Barnfield have recently studied the evidence for the birth date of Richard III's son Edward and assigned it to 'the period between mid-June and early September 1476' ('Edward of Middleham's Birth', *Ricardian Bulletin*, September 2016, pp. 53-5). There was thus a considerable gap between their ages.

141/29-34. See above, n. 54/50-55/9 for discussion of what threat they posed to Richard.

141/49-142/5. Clearly there was some such fear, since in Henry IV's 1407 confirmation and exemplification of the charter of the Beauforts' legitimation there was an interlineation indicating specifically that they were not to be held capable of the crown (see n. 80/23-33 above).

142/5-6. On the other hand, Henry VII may have put to death Richard's bastard son John of Gloucester, and if the mysterious 'Richard Plantagenet' (see note 192/49-193/3 below) was really Richard's son, he took great care to stay out of harm's way. Even if he were not, his story reflects knowledge of the royal attitude toward kings' bastards.

142/17-20. More, p. 82, quoted above, n. 138/50-139/10.

142/mar. n. Holinshed, III, 484; also Hall and Grafton. For Polydore, see above, n. 138/50-139/1016.

142/42-143/6. More has Buckingham say, 'is it not likelye ynoughe that she shall sende him [York] somme where out of the realme? Verely I looke for none other' (p. 29). Later he has the Archbishop say to the queen, 'So much drede hath my Lorde his vncle, for the tender loue he bereth him, lest your grace shold hap to send him awaye' (p. 37). Crowland, p. 162 mentions a suggestion by the Woodville party that the daughters of Edward IV be shipped out of the country to be preserved in case anything happened to their brothers.

143/7-9. The idea of York's being sent into Flanders parallels a curious accusation in the indictment of the Duke of Clarence: that he tried to have a strange child brought to Warwick Castle and substituted for his son while he sent his son to Ireland or Flanders to serve as a figurehead in raising forces against Edward IV. (See *PROME*, XIV, 402, Appendix, n. 1: 'He planned to send his son and heir abroad to win support, bringing a false child to Warwick castle in his place'.) If Perkin Warbeck was actually the Duke of York sent to Flanders, this precedent might have given the idea to whatever person sent him.

143/mar. n. and 21-22. Grafton, II, 202f, copied from Hall, pp. 473f, and thence derived from Polydore, pp. 596f and embellished: the oration of Perkin to James IV of Scotland. The Biblical reference, from II Kings 11, is in the speech.

143/29-35. Charles, Duke of Burgundy died in 1477. Buc seems particularly vague in his information on the House of Burgundy, calling Margaret aunt rather than sister to Clarence and Richard (see above, text, p. 17 and note thereto).

143/43-45. There exists a letter (Ex. Orig. inter Chart. Antiq. et Miscellan. in Bibliothec Lambethan, Vol. XII, quoted by Gairdner in *Memorials*, Appendix A, pp. 393-9) from Margaret of Burgundy to the Pope asking assistance in favour of Perkin against Henry Tudor, who holds the crown by right of conquest and pretends he is of the blood of Lancaster, knowing full well that he is illegitimate on both sides and that his nomination by the Three Estates in a Parliament called by himself is illegal. She states that he invaded and seized the kingdom just after the house of York had acquired safe possession of it. When Henry took the throne Margaret had other reasons for grievance, since her dowry had never been paid in full, and with Henry's accession the payments stopped.

144/11-15. Shortly after the siege of Boulogne in 1492 Perkin was received in France and Burgundy.

144/26-28. Lambert Simnel in 1487 is said to have pretended to be Richard, Duke of York, or Edward, Earl of Warwick, who was still alive in the Tower, or first one then the other. See Gordon Smith, 'Lambert Simnel and the King from Dublin', *The Ricardian,* CXXXV (1996), 498-536, which comprehensively analyses all reports of his identity and whom he was pretending to be and suggests the possibility that he may have been impersonating Edward V or may actually have been Edward V.

145/13. 'Sir Simon Priest' is an error for Sir Richard Simon, who was a priest. This passage is burnt away in the original, so we do not know whether the error is Buc's misreading or that of George Buck Esq. or his scribe. Hall, p. 428, Grafton, II, 169, and Holinshed, III, 484 all read 'Sir Richard Symond [or Simond] priest' without punctuation).

145/13-14. Bernard André, pp. 49-52, claims that Margaret of Burgundy believed this pretender to be a son of Edward IV, sent for him and he came. His nominal supporters, John, Earl of Lincoln and Francis, Viscount Lovell were granted aid by Margaret, Duchess of Burgundy. Buc seems again to be assuming, erroneously, that Charles, Duke of Burgundy, was still alive.

145/1st mar. n. Dion Cassius, LVII, 16.3; Tacitus, *Annales*, II, xxxix and Suetonius, Tiberius XXV all speak of 'pseudo Agrippa'. 'Pseudo-Nero' is referred to only by Dion Cassius LXIII, 9 and LXVI, 19, and Sextus Condianus only by Dion Cassius, LXXIII, 6.

145/33-35. Velleius Paterculus, *Historia Romana*, I, xi, 1.

145/50-146/1. The shoemaker's son who impersonated Warwick was Ralph Wilford. His parentage is given by Stow, *Annales*, p. 805 and Holinshed repeats it (III, 523) with reference to Stow. Fabyan, p. 686 calls him 'sonne of a cordyner'.

146/11-12 and 1st mar. n. Ovid, *Epistulae Heroides*, XVI, 130 [Belief in great matters is apt to come slowly].

146/19-26 and 34-36. Livy, I, iv (Romulus and Remus). Diodorus in fragmentary books VII (5.1) and VIII (3-6) refers to Romulus and Remus.

146/27-33. Herodotus I, 108-13; Trogus Pompeius, *Historiae Philippicae*, I, fragment 24.

146/49. There is no reference to Moses in Perkin's speech as the chroniclers record it.

147/17-19. Hall, p. 463, Frederic Madden, 'Documents Relating to Perkin Warbeck', *Archaeologia*, XXVII (1838), p. 176, says the conspirators planned to attach white roses to their garments if they succeeded.

147/35-40. The message Henry's ambassadors gave was not an indication or proof of Perkin's real identity, but merely a statement that he was obviously an imposter because everyone knew Richard had killed his nephews, and to believe otherwise was the height of insanity (Polydore, p. 591). Here Henry's historian speaks better for Perkin than does Buc, in giving him a very flimsy argument.

148/2nd mar. n. Grafton, II, 215, derived from Polydore, p. 606. Also in Hall and Holinshed.

149/19-20. Polydore, p. 603 gives 'Petrus Hyalas'; Hall, p. 482 and Grafton, II, 211, 'Peter Hyalas'; Stow, *Annales*, p. 803, 'Peter Helias'; Holinshed, III, p. 517, 'Peter Hialas'; and Gainsford, p. 88, 'Peter Hialos'.

149/35-39 and 2nd mar. n. According to Perkin's confession, the sole source for which is Hall, p. 488f, ambassadors Loyte Lucas and Stephyn Fryan were sent from the French king to invite him to France. Frion – as his name is given in Pat. Rolls (1485-94), pp. 118 and 344 – was Henry's Clerk of the Signet and Secretary of the French Tongue from 1486 until 1491 at the latest.

149/44-150/2. This French visit actually occurred earlier. At this stage Perkin went directly from Ireland to Cornwall, where he was captured. His stay in France had followed his first visit to Ireland. After his expulsion from France because of the Treaty of Etaples, he returned to Flanders then set out for Kent, Ireland again, and Scotland.

151/44-152/17. Polydore admits that Henry VII, despite his underplaying his concern about Perkin, was frightened (*The Anglica Historia of Polydore Vergil,* ed. Denys Hay, *Anglica Historia,* Cam Soc. 1st ser. 29, London, 1844, p. 66). It is clear that he did not know what happened to Edward V or Richard of York. Henry signally failed to confront Perkin with his queen, who was York's sister, or with any of the family. Polydore has included statements he alleges were made by Perkin, having him say that Richard ordered the brothers murdered, but the murderer relented and killed only Edward, sparing York and transporting him out of the country (Polydore, p. 596). This loses credibility if we bear in mind how unlikely it would be for the figurehead of the Yorkist movement to denigrate the last Yorkist king. But actually, in his proclamation, of which there is a reliable record, he does *not* mention an attempted murder – in fact does not mention Richard at all – but says 'we in our tender age were secretly conveyed over the sea into other divers countries, there remaining certain years as unknown' (quoted by Spedding, *Works of Francis Bacon*, VI, Appendix II, p. 252).

Perkin was said to have confessed, but the confession, if it was not a fiction, was made in private, as Richmond Herald indicated to Raimondo de Soncino (letter to the Duke of Milan, *CSP* Milan, pp. 329-31) and André seems to confirm (p. 72f), saying that the king ordered the confession published. But neither Polydore nor Fabyan mentions it, and Hall is the sole author who gives a text for it (p. 488f), saying Perkin was compelled to read it on the scaffold. The inconsistencies within the confession and with earlier statements made by and about Perkin, and also the complete disregard of its details not only by foreign powers but by Henry's official historian lead one to believe its authorship doubtful, its details unsupported, its recitation not voluntary and its circulation, if any, minimal.

For a very thorough discussion of Perkin Warbeck and his identity, see Ann Wroe, *Perkin. A Story of Deception*, London, 2003. At the end of this long, carefully researched book the author finds herself unable ultimately to determine whether or not he was the Duke of York.

151/48-49. Grafton, II, 218; Hall, pp. 488f; also in Holinshed.

152/12. [Varying and changeable multitude]

152/25-26. Seneca, *Controversiae*, X, 8.

152/30-31 and 3rd mar. n. [If one who is tortured cannot stand the torment any longer he will confess that he has done something he hasn't] Augustine, *De Civitate Dei*, XIX, vi paraphrased.

153/4-8. Psalm 22, Matthew 27, and Mark 15.

154/12, 170/35, 172/45 and 212/28. See n. 170/34-43. The son of Richard's referred to here is John of Gloucester.

154/23-24. Buc is recurring here to imagery on which he based his long poem *Daphnis.*

154/24-25. Gainsford parallels Simnel and Warbeck.

155/21-23. *crimen alienum*: someone else's crime; *crimen proprium*: one's own crime. Polydore, p. 608, 'cùm nullo suo delicto supplicium quaerere posset, alieno ad id tractus est' [although he deserved no punishment for a crime of his own, he was brought to it by someone else's].

155/29-30. [suspicion of flight, which is not normally taken to be detrimental to the state, is not adjudged a crime]; I have not succeeded in locating this sentence in the *Institutes* or *Digest.*

155/2nd mar. n. William Staundford, *Les Plees del Corone* (London, 1607), I, 27 and 33v. Ch. 26 covers 'Escape Voluntary' and Ch. 27 'Negligent Escape'.

156/14-16. Gainsford, Preface, sig. B2.

156/19-158/21. Sebastian, King of Portugal, who reigned 1557-78, after his death in battle in somewhat confusing circumstances became the focus of a messianic hero image associated with millenarian prophecies. There were four main contenders for Sebastian's identity. (See H. V. Livermore, *A New History of Portugal*, 2nd ed., London, 1976, p. 167.)

156/43. Quintilian, *Instituto Oratoria*, I, ii, 19: 'caligat in sole' [can't see in the sun]. Erasmus, *Chiliades*, p. 513 gives this quotation with the explanation: 'in clarissima caecutire' [to be blind when it is brightest].

157/1-4. Gainsford, p. 60. In context, and taken with other similar remarks by Gainsford, this assumes an aspect of sarcasm rather than factual statement (p. 42: 'this misnamed *Richard*'.)

158/24-25. [Your uncle has done a deed most unworthy of himself] I cannot find the source of this quotation.

157/mar. n. [This ambassador told this to Baron Darcy]

158/25-26. At this point the editor of the printed version of Buc's *History* inserts some supplementary material appearing in no other version, a letter from Dr Stephen de Sampugo to Joseph Texere giving evidence from Venice that Don Sebastian is not a counterfeit.

159/35-43. Buc seems, by attacking Morton, to be deflecting blame from Henry VII. There is no reference in his sources to Morton's complicity in the death of Warwick. Hall says, 'The fame after hys death springe abroade, yt Ferdinand kyng of Spayne woulde neuer make full conclusion of the matrimony to be had betwene prynce Arthur and the lady Katheryn hys daughter nor sende her into England aslong as this erle lyued' (p. 491) and is followed in this by Grafton and Holinshed. Warwick and Warbeck were executed in 1499 and Morton died in 1500, ten months later.

160/7-8. This book is no longer extant. It was probably in manuscript privately circulated among Hoby's friends, of whom Buc was one (see above, p. cxxii).

160/36. [Abundant caution doesn't hurt]

160/mar. n. This is not in More, Holinshed, Stow or Gainsford. This oath is mentioned only in Hall, p. 251.

160/50-161/1. There is no evidence of Sir Robert Clifford's following the house of York except for a very few minor grants to a Robert Clifford, Esq. under the Yorkist kings in *Pat. Rolls*. Buc presumably uses for his evidence the fact that Clifford is expected to have known the Duke of York well enough to identify him.

161/1st mar. n. This does not appear in More. Buc imagines it does because these authors include his work verbatim in theirs. These followers are recorded *passim* in Holinshed, Grafton, Stow, and Hall under Henry VII, and in Gainsford *passim*.

161/13-18. Sir William Stanley was executed in 1495 for treason in complicity with Perkin Warbeck. Sir Robert Clifford, who informed against him and received a substantial reward from Henry VII for so doing, reported that Stanley had said if Perkin really were the son of Edward IV he would not fight against him (Polydore, p. 593). For further information on Sir William Stanley, see above, n. 29/29-36.

161/19-20. George Neville was not the brother of the Earl of Westmorland. He is cited in Hall, p. 463 as 'syr George Neuell bastard'. *PROME,* Henry VII: Oct.1495, XVI, 230 records an Act of Attainder passed against 'George Neville, late of London knight, otherwise called George Nevile bastard, comenly called bastard sone to Sir Thomas Nevile'.

161/24. Grafton, Hall, Holinshed and Stow give 'Thomas Astwood' instead of Thomas Bagnol. According to Stow, *Annales*, p. 799, Bagnall was executed the next year for an unstated offence. Hall, p. 467, Grafton and Holinshed give 'Cressenor' and Stow, p. 798 gives 'Chressenor' where Buc has 'Challoner'. Possibly this is a misreading of 'Chressenor', since at a glance long 's's might look like 'l's.

161/29. Gainsford, p. 49, spells the name 'Rochford'. It is given as Richeford in the chroniclers.

161/44. This section no longer exists in Buc's original manuscript but only in the Editor's copies, so we have no means of knowing what spellings Buc gave for these names. He evidently got them from Gainsford, p. 62, where '*Moumford*, *Corbet*, *Whight*, *Bets*, *Quintine*, or *Geuge*' are listed; George Buck Esq. and his scribe probably garbled them further in copying. The chroniclers give them rather differently: for example, Hall gives 'Mountforde, Corbet, white belt, quyntine or otherwise Genyn', p. 472. Interestingly, More refers to them in *The Debellation of Salem and Bizance*, 1553 (in *Workes*, 1557, p. 990, sig. R3v) as an example of felons put to death for treason without indictment and calls them 'captaine Quintyn, captein Genyn, Corbet & Belke'. I can find no other record of these men, nor can I locate Buc's source for Serjeant Ferior and the yeoman Edwards, which again may have been confused by misreadings or incorrect copying by George Buck Esq. and his scribe. Buc seems to have misunderstood the statement about the executions: there were, Hall states, 160 prisoners taken, but only the five captains noted above were put to death. Hall says later that 200 of Perkin's soldiers were slain at Exeter (p. 484).

162/1st mar. n. Holinshed, III, p. 505; Grafton, II, 193; Hall, p. 464; Stow, *Annales*, p. 797.

162/2nd mar. n. More, p. 82, quoted above n. 139/3-10.

162/17-22 and 3rd mar. n. Camden, *Britannia,* p. 148. This reference speaks only of the sieges of Exeter, does not say who was convinced by Perkin, and calls him a base pretender. However, Buc seems to be giving *viva voce* information here, suggesting that Camden's opinions were changing or, as was the case with Stow, differed from those he had published.

163/44-48. For Richard's naming John de la Pole his successor, see above, n. 74/3-8.

163/10-11. This is probably intended to refer to Richard's bastard son John of Gloucester. No one is recorded as suggesting that Richard's son Edward died other than naturally.

163/29-30. [tricks and deceit]

163/35-38. I have been unable to trace this manuscript, which may no longer be extant. The countess referred to is undoubtedly the Countess of Richmond. How plausible this suggestion is David Johnson shows in his speculative article 'Sir George Buck and the Beaufort Plot to Kill the Princes', *Ricardian Bulletin*, Spring 2006, pp. 36f.

164/5. [of infernal rule]

164/38-40. See above, n. 54/50-55/11.

164/42. [origins]

164/46. [evil genius]

164/48. *Aeneid*, VI, 430 [condemned to death by false accusation].

165/5. [it is lovely to repeat often]

165/7-9. See above, n. 138/50-139/10.

165/11. [from their own knowledge]

165/19-20 and 1st mar. n. [a liar needs to have a good memory]: I have been unable to find this reference in Aristotle. However, Quintilian quotes it as an already well known saying: 'verumque est illud, quod vulgo dicitur, mendacem memorem esse oportere' [and it is true, as is commonly said, a liar should have a good memory] (*Institutiones*, IV, ii, 91).

165/24-26. See 139/25-31.

165/34. [Those who confess are taken to be condemned]

166/25-167/2. [A wound or a bite or a sword blow will heal, but a scar will remain]. This story is in Plutarch, *Moralia*, 65D. Buc has invented the detail of the conversation.

167/ 1st mar. n. Ausonius, *Opuscula* II, iii, 63-4 ('Oratio').

167/11 and 2nd mar. n. odium et contemptus [hatred and contempt] Aristotle, *Politics*, V, 1311a.

167/16-17 and 3rd mar. n. [Those whom people hate they wish to die] Cicero *De Officiis*, II, vii. This quotation is given above, text, p. 34, as well. Buc has made a translation which he crossed out first in pencil then in ink: 'Men wish to see the finall fate / of him, whome they doo loothe, & hate' (Tib. f. 206).

167/22-23. [transference of a crime]

167/4th mar. n. ['perisse' is an old form for 'perire']

167/36-44. See quotation in 139/25-31 above, More, p. 87. Also in Holinshed, III, p, 402, Stow, *Annales*, p. 770, and in Hall and Grafton. There exists no documented or reported confession by Tyrell relating to the sons of Edward IV, nor is there any contemporary report of one. Presumably had there been a real confession it would have been published at the time.

169/23-25. Warwick was tried before Oxford as High Constable of England (Hall, p. 491 and followers). There is no other suggestion of Oxford's persecuting Warwick or Warbeck.

169/27 and 29. Heveningham = Hedingham Castle.

169/35-40. Buc seems to have been the first person to tell this story of Oxford's fine. Bacon repeats it as hearsay ('there remains to this day a report') and with more detail in *Henry VII*, p. 209. The fine, imposed by Henry VII, was for retaining, and the amount 15,000 marks, according to James Ross, *John de Vere, Thirteenth Earl of Oxford* (Woodbridge, 2011), p. 141f. It is true that Oxford had no direct heir: he was succeeded by his nephew. Buc's informant is the Earl of Arundel, to whom he dedicates this work.

169/44. [Like salt in water]: I cannot trace the song or poem to which this is a refrain.

170/11. All George Buck Esq.'s copies give '12.m^{li}'. Since this is burnt away in the original manuscript, it is impossible to tell whether it was an error by Buc or of his great-nephew or the latter's scribe. I would guess the last is most likely. Having followed this reading in the first two editions, I am very grateful to Alan H. Nelson (see http://www.oxford-shakespeare.com) and Christopher Paul for pointing out to me separately this clear error and for the latter's suggestion that the great-nephew or his scribe may have misread "ij" as "12".

170/29. Erasmus, *Chiliades*, p. 208 gives the Greek version and translates it 'Heroum filij noxae'.

170/2nd mar. n. There is no such reference in Grafton. The manuscript chronicle cannot be identified and may no longer be extant.

170/33-40 and 4th mar. n. Gainsford, p. 108, Perkin's confession mentions that the Irish welcomed him first as the Earl of Warwick, then as Richard's bastard son, who was in Henry VII's keeping at the time. The chroniclers do not mention Richard's bastard son here.

170/34-40. It is unfortunate that Buc's main source for John of Gloucester's execution is lost. The only other intimation we have of Henry's treatment of John is in the chronicles, where Perkin in his confession reports that the Irish tried to induce him with threats to pretend to be Warwick, but when he refused suggested he was a bastard son of Richard III, which he denied. On the other hand, perhaps John managed to escape the net after all, since *Pat. Rolls* (1494-1509), pp. 447f, records a pardon on 27 November 1505 to the Mayor of the Staple of Calais and to a long list of merchants of the same, among whom one is 'John Gloucestre'.

170/40-42. Richard, Duke of York, father of Edward IV and Richard III, was Lieutenant of Ireland 1447-53.

171/17-19. Piers Gaveston was Edward II's favourite, executed by Edward's nobles because of objection to his power with the king. Andrew Harclay was a leader against the Scots under Edward II, who objected to his taking too much authority into his own hands. Dr Lopez was executed, though he protested innocence, for a plot to poison Queen Elizabeth whose doctor he was.

171/30-31 and 2nd mar. n. [Let your hurt mind be open to your guardian spirits]: this quotation, lacking a dactyllic foot before *manes*, is actually in Ausonius, *Opuscula*, II.iii.57.

171/48-49 and 3rd mar. n. [Greek: You cannot kill me, because it is not my destiny. Latin: You cannot kill me because I am protected by fate.] This is not from Suidas but from Philostratus, *Vita Apollonii*, VIII, viii. Suidas in its entry for Apollonius refers to Philostratus's account but does not quote it.

171/37-42. Shakespeare was equally familiar with this assumption: 'And under him / My genius is rebuked as it is said / Mark Antony's was by Caesar' (*Macbeth* III, i). Its source is Plutarch's *Life of Marcus Antonius*, XXXIII, 2-3.

172/1. [the majesty of Apollonius] Flavius Vopiscus, 'Divus Aurelianus', XXIV, 7, in *Historia Augusta.*

172/25-26. Hebrews. 10:31.

172/26.[God is terrifying]: there are several biblical quotations to this effect.

172/29-30. [No grief is useful unless for sin, no fear unless of God]: I have not located this quotation. Margins are completely burnt away here, along with all references, and there is no representation in the copies.

172/32. Psalms, 52:6.

173/19. Grafton, Hall, Holinshed and Stow agree because they all incorporate More's work in their histories. It is interesting that in this as in other matters Stow's personal researches are more favourable to Richard than what he published.

173/25-26 and mar. n. [What was said is unsaid, what was agreed is in measure unagreed] Terence, *Phormio*, 951.

173/33-36. This is the gist of Perkin's statements about himself as given in Polydore, pp. 596f and Hall, pp. 473f. There is no evidence that a report of a speech by Perkin to the king of Scots ever existed, but there does exist a copy of a proclamation made while he was with King James (Harl. 283, copied from an original once in the Cotton collection; it is printed by Spedding in Bacon, *Henry VII*, Appendix II, pp. 252-5. This does say that Perkin escaped from the Tower and was conveyed abroad where he remained a number of years but mentions no attempt by Richard against his life, as Hall and his followers do.)

BOOK IV

174. Buc has followed his outline rather closely. Two items are out of place: 'Kings must not marry . . . without consent of the barons' (a topic barely touched on) should follow 'His wooing the Lady Eleanor . . . and his marriage with her'. 'King Edward's death' should follow 'Dr Stillington . . . imprisoned'. 'The mortality of Plantagenets' is not dealt with in this book (he has discussed the early deaths of Edward IV's daughters in the previous book), and the three final headings have been discussed near the beginning of Book III.

175/mar. n. More, p. 72:

> For no woman was there any where yong or olde, riche or pore, whom he set his eie vpon, in whome he any thinge lyked either person or fauour, speche, pace, or countenance, but w[t]out any fere of god, or respect of his honour, murmure or grudge of y[e] worlde, he would importunely

pursue hys appetite, and haue her, to the gret destruccion
of many a good woman.

175/14. 'Amasia' [lover] is a post-classical word, found normally in the masculine.

175/24-33. The key to this double-entendre lies in the separation of 'faucon' into 'faux' and 'con' [false cunt]. 'Serrure' is a lock. The fetterlock was a traditional badge of the house of York (see Frederic Madden, 'Political Poems of the Reigns of Henry VI and Edward IV', *Archaeologia*. XXIX (1842, 332). Kendall (*Richard III,* p. 28) mentions the towers at Fotheringhay rising in the shape of a fetterlock. Camden, *Remaines*, p. 215, notes that Edmund of Langley 'Bare also for an Impresse a Faulcon in a fetter-locke, implying that he was locked vp from all hope and possibility of the Kingdome . . . [H]is great Grandchilde King *Edward* the fourth reported when hee commaunded that his yonger sonne *Richard* duke of *Yorke*, should vse this deuice with the fetter-locke opened . . .' Buc several times mentions these 'speaking pictures' in *The Third Universitie*, using interchangeably the words 'Ierogliffe', 'Hieroglyphick', and 'Rebus'. Camden, *Remaines*, p. 164, notes that the idea came from France, and they are called 'painted Poesies': 'they which lackt wit to expresse their conceit in speech, did vse to depaint it out . . . in pictures, which they called *Rebus* . . .' Sir James Lay's discourse on 'Motts' in Hearne's *Curious Discourses*, I, 123, says their purpose is 'First, in a word to contain a world. Secondly, when thereby a dumb beast, or bird, or dead creature doth, as it were, speak, and bewray his own primary quality. Thirdly, when the simple cannot understand it, and yet the wise cannot but understand it'.

176ff. For Edward's marriages and the illegitimacy of his children see above, n. 39/4th mar. n.

176/5. Properly Sir Thomas, son of Lord Butler.

176/9. Stillington's name was not Thomas but Robert.

176/1st mar. n. and 8-19. Commynes, II, 305 (Bk. VI, ch. 8): 'ung evesque de Bas . . . qui autresfoys avoit eu grand credit avec . . . roy Edouard . . . disoit que ledit roy Edouard avoit promys foy de mariage à une dame d'Angleterre (qu'il nommoit) . . . et en avoit faict la promesse en la main dudict evesque' [a bishop of Bath, who earlier had great credit with King Edward, stated that the said King Edward had promised marriage to a lady of England, whom he named, and had made the promise in the presence of the said bishop]. The ed. of 1576, f. 307, says, 'entre les mains' [between the hands]. Buc has combined this with an earlier passage, which he later quotes in its context, text, p. 183: 'Et dict cest evesque qu'il les avoit espousez, et n'y avoit que luy et eulx deux' [And the said bishop said that he had married them, and there were present only himself and the two of them] (II, 232, Bk. V, ch. 20). Only Commynes, writing thirty years after these events, tells us that Stillington – who had been Edward IV's Chancellor – married them and later was responsible for revealing the secret to Richard. There is no proof of Buc's suggestion that Stillington's brief imprisonment under Edward IV was connected with his revealing the precontract (see n. 183/45-184/9). He was immediately imprisoned by Henry VII on his accession.

Titulus Regius, the document in *PROME*, Richard III: Jan. 1484, XV, 15-18 setting out Richard's title to the throne, using as part of its evidence Edward's precontract with Lady Eleanor before he married Elizabeth Woodville, said,

> at the tyme of contract of the same pretensed mariage, and bifore and longe tyme after, the seid King Edward was and stode maried and trouthplight to oone Dame Elianor Butteler, doughter of the old erle of Shrowesbury, with whom the same King Edward had made a precontracte of matrimonie longe tyme byfore he made the said pretensed mariage with the said Elizabeth Gray . . .

(Elizabeth Woodville was widow of Sir John Gray.)

176/9-12. See above, text, p. 35. Buc has given Robert Stillington's first name erroneously as 'Thomas'. As Buc says, he was a man of substance, as Edward IV's Chancellor.

176/28. Hugh Ross Williamson says that Edward IV had a son, Edward de Wigmore, by Eleanor Butler, deriving this information from a family tradition of Edward de Wigmore's descendants (*The Butt of Malmsey*, London, 1967, p. 90).

177/1st mar. n. *El Reusuerq* seems no longer extant. Buc also uses it once in *Comm.*

177/8-178/8. In text, p. 177-78 Buc follows More's account of the marriage (p. 61). He adds the lodge or forest-house, having a tendency to visualize scenes. He is elaborating on Fabyan (p. 654), who says Edward pretended to go hunting when he went to marry Elizabeth, and that only the bridegroom, the bride, her mother, the priest, two gentlemen, 'and a yong man to helpe the preest synge' were present. The story of his having seen her first in the place where he married her comes from Hall, p. 264, and is repeated by Grafton and Holinshed: while hunting in the Forest of Wychwood, Edward stopped at her family's manor at Grafton and soon after married her there, 'where he first phantasied her visage'.

177/19-21. Commynes, II, 232 [And afterwards the said King Edward married for love the daughter of an English knight, a widow who had two sons].

178/2-7. Buc follows here very closely the wording of *Titulus Regius* (*PROME*, Richard III: Jan. 1484, XV, 15): 'the said pretensed mariage was made privaly and secretely, without edicion of bannes, in a private chambre, a prophane place, and not openly in the face of the church, aftre the lawe of Goddes churche, but contrarie therunto . . .'

178/9-19. The marriage, said to have taken place 1 May 1464, was concealed by Edward until 29 September when negotiations for the French marriage forced him to reveal it (Fabyan, p. 654; and *The Historical Collections of a Citizen of London* ['Gregory's Chronicle], ed. James Gairdner, London, 1876, Cam. Soc. 2nd ser. 17, pp. 226f). All sources report the nobility's resulting anger, for example Crowland, Fulman ed., I, 539; Fabyan, p. 654; Mancini (Arm: 60ff, Car: 42-5).

178/20-38. At the basis of the breach between Edward IV and Warwick seems to have been their difference over the question of alliance with France or Burgundy. 'Hearne's Fragment' (*A Remarkable Fragment of an Old . . . Chronicle . . . of the Affairs of Edward the Fourth* . . . in Thomas Sprott, *Chronica*, ed. Hearne, Oxford, 1719), p. 299, says that Warwick's councils with the French king aroused his greed. The Crowland continuator (p. 114), who favours the Woodvilles, goes to some length to say that he considered the previous continuator wrong in attributing the breach to Edward's marriage and blames instead the marriage of his sister Margaret to the Duke of Burgundy.

178/2nd mar. n. [The indignity of this marriage of King Edward with a simple gentlewoman so displeased the Earl of Warwick and the principal lords of England and so offended King Louis XI that they formed a confederation against King Edward] Du Tillet, *Traictez*, p. 246. Buc has altered word order somewhat for compression and clarity.

179/5-9. Crowland Chronicle, Fulman ed., I, 539 [After this King Edward, driven by his own will, chose to marry secretly Elizabeth, the widow of a certain knight, and after had her crowned queen. This the aristocracy of the kingdom took ill, that a woman of such base stock should be raised to the height of queen consort] (my translation).

179/22-25. In 1470, Warwick and Clarence with French assistance drove Edward from the kingdom and restored Henry VI. The next year Edward killed Warwick at the battle of Barnet, defeated Henry's forces at Tewkesbury, and resumed the throne.

179/28-180/12. The story that Edward's mother was mortally offended by the marriage is reported by Mancini: 'she offered to submit to a public enquiry, asserting that Edward had not been conceived from her husband the Duke of York but was begotten in adultery, therefore was by no means worthy of the eminence of kingship' (Car: p. 43). More twists this by writing that she tried to prevent it: he and the chroniclers who follow him allege she charged him with a prior impediment, a relationship with 'Elizabeth Lucy', and there is agreement that her objections involved a charge of illegitimacy or bigamy (More's word 'bigamy' not used in the modern sense but referring to Elizabeth's having been married before). See n. 135/32-136/32 above. More and his followers overlook the fact that the marriage was secret, so neither the Duchess of York nor anyone else could have known it was intended.

179/28-180/36. This is largely indirect discourse in More (pp. 62f) and has been turned into speeches by Buc, who has added some expansion and repetition, though More's organization and the skeleton of his wording remain. More does not shift into direct discourse until 'And I doubt not' (p. 181, l. 15). Buc makes few changes. These involve expanding More's verbal compression: p. 180, l. 47, 'love mutually and virtuously' is 'loue together' in More; p. 180, l. 50, 'and being considered even after the worldly accompt' is in More 'euen worldly considred'; p. 181, ll. 3-4, 'love and favour' is in More 'herty fauor'.

179/38. Buc has accidentally given 'Elizabeth' for 'Eleanor'.

181/43-47. More, pp. 64f (also Hall, p. 367, Grafton, II, 105 and Stow, *Annales*, p. 756). It is 'Elizabeth Lucy', not Edward, who is asked to and does deny the marriage.

181/47-182/1 and 182/14-16. More, p. 56, 'The king wold say that he had .iii. concubines, which in three diuers properties diuersly exceled. One the meriest, another the wiliest, the thirde the holiest harlot in his realme, as one whom no man could get out of ye church lightly to any place, but it wer to his bed'. More identifies Mistress Shore as the merriest. There is no mention of one called the 'wittiest', but the appellation would seem to agree with his description of her: 'a proper wit had she, & could both rede wel & write, mery in company, redy & quick of aunswer, neither mute nor ful of bable, sometime taunting w[t]out displeasure & not w[t]out disport'. Buc's description of 'Elizabeth Lucy' agrees in all other respects with More's.

Mistress Shore's first name was Elizabeth. On the annulment (for non-consummation) of her marriage she reverted to her maiden name, Lambert. She almost certainly came to be known as 'Jane Shore' from Thomas Heywood's two-part play, *Edward IV* (1594), in which she is a major character.

182/1st mar. n. [Love is a credulous thing] Ovid, *Epistulae Heroides*, VI, 21.

182/2-13. Arthur Plantagenet was created Viscount Lisle in 1523 and died in 1542. See above note to 39/4th mar. n. for discussion of who might really have been his mother.

182/29. See above n. 176/5.

182/42-43 and 4th mar. n. [credulity is apt to be a maiden's downfall] Ovid, *Epistulae Heroides*, XVII, 41.

183/17-40. I have been unable to find a source for this story. Buc or a *viva voce* informant (Stow?) may have pieced together a plausible sequence of events from a work no longer extant. On the other hand, Buc may be indulging his taste for elaborating dramatic scenes from a meagre suggestion.

183/41-44 and mar. n. Commynes II, 305. See above nn. 176/1st mar. n. and 8-19.

183/45-184/9. There is no evidence of the bishop's revealing the marriage before Edward IV's death or that his imprisonment sprang from knowledge of it. Coming so close to Clarence's execution, it may have been for suspicion of aiding or associating with Clarence, which may or may not have consisted in revealing the bigamous marriage. In his general pardon on 20 June 1478 is a 'Declaration that Robert, bishop of Bath and Wells, has been faithful to the king and done nothing contrary to his oath of fealty, as he had shown before the king and certain lords' (*Pat. Rolls*, 1476-85). If Stillington did tell Clarence of the precontract, this may explain why he needed a pardon. Mancini (Arm: 62, 68, Car: 44, 48) says that the Woodvilles were thought to be responsible for Clarence's death, seeing him as an impediment to the succession of Edward's sons: 'regina, memor contumeliarum in genus suum et criminum in seipsam obiectorum, quod scilicet more maiorum legitima regis uxor non esset, existimavit, numquam prolem suam ex rege iam suscepam regnaturum, nisi dux Clarentie aufferretur . . .' [The queen . . . remembered the insults to her family and the calumnies with which she was reproached, namely that according to established usage she was not the legitimate wife of the king. Thus she concluded that her offspring by the king would never come to the throne, unless the Duke of Clarence were removed] p. 62.

Mancini is at least aware that the objection to Edward's marriage has to do with his being already married, but he guesses incorrectly that this indicates he was married by proxy to a lady on the Continent, presumably Bona of Savoy (Arm: 96-7, Car: 66-7).

184/3-4. Godwin, p. 307 actually says Stillington 'died a prisoner in the Castle of Windsor, whether he was committed for foure yeeres before his death (for what cause I know not) in the moneth of October 1487'. The Godwin reference is to imprisonment, not to redemption from imprisonment. He is referring to a much later period in Henry VII's reign.

184/6-7. Commynes, II, 305, slightly paraphrased without changing sense [King Edward dismissed the bishop and kept him in prison and held him to ransom for a goodly sum].

184/10-7 and 3rd mar. n. Polydore, p. 539. The reference to Book 24 is correct. Crowland, p. 150, says 'rex ille neque senio, neque quovis intellecto certo genere morbi cuius cura in minore persona facilis non videretur affectus esset' [the king, though he was not affected by old age nor by any known type of disease which would not have seemed easy to cure in a lesser person']. Mancini says Edward IV's death was caused by depression over French hostility, aggravated by a stomach chill caught while he was in a boat watching his party fishing (Arm: 58-9, Car: 40-3). Armstrong regards this account as not improbable but also summarizes other accounts of the king's death, noting that its causes were not mentioned in English sources until the sixteenth century; by which date, he generalizes, 'sudden death in noble or princely families usually aroused . . . suspicion' of poison (in Mancini, notes, p. 107). See also above, n. to p. 23/6.

184/4th mar. n. Bouchard, f. ccvi, says: 'En lan dessudit lxxxii [*sic*] en apuril, le roy da*n*gleterre fut frappe dune appoplexie: do*n*t mourut soubdamenme*n*t sansparler. Aucuns disoyent que il auoit este empoysonne' [In the year 82, in April, the king of England was struck down by an apoplexy, from which he died suddenly without speaking. Some said he had been poisoned].

184/5th mar. n. Monstrelet, 'Nouvelles Chroniques', f. 76v, 'le Roy Edouard d'Angleterre, mourut audit Royaume d'vne apoplexie qui le print. Autres dient qu'il fut empoisonne en beuua*n*t de bo*n* vin du creu de Chaluau, que le Roy luy auoit donné'. Buc has mistaken 'creu' for a place [King Edward of England died in the said kingdom of an apoplexy which killed him. Others say he was poisoned by drinking the good wine of Chaluau which the king gave him']. Presumably the king of France is meant.

184/20-25. Commynes, II, 304, 'il tomba malade et bien tost après mourut, aucuns dient d'ung quaterre' [He fell ill and shortly after died, some say of a catarrh'].

184/36. Buc seems here to be going back on his earlier arguments about Edward IV's sons.

185/1st mar. n. This reference is not in More but in Hall, p. 387, Grafton, II, 126, Holinshed, III, 409 and Stow, *Annales*, p. 775, in a section invented by Hall immediately following More's narrative.

185/6-9. This refers to Dr Shaw's (Shaa's) sermon, 22 June, on the theme 'bastard slips shall not take deep root' (see above n. 130/31-32).

185/7. By Friar Pynk Buc means Friar Penketh (More, pp. 58f). The chronicles sometimes give the name as Pynk.

185/9-11. The petition incorporated in *Titulus Regius* is not from the North but from the Three Estates of the realm. Buc misreads Crowland, pp. 158-60 (quoted above in n. 46/3-16), which habitually denigrates the North.

186/3-4. Henry VIII.

186/9-12. Polydore, pp. 524 and 547 attributes the death of Edward IV's sons to this sin of their father.

187/10-11. This resembles the beginning of Psalm 1.

187/45. [Great and stronger than all things is truth, great is truth and prevails]; Apocrypha III Esdras, 4:41 says just 'Magna veritas et praevalet'.

187/45-6. There is a gap in the ms. here, and I have supplied the quotation directly from Cicero, *Tusculian Disputations*, V.xxiv, 68, 'in quo inest omnis cum subtilitas disserendi tum veritas iudicandi' [in which, then, inheres all the subtlety for discernment and truth of a judgment].

187/47. [counsels of the impious and throne of iniquity]

188/34-40. *PROME.* Henry VII: Nov. 1485, XV, 102: Pembroke, Morton, Knevet, Thomas Nandyke [*sic*], late of Cambrigge. Nigromancer', Lewkenor, John and Richard Guildford, Fogg, Poynings, Haute, Fiennes, Gainsford, the bishops of Salisbury and Exeter and many more had their attainders reversed.

188/45-46. [Sorcerers and enchanters, a kind of people that even for their simply renouncing of God, the Best and Greatest, should suffer capital punishment]: I have not found the source of this quotation.

189/8-11 and 2nd mar. n. This is not in More. It is in Polydore, p. 557f, Hall, p. 389, Grafton, II., 144, Stow, *Annales*, p. 782, and Holinshed, III, 431.

189/3-4. The source for Richard's having plans to marry his niece is Crowland, pp. 174-6, which presents it as a fully formed scheme that he was forced through opposition of his own party to abandon, making public denial of this intent. Such a scheme is highly unlikely, if only because around this time Richard was negotiating matrimony with the Portuguese royal house, sending an embassy to sound out a double marriage: for himself with Princess Joana, and for his niece Elizabeth with Don Manuel, Duke of Beja. Negotiations for these marriages were progressing between March and August 1485 (see Barrie Williams, 'The Portuguese Connection and the Significance of "the Holy Princess"', *The Ricardian*, VI, 1983, 141). Richard's negotiations with Portugal were still spoken of in Aveiro when I taught at its university around forty years ago, and they are recorded by Domingos Mauricio Gomes dos Santos, *O Mosteiro de Jesus de Aveiro,* Lisbon, 1963, pp. 92ff (I am grateful to Drª Joana Vaz and Møns. Aníbal Ramos for calling my attention to this source). Barrie Williams in the article cited above later picked up on it too.

Evidently, Richard was concurrently looking into the possibility of a match for himself with the Infanta of Spain (I am grateful to Annette Carson for calling this to my attention). This is recorded around 1488 in an account by Álvaro Lopes de Chaves, secretary to Kings Afonso V and John II of Portugal, of meetings of the Portuguese Council of State held in Alcobaça in 1485 (A.J. Salgado, Álvaro Lopes de Chaves, Livro de Apontamentos (1438-1489), Códice 443 da Colecção Pombalina da B.N.L, Lisboa 1983, p.255). Chaves reported alarm expressed in the Council that Richard would marry the Infanta Isabella of Castile, thus forming an alliance with Spain which would result in England becoming the enemy of Portugal, rather than offering the military support for which they hoped. This alternative possibility necessitated hastening the arrangement of his projected match with the Holy Princess, Joana of Portugal. It is quite possible, as Carson suggests in *Maligned King*, p. 303, that Elizabeth of York's wish for the Portuguese match, which also provided a royal marriage for her, and the danger of a Spanish one which did not, occasioned her appeal to Norfolk cited in text p. 191. That Princess Joana, who was famous for being devout and serious, looked favourably on the idea of marrying Richard – having refused other royal suitors – speaks well for him and his contemporary reputation. Given that Queen Anne was already ill with the sickness that would soon end her life, it is not surprising that embassies may have sounded out the subject of his remarriage before her death, due to the urgency of producing an heir. On this depended the stability of his kingdom, which was his primary responsibility as king.

189/8-9. Polydore reports in manuscript, though not in print, that Elizabeth said she would prefer suffering the torments of St Catherine for love of Christ rather than marry an enemy of her family (*Anglica Historia,* Hay ed., p. 3). This has been interpreted as a reference to Richard but seems much more likely to refer to Henry, who was an enemy of the house of York; perhaps the awareness that this interpretation could be placed on it determined Polydore against printing it. It is in Hall (p. 157), and copied by the chroniclers who followed him, who gave the projected contract the colouring and tone Buc notes. Recent authors have picked up and run with it, saying that Richard

> compased all the meanes and waies y[t] he coulde inuent how to stuprate, and carnally to know his owne nece vnder the pretence of a cloked matrimony. . . . At whiche most importunate and detestable co*n*cupiscence the common people . . . grudged and maligned. . . . But God of his only goodnes preserued y[e] Christe*n* mynde of that verteous and immaculate virgin, and from their flagicious and facinerous act*es*, did graciously protect and defend.

Alison Weir in *The Princes in the Tower* (London, 1992) has suggested Richard and Elizabeth went to bed together, though by the time she wrote *Elizabeth of York* (London, 2013) she had changed her mind. It is this angle, which comes only from the pro-Tudor chronicles considerably postdating Richard's reign, that now seems most to intrigue people about the letter cited below, text, p. 191, though it makes no such suggestion.

189/9-11. There is no suggestion in Crowland's account of the queen having been murdered, but rather of an illness, during which his doctors would naturally have advised Richard not to share her bed for fear of contagion. A.J. Pollard in *Richard III and the Princes*, p. 165, oddly reads this as 'apparent lack of concern'. However, if he did cease to share her bed when so advised, this seems to display his sense of responsibility to his kingdom. To risk his own life, especially without an heir, was to risk civil war should he die of an illness thus contracted. The idea of Richard being complicit in Anne's death appeared first in print in Rous, p. 215, who also invented legends of his being born with teeth and shoulder-length hair, followed by Commynes (II, 235) and Polydore (p. 557), followed by Hall, Grafton, Stow and Holinshed. These sources claim he killed her with sorrow through shunning her bed, complaints of her barrenness, and spreading rumours of her death and are presumably Pollard's sources for interpreting his shunning her bed as cruelty.

189/14-19. Richard and other leading members of the Council had been attempting since 23 May 1483 to persuade Elizabeth Woodville and her family to leave sanctuary (see above n. 23/41–24/5). Finally she sent her five daughters to court on Richard's promise to protect them, treat them as his kinswomen, see them honourably married, and to pay her a generous annual pension (Harl. 433, f. 308f; in Vol. 3, p. 190 of Horrox and Hammond edition). Her coming out of sanctuary could not have anything to do with any scheme of marrying her daughter to Richard, for she left sanctuary in March, 1484, at least a month before Richard's son died and a year before his wife's death. Buc, assuming that Richard's nieces did not come to court until Christmas, is erecting a theory based on the queen's demise near that time.

189/26. 'Queen Blanche' is an error for 'Queen Elizabeth', probably one of absent-mindedness. Buc (if indeed the error is his and not his great-nephew's – this short segment is missing in the original manuscript) may be thinking of John of Gaunt's wife Blanche.

189/34-36. This report of Queen Anne and Lady Elizabeth wearing matching dresses is taken from Crowland, p. 174, which mentions 'vana mutationiis vestium Annae, reginae, atque Dominae Elizabeth' [vain exchanges of clothing between Queen Anne and Lady Elizabeth]. This seems to have fuelled the rumour that Richard intended to marry his niece. However, Baldwin mentions in *Elizabeth Woodville*, p. 114, that Margaret Beaufort wore 'the same clothes as the Queen' at the 1487 Christmas festivities, evidently merely signalling that these two were the most important women in the kingdom, as presumably Queen Anne's kind gesture toward her oldest niece was intended to do.

189/50. Buc has made a mistake, saying 'in April following' when he means 'the preceding April'.

190/6-43. Discussion of divorce in this connection originates with Crowland, p. 174f: 'aut expectata morte reginae, aut per divortium cujis faciendi sufficienes causas se habuisse ' [either after the death of the queen, or by means of a divorce for which he believed he had sufficient grounds'. Cornwallis, p. 21, picks this up.

190/1st mar. n. Hermann Vulteius, *Jurisprudentia Romana*, I, xxi. Buc has here confused Hermann Vulteius with his father, Justus.

190/9-13. Valerius Maximus, VI, iii, 9-12.

190/25-26 and 2nd mar. n. [There being no obstruction of human or divine law, nor any constitutional opposition or statement to the contrary]: this Bull is in Cotton Vitellius B.X., ff. 109-112. Though it addresses this point and includes a similar statement it is not in the words Buc gives.

190/3rd mar. n. This appears as an annotation to Matthew 5:31 on f. 20 of a book called *Euangelium Secundum Matthaeum, Marcum, et Lucam* (Paris, 1553), printed and possibly compiled by Robert Stephens. At the end of it is printed Andreas Osiander's *Harmoniae Evangelicae Libri IIII*, but there is no indication that the earlier portions of the book, from which the quotation comes, are by Osiander too. Buc's quotation makes few changes other than deletions of subsidiary material. There is no point in translating this, since it is merely the form of divorce according to the law of Moses and the Israelites, the man repudiating the woman and giving her back her freedom.

191/1-25. Much more careful study of the original manuscript page dealing with this matter (see Plate II, which represents the not very legible scribal folio), has convinced me that the wording is not as I gave it previously. This time I devoted several whole days to it, as opposed to the original few hours. Previously, entangled with the impossible syntax and led astray by the Editor's (George Buck the Younger's) attempt to clarify it, based on his own I believe incorrect assumption of its meaning, my original reading of it was 'she prayed him . . . to be a mediator for her in the cause of the marriage to the king' (lines 10–11). It rather reads 'she *prayed* him . . . to be a mediator for her to the k[ing] in the cause of [the marria] ge'. The letter as Buc cites it is ambiguous. He seems to have understood it as referring to a plan for marriage between Richard and Elizabeth, but this is not completely clear. It is interesting to note how the Editor, seeking to clarify the letter, does away with the inherent ambiguity and settles firmly on the interpretation that it did refer to a projected marriage of Elizabeth with the king: 'shee desires hym, to bee a mediator to [hym] \the king/ for her, in the behalf of the marriage propounded betweene them . . .' (Egerton, f. 267). Malone and Fisher read the same, with a minor shift in Fisher to 'to be a mediato^{r} for her to the kinge' (f. 273^{v}). The younger Buck's printed edition (p. 128), whose object was to compress and shorten wherever possible, reads 'the King . . . was her only joy and maker in this world, and she was his in heart and thought'.

See above, Introduction, Chaper VI, for discussion of this letter's treatment over the centuries. It need not be read as Buc perhaps interprets it, and as his great-nephew, taking the cue from him, certainly does. The most likely intention of Elizabeth, it seems to me in view of what we know of the Portuguese/Spanish marriage options, is that she was asking Norfolk to mediate with the king to bring about a marriage for her with someone else; probably to influence the king against Spain and in favour of Portugal with its concomitant match for her with the Duke of Beja (see above 189/3-4). In short, Norfolk was to mediate with the king about the marriage, not that he was to mediate with the king about her marrying him (which sounds, frankly, absurd). What some people read as effusions of passion for Richard can, and with historical perspective *must* be read as formal expressions of fealty and dependence. Since Elizabeth was entirely dependent on him for both her day to day support and any permission to marry, he was *in fact* her 'only joy and maker in the world': her future lay entirely in the hands of her king. She was also his in heart, mind and body, as any subject would express him- or herself. The subject belonged to the prince and was obliged to give him support with all his being, if a man to support him physically as well as in mind. Thus Prince Charles, on his investiture as Prince of Wales in 1969, swore to be the queen's 'liege man of life and limb'.

A great deal of unnecessary nonsense has been made of this expression (even to the point of someone's essentially accusing me of inventing and inserting the word 'body' into the text, disguised as being from an early manuscript, since the word does not appear in the 1646 printed edition!). Because of the unaccountable interest in this letter, apparently exacerbated by my edition of it, I am providing a reproduction of the version from Tiberius (see above, Plates II and III). Unfortunately the first page (Plate II) is in the hand of Buc's scribe, and, quite apart from the burning, the many corrections by the author make it in places nearly illegible. There is no sign of tampering of any sort anywhere in the three manuscripts or indeed in the original. The burnt-away portion of Tiberius would allow for a word the length of 'bodie' or 'body', and the sole remaining stroke of the word that is burnt out here looks like the beginning of a 'b'. That the manuscript copies all give the word 'body' at this point would seem to indicate that it was in the original. The Editor is not given to making substantive changes or additions this early in his revision process, and there is no more reason to suspect that either he or Sir George made it up than to suspect I did. It would have been extremely embarrassing if he had, and someone had asked Arundel for a sight of the letter itself! Despite the illogic of which, many people are anxious to say (or at least to suspect) the letter never existed.

See also Hanham, 'Sir George Buck and Princess Elizabeth's Letter', *The Ricardian*, VII (1987), 398-400 and Kincaid, 'Buck and the Elizabeth of York Letter', *Ricardian* (1988), 46-49. There have been subsequent discussions of it in *The Ricardian*.

191/46-7 and 3rd mar. n. [that this thing, the desire to contract matrimony with a close blood relation, never entered his mind] (my translation), Crowland, p. 174. Buc compresses a slightly longer section, hence I have not been able to use Pronay and Cox's translation.

192/6-9 and 1st mar. n. [King Richard saw no other way of confirming his crown or thwarting the hopes of his rival than by contracting marriage with the said Elizabeth or pretending to do so] (my translation), Crowland, p. 174f. Buc has indicated by the brackets in his manuscript that 'vel simulando' is his own addition. He makes other additions to fill in necessary information, and thus I have again been unable to use the now standard translation.

192/19 and 3rd mar. n. [with no less honour than befitted the burial of a queen] Crowland, p. 174.

192/4th mar. n. This reference is not in More. Holinshed (who copies Hall) says, III. p. 430f, 'But howsoeuer that it fortuned, either by inward thought and pensiuenesse of hart, or by infection of poison (which is affirmed to be most likelie) within few daies after the queene departed out of this transitorie life . . .' The reference to the Lent season is from Stow, *Annales*, p. 782.

192/49-193/3. Richard's bastards were John of Gloucester, who in childhood was made Captain of Calais by his father; Katharine Plantagenet, who was married to William, Earl of Huntingdon in 1484 (Harl., 258, ff. 11v-12 and Pat. Rolls, 1476-85, p. 538); and possibly Richard Plantagenet who, according to Peck, II, 13-15, was told of his identity only on the eve of Bosworth and lived a long and quiet life as a master mason in Eastwell, Kent. (For another intriguing suggestion of his identity, see Baldwin, *The Lost Prince*). The little that is known of John and Katharine suggests they were born before Richard's marriage. (There is at least one other whisper of an illegitimate child of Richard: the wife of a teacher in my school spoke of a tradition in her family that a forebear of theirs, the poet Stephen Hawes, was an illegitimate son of Richard. This is a story which

Hilda Lamb, a member of the same family, used in her novel *The Willing Heart*, London, 1958.)

193/1st mar. n. [Suspicion comes from bad opinion and flimsy evidence] Aquinas, *Summa Theologica*, pt. II^{a}II^{ae}, quest. LX, art. 3.

193/2nd mar. n. [Suspicion is an act through which doubt is transmitted] Pardulphus Prateius, *Lexicon Juris* (Frankfurt, 1581), entry under 'Suspicio'. p. 549.

193/28-9. Publius Syrius, *Sententiae*, II, 4 [Suspicion is seriously bad for people].

193/30. [Suspicion is to be borne, not inflicted] I have not been able to trace this quotation.

193/3rd mar. n. I have been unable to trace this verse or this work.

194/4. [The innocent is happier if without suspicion]: this is not in Seneca but from a declamation regarded as pseudo-Quintilian, *declamatio maior* 17, 8, where 'suspiciones' is given in the plural.

194/mar. n. Suetonius, *Divus Julius*, LXXIV.

194/11. Erasmus, *Chiliades*, p. 55, 'Polypi mentem obtine' [Acquire the mind of a polyp (i.e., change colours)].

BOOK V

195. There are a few matters out of order in this list of contents: the second, third and fourth headings follow 'All the Plantagenets put to death by his successors'. 'The character of King James' appears in the midst of the discussion regarding Richard's tyranny or lack of it. 'The author's scope, peroration, et *votum*' may be Buc's diffuse summing up of Richard's case (pp. 213-18), unless, perhaps more logically, it followed the two verses that now conclude the work and was, like them, burnt away. George Buck Esq., possibly unable to find a justification for this heading, deletes it in the manuscript copies, but in the printed version has come to the conclusion that it must refer to this information, which he compressed and brought together in a single page, given the prominence of larger type at the end of the book, immediately preceding the two verses, and he restored the subject heading to the list of Book V's contents. It is worth noting once again that Buc's manuscript was still in process of revision when he left it, not a finished work. It seems unlikely that he would have ended his book with two poems not particularly complimentary to Richard. Indicating that he will conclude with 'The author's scope, peroration, et votum', he would most likely have summed up his arguments in favour of Richard and indicated how he has proved them, hoping that he has pleased the reader.

195/13. [Skills of the palace, royal crime]

195/21. [Stone of the kingship's destiny]

195/23. [. . . and wish]

196/16-19. This is evidently a *viva voce* reference: it exists in none of Stow's works.

196/24-25 and 2nd mar. n. [The man is a tyrant who looks after his own interest at the expense of the public's] Aristotle, *Ethics*, VIII, x, 2.

196/26 and 3rd mar. n. This is similar to a statement in *Ethics*, VIII, x, 3 [That man is a tyrant who cruelly abuses his power].

196/4th mar. n. Proverbs 19:12.

196/28-29. Plato, *Republic*, VIII, xvi, 566.

196/32-33. I have been unable to locate this reference. Cf. Erasmus, *Institutio*.

197/1st mar. n. Plutarch, *Moralia*. This remark occurs twice, in 61C and 147B.

197/12 and 2nd mar. n. [Tyrants envy those who are brilliant (famous) and kill those who are strong]: this is not in Lucan. It is in C. Claudianus, *Panegyricus de quarto consulatu Honorii Augusti,* l. 310, in another tense: 'invideant claris fortesque trucident' [let them envy . . . and kill].

197/12-13 and 3rd mar. n. [The tyrant forbids the unhappy to die, commands the happy to] Seneca, *Hercules Furens*, 513.

197/15-16 and 4th mar. n. [A tyrant's generosity is nothing but transferring money from its proper owner to other unworthy ones]; this is not Demosthenes but is very close to Cicero, *De Officiis*, I, 43, which must be its immediate source.

197/23-24 and 5th mar. n. [Precious Tagus's rushing waters at Tartessias would not satisfy him, nor the golden pools of blushing Pactolus; and if he drank the whole of Hermus he would burn with greater thirst, etc.] Claudian, *In Rufinum*, I, 101-3. Buc ignores the line endings.

197/26-27 and 6th mar. n. [Whatever is conspicuous and beautiful in all the water belongs to the treasury] Juvenal, Satire IV, 54-5: an exact quotation.

197/40-43. *The Statutes at Large from the First Year of Edward the Fourth to the End of the Reign of Queen Elizabeth* (London, 1770), II, 54, 23 Jan. 1484, Cap. II. This tax had been introduced by Edward IV.

197/8th mar. n. *PROME*, XV, 58. Parl. 1 Richard III, Jan. 1484.

197/9th mar. n. More, p. 70.

198/1-2. [It is not easy for a ruler to be pious] Sophocles, *Ajax*, 1350.

198/3. [The gates of happiness are closed to the tyrant]: I cannot find the source of this quotation.

198/5-6. More, p. 78. This is said in an ironic context.

198/11-20. Commynes, II, 233 lists the death of Buckingham among the cruelties leading to Richard's overthrow. Polydore, p. 553, Hall, Grafton and Holinshed point out the irony of Buckingham's death in such a way as to make it appear to represent ingratitude in Richard: 'This death (as a reward) the duke of Buckyngham receaued at the handes of kyng Richard, whom he before in his affaires, purposes and enterprises had holde*n* [Grafton and Holinshed read 'holpen'] susteyned and set forward above all Godes forbode' (Hall, p. 395). Cornwallis, p. 25f says:

> was it a fault to punish his p*er*iurye, whoe had sworne true alleageance, then the execution of Lawe is a sinne: if soe, let transgressors be accounted inocent, and magistrat*es*, & Iudges, be accounted guiltye of transgression – but had this bene the acction of some other Prince, it had bene good, iust and necessarey, – but being his it is Censured the Contrarey . . .

198/21-28. Polydore, p. 565, and his followers say that Richard kept Edward, Earl of Warwick a prisoner in Sheriff Hutton during his reign. In fact he probably resided at Sandal Castle, as did Richard's older nephew and heir, John de la Pole. Both were members of the Council of the North. There is certainly no evidence of Warwick's imprisonment, though Henry VII sent men to seek him at Sheriff Hutton. More does not mention his treatment by Richard.

198/28-32. After Henry secured the throne, Warwick was for a time a ward of Margaret Beaufort, kept under strict guard (Michael K. Jones and Malcolm G. Underwood. *The King's Mother, Mother, Lady Margaret Beaufort,* Cambridge, 1992, p. 67). Henry then imprisoned him in the Tower. Simnel's revolt forced Henry to show Warwick in public. Difficulties with pretenders and desire for alliance with the Spanish royal house led him to destroy Warwick at last. Polydore explains that Ferdinand exacted Warwick's death, because he posed danger to the succession, as a condition for the marriage of Catherine of Aragon with Prince Arthur. Henry executed Warwick in November, 1499, on the pretext that he had entered into a conspiracy with Perkin Warbeck to escape. Even the chroniclers favourable to the Tudors unanimously deplore this act of Henry's.

198/33-45. James did imprison for life his cousin Arabella Stuart who married William Seymour so that the pair, both of whom had a claim to the throne, would remain childless.

199/2-5 and 1st mar. n. [Edward Balliol, King of Scotland, transferred the kingdom and crown of Scotland to Edward, King of England, by his letters patent and authentic which was done in the 33rd year of his reign, A.D. 1356] Walsingham, *Historia Anglicana*, I, p. 281.

199/19-25. 'Mistress Shore' was arrested in connection with Hastings's and the Woodvilles' plots against Richard and made to do public penance as a harlot. More (p. 54) arouses sympathy for her by describing her reputed beauty and dignity and the pity of the populace at her penance. According to the *Great Chronicle* (p. 233), she was attached so that Hastings's goods could be accounted for. Richard's treatment of her was far from harsh. He had her released into her father's custody (Harl. 433, f. 340v, Horrox and Hammond edition III, p. 259) and expressed willingness to allow her marriage to his solicitor, Thomas Lynom, though he hoped that the Bishop of Lincoln would dissuade Lynom from the marriage.

199/21-23. This reference occurs in the oration given to Buckingham by More, p. 71, and is obviously manufactured to suit character and occasion. Buc quotes it exactly.

199/31-34. Quoted without material alteration from (*Foedera*, V, Pt. 3, 138, [XII 204] 'De Proclamationibus faciendis pro Morum Reformatione' [About proclamations making for reformation of morals]. The proclamation was issued October 1483 in connection with 'Buckingham's rebellion'.

199/35-40. Holinshed, III, 422f, has copied the indictment against Colingbourne for treason. He had been intriguing with Henry Tudor since July 1484 and had published writings to stir up the people against the king. The one rhyme of Colingbourne's which has come down to us is 'The Rat, the Catte and Louell our dogge / Rule all Englande vnder the hogge' (Hall, p. 398), referring to Ratcliffe, Catesby, Lovell, and Richard. James H. Ramsay, *Lancaster and York* (Oxford, 1892), II, 528, suggests that this was revenge for Colingbourne's being deprived of his appointment as Richard's mother's officer in Wiltshire in favour of Lovell (Harl. 433, f. 2[v], Horrox and Hammond edition, I, 3). Fabyan, p. 672, describes Colingbourne's arrest and execution as he does many minor cases of scandal, complete with grisly anecdote, yet clearly says that he was executed for treason as well as for a rhyme in derision of king and Council. In time the accusation regarding the rhyme completely obscured the accusation of treason. Harington, under the influence of *A Mirror for Magistrates*, uses Colingbourne as an example of evil fortune befalling poets: 'one Colingbourne, that was hanged for a distichon of a Cat, a rat, and a dogge' (*A New Discourse of a Stale Subject, Called The Metamorphosis of Ajax*, ed. Elizabeth Story Donno, London, 1962, p. 100). The information that Colingbourne was actually put to death for treason was first given in Stow, *Annales*, p. 780.

199/3rd mar. n. See above, pp. pp. cxxii-cxxv for discussion of this manuscript. Cornwallis, p. 22: 'how falsely doth our Cronicler seeke to Cleare Collingbourne whoe noe doubt was (as may app*ere* by his Inditem*ent*) executed for treason againste the state, not for that silly folish ridiculous libell'.

199/41-42. [A tyrant is inimical to the citizens, hostile to the laws] Demosthenes, 2nd Philippic, 25.

199/4th mar. n. See above, n. 28/5th mar. n.

200/1-4. [by nature generally secretive and plotting, and they try by artfulness and cunning to hide and dissemble the things they do, communicating nothing of their plans or affairs to others and not seeking advice from others or accepting it, but following only their own counsel]

200/6 and 1st mar. n. [The best man needs advice]: I have been unable to locate the source of this quotation, which sounds proverbial.

200/7-8 and 2nd mar. n. [It is a tyrannical act to undertake a great venture without advice] I have not found this quotation.

200/15-17 and 3rd mar. n. More, p. 27. This is slightly but not materially paraphrased. More means it to be taken ironically in the context of his characterization of Richard.

200/18-29. The view of Richard as a spendthrift comes from More's statement 'Free was hee called of dyspence, and sommewhat aboue hys power liberall . . .' (p. 8) quoted above at greater length, 126/37-45. He inherited a treasury which the Woodvilles had plundered on the death of Edward IV, then he had to face a rebellion shortly after he took office, but unlike Edward IV, who established 'benevolences' ('not what every man list to pay, but what the king list to take'), Richard sought loans. Horsfall, p. 215 points out that 'Only if we begin from a position of settled hostility to Richard (like the Crowland chronicler) does it follow that this measure was a rank hypocrisy'.

200/4th mar. n. Suetonius, *Caligula*, XXXVII, where the figure is given as 270 million, and *Nero*, XXX.

200/21. [monstrosities and prodigies and plagues of sovereignty, pests of the republic]: I have been unable to locate this quotation.

200/23-24. Richard's enemies confess his temperance but ascribe it to a sense of guilt and an attempt to win friends by deceit. See Polydore, p. 548, Hall, pp. 380f and Bacon, VI, 28.

201/21-29. See above, n. 55/36-56/36. Later black legends accumulated around Sir Ralph Ashton which seem at variance with Buc's assessment of him. See above, n. 55/36-56/36.

201/50-202/1. Many of Richard's enemies refer to his excellent legislation. Polydore, p. 548, Hall, pp. 380f and Bacon, VI, 28. A.J. Pollard in several works mentions his concern with the administration of justice before 1483. This would suggest that such concern persisted into his kingship. Indeed his Parliament begins with the preamble: 'ne that justice so procede, that benignite and pitie have no place, but that a due moderation and temperament be observed . . .' (*PROME*, Richard III: Jan. 1484, XV, 24). However, many recent writers have been at pains to point out that all that can be said for his legislation is that his successor did not undo it all, and that it is impossible to tell how much legal reform was actually due to him personally rather than to his council. On the other hand, most commentators note his personal interest in law, which would seem to suggest that he took responsibility for a fair amount of the legislation passed during his reign. This personal interest seems clear from his summoning his judges to a meeting on 26 June 1483 and commanding them 'in Rigth streygth maner that they Justly & duly shuld mynystir his law w[t]owth delay or ffavour' (*Great Chronicle* pp. 232). In addition, after his coronation he charged the attending lords when they went home to see to it that their domains were 'wel guydid', to administer the law swiftly and impartially and see to it that no extortions were made (*Great Chronicle*, pp. 232f).

He seems to have wished to be a 'hands-on' king, as can be seen, for example, in his proclamation in Kent after Buckingham's uprising (Harl. 433, f.128v, Horrox and Hammond II, p. 48) and in that of 8 December 1484:

> The kinges grace willeth that for the love that he hath for the ministracion and execucion of Justice for the comowne welthe of this Royaulme the whiche he moost tendrethe that if any persone fyndethe him greved of murdre manslaughter extorcion oppression of any othre Iniurie or wrong contrary to iustice, doon by any Officer or any othre persone that he or they shewe it to the kinges grace and according to Justice and his lawes they shal have Remedy.
>
> (Harl. 433, f. 273; Horrox and Hammond III, 124)

He seems committed to making the law more accessible and less complex for those without means, e.g. by using the English language. Keith Dockray in *Richard III, a Sourcebook* (Stroud, 1997), p. 96 indicated that one way in which he made justice more accessible was by designating John Harrington Clerk of Council of Requests and Supplications (see also Hannes Kleineke, 'Richard III and the Origins of the Court of Requests', *The Ricardian*, XVII (2007), pp. 22 – 32). He did away with Edward IV's 'benevolences', provided for bail bond, sought clarity in land ownership, and protected native merchants from unfair foreign competition.

The authority on Richard's legislation used to be H.G. Hanbury, 'The Legislation of Richard III', American Journal of Legal History, VI (1962), 95-

113. However, Charles Ross in Richard III attacked Hanbury for pro-Ricardian bias (p. 187), arguing that he failed to take into account Richard's status as a usurper, which Ross thinks would certainly have affected his motivation: i.e., he passed good laws in order to make himself popular with his subjects (p. 189) – though it is not at all clear why any king should not wish to be approved by his subjects. But whatever Richard's motive, which it is not possible to determine at this distance in time, his legislation remains good and forward-looking. Ross seems to have contradicted himself to a degree by saying, some pages before, 'It is not wholly unlikely that Richard's personal interest in legal matters had something to do with the pronounced emphasis on law reform which runs through the legislation of his only parliament' (p. 174). There is an excellent article on Richard's legislation by Anne F. Sutton, 'The Administration of Justice whereunto We Be Professed', appears in *Richard III, Crown and People*, pp. 359-70. His laws themselves appear in *PROME*, Richard III: Jan. 1484, XV.

202/1st mar. n. Stow, *Annales*, p. 882. Justice Shelley is identified there not by name but only as 'a counsellor'. Stow has taken the reference from Hall, p. 698: 'The Cardinall hard this saiyng verie paciently, and answered: Sir I maruell that you speak of Richard the third, which was a vsurper and a murderer . . . , then of so euill a man, how can the actes be good. . . . And it please your grace said the cou*n*sailer, although he did euill, yet in his tyme were many good actes made not by hym onely, but by the consent of the body of the whole realme, whiche is the parliament'. This, of course, is another remark in support of Parliament.

202/2nd mar. n. I have been unable to locate this manuscript, which was probably burnt in the Cotton fire. Fabyan is the only other author to give this information: see above, n. 51/45-48.

202/11-15. See above, n. 201/50-202/1.

202/23-24. See above, n. 19/16-18.

202/26-29. See above, text, p. 22.

202/35-36 and 3rd mar. n. More, pp. 7f. This is a very close paraphrase.

202/41-43 and 4th mar. n. *PROME.,* Richard III: Jan. 1484, XV, 16, a very close paraphrase.

203/1st mar. n. More says only that 'ye duke first began to praise & bost the king, & shewe how much profit ye realm shold take by his reign' (p. 92). Stow follows the continuation of this conversation which Hall invents in his version of More: '. . . whome I thought to bee as cleane without dissimulation, as tractable without iniurie, and so by my meanes hee was made Protector', *Annales*, (pp. 774f). Far from thinking Richard honest, Buckingham is in this speech expressing disillusionment with him

203/2nd mar. n. [Eloquence in princes is their greatest ornament] Cicero, *De Finibus*, IV, xxii, 61.

203/16-20. [As a result so much disputation arose between the brothers and so many keen arguments were put forward on either side with the greatest acuteness in the presence of the king, sitting in judgement in the council-chamber, that all who stood around, even those learned in the law, marvelled at the profusion of arguments which the princes produced for their own cases] Crowland, p. 132f.

Buc has made changes to adjust the source to his grammatical construction and makes a few paraphrases. Carson and Barnfield in 'The Marriage of Lady Anne Neville and Richard Duke of Gloucester', p. 50 calculate that this disputation probably took place in the autumn of 1473 and was settled by the king around March 1474.

203/20-24. [These three brothers moreover, the king and the dukes, possessed such outstanding talent that if they had been able to avoid dissension that triple cord could have been broken only with the utmost difficulty] Crowland, pp. 132f. Buc has paraphrased it very slightly.

203/25-204/45. Of Richard's achievements, Rous notes (p. 215) that he was to be praised for his building at Westminster, Nottingham, Middleham, and Barking, gifts to the commons of London, Gloucester, and Worcester, and endowment of Queens' College, Cambridge. Stow, *Annales*, p. 787f, says:

> He founded a colledge at Midelham beyond Yorke, and another at London beside the Tower, in a chappell called our Ladie of Barking: he also endowed the Queenes Colledge at Cambridge with fiue hundred markes of yeerelie rent. He deforested the great field of Wichewoode, betweene Woodstocke and Bristowe, which king *Edward* the fourth had incorporated before to the forrest, &c.

In his *Survey of London*, I, 131, Stow notes again Richard's association with Barking: 'he new builded and fonded therein a colledge of Priestes'. *John Leyland's Travels in Tudor England*, ed. John Chandler (Stroud, 1993), cites building works by Richard III according to shire.

203/29-32. Stow, as above, and Rous, p. 215. Also Stow, *Survey*, I, 131.

203/33-38. Richard's grant for building of a chapel near Towton, 28 November 1483, is recorded in Harl. 433, f. 38 (Horrox and Hammond ed., I, 119) and f. 124v (Horrox and Hammond ed., II, 39).

203/39-40. Rous, p. 215, and also Polydore, p. 538: 'Instituit Eboraci collegium centum sacerdotu*m*' [He instituted at York a college of a hundred priests].

203/44-45. Stow, *Survey*, II, 122: Richard built the tower at Westminster 'a great height, and many faire lodgings in it, but left unfinished . . .'

203/45-46. Camden, *Britannia*, p. 641 mentions Richard's repairs to Carlisle Castle. His badge can still be seen carved on a tower he built there.

203/46-47. Richard was not the founder or original builder of Penrith Castle, which was one of the seats he acquired with the Warwick inheritance, but he did considerable building there. The foundations of a stairway he added can still be seen. Recent research by Henry Summerson published by D.R. Perriam, in 'William Strickland's Tower in Penrith: Penrith Castle or Hutton Hall?', *English Heritage Historical Review*, vol. 3 (2008), pp. 36-45, shows that Ralph Neville, 1st Earl of Westmorland (1345-1424), was the builder of the castle in around 1386 and that Bishop Strickland's earlier works in Penrith, previously thought to have originated the castle, were on a separate site.

203/48. This may refer to Richard's bail bond law, listed as item 21 in *PROME,* Richard III: Jan. 1484, XV, 61f under the title, 'An act for baylyng of persons suspected of felony'.

203/49-204/1. This reference is not in Polydore but in *PROME*: Richard III: Jan. 1484, XV, 10-13. It consists of a levy of tonnage and poundage to be applied to safeguarding the seas, but stipulates that this is not to be prejudicial to the Hanseatic merchants or to Spain.

204/1st mar. n. *Foedera*, V, Pt. 3, 142 [XII, 215f], 2 March 1484.

204/1-37. Buc, *Third Universitie* Oooo3v) says 'I will not say that they were any collegiate societie here in England, vntill the time of King *Richard* the 3. but it is certaine that he by his charter made them a company and corporation, and setled the office in Cole-herbert'. As Constable of England while he was Duke of Gloucester, Richard 'had shared with the Marshal the supervision of the heralds' activities' (Wagner, p. 9). In Cotton MS. Julius C. IX, ff. 150-51 is a record of Richard's orders as Constable and Marshal for the officers of arms. Harl. 433, f. 39v (Horrox and Hammond ed., I, 125) mentions Richard's grant of incorporation to the heralds: 'Garter king of Armes & to other kings of Armes / the king hathe graunted to be corporate . . .And also a place in Londone called coldearbere . . .'. Stow, *Survey*, I, 237, mentions the grant to the heralds of Cold Harbour.

204//4-5. [as they shall be in perpetuity a corporate body in actuality and in name, having succession perpetually]

204/13. Stow says in *Survey*, I, 236 that Cold Harbour was originally called Poultney's Inn.

204/35-37. The signature 'Barowe' is that of Sir Thomas Barowe, referred to in text, p. 56f as Master of the Rolls. Because all copies misread the name as 'Baron' or 'Barone' (this is not difficult to do), Yarnold (Egerton 2217, f. 134v) mistook it as a reference to Buc's *Baron*.

204/38-41. Stow, *Survey*, I. 49 notes Richard's repair of the Tower.

204/42-45. Polydore, Bk. XXV, *passim* [Richard III began many public and private works, which by his early death were interrupted and not completed].

205/21-22. Buc erroneously cites James IV for James III.

205/29-30. See above, n. 58/13-15.

205/40-206/30. [Most serene Prince: one thing consoles me, your most celebrated fame disseminated through the whole compass of the world in every kind of virtue, and your innate kindness, very clear humanity, your mildness, liberality, loyalty, tremendous justice, incredible breadth of spirit, your not human but almost divine wisdom, because of which you are at ease not only with important people but comfortable with the common people too, you show such affability to the people – and with what virtues and great prudence – so that you make better everything that is pronounced and spoken.

[The most serene Prince, the King of Scots, my lord, who holds you in great love, seeks your friendship and affinity above the reach of my thought. If I have made any error, let it be attributed to your divine virtues, your communications and commerce with celestial presences. I behold in your countenance lordship and dignity in command, which shows moral and heroic virtue: about you I can pronounce the words of the poet Statius about the most famous Theban prince: 'Never has nature enclosed in a smaller body so great a spirit, such great strength'.

[For in you is military strength, expertise, good fortune and authority, which Cicero required in a leader of armies. In you, most Serene Prince, thus concur the requisites of a most noble king and general, so that no orator's words can add to your military or domestic virtue. Therefore, Most Serene Lord and Prince, act so that between yourself and our prince may come affection and friendship, so that no distinction may appear between the English and the Scots, but with a single unified bond of love and benevolence they may be seen to be joined together. Thus shall unlimited advantage arise between your people and ours, in a union of sweet affection, association, marriage, and affinity.

['While rivers run to the sea and rains cultivate the curves of the mountains, while the sky shall feed the stars, while the boar shall love the mountain ridge and the fish the rivers, while bees feed on thyme and cicadas on dew, always may your honour and your praise endure'.]

These last lines are a conflation two passages of Vergil which share a line: *Aeneid* I, 607-9 (the first two and last lines) and Eclogue V, 76-8 (the last three lines). Buc's text contains some inferior readings: 'imbres' [showers] for Vergil's 'umbrae' [shadows] and 'sint arati' [cultivate] for 'lustrabunt' [purify, encircle].

Buc presumably has the union of England and Scotland under James I in mind in quoting this speech. He derived its text from B.L. MS. Cotton Vespasian C. XVI, ff. 75-9, headed 'Scotia An*no* 2 Ricardi 1484 ***tember "Or*ati*o Scotoru*m* ad rege*m* Ric 3[ii] p*er* pace firma*n*da int*er* anglos & scotos"'. It is continued in MS. Cotton Caligula B.V, ff. 151-152[v]. Buc's crosses may be seen in the margins of the former, where he begins quoting and elsewhere. He excerpts the speech and makes minor transpositions. His grammatical changes seem intended as improvements, but because the portions derived from Egerton are corrupt, and because the manuscript from which Sir George Buc derived it is also corrupt, it is difficult to make a definite pronouncement. (For example, 'carissima' in line 4 is a mistake, probably by Buc's great-nephew's scribe, for 'clarissima'.)

Livia Visser-Fuchs has written an interesting article on this speech, as well as including a text of it from Vespasian C.XVI: 'Richard III, Tydeus of Calydon and Their Boars in the Latin Oration of Archibald Whitelaw, Archdeacon of St Andrews, at Nottingham on 12 September 1484', *The Ricardian*, XVII (2007) 1-32. She also provides a translation of the whole speech and comments on its concealed reference to Richard's boar emblem. However she confuses the reader by referring sometimes as *Georgics* to Vergil's *Bucolica*, known in English as '*Eclogues*'. This does not work, at least in an article in English, since, though 'Georgics' may be a reasonable translation of 'Bucolica', it is not the title by which that book is generally known in English. More important, there is no *Georgics* V, while there is a – very famous – fifth Eclogue, which is the source of part of Quhitlaw's quotation.

There is another translation by David Shotter of the whole speech in A.J. Pollard, ed. *The North of England in the Age of Richard III* (Stroud, 1996). He misses annotating the Vergil quotation as combining two separate sources and attributes it all (inaccurately) to Eclogue V. Shotter takes his text from the version printed in *The Ballantyne Miscellany*, II, ed. D. Laing (Edinburgh, 1936), pp. 41-8.

207/mar. n. [It appears that the best men have been swallowed up by violent death] Aelius Lampridius, *Alexander Severus*, LXII in *Historiae Augustae*

Scriptores.

207/37-38. Richard was 32. He was born 2 October 1452.

208/28-29 and 1st mar. n. [If one must act unjustly, it is best to act unjustly for the sake of a kingdom, and in other things to behave morally] Euripides, *Phoenisses*, ll. 524f.

208/2nd mar. n. Cicero, *De Officiis*, III, 82, quoting from *Phoenisses* lines cited above. It is given in verse, but Buc's manuscript ignores the line endings. See also Suetonius, *Julius*, *passim*. Shakespeare, too, was impressed with this quotation (3 *Henry VI*, I, ii).

209/3-4 and 1st mar. n. [The prince is above the law] *Digest*, I, 3, 31: Ulpian *Legem Iuliam et Papiam*, XIII.

208/49. [Arts of empiry or arts of rule]

209/1-2. [Holy crime or royal crime, or crime of sacred ambition]

209/2nd mar. n. [Whoever allows himself to be governed by honesty is precariously ruled] Seneca, *Thyestes*, 214-5. The line ending is ignored.

209/6-9. In Seneca Polyneices does not say he would do the things he mentions but merely asks Eteocles if he would consign his own household gods to the flames.

209/3rd mar. n. The quotation is actually: 'Imperio pretio quolibet constat bene'. [Rule is well purchased whatever the price. (Buc's version says 'cheaply purchased'.)] This is actually from Seneca, *Phoenissae*, I, 664, an unfinished play for which an original title is thought to have been *Thebaid*, and the speaker is Eteocles, not Polyneices. Euripides wrote a play, *Phoinissai*, which influenced Seneca, in which Eteocles, in ll. 553-5, speaks the words quoted *supra* on p. 208, ll. 28-29.

209/42-26. Edward III cannot be accused of complicity in the death of either his father or the Earl of Kent, being a child at the time, under the control of his mother and her lover Mortimer. He punished the offenders when old enough to wield power.

209/48-9 and 7th mar. n. [Crimes must be protected by crimes] Seneca, *De Clementia*, I, xiii, 2: 'Scelera enim sceleribus tuenda sunt'.

210/6-8 and 3rd mar. n. Camden, *Britannia,* p. 430: he refers to the inhabitants of Warwickshire, Worcestershire, Shropshire, Cheshire, and Staffordshire as 'Cornavii'. There has been slight paraphrase to adapt this to context, but no change of sense. There are scribal errors in Egerton, one of them no doubt being 'purum' (pure) for 'puerulum' (boyish). ['His yoong sonne *Edward* . . . being but a very child was beheaded by King Henry the Seventh to secure himself and his posterity'] (Holland, trans., p. 570). The Buc/k text is literally translated, 'Edward son of the duke of Clarence, pure and innocent, for his own and his descendants' security was punished by (losing his) head'.

210/4th mar. n. Grafton, II, 228f and Holinshed, III, 533f, derived from Polydore, pp. 613f.

210/5th mar. n. Geronymo Çurita, *Anales de la Corona de Aragon* (Çaragoça, 1610), VI, f. 42-42v, and Esteuan de Garibây, y Çamálloa, *D'el Compendio Historial de las Chronicas y Vniversal Historia de Todes les Reynos d'Espana* (Antwerp, 1571), II, 1448-50. Garibây's account, using Polydore as a source, is closer to Buc's.

210/25-211/6. This incident occurred in 1506 and is recorded in CSP (Venice), I, 312ff and CSP (Spain), I, 385.

211/13-14. [Human right and the sacred faith of hospitality]

211/32-42. Holinshed, III, 536, notes that Henry kept his word about not putting Suffolk to death, 'keeping him in prison so long as he liued, and afterwards was beheaded vnder the reigne and commandement of his sonne' (in 1513).

212/3-6. John de la Pole, Earl of Lincoln, was killed in the battle of Stoke, 1487, leading an army ostensibly to support Simnel's uprising.

212/6-8. Buc's information probably came from Glover, p. 539: '*Katherine*, married to *William* Lord *Sturton*, widdow to the Lord *Grey*, and dyed in the Tower of London, in the 17. year of *Henry* the seauenth'. CP XII, i, 304 refers to this marriage to Lord Stourton, but a note indicates that it has been doubted. *Debrett's Peerage and Baronetage,* ed. Charles Kidd and David Williamson, London, 1995 supports it.

212/1st mar. n. Grafton, II, 79, from More, p. 3.

212/9-18. Lady Anne's marriage to Thomas Howard, later 3rd Duke of Norfolk, was allowed by Henry VII in 1495, but they had been contracted under Richard III. Henry would give his sister-in-law no dower and the queen was forced 'from very shame' to settle an annuity on her from her private estate (Brenan, I, 119f). Catherine's marriage to William Courtenay, Earl of Devon, took place in 1495, not under Richard III, as Buc states. Cecily was married not to a base fellow but to John, Viscount Welles, a relation of Henry VII, around 1487, and on his death married (without the king's permission) Thomas Kyme of Friskney, who was, according to Rosemary Horrox in the *ODNB*, a Lincolnshire esquire and landowner. Dying unmarried were Mary (d. 1482), Margaret (d. 1472), and Bridget (d. 1517).

212/2nd mar. n. Polydore, p. 559, actually from Book 5.

212/3rd mar. n. Glover, p. 205.

212/19-20. Although Buc does not mention Bacon, it seems likely from this and a few other references that he used Bacon's history of Henry VII, which says about the king's marriage relationship, 'he shewed himself no very indulgent husband towards her . . . his aversion toward the house of York . . . found a place not only in his wars and counsels, but in his chamber and bed' (VI, 41f). And 'Towards his Queen he was nothing uxorious; nor scarce indulgent; but companionable and respective, and without jealousy' (p. 242). More recent writers have found the relationship between Henry and Elizabeth gentler than did Bacon. See for example Thomas Penn, *Winter King*, pp. 70f.

212/21-27. On his accession Henry VII gave Elizabeth Woodville all possessions and rights of Queen Dowager (*PROME,* Henry VII, Nov. 1485, XV, 133). But Campbell, *Materials*, II, 148f records a document whereby all her lands and fees were taken from her in May 1487 and assigned to her daughter. Polydore, p. 571 gives as the reason for this that she had submitted herself and her daughters into Richard's hands contrary to her promise to Henry VII and his supporters, but if this was the cause the delay seems incredible. In 1487, however, she is rumoured to have supported Lambert Simnel. She retired to Bermondsey Abbey, perhaps voluntarily, being an heir to one of its benefactors, perhaps not, and died in 1492.

212/5th mar. n. Gainsford, p. 111.

212/6th mar. n. Joel, 1:4.

212/42-46. The horrific execution of the Countess of Salisbury, who was born in 1473, occurred in 1541 on pretext of treasonable correspondence with her son Cardinal Reginald Pole, who was attempting to restore Catholicism to England.

212/47. Henry, Lord Montagu, the eldest surviving son of the Countess of Salisbury, was executed in 1539, he and Henry Courtenay, Marquess of Exeter, having become 'victims of the King's fears that one of them might be chosen in his place if he were dethroned' (CP IX, 96).

212/48-213/4. Reginald Pole, born in 1500, second or third son of the Countess of Salisbury, became Cardinal in 1536 and was Archbishop of Canterbury from 1555 until his death two years later. Living abroad, he intrigued for Henry VIII to be deposed and Catholicism to be restored in England, remaining abroad until after Mary's accession. (*ODNB*, vol. 44, pp. 715-26, article by T.F. Mayer). Chapuys suggested him to Charles V as a suitable candidate for the English throne (*Letters and Papers, Foreign and Domestic, of the Reign of Henry VIII*, ed. J.S. Brewer, London, 1862-1932, VI, pp. 486f and VII, pp. 591f). He was attainted with the rest of his family in 1539.

213/5-8. A fugitive pretender in France, Richard de la Pole took over the title 'White Rose', styled himself Duke of Suffolk even in his brother's lifetime and was backed by Francis I as candidate for the English throne. He was attainted in 1504 with his brothers William and Edmund and, with them, excepted from Henry VIII's general pardon. He fled abroad in 1501 and died in the Battle of Pavia, 1525. These Yorkist claimants sought French support just as the Lancastrian claimant, Henry VII had done.

213/14. [such as was not said and written for the sake of defamation and special advantage]

213/30-31. See above, text, pp. 87-9 and notes thereto.

214/13. [triple cord]

214/mar. n. Curtius, VIII, viii, 11. [Possession got by the sword does not last long]

214/19-23. The story is that Edward the Confessor nominated William as his heir if he were to die without a son, and Harold when he was William's prisoner promised to help William to the throne but broke his promise and seized the throne himself on the death of King Edward (Matthew of Westminster, *Flores Historiarum*, ed. Henry Richards Luard, R.S. 95, London, 1890, I, 579 and 590f; William of Malmesbury, *De Gestis Regum Anglorum*, ed. William Stubbs, R.S. 90, London, 1887-9, I, 278-80; Polydore, pp. 141-4). It was not customary at this time for kings to choose their successors, who were chosen by the barons. In this case they chose Harold.

214/27-38. It was the practice during the genealogical fervour of the Tudor and early Stuart period to trace genealogy back as far as possible. In the Grenville copy of *Daphnis* in the British Library, Buc's genealogical tree traces the royal line from Egbert to Henry II.

214/39-43. See above, n. 82/15-18.

214/43-215/12. Citing Henry's and his heirs' title as being established by Parliament – just as he had shown Richard III's to be – is another of Buc's comments supporting Parliamentary authority in establishing the king's title. See Baker, p. 317.

215/1st mar. n. *PROME*, Henry VII: Nov. 1485, XV, 97.

215/13. See text, pp. 87ff.

215/3rd mar. n. Buc is evidently confusing the names of Edmer and Ailred, two abbots of Rievaulx who wrote history. This material is not found in any of present volumes of the Cotton collection, which contains only Ailred's histories of King David of Scotland and Henry II of England. But listed in early Cotton catalogues was a life of Edward the Confessor by Ailred. This is cited as missing in David Casley's survey of the library (*A Catalogue of the Manuscripts in the King's Library: an Appendix to the Catalogue of the Cottonian Library; Together with an Account of Books Burnt or Damaged in the Late Fire*, London, 1734). An extant copy, B.L. MS. Arundel 63, Ch. 29, ff. 15v-16, entitled 'De anulo que*m* dedit beato ioha*nn*i . . .', contains this information.

215/20-21. [oracles of sovereignty . . . instruments and monuments pertaining to kingship and power]

215/36-39 and 4th mar. n. Hector Boethius*, Scotorum Historiae* (Paris, 1575), Bk. I, f. 2: 'Fuit is lapis cathedrae instar fatalis, vt qui vbicunque inueniretur, Scotis regnum portenderet' [This stone in the chair was essentially fateful, wherever it was found']. Bk. XIV, f. 298: '. . . cathedram lapideam, quibus insidentes coronari Scotorum reges consueuerant, è Scona Londinium secum attulit, atque in Vestmonasterio, vbi & hodie visitur, deposuit' [the chair's stone, sitting on which the kings of the Scots were crowned, was carried away from Scone to London and placed in Westminster, where it can be visited today']. George Buchanan, *Rerum Scoticarum Historia* (Edinburgh, 1538), Bk. VIII, f. 76v: '. . . lapidem marmoreum rudem, in quo fatum regni contineri, vulgo persuasum erat, Londinum misit' [the rough marble stone, in which was contained, as the common persuasion is, the fate of kingship, he sent to London].

215/38-46 and 5th mar. n. [King Edward I transferred the stone from Scone to London and placed it where it is visited today] Holland trans., 'Scotia', p. 42. Camden (p. 709) says that King Kenneth established a stone enclosed in a chair at the monastery of Scone for coronation of the kings of Scotland. Edward I transported it to Westminster. He then quotes a prophecy which has now come true. Camden's words, which Buc paraphrases, are:

> Rex Edwardus Primus Angliae Westmonasterium deferendum curauit. De quo vaticinium vulgo iactitatum, quod cùm nunc fidem inuenerit, vt id genus paucula, subiungendum curaui.
>
> Ni fallat fatum, Scoti quocunque locatum
> Inueniunt lapidem, regnare tenentur ibidem.

The prophecy appears infra p. 216/3-4.

[Holland trans. 'Scotia', p. 42:

> which stone Edward the First, King of England, caused to be conveied unto Westminster. Touching which I haue put

downe this prophesie so rife in every mans mouth, since it hath now proved true and taken effect, as very few of that sort doe.

Except old sawes be vaine,
And wits of wisards blind:
The Scots in place must raigne:
Where they this stone shall finde.]

215/42-46. [If there is faith or trust in the ancient chronicle, / This noble cathedral encloses that stone; / Jacob, the distinguished head, once a Patriarch, / Discerning the spirit of this miracle-city, placed this, / Which king Edward first brought from Scotland.] The existence at one time of this inscription is corroborated by William Brenchley Rye, *England as Seen by Foreigners* (London, 1865), p. 132. He includes the description of Westminster Abbey in 1610 by Justus Zinzerling which notes that 'One of the curiosities is the stone on which Abraham rested; the chair or throne bears an inscription'. This does not prove that the inscription on the chair or stone was the same Buc later quotes, though the date would suggest it was. That it gave the chair's legendary history is suggested by Zinzerling's association of it with Abraham, in error for Jacob. It is unclear in this recollection whether the inscription was on the chair or the stone. That engraved on the chair is identified by John Speed, The Historie of Great Britaine London, 1628), p. 654, with the quotation Buc cites, text, p. 216, ('Ni fallat fatum Scotus . . .'). That this says nothing about the stone's Biblical association leads one to interpret Zinzerling's account as suggesting that there was a legend to this effect somewhere in the vicinity of the chair. Buc had previously referred to the stone in *Daphnis*: 'You (most sacred Prince) the great IACOB, enthronized vpon the Patriarke *Jacobs* fatall stone, and vpon Saint *Jacobs* Festivall espoused solemnly faire *England* her selfe' (f. A3^{v}).

215/6th mar. n. See above n. 215/4th mar. n. [In this stone the fate of the kingdom of Scotland is contained].

216/3-4. Camden, *Britannia,* p. 709 ('Perthia'). Buc, to make the prophecy seem to refer to James I, makes Scoti' singular but makes no other changes [The fortune of the Scots king shall not fail; wherever he finds that same stone he shall hold the throne] Holland trans., Scotland, p. 42.

216/6-7. Ecclesiastes 4:12.

216/9-10. Luke 1:33.

216/16-18. I Kings, 11.

216/19-20. [The kingdom is transferred from people to people because of injustices and injuries and deceits] Ecclesiasticus (Sirach), 10:8.

216/24-29. Gildas, *De Excidio Britanniae*, ed. Joseph Stevenson (London, 1838), *passim*.

216/29-31. Huntingdon, p. 173.

216/2nd mar. n. William of Malmesbury, I, 277.

216/39. [at the point of death]

216/41-45 and 3rd mar. n. [For it is not so much as an honour that inheritance of the kingdom of England comes, but through dire conflict and much effusion of human blood, etc. The royal diadem, which not one of my predecessors bore, I obtained by divine grace only, not hereditary right] B.L. MS. Cotton Vespasian A. XIX. The first sentence is from f. 113, the second from f. 110v. This work was listed among the entries in Cotton's library in all the earliest catalogues but is now erroneously described as lost. Buc used it in *Daphnis* as well. Camden quotes these passages (*Britannia*, p. 104), placing the second one first, as Buc does, but Buc obviously derived his use of it from the original, whereas Camden's 'sanguinis humani' is divergent. Moreover, Buc's pencilled 'X's in the margins throughout the manuscript, indicating his interest in certain passages, including the ones he quotes, reflect his practice in other books from which he derives information.

217/4-12. Polydore, p. 547. The brackets (which I have slanted to distinguish them from those used to offset insertions from the copies) – one of which appears in Tiberius, the other would have been in a burnt out section – are Buc's indication of material he has added to the extract, otherwise closely followed. [That perhaps happened to those two innocent boys because Edward their father committed a crime neglectful of religion, deceiving by violating a most holy promise made at the gates of York intending something different from what he pledged verbally and afterward by the death of his brother the Duke of Clarence */and King Henry, and the death of his son, and for violating his marriage with Lady Eleanor, etc./* he rendered himself and his sons liable to God's punishment.]

217/13-19. See above, n. 135/7-137/48.

217/33-218/7. [Epitaph of King Richard III, buried by command and at expense of blessed King Henry VII: I, whom the earth encloses here under varicoloured marble, was by just voice Richard III, Protector of my country, as uncle for the right of my nephew. By broken faith I held the kingdom of Britain; I then bore the sceptre two summers and sixty days minus two. Contending bravely in battle, surely deserted by the English, King Henry VII, I fell to you. But you yourself, in piety, honour my bones at your own cost, giving kingly honour to one who was once a king. Three hundred times five years of salvation had passed, only excluding four (and) twice five years, on the eleventh day before the September Kalends, when I had rendered to the red rose the rights which it sought. But whoever you are, pray for my sins, alleviating my punishment with your prayers. Let there be eternal glory to God, the best, greatest, three and one.]

Francis Sandford, *A Genealogical History of the Kings of England* (London, 1677), p. 410, says, 'His Epitaph registered in a Book in the Colledge of Arms (differing not much from that mentioned in Mr *George Buck*'s History of this King) . . . I have here inserted'. Because the end of Cotton Tiberius E.X is entirely burnt away, no part of the epitaph remains there: this entire text is derived from the Editor's copies. The Editor is not given either to consulting manuscripts or to making additions to Sir George's work this early in his revision process, so it is probably safe to say that the epitaph, as well as the poem that follows it, did appear in Sir George's original before the Cotton fire. Though one might wonder whether he would have chosen to conclude his work in defence of Richard with writings uncomplimentary to him, he did not plan to end it so: the list of contents for Book V cites his intended conclusion as 'The author's scope, peroration, et votum'. Further support for his authorship is the softening of attitude toward Richard, characteristic of Sir George (note that I am not listing all the variants from the Sandford version, but just those which illustrate the more favourable attitude to Richard): 'iusta' is substituted in l. 36 (p. 217) for 'multa', 'certans' in l. 41 for 'merito', 'petita' in l. 1 (p. 218) for 'debita', l. 3 'levata' for 'fienda'.

John Ashdown-Hill in 'The Epitaph of King Richard III', *The Ricardian*, XVIII (2008), pp. 31-45, prints other versions of the epitaph: BL. Add. MS. 45131 f. 10v (dated 1495-1534) and College of Arms MS I 3, f. 4 (1509-1557). He points out that the final couplet does not, in context of its composition ('the late medieval preoccupation with purgatory') imply that Richard was more in need of prayers than other people (p. 39). He also suggests that it was the threat of Perkin Warbeck that caused Henry VII in 1593-4 to set up this monument to his conquered enemy, 'which is far less hostile [even in the versions other than Buc's] than might have been expected'. Though 'previously it had suited Henry to call Richard a usurper and treat Edward IV's sons as legitimate claimants . . . now that one of Edward's sons was reputedly moving against him, it may have seemed preferable to take a more equivocal stance. After all, Richard III was safely dead' (p. 40).

All three of the Editor's manuscript copies of Buc's work give in their marginal notes on this epitaph '(A) Annos 2 et 52 days [i.e., 22 August] and '(C) die 22 Augusti'. The 1646 printed edition by the Editor, though he changes these dates to '*Annos* 2. & 51. Dies.' and 'Die 21. Aug.', intentionally predating them to accord with Henry VII's dating of his reign from the day before the battle. All the Editor's versions give the year as 1484, which presumably is simply a mistake, not one Sir George Buc would have made. See also Kincaid, 'Researching Richard III's Epitaph', *The Ricardian*, XXIV (2017), p. 117-29.

218/8-28. [Epigram on three Richards, Kings of England, transcribed from an old manuscript book: There were three Richards whose fortunes were alike in three things, but in others the fate of each was his own. For they were alike in dying without posterity, in rapacious lifestyle, and in violent death, but it was the greater glory of the first that he fought in the Holy Land, and returning home was struck by a catapult in a distant land. The second, deposed from his kingdom, after being shut in prison for some months, chose to perish from hunger rather than bear opprobrium. The third, exhausting Edward's ample accumulation of wealth, proscribing his [Edward's] supporters, at last, after two years the adherents of Henry having taken the kingdom in battle, he lost his earthly life and his crown. In the year one thousand four hundred and eighty-five, the sixth month ['Sextilis' was the old name for 'August', which, in the old-style calendar, was the sixth month], the twice-eleventh day, the teeth of the boar were blunted and the red rose, champion of the white, flourishes again in the world.]

This epigram appears in Crowland, p. 184, with few differences. Buc may have copied it from there, though Julian M. Luxford in '*Tres Sunt Ricardi* and the Crowland Chronicle', *The Ricardian* XVIII (2008), 21-9, who prints a version from an Eton manuscript, feels there are too many divergences for that to be the case. I disagree and feel that the changes fall within the parameters of Buc's tendency both to paraphrase and to soften harshness to Richard in his citations. These changes include substitution of 'Mundanum' [worldly] in l. 16 for '[Ille] trucem' [violent], and reference to his suppressing Edward's progeny is entirely deleted. The other variants are insignificant. The loss of Buc's reading makes it impossible absolutely to determine responsibility for these divergences, but such softenings of harshness to Richard are consonant with his tendency elsewhere. Besides, his great-nephew did not make substantive changes of this sort in his manuscript copies.

APPENDIX
FOLKLORE AND HISTORY

Humankind has a need for icons to represent various things, most basically good and evil. The need of English speakers to hang onto Richard III as a representative of evil has been present nearly since his death and has recently shown its strength again in the discovery of his skeleton. T.G. Heath nearly nails the situation when he says, 'The figure of Richard III hovers like a medieval incubus over English history, – an evil spirit that has absorbed not only the imputations by his contemporaries of dissemblance, treachery, and murder but also each generation's fear of royal tyranny . . .'[1] But the fear goes much deeper than could be accounted for merely by royal tyranny. It is particularly significant that he was rumoured to have been responsible for the death of children: this connects to the mythical archetype of the Wicked Uncle. Death of children, especially at the hands of a close relation, is an emotive subject. A.J. Pollard cites Chaucer's Clerk's Tale and the story of the Babes in the Wood as other stories with a child or children as victim.[2] Projecting ourselves back to childhood, we focus on our sense of vulnerability. Richard III represents a potential threat to us at our most vulnerable. We feel a need to neutralize that threat.

A strand in the image Henry VII built of Richard III is linked to the death of children: Herod's Slaughter of the Innocents. Herod became a highly popular comic villain figure in mediaeval drama, as can still be seen in the extant portion of the Coventry mystery cycle. When Henry VII in his Parliament of November 1485[3] vaguely refers to Richard's 'shedding of infants' blood', this can only be a reference to Herod. It summons up all the horror of the mass slaughter of male babies near Bethlehem in an attempt to kill the infant Jesus. There is no reference at all in Henry's Act of Attainder to Edward V and his brother. Had he known that Richard had had them killed he would certainly have said so, provided details, held a requiem mass for them. That he did none of this proves he was as ignorant of the matter as we are now, as does his later uncertainty about the identity of Perkin Warbeck.

Another prominent strand of the image of Richard as evil archetype has to do with physiognomy. Abnormal physiognomy and curiosities of nature fascinated mediaeval and early modern chroniclers, who avidly recorded the appearance of monstrosities: the giant fish washed up on the beach or the baby born with two heads. A specific caveat concerning hunchbacks stems from Leviticus 21, which

1 T.G. Heath, 'Another Look at Thomas More's *Richard*', *Moreana* XIX-XX (1968), 11.
2 *Richard III and the Princes in the Tower* (Stroud, 1991). pp. 17-20.
3 PROME, VI, 275-8.

says that no one with a blemish – and that includes a humped back (21:20) – may approach the altar for fear of defiling it. It was a mediaeval commonplace that an evil mind, indeed an evil *soul,* accompanied a deformed body: the soul was thought to be cause of 'al the natural mevnges [movings] of the body'. This is a quotation from a book called *Secreta Secretorum*,[4] very popular in the Middle Ages, a compendium of physiognomy and its significance. When the shoulders are, it says, 'moche uprerid, thei tokenyth orribill kynde [nature] and vntrought [untrustworthiness] . . .' (p. 235). It also states that a man 'that . . . hath . . . the lymes [limbs] dyfformyd out of kynde [nature]: Suche bene to enchue [such should be avoided] as enemys, for to wickednesse they bene enlcynet' (p. 232). Basically this means that anyone with a physical abnormality is inclined to evil.

A humped back had a visual association with the devil: Samuel Harsnett in his *Declaration of Egregious Popish Impostures* (London, 1603) says, 'It was a pretty part in the old Church-playes, when the nimble Vice would skip into the deuils necke, and ride the deuil a course'. This action is echoed in Shakespeare's *Richard III* when little York says to his uncle, 'Because that I am little, like an ape, / He thinks that you should bear me on your shoulders' (III, i): the ape, apparently a travesty of the human form, was associated with the devil, and is envisioned as sitting on his shoulder. The 'ape' on Richard's shoulder is manifested in his traditional hump (scoliosis is no use, producing no hump). As well as with the devil, Richard is aligned with the figure of the Vice, who was sometimes portrayed as deformed and who always wooed the audience to be on his side, trying to lead them astray.

The originators of the monstrosity myth associated with Richard were John Rous, who invented the story that he was born with hair to his shoulders and a full set of teeth, having spent two years in the womb,[5] and Sir Thomas More.[6] Rous limits Richard's physical imperfection to what would have been visible when he was clothed: one shoulder was higher than the other. Rous had probably seen Richard. More, who had not, added that he was 'ill fetured of limmes' (p. 7) and more specifically that he had a 'werish withered arme and small' (p. 48), a deformed limb fulfilling the requirement of a man 'that . . . hath . . . the lymes [limbs] dyfformyd out of kynde' (see above). Equally incorrectly, as the discovery of his skeleton proved, More cites Richard's left shoulder as higher than his right. This is neither an error nor a wish to assimilate Richard's to his own raised shoulder (the left, as Erasmus tells us) but a symbol of the prominence of evil, traditionally associated with the left side (as in 'sinister').

That Rous gives him no physical imperfections other than uneven shoulders seems to indicate that during his lifetime no one was aware of his scoliosis. And indeed while he lived no one mentions any malformation, only describing him as short with thin arms and legs. So clearly nothing of that sort was evident to anyone who saw him dressed. In the photograph of the model carefully constructed by measuring each vertebra (*The Lancet*, CCCLXXXIII, 2014, p. 1944), we can

4 Three Prose Versions of the Secreta Secretorum, I. ed. Robert Steele, EETS, extra ser. 74 (London, 1898), p. 218.
5 John Rous, *Historia Regum Angliae*, 2nd ed. (Oxford, 1745), p. 215.
6 *The History of King Richard III*, by Richard S. Sylvester, The Complete Works of St Thomas More, II, New Haven, 1963.

ourselves see that the bend was indeed slight and well-balanced. We may assume that Richard's scoliosis first became public when his body was transported naked, slung face-down over a horse from the battlefield to Leicester: there is an effect of scoliosis visible only when bent forward, when the lateral twist of the spine can cause protrusion of the shoulder-blade or ribs on the affected side.[7] Presumably no one of that time would have distinguished between scoliosis and kyphosis, the configuration of the humped back, which has a radically different effect of producing a visible hump and causing the head to bend forward when standing. One might assume that scientific observation had progressed since the Tudor period, but there is doubt when emotions take over.

In the comic strips of my childhood villains were either deformed, exceptionally ugly or foreign. But I would have assumed that by now political correctness and a scientific approach would have done away with the traditional link between ugliness or physical abnormality and character, specifically that a physical disorder and a propensity for evil necessarily went hand in hand. I thought it more likely that those who overcame a physical disorder to become outstandingly effective were likely nowadays to be generally regarded as nearly heroic (viz. the Paralympics). But there does evidently remain a very strong psychological need for a figure of evil, including an 'evil' body deformed in a specific, extreme, traditional manner. And people simply won't wear scoliosis, perhaps because it is too common, perhaps because it can be concealed, perhaps because it is simply not dramatic enough. They *insist* on Richard's being a hunchback, no matter what the evidence to the contrary. The gleefulness with which the discovery of his scoliosis was greeted – because, the clamour went, it PROVED he was a hunchback (when it proved precisely that he was not) and thus PROVED that he was a moral monster (a connection I fail to perceive) – suggests that the extra-rational need for a villain figure quite specifically disfigured, perhaps as a sort of scapegoat, is very strong indeed.

This need to retain Richard as a figure of monstrous inhumanity, both physically and morally, clearly affected the reception of the discovery of his bones. That he had scoliosis, whose sole noticeable effect when he was clothed would have been to raise one shoulder (the right), has been – now it can only be wilfully – misread as proving that he was in real life the hunchback of tradition, and that *therefore* all the other tales about him are true. In fact the discovery of his bones *disproved* two major myths about the traditional physical picture of him: (1) he was not a hunchback, though he did have a curved spine, (2) he did not have a withered arm or a short leg, as depicted in the play (everyone has been totally silent about the latter discovery). Antony Sher in his book *Year of the Fat Knight* (London, 2015), p. 48, says that when he played Richard at the RSC in 1984 the Richard III Society had badgered him for distorting their hero. However, 'In Sept. 2012 they helped fund the excavation of Richard's skeleton . . . and were disappointed to discover that he really was a hunchback. They'd always claimed that it was part of Shakespeare's distortion'. (This is the only comment I have encountered citing such disappointment among the Richard III Society, which I take leave to doubt.)

7 I owe this observation to Philippa Langley in a lecture at the Middleham Festival, 2016. See also *The King's Grave*, p. 212.

E. Jane Dickson in her article 'The King and I', in *Radio Times* for the week of 14-20 May, 2016, citing Benedict Cumberbatch in the role of Shakespeare's villain, claims that 'the exhumation . . . of the remains . . . allowed unprecedented authenticity in the matter of the king's hump . . .' (p. 13). Which in fact it proved he did *not* have. And although Rupert Goold's Almeida production as shown in the cinema began with the discovery in the car park, it showed a picture of a grossly over-bent spine, and Ralph Fiennes's Richard was given a monstrously distorted back. Though Shakespeare's villain is perhaps monstrously deformed, one really cannot look to the bones of the historical Richard for support of this. A play is not fact. It is interesting that Richard's scoliosis should be accepted as proof that he had a quite different, much more dramatic physical malformation. This suggests that the need for him to be *monstrously* deformed is very strong indeed. To attempt to defend the historical Richard, in contrast to the literary versions, seems somehow threatening to a lot of people. They can apparently ignore (silently) the knowledge that he had no withered arm, but that he didn't have a humped back is too much. Scoliosis is near enough: a humped back by adoption, and interestingly still a manifestation of an evil soul rather than a mild disorder whose effects he overcame in both appearance and action.

As soon as the scoliosis was discovered, *The Guardian* of 4 February 2013 said: 'it was not, after all, simply Tudor propaganda which had portrayed the king as a twisted psychopath". Sir Stanley Wells, eminent Shakespeare scholar, called upon to consider the effect of the discovery on Shakespeare, both in an article for *The Stage* on 5 February 2013 ('Richard's Skeleton – What Does It Mean for Shakespeare?') and in his Shakespeare blog of 14 February 2013, claimed that the discovery of the skeleton was 'confirmation that he was indeed physically as well as morally deformed': the two attributes still – it seems necessarily – go hand in hand, the twist in the spine somehow confirming moral deformity, even in the minds of highly educated and intelligent people. What an historical discovery could conceivably 'mean for' a play, which is by definition fiction, is incomprehensible. And how do the people who insist he was a hunchback, despite physical evidence to the contrary, explain the fact that we have no reports, including those of his enemies, that mention this during his lifetime? A humped back could not possibly have been concealed.

Later the review by Nigel Jones of *The Search for King Richard III: the King's Grave* (London, 2011) by Philippa Langley and Michael Jones, *Sunday Express*, 6 Oct. 2013 took a similar view more unpleasantly phrased – the excess of its phrasing showing that the author feels a very strong vested interest in the retention of an evil Richard III:

> Finding Richard's long-lost remains, though hugely historically important, did nothing to change these inconvenient truths. In fact, uncovering the skeleton proved that one Shakespearian caricature, that 'crook-back Dick' had a deformed spine, which the Ricardians had always scoffed as 'Tudor propaganda' was, ahem, a cold fact. His spine twisted by the bone disease scoliosis,Richard in life was

essentially as the Bard portrayed him on stage.[8]
The Ricardians will never believe it but history tells us that his dark soul was as warped as his misshapen body.[9]

The fact is that 'history tells us' nothing of the kind. Logically, since Richard reigned only two years, he should have been all but forgotten, a footnote to history. And indeed, according to a recent study by Barrett J. Beer, this is how lower-status histories of the mid-sixteenth century did in fact treat him: their non-elite readers, who 'comprised the majority of the reading public at this time . . . would have concluded that Richard was an insignificant and colourless king scarcely worthy of mention'.[10] Probably his short reign is the main cause of the focus on him for archetypal figure of evil: that he reigned such a short time left less information about him, less emotional residue surrounding him than other kings. It is no wonder that Henry VII (a master publicist with essentially no title to the crown) managed to establish a negative reputation for someone who had reigned only two years. Henry's own recorded actions in pursuit of security on his throne demonstrated a degree of tyranny that far surpassed the tendentious allegations his supporters fostered against Richard III, yet Henry (who evidently was physically 'perfect') is not remembered as a monster. He reigned much longer and would not have been so easy a candidate for blanket vilification, and besides, his dynasty continued after his death. Richard had reigned almost no time at all, left no direct heirs, and is thus in a way a blank canvas for the role of evil monster. And as the gothic cult of the monster through the ages (e.g. Frankenstein's Creature, Edward Hyde) shows, something in the human animal needs a figure to occupy that role.

At the time the Tudor dynasty was beginning, the style of history writing was changing. Mediaeval history had been either annalistic or providential. The former, organized by mayoral years, was in the form of something nearing a list, citing monstrous births side by side with decisive battles. Providentialism organized history with a didactic viewpoint: it was written to show how God worked to reward good and destroy evil people. Facts were chosen or discarded or distorted to support this view. According to Edward Hall's *schema* of English history, which Shakespeare follows, Richard III came last in a long line displaying divine retribution exacted for the deposition of Richard II.

The negative view promoted by the Tudors and their followers was so remarkably successful because (a) they had first rate writers to assist it, (b) printing, introduced to England in 1476 and patronized by Richard III, was burgeoning by Tudor times. The Italian Polydore Vergil, Tudor official historian, followed the providential bent and also accepted the Continental view that it was

8 Scoliosis is medically classed as a disorder, neither a disease nor indeed a disability.

9 There is another side to all this: some denizens of Leicester attributed to Richard the unlikely football win in the spring of 2016 – he seemed to be accepted as the patron of the football team. And according to a feature on the big TV screen set up in Leicester town centre at the time of his re-interment, local gays, regarding themselves as fellow outsiders, were adopting him as their patron saint. So perhaps his image changed briefly in Leicester. In addition Middleham, which has always been pro-Richard, now proudly sports a Richard III Hotel.

10 Barrett J. Beer, 'Richard III: The Image of the King in Small Mid-Tudor Chronicles: 1540-1560', *Notes and Queries*, LXII (2015), pp. 44-5.

the historian's task to glorify the ruler who was his patron. He introduced to English history writing the continuous narrative, illustrating it with invented orations to create drama and immediacy. Thomas More's 'history', seems to rely on Polydore for some details. He also intended it to convey a moral message and uses invented orations. More, though, was more inventive, juggling a number of balls at once. Primarily he was giving a picture of a tyrant, basing his portrait on classical models, following the mediaeval *de casibus* tradition, also a providential technique. Starting with a portrait of a model king, he shows a tyrant's rise and the beginning of his fall (the work is unfinished). He was, at the same time as he was presenting it, satirizing his own portrait. James R. Siemon points out that it is More's tendency first to report something, then, on the verge of taking it back, introducing 'reporters and wise men to attest to claims that eventually he drops as conjectural anyway'. With the 'self-cancelling nature of such passages' he 'performs handsprings of irony around its assertions, giving with one hand, taking back with the other'.[11] More uses irony throughout in such a way that if you remove it you have a picture of an innocent and even noble Richard. Buc sometimes takes More's ironic statements in all seriousness because, ignoring the irony, they work well on the side of the defence.

By Shakespeare's time printing had ensured that 'the abstracts and brief chronicles of the time' (the words 'abstract' and 'brief chronicle' actually formed part of their titles) were in everyone's hands. More's *Richard III* had proliferated: writers and publishers dealing with the period it covered adopted it almost wholesale, word for word incorporating it in the composite histories that bore their names: Hardyng, Grafton, Hall, Holinshed, Stow. No longer are things right or wrong just because More says them: they are now *much more* right or wrong because More, Hardyng, Grafton, Hall, Holinshed, and Stow ALL say them! Most influential is that Shakespeare, using Hall and Holinshed as the sources for his history play series, consequently used More. Hence the monstrous Richard was transferred, with structural alterations and different focus, to Shakespeare's frequently performed play.

What is most surprising is the extent to which historians still accept More's tale as fact. Colin Richmond observes, 'It is . . . a book that should not, indeed must not, be used by historians. . . . [I]t is impossible to discern in his *History* what is history'.[12] More was creating a moral exemplum, not trying to relate historical facts. He slants and moulds the portrayal of his central character to fit this aim, using irony for stress. More is a slippery author. Arguments abound as to the meaning of his *Utopia*, and no definitive explanation of it has yet been widely accepted. Equally, his *Richard* remains open to interpretation. And there have been many widely differing interpretations of it. To cite a few, one is that it is a satire,[13] another that it represents epideictic rhetoric,[14] another that it encourages

11 'Reconstructing the Past: History, Historicism, Histories', in *A Companion to English Renaissance Literature and Culture*, ed. Michael Hattaway (Oxford, 2012), II, p. 530.

12 '1483: the Year of Decision (or Taking of the Throne)' in *Richard III: a Mediaeval Kingship*, ed. John Gillingham (London, 1993), p. 40.

13 Alison Hanham, *Richard III and His Early Historians* (Oxford, 1975), Ch. 7. Regrettably she also tries to show that it is in five acts. With there being no concept in More's time of a five-act play, this cannot really make sense.

14 Elizabeth Story Donno, 'Thomas More and Richard III', *Renaissance Quarterly*, XXXV (1982), 401-47.

moral virtue and political reform.[15] A.J. Pollard in 'The Tyranny of Richard III',[16] points out that in the sixteenth century 'a function of history was to supply moral lessons', so the historical writer 'was guided by a preconceived notion of what a tyrant was and presented the "facts" in such a way as to achieve this': this was a fact of literary criticism of the time, not an aspect solely of Tudor propaganda.

Richard's monstrous reputation and its tenacity owe their prominence to the fact that two of the most brilliant authors in the English language, More and Shakespeare, chose his reign as a subject for their works. The most obvious harm to the way he is viewed today still comes from Shakespeare's history plays, which people have always taken the liberty of regarding as historical fact: it is much easier to learn history from a play, a visual, auditory and participatory representation of life, than from a history book. The play has several things going for it: the main ones are it is a gift to a leading actor, and its structure is deeply satisfying to an audience: they get not only to watch and delight in Richard's villainies, but, since he takes them into his confidence, to be complicit in them. This is cathartic in the most basic way: carefully controlled, we can let loose our propensity to enjoy and share in Richard's evil-doing: up to a point all the people he destroys are immoral or stupid, and he runs rings around them. He invites us to be complicit in his cleverness, and so we are. Then we are forced to turn against him: we can see when he goes too far, while he can't, so he ceases to manipulate us, and we are free to condemn him and save our own souls in damning his.

Brian Walsh reminds us that performance of the play is basic to the persistence of Shakespeare's Richard. It is not the text 'that has sustained the Richard of Rous, More et al. against revisionist claims that suggest a different historical Richard. It is the Richard of More, et al. given a body and a stage/film set to "bustle" upon that energizes and perpetuates that dialectic'.[17] There have been periods when *Richard III* was Shakespeare's most popular play, notably the nineteenth century. The play has had more recent life as political comment on the period in which it was being performed. In the twentieth century the focus was on current or recent dictators.[18] Particularly, from around 1937 to the Loncraine/McKellen film in 1996, the subject was Adolf Hitler.

This is not a play that we would willingly surrender. But why should we have to? Is it impossible to adopt a vision that sees fiction as not representative of fact? After all, that is what the term 'fiction' is supposed to mean: something made up. Evidently this is difficult. The stage portrayal and its popularity are not going to disappear. And even today we may meet someone who will reply, when one questions the approach to this play as historical fact, 'But didn't he kill an awful lot of people?' Archetypes exist because there is a need for them.

Misinformation about Richard keeps appearing in historical writing, evidently through tradition. A factual error which Polydore Vergil[19] and More began (p. 23)

15 Dan Breen, 'Thomas More's "History of Richard III": Genre, Humanism, and Moral Education', *Studies in Philology*, CVII (2010), 465-92.

16 *The Journal of Medieval History*, III (1997), p. 148.

17 *Shakespeare and the Queen's Men, and the Elizabethan Performance of History* (Cambridge, 2009), p. 169.

18 See M.G. Aune, 'The Uses of Richard III: from Robert Cecil to Richard Nixon', *Shakespeare Bulletin*, XXIV (2006), 23-47.

19 *Anglica Historia* (Basle, 1599), p. 539.

that he was protector of the sons of Edward IV, when he was in fact named protector of the kingdom, not of the princes, will not lie down, nor will the disapproving remarks, continuing right up to the present day[20] that he failed to convince the Council to sentence Rivers and Gray to execution, as if he were under obligation to do so. He was under no such obligation: the office he held of High Constable was structured so that his Court's proceedings were sufficient, its summary judgement being designed to avoid delay when stamping out rebellion and treason.[21] Of course if such facts are ignored he can be made to seem to contravene the bounds of legality.

Recent and current historians use several techniques to retain, uphold and 'improve' the traditional picture of Richard as a monster. One is to treat all uncomplimentary statements about Richard as factual, whatever the motive was in making them. Henry's attacks on him in his first Parliament are treated as unique (it is important that Richard be *uniquely* evil), whereas it was in fact the practice of kings of the period to begin their reign as new brooms, by denigrating or disapproving of the previous one: this is clear in the statements made by both Edward IV and Richard III, for example (Edward's 'shedding of innocent blood'[22] is not very different from Henry's 'shedding of infants' blood'). Another technique is to state that anything that does not fit their negative picture someone made up. An example of this is the Elizabeth of York letter, which Buc is often blamed, either directly or by innuendo, for inventing: its failure to be found appears in some way suspicious, despite only a small fraction of the manuscript material which existed in the fifteenth to seventeenth centuries surviving (one keeps wondering how so many people seem to have missed this fact, which is certainly pertinent in all narrow fields of specialization). As blinders they use a stock phrase 'No one has ever seen' such and such a quoted source – something which they cannot prove nor anyone else disprove – so they remain without egg on their faces until in some cases someone actually locates it. Similarly, when they find something inconvenient they insist that someone made it up: for example, they state that Bishop Stillington was (of course) lying when he testified to Edward's having been bigamously married. Their bare statement is assumed to be enough – they are, after all, the experts. They also lay disproportionate stress on any niggling imperfection or accusation against Richard, sometimes even in the face of irrefutable proof to the contrary. Michael Hicks's 'serial incestor' accusation (see above, pp. cxv-cxvi) is a case in point. (David Horsfall, who is not a defender, comments, 'Richard as "serial incestor" turns out to be an ingenious modern version of the bottled spider, the duke whose every move conceals a dastardly motive, with as much basis in reality', p. 107).

Anne Sutton warns

> The greatest problem confronting any study of Richard of Gloucester is the 'attitude' expected from authors, both the

20 See David Horsfall, *Richard III: a Ruler and His Reputation* (London, 2015), p. 154.

21 See Annette Carson, *Richard Duke of Gloucester as Lord Protector and High Constable of England* (2015); cf. Sutton, 'The Admiralty and Constableship of England in the Later Fifteenth Century' in *Courts of Chivalry and Admiralty in Late Medieval Europe* (2018), p. 205.

22 PROME, XIII, 1 Edward IV, p. 13.

> popular non-historian biographers and those employed to teach history at universities. It is a tradition that Richard was somehow 'different' from any other fifteenth-century duke or king and the authors' attitude should be hostile. As a consequence any study that seeks to find out the facts, read them correctly and be as neutral as possible, must be fully explained and referenced . . . this detailed level of enquiry, motivated by curiosity, is the best way to enlarge our understanding.[23]

If we were willing to do that, however, we would risk losing something for which clearly we have a very deep-seated need.

23 'Richard of Gloucester 1461-70: Income, Lands and Associates. His Whereabouts and Responsibilities', *The Ricardian*, XXVI (2016), p. 85.

GLOSSARY

accabled (67)	overwhelmed
accol (118)	embrace
acolasts (200)	prodigals
affied, affying, affiance (27, etc.)	trust(-ed, - ing)
ambit (141, 152)	scope
appanage (20)	provision (land, office) for younger son of royalty
assentation (121)	assenting, flattery
Bashaes (42)	imperious people
battologies (7)	excessive and extensive repetitions
captate, -ion (35, 64)	endeavour to get
carnifices (105)	slaughterers
cognation (110)	relationship
commorient (141)	dying together
compatient (141)	sympathetic
copy (6)	copiousness
crapauds (38)	toads
deturpation (83)	making vile or base
disertly (27, etc.)	eloquently
emules (29)	rivals
facinorous (41)	excessively wicked
fastigious (86)	culminating
idoneous (193)	suitable
ierogliffs (175)	hieroglyphs, symbols
illuded (146)	mocked
inchantally (206)	by enchantment
largitions (197)	bounties
leames (86)	drains
mome (122)	dolt, fool

monomachy (104)	single combat
mott (175)	motto
naves (48)	hubs
novercal (67)	stepmother-like
obnoxious to (89, 197, 200)	subject to injury by
opiniasts (117)	opinionated people
palliardise (199)	debauchery
parachronism (172)	erroneously assigning a later date
parergon, -a (56, 172)	digression
pasquillants (117)	writers of satire
patrociny (4)	patronage, protection
perduells (95, 96)	enemies
philautists (199)	self-lovers
placentine (124)	ingratiating
posters (16, etc.)	descendants
precony (202, 203)	extolment
prosopolepsies (4)	partialities
quadruplators (193)	informers
rebus (175)	a picture or device signifying a word or concept
refell (8)	refute
refricated (63)	restimulated
reginists (26)	queen's adherents
rhodomontados (26, 42)	extravagant boastings
ritrat (56)	portrait
sicaries (166)	assassins
sobriquets (9, etc.)	nicknames, epithets
suppeditated (6)	supplied
surquidry (101)	pride
tirociny (6, 9)	training, apprenticeship
truhanes (88,192)	vagabonds
viaticum (121)	money or provision for travel
vitilitigators (120)	contenders
wast (140)	desolate

BIBLIOGRAPHY

LIST OF PRINTED SOURCES AND THESES

Adams, Joseph Quincy, 'Hill's List of Early Plays in Manuscript', *The Library* XX (1939).

Ailredus, Abbot of Rievaulx, *The Chronicle of the Reigns of Henry II and Richard I*, ed. William Stubbs, 2 vols., R.S. 49, 1867.

Albright, Evelyn May, *Dramatic Publication in England, 1580-1640*, New York, 1927.

Allen, John J., 'The Spanish *Corrales de Comedias* at Almagro and the London Playhouses and Stages', *New Issues in the Reconstruction of Shakespeare's Theatre*, ed. Franklin J. Hildy, New York, 1990.

André, Bernard, *Historia Regis Henrici Septimi*, in *Memorials of King Henry the Seventh*, ed. James Gairdner, R.S. 10, London, 1858.

Anglo, Sydney, 'The *British History* in Early Tudor Propaganda', *Bulletin of the John Rylands Library*, XLIV (1961).

_______, *Spectacle, Pageantry, and Early Tudor Policy*, Oxford, 1969.

Appleby, Jo, Piers D. Mitchell, *et al.*, 'The Scoliosis of Richard III, Last Plantagenet King of England: Diagnosis and Clinical Significance', *The Lancet*, CCCLXXXIII (31 May 2014).

Armstrong, C.A.J., 'The Inauguration Ceremonies of the Yorkist Kings and Their Title to the Throne', *Transactions of the Royal Historical Society*, 4th ser., XXX (1948).

Ashdown-Hill, John, *Eleanor, the Secret Queen*, Stroud, 2009.

_______, 'The Epitaph of King Richard III', *The Ricardian,* XVIII (2008).

_______, *The Last Days of Richard III and the Fate of His DNA,* Stroud, 2013.

Aune, M.G., 'The Uses of Richard III: from Robert Cecil to Richard Nixon', *Shakespeare Bulletin*, XXIV (2006).

Bacon, Francis, *History of the Reign of Henry VII, The Works of Francis Bacon,* VI, ed. James Spedding, Robert Leslie Ellis, and Douglas Denon Heath, London, 1938.

Baker, David Weil, 'Jacobean Historiography and the Election of Richard III', *Huntington Library Quarterly*, LXX (2007).

Baker, Richard, *A Chronicle of the Kings of England*, London, 1643.

Bald, R. C., 'The *Locrine* and *George-a-Green* Title-Page Inscriptions', *The Library*, XV (1934).

_______, 'A Manuscript Work by Sir George Buc', *Modern Language Review*, XXX (1935).

_______, 'A Revels Office Entry', *Times Literary Supplement*, no. 1,311 (17 March 1927).

Baldwin, David, *Elizabeth Woodville*, Stroud, 2002.

_______, *The Lost Prince*, Stroud, 2007.

_______, *Richard III,* Stroud, 2013.

Bale, John, *Scriptorum Illustrium Maioris Brytanniae*, Basle, [1557-9].

Barnfield, Marie, 'Diriment Impediments, Dispensations and Divorce: Richard III and Matrimony', *The Ricardian*, XVII (2007).

_______ and Stephen Lark, 'The Paternity of Lady Lumley, Some New Evidence', *The Ricardian*, XXVI (2016), and corrigendum XXVII (2017).

Bawcutt, N.W., 'New Revels Documents of Sir George Buck and Sir Henry Herbert, 1619-1662', *Review of English Studies* XXXV (1984).

Beaumont, Francis and John Fletcher, *Comedies and Tragedies*, London, 1647.

Beer, Barrett J. 'Richard III: The Image of the King in Small Mid-Tudor Chronicles: 1540-1560', *Notes and Queries*, LXII (2015).

Bellamy, J.G., 'Justice under the Yorkist Kings', *American Journal of Legal History*, IX (1965).

Benedict of Peterborough, *The Chronicle of the Reigns of Henry II and Richard I A.D. 1169-1192*, 2 vols., ed. William Stubbs, R.S. 49, London, 1867.

Bennett, Josephine Waters, *The Evolution of the 'Faerie Queene'*, Chicago, 1942.

Bennett, R.E., *The Life and Works of Sir William Cornwallis*, unpublished doctoral dissertation, Harvard, 1931.

_______, 'Sir William Cornwallis's Use of Montaigne', *PMLA*, XLVIII (1933).

Bentley, Gerard Eades, *The Jacobean and Caroline Stage*, 7 vols., Oxford, 1941-68. *Biographia Britannica*, 7 vols., London, 1748.

_______, corrected and enlarged by Andrew Kippis, 5 vols., London, 1780.

Biographia Poetica, London, 1802.

Boethius, Hector, *Scotorum Historiae*, Paris, 1575.

Bouchard, Alain, *Les Grandes Cronicques de Bretagne*, [Caen, 1518].

Bracton, Henricus de, *De Legibus et Consuetudinibus Angliae*, 6 vols. ed. Sir Travers Twiss, R.S. 70, London, 1878-83.

Breen, Dan, 'Thomas More's History of Richard III: Genre, Humanism and Moral Education', *Studies in Philology*, CVII (2010).

Brenan, Gerald and Edward Phillips Stratham, *The House of Howard*, 2 vols., London, 1907.

British Library Harleian Manuscript 433, edited by Rosemary Horrox and P.W. Hammond, 4 vols., Gloucester, 1979-83.

Brixius, Germanus, *Antimorus*, Basle, 1519. [Brooke, Ralph], *A Discoverie of Certaine Errours Published in Print in the Much Commended Britannia, 1594*, [London, 1596].

_______, *A Catalogue and Succession of the Kings, Princes, Dukes, Marquesses, Earles, and Viscounts of this Realme of England*, London, 1619.

Brooks, F.W., *The Council of the North*, Historical Association Pamphlet 25, London, 1966.

Brusonius, L. Domitius, *Rerum Memorabilium*, 7 vols., Frankfurt, 1600.

B[uc], G[eorge]. Knight, *Δαφνις Πολυστεφανος. An Eclog Treating of Crownes and of Garlandes, and to Whom of Right They Appertaine*, London, 1605.

Buchanan, George, *Rerum Scoticarum Historia*, Edinburgh, 1583.

Buck, George, Gent., *The Great Plantagenet*, London, 1635.

_______, *The History of the Life and Reigne of Richard the Third*, London, 1646.

_______, *The History of the Life and Reigne of Richard the Third*, London, 1647.

_______, *The History of the Life and Reigne of Richard the Third*, Wakefield,1973.
Burton, William, *The Description of Leicester Shire,* London, [1622].
Butler, Sophie P., *Sir William Cornwallis the Younger (c.1579-1614) and the Emergence of the Essay in England*, unpublished doctoral dissertation, Oxford 2013.

Calendar of the Charter Rolls Preserved in the Public Record Office, Vol. VI: *5 Henry VI-8 Henry VIII*, London, 1927.
Calendar of Letters, Despatches, and State Papers, Relating to Negotiations between England and Spain, I, ed. G.A. Bergenroth, London, 1862.
Calendar of the Patent Rolls: 1461-7; 1467-77; 1476-85;1485-94, 1494-1509, London, 1897-1916.
Calendar of State Papers and Manuscripts, Relating to English Affairs, Existing in the Archives and Collections of Milan, I, ed. Allen B. Hinds, London, 1912.
Calendar of State Papers and Manuscripts, Relating to English Affairs, Existing in the Archives and Collections of Venice . . . , I: 1202-1509, ed. Rawdon Brown, London, 1864.
Calmette, Joseph, *Le Moyen Age*, Paris, 1948.
_______, et G. Périnelle, *Louis XI et l'Angleterre (1461- 1483),* Paris, 1930.
Cambrensis, Giraldus, *Topographia Hibernica*, V in *Opera*, ed. James F. Dimock, R.S. 21, London, 1867.
Camden, William, *Britannia*, London, 1600.
_______, *Britannia*, London, 1607
_______, *Britain*, trans. Philemon Holland, London, 1610.
_______, *Remaines*, London, 1605.
_______, *Remaines*, London, 1614.
Carson, Annette, *Richard III: The Maligned King*, Stroud, 2013.
_______, 'Notes Towards the Definition of a Tyrant', *Ricardian Bulletin* (December 2013).
_______, *Richard Duke of Gloucester as Lord Protector and High Constable of England*, Horstead, 2015.
_______, J. Ashdown-Hill, D. Johnson, W. Johnson and P.J. Langley, *Finding Richard III: the Official Account of Research by the Retrieval and Reburial Project*, Horstead, 2014.
_______, and Marie Barnfield, 'Edward of Middleham's Birth', *Ricardian Bulletin* (September 2016).
_______, and Marie Barnfield, 'The Marriage of Lady Anne Neville and Richard Duke of Gloucester', *Ricardian Bulletin* (December 2016).
Carte, Thomas, *A General History of England*, 4 vols., London, 1686-1754.
Casley, David A., et al., *A Catalogue of the Manuscripts in the King's Library: An Appendix to the Catalogue of the Cottonian Library; Together with an Account of Books Burnt or Damaged by a Late Fire*, London, 1734.
Catalogue of the Library of Sir Edward Coke, ed. W.O. Hassall, Yale Law Library Publications, 12, New Haven, 1950.
Catalogue of the Library of the Late Charles Yarnold, Esq., London, 1825.
A Catalogue of the Manuscripts in the Cottonian Library Deposited in the British Museum, London, 1802.

Cavendish, George, *The Life and Death of Cardinal Wolsey*, ed. Richard S. Sylvester, EETS 243, London, 1959.

Cely Letters 1472-1488, The, ed. Alison Hanham, EETS 273, London, 1975.

Challen, W.H., 'Sir George Buck, Kt., Master of the Revels', *Notes and Queries* (1957).

[Chalmers, George], *An Apology for the Believers in the Shakespeare-Papers*, London, 1797.

_______, *A Supplemental Apology for the Believers in the Shakespeare-Papers*, London, 1799.

Chamberlain, John, *The Letters of John Chamberlain*, ed. Norman Egbert McClure, Philadelphia, 1939.

Chambers, E.K., *The Elizabethan Stage*, 4 vols., Oxford, 1923.

_______, *Notes on the History of the Revels Office under the Tudors, 1610-1622,* London, 1906.

_______, Review of *The King's Office of the Revels, Review of English Studies*, I (1925).

Chambers, R.W., *Thomas More*, London, 1935.

Chartrou, Josèphe, *L'Anjou de 1109 à 1151 – Foulque de Jerusalem et Geoffroi Plantagenet*, Paris, n.d.

Chrimes, S.B., *English Constitutional Ideas in the Fifteenth Century*, Cambridge, 1936.

_______, *Henry VII*, London, 1972.

_______, *Lancastrians, Yorkists, and Henry VII*, London, 1966.

Christ Church Letters, ed. J.B. Sheppard, Cam. Soc., 2nd ser. 19, London 1877.

The Chronicle of the Rebellion in Lincolnshire, 1470, ed. John Gough Nichols,

Camden Miscellany, I, ed. William Stubbs, 2 vols., R.S. 49, London, 1847.

Clare, Janet, *'Art Made Tongue-Tied by Authority': Elizabethan and Jacobean Dramatic Censorship*, Manchester, 1990.

Clarke, Peter D., 'English Royal Marriages and the Papal Penitentiary', *English Historical Review*, CXX (2005).

Coggeshall, Radulphus de, *Chronicon Anglicanum*, ed. Joseph Stephenson, R.S. 66, London, 1875.

C[okayne,] G[eorge] E[dward]. *The Complete Peerage*, ed. Vicary Gibbs *et al.*, 13 vols., London, 1910-59.

_______, *The Complete Peerage,* 14 vols. compressed in 7, Gloucester, 1982-1998.

Coke, Edward, *The First Part of the Institutes of the Laws of England*, 4 vols., ed. Frances Hargrave and Charles Butler, London, 1794.

Colie, Rosemary L., *Paradoxia Epidemica*, Princeton 1966.

Colley, Scott, 'Richard III and Herod', *Shakespeare Quarterly*, XXXVII (1986). *A Collection of Curious Discourses Written by Eminent Antiquaries upon Several Heads in Our English Antiquities*, ed. Thomas Hearne, 2 vols., London, 1773.

Commynes, Philippe de, *Mémoires*, 3 vols., ed. Joseph Calmette, Paris, 1924-5. *A Complete History of England*, I and II, [ed. John Hughes], London, 1706.

________, 2nd ed. I and II, [ed. John Hughes], London, 1719.

Conway, Agnes Ethel, 'The Maidstone Sector of Buckingham's Rebellion', *Archaeologia Cantiana*, XXXVII (1925).

Cornwallis, Sir William, *The Encomium of Richard the Third*, ed. A. N. Kincaid with introduction by J.A. Ramsden and A.N. Kincaid, London, 1977.

_______, *Essayes of Certaine Paradoxes,* London, 1616.

The Coronation of Richard III, the Extant Documents, ed. Anne F. Sutton and P.W. Hammond, Gloucester, 1983.

Cothi, Lewis Glyn, *The Poetical Works*, Oxford, 1837.

Crowland Chronicle Continuations, The, 1459-1486, ed. Nicholas Pronay and John Cox, [London], 1986.

[The Crowland Chronicle] in *Rerum Anglicarum Scriptorum Veterum*, I [ed. William Fulman], Oxford, 1684.

Çurita, Geronymo, *Anales de la Corona de Aragon*, 6 vols., Çaragoça, 1610.

Dean, Leonard F., 'Literary Problems in More's *Richard III*', *PMLA*, LVIII (1943).

Debrett's Peerage and Baronetage, ed. Charles Kidd and David Williamson, London, 1995.

De la Haye, Jean, *Les Memoires et Recherches de France, et de la Gaule Acquitanique,* Paris, 1581.

De Ricci, Seymour, *English Collectors of Books and Manuscripts (1530-1930)*, Cambridge, 1930.

Dockray, Keith. *Richard III: a Sourcebook*, Stroud, 1997.

_______, *William Shakespeare, the Wars of the Roses and the Historians,* Stroud, 2002.

Donno, Elizabeth Story, 'Thomas More and Richard III', *Renaissance Quarterly*, XXXV (1982).

Dos Santos, Domenigos Maurício Gomes, *O Mosteiro de Jesus de Aveiro*, Estudos de Historia (Ultramarina e Continental), Lisbon, 1963.

Drake, Francis, *Eboracum*, London, 1936.

Du Boulay, F.R.H., *An Age of Ambition, English Society in the Late Middle Ages*, London, 1970.

Duff, E. Gordon, *Fifteenth Century English Books*, Oxford, 1917.

Dugdale, William, *The Baronage of England*, London, 1676.

_______, *Monasticon Anglicanum*, VI, i, London, 1830.

Du Haillan, Bernard de Gerard, *L'Histoire de France*, [Paris], 1577.

Duncan-Jones, Katherine, *Shakespeare: an Ungentle Life*, London, 2010.

Dunham, William Huse, *Lord Hastings' Indentured Retainers, 1461-1483*, Transactions of the Connecticut Academy of Arts and Sciences, 40, New Haven, 1955.

_______ and Charles T. Wood, 'The Right to Rule England: Depositions and the Kingdom's Authority, 1327-1485', *American Historical Review*, LXXXI (1976).

Du Tillet, Jean, *Recueil des Roys du France*, Paris, 1602.

Dutton, Richard, *Mastering the Revels: The Regulation and Censorship of English Renaissance Drama*, London, 1991.

Eccles, Mark, 'Sir George Buc' in 'Brief Lives, Tudor and Stuart Authors', *Studies in Philology*, LXXIX (1982).

_______, 'Sir George Buc, Master of the Revels' in *Thomas Lodge and Other Elizabethans*, ed. Charles J. Sisson, Cambridge, Mass., 1933.

Edwards, J.G., 'The "Second" Continuation of the Crowland Chronicle', *BIHR*, XXXIX (1966).

Edwards, Rhoda, *The Itinerary of King Richard III, 1483-1485*, London, 1983.

Emden, A. B., *A Biographical Register of the University of Cambridge to 1500*, Cambridge,

1963.

English Historical Scholarship in the Sixteenth and Seventeenth Centuries, ed. Levi Fox, London, 1956.

English Library before 1700, The, ed. Francis Wormald and C.E. Wright, London, 1958.

Erasmus, Desiderius, *Adagiorumi Chiliades*, Basle, 1536.

_______, *Institutio Principis Christiani*, Basle, 1540.

_______, *Opus Epistolarum Des. Erasmi Roterodami*, 12 vols.. ed. P.S. Allen, Oxford, 1904-58.

_______, *Proverbs or Adages*, trans. Richard Taverner, facsimile of 1569 ed., ed. De Witt T. Starnes, Gainesville, 1956.

Euangelum Secundum Matthaeum, Marcum, et Lucum, Paris, 1553.

Evans, Howell T., *Wales and the Wars of the Roses*, Cambridge, 1915.

Evans, Joan, *A History of the Society of Antiquaries*, Oxford, 1956.

Excerpta Historica, compiled by Samuel Bentley, London, 1831.

Extracts from the Municipal Records of the City of York during the Reigns of Edward IV, Edward V and Richard III, ed. Robert Davies, London, 1843.

Fabyan, Robert, *The New Chronicles of England and France, repr. from Pynson's edition of 1516*, ed. Henry Ellis, London, 1811.

Faction in Parliament: Essays on Early Stuart History, ed. Kevin Sharpe, Oxford, 1978.

Fifteenth Century England, ed. S.B. Chrimes, C.D. Ross and R.A. Griffiths, 2nd ed., Stroud, 1997.

Financial Memoranda of the Reign of Edward V: Longleat Miscellaneous Manuscript Book II, ed. Rosemary Horrox, Cam. Fourth Ser. Miscellany XXIX, London, 1987.

Foard, Glenn and Anne Curry, *Bosworth 1485: a Battlefield Rediscovered*, Oxford, 2013.

Foedera, Conventiones, Literae, et Cujuscunque Generis Acta Publica, inter Reges Angliae, compiled by Thomas Rymer, VII-XII, London, 1709-11.

_______, III and V, 3rd ed. reprinted, Farnborough, 1967.

Foxe, John, *The Ecclesiasticall Historie, Conteining the Acts and Monuments of Martyrs*, London, 1583.

Fuchs, Leonhard, *De Historia Stirpium Commentarij Insignis*, London, 1551.

Fuller, Thomas, *The Church History of Britain*, ed. J.S. Brewer, II, Oxford, 1845.

Fussner, F. Smith, *The Historical Revolution: English Historical Writing and Thought 1580-1640*, London, 1962.

Gainsford, Thomas, *The True and Wonderfull History of Perkin Warbeck*, London, 1618.

Gairdner, James, *History of the Life and Reign of Richard the Third*, Cambridge, 1898.

Garibay y Çamálloa, Esteuan de, *D'El Compendio Historial de las Chronicas y Universal Historia de Todos los Reynos D'España*, Antwerp, 1571.

Gibbon, Edward, *Miscellaneous Works*, III, London, 1815.

Gildas, *De Excidio Britanniae*, ed. Joseph Stevenson, London, 1838.

Gildersleeve, Virginia Crocheron, *Government Regulation of the Elizabethan Drama*, New York, 1908.

Glover, Robert, *The Catalogue of Honour*, ed. Thomas Milles, London, 1610.

G[odwin], F[rancis], *A Catalogue of the Bishops of England*, London, 1601.

Goodman, Anthony and Angus MacKay, 'A Castilian Report on English Affairs, 1486',

EHR, LXXXVIII (1973).
Goodman, Tony, 'The Man Himself: Richard III and the Miraculous', *Ricardian Bulletin* (Summer, 2007).
_______, 'The Man Himself: Some Favourable Sixteenth-Century Views of Richard III', *Ricardian Bulletin* (June 2010).
Grace, Damian, 'More's *Richard III*: a Satirical Drama?', *Moreana*, XV (1978).
Grafton, Richard, *Grafton's Chronicle; or, History of England*, 2 vols., London, 1809.
Grants, etc. from the Crown during the Reign of Edward the Fifth, introd. by John Gough Nichols, Cam. Soc., 1st ser. LX, London, 1854.
Great Chronicle of London, The, ed. A. H. Thomas and I. D. Thornley, London, 1938.
Green, Richard Firth, 'Historical Notes of a London Citizen, 1483-1488', *EHR*, XCVI (1981).
Greg, W.W., 'Three Manuscript Notes by Sir George Buc', *The Library*, XII (1931).
Griffiths, R.A. and R.S. Thomas, *The Making of the Tudor Dynasty*, Stroud, 1985.
Guicciardini, Ludovico, *Descrittione de Tutti i Paesi Bassi*, Antwerp, 1581.

Hall, Edward, *Chronicle*, ed. Henry Ellis, London, 1809.
Halsted, Caroline A., *Richard III as Duke of Gloucester and King of England*, 2 vols., London, 1844.
Hanbury, H.G., 'The Legislation of Richard III', *American Journal of Legal History*, VI (1962).
Hanham, Alison, 'Hastings Redivivius', *EHR*, XC (1975).
_______, 'Honing a History: Thomas More's Revisions of His "Richard III", *Review English Studies*, n.s. 59 (2008).
_______, 'The Mysterious Affair at Crowland Abbey', *The Ricardian*, XVII, 2008.
_______, *Richard III and His Early Historians, 1483-1535*, Oxford, 1975.
_______, 'Richard III, Lord Hastings and the Historians', *EHR*, LXXXVII (1972).
_______, 'Sir George Buck and Princess Elizabeth's Letter: a Problem in Detection', *The Ricardian*, VII (1987).
Harbage, Alfred, *Annals of English Drama, 975-1700*, rev. S. Schoenbaum, London, 1964.
Hardyng, John, *The Chronicle of Iohn Hardyng . . . together with the Continuation by Richard Grafton*, ed. Henry Ellis, London,1812.
Harington, John, *A New Discourse of a Stale Subject, Called The Metamorphosis of Ajax*, ed. Elizabeth Story Donno, London, 1962.
_______, 'A Brief Apologie of Poesie', *Elizabethan Critical Essays,* ed. Gregory Smith, 2 vols., London, 1904.
Harpsfield, Nicholas, *The Life and Death of Sr Thomas Moore, Sometimes Lord High Chancellor of England*, ed. Elsie Vaughan Hitchcock, London, 1932.
Hay, Denys. 'The Manuscript of Vergil's "*Anglica Historia*"'. *EHR*, LIV (1939).
Hazlitt, W. Carew, *Collections and Notes*, ser. 1, London, 1876.
Helmholz, Richard, 'The Sons of Edward IV: a Canonical Assessment of the Claim that they were Illegitimate', in *Richard III: Loyalty, Lordship and Law*, London, 2000.
Hervey, Mary F.S., *The Life, Correspondence and Collections of Thomas Howard, Earl of Arundel*, Cambridge, 1921.
Heuterus, Pontus, *Rerum Burgundicarum*, Antwerp, 1584.

Hicks, Michael, *Anne Neville, Queen to Richard III*, Stroud, 2007.

_______, *The Family of Richard III*, Stroud, 2015.

_______, *Richard III and His Rivals: Magnates and Their Motives in the Wars of the Roses*, London, 1991.

_______, *Richard III: the Man Behind the Myth*, London, 1991.

_______, 'The Second Anonymous Continuation of the Crowland Abbey Chronicle, 1459-86 Revisited', *EHR*, CXXII (2007).

_______, 'Unweaving the Web: the Plot of July 1483 against Richard III and Its Wider Significance, *The Ricardian*, IX (1991).

Hildy, Franklin J., 'The Corral de Comedias at Almagro and London's Reconstructed Globe', *Shakespeare and the Mediterranean: the Proceedings of the Seventh International Shakespeare Association Valencia 2001 World Congress*, ed. Tom Clayton, Susan Brock, and Vicente Forés, Newark, 2004.

_______, '"Think when We Talk of Horses that You See Them", Comparative Techniques of Production, New Issues in the Reconstruction of Shakespeare's Theatre in the Elizabethan and Spanish Golden Age Playhouses', *Text and Presentation,* XI (1991).

The Historical Collections of a Citizen of London in the Fifteenth Century [Gregory's Chronicle], ed. James Gairdner, Cam. Soc., 2nd ser. 17, London, 1876.

Historie of the Arrivall of Edward IV in England, ed. John Bruce, Cam. Soc. 1st ser., I, London, 1838.

Holinshed, Raphael, *Holinshed's Chronicles of England, Scotland, and Ireland*, 6 vols., London, 1807-8.

Hooper, Samuel, *A Catalogue of the Manuscripts in the Cottonian Library*, London, 1777.

Hope, W.H. St John, 'The Discovery of the Remains of King Henry VI in St George's Chapel, Windsor Castle', *Archaeologia*, LXII (1911).

Horrox, Rosemary, *Richard III: a Study of Service*, Cambridge, 1989.

_______, 'Richard III and London', *The Ricardian*, VI (1984).

_______, and P.W. Hammond, eds., *British Library Harleian Manuscript 433*, 4 vols., Gloucester, 1979-1983.

_______, 'Financial Memoranda of the Reign of Edward V: Longleat Miscellaneous Manuscript Book II', *Camden Fourth Series Miscellany XXIX*, vol. 34, Royal Historical Society (1987).

Horsfall, David, *Richard III: a Ruler and His Reputation*, London, 2015.

Hotson, Leslie, *The Last Night of Twelfth Night,* London, 1954.

Hoveden, Roger de, *Chronica*, 4 vols., ed. William Stubbs, R.S. 51, London, 1868-9.

Howard, Henry, *A Defensatiue against the Poyson of Supposed Prophesies*, London, 1583.

Howard, Henry, *Indication of Memorials, Monuments, Paintings, and Engravings of Persons of the Howard Family . . .*, Corby, 1834.

Howard-Hill, T.H., 'Buc and the Censorship of Sir John Van Olden Barnevelt', *Review of English Studies,* XXXIX (1988).

Hume, David, *The History of England*, London, 1763.

Huntingdon, Henry of, *The History of the English*, ed. Thomas Arnold, R.S. 74, London, 1879.

Hutchinson, William, *The History of the County of Cumberland*, 2 vols., Carlisle, 1794.

Hutton, William, *The Battle of Bosworth Field,* London, 1813.

Ingulph's Chronicle of the Abbey of Croyland with the Continuations by Peter of Bois and Anonymous Writers, trans. Henry T. Riley, London, 1834.

Ives, E.W., 'Andrew Dymmock and the Papers of Anthony, Earl Rivers, 1482-1483', *BIHR*, XLI (1966).

Jacob, E.F., *The Fifteenth Century, 1399-1485*, Oxford, 1961.

Jacob, John, *Publicanus Vindicatus*, London, 1654.

_______, *et al.*, *A Remonstrance of the Case of the Late Farmers of the Customes, and Their humble Petition to the Parliament,* [London], 1653.

James, Montague Rhodes and Claude Jenkins, *A Descriptive Catalogue of the Manuscripts in the Library of Lambeth Palace,* 2 vols., Cambridge, 1930-2.

Jenkins, Gladys, 'Ways and Means in Elizabethan Propaganda', *History*, new ser., XXVI (1941).

Jesse, John Heneage, *Memoirs of King Richard III and Some of His Contemporaries*, London, 1862.

Johnson, David, 'The Real Reason Why Hastings Lost His Head,' Parts 1 and 2, *Ricardian Bulletin* (Winter 2007 and Spring 2008).

_______. 'Sir George Buck and the Beaufort Plot to Kill the Princes', *Ricardian Bulletin* (Spring 2006).

Jones, Michael K. and Malcolm G. Underwood. *The King's Mother, Lady Margaret Beaufort, Countess of Richmond and Derby*, Cambridge, 1992.

Jones, W. Garmon, 'Welsh Nationalism and Henry Tudor'. *The Transactions of the Honourable Society of Cymmrodorion* (1917-18).

Kalckhoff, Andreas, *Richard III. Sein Leben und Seine Zeit*, Bergisch Gladbach,1980.

Kamps, Ivo, *Historiography and Ideology in Stuart Drama*, Cambridge, 1996.

Kearns, Emily, 'Richard's Epitaph Revisited', *The Ricardian*, XXIV (2014).

Kelly, Henry A., 'The Case against Edward IV's Marriage and Offspring: Secrecy; Witchcraft; Secrecy; Precontract', *The Ricardian,* XI (1998).

_______, 'Incest and Richard III. Bigamy and Edward IV', *Ricardian Bulletin* (2007).

_______, 'The Last Chroniclers of Croyland', *The Ricardian*, VII (1985).

Kendall, Paul Murray, *Richard III*, New York, 1955.

Kendrick, T. D., *British Antiquity*, London, 1950.

Kincaid, A.N., 'Buck and the Elizabeth of York Letter: a Reply to Dr Hanham', *The Ricardian*, VIII (1988).

_______, 'The Dramatic Structure of Sir Thomas More's *History of Richard III*', *Studies in English Literature*, XII (1972) [repr. *Essential Articles for the Study of Thomas More*, Hamden, CT, 1977 and in *More*, vol. I, *Great Political Thinkers* 6, ed. John Dunn and Ian Harris, Elgar Reference Collection, Cheltenham, 1997.]

_______, 'Researching Richard III's Epitaph', *The Ricardian*, XXVII (2017).

_______, 'Sir Edward Hoby and "K. Richard": Shakespeare Play or Morton Tract?', *Notes and Queries*, XXVIII (1981).

Kingsford, Charles Lethbridge, *English Historical Literature in the Fifteenth Century*, Oxford, 1913.

Kinney, Daniel, 'King's Tragicomedies in More's *Richard III'*, *Moreana*, LXXXVI, (1985).

Kleineke, Hannes, 'Richard III and the Origin of the Court of Requests', *The Ricardian*, XVII (2007).

Lander, J.R., 'Council, Administration and Councillors, 1461-1485', *BIHR*, XXXII (1959).

Langley, Philippa and Michael Jones, *The King's Grave: The Search for Richard III*, London, 2013.

['Leicester's Commonwealth']: *The Copie of a Leter, Wryten by a Master of Arte of Cambrige, to His Friend in London; Concerning Some Talke . . . about the Present State, and Some Procedinges of the Erle of Leycester . . .*, n,p., 1584.

Le Neve, John, *Fasti Ecclesiae Anglicanae*, 3 vols., Oxford, 1854.

Letters and Papers, Foreign and Domestic, of the Reign of Henry VIII, ed. J.S. Brewer, *et al.*, 23 vols. in 35, London, 1862-1932.

Letters and Papers Illustrative of the Reigns of Richard III and Henry VII, ed. James Gairdner, R.S. 24, London, 1861-3.

Levine, Joseph M., *Humanism and History*, Ithaca, 1987.

Levine, Mortimer, 'Richard III – Usurper or Lawful King?' *Speculum*, XXXIV (1959).

Levy, F.J., 'The Making of Camden's *Britannia*', *Bibliothèque de Humanisme et Renaissance*, XXVI (1964).

_______, *Tudor Historical Thought*, San Marino, 1967.

Leyland, John. *John Leyland's Travels in Tudor England*, ed. John Chandler, Stroud, 1993.

Liber Eliensis, ed. E.O. Blake, Cam. Soc., 3rd ser. 92, London, 1962.

Livermore, H.B., *A New History of Portugal*, 2nd ed., London, 1976.

Lowe, D.A., 'Patronage and Politics: Edward IV, the Wydevilles, and the Council of the Prince of Wales, 1481-83', *Bulletin of the Board of Celtic Studies*, XXIX (1980-2).

Luxford, Julian M., 'Tres sunt Ricardi and the Crowland Chronicle', *The Ricardian*, XVIII (2008).

McDonald, Ross, *Shakespeare and the Arts of Language*, Oxford, 2001.

MacGibbon, David, *Elizabeth Woodville (1437-1492), Her Life and Times*, London, 1938.

McKisack, May, *Medieval History in the Tudor Age*, Oxford, 1971.

MacLagan, Michael, 'Genealogy and Heraldry in the Sixteenth and Seventeenth Centuries', *English Historical Scholarship*, ed. Levi Fox, London, 1956.

Macray, William Dunn, *A Register of the Members of St. Mary Magdalen College, Oxford*, new ser. I, London, 1894.

Madden, Frederic, 'Documents Relating to Perkin Warbeck, with Remarks on His History', *Archaeologia*, XXVII (1838).

_______, 'Political Poems of the Reigns of Henry VI and Edward IV', *Archaeologia*, XXVII, 1838.

Maitland, William, *The History and Survey of London*, 2 vols., London, 1756.

Mancini, Dominic, *The Usurpation of Richard III*, trans. and ed. C.A.J. Armstrong, 2nd ed., Oxford, 1969.

Mancini, Domenico, *de occupatione regni Anglie*, trans. and ed. Annette Carson, Horstead, 2021.

'The Manuscripts of the Corporation of Southampton and Kings Lynn', Historical

Manuscripts Commission, 11th Report, Appendix, iii, London, 1887.
Marcham, Frank, *The King's Office of the Revels, 1610-1622*, London, 1925.
_______, 'The King's Office of the Revels, 1610-1622', *Review of English Studies*, II (1926).
Marchegay, P. and A. Salmon, *Chroniques des Comtes d'Anjou*, Paris, 1871.
Markham, Clements R., *Richard III: His Life and Character*, London, 1906.
Martin, Thomas, *The History of the Town of Thetford*, London, 1779.
Materials for a History of the Reign of Henry VII, 2 vols., ed. William Campbell, R.S. 60, London, 1873-7.
Matthew of Westminster, *Flores Historiarum,* 3 vols., ed. Henry Richards Luard, R.S. 95, London, 1890.
Maurer, Helen, 'Bones in the Tower: a Discussion of Time, Place and Circumstance', Parts 1 and 2, *The Ricardian*, VIII and IX, 1990 and 1991.
Memorials of Henry VII, ed. James Gairdner, R.S. 10, London, 1858.
Meyer, Johannes, *Annales, sive Historiae Rerum Belgicarum*, Frankfurt, 1580.
Millican, Charles Bowie, *Spenser and the Table Round*, Cambridge, MA, 1932.
Molinet, Jean, *Chroniques*, 3 vols., ed. George Dutrepont and Omer Jodogne, Brussels, 1935-7.
Monstrelet, Enguerran de, *Chroniques*, 3 vols., Paris, 1595.
More, Thomas, *The Correspondence of Sir Thomas More*, ed. Elizabeth Frances Rogers, Princeton, 1947.
_______, *The Debellation of Salem and Bizance*, *Workes*, London, 1557.
_______, *Historia Richardi Tertii*, ed. Daniel Kinney, *The Complete Works of St Thomas More,* XV, New Haven, 1986.
_______, *The History of King Richard the Third*, ed. George M. Logan, Bloomington, 2005.
_______, *The History of King Richard III*, ed. Richard S. Sylvester, *The Complete Works of St Thomas More*, II, New Haven, 1963
_______, *The Latin Epigrams of Thomas More*, ed. Leicester Bradner and Charles Arthur Lynch, Chicago, 1953.
_______, *Latin Works*, Basle, 1563.
______ , *Translations of Lucian*, ed. Craig R. Thompson, *The Complete Works of St. Thomas More*, III, pt. 1, New Haven, 1974.
_______, *Workes . . . in the Englysh Tonge*, London, 1557.
Myers, A.R., 'The Character of Richard III', *History Today*, IV (1954).
_______, 'Richard III and Historical Tradition', *History*, LIII (1968).

Nelson, Alan H. 'George Buc, William Shakespeare, and the Folger *George a Greene*', *Shakespeare Quarterly* XLIX (1998).
Newburgh, William of, *Historia Regum Anglicarum,* I and II in *Chronicles of the Reigns of Stephen, Henry II, and Richard I*, ed. Richard Howlett, R.S. 82, a & b, London, 1884-5.
Nichols, John, *History and Antiquities of the County of Leicester,* 4 vols., London, 1795-1815.
Nicolas, Nicholas Harris, *Privy Purse Expenses of Elizabeth of York,* London,1830.
Nicot, Jean, *Trésor de la Langue Française,* Paris, 1606.

Nokes, E.M. and G. Wheeler, 'A Castilian Report of the Battle of Bosworth', *The Ricardian*, II (1972).

Norland, Howard B., 'The Role of Drama in More's Literary Career', *The Sixteenth Century Journal*, XIII (1982).

Original Letters Illustrative of English History, ed. Henry Ellis, 3rd ser., I of each series, London, 1825-46.

Oxford Dictionary of National Biography, ed. H.C.G. Matthew and Brian Harrison, Oxford 2004.

Palliser, David, 'Richard III and York', *Richard III and the North*, Hull, 1986.

Paradin, Claude, *Alliances Genealogiques des Rois et Princes de Gaule*, [Geneva], 1606.

Paris, Matthew, *Chronica Majora*, 7 vols., ed. Henry Richards Luard, R.S. 57, London, 1872-83.

Parliament Rolls of Medieval England, The, ed. Chris Given-Wilson, 16 vols., Woodbridge, 2005.

Parsons, Robert, *Leycesters Common-wealth*, London, 1641.

Paston Letters and Papers of the Fifteenth Century, 3 vols., ed. Norman Davis, Richard Beadle, and Colin Redmond, Oxford, 2014.

Patronage, Pedigree, and Power in Late Mediaeval England, ed. Charles Ross, Gloucester, 1979.

Peck, Francis, *Desideria Curiosa*, II, London, 1732.

Penn, Thomas, *Winter King*, London, 2012.

Perriam, D.R., 'William Strickland's Tower in Penrith: Penrith Castle or Hutton Hall?' *English Heritage Historical Review*, III (2008).

Planta, Joseph, *A Catalogue of the Manuscripts in the Cottonian Library*, [London], 1802.

Plumpton Correspondence, ed. Thomas Stapleton, Cam. Soc., IV, London, 1839.

Pollard, A.F., *Henry VIII*, London, 1951.

_______, 'The Making of Sir Thomas More's Richard III', *Historical Essays in Honour of James Tait*, Manchester 1933.

_______, *The Reign of Henry VII from Contemporary Sources*, 3 vols., London, 1913-14.

_______, 'Sir Thomas More's 'Richard III'', *History*, XVII (1933).

Pollard, A.J., *The Middleham Connection: Richard III and Richmondshire 1471-1485*, Middleham, 1983.

_______, ed., *The North of England in the Age of Richard III*, Stroud, 1996.

_______, 'North, South and Richard III', *Richard III Crown and People*, ed. J. Petre, Gloucester, 1985.

_______, *Richard III and the Princes in the Tower*, Gloucester, 1991.

_______, 'The Richmondshire Community of Gentry during the Wars of the Roses' in *Patronage, Pedigree and Power in Late Mediaeval England*, ed. Charles Ross, Gloucester, 1979.

_______, 'The Tyranny of Richard III', *Journal of Medieval History*, III (1977).

Pollard, A.W. and G.R. Redgrave, *A Short-Title Catalogue of Books Printed in England, Scotland, and Ireland and of English Books Printed Abroad, 1475-1640*, 3 vols., London, 1986.

Portal, Ethel M., 'The Academ Roial of King James I', *Proceedings of the British*

Academy, VII (1915-16).
Potter, Jeremy, *Good King Richard?* London, 1983.
Pugh, T.B., *Henry V and the Southampton Plot of 1415* [Stroud,] 1988.
_______, 'The Marcher Lords of Glamorgan and Morgannwg, 1317-1485', *Glamorgan County History,* III, ed. T.B. Pugh, Cardiff, 1971.

Ramsay, James H., *Lancaster and York*, 2 vols., Oxford, 1892.
Rapin Thoyras, Paul de, *The History of England,* trans. N. Tindal, VI, London, 1728.
Rastell, John, *The Pastime of People*, ed. T.F. Dibdin, repr from 1529 ed., London, 1811.
Reese, M.M., *The Cease of Majesty*, London, 1961.
Report from the Committee Appointed to View the Cottonian Library, A, London, 1732.
Reynolds, E.E., *The Trial of St. Thomas More* , London, 1964.
Ricart, Robert, *The Maire of Bristowe Is Kalendar*, ed. Lucy Tolmin Smith, Cam. Soc., 2nd ser. 5, London, 1872.
Richard III: the Great Debate, ed. Paul Kendall, London, 1965.
Richard III and the North, [ed. Rosemary Horrox], Hull, 1986.
Richard III, Crown and People, ed. J. Petre, Gloucester, 1985.
Richard III: Loyalty, Lordship and Law, ed. P.W. Hammond, London, 2000.
Richmond, Colin, '1483: the Year of Decision (or Taking of the Throne)', *Richard III: a Mediaeval Kingship*, ed. John Gillingham, London, 1993.
Roper, William, *The Lyfe of Sir Thomas Moore, Knighte*, ed. Elsie Vaughan Hitchcock, EETS, orig. ser. CIXVII, London, 1935.
Roskell, J. S., 'The Office and Dignity of Protector of England, with Special Reference to Its Origin', *EHR*, LXVIII (1953).
_______, William Catesby, Counsellor to Richard III', *Bulletin of the John Rylands Library*, XLII (1959).
Ross, Charles, *Edward IV*, London, 1974.
_______, *Richard III*, Berkeley, 1981.
_______, *The Wars of the Roses*, London, 1976.
Ross, James, *John de Vere, Thirteenth Earl of Oxford*, Woodbridge, 2011.
Round, J. Horace, *Family Origins*, London, 1930.
Rous, John, *Historia Regum Angliae*, 2nd ed. Oxford, 1745.
_______, [*The Rows Roll or Warwick Roll*], London, 1845.
Rye, William Brenchley, *England as Seen by Foreigners in the Days of Elizabeth and James the First*, London 1865.

Salgado, A.J., *Álvaro Lopes de Chaves, Livro de Apontamentos (1438-1489), Códice 443 da Colecção Pombalina da B.N.L*, Lisboa 1983.
Salisbury, John of, *Letters*, ed. W.J. Millor and H.E. Butler, revised by C.N.L. Brooke, 2 vols., London, 1955.
_______, John of [Sarisberiensis, Johannes], *Policraticus*, ed. Clement C. J. Webb, 2 vols., Oxford, 1909.
Sandford, Francis, *A Genealogical History of the Kings of England, and Monarchs of Great Britain*, London, 1677.
Schwyzer, Philip, *Shakespeare and the Remains of Richard III,* Oxford, 2013.
Scofield, Cora L., *The Life and Reign of Edward the Fourth*, London, 1967.

Scott, J.R., 'Letters Respecting Fauconberge's Kentish Rising in 1471', *Archaeologia Cantiana* XI (1877)

Serres, Jean de, *Inventaire General de l'Histoire de France*, 3 vols., Paris, 1600.

Shakespeare, William, *The Tragedy of King Richard III*, ed. Horace Howard Furness, Philadelphia, 1908.

_______, _______, ed. Anthony Hammond, London, 1981.

_______, _______, ed. James R. Siemon, London, 2009.

Sharp, Thomas, *A Dissertation on the Pageants of Dramatic Mysteries Anciently Performed at Coventry*, Coventry, 1825.

Sharpe, Kevin, *Sir Robert Cotton, 1586-1631: History and Politics in Early Modern England*, Oxford, 1979.

Sher, Antony, *Year of the Fat Knight,* London, 2015.

Short-Title Catalogue of Books Printed in England, Scotland, Wales and British America, 1641-1700, 2nd ed., compiled by Donald Wing, revised and edited by John J. Morrison, *et al*., New York, 1994.

Siemon, James R., 'Reconstructing the Past: History, Historicism, Histories', in *A Companion to English Renaissance Literature and Culture*, ed. Michael Hattaway, 2 vols., Oxford, 2012.

Skidmore, Chris, *Richard III*, London, 2017.

Smith, Gordon, 'Lambert Simnel and the King from Dublin', *The Ricardian,* CXXXV (1996).

Smith, Thomas. *Catalogus Librorum Manuscriptorum Bibliothecae Cottonianae*, Oxford, 1696.

Speed, John, *The Historie of Great Britaine*, London, 1628.

Spelman, Henry, *Reliquiae Spelmanniae*, Oxford, 1698.

Sprott, Thomas, *Chronica*, ed. Thomas Hearne, London, 1719.

State Papers Published under the Authority of Her Majesty's Commission, I-XI: Henry VIII, London, 1830-1952.

The Statutes at Large, from the First Year of Edward the Fourth to the End of the Reign of Queen Elizabeth, London, 1770.

Stauffer, Donald A., *English Biography before 1700*, Cambridge, MA, 1930.

Staunford, William, *Les Plees del Corone*, London, 1607.

The Stonor Letters and Papers, 1290-1483, 2 vols., ed. Charles Lethbridge Kingsford, Cam. Soc., 3rd ser. XXIX and XXX, London, 1919.

Storey, R.L., 'The North of England' in S.B. Crimes, C.D. Ross and R.A. Griffiths, eds., *Fifteenth Century England*, 2nd ed., Stroud, 1997.

_______, 'The Wardens of the Marches of England towards Scotland, 1377-1489', *EHR,* LXXII (1957).

Stow, John, *The Annales of England*, London, 1601.

_______, *The Annales or Generall Chronicle of England*, London, 1615.

_______, *Survey of London*, ed. Charles Lethbridge Kingsford, Oxford, 1908.

Streitberger, W.R., *Edmond Tyllney, Master of the Revels and Censor of Plays: A Descriptive Index . . . to His Diplomatic Manual on Europe*, NY, 1986.

_______, 'On Edmond Tyllney's Biography', *Review of English Studies* 29 (1978).

_______, *Jacobean and Caroline Revels Accounts, 1603-42*, Malone Society Collections, Vol. XIII, Oxford 1986.

_______, *The Masters of the Revels and Elizabeth I's Court Theatre*, Oxford, 2016.
Strype, John, *Historical Collections of . . . John Aylmer*, London, 1701.
Sutton, Anne F., 'The Administration of Justice whereunto We Be Professed', *Richard III, Crown and People*, ed. J. Petre, Gloucester, 1985.
_______, 'Richard of Gloucester 1461-70: Income, Lands and Associates. His Whereabouts and Responsibilities', *The Ricardian*, XXVI (2016).
_____, 'The Admiralty and Constableship of England in the Later Fifteenth Century', *Courts of Chivalry and Admiralty in Late Medieval Europe*, Anthony Musson and Nigel Ramsay, eds, Woodbridge, 2018.

Tannenbaum, Samuel A., *Shakespearian Scraps and Other Elizabethan Fragments*, New York, 1933.
Tanner, Lawrence E. and William Wright, 'Recent Investigations Regarding the Fate of the Princes in the Tower', *Archaeologia*, LXXXIV (1935).
Thomson, J.A.F., 'Richard III and Lord Hastings – a Problematical Case Reviewed', *BIHR*, XLVIII (1975).
Three Prose Versions of the Secreta Secretorum, I, ed. Robert Steele, EETS, extra ser. LXXIV, London, 1898.
Thrush, Andrew, 'The Personal Rule of James I, 1611-1620', in *Politics, Religion, and Popularity in Early Stuart Britain: Essays in Honour of Conrad Russell,* eds. Thomas Cogswell, Richard Cust, and Peter Lake, Cambridge, 2002.
Torrey, Michael, 'The Plain Devil and Dissembling Looks', *English Literary Renaissance*, XXX (2000).
Treswell, Robert, *A Relation of Such Things as Were Observed to Happen in the Journey of the Right Honourable Charles Earle of Nottingham, His Highnesse Ambassadour to the King of Spaine,* London, 1605.
Tucker, Melvin J., *The Life of Thomas Howard, Earl of Surrey and Second Duke of Norfolk, 1443-1524*, London, 1964.
Tudor-Craig, Pamela, *Richard III*, London, 1973.
Twysden, Roger, *Certaine Considerations upon the Government of England*, ed. John Mitchell Kemble, Cam. Soc., 1st ser. XLV, London, 1849.

Ungerer, Gustav, 'The Spanish and English Chronicles in King James's and Sir George Buc's Dossiers on the Anglo-Spanish Peace Negotiations', *Huntington Library Quarterly* LXI (1998).

Van Norden, Linda, *The Elizabethan College of Antiquaries*, unpublished doctoral dissertation, University of California at Los Angeles,1946.
_______, 'Sir Henry Spelman on the Chronology of the Elizabethan Society of Antiquaries', *Huntington Library Quarterly*, XIII (1949-50).
Vergil, Polydore, *Anglica Historia*, 2nd ed., Basle, 1555.
_______, *The Anglica Historia of Polydore Vergil, A.D. 1485-1537*, ed. and trans. Denys Hay, Cam. Soc. 74, London, 1950.
_______, *Three Books of Polydore Vergil's English History*, ed. Henry Ellis, Cam. Soc. 1st ser. XXIX, London, 1844.
Vincent, Augustine, *A Discouerie of Errours in the First Edition of the Catalogue of the*

Nobility, Published by Raphe Brooke, Yorke Herald, 1619, London, 1622.
Visser-Fuchs, Livia, '"He Hardly Touched His Food, but Talked to Me All the Time": What Niclas von Popplau Really Wrote about Richard III', *The Ricardian*, XI (1999).
_______, 'Richard III, Tydeus of Calydon and Their Boars in the Latin Oration of Archibald Whitelaw, Archdeacon of St Andrews, at Nottingham on 12 September 1484', *The Ricardian* XVII (2007).

Wagner, Anthony Richard, *A Catalogue of English Mediaeval Rolls of Arms*, 2 vols., Oxford, 1950.
_______, *The Records and Collections of the College of Arms,* London, 1952.
_______, 'Sir Henry Spelman on the Chronology of the Elizabethan Society of Antiquaries', *Huntington Library Quarterly*, XIII (1949-50).
Walpole, Horace, *Historic Doubts on the Life and Reign of King Richard the Third*, London, 1768.
Walsh, Brian, *Shakespeare and the Queen's Men, and the Elizabethan Performance of History*, Cambridge, 2009.
Walsingham, Thomas, *Historia Anglicana*, 2 vols., ed. Henry Thomas Riley, R.S. XXVIII, London, 1863-4.
_______, *Ypodigma Neustriae*, ed. Henry Thomas Riley, R.S. 28(7), London, 1876.
Warkworth, John, *A Chronicle of the First Thirteen Years of the Reign of King Edward the Fourth*, ed. James Orchard Halliwell, Cam. Soc. 10, London, 1839.
Watson, Thomas, *The* Ἑκατομπαθια *or Passionate Centurie of Loue*, London, [1581].
Wendover, Roger de, *Flores Historiarum*, 3 vols., ed. Henry G. Hewlett, R.S. LXXXIV, London, 1886-9.
William of Malmesbury, *De Gestis Regum Anglorum*, 2 vols., ed. William Stubbs, R.S. XC, London, 1887-9.
William of Newbergh, *Historia Regum Anglicarum* in *Chronicles of the Reigns of Stephen, Henry II, and Richard I*, ed. Richard Howlett, R.S. LXXXII, 4 vols., London, 1884-5.
Williams, Barrie, 'The Portuguese Connection and the Significance of "the Holy Princess"', *The Ricardian*, VI (1983).
Winstanley, William, *England's Worthies*, London, 1684.
Wolffe, B.P., 'Hastings Reinterred', *EHR*, XCI (1976).
_______. 'When and Why Did Hastings Lose His Head?', *EHR*, LXXXIX (1974).
Woolf, D.R., *The Idea of History in the Early Stuart England,* Toronto, 1990.
Wood, Charles T., 'The Deposition of Edward V', *Traditio* XXXVII (1975).
Worcester, William, *Annales Rerum Anglicanum* in II, *Liber Niger Scacarii*, ed. Thomas Hearne, London, 1771.
Wormald, Francis and C.E. Wright, *The English Library before 1700*, London, 1958.
Wroe, Ann, *Perkin: A Story of Deception*, London, 2003.
Wylie, John A.H., 'The Princes in the Tower, 1483 – Death from Natural Causes', *The Ricardian*, VI (1985).

York Civic Records, ed. Angelo Raine, Yorkshire Archaeological Soc., CIII, Wakefield, 1941.
York House Books, 1461-1490, The, ed. Lorraine C. Attreed, 2 vols., Stroud, 1991.

Zeeveld, W. Gordon, 'A Tudor Defense of Richard III', *PMLA*, LV (1940).

INDEX

Note: As in previous editions, entries generally exclude references in footnotes/marginalia

C